BRAINS OF THE NATION

MW01169655

BRAINS OF THE NATION

PEDRO PATERNO, T. H. PARDO DE TAVERA, ISABELO DE LOS REYES
AND THE PRODUCTION OF MODERN KNOWLEDGE

RESIL B. MOJARES

ATENEO DE MANILA UNIVERSITY PRESS

ATENEO DE MANILA UNIVERSITY PRESS
Bellarmine Hall, Katipunan Avenue
Loyola Heights, Quezon City
P.O. Box 154, 1099 Manila, Philippines
Tel.: (632) 426-59-84 / FAX (632) 426-59-09
E-mail: unipress@admu.edu.ph
Website: www.ateneopress.org

Copyright 2006 by Ateneo de Manila University
and Resil B. Mojares

Book and cover design by JB de la Peña

All rights reserved. No part of this publication may be reproduced,
stored in a retrieval system, or transmitted in any form or by any means,
electronic, mechanical, photocopying, recording, or otherwise,
without the written permission of the Publisher.

The National Library of the Philippines CIP Data

Recommended entry:

Mojares, Resil B.
    Brains of the nation : Pedro Paterno, T. H. Pardo de
Tavera, Isabelo de los Reyes and the production of
modern knowledge / Resil B. Mojares.
- Quezon City : Ateneo de Manila University Press,
c2006.
    p. ; cm.

Includes bibliographical references.

    1. Paterno, Pedro Alejandro, 1857-1911. 2. Pardo de
Tavera, Trinidad Hermenegildo, 1857-1925. 3. De Los
Reyes, Isabelo, 1864-1938. 4. Philippines-History-
1898- -Biography. I. Title.

DS676.8A1 959.903'092 P272 2006 P061000320
ISBN 971-550-496-6

. . . if today the enlightened class
constitutes the brains of the nation,
within a few years it will constitute its entire nervous system
and manifest its existence in all its acts.

JOSE RIZAL
31 October 1889

CONTENTS

PREFACE

THIS BOOK TRACES the formation of modern knowledge in the Philippines through the lives of three pioneering Filipino intellectuals, Pedro Paterno, Trinidad Pardo de Tavera, and Isabelo de los Reyes.

I have chosen to ground the study in *lives* for three reasons. The most immediate is personal inclination: I am more comfortable with local, human detail, and the narratives into which lives can be shaped, rather than the philosophical investigation of disembodied ideas. The second is the need for a biographical archive since the three men in this study are obscured figures whose careers have not been fully studied and whose works are now mostly unread. The third is a theoretical afterthought. At a time when so much scholarship is (Western) theory-driven, it is wise to recall novelist N.V.M. Gonzalez who, reflecting on his career as a writer, gently warned, "an imagination—a sensibility—that emerges out of a Third World environment must fend for itself, for it is easy prey to the rabid charity of other worlds."[1] Locating the study in particular lives provides one with a specific, historicized cultural site from which one can look out into the world. Even as one must acknowledge that it is a position neither pure nor unassailable, it is ground under one's feet, mooring and haven in which one can orient oneself in relation to the territory covered or yet to be traversed.

These essays can be traced back to the generosity of Rudolf Rahmann, SVD, and Josef Goertz, SVD, who decided in 1973 I should become an anthropologist and took me in as a student in a series of unlisted, postgraduate courses in anthropology. I suspected it was their way of setting a young academic on track, and keeping me out of trouble. It was the first year of martial rule under Ferdinand Marcos and I had just emerged from political detention for my work as a journalist. Yet, theirs was as well the gesture of a genuine commitment to mentorship and the intellectual life. Rahmann and Goertz (then president and research director, respectively, of the University of San Carlos in Cebu City) came out of the early twentieth-century German ethnological tradition. An anthropologist, Rahmann studied under Wilhelm Schmidt, SVD, and served as editor of the venerable *Anthropos* in Germany. Goertz trained as a psychologist in Prague, Vienna, and Rome, and taught in St. Augustine in Germany. Both followed a mission as educators in China before, history intervening, they found themselves relocated to the Philippines.[2] I now vaguely recall the courses I took but I remember the zeal for scholarship the two fathers imparted. I have kept the almost cultic image of Father Goertz taking out of a folder yellowing sheets of lecture notes on Wilhelm Wundt and Lucien Levy-Bruhl the first time I sat in his office for my lessons. I imagined a sheaf that had traveled all the way from St. Augustine to Peking to Cebu.

As it turned out, I had to leave anthropology to take up a Ford Foundation fellowship in comparative literature that was supposed to turn me into a specialist on Indonesian literature. Though the fellowship was meant for study in another Southeast Asian country, I stalled, asking that I do my course work at the University of the Philippines instead, leaving Indonesia for afterwards for field research. These were interesting times in the Philippines and I did not want to leave. As again it turned out, though I eventually earned my doctorate, political and bureaucratic reasons prevented me, a former detainee, from going to Jakarta to train as an Indonesianist. (I thank Jose V. Abueva, then Ford representative and now a friend, for the kindness in allowing my program changes midstream.)

Irrevocably set on an academic career and ensconced as founding director of my home university's Cebuano Studies Center, I pursued a variety of interests. In 1990, during a stint as visiting professor at the University of Hawaii, I first thought of embarking on a study of Filipino ethnological writings in the nineteenth century. I was intrigued by the works of Paterno, Pardo, and de los Reyes on "ancient Filipino civilization," beguiled by the thought that these writings seemed central but had been largely ignored in Philippine scholarship. Such, however, are the vagaries of intellectual work in the Philippines that while the project quietly percolated I never had the occasion to pursue it. It was not until 2000, during a six-month fellowship at Kyoto University's Center for Southeast Asian Studies, that I thought again of exploring the problem of early Filipino ethnology and, more broadly, the emergence of the disciplines in the Philippines. Stimulation came from discussions with sojourning colleagues in Japan (particularly, Patricio Abinales and Caroline Hau) on the prospects of tracing the genealogies of Philippine studies. It was sometime after that I decided to write on my "three figures of the Filipino Enlightenment." (There is Jose Rizal, of course, but he is the best-studied of his generation and I had done a piece on him during the Kyoto sojourn.[3]) Not quite sure whether I would have the time to finish the entire study I decided on a building-block approach of writing a series of monographic essays. The final section of the book is a late addition occasioned by the need to pull together strands of the text by taking a long view of the historical formation of intellectuals in the Philippines.

I wish to thank the various libraries consulted, particularly Ateneo de Manila University's Rizal Library and T.H. Pardo de Tavera Special Collections Archives, Lopez Memorial Museum, National Library, and the libraries of St. Andrew's Theological Seminary and the University of San Carlos. Prudenciana Cruz, director of the National Library, was particularly helpful in the final stages of the work.

A year-long fellowship at the Asia Research Institute of the National University of Singapore (2003–2004) hastened the completion of and hopefully deepened the study, for which I have many to thank, Anthony Reid, Jim Warren, my fellow *arivistes*, and the staff at ARI. I thank Takashi Shiraishi, Reynaldo Ileto, and Jose Cruz, SJ, for recommending me for the fellowship.

There is admittedly a measure of fiction in this brief narrative. Beginnings are inventions of the present moment, and the moment does not stand still. This does not of course make them untrue. It is the tracing of beginnings (a theme of the present book) that enables us to satisfy the unrelenting need to embrace widths of time and space, to feel their coherence even if this must be configured again and again.

NOTES

1. N.V.M. Gonzalez, "Moving On: A Filipino in the World," *Foreign Values and Southeast Asian Scholarship*, ed. J. Fischer (Berkeley: University of California, Center for South and Southeast Asian Studies, 1973), 124.

2. See Eric S. Casiño, "Father Rudolf Rahmann, SVD, and the European Connection in Philippine Anthropology," *Philippine Quarterly of Culture & Society*, 13:4 (1985), 253–61.

3. Resil B. Mojares, "Rizal Reading Pigafetta," *Waiting for Mariang Makiling: Essays in Philippine Cultural History* (Quezon City: Ateneo de Manila University Press, 2002), 52–86. Recent additions to Rizal scholarship are Benedict Anderson's highly absorbing essays of intellectual detection: "Nitroglycerine in the Pomegranate," *New Left Review* 27 (2004): 99–118, and "In the World-Shadow of Bismarck and Nobel," *New Left Review* 28 (2004): 85–129.

PEDRO PATERNO

ᴸORD OF LUZONICA

HISTORY HAS NOT BEEN KIND to Pedro Paterno. A century ago, he was one of the country's premier intellectuals, blazing trails in Philippine letters. Today, he is ignored in the fields in which he once held forth with much eminence, real and imagined. No full-length biography or extended review of his corpus of writings has been written, and no one reads him today.[1]

That Paterno has sunk to insignificance has to do in part with his politics. Nationalist historiography has cast him as symbol of the class that betrayed the Philippine Revolution. Reduced to a convenient sign (Traitor to the Revolution or, kindly, Peacemaker, Father of the Malolos Constitution), the motions, depth, and shadows of the living person have dissolved in the flat light of ritualized remembrance. Paterno's disappearance can be traced as well to his delusional personality and the eccentric texts he produced. His books on Philippine culture and history were judged an embarrassment by his contemporaries almost from the day they saw print. Few authors since have anything good to say about him. Aiming to be evenhanded, Leon Ma. Guerrero can only offer a backhanded compliment. Saying Paterno "was not an unkind or an untalented man," he concludes: "Posterity has been rather harsh with him because he was an incorrigible snob."[2]

Paterno's ghost inhabits an important phase in the national history. It is time to put it to rest by locating it more clearly in the context of that history. At a time when there is a need to go beyond the reductionism of early nationalist historiography, a reevaluation of such occluded figures as Paterno should reward us with a denser, more textured understanding of the past. At a time when there is interest in defining the local ground for Philippine studies, it is necessary and instructive to recall the work of a scholar who was unreservedly a pioneer in this field.

ENCHANTED BY KABBALISTIC CODES, Oriental secrets and the "poesy of the past," he blurred boundaries between what was in the world and in the mind. Paterno could have been invented by Miguel de Cervantes or Jorge Luis Borges. It is amazing that he has not attracted a biographer.

Pedro Alejandro Paterno (1857–1911) was a child of privilege in a society of limited opportunities.[3] He was born in Santa Cruz, Manila, on February 27, 1857, to the wealthy Chinese-Filipino couple Maximo Molo Paterno and Carmen Devera (de Vera) Ignacio. According to tradition, the family "began" when a Chinese apothecary of mandarin origins, Ming Mong Lo, married a local woman with "blue blood" in her veins, she being "the direct descendant of the Great *Maguinoo*, or Prince of Luzon, a title hereditary, according to tradition" (or so Paterno boasted to the English author John Foreman).[4] The "Chinaman" adopted the name Jose Molo upon Christian baptism and prospered as a merchant in the premier commercial district of Binondo. It is said that he had five children, one of them Paterno Molo y San Agustin (1786–1853), a proprietor of merchant boats that carried goods to as far as Aparri. Paterno Molo's image has been preserved in what is regarded as the earliest known dated oil portrait of a Filipino, executed by the painter Severino Pablo in 1836. It shows a man in a blue *barong Tagalog* striking the pose of a confident and prosperous burgher.

Paterno Molo had nine children, the sixth being Pedro Paterno's father, Maximo (Maximo Molo Agustin Paterno y Yamson) (1830–1900). By 1849 the family had changed their surname from *Molo* to *Paterno* in honor of the family's patriarch. It was not uncommon for Chinese mestizos and indios to take a parent's first name as a surname, but Pedro Paterno had a more fanciful explanation for the change. He told Foreman that the name change came because his father's "placidity and solicitude for others" had earned from his friends the nickname *paterno* ("paternal").[5]

Called *Capitan Memo*, Maximo built the family wealth by running a lighterage service for ships entering the Manila port, operating a store on the Escolta, brokering between foreign trading houses and provincial producers, and acquiring agricultural land in Batangas. Capitan Memo married thrice. The first was to Valeriana Pineda, daughter of Silvino Pineda and Petrona Andrea, on January 22, 1848. She died shortly after bearing him a son, Narciso. Maximo then married Carmen Pineda Devera Ignacio (possibly a cousin of Valeriana), daughter of Potenciano Devera Ignacio and Maria Pineda. Maximo and Carmen had nine children: Agueda, Dolores, Jose, Pedro, Jacoba, Antonio, Maximino, Maria de la Paz, and Trinidad. After Carmen died, Maximo married her sister Teodora and had five more children, Mariano, Concepcion, Feliciano, Rosenda, and Adelaida.

By the time Pedro was born Chinese mestizos were a dominant social group. Outside *indios* (indigenes), they constituted the largest of the race-based administrative and cultural categories in colonial society by the mid-nineteenth century, numbering 240,000 against 20,000 Spanish mestizos, 10,000 Chinese, and 5,000 Spaniards.[6] While small compared to the more than four million indios, their concentration in the urban centers and strategic access to both the inside and outside of colonial society earned them social and economic prominence. Regarded as indigenous subjects of Spain rather than as Chinese, they had the same tribute-paying obligations and legal rights as the indios. With their resources and position, they were the cultural vanguards of "native" society, leading creators of a "Filipino-Hispanic" identity in the nineteenth century.

The Paterno ancestral home, on family land that extended up to the banks of the Pasig River, stood on Calle San Sebastian (later R. Hidalgo) in Quiapo, an elegant street where lived such patrician families as the Aranetas, Ocampos, Legardas, and Genatos. It was one of Manila's most fashionable residences, designed by Felix Roxas, the first Filipino architect, a large two-story, stone-and-wood house with an inner courtyard and a façade decorated with such neo-classic features as Tuscan columns.[7] The Paternos also owned residences and *accesorias* (apartments) elsewhere in the city.

The prominence of the interrelated families of Paterno, Molo, and Agustin is indicated by the appearance of their names in rosters of *gobernadorcillos* of Santa Cruz. Santa Cruz was one of Manila's richest districts, home to Chinese-mestizo families grown prosperous in the wake of expanding colonial commerce in the nineteenth century. They had grown as well in the confidence to display the status that came with wealth. The borough was famous not only for its goldsmiths and silver-smiths, Nick Joaquin writes, "but most of all for the vanity of its women, of whom it is said that they walked in the festive procession of their patroness, Nuestra Señora del Pilar, covered with jewels from head to foot."[8]

Pedro Paterno was raised in an environment that cultivated wealth, status, and the arts. The Deveras and Pinedas did not only own jewelry shops (*joyerias*) in Santa Cruz, both Paterno's mother Carmen and step-mother Valeriana designed and fabricated jewelry for local and foreign buyers. Paterno relatives included the Asuncion brothers, among them Mariano (1804–1885) and Justiniano (1816–1896), acclaimed portrait-ists and sculptors in nineteenth-century Manila. Pedro Paterno's sisters and stepsisters were accomplished in the arts of painting, embroidery, music, and jewelry-making. Dolores Paterno (1854–1881) was a com-poser of some repute. Agueda, Jacoba, Paz, Concepcion, and Adelaida produced paintings and jewelry that were exhibited at the *Exposicion Regional de Filipinas* in Manila in 1895 and the St. Louis Exposition in 1904.

Extant portraits of Paterno's mother and sister Dolores, done by Justiniano Asuncion, show fine-featured women, bejewelled and garbed in intricately-embroidered *piña*. A portrait of Maximo Paterno (1852) by Severino Pablo has also survived. Possession of these portraits was a mark of the family's high status in local society.[9]

After an early education under the tutorship of Florentino Torres (who would, in later years, become a member of the Philippine Su-preme Court), the young Pedro Paterno attended the Jesuit-run Ateneo Municipal where (it is said) he earned "unusually high ratings" and fin-ished his secondary studies in 1871.[10] Upon graduation, he was sent to

Spain for higher studies, one of the first in what would be an exodus of sons of the Filipino bourgeoisie seeking education in the cities of Europe. This exodus included Paterno's younger brothers Antonio and Maximino, who also studied in Spain and earned degrees in medicine and law, respectively.

Paterno studied philosophy and theology at Universidad de Salamanca and then moved to Universidad Central de Madrid where he earned a doctorate in civil law in 1880. He stayed on in Spain in a sojourn that lasted some twenty-two years, practicing law and, mostly, living off a splendid pension from his family. Political circumstances may have occasioned his protracted residence in Madrid. Shortly after he left for Spain—a lad of around fourteen—his family was dealt a harsh lesson in colonial realities.

Nineteenth-century economic and social changes had created an urban elite of mostly creole and Chinese-mestizo merchants, landowners, civil servants, and priests, empowered by their new status and wealth and inspired by late Enlightenment currents emanating from Europe. A new liberalism manifested itself in the debate over the rights of the secular clergy vis-à-vis the dominant religious orders, the expression of secular, *progresista* ideas in the emerging local press, and the assertion of a "civil sphere" apart from the hegemonic claims of the Church.

The Spanish revolution of 1868 and the assumption of Carlos Maria de la Torre as governor-general in 1869 created the opening for these various tendencies to come together.[11] A reform movement led by a multiracial elite of priests, professionals, merchants, and bureaucrats openly campaigned for *asimilacion*, the empowering of Filipinos with civil and political rights equal to those enjoyed by peninsular Spaniards. Maximo Paterno, Pedro's father, joined such notables as Joaquin Pardo de Tavera, Antonio Regidor, and Father Jose Burgos in a *Comite de reformadores* and was among those who participated in the historic public manifestation that called for reforms and support for the new, reputedly liberal governor-general at the plaza of Santa Potenciana in Intramuros on July 12, 1869.

The display of public assertiveness unsettled church and civil authorities. Seizing upon a mutiny of soldiers in the fort of Cavite on January 20, 1872, they launched a mass crackdown on alleged separatist conspiracies and executed the priests Jose Burgos, Mariano Gomez and Jacinto Zamora. Maximo Paterno was one of the victims in the crackdown. He was arrested on February 20, 1872, imprisoned in Fort Santiago, and sentenced by a military tribunal to imprisonment in the Marianas for eight and six years, respectively, for the double offense of "conspiracy against the national integrity and conspiracy against the constitution of the State." The particulars of the charges were vague. A person described as "peaceful and calm to excess (if excess is possible in this respect)," Paterno was accused of having contributed money to the founding of a liberal Madrid newspaper called *El Correo de Ultramar* (the existence of which had not been verified); that he received a copy of the reformist *El Eco Filipino* by mail; and that a witness (a person in jail for falsification and robbery) reportedly testified that Paterno adhered to "separatist ideas."[12]

In the company of prominent citizens, Paterno was shipped to the Marianas on March 14, 1872. A petition for amnesty in his behalf—and that of Antonio Regidor, Joaquin Pardo de Tavera, Jose M. Basa, and Agustin Mendoza—was filed with the Spanish prime minister on July 30, 1873 but was granted only on November 28, 1874. When news of the amnesty reached Guam, Paterno promptly paid eight thousand pesos to charter a Spanish merchant steamer, *Legazpi*, that took him and fellow *deportados* from Guam to Hong Kong on January 16, 1875.[13] Like the other deportees, he was initially forbidden to go back to the Philippines by the terms of the amnesty. He eventually returned to Manila around 1882 and remained active in business. He was one of the investors, led by Jacobo Zobel and Pedro Roxas, who formed Compania de Tranvias de Filipinas which started operating a tramway concession in Manila in 1883.[14]

We do not have word on how these events affected the young Pedro Paterno. What we know is that he led the life of a gentleman of leisure, haunting Madrid's salon society, taking up such hobbies as fencing, and devoting himself to literary and scholarly pursuits. Gaining entry into aristocratic circles in metropolitan Spain, he proudly claimed the friendship of Spanish president Emilio Castelar, Overseas Minister Victor Balaguer, poet-politician Gaspar Nuñez de Arce, and assorted members of the nobility. His house at 16 Sauco, in front of Paseo de Recoletos in the center of Madrid, was the scene of frequent *reuniones artisticas*, of which the Filipino artist Miguel Zaragoza reminisced:

Those reunions were most agreeable and delightful. They would make music there, as the French would say; there, novice poets, who are now worthy figures, would read their brilliant nocturnal studies; and not a few painters would adorn the walls of the beautiful entresuelo (mezzanine) with small paintings and studies.

The gatherings attracted such a selection of luminaries, including the poets Ramon de Campoamor and Manuel del Palacio, that the famous Jose Zorrilla, Spain's national laureate, complimented Paterno (so Zaragoza reports) by saying:

Dear grandson (that was how he called him), you should be satisfied. You have succeeded in bringing together in your house heads of different political parties and writers and poets who fall all over themselves to get to the temple of glory.[15]

Paterno's first book, *Influencia Social del Cristianismo* (1876), a lecture before the Academia de Teologia Dogmatica y Polemica in Salamanca's Central Seminary, shows how Paterno consciously located himself in the stream of metropolitan Spanish culture. Extoling Christianity's exalted role in the march of civilization, the speech makes no reference to the Philippines and could very well have been delivered by a Spanish politician or theologian. It sketches the grand themes that underlie Paterno's subsequent work: the law of social evolution, the value of reason, human perfectability, and the synthesis of an essentialized "Orient" and "Occident" in a Christianity that stands at the most advanced stage of world civilization.[16]

In 1880, Paterno published two books of literary musings in which he began to speak, if delicately, to his nationality. *Sampaguitas* (1880), dedicated to Balaguer, compiled twenty poems that showcased Paterno's lyric gift, crafted in the idiom of such Spanish poets as Campoamor and Gustavo Becquer.[17] The book was announced as the first volume of a planned series called "Biblioteca Filipina" which aimed to make known to the public "the mature fruits produced by the Filipino youth." What slight references there are in Paterno's poetry to the Philippine scene are distanced, exoticized. *Poesias Liricas y Dramaticas* (1880), which contains dedicatory verses and the fragment of a play, is in the same vein.

The Spaniard Wenceslao Retana remarks that Paterno's poetry cultivated a "vague refinement" (*vaga delicadeza*) and offered nothing original either in form or substance.[18] Equally unimpressed by the poetry, historian John Schumacher concedes however that *Sampaguitas* is "the first conscious attempt to create a *Filipino* literature," "to project a Filipino national personality and to present to the public the work of a Filipino, specifically as such."[19]

In turning to the Philippines, Paterno joined other Filipino intellectuals in the 1880s in projecting *Filipinas* and its "better classes" in the consciousness of metropolitan Spain. It was in this spirit that Filipinos in Spain formed societies, Jose Rizal proposed the production of a book to showcase Filipino talent in a meeting held in 1884, and *La Solidaridad* (1889–1895), the Filipino organ in Spain, featured articles on Filipino history and culture. Paterno's turn to the homeland may have been occasioned as well by his awareness that it was in speaking *of* and *for* the country that he could be a consequential voice in the metropole.

TOWARD THE END of 1882, Paterno returned to the Philippines for a vacation. The colony was quiet but memories of the tragic events of 1872 were alive. Paterno's father had just returned to Manila from Hong Kong after ten years of exile.

All was not quiet in the colony. Paterno must have noted how, despite the restraints, native Filipinos had grown increasingly visible and vocal as participants in Manila's intellectual life. Young men like Isabelo de los Reyes were entering careers as scholars and publicists. A partly Tagalog newspaper, *Diariong Tagalog*, had just been launched and Marcelo H. del Pilar was beginning to test the limits of dissent. One of Paterno's callers during his home visit was Jose Rizal, on his way out of the country for the first time, one of the young men who probably would not have left were it not for the ghosts of 1872. It was their first meeting.

After a year, Paterno left and toured China, Japan, Europe, and the United States, before settling back in Spain to resume an active social and literary life. Paterno's home visit must have whetted his appetite to be an authority on his country. In 1885, he published *Ninay*, which has come to be regarded as "the first Filipino novel." Turning to a more direct form of cultural advocacy, he produced a series of ethnological treatises on the Philippines: *La Antigua Civilizacion Tagalog* (1887), *Los*

Itas (1890), *El Cristianismo en la Antigua Civilizacion Tagalog* (1892), *El Barangay* (1892), *La Familia Tagalog en la Historia Universal* (1892), *El Individuo Tagalog y su Arte en la Exposicion Historico-Americana* (1893), and *Los Tagalog* (1894).

These works established Paterno's visibility as a gentleman-scholar. He was the first to theorize, in the idiom of European scholarship, a grand precolonial civilization for the Philippines. Many of his fellow Filipinos in Europe, however, regarded him and his work with a mix of amusement, envy, and contempt, calling him the *Sampaguitero*, an allusion to his first book and the trade of vending exotic flowers. *Solidaridad* gave his works respectful but less than enthusiastic notice. Wenceslao Retana snidely remarked that Paterno owed his fame more to his *tertulias* than his literary merit.[20]

Paterno invited such sarcasm. He kept aloof from other Filipinos in Spain, conscious that he was wealthier, better connected, and more "assimilated" than the rest. Claiming descent from Tagalog nobility, he affected the title of *Maguinoo* ("lord"), aspired to the manners of a Spanish *hidalgo*, and grandly signed his *Antigua Civilizacion*: "Pedro Alexandro Molo Agustin Paterno y de Vera Ignacio (*Maguinoo* Paterno). Doctor en Jurisprudencia." He dressed in style and traveled around Madrid in a coach that carried his personal coat of arms—a sun, above it a *salakot* (a native Filipino headgear) surmounted with a ducal crown and a bird, and below, interlaced with the cords of the salakot, two crossed bolos. This shield decorated—painted, embroidered, engraved in silver—the harness of his horses, blanket, cards, and other personal effects.[21] Retana wrote: "Paterno cultivated an image of munificence; some took him for an authentic potentate."[22] Paterno is reported to have remarked "that if he looks like a Filipino, it is not by choice but because of his color that he cannot erase."[23] He was, in his mind, a class to himself.

Intellectual circles in nineteenth-century Spain were hierarchical and status-conscious.[24] State patronage and clientilist networks were important for those desirous of recognition in the royal academies and select circles of intellectuals. Though the character of Spain's intelligentsia was changing during Paterno's time in Madrid it is clear that he molded himself in the feudal manner of traditional intellectuals schooled in the highminded style of addressing the state and their fellows rather than the vulgar public. Paterno fancied Spanish royalty. He would later boast to John Foreman that "under the protection and tutelage of the Marquis de Heredia," he was introduced into aristocratic circles "in which he became a great favorite." The "Marquis de Mina" was his college companion, he said. It was proposed at one time that he should wed the daughter of the "Marchioness de Montolibar" but he disregarded the suggestion, Paterno told Foreman, because "his heart already inclined towards the Filipina who is now his wife."[25] What in fact happened was that in 1890, Paterno married Luisa Pineyro y Merino. The bride was, he announced in the wedding invitation he sent Rizal and other Filipinos, "cousin of a marquis" and descendant of the "old and famous" Pineyro de Lugo and Merino families.[26] Luisa's sister, Antonia, was also married to the successful London-based creole lawyer Antonio Ma. Regidor. It was a marriage that boosted Paterno's peninsular ambitions.

Established in Spain over a decade ahead of Rizal, Marcelo del Pilar, and Mariano Ponce, Paterno styled himself the most illustrious Filipino in Spain. He organized Filipinos in Madrid for a banquet on December 30, 1881, to honor Overseas Minister Fernando Leon for his work in the abolition of the Tobacco Monopoly. It was on his initiative, he claimed, that a well-attended banquet was held in Madrid's *Restaurante Ingles* to honor Juan Luna and Felix Resurreccion Hidalgo for winning top honors at the 1884 *Exposicion Nacional de Bellas Artes* in Madrid.

A patron and friend of Luna and Hidalgo, Paterno promoted their works and provided for a studio and equipment for Luna, Hidalgo, and Miguel Zaragoza when they were in Rome and hosted several feasts for them when he came to visit.[27] Paterno gloried in their feat of breaking into the European art world with paintings that demonstrated Filipinos could "out-European" the Europeans. While Luna himself may have intended other messages (as critics argue) to such works as *Spoliarium* (1884), Paterno surely took the benign view of the colony's relations to the metropolis visualized in Luna's *La Madre España Llevando a su Hija Filipinas al Camino del Progreso* (1888), an allegorical piece commissioned by the Spanish Overseas Minister which showed "Mother Spain" leading her ward, "Filipinas," up a flower-strewn marble stairway as she points to the Future. An earlier version of this painting was in fact given by Luna to Paterno.[28]

An avid collector of Orientalia, Paterno turned his Madrid residence into a museum of antiquities. The collection included an assortment of

Philippine hats and earthenware, Chinese fans, ivory pieces, porcelain, weapons, fabrics, and even varieties of coconuts he collected in his travels in Oceania and Asia. In 1883, he opened this museum to members of the Spanish press in what he called *Veladas y exposiciones de objetos artisticos y arquelogicos de Filipinas*. He and his wife Luisa also showcased their prize possessions in the 1887 *Exposicion General de las Islas Filipinas* in Madrid's Parque de Retiro and the 1893 Madrid *Exposicion Historico-Natural y Etnografica*. At the *Exposicion Historico-Americana* in 1892–1893, Paterno displayed his exquisite Philippine selection of pre-Spanish goldwork, early-colonial jewelry and *salakot* adornments, silverware and ceramic pieces, and old books on the Philippines (including his own works).[29]

Initiated by Overseas Minister Balaguer, the 1887 *Exposicion de Filipinas* was condemned by Rizal and other nationalists. The exhibition of "living specimens" of non-Hispanized natives was attacked by the nationalists as a grave affront to the dignity of those who were displayed and part of a conspiracy of the friars and other reactionaries to represent Filipinos as an inferior race. Paterno, however, actively participated in the exposition, taking the official view that it was meant to publicize the Philippines and its resources.[30] While he promoted an appreciation for Philippine artistic achievements, he did so out of dilletantism, exoticism, and vague sentiments of patriotism.

Paterno stood outside what came to be called the "Propaganda Movement," the Filipino reform movement of the 1880s and 1890s. While historians have since viewed his writings as part of the movement, Paterno distanced himself from the organizing activities of Filipinos engaged in the campaign for colonial reforms. Outside a few pieces, he was not an active contributor to *Solidaridad*. While he played host to Rizal, the Luna brothers, Graciano Lopez Jaena, and others in his Madrid residence, he did not share the views of the militant autonomists among the expatriates. He did not involve himself in Masonic activities as Rizal, Lopez Jaena, and Marcelo del Pilar did.

Nineteenth-century Spain was a cauldron of political conflict.[31] Insurrections and frequent changes of government marked the internecine struggles between monarchists and republicans, Left and Right, Federalists and Unitarians, secular and clerical factions, Carlists (supporters of Carlos VII's claim to the throne) and Alfonsists (partisans of Alfonso

XII). Divisions within Spanish society provided Filipino émigrés with openings for propaganda work. While del Pilar and others aggressively lobbied with Spanish politicians on Philippine causes, Paterno kept his dealings with these officials on a high, ceremonial plane. While Filipino propagandists gravitated towards liberals and socialists sympathetic to Philippine autonomy—like the militant Federalist Francisco Pi y Margall, Cuban autonomist Rafael Ma. Labra, and Masonic leader Miguel Morayta—Paterno cultivated friendship with such conservatives as Emilio Castelar and Victor Balaguer.

Paterno would name Emilio Castelar his intellectual inspiration. The son of a Cadiz merchant, Castelar (1832–1899) was a leading champion of Spanish Republicanism. Ousted as history professor at Universidad Central de Madrid because of his speeches against the monarchy, he escaped to France, returned after the Revolution of 1868, joined the Parliament, and became president of the first Spanish Republic (1873–1874). Having alienated hardline Republicans, he lost the presidency, went into exile after a military coup in 1874, returned after the accession of King Alfonso XII in 1875, and was elected once more to the Parliament. At the time Paterno was a student in Madrid, Castelar had become a right-wing Liberal. Renouncing the socialist and federalist doctrines of people like Pi y Margall, he courted—in the name of "national unity"—the support of the army, the monarchists, and the Catholic Church.

It was not just Castelar's stature that attracted Paterno. There was a great deal in the poet-politician Castelar that one finds in Paterno: advocate of nonviolent political evolution, a chameleonlike hero of the Conservatives, a vain and exuberant writer in the manner of Lamartine and Michelet, and a politician the historian Raymond Carr calls "the mildest of the new generation, yet a power through the humourless vanity which made him the greatest orator of his day." Called "the last of the Romantics" because of the lyrical egotism of his writings, he inspired a cult of followers with the brilliance of his oratory. Castelar once boasted, "With one speech, I have freed two hundred thousand Negroes."[32] Compared to the austere Pi y Margall, the flamboyant Castelar appealed to Paterno.

Serious and reserved, Rizal did not warm up to Paterno. In a speech at the banquet of Filipino students at Café de Madrid on December 31,

1883, Rizal hailed Paterno (who had just returned from his Philippine trip) by referring to him as "the indefatigable Mr. Pedro Paterno, the personification of longing and activity, a son of the mother country, and a favorite of the Muses." One hears the trace of tolerant amusement in the toast.[33] Writing to Ferdinand Blumentritt on March 29, 1887, Rizal remarks: "Pay no attention to what Paterno says of *Bathala* in his work. P.A. Paterno is ... I can't find a word for it but only a sign thus: [there follows a spiral-like scrawl]."[34] Apparently, Blumentritt agreed. While the Austrian scholar liberally cited Filipino scholars in his works, he virtually ignored Paterno.

Other Filipinos shared Rizal's view of Paterno. Writing to Rizal on August 13, 1890, Juan Luna expressed an amused, mocking view of his occasional patron. Remarking on the Filipino fondness for martial sports and alluding to Paterno's Egyptomania, Luna suggested to Rizal that they should organize a tournament "so that this kind of sport would make of the Filipino youth a bunch of ready fighters for the honor of the much reviled Egyptian race, as our immortal poet Mr. Pedro (P.A. Paterno) said."[35]

T.H. Pardo de Tavera regarded Paterno's scholarship with scorn. He called him a plagiarist and "vulgar impostor" who made false claims about his sources and advertised non-existent books among his works. He dismissed *Antigua Civilizacion* as "a work of pure fantasy full of extraneous and incredible assertions." He judged *Los Itas* a book of "buffooneries" and *Cristianismo en la Antigua Civilizacion Tagalog* a piece of work "full of surprises for history, science, and reason!"[36] Though restrained in his criticism of Filipino colleagues, Isabelo de los Reyes similarly remarks on Paterno's credulity and exaggerations.[37] As usual, Wenceslao Retana had his own choice remarks. While acknowledging the labor that went into Paterno's books, he rejected their arguments as "the dreamy fantasy of a poet" devoid of all "scientific value."[38]

It is doubtful whether the opinions of his fellow-emigres made a dent on Paterno's sense of his own importance. In 1892, he was awarded a gold medal for his participation in the Historico-Americana Exposition. In 1893, in recognition of his literary and scholarly contributions, he was conferred the *Gran Cruz de Isabel La Catolica* and an appointment from Overseas Minister Antonio Maura as director of the *Museo-Biblioteca de Filipinas*, the first public library in the Philippines.

In 1893, Paterno published *El Regimen Municipal en las Islas Filipinas*, a commentary on the newly promulgated Maura Law of 1893 in which he gives lavish praise to Segismundo Moret and Antonio Maura for their work in the "social redemption" of the colony. He hails the Maura reforms in municipal government as the realization of his own ideas on the barangay as the political basis of the archipelago. Waxing eloquent on this confluence of Spanish and Filipino ideals, Paterno declares:

> The grand desire that agitates our soul, the ideal that we tirelessly pursue in our journey, is the eternal union of Spain and the Philippines, the indissoluble union of two races, union of fraternity and equality at the foot of one altar, with eyes raised to the same God.[39]

Recalling his own ideas on the *pacto de sangre*, the blood compact between Spaniards and native chieftains at the time of the Spanish coming, he says that he looks forward to the day when Filipinos and Spaniards can say, "We are of one blood" (*Somos los del sangdugo*). Praising Spain, he concludes: "We desire and can be Spaniards, with honor and dignity."[40]

PATERNO RETURNED TO MANILA in 1893 mantled with his accomplishments in the metropolis. Settling into the colony, he led the life of art and leisure he enjoyed, gracing the *tertulias* of Manila society, declaiming his lyrics, and delivering brilliant speeches in the Castelarian manner. High officials like governor-general Ramon Blanco and his successor Fernando Primo de Rivera consulted him on Philippine affairs. He relished his importance. A curious studio photograph of Paterno, which must have been taken around this time, shows him wearing a Roman-style tunic and carrying a feather-topped mace.[41]

Though his position as director of Museo-Biblioteca de Filipinas was largely honorific and carried no emoluments, it was congenial to his interests as bibliophile and connoisseur of Filipino *objets d'art*. Inaugurated on October 24, 1891, Museo-Biblioteca was in the process of being organized when Paterno assumed as director on March 31, 1894. It was housed in modest quarters on 12 Gunao Street in Quiapo. Paterno built its collections, underwrote the publication of its short-lived, monthly *Boletin* (1895), and collaborated in organizing the *Exposicion Regional de Filipinas* in Manila in 1895. (The library-museum closed down at the onset of the U.S. occupation in 1898. Paterno took its collections to his residence and parts of these were later transferred to public libraries the Americans put up in the early 1900s. Paterno had the satisfaction years later, as member of the Philippine Assembly, of sponsoring Act No. 1849 [June 3, 1908] which established the Philippine Public Library, today's National Library.)[42]

Paterno had an untroubled view of his location betwixt colony and empire, between what many colonials at the time called *patria chica* (Philippines) and *patria grande* (Spain). When the *Boletin* was criticized in the Spanish press of Manila in 1895 for its masthead illustration showing the figure of the Filipino Woman, nativizing, it was said, the representation of Spain the Motherland, Paterno expressed wonderment that such a distinction should be made. (*Boletin* falsely attributed the amateurish masthead sketch to Juan Luna.) He sees no contradiction, Paterno says, between his love for "motherland" (*patria*) and "homeland" (*hogar*). They are one.

> I have spent fourteen years of my existence in Manila and the remaining twenty-two in the Iberian peninsula. It was by luck that my birth, my childhood, my material life, for lack of a better name, belongs to the Philippines. But my youth, my studies, my social relationships, that is to say, my intellectual life, is from Spain. It is not surprising therefore that these islands as well as that peninsula should be equally loved by me and united in my mind under one idea; in my breast under one sentiment; and in my lips, under one word: motherland.[43]

In this idealized view, however, it was clear which had been subordinated to the other. Paterno ends his peroration by declaring: "Ah, may God preserve my motherland and in her, always, always, my homeland." To which the editors of *Solidaridad* appended the slyly sarcastic note: "Our comment: Very good, Mr. Paterno."[44]

A year later, the Philippine Revolution began. Paterno found himself faced with choices he did not wish to make. His fine conflation of *patria* and *hogar* had collapsed. As with many of his contemporaries, the revolution shook the ground on which, only a while earlier, he had so confidently stood.

The outbreak of armed hostilities in August 1896 shocked the Spanish authorities and, as in 1872, fed a paranoia about secret societies and separatist conspiracies. Prominent residents in Manila and elsewhere were arrested on the merest suspicion that they were the brains and financiers of the insurrection. Among the *principales* arrested in September—together with Pedro Roxas, Ambrosio Rianzares Bautista, Luis Yangco, and Antonio Luna—was Paterno's younger brother, Maximino. Pedro Paterno himself was investigated for possible complicity in the insurrection. His house was among the many residences ordered searched by Spanish authorities in the weeks prior to the exposure of the "Katipunan conspiracy" in August 1896.[45] For the authorities it was inconceivable that a mass uprising could take place without elite leadership and support. Stricken by a siege mentality, Spaniards blamed the uprising on the innate excitability of the masses (what a Spanish writer theorized as "Malay fever," *fiebre Malaya*) and the "jingoism" of the local elite who had undermined Spanish authority by, among others, propagating "doctrines exalting the ancient Tagalog civilization."[46]

Paterno's connection to the revolution was raised in the trial of Jose Rizal in 1896. A brief for the Spanish prosecution on December 22, 1896, states that Paterno's *Antigua Civilizacion* "echoed" Rizal's "false and pernicious doctrine" exalting Tagalog civilization at Spain's expense. Ideas which had "consequences both erroneous and injurious to Spanish sovereignty" included—so the Spaniards believed—the argument that "sovereignty rests not on the right of conquest but on certain so-called pacts or treaties contracted between our predecessors and the kinglets of these Islands, and that the municipal reforms of Senor Maura were nothing but the restoration of the ancient Tagalog barangay."[47] Reference is made to Paterno's speech at the inauguration of a monument to Antonio Maura in Pagsanjan, Laguna. (I have not seen the text of this address but Paterno's views on the relation between the Maura Law and the traditional concept of the barangay are contained in his *Regimen Municipal en las Islas Filipinas* [1893].) In looking for the intellectual conspiracy behind the revolution, some Spanish authors fastened on the symbolism and use in Katipunan initiation rituals of the *pacto de sangre*, which a Spanish writer called "the anchor (*ancora*) of the revolution."[48] For having theorized on the subject, Paterno was seen as complicit in the events. A racist, pseudonymous tract on the revolution claimed that Paterno's

18

"fantastic doctrine" of a Tagalog civilization ("on the plane of the Aztec and ancient Peruvian Indians") contributed to the insurrection. It mockingly suggested that Paterno had ambitions to be "Emperor Pedro I."[49]

All these accusations had more to say about Spanish paranoia than Paterno's role in the events. These provided basis, however, for Paterno's later boast that the friars suspected he was "the real archplotter" of the revolution but that they could not move against him since the highest civilian and military officials, with whom he was on intimate terms, could vouch for him. Yet, at the time, it must have surprised him that he could be suspected of preaching ideas inimical to Spain. It must have rankled too that despite his identification with Spain he was still, in Spanish eyes, a "native."

Like others of the Manila elite, Paterno kept his distance from the events. Towards the end of July 1897, however, he voluntarily presented himself to governor-general Fernando Primo de Rivera (an acquaintance while he was in Spain) and offered his services as a mediator. Despite Spanish suspicions of his nativist ideas, highly placed Spaniards still believed he was "a great authority" who exercised great influence among the natives.[50] Primo de Rivera accepted his offer of mediation.

On August 4, 1897—accompanied by a manservant and twenty porters who took turns in carrying him in a hammock—he left Manila to look for Emilio Aguinaldo, the supreme head of the revolution. After a circuitous trek of five days, he entered Aguinaldo's headquarters in the remote barrio of Biyak-na-Bato in San Miguel, Bulacan, where he began talks with Aguinaldo on terms for peace.[51] He was well-received although, General Artemio Ricarte reports, there was a tense moment when at an inopportune remark by Paterno that "he did not wish to take part in any rebellious act as that would lead the country not to progress but to certain ruin," Aguinaldo reportedly shouted back: "You who, with your superior education, should be guides to us blind ones who gladly struggle to reconquer the liberty of the land, are the ones who put most obstacles in the way and are the worst enemies of the insurrection." Feeling his pride injured, Paterno bluffed in the same tone, saying: "Before you had conceived your idea, we had already done so; before you took up arms, we had already taken them up; but we were unsuccessful and you, too, will not succeed if you continue in your weak efforts."[52] Paterno was led out of the room to prevent the situation from turning violent and Paterno and Aguinaldo were shortly reconciled. There were rumors in Manila that he had been taken prisoner and that Aguinaldo had been deposed because of internal dissension.

In the next three months, Paterno held meetings in his house in Manila and shuttled between the city and surrounding provinces, visiting Biyak-na-Bato several times, contacting revolutionary chiefs in central and southern Luzon, using appeals to patriotism—even bribery and cajolery—to hammer out a peace agreement. Paterno doggedly pursued a settlement in the field even though his wife, Luisa, was gravely ill at the time. She died on November 27, 1897.

Through his efforts, the Pact of Biyak-na-Bato was signed on December 14–15, 1897, and, on Christmas Day, Aguinaldo officially proclaimed an end to the revolution. As part of the agreement, Aguinaldo and selected revolutionary leaders left Biyak-na-Bato for the port of Sual (Dagupan) where, to the cheers of local residents, they sailed to exile in Hong Kong on December 27. Paterno accompanied the group and returned to Manila on January 11.

The end of the war was marked in Manila by concerts, theatrical performances, regattas and horse races, and fireworks from January 30 to February 2, capped by a grand reception at the *Palacio del Ayuntamiento*.[53] Though the diversions enthralled Manilans it was, above all, an orgy of Spanish self-congratulation. The celebration was a proud moment in Paterno's career. Whether motivated by a desire for fame or a genuine love for both "homeland" and "motherland," he had claimed the unique role of "speaking for" both Spain and the Philippines. In his 1910 account of the negotiations, Paterno wrote with customary flourish: "I ask for nothing and hope for nothing; perhaps a spray of sampaguitas for my grave, a smile from my sweet country." Capping his valedictory, he adds: "And let my corpse be enshrouded with the flag, that same flag, thrice holy, which I have kissed a thousand times with my lips."[54] (What flag Paterno had in mind is conveniently vague.) Primo de Rivera was contemptuous and condescending, saying that Paterno was out to gain "notoriety and honors."[55]

Flushed with success, Paterno (so it was later revealed) sent a confidential letter on February 23, 1898, to Miguel Primo de Rivera, the governor-general's nephew, seeking his intercession with the Spanish Cortes for remuneration for Paterno's services as peacemaker.[56] Having heard that he was to be given a Spanish title for his services, Paterno wrote that he would not accept a petty title that would only make him a "laughing-stock" in a place as "materialistic and mercantile" as Manila. He set forth his desire that (1) belonging as he does to "the family of the *Maguinoong* Paterno," he would not settle for a title less than that of a *Duke* "because the natives have obeyed me as the great Maguinoo or Prince of Luzon (*gran Maguinoo o Principe de Luzon*), and the ex-revolutionists call me the arbiter of their destinies"; (2) that he wished to be made "Grandee of Spain of the First Class" with the right to a seat in the Spanish Senate "to defend the interests of the Colony" (adding that he qualifies for the said post as he can show that he possesses an income of $25,000 "and more if necessary"); (3) that these honors must come in the nature of a gift and not a purchase; and (4) that his services as pact maker must be properly valued in [Mexican] dollars (he cites the sum of $1,000,000 in a postscript), saying that anything less would expose him to contempt from a public that knows of the liberality with which he dispenses his wealth. He mentions in this connection that he distributed with "abundant profusion pecuniary and material recompenses to buy over the wills and unite all the insurgent chiefs to bring them to surrender to Spain."

> . . . I, who, amidst inundations and hurricanes have assaulted and conquered the barracks and military posts of the enemy, causing them to lay down their arms to Spain without bloodshed and at my command surrender all their chiefs and revolutionary Government with their brigades and companies, I think I have good right to ask Spain, if she wishes to show herself a mother to me, to give me as much as she has given to other sons for lesser services.[57]

This shamelessly self-serving letter (in which he also recommends that his brother Maximino be named *Count*) was published by governor-general Primo de Rivera in 1898 and picked up by other writers. Ignored by the Spanish authorities, the letter exposed Paterno to ridicule. Yet his petition, while shameless, was not wholly unreal. Creating novel titles named after places in the empire was a practice started by Carlos III as boon to loyal subjects. Between 1761 and 1897, eight titles of nobility were in fact awarded based on Philippine achievements and place names, including one to the Philippine Creole poet Luis Rodriguez Varela who was named *Conde Filipino* in 1795. None, however, had been given to an indio or mestizo.[58] In asking for a title, Paterno was thinking of other precedents: the titles of "Prince of Peace" given to Manuel Godoy for his intervention in the Peace of Basilea and "Duke of Victory" and "Prince of Vergara" given to Baldomero Espartero for ending the Carlist War with the Treaty of Vergara in 1839. Paterno's petition, however, was taken either as proof of monumental naivete or a case of calculating self-aggrandizement.

After the initial euphoria over the restoration of peace, there was a lot of bad blood over the terms and implementation of the Pact of Biyak-na-Bato. There were controversies over reforms allegedly promised and the disposition of money payments. Speaking of these events in 1899, T.H. Pardo de Tavera criticized Paterno for being dishonest and manipulative, glossing the relative strength of Spanish and Filipino forces depending on who he was talking to and telling the Spaniards that the Filipinos wanted a financial settlement bigger than what was actually demanded. Paterno always inflated his own role and, Pardo suggests, may have pocketed some of the money.[59]

We have no information on Paterno's response to the publication of his letter to Miguel Primo de Rivera but, as subsequent events show, Paterno survived the damage to his reputation.

When the Spanish-American War broke out, the besieged colonial government tried to rally Filipinos to Spain's defense. Paterno was named president of the *Asamblea Consultiva* (Consultative Assembly), a body of leading conservatives that governor-general Basilio Augustin convoked on May 28, 1898, four weeks after the Spanish debacle on Manila Bay. Three days later, Paterno issued a manifesto, *Al Pais*, in which he warned Filipinos that the United States would parcelize and sell the Philippines to the British, Germans, French, Russians, or Chinese. He rallied local support for Spain, invoking the historic ties of Spain and the Philippines and raising the promise of Filipino "home rule." Congenitally self-referring, Paterno spoke of his own patriotism and sacrifices for peace and called his proposals "the result of study and political experience."[60] With Spain *in extremis*, Paterno saw that the only way to muster Filipino support was to push for "home rule" under Spanish sovereignty. He led a delegation to discuss reforms with Augustin on June 13 and drafted a

Philippine autonomy plan that was issued on June 19 from the office of the governor-general.

The appeal came too late and Paterno grandly overestimated his influence. His scheme of autonomy was unrealistic (American historian John Taylor writes), "a bit of molten glass [that] expands under the breath of a skillful blower into a glowing and iridescent bubble."[61] In a sharp response from Cavite on June 9, the revolutionaries ridiculed Paterno's patriotism. They chided him as an unworthy son to his father, a "virtuous grand old man" who suffered exile for the national cause. They reminded everyone that Paterno had made no sacrifices but led an easy life in Spain "by dint of lavish expenditure," that his "honors" were no gain to the country, and that he bungled the Pact of Biyak-na-Bato.[62]

The Consultative Assembly was dissolved after just one or two meetings as the local elite began to defect to Aguinaldo. As his plans for an orderly transition collapsed, Paterno explored other alliances. He joined prominent Manilans in an association called *Club Independiente*, organized after the Spanish debacle in Manila Bay as a patriotic forum for local opinion on the fast-developing events. (The club helped mount the first civic commemoration of Rizal's death on December 30, 1898, the first "Rizal Day." Dissolved at the outbreak of the Filipino-American War, it reemerged to become the forerunner of today's Club Filipino.)[63]

Events were moving too fast for Paterno. The empire on which he had lavished fulsome praise was disintegrating.

ON A WET AND GLOOMY DAY in August 1898, U.S. troops entered and seized Manila. The city had been blockaded for weeks by an uneasy alliance of Filipino and American forces. Unknown to Filipinos, secret negotiations had taken place between the Americans, under Commodore George Dewey and General Wesley Merritt, and Spanish governor-general Fermin Jaudenes for the surrender of the city to the United States after a mock battle meant to salvage Spanish honor and, more important, keep the Filipino revolutionaries out of the city. Thus, on August 13, the Stars and Stripes was raised over Fort Santiago, signaling the beginning of U.S. occupation.

Paterno was forced to cast his lot with the revolutionaries. He had little choice. The Spanish government to which he had sworn allegiance had been terminated and Paterno was not one who would stay outside the center of events. A journalist at the time wrote that Paterno had learned that a Filipino national congress was to be convened and who better to preside over it but he, Paterno?[64]

Around August 19, with a group that included Antonio Luna, Felipe Calderon, and Leon Guerrero, Paterno crossed over from Manila to Cavite to confer with Aguinaldo. Though he was a late-joiner and avowed *Hispanista*, and despite questions over his role in the treaty of Biyak-na-Bato, such was Aguinaldo's need for a "respectable" national front that, on September 4, 1898, Aguinaldo appointed him to the Revolutionary Congress that was convened in Malolos on September 15.

In the inaugural session, Paterno was elected president of the Congress, winning over rival Antonio Luna. Paterno presided over the assembly, dazzled Aguinaldo with his martial oratory, and organized lavish social events aimed at creating for the Republic an aura of pomp and circumstance. He founded the republican organs *La Republica Filipina* (1898–1899) and *Gaceta de Filipinas* (1899), and played an active role in framing the Malolos Constitution. In the session on September 29 that ratified Philippine Independence, Paterno declared:

> We are laying today the foundation of a new political order in our country. This day is a beacon light on the eternal path of the centuries. It marks the separation of our past from our future. A past, the era of cruelty, of chicanery, of slavery, has ended. We are to rewrite the history of the Philippines. Today we are inditing the first page; and you all know that the golden age is not gone; it is not behind us; it is before us, in the future.[65]

Paterno's bravado did not completely mask the fact that just three months earlier he had avidly campaigned for the preservation of Spanish sovereignty in the islands.

From its inception, the Malolos government was riven with tensions between conservative plutocrats led by Paterno and militant elements represented by Apolinario Mabini, Aguinaldo's adviser and premier of the Cabinet. There were fierce disagreements on issues like the constitution, the relative powers of the executive and legislative branches of government, and the management of the Treasury. Mabini judged that it was the intent of Paterno and his allies to control Aguinaldo and the government. He despised the opportunism of the Manila elite and wrote that "Congress would be capable of even hanging itself if the clique of Paterno will be in the majority."

> Paterno and [Felipe] Buencamino are after honors in their plans and want to appear the idol of the people. But they are pliant (*malalambot ang ilong*), easily frightened, and cannot endure pains and the heat of the sun. That is why they immediately rush to the shade of a robust tree.[66]

Indeed, as U.S. military action intensified, Paterno pushed for conciliation with the Americans. He called for a policy of diplomacy (as he did in Biyak-na-Bato) and tried to rally support for a limited goal of autonomy (as he did in the negotiations with Augustin), this time under U.S. protection. When this was vigorously opposed by Mabini, Paterno and the "capitulationists" maneuvered to have Aguinaldo dissolve the Mabini Cabinet and replace it with a Paterno-led "peace Cabinet" on May 8, 1899. Sometime in May, Paterno sent an emissary to the Schurman Commission with a copy of the "Autonomy Plan" he drafted for the Spanish government on June 19, 1898. Paterno's message to the Americans was that republican leaders were ready to drop the idea of independence and make peace on the basis of Filipino "home rule" under U.S. sovereignty.[67]

Paterno's mood at this time is expressed in a letter he wrote to his brothers and sisters in which he voiced confidence that a settlement with the Americans was imminent. "I shall soon rest in Manila," he said.

> After a month's fight, I have been forced to take over the reins of the government by reason of patriotism; it is impossible to have peace with Mabini; and in order to come to an end it was necessary to have my presence in the Council of Ministers. There is much probability, almost certainty, that we are going to have peace with the Americans.[68]

Paterno's takeover so infuriated General Antonio Luna that he ordered Paterno and his allies in the Cabinet arrested. Though Paterno was not jailed, the conflict between Luna and the Paterno Cabinet was one of the events that precipitated Luna's assassination on June 5, 1899. In the meantime, negotiations for an agreement with the Schurman Commission failed to gain support from either republican leaders or the Americans. Boxed into the role he had taken in the Aguinaldo government, Paterno was forced to issue a manifesto on June 2, 1899, urging the people to pursue the war against the Americans.[69] But, as Pardo de Tavera confided to a friend on October 3, 1899, Paterno's display of intransigence was just show; in truth he sorely wanted to return to Manila.[70]

The war was not going well. The Aguinaldo government retreated northwards as the Americans advanced. Fleeing with other leaders, Paterno sought refuge in Benguet under the protection of the powerful Cariño family of Baguio. The Americans tried to get him to surrender through the mediation of German scientist and Baguio resident Otto Scheerer, who knew Paterno, but negotiations broke off as Scheerer himself fell under suspicion as an insurgent sympathizer. On March 2, 1900, Paterno sent out surrender feelers but before a surrender could be effected, he was captured on April 25 when soldiers of the 48th U.S. Infantry surrounded the house where he was convalescing in Antamok. (There were rumors, probably malicious, that he was captured disguised as a female Igorot servant and had been brought back to Manila "at the point of death.") Paterno was detained in the police station on Anda Street in Intramuros, along with Felipe Buencamino and other political prisoners.[71]

Around this time he wrote a personal testament worth quoting at length for what it reveals of Paterno's mind and personality. Addressed to U.S. authorities, the document is a self-interested presentation of Paterno's political sympathies. Paterno begins by tracing his privileged lineage and formative years in Spain:[72]

> Being possessed of ample income, I could afford to gratify my every taste in literary and artistic pursuits, and was soon upon terms of the closest intimacy and friendship with all the great men of that period in Madrid. My salon was a place of reunion for the brightest lights in politics, in literature, in art, in science, and religion. And the very foremost among this number was Emilio Castelar, to my mind, first and last, the greatest of all Spain's great men. He was my friend and counselor, and from him I drew all the best inspirations of my youth.

From this environment, while in Madrid, I drew the very best inspirations for my own works, and there I imbibed a social and moral philosophy which has shaped the ends of my subsequent life. If I have attained any eminence in the field of letters, whatever success that may spell, I must attribute to the impressions instilled in me in those golden days of intellectual companionship in dear old Madrid.

Depicting himself as a man of principle thrust into the center of events, he narrates his relations with Rizal and the role he played in the revolution and the war against the Americans.

From Madrid I returned to the Philippines toward the end of 1882, being then brought in contact for the first time with Dr. Rizal, to whom I gave letters of introduction to Señor Sagasta Moret [sic], the present prime minister, [Fernando de] Leon y Castillo, now the Spanish minister at Paris, and to numerous others. Rizal was extremely radical in his views, and to him my unfailing text was moderation, my best judgment being always to avoid the extremes of demagogy and cultivate a spirit of conservatism. Rizal, in opposition to my repeated counsels, at this time wrote his famous work "Noli me tangere," and had openly proclaimed therein many opinions set forth by myself in a work written by me some little time previously, "Ninay"—and which opinions I had, upon mature consideration, deemed it best to suppress. These expressions of view were distinctly not favorable to the methods of the Religious Orders and to a further continuance of their presence in the Philippines. Subsequent to this, in 1891, and again contrary to my advice, Rizal returned to Manila, and shortly thereafter, at the instigation of the friars, was imprisoned by the authorities and deported to Dapitan . . .

I myself was in no little danger at this time, as Archbishop Nozaleda and the friars generally were clamoring for my execution likewise, upon the ground that I was the real arch-plotter and Rizal the tool. They accused me to [Ramon] Blanco[,] [Camilo] Polavieja and [Fernando] Primo de Rivera as being a "filibuster" and the head of all the insurrectionists and revolutionists in the country, but these charges had no weight with the Spanish commanders, the latter having known me in Spain and also in the Philippines, and being thoroughly familiar with my life, belief, and theories.

And not only they, but all my friends in Spain likewise, defended me, well knowing that I had never been a revolutionist, and that whatever ideas I had held in regard to reform for the Philippines had been consistently proclaimed before the Spanish Government, in the broad light of day; and in consequence all these false accusations proved futile to harm me.

The revolution broke out, and the Spanish Governor Rivera endeavored, first through himself and General Polavieja, then through the Jesuits, and finally through the medium of the Spanish Casino, by its president, Don Rafael Comenge, to pacify and bring to terms the insurgents; but all attempts in this direction were abortive. Then Rivera confided the mission to me; and, in August 1897, I started out on a quest from mountain to mountain, and through forest after forest, to seek out and meet for the first time Aguinaldo and his followers, none of whom I had ever seen or had any dealings with. I managed, by good fortune, not only to find, but to triumph. It was only after five months' effort, but finally I did succeed in inducing them to consent to a peace, notwithstanding their repeated declarations that they would prefer to die rather than to ever consent to a surrender of any kind; and the result was that, in January 1898, the treaty of peace of Biac-na-Bato was signed.

This peace was maintained until the declaration of war by the United States in April 1898. Then followed the events of the American occupation. On September 29, 1898, the Ratification of Filipino Independence was proclaimed at Malolos and I was elected president of the Congress. The Constitution of the Philippines was drafted and the Filipino Republic was proclaimed in January 1899. I was empowered by a meeting of the Congress held in San Isidro to propose to General [Elwell] Otis a plan of Filipino autonomy, under an American protectorate, in order to put an end to the war, but was prevented by General Luna from coming to Manila to undertake the negotiations. I was then named president of the Council of Ministers by Aguinaldo, and sent as one of the commission presided over by Señor [Gracio] Gonzaga, and among whose members was General [Jose] Alejandrino, to confer with General Otis in reference to this matter, but there was no result; and I retired to the mountains of Benguet, where I was concealed from the Americans, and the war followed.

Editing the events, Paterno simultaneously builds up his preeminence as well as innocence. He reinvents and embellishes his political views in a way that aligns him with the new order. Claiming he had long foreseen the ascendancy of the United States, he endorses its claim to power.

I wish to say, in conclusion, that I have never been an *insurrecto*. I have always believed in reform by evolution—never by revolution. I was never in insurrection against Spain, believing as I do that fidelity to those at whose hands benefits have been received is a simple due on the part of those who have received; and having received my education, and whatever it may have done for me, from Spain, I could never have turned on her, my alma mater. I would have been faithful to and followed her to the end, accepting, had she seen fit to grant it, independence at her hands and under her protection. Likewise, and in accordance with my life-long principles, do I feel toward the American Republic.

In 1883–1884, in a tour of the world, comprising China, Japan, Europe, and the United States, I visited and spent some time in all of the larger cities of the Republic: San Francisco, from which point I visited the wonders of the greatest of valleys—the Yosemite— and the giant redwood trees, Salt Lake City, Chicago, New York, Boston, Washington, Baltimore, Richmond, Virginia, Philadelphia, and in fact the principal centers. I had also the pleasure of marveling at that most colossal of structures, the Brooklyn Bridge.

But in the midst of the vastness, the bustle and activity that I encountered upon every hand, and in spite of my enthusiasm, there ever lurked in my mind a sense of something lacking. In my hours of rest I was always seeking the "gusts of time," something old, antique, and time-worn—something to call to mind that to which all my life I had been accustomed in the cities of Europe, the only one which I had hitherto known. Impossible not to be amazed at the striking evidences of physical and mental progress on every hand, visible to the same extent and degree in no other part of the globe;

but, in spite of it all, I was ever seeking the antique ideal, the illusion and poesy of the past, the glamour of the olden time. For to me olden time has always seemed the most poetical. I perceived, however, that the practical advantages more than compensated; that, in America, Christianity was a practical reality—something I had never seen nor known in Rome nor elsewhere; that right was realized in practice; that liberty was fulfilled in practice; political ideals, which had been considered the grandest in theory, realized in practice in America; that things which would be considered the most radical and subversive in any other part of the world were, in America, the most advanced and the most matter of course, what in the Old World might appear the most "unrealizable" was to be found in its most realizable perfection in the United States.

As I said to Emilio Castelar and friends in Spain in 1880: "The history of the oceans is the history of civilization: as the waters of the Mediterranean Sea bear in their depths the reflection of the civilization of ancient Greece and Rome, as the great Atlantic Ocean has long typified the progress of modern times, so shall the still vaster Pacific witness and exemplify the irresistible onward and upward advance of the future. For on her waters shall meet the greatest nations of the earth and the most powerful engines of war; Russia, China, Japan, the United States, Great Britain and the continental powers. Filipinas is weak, but she is the key to the circumnavigation of the globe—a powerful factor in all the coming conflict."

They termed me the "child prophet," but the prophet was not then in his own country. The Philippines are weak, I then told them, but they are the key to the coming kingdom. Shall you be found strong enough to hold that key? I did not believe so, and my belief at that time was that the eventual destiny of the Philippines was to lie between Great Britain and the United States with the greater chances in favor of the United States, the latter being the daughter growing up and Great Britain, the mother, already advancing in age.

Paterno's brazen, self-dramatizing presentation of his life and thoughts—at once mendicant and vain—did not impress the Americans. John Bancroft Devins, the American newspaper editor who published the document in 1905, wrote: "Señor Paterno, as the sketch shows, is not the victim of undue modesty. It is not fair to infer from this estimate, however, that all Filipinos are egotists, but it illustrates the danger of educating natives in a new environment."[73]

THE MONTHS THAT FOLLOWED his capture in Antamok proved to be a hectic time for Paterno. Around mid-June, General Arthur MacArthur, military governor of the Philippines, allowed him to leave the Anda Street jail, returning only at night for confinement, to help the newly released Felipe Buencamino in drumming up public support for U.S. pacification efforts.[74]

Buencamino and Paterno went into a series of discussions with prominent Manilans and formed *Comision de la Paz*, a citizens' commission to help effect peace with the Americans (with Paterno as head and Buencamino, Leon Guerrero, Ambrosio Flores, and Maximino Paterno among its members). On June 21, 1900, MacArthur issued a proclamation offering amnesty to all who renounced loyalty to the Republic and swore allegiance to the United States. On this same day, Paterno and Buencamino convened a meeting in Paterno's house on Calle San Sebastian, attended by "about two hundred well-known revolutionists," including thirty men MacArthur had liberated from jail so they could attend the meeting. Among those present were, in addition to Paterno and Buencamino, four ex-members of the Aguinaldo Cabinet.

Agreement was reached at this stormy meeting on terms for peace with the U.S., which included a complete and general amnesty, guarantee of individual rights, the expulsion of foreign religious communities, and the immediate establishment of civil government. These conditions were presented to MacArthur but the military governor did not respond right away either because he was ill at the time (as was reported) or because he judged that drawing out the debate would keep Filipinos from making war. With this delay, however, to quote an American newspaper report:

Paterno sprang his coup d'etat in the form of a most remarkable and impertinent document, without reason, without sequence, without head or tail, which began with quotations from European statesmen like [William] Gladstone, [Helmuth Karl] Von Moltke, etc. Paterno's plan was nothing less than a seditious plea for Philippine independence, and it had a disquieting effect upon the people. It was published simultaneously in all of Manila's Spanish papers, a method of publicity which insured its spread throughout the entire archipelago.[75]

Paterno was reenacting the days of Biyak-na-Bato when he single-handedly brought an end to the war. What he published on June 28—which he also caused to be printed and distributed as a pamphlet entitled *El Problema Politico de Filipinas* (1900)—was a rehashed version of the autonomy plan he submitted to the Spanish government two years earlier.[76] Paterno proposed protectorate status for a "free Filipino state under the direction of the United States of America," one in which the Philippines would enjoy sovereignty in its internal affairs but cede to the United States control of foreign affairs and national security. In typical style, Paterno did not only outline a proposed structure of government but dressed up his plan with citations of international law and political thought and, for good measure, a comparison of the governments of France and the United States.

What must have riled the Americans was his fundamental argument that the Filipinos constituted a "nation" (*nacion*) and had established a "state" (*estado*) when they declared independence on June 12, 1898, and formed their government. For this reason, Filipinos neither recognized the Spanish surrender of Manila to the Americans nor the Treaty of Paris. Thus, Paterno pronounced, it was only through the autonomy plan he was proposing that the war could be brought to an end.

The Americans did not quite know what to make of Paterno—whether to consider him audacious or impertinent, sinister or comical. In enemy-occupied, politically charged Manila, however, Paterno's stock rose as rumors circulated that Paterno had the ear of MacArthur himself and that the United States had conceded to Filipinos all that Paterno demanded. For causing the publication of his protectorate plan, Paterno was sent back to the Anda Street jail and kept incommunicado. Though he was amnestied upon taking the oath of allegiance to the U.S. on July 2, Paterno refused to leave jail, styling himself a political martyr in the cause of independence. He reportedly announced he would not leave jail until every Filipino political prisoner had been set free.

Apparently, playing the jailed martyr did not suit Paterno's character. He was shortly out of jail and, though he had been warned by

MacArthur to stay clear of politics, he continued to confer with other Filipino leaders. His house on Calle San Sebastian became a regular rendezvous for Filipino leaders perturbed by rapidly unfolding events. Then, on July 18, in a meeting at his house, Paterno hatched his plan for a popular festivity to be held on July 28 and 29. Billed as *fiestas de la amnistia*, it would demonstrate the people's gratitude for MacArthur's amnesty proclamation. Recalling the fiesta that celebrated the treaty of Biyak-na-Bato in 1897, Paterno envisioned a citywide celebration featuring triumphal street arches, parades, fireworks, and sporting races.

The Americans granted permission for the festivity with the proviso that nothing of a "political" nature would be carried by the celebration and that it would simply be a public manifestation of gratitude for the U.S. offer of amnesty. Paterno, however, clearly meant to have the festivities drum up public support for his protectorate plan, and there were perhaps others who were interested in conveying more radical messages. The climax of the fiesta was to be a banquet at Teatro Zorrilla to which MacArthur and members of the Taft Commission were invited. Paterno planned on delivering a banquet speech that would call for the "independence of the nation under the protection of the United States." It was a speech aimed (in James LeRoy's sarcastic comment) at "eclipsing all previous Philippine records for oratory."[77]

What followed spooked the Americans. Paterno had advance copies of his speech printed. When MacArthur objected, Paterno allayed the general's fears by telling him: "We will decorate the hall beautifully. Great, big American flags and little Filipino flags!"[78] Yet, pictures of Aguinaldo suddenly materialized on street arches and Philippine flags and pro-protectorate and pro-independence slogans appeared. The U.S. military stepped in and ordered all political symbols removed. There were rumors in the American community that the banquet was a cover for a mass uprising and that the American dinner guests would be murdered.

In the evening of the banquet, Paterno received a letter from William Howard Taft saying that the members of the Commission, having learned that political speeches would be delivered, were not attending the banquet because they did not wish to be a party to the misrepresentation that the U.S. was open to the idea of a protectorate. MacArthur sent a letter scolding Paterno for reneging on his assurances that nothing of a political nature relating to the future form of government be taken up.[79] There was confusion among those gathered at Teatro Zorrilla. Conflicting rumors spread that Taft and the U.S. military had instructed that no speeches were to be delivered, that the banquet should not take place unless a member of the Commission was present, and that the Americans were not attending the affair.

Since the banquet could not commence in the absence of the Americans, Paterno rushed to Taft's residence and "with tears and on bended knee, so to speak," implored Taft to come, promising that there would be no speeches. Taft finally condescended to make an appearance, with commissioner Luke Wright in tow, arriving at the banquet room about 9:30 P.M. to the immense relief of the famished guests who had waited for over two hours. The patriotic after-dinner speeches stayed in their speakers' pockets. The most politic Taft, with Wright, endured the dismal dinner. "They sat through a couple of silent, weary hours, took a few sips of wine, smiled a few smiles, shook a few hands, and then went home."[80]

Reprising his role as peace broker in 1897, Paterno was reliving Biyak-na-Bato in very personal terms. As his wife Luisa died while he was in the thick of truce negotiations in 1897, Don Maximo passed away on July 26 while his son was concocting terms for ending the war in 1900. The tragedy must have lent a particular intensity to Paterno's thoughts at this time. In the speech he was prevented from delivering at the Zorrilla banquet, Paterno addressed Filipinos:

Fear nothing, beloved people, for I have consecrated to you my entire existence. I have defended and will defend your ideals in the fields, upon the mountains, and in the cities,—everywhere. It matters not that I succumb and die, for just as the sun dies as the shades of night fall, to arise again with new heat and splendor on the following morn, so shall I arise again to impart to you all the fire of my new life, all the energies of my new existence. And to thee, beloved country,

"Give me in turn, O Flower of my love,
A grave to sleep among thy flowers."

Let my last glance fall upon thy splendid sky, my last sigh be lost amid the echoes of thy triumph, my body rest in this beloved soil, that my lips may forever kiss it, that my body may feel thy patriotic fire, and my spirit thy immortal nationality.[81]

We do not know what Paterno thought would be accomplished by his speech. He apparently imagined that a stirring valedictory in the style of one about to be executed— a somber reprise of Rizal's *Mi Ultimo Adios*—was both dramatic and appropriate. Sadly, there was a wide gulf between Paterno's visions of himself and realities on the ground.

Americans judged him a caricature of the Machiavellian *politico*, more an irritant than a threat. Reflecting what Taft thought of Paterno, a mocking, bemused Mrs. Taft (to whom Paterno gallantly dedicated an English edition of his *Ninay* in 1907) called him "an unctuous gentleman" who played both sides of the political fence ("carrying water on both shoulders").[82] In private, Taft was quite blunt in his opinion of Paterno. In a letter to Elihu Root on October 21, 1900, he branded Paterno "a great deal of an ass" but added, typically, "he seems to have a good deal of influence in certain circles among the Filipinos. . . . If he is not trusted in any way he may be useful hereafter."[83]

Charles Burke Elliott, an American author, saw Paterno as a reincarnation of the scheming and childishly ostentatious nineteenth-century Spanish minister Manuel Godoy:

His Excellency, Don Pedro Paterno, a distinguished citizen of Manila and Madrid, wearer of the Grand Cross of Isabela the Catholic, suave, resourceful, diplomatic, friend of the people, intimate of Grandees, ready at a moment's notice to furnish a treaty, a drama, an opera, a form of government or a system of philosophy, and, like Godoy, ambitious to win the title of Prince of Peace.[84]

To many, his amnesty banquet was "a Gilbert-and-Sullivan opera," a fiasco that exposed him to public ridicule. Aguinaldo was not amused. He called the amnesty festival "a crime of high treason" and "the greatest act of contempt" for the revolution's goal of independence. Republican leaders still out in the field condemned Paterno as an intriguer and were disgusted over his moves to style himself as the nation's spokesman. Galicano Apacible called the "protectorate" proposal one of Paterno's *paternadas* (a word coined by Paterno's contemporaries to refer to his extravagances). He ridiculed the proposal as a call to "national suicide" and branded Paterno "unbalanced" and "dangerous" because "a great part of our people still respect him and believe in him."[85] Asked for his views on Paterno's festive production, Apolinario Mabini remarked: "Paterno has always distinguished himself for his love of premature fiestas. When he was elected President of the Malolos Congress he occupied himself primarily with the organization of a fiesta he labeled *popular* to celebrate Philippine independence even if it was not yet officially recognized." For occasions like the first anniversary of the Malolos Congress and the baptism of Aguinaldo's daughter, he staged fiestas even when the war was going on, squandering resources badly needed for ammunition, shoes and uniforms for Filipino soldiers. Mabini bitterly remarked that Paterno's *fetes* only resulted in "funerals" and the "decomposition" of the Republic.[86]

It simplifies Paterno's character to reduce his deeds to naked ambition. Part Don Quixote, part Sancho Panza, his actions appear driven by an obtuseness and earnestness that draw from an untroubled belief in his intellectual prowess and the power of symbols. Did he sincerely believe—as his idol Castelar apparently did—that he could free a nation with one speech? Even the historian Teodoro Agoncillo, who casts Paterno as a leading traitor to the revolution, concedes a curious duality in the man's motives.

> There was in him a strange blending of the dreamer and the man of practical affairs, of the poet and the businessman. As a poet, he dreamt of the Philippines as an Olympus where little gods, brown gods and white gods, playfully led happy and quiet lives. As a businessman, he envisaged his country as the stepping stone to his lofty ambition—that of a bemedalled Maguinoo, a Nobleman, to whom the brown gods and the white gods owed their peace and contentment.[87]

THE WAR WAS AT AN END. In the isolated mountains of Isabela, the death of the Republic was sealed with the capture of Aguinaldo on March 23, 1901. There were new rulers in the land who worked out of an ethos that gave less importance to the trappings of tradition as Spain did. The turbulence of the century's turn created an intellectual divide that stranded Paterno despite his efforts to retool himself. Only forty-four years old, the gusts of time were hurrying him into the past rather than the future.

Paterno was back in his home in Santa Cruz. The residence occupied a large section of the block, its spacious, frescoed interiors decorated by chandeliers, velvet curtains, Venetian glass mirrors, oil portraits of family members, and a bronze bust of Paterno done by the Madrid sculptor Mariano Benlliure. An American visitor to the house wrote: "Paterno lived like a duke, even though he failed to receive the title. . . . The Paterno family own large steamships and plantations, and are holders of much real estate. Had the Philippine republic succeeded, the Paternos would have been the Rockefellers of the Archipelago."[88]

In 1902, in recognition of his experience with Philippine exhibitions in Spain, he was named the only Filipino member of the board that laid the preparations for Philippine participation in the 1904 Louisiana Purchase Exposition in St. Louis. In private, the Americans averred that the appointment was made for "effect in the islands."[89] He was consigned to a peripheral role and was not part of the "Honorary Board of Philippine Commissioners" that traveled to St. Louis to showcase before the American public specimens of "intelligent Filipinos."[90] Though Paterno tried to build his influence in the new order, it was clear the Americans were not keen on giving him the prominence he once had. The genial Taft privately sneered at such *hispanophiles* as Paterno and Buencamino as "turncoats of long experience." "They are born politicians, are as ambitious as Satan, and as jealous as possible of each other's preferment."[91]

Paterno kept himself in the public eye with literary and scholarly pursuits. He founded *La Patria* (1902–1903) to support U.S. rule as a *fait accompli*, work for eventual home rule, sustain a feeling of gratitude towards Spain for her civilizing contributions, and foster Roman Catholic unity. He published chapbooks and reprints of his works from what appears to be the family-owned *Imprenta La Republica* in Santa Cruz. He lectured at Liceo de Manila and produced one of the first textbooks on the Philippine system of government under the Americans, *Gobierno Civil de las Islas Filipinas o Manual del Ciudadano Filipino* (1910).[92] He also produced *Synopsis de Historia de los Estados Unidos (Apuntes)* (1909), a textbook compilation of facts about American history from aboriginal times to the present.[93]

As vernacular theater surged in popularity at the turn of the century, Paterno also wrote plays, choosing the eminently aristocratic form, opera. Since he did not write in Tagalog (it is said that he could not even passably speak the language) he had them translated into Tagalog. In August 1902, his play *La Alianza Sonada* (*Sangdugong Panaginip*) was staged in Teatro Zorilla, had a modest run of at least eight performances, and was attended by no less than Governor Taft. Billed as the first original "Filipino opera," the one-act, five-scene play tells of a mythical Muslim invasion of Luzon in the sixteenth century.[94] Uniting to resist the Muslim aggressors—who have demanded women for their harems as tribute from the towns of Pasig, Kainta, and Antipolo—the people enter into a blood compact (*tandaang dugo*) under their leader Lapu. In the course of the resistance, asleep in the cave of the mythical Doña Jeronima, Lapu dreams of seeing a rainbow ("path to paradise") and a constellation of "American stars" (*bituin Americana*), signs of the coming of the United States and the fated union of Filipinos and Americans for the greater glory of "Bathala's country" (*bayan ni Bathala*).

The play telescopes three imagined stages of Tagalog history: the time of Muslim rule, Spanish colonialism, and the "dreamed alliance" with the Americans. Paterno garnishes his libretto with such plot elements as threats of rape and a lovers' death scene that evokes, it is claimed, Wagner's *Tristan und Isolde*. These are, however, of less moment than the play's heavily symbolic vignettes: a Greek-like chorus of deities, mythological creatures, female spirits dancing, characters borne by clouds, the townspeople embracing a representation of the Statue of Liberty, and the joint orchestral renditions of the "Star-Spangled Banner" and the Filipino "Marcha Nacional" played as two women, dressed as "America" and "Filipina," embrace.

The pretentious spectacle combines conventions of the *moro-moro*, local mythology, and French and Italian operas, with a musical repertoire that ranges from European arias to local *balitao* and *kundiman* melodies (including tunes from *La Flor de Manila*, a popular composition by Paterno's sister, Dolores). Paterno himself praises the "Wagnerian" qualities of the music—composed by the Tagalog musician Ladislao Bonus (1854–1908)—which, Paterno says, is "saturated with Italian sentimentalism combined with oriental voluptuosity."[95] In Lapu, Paterno writes himself into the text: a hero whose "intelligence" and "inventions"— cryptic writings on a board and a secret philter for the blood compact—aid the people in their liberation. The play ends with the grand chorus:

> Shine forever, our eternal alliance
> with the Grand Republic of the
> United States of America! Shine
> from an untarnished sky, the great
> constellation of the American stars![96]

This unabashed endorsement of U.S. rule was financed by Paterno. Its gala performance on August 27 was attended by "some 1,500 people," including many Americans led by Taft. It was "well-applauded," so reported Manila's American press. During the intermission, Paterno appeared on stage to present to Taft a large silver and gold vase with the inscription, "To the Honorable Civil Governor of the Philippine Islands, in memory of *Sangdugong Panaguinip*." At the close of the performance, Paterno formally handed to Taft a sack containing the entire receipts of the performance though it is not clear what the money was for.

Paterno went on to stage *Magdapio o Fidelidad Premiada*. While it initially ran into some trouble with American censors, it opened on February 1, 1904, in a performance honoring the man who had succeeded Taft, Luke Wright. Allegorical in the manner of political plays at the time, *Magdapio* introduced a nature mythology of Thunder, Tempest, and Sun gods and sketched an ancient history in which Aetas and Malays fight for the love of a beautiful earth maiden, Magdapio, born out of a cleaved mountain of gold, silver, and other precious metals. Magdapio proves faithful in her love for the Aeta hero by casting herself to the bottom of the lake and is rewarded by the deities with the honor of being called "Pearl of the Orient."

Magdapio appeared at a time when there was public enthusiasm and anxiety on the part of the authorities over anti-U.S. "seditious plays." While the public was primed to read subversive messages in the play (and such messages may have been imagined by Paterno himself), the play was touristic-burlesque rather than political in its effects. It was badly mangled by the Manila press and failed to draw much of an audience. What Paterno may have imagined as an artistic and erudite performance left his audience amused, exasperated, and bored. An American in the audience wrote that people chattered, hissed, and turned rowdy when "a stiff and ungainly ballet of six" degenerated into "a disgusting and silly hoochee-hoochee, done by young women who were egged on by the frantic howls and hoots of the crowd." It was, he said, "the queerest operetta ever perpetrated."[97] The American was not an unbiased reporter but, by all counts, *Magdapio* was a pathetic coda to Paterno's career.

On the political front, Paterno tried to position himself as leader of the conservative opposition to the Federalistas who had become the most influential Filipinos at the time because of their closeness to American officials.[98] Failing in this, Paterno joined the Federal Party but, disappointed at the minor role he had in the group, left it to form in November 1901 *Asociacion de la Paz* as nucleus for a new party. It counted among its leaders Leon Guerrero, Joaquin Luna, Isabelo de los Reyes, Alberto Barretto, Justo Lukban, and Rafael Palma.

In 1902, he ran a vigorous campaign for governor of Rizal Province against former revolutionary general Ambrosio Flores but lost by forty-two votes. He drifted back to the Federalistas but again left and founded *Partido Liberal*, a small group organized in November 1902 and then renamed *Partido Independista* to capitalize on pro-independence sentiments. Locating himself in a middle ground between the Federalistas and the advocates of immediate independence, he joined a new party called *Union Nacional* in 1906 and won a seat in the first Philippine Assembly, representing the first district of Laguna. Paterno made a move for the Speakership of the Assembly but withdrew when he realized he had no chance of winning against the young, highly skilled politician from Cebu, Sergio Osmeña. Even his own partymates did not support his bid. Rafael Palma explains: "[Paterno] was not popular with the new government. His education was too Spanish, his temper, his poor health as well as his activities in the early years of peace made him undesirable to some of the delegates."[99]

He had been an *Hispanista* for so long he could not quite find his place in the new colonial order. Weeks after the opening of the Assembly in 1907, he insinuated himself as a leader of the opposition to Osmeña and the dominant Nacionalista Party by joining others in forming the Liberal Party. It was clear, however, that, since the *fiestas de la amnistia* fiasco of 1900, his political career had gone downhill. Younger, more aggressive politicians had taken over the debating floor of the Assembly. Factional alliances, electoral base-building, realpolitik—instead of intellectual titles, lineage, or Spanish oratory—had become the new instruments of power.

Paterno continued to write Spanish-language novels and plays that did little to enhance his reputation as an intellectual. He no longer did anything as bizarre as *Magdapio*. A more somber Paterno produced a political play entitled *Pagdating ni Taft* to mark the visit of William Howard Taft (now Secretary of War) and a U.S. congressional delegation in August 1905. In the play, a group of Pasig River boatmen (*banqueros*), formerly wealthy *principales* who had fallen on hard times, discuss the problems of the country. Unable to reach a consensus they consult an old sorcerer named Lapu (the hero's name in *Sangdugong Panaginip*) who advises them to keep their peace and cooperate in making Taft's visit a success. Thus, with Lapu's counsel, the boatmen organize groups to present to Taft resolutions asking not only for Philippine independence but such benefits as agricultural banks and a school for the arts.[100]

Quietly taking his place in the new order, Paterno turned towards past accomplishments. He reprinted his works and planned new titles that recycled his theories on ancient Tagalog civilization: *Bathala, el Dios grande y unico del tagalismo, comparado con el Aj, Ra, Brahma y Jehova*; *Los Anitos o santos tagalos*; *Arco iris, camino del Paraiso Tagalo*; *Absolucion de los pecados por el Sonat, obispo de la antigua religion Tagalo*. To the end, Paterno stayed cast in the image of the Victorian gentleman-scholar enchanted by what he had called the antique "gusts of time." Evoking the halcyon days of a surer, more confident Science, he was reported to be at work on books in natural history, *Ornitologia de las orillas del Pasig* and *Las plantas de mi jardin*, and a treatise in astronomy, *Las constelaciones de Manila*.[101]

Eclipsed and in poor health, Paterno died "unloved" on March 11, 1911. His remains were interred in Manila's Cementerio del Norte in ceremonies that did not quite have the pomp of circumstance that surrounded him at the height of his career. The eulogies at his death had to remind the public that he had after all dedicated much of his life to the country and that his virtues "were not few nor his patriotism small." In a tribute, Jaime de Veyra praised him (too generously) as a polymath who surpassed Rizal and Isabelo de los Reyes in the fecundity of his scholarship and the "variety of applications to which he put his talent, energy, and learning."[102] Rafael Palma, however, sounded the ambivalence with which Paterno was regarded when he said on Paterno's death: "Let us forget the errors and weaknesses that, as human, he incurred."[103]

History has not quite forgotten, yet neither has it wholly remembered.

CONJURING A CIVILIZATION

NO ONE READS Pedro Paterno today. Historian John Schumacher dismisses the value of Paterno's writings as scholarship. While he acknowledges Paterno's value as an index to the interest in national identity among late nineteenth-century Filipinos, he finds Paterno's writings overblown, fantastic, and inept. As a prototype of "nationalist history," Schumacher says, Paterno's "eccentric and ingenious lucubrations" on Philippine civilization undermined the national cause. "Reconstructing a Filipino past, however glorious in appearance, on false pretenses can do nothing to build a sense of national identity, much less offer guidance for the present or the future."[104]

Yet, one has to come to terms with Paterno and his work. With contemporaries like Jose Rizal, Gregorio Sanciangco, and T.H. Pardo de Tavera, he stands at the beginning of the history of Filipino scholarship. No matter how flawed, his work in the cultural sciences must be accounted for in any history of Philippine studies. It is part of the archive of our consciousness of being a nation among nations in the world.

PATERNO'S WRITINGS were driven by two impulses: the Renaissance desire in "self-fashioning," the cultivation of the self and image of the erudite gentleman, and the desire to render visible in the world the Philippines as the seat of a distinctive civilization.

Ninay (1885) expresses these impulses. A contrived romance of ill-fated love set in Manila in the 1880s, the novel follows Spanish *costumbrista* tradition in portraying the customs of a place. In a manner not unfamiliar in novels of the period, Paterno weaves into the book a miscellany of information on local geography, natural history, and ethnology in the form of editorial asides, footnotes, and appendices.

A double movement marks the novel's representation of the country: on one hand, a voyeuristic pleasure in the quaint and local; on the other, a universalizing impulse that connects the local to cultural phenomena elsewhere in the world. In copious footnotes, Paterno relates Tagalog family values to ideas in the Hindu *Bhagavata Purana* and the mores of the French nobility; he cites parallels between Filipino and Arab uses of the cinnamon; he compares local pottery and Japanese ceramics; he conjures the magical qualities of the Pasig River by evoking the *apsaras* (nymphs) and *devas* (deities) of the Ganges.[105] The move to document the particular and "universalize" it lies at the heart of Paterno's effort to render the Philippines visible in the world of "civilizations." It is a move at once patriotic as well as self-interested.

Ninay is more *romance*, with its idealization of reality, than *novel*, with the robust social realism that had become its hallmark in Europe at the time Paterno was writing. Unlike Rizal's novels (which it precedes by only a few years), *Ninay* glosses realities of colonial life by subsuming questions of power in a melodrama of fate and chicanery (to the extent of casting a Portuguese as the novel's villain). Paterno's Tagalog society is distilled as an elite of charm, gentility and wealth. It is a society of a distinctly upper-class cast: the Spaniard Don Evaristo and his native wife, their daughter and her suitors, the young and wealthy Don Carlos Mabagsic, and Federico Silveyro, the son of an affluent Portuguese landowner. Even the lowly fugitive Berto is "of a good family." In the novel, the wealthy go on festive excursions to Antipolo in gaily decorated riverboats and carriages, and revel in the Parnassian delights of music, poetry, and good food. Don Evaristo's house is filled with precious vases from Kyoto, fine Philippine ethnic crafts, and rare European books on botany and conchology; his daughter Ninay speaks four languages, paints, and plays the piano; local discourse is decorated with lines from Spanish poets Jose Selgas and Ramon de Campoamor.

Paterno the *auteur* presents himself as an exemplar of the culture he depicts. He annotates his text with citations of the travel accounts of Antoine Francois Prevost and ornithological studies of John Edward Gray. An episode in the novel where the hero is marooned in the company of a tribe on an exotic and indeterminate island occasions comparative notes on India and Africa and esoteric topics like music and costume, culled from European authors like Auguste Racinet, Louis Ferdinand Maury, and Francois-Joseph Fetis. Paterno's exotic island episode seems inspired by late eighteenth-century European travel writing on the Pacific (Denis Diderot's 1772 *Supplement au Voyage de Bougainville*, for instance) rather than a personal knowledge of local geography.

Paterno positions himself outside his subject. He does this by layering the narrative, choosing as his first-person narrator someone who has returned to the country after years of absence and framing Ninay's story as a narrative told by a local informant on the occasion of a nine-night wake (*pasiam*). More important, the "outsideness" is shown in Paterno's bookish annotations. Virtually all his annotations on Philippine life are extracts from European authors, from observations on local religion by the missionaries Juan Francisco de San Antonio and Juan de la Concepcion, to data on geography and botany from Manuel Blanco, Manuel Buzeta and Felipe Bravo, to the observations of authors like Paul de la Gironiere and Fedor Jagor.

Writing in Spanish in Spain for Spaniards, Paterno objectified the Philippines. This was not an exceptional move. *Ninay* was not too different in its exoticizing "outside" stance from the *novelas de costumbres* published by Spaniards in the Philippines at the time. Neither was it completely divorced from the proto-nationalism of nineteenth-century Filipino émigrés. Putting the country in the map of European consciousness was central in the discourse of nationality among these émigrés.

While *Ninay*'s novelistic value is slight and its author's show of erudition superfluous and exhibitionary, the book embodied the spirit of early nationalism. Against a background of racist, colonialist denigrations of Filipino culture, Paterno claims for it distinctness, comparability with other cultures in the world, and a dynamic history antedating Spanish colonialism. In an appendix on the state of the Philippines at Spanish contact (desultorily thrown in with appendices on the history of the Virgin of Antipolo, the ancient mourning custom of *pasiam*, and the art of dance in India), Paterno sketches a pre-Spanish society dynamized by migrations and cultural infusions from Arab, Chinese, and Japanese civilizations. As with his other writings, however, Paterno's patriotism is forged in the medium of his own personal ambition.

After *Ninay*, Paterno produced a series of ethnological treatises on what he called "ancient Tagalog civilization." He was concerned, he says, by his having read in works on the Philippines many errors copied and repeated as incontrovertible truths. While he does not presume to be "omniscient or infallible," he has taken up the pen to help writers "of good faith" to set the accounts of his country straight.[106] He writes that from the time he was a student in Salamanca, studying theology under the Jesuits, he had always been intrigued by correspondences between indigenous Tagalog concepts and Christian theological themes. This inspired him to "assiduously discover hidden facets of history, which illumined by recent data in ethnography, philosophy and sociology, tend to crystallize my sincere opinions that Buddhism once dominated the Archipelago and that its horizons were brightened by the brilliancy of the first rays of Christianity, much earlier than the Spanish conquest."[107]

Antigua Civilizacion Tagalog (1887) outlines a broad evolutionary framework in which the history of the Philippines—or what Paterno calls *las islas Luzonicas*—is divided into "mythological" and "historical" periods, with the latter subdivided into the three epochs of the *aborigines, civilizacion tagala*, and *civilizacion catolica*. Through these stages, the interrelated development of religion, morality, law, and social organization in the archipelago followed a universal, unilineal process of evolution. "All societies passed through a period of primitive barbarism before they advanced to that of civilization. The Luzonic isles, in the same manner as Spain, England, and Germany, gradually evolved from one period to the next."[108]

Paterno sketches the "aboriginal" period by describing the racial, social, and moral character of the *Itas* (*Ayta*; people the Spaniards called *Negrito*), the archipelago's "first inhabitants." A "race of pure blood," nomadic and isolated, Itas led a static, primitive existence since races that do not mix (*mezcla*) degenerate in time and disappear. It is in the

46

mixture of races that a people becomes robust and powerful (*robustas y poderosas*) as in the case of "the Spanish, French, German, English; in general, those of the occidental nations of Europe."[109] Driven to the mountains by peoples of a more "robust complexion" and "a higher grade of culture," these aborigines are close to extinction though their beliefs, by dint of "oriental tenacity" (*caracter oriental de tenacidad*), have survived in the present.

Paterno characterizes aboriginal religion, the *doctrina de los Nonos* ("doctrine of the Ancestors"), through a catalogue of myths and superstitions extracted from Spanish histories and missionary accounts. He pastes together this material scrapbook-style, presenting the data with little analysis or comment. Where he comments, he does so to point out parallels with culture traits in other parts of the world. On ancient "tree-worship," for instance, he says that the *balete* (the local name given to various species of *Ficus*) is a dwelling place of the gods as Olympus is to the Greeks and Mt. Fuji to the Japanese. The worship of *nonos* in the balete is an example, Paterno says, of animist beliefs found among prehistoric and "backward" (*atrazados*) peoples in Europe, Africa, Asia, and America. The native veneration of the crocodile has Egyptian analogues and can be traced back to the "Turanian mode" of seeing the world (alluding to the Ural-Altaic nomads who antedated the Aryans in Europe and Asia).

In describing the archipelago's aboriginal culture, Paterno argues that the Philippines (*Luzonica*) evolved out of a matrix common to all civilizations. More important, he sets the ground for the emergence of his primary object: the "Tagalog civilization" that began with the arrival of the Malays, Chinese, Japanese, and *Musulmanes* (Muslims, Arabs) and ended with the coming of the Spaniards, who inaugurated the "third epoch" by bringing to the islands knowledge of "the true God."

Discussing Tagalog religion, for which he invents the terms *Tagalismo* or *Bathalismo*, Paterno shifts to a more polemical mode. He suggests that the religion of *Bathalismo* can no longer be appreciated in its fullness but seen only in its traces. Raising a theme that would be popular in early nationalist writings, he says that the destruction by the missionaries of native idols and shrines may have destroyed arcane inscriptions and symbols such as found in other parts of the world. Hence, European chroniclers have mistakenly characterized the *indio* as "a savage without beliefs, without God, and without religion." To counter this misrepresentation, Paterno says, he has taken up the task of rescuing from oblivion the "luminous ideas" of Tagalog religion, the lost *codice tagalo* of the ancestors.

Paterno engages in philosophical and philological speculation in claiming for Tagalog religion the basic ideas of the world's "great religions." Tagalogs are neither idolaters nor pantheists; they are monotheists possessed of sublime moral and theological ideas. In certain respects, he asserts, Tagalismo is even superior to other religions in the world. He illustrates with an extravagant deconstruction of the Tagalog word for God, *Bathala*, a word so sacred (he says) the natives pronounce it only in the most solemn moments (thus occasioning the outsider's error that Tagalogs either have no God or many). He breaks down the word to its constituent syllables and scriptological marks, reading into them the semantic plenitude of the Tagalog conception of God.[110] He interprets for instance ◯〇Ꞇ (*BHL* or *BaHaLa*) as ideographic signs for the concepts of totality, providence, spirituality, and the generative union of Man and Woman in the Spirit of God. Working out of such kind of philological "evidence," Paterno constructs a fairly coherent, if sketchy and impressionistic, metaphysics of Tagalismo in which such symbols as the sun (*arao*), sky (*langit*), rainbow (*balangao*), and entities like *Lauon* ("the ancient") and *anitos* (good spirits), are ways into the believer's immersion in "the immensity of *Bathala*."

Paterno's definition of the core ideas of Tagalismo is impelled by the desire to connect indigenous religious beliefs to world religions with their elaborately articulated doctrines, standards of morality, and claims to universality. He sketches parallels between Tagalismo and such religions as Brahmanism, Buddhism, Taoism, Shintoism, Zoroastrianism, and Christianity. His method is to select and interpret practices and ideas in these religions (reincarnation, cult of saints, Heaven and Hell, immortality of the soul, existence of one God) and then cite resemblances or similarities (*semejanza o identidad*) in Tagalismo.

Paterno claims for the Philippines a long history embedded in the evolutionary progress of mankind. Tagalismo developed out of earlier civilizations and, like other religions, underwent stages of incubation (*incubacion*), infancy, and youth in its development. Paterno acknowledges that idolatry still exists in the country, that there are errors, "backwardness and confusion" as would be expected in the history of any religion. There are differences in the practice of city and country and across social classes. "Each human society is like an army that has its vanguard and rearguard, between whom march the mass of the army." But he says, "Tagalismo, in its doctrine and practices, in religion as in civic life, represents a genuine advance."[111]

In the second half of *Antigua Civilizacion*, Paterno turns to the moral and political features of Tagalog society. His sources range through the published works of missionaries (like Gaspar de San Agustin and Juan de Plasencia), colonial officials (Antonio de Morga, Sinibaldo de Mas), and travelers (Alfred Marche, Juan Alvarez Guerra). From this material he builds his picture of the archipelago. The Philippines, he says, was once part of a single land mass—which he vaguely refers to as an *imperio*—before ancient cataclysms fragmented it into many islands and dispersed its population into many races confounded by successive migrations and invasions. An "ancient civilization," however, has been conserved in a *nacion tagala* encompassing what is now Luzon and Visayas. This realm is divided into little states (*estados*) called barangay, each with its king (*hari*) and a powerful "aristocracy of *Principes* or *Maguinoo*." These petty states, however, failed to unite into a single political unit and thus fell prey to Mohammedan and Spanish invasions.

Tagalog society was divided into three social formations: *mahaldicas* (nobles), *timauas* (freemen, *plebeyos*), and *alipin* (servants, *siervos*). At the apex were the king and the *maguinoos* who constituted an aristocracy internally differentiated in rank or title (such as that of *Gat*, a "grand duke" or "first lord"). This aristocracy was governed by elevated principles of equality, liberty, and hierarchy. It was not a hereditary caste but a status merited through service, bravery, virtue, and wealth. The *maguinoo* class, Paterno boasts, does not only favorably compare with aristocracies "in Persia, Italy, England, and France" but has imbibed "luminous ideas" of a chivalric and martial nobility that came from China and Japan and "reverberated splendidly in Luzonic soil."[112] Tagalog society, Paterno concludes, is an aristocracy rather than a monarchy or democracy. The *masas populares* are lacking in understanding, driven by instinct and passion, while the king is mortal and subject to prejudice and whim. It is the aristocracy that provides society with its fulcrum and guide.

Tagalog society was a *moral* society governed by custom and law. Women enjoyed respect and equality. Prostitution, concubinage, and licentious sexual conduct are unknown in "ancient times" and, where found, are later influences from the "Asiatic continent."[113] Contrary to what Spanish observers have said, slavery (*esclavitud*) does not exist in the Philippines. What has been mistaken for slavery, Paterno says, is a complex system of servitude (*servidumbre*) made up of two principal categories, *alipin* (*siervos*) and *alila* (*criados*), further subdivided into various kinds according to the rights enjoyed, services or goods owed to lords, and conditions under which a person enters or leaves servitude.

Following categories in European ethnologies of the time, the rest of the treatise takes up marriage practices, inheritance and succession rules, dispute settlement, mourning customs, dress, and a miscellany of other items. Underlying this presentation is Paterno's basic argument that Tagalog culture is characterized by what makes for a civilized society, principles of structure, norms, and rules.

FOR PEDRO PATERNO, Christianity represents the most advanced stage in the history of religion. This assumption drives his claim that Tagalismo partakes of the character of a high religion on the basis of the features of Christianity found in it. What European observers have mistaken for idolatry, he says, are in fact Christian or proto-Christian beliefs and practices. The native *anito* (ancestral spirits that mediate between the people and *Lauon*, the Eternal) are equivalents of Christian saints. The functional diversity of anitos parallels the specialized powers attributed to Christian saints, as in the protective efficacies of San Roque for cholera, Sta. Barbara for thunder, or Sta. Lucia for blindness. Local veneration of such phenomena as the balete tree, rainbow, and sun is in the order of Catholic reverence for such sacred relics as wax figurines, crosses, triangles, and images of saints.

Paterno draws other parallels between Christian and Tagalog practices. The institution of priesthood, and such functions as ordination, confession, and remission of sins, has its Tagalog analogue in the *Sonat* (the "bishop" who ordains priests), *catalonan* (priest), and *pangatahoan* (seer). Tagalogs did not only have the *sibi* or impermanent oratories mentioned by missionaries, they had for "churches" caves in rocky promontories and high mountains, places expressive of mystery and eternity. Christian ideas

50

of church and sacrifice are inscribed in the Tagalog words *simba* (sacrifice) and *simbahan* (place of sacrifice and adoration). If, Paterno continues, Tagalogs did not have pictures or images of God it is because, like Shinto believers, they consider the divine too majestic to be rendered in material form. (Elsewhere, however, he says that the Catholic *estampa* and *imagen* have their counterparts in the native *licha* and *larauan*.)

Antigua Civilizacion is more polemical sketch than ethnographic treatise in its source-mining, positional shifts, play on surface resemblances, and bald assertions. Paterno does not even balk at inventing data. He stylistically recounts an Ovidean origin myth he claims to have heard from an "ancient Tagalog" (*nono*):

There was once a beautiful youth named Daga who so loved the Sun she consecrated her virginity to it. One hot day, she bathed in a secluded spring and then rested in the canebrake where she fell asleep. While she was sleeping, a ray of sun came down and impregnated her and she gave birth to a male child amid the birdsongs of the canebrake.

When she showed the child to her father, the stern parent cast her out of the house and, furious, wrote the sign for male ꜩ (la) in the middle of her name, hence *Dalaga*.

Unable to suckle her child, the girl left him in a bed of thick leaves and white flowers. The white sampaguitas opened their bosom to the infant.

The girl, who had been taken back into her father's house after she was found out to be still a virgin, went back to where she had left the child. But as she held him close to her breast an eagle snatched the child and flew to the mountain peaks.

She fainted with grief. When she awakened she found herself surrounded by spirits and was transported to heaven.

The boy-child grew up in the mountains and, from the age of twelve, started to perform great miracles. He founded a new religion, its doctrines distilled in the idea that God is the "All-Provident, the Providence, *Bathala*."[114]

This foundation myth of *Bathalismo*, Paterno says, recalls myths in India and China and the story of Jesus Christ. He asks: "Was the life of

Jesus already contained (*recogida*) in Hindu and Tagalog traditions, or did the Holy Gospel reach India and Luzon before the coming of the Spaniards?"[115] Elsewhere, drawing parallels between Tagalog beliefs and Chinese thought, he also wonders whether Christian elements are already present in the Chinese philosophy of Lao Tzu and Confucius.

Paterno elaborates on Christian elements in Tagalog religion in *El Cristianismo en la Antigua Civilizacion Tagalog* (1892), written in response to Oveido bishop R. Martinez Vigil's article, serialized in the Ibero-American review *La España Moderna* (1891), which debunked exaggerated claims made about an old Philippine civilization. Paterno felt alluded to but had delayed his response, he says, because he was laid low by an illness at the time.[116]

In his response Paterno theorizes that Philippine civilizational origins may be traced back to the time of Solomon and Alexander the Great. He quotes Biblical passages on the voyage of Solomon's men to Ophir and Tharsis, which, he speculates, refers to points in India and Oceania. He argues that there was contact between the Philippines and pre-Christian Europe from the time of the ancient Greek traveler Iambulus and the geographer Ptolemy. There was closer contact with India and, through India or directly, the ancient Near East. By this route the islands were exposed to Egyptian, Persian, and early Christian influence, perhaps as early as the beginning of the Byzantine Empire in the fourth century. Paterno further raises the possibility that Philippine inhabitants who traveled to India and China may have heard the Christian doctrines from St. Thomas the Apostle who was proselytizing in Asia in the first century A.D. This link was severed with the rise of Mohammedanism but Buddhist and Christian influences had already found their way to the archipelago. Buddhist influence, in particular, was important until its decline in the mid-fourteenth century, as attested to by Sanskrit elements in Tagalog and the reference in Chinese sources to Buddha statues found in areas around Manila.

In making these arguments, Paterno stitches together assorted citations of sometimes dubious relevance, such as Biblical passages, speculation by missionaries like Francisco Colin and Rodrigo de Aganduru Moriz on precolonial contact with Europe and the Near East, and studies on Chinese sources by Friedrich Hirth and Sanskrit by Eugene Burnouf and Hendrik Kern.

Combining Christian commentaries and philological analysis, Paterno produces a "Tagalog theology." He mines the nineteenth-century Jesuit letters of Mateo Gisbert and Pablo Pastells to show native equivalents to such figures as the Holy Trinity, Virgin Mary, and Lucifer in the mythology of the Bagobo and Mandaya on the basis of the etymology of the names of deities and their relations and functions. He extracts missionary statements about the ethical conduct of precolonial natives and argues that this could only mean that their values were already "Christian." Citing the ease of Christian conversion in the islands, he theorizes that their inhabitants were already predisposed to the Gospel because of the prior existence of a primitive Christianity. While he admits that local beliefs seem "garbled and confused" (suggesting this may have been occasioned by imperfect transcription by missionaries), he insists that local theological understanding reveals "clear and definite concepts like the Hebrews, Greeks and Latins had," and that differences are a matter of difference in customs, language, and mode of expression.[117]

Paterno's principal method is philological. He selects (and invents) key native terms, breaks them down to their letters and vocables, and unlocks the concepts they contain. He says that Tagalogs followed "ancient natural custom observed also among Assyrians, Medes, Persians, and Hebrews in forming a word which condenses entire phrases, preserving profound ideas."[118] Much of his treatise is taken up by linguistic analysis, "in the light of (Christian) theological doctrines," leavened with comparative data from a wide range of world cultures. At the most extreme, Paterno's strategy of proof is shown in his Kabbalistic analysis of the four letters *BTHL* in *Bathala* to show how this Hebraic tetragram conveys the entire mystery of the Holy Trinity. He embellishes his analysis by parading analogues in the names of deities from universal mythology, such as the gods of the Batak, Tamil, Maori, Tonga, Iroquois and "a hundred more names of gods the enumeration of which would be tedious."[119]

I believe that the aforesaid will be sufficient to demonstrate to the readers that the Tagalog language possessed, since remotest times, we shall not say phrases, expressions and synonyms but simple vocables, for expressing properly and with concision the mysteries and the miracles of Him who resuscitated the dead, to prove the truth of his doctrine. . . . *Thus spoke the Tagalog. And thus he also thought.*[120]

Paterno was aware of the skepticism with which his *Antigua Civilizacion* was received.

> Some have taken the interpretations I give of *Bathala* as products of my imagination and that I, according to them, wish to inject into simple letters entire phrases of profound ideas. However, such critics, no matter how respectable they are, doubtless ignore the primitive oriental languages and, in this instance, the Tagalog language in the roots of which are preserved on the whole the purity of the elements of the most ancient ones; or perhaps the first words of the language of man, elements religiously preserved by generations of Tagalogs.[121]

It is clear that the theology he excavates from words is mostly of his own making. His analysis is selective, conjectural, and based on words mostly taken from books, isolated and without adequate context. He deploys Bagobo and Mandaya words and myths even though he has excluded Mindanao from the *Luzonica* he stakes out as his field. He invents concepts by converting minimal vocabulary entries into complex ideas through pseudo-etymological elaboration, taking liberties as he ascends from local facts to philosophic possibilities. For instance, citing the authority of *Vocabulario de la Lengua Tagala* (1860), by Juan Noceda and Pedro de Sanlucar, he claims that Tagalogs had an equivalent for Christ in *Anac-Hala* (or *Anac-Ala*) and the Holy Ghost in *Lacanpati*. In fact, the Noceda-Sanlucar dictionary simply defines *anac ala* or *acala* as "to think, probe." It does not have an entry for *Anac-Hala* that Paterno says is the "real name of [the] first anito" and the local equivalent for Christ. Paterno freely extrapolates in identifying the Holy Ghost with *Lacanpati*, which Noceda-Sanlucar merely defines as "an idol the natives have as protector of the fields" and other sources describe as a hermaphroditic deity.[122]

He invents sources. He alludes to doing research in the province of Bay (Laguna), during his 1882 vacation in the Philippines, where he purportedly learned of the ancient Tagalog equivalent of the Holy Communion in the sacrificial rite called *pandot*. Rite worshippers (Paterno reported) partook of thin, white hosts called *calantipas* and the vegetable juice called *gayoma*, converted to "divine essence" through the exorcistic act called *mandala*. Taking off from the simple entry *Pitho* in the Noceda-Sanlucar *Vocabulario* ("the name of an ancient man who was believed to be a prophet"), Paterno proceeds to attribute a direct quote to this "Tagalog prophet" about an origin myth that echoes the Biblical story of the Garden of Eden. The myth tells (Paterno writes) that the god *Ha* (later transformed to *Bathala*) created *Tao*; that *Tao* sinned and was cast out of the country; and two other deities co-equal to *Ha*, named *Hayin* and *Hib*, decreed that *Tao* be redeemed through *Bathala*'s son, *Anac-Hala*.[123]

In theorizing a "Tagalog civilization," Paterno is engaged in a move that others (like Rizal) would make, carving out a history and identity apart from and antecedent to Spanish colonialism. He made the radical (if specious and overblown) claim that what Spain claimed to be her greatest contribution to the civilizing of the country was something Filipinos possessed even before the Spanish conquest. He remained politically conservative, however. He does not, he carefully points out, advocate either a return to the past or disengagement from Spain.

> I do not advocate the return to the past. I know the valuable effect of time on institutions and popular attitudes. My goal is that these excellent qualities of our past, these precious gems of what had been, these impressions of beauty of the remote past will cause to shine, augment and embellish those of the present, well assured of finding in the products of universal progress, in the clean, brilliant, transparent, crystal clarity of our days, better means of showing the true images of things, so that the eternal beauty may be admired today with greater enthusiasm.[124]

Paterno imagines an evolutionary progression in which the Tagalog legacy is perfected in the best that Spain and Christianity represent. Of his *Antigua Civilizacion*, he writes:

> My book may be bad, because it is mine, but no one can deny that in it I gave recognition to what others have written or will write later; nobody can prove that I have shamelessly glorified the Taga-

logs, for whom three hundred years were enough . . . to transform them from savages to civilized Christians, [thus] accomplishing in three centuries what outstanding European nations could not do in one or two thousand years.[125]

Paterno takes the stance of the loyal subject. His is not a "nationalist" treatise, it is a call to Spain to recognize the glories of one of her possessions. The project to recover indigenous culture is not "anti-patriotic," he says. Spaniards should not begrudge him the fortune of being a Filipino born in the nineteenth century, the child of Mother Spain, "my soul [is] filled with her generosity, nobility, frank willingness, courage, zeal." Being Filipino does not exclude him from participating in Spain's "historic attempts to contribute a brick to the edifice of universal culture."[126]

PATERNO PURSUED his theory of ancient Tagalog civilization in *Los Itas* (1890), *El Barangay* (1892), *La Familia Tagalog* (1892), and *El Individuo Tagalog* (1893). The last three-mentioned works were also put together in a single volume entitled *Los Tagalog* (1894).

In the preface to *Los Itas*, he makes explicit the overarching purpose of his studies: to locate the Philippines in the flow of universal history (*Historia Universal*). A significant vacuum needed to be filled, he says, by going beyond the scattered, unorganized data in foreign commentaries, travelogues, and missionary chronicles to discover the genesis of Philippine culture and its relations with other cultures in the world. In this endeavor he claims the privilege of speaking from the higher vantage point of world-knowledge:

Authentic History does not so much consist of the succession of events as in the manifestation of human activity, encompassing in the universality of research all thought, all languages, all traditions of man, his beliefs, customs, laws, sciences, arts, letters, in all places and all times.[127]

Tagalog civilization belongs to this history. His aim, Paterno says, is to promote an appreciation of this fact, not so much "to enrich with one more stone the edifice of [Universal History] but to contribute to it an endeavor, a humble effort to form the foundation on which to build the History of [a] forgotten people."[128]

Los Itas elaborates on the aboriginal basis of Philippine society. Paterno grandly announces that he is drawing from current knowledge in anthropology, geology, psychology, and prehistory in treating questions of race, religion, social organization, morality, and the arts. To ascertain the history of a people, he says, it is necessary to study the diverse causes that determine the state of their civilization. These include the "necessities of existence," environment (such as the effect of hot and cold climates), inherited sentiments and ideas, as well as various external and internal pressures (such as war and migration). Social and cultural evolution proceeds in sequential stages and unfolds in the long duration, from the simple and rudimentary to the complex and articulated. Morals, for instance, evolve in a process in which life's necessities create ideas and sentiments, which are enacted and then develop into customs that in turn evolve into morals and laws.

Paterno works with a classic evolutionist outline that he illustrates with local data drawn from missionary letters, travel accounts, dictionaries, and the studies of scientists like Rudolf Virchow, A.B. Meyer, and Hendrik Kern. He interposes at certain turns his own "data" and observations. The local material is fragmentary and discontinuous, often appearing in the form of long quotations from secondary sources that are minimally situated and analyzed. The universalizing ambition of Paterno's work is such that the text is heavily overlaid with comparative notes from cultures all over the world as well as theoretical speculation in the emergent disciplines of anthropology, linguistics, and psychology. The work is impressive in the range of its bibliographic citations but Paterno's "theory" overwhelms his local data.

Paterno characterizes the development of Tagalog society in terms of successive stages that proceed from the earliest world civilizations. Expanding his earlier division of three historical stages (*aborigines, tagala, catolica*), he claims three phases of influence in Tagalog history: *civilizacion indostanica* (represented by contacts with India and the Near East that drew the islands into the orbit of Brahmanic and Buddhist influence), *civilizacion mahometana* (Muslim influence in the fourteenth and fifteenth centuries), and *civilizacion cristiana* (which began in the sixteenth century with the coming of Spain).

While Paterno's "deep" history (with its references to Phoenician voyages and medieval geography) is an exercise in fantasy and guesswork, the claim to antiquity is moved by his desire to create for Tagalogs a genealogy that goes back to the cradle of human civilization. In the same manner, his discourse on race incorporates the Ita into a universal history. He surveys the literature on race classification and the geographic distribution of the "Negro" or "Ethiopic" race (from Linnaeus and Georges Cuvier to James Cowles Prichard and Armand de Quatrefages) and concludes that the origins of the Ita can be traced back to the *raza negra* in India, Egypt, and Mesopotamia.[129]

Paterno frames aboriginal and Tagalog cultures in evolutionary terms. Invoking Lamarck and Darwin, he plots Philippine prehistory according to a European-derived sequence of Stone Age (palaeolithic and neolithic), Bronze Age, and Iron Age. He characterizes the development of early religion in the islands as an evolutionary advance through stages of atheism (*ateismo*), fetishism (*feticismo*), animism (*animismo*), polytheism (*politeismo*), and idolatry (*idolatria*). Putting together data from various writers on the Philippines (such as Antonio Mozo, Pedro Chirino, and Alfred Marche), he posits the evolution of the Ita family from communism (*comunismo*, the state of "primitive promiscuity") to matriarchy (*matriarcado*), then patriarchy (*patriarcado*), characterizing various Ita groups on the basis of loose and random evidence for such practices as polyandry, couvade, exogamy, endogamy, and adelphogamy. He uses the same unilinear, quasi-biological framework in describing morals, laws, and the arts, sketching the features of a wide range of culture items, from weapons and dwelling types to moral ideas and sentiments.

Acknowledging there are physical and cultural differences among Itas, he explains these as the result of culture contact and racial mixture, distinguishing between "pure negritos" and "mestizos negrito-malayos." Sketching broad distinctions among Itas in Mindanao, Visayas, and Luzon, he states that various groups have been stranded at different evolutionary stages. He concludes, for instance, that "communism" survives in Mindanao where the Itas are lowest in the evolutionary scale, while "patriarchy" is ascendant among the Luzon Itas who are the most advanced aboriginal groups in the archipelago. He considers the "pure" Ita a primitive survival, a degenerative and lethargic race (*raza estacionaria*) that will die out due to isolation, biological limitations, and the effect of such factors as changes in diet and climate. While he cites names of the numerous groups he considers part of the Ita population, his interest in universal categories leaves the description of these groups underspecified in terms of time and location.

Driven by a totalizing approach, the treatise is packed with statements on topics current in nineteenth-century ethnology, from kinship and property systems to practices of infanticide and cranial deformation. He loads the book with a plethora of notes on supposed parallels with other cultures. Remarking that Ita artistic conceptions are stagnant, he alludes to the mentality of the "Cro-Magnon race" and primitive African and Amazonian tribes. He supplies Ita words and characters with equivalents not only in other Philippine languages but obscure examples from such widely separated languages as Quechua (Peru-Ecuador), Eskimo (Arctic), Dahomey or Ewe (North Africa), and Serpa (Tibet). Paterno's display of knowledge is mostly extraneous and merely self-indulgent.

From the privileged vantage point of "modern science," Paterno surveys his country. It is a project caught in the discordant impulses of inscribing difference and, at the same time, privileging a universalism that erases difference. It is clear in what direction the balance is tilted. Paterno had an untroubled view of his goal of inserting his country into a "universal history of mankind." The formation of nations, he says, is governed by the same laws.

> Nations are the result of the labor of centuries; they are not formed except piece by piece, and the annexation of component provinces is done one after another. What is necessary in the formation of the whole is a durable unity, assimilation of elements, coordination of parts. When these conditions are lacking, the product is ephemeral; it is like one of those vast constructions of wood that a spark suffices to reduce it to ashes.[130]

Paterno focuses on some of these "components" in subsequent writings on Tagalog political organization, family, and notions of personhood. These texts, however, are repetitive and do not substantially expand or deepen his ethnographic material and underlying arguments. *El Barangay* (1892) is a slight, didactic monograph that, while repeating arguments already made in *Antigua Civilizacion*, may be the first to theorize on the barangay at some length. Paterno claims political homogeneity and temporal depth for *el Reino Tagalog*. He mentions, for effect, Recollect Rodrigo de Aganduru Moriz's estimate that Philippine history stretches back "3,027 years." (This is obviously drawn from estimates of the age of the world based on Biblical time scales, the most famous of which was the seventeenth-century Irish bishop James Ussher's thesis that God created the universe on October 22, 4004 BC. Most educated Europeans, including the young Charles Darwin, believed as late as the first half of the eighteenth century that the world was just six thousand years old. Advances in geological science, however, had already demolished these Biblical chronologies by the time of Paterno.)[131]

Paterno claims for the Tagalog political system the features of such European categories as monarchy, aristocracy, and democracy. He idealizes native polity by asserting that its basic unit, the barangay, guided by the philosophy of *Bathalismo*, partakes of the character of an enlightened aristocracy. Slavery and hereditary castes do not exist; the king (*hari*) rules with the advice of "a council of elders and lords" (*consejo de nonos y maguinoos*) who are distinguished by their wisdom and virtue. The *sangdugo*, the principle of "equality and universal fraternity" expressed in the practice of the blood compact, constitutes the moral "doctrine" of the community.

La Familia Tagalog en la Historia Universal (1892) places the development of the Tagalog family and kinship system in the context of "universal history."[132] As in his other works, Paterno starts out from European categories of social evolution, liberally citing the authority of such authors as Johann J. Bachofen, John Lubbock, John Ferguson McLennan, and Charles Letourneau, plotting out a sequence in which the family evolves from "communism" or "hetairism" through the stage of matriarchy to the more advanced stage of patriarchy. His reliance on European categories is illustrated in his speculative statements on such topics as bride-capture, polyandry, gynocracy, and polygamy. He provides local evidence for these practices by selectively deploying statements from Spanish-colonial accounts and mining old Tagalog dictionaries for relevant concepts. He thickens the account with a wealth of loosely connected comparative data on marriage and family from diverse world cultures.

Of particular interest is Paterno's gloss in reading Tagalog culture. His basic argument is that when the Spaniards arrived in 1521, the Tagalog family had already evolved into the advanced stage of patriarchy founded on an institution of marriage that was monogamous and dissoluble (*monogamico y disoluble*). Tagalogs had developed kinship and interpersonal relations founded on values of social mutuality and individual liberty. These values, Paterno says, were expressed in the ancient Tagalog institutions of divorce and the blood compact (*pacto de sangre*). Divorce was a logical consequence of the doctrine of individual liberty; the blood compact symbolized the mutual love Christians call charity (*caridad*) and that universal fraternity proclaimed in Voltairean philosophy (*filosofia volteriana*).[133] He dilates this argument by invoking the unimpeachable authority of the science of evolution, by quoting the evidentiary statements of Spanish chroniclers, and by illustrating with examples from the highly developed Tagalog vocabulary for marriage customs and kinship relations. Parading around a hundred Tagalog kinship terms, he conveys an image of empirical depth and moral thickness to the native family. Though he does not quite make the connection explicit, he insinuates the basis for an extensive and coherent polity in the articulation of an elaborate family system.

Paterno's claim to originality lies in the following moves. He reframes the statements of Spanish-colonial writers by accenting the positive and by relocating them in the classificatory systems of evolutionist theory. He assumes "insider" knowledge by reinterpreting or elaborating evidence from Tagalog and local languages. He builds the overarching argument that Tagalog culture does not only have a "deep" base in ancient civilizations but has evolved into a stage higher than has been recognized by foreign writers on the Philippines.

El Individuo Tagalog y su Arte en la Exposicion Historico-Americana (1893) is a notable essay on Tagalog notions of personhood, gender relations, art and psychology.[134] The fact that these topics did not receive as much attention from Spanish chroniclers as religion or social organization made for a fresher work since Paterno had to improvise his own data to build his arguments. Pursuing the same theme of Tagalog advancement, Paterno constructs the Tagalog person as one complex and distinctly moral. The human individual, he says, is formed out of "natural" capacities and the influence of environment. He classes as natural sentiments a

61

person's desire for well-being (*hangad guminhaua*), dignity, worth, and self-esteem (*cadangalan, camahalan, cahalagahan*). These sentiments assume their particular form under the influence of environmental factors such as he illustrates in the differences between Itas and *Igorrotes*, on one hand, and Tagalogs, on the other.

He characterizes the Tagalog person as one who possesses individualism (*individualismo*) in all its purity (*en toda su pureza*). He localizes "individualism" in the Tagalog notions of *catagalasican*, "being a free, unfettered person," and *calabusaquitan*, the quality of "putting force in the maintenance of one's essence, liberty, and independence" (*poner teson en el mantenimiento de su esencia, de su libertad, de su independencia*). He claims for the Tagalog a well-developed sensitivity to material and spiritual realities. The Tagalog unites in himself a trinity of "souls" (*espiritus*): *calulua, diwa,* and *lagyo,* which correspond, respectively, to the *alma intelectiva* (the faculty that allows one to understand spiritual matters), *alma sensitiva* (the faculty for knowing corporal things and sense experiences), and *alma vegetativa* (the soul that animates the physical body).

Paterno dilates on the basis of entries and minimal definitions in Spanish-colonial dictionaries. He offers, for instance, a theory of Tagalog individualism out of lexical items: *Labusaquit: Poner teson en algun negocio,* "Showing tenacity or determination in an undertaking"; *Tagalasic: Persona libre, desenfrenada,* "A free, unbridled person." He isolates words from living speech and does not provide examples of actual use. In his excursus on the Tagalog's finely developed "natural sentiments," he draws general support from the rich local vocabulary for spiritual and moral ideas, citing the plurality of Tagalog terms for such categories as will (*voluntad*), memory (*memoria*), sight (*mirar*), and thought (*pensar*). He parades a local vocabulary that cannot be adequately translated, he says, because of the relative poverty of Spanish and European languages.

On gender relations in Tagalog society, Paterno relies on a selection of evidence from published sources, fanciful elaboration, and deductions from Western theory on the evolution of sexual relations and the family. While holding to the orthodox view on male superiority, Paterno claims moral high ground for Tagalog culture by arguing that while early society (including the Philippines in its primitive stages) regarded woman as a domestic animal, slave, servant or child, the Tagalog woman has been treated as man's civil equal. Woman's high status, he says, is

62

shown in the high value given to chastity in local culture, as illustrated in such venerated cultural figures as *Lacanbini,* "Immaculate Virgin of the ancient Tagalog civilization," and *Todlibon,* the Bagobo "goddess of Chastity." Interpreting chastity as sign of woman's high status, Paterno characteristically resorts to argument by rhetorical effect:

> In this manner Tagalog civilization raised woman above the whirl-winds of the grosser passions, and crowned her with the brilliant aureole of total abstinence from sensual pleasures: *virginity.* Certainly, virginity is not a necessary condition for chastity, but it is its most fair embodiment, its ideal perfection.[135]

Writing in a loose, speculative style, Paterno does not develop his ideas on personhood in a sustained and coherent fashion. He begins with a thesis and then proceeds to support it with isolated, selective, and dubious evidence. His philological exercises in the semantics of personality, while fanciful, are, however, important in pointing to the value of language as resource for understanding native epistemology.

Paterno's discussion of Tagalog art in *Individuo Tagalog* is limited to a concatenation of occasional notes. He defends the musical-and-dance form called *comintang* against malicious characterizations in the Spanish press that it is a lascivious "belly dance." A form that derives its name from the ancient state of Kumintang, now Balayan in Batangas, the dance dates back to "matriarchal" times, Paterno says. Its dance movements and music express "the different agitations of an enamoured soul" and convey qualities akin to those of Hindu sacred chants and the Javanese *gamelan.* Speaking as patriot and connoisseur, he inserts a brief catalogue of Philippine arts and antiquities exhibited at the 1892–1893 *Exposicion Historico-Americana.* He praises Filipino *objets d'art* in the same vein that he writes of other aspects of Philippine civilization. They manifest, he says, traits reminiscent of Greco-Roman, Persian, Arabic, Indian, Japanese, and Chinese art but combine them in an overall harmony that is "Oriental."

In a related article in *La Solidaridad* in 1895, he would say more about Philippine art, explaining its virtues in the romantic-mimetic terms familiar at the time.[136] He asserts (though he does not quite explain how) that the specific character of native art is influenced by the particular flora, fauna, and "anthropology" of the archipelago. These are the wellsprings that give to Filipino art that "originality" that Filipinos demonstrate in their alphabet, language, and barangay form of government. Except for a few desultory and impressionistic observations, Paterno does not go into Tagalog aesthetics at any length.

HIS WRITINGS on "ancient Tagalog civilization" form the core of his scholarly work. After he became increasingly involved in Philippine politics he also published on law and government. In *El Regimen Municipal en las Islas Filipinas* (1893), his commentary on the Maura Law of 1893, he exhibits his knowledge of law (he was one of the first Filipinos to earn a doctorate in civil law), curries favor with high Spanish officials, and claims that the Maura Law expressed the spirit of his own ideas on barangay government in the Philippines. *El Problema Politico de Filipinas* (1900), his autonomy plan for the Philippines, advertised his knowledge of Western political thought and constitutional systems. Under the Americans, he published the textbooks *Synopsis de Historia de los Estados Unidos* (1909), a very rudimentary sketch of U.S. history, and *Gobierno Civil de las Islas Filipinas* (1910), a primer on the Philippine government introduced by a discussion of political science principles drawn from Spanish translations of such authors as Richard Hooker (1553–1600), Francois Guizot (1787–1874), and Arthur Helps (1813–1875). Despite their patchwork character and motive of self-promotion, these works, together with the earlier *El Barangay* (1892), place Paterno as one of the pioneers of Philippine political science.

The turn into the twentieth century was a distinct divide in Philippine history. The establishment of a new colonial order in the wake of a destructive war brought with it radical reorientations in political system, foreign relations, and models of intellectual work. The country witnessed a generational change of leadership, new avenues to political power, a shift in the prestige language from Spanish to English, and the eclipsing of Spain (and Europe) by the United States as source of symbolic power. These changes rendered Paterno and his scholarship anachronistic.

In his last years, Paterno published an account of his travels in Laguna during his campaign for an assembly seat in 1907, *En Automovil por el Primer Distrito de la Laguna de Bay* (1907), and an interesting if self-serving memoir of the Biyak-na-Bato negotiations, *El Pacto de Biyak-na-Bato* (1910). He wrote undistinguished, Spanish-language plays and novels that became archaic almost from the time he wrote them. Spanish had declined as a medium and literary talents more robust and contemporary than Paterno occupied the field. He never lost his self-assurance, however. He never retracted nor revised the basic arguments on history and culture he first set forth in *Antigua Civilizacion Tagalog* in 1887.

At a time when U.S.-guided "nation building" was the watchword, Paterno produced his eleven-volume *Historia de Filipinas* (1908–1912). It went largely ignored and unread. *Historia de Filipinas* is a sad monument to the man. For one who had always thought of Philippine history as an episode in a universal history, the writing of a *national* history must have been quite a challenge. In the Philippines, it was a concept not only relatively new but one compromised by the fact that its subject, the Filipino nation, was not sovereign and free. Paterno was aware that writing a national history required a shift of perspective. In his preface to *Synopsis de Historia de Filipinas* (1911), he defines Philippine history as "the narration of events that have transpired in the Filipino Nation" (*narracion de los sucesos acaecidos en el Pueblo Filipino*) and that its subject is the *Pueblo Filipino*.[137] The book opens with an interrogatory:

> What is the history of Filipinas? . . . the narrative of events that happened in the Filipino Nation.
>
> How is it divided? . . . (1) that of the Indigenes, (2) the Spaniards, (3) the Revolution, (4) the Filipino Republic, and (5) the Americans.
>
> What is its subject? . . . the Filipino People (*Pueblo Filipino*).
>
> What is its object? . . . the study of the deeds realized by Filipinos and the proven events (*acontecimientos verificados*) in these islands.[138]

He distinguishes between *prehistoria* and *historia*, saying that the latter is based on documentary sources while the other mostly conjectures on the "deeds, ideas, and practices of *antiguo tagalismo* as vestiges of the primary evolutionary stages of human society." *Tagalismo*, he says, is a generic term that encompasses all the varieties of the Malay race present in the archipelago. Hence it embraces all ethnic communities, including those of Mindanao, the *joloanos mahometanos*, and others that have intermixed with the local population through history. "All are Tagalogs," Paterno says.[139]

Paterno was, however, on unfamiliar ground. The history he writes is a jerry-built compendium of his previous writings. He recycles his ethnological studies on ancient Philippine culture into a three-volume, non-narrative *Historia Critica de Filipinas* (1908), produces a dreary annalistic chronicle of Spanish rule in the seven-volume *Historia de Filipinas* (1908–1912), and vainly attempts a summary in *Synopsis de Historia de Filipinas* (1911). Due to the "documentary" sources available, the Spanish period is the most packed in factual information. He draws from familiar Spanish sources, with only a few footnotes and no bibliography.

Paterno's hybrid *Historia* does not present a coherent view of the nation. In what is part speculative treatise, part civic chronicle, part self-advertisement, Paterno hammers together fragments of his and the country's past in a project of historical salvage. Particularly pathetic is Paterno's effort to insert himself into the plot of an emerging national narrative that had consigned him to a peripheral and disreputable role.

In a truncated sketch of the origins of the nationalist movement, he credits his father Maximo Paterno as the one who initiated the move among Filipinos to send their sons to Europe after the opening of the Suez Canal. He assigns him a leading role in the reform movement during the Carlos de la Torre administration. He reduces the story of the Propaganda Movement into a list of his own activities (ostensibly sourced from "various manuscripts" of Mariano Ponce and Isabelo de los Reyes). Inflating his accomplishments, Paterno cites his lectures, journalistic pieces, and "renowned and transcendental" *veladas* as seminal events in raising awareness of Philippine history and culture. It was on his initiative, he says, that the *Circulo Hispano-Filipino* was organized in 1881 to seek Filipino representation in the Spanish Cortes. It was the public viewing of his Philippine collection in Madrid in 1883 that led to the *Exposicion de Filipinas* in 1887 and creation of the *Museos y Bibliotecas de Ultramar* in Madrid and Manila. He was the benefactor who paid for the trip that allowed Juan Luna, Felix Resurreccion Hidalgo, and Miguel Zaragoza to travel from Madrid to Rome to pursue their art studies. It was he who convinced Jose Rizal (during his Philippine visit in 1882) to study in Spain and then "furnished him with the means to pay for the trip to the Peninsula" that opened doors to Rizal's achievements.[140]

His *Ninay* and *Antigua Civilizacion* are texts into which he smuggled—"as a practical procedure in that time of darkness"—"occult" meanings, conveying the need for freedom, independence, and cultural conservation, for which reason, he says, the Spanish authorities prohibited the Tagalog translation of his works. His enunciation of the doctrines of *Bathalismo* (inculcating, he says, the nobility of fighting for one's country) and *pacto de sangre* (symbol of brotherhood and fraternity) provided "the basis of the Katipunan." His books, Paterno says, inspired Rizal's own writings and led to the Revolution.[141]

It is difficult to believe an author would be capable of such self-aggrandizing fiction. One can understand why Paterno, as scholar and author, has been conveniently ignored as an embarrassment.

RIZAL'S FABLE of the moths can be read as a tale of colonial intellectuals. Rizal recalls that as a child he was enchanted by the sight of moths fluttering in "playful and uneven flight" around the flame of an oil lamp. Saddened by the sight of a young moth that is singed by the flame and dies, the young Rizal listened to his mother's cautionary tale of disobedience, of the young and reckless moth that perished because he did not heed the wise old moth's warnings about the dangers of illusions. It was a different insight that stirred Rizal in remembrance: "Light is the most beautiful thing there is in creation and that it is worthy for a man to sacrifice his life for it."[142]

Rizal was drawn to the flame of knowledge but fully appreciated its perils. It was not an easy flight. The nineteenth century witnessed an unprecedented expansion in the production and circulation of knowledge. The rise of publishing, new economic opportunities, accelerated travel, and proliferation of such media for knowledge-promotion as schools, learned societies, museums, and exhibitions, stimulated public appetite for new learning. All these had a particular, powerful appeal in colonial societies where knowledge had been suppressed by a lack of opportunities and a culture of intellectual disenfranchisement. The privileged few in these societies who attended universities and traveled to Europe must have been whelmed by abundant knowledge.

In telling the fable of the moths Rizal was speaking about himself. One can well imagine Paterno as the moth who—seduced by light, drunk in the "magical exhalation" of it all—was consumed in his own sad fashion. Yet this is an obvious simplification. It does not account for the fact that, in negotiating the colonial difference, he traced his own distinctive orbit and exercised his own kind of agency.

Pedro Paterno seems the quintessential victim of Orientalism. He is the ambitious native who assumes the white man's face, mimics his learning, and surveys the native land with an imperial gaze. This is a reductive characterization. It concedes to Orientalism greater powers than one should; it denies the possibility that even what may seem mere rearticulations of its premises may have disruptive, dislocative effects.

While Orientalism has been much studied, much more remains to be done on how "Orientals" themselves engaged it—and engaged it not afterwards but almost at its birth. This is illustrated, among many examples that can be cited, in current studies on the construction of primitives in imperial expositions and "world fairs." What has not been given sufficient notice is that "natives" were vocal participants and interlocutors of these Orientalist spectacles. Graciano Lopez Jaena mounted a vigorous public critique of the 1887 *Exposicion de Filipinas* in Madrid. Jose Rizal boldly attempted the staging of an international scholarly conference on the Philippines as part of the 1889 International Exposition in Paris.[143] And Pedro Paterno was involved in Spanish exhibitions and the St. Louis Exposition of 1904. Filipinos were active agents in the politics of their representation.

Pedro Paterno took the high ground of modern science. He was not an indigenist. His claim was that he was a more enlightened exemplar of modernity than the foreigners (in particular, the Spaniards) who had written about the Philippines. His suit was that he spoke out of a broader view of world civilization and a better theoretical understanding of the historical dynamics of cultural progress. Appropriating the authority of Europe, he carved out "Tagalog civilization" as object of knowledge and distanced it from the negative descriptions of foreign observers by putting it on an idealized plane.

His work may be "fiction" but from such fictions is history made.

CANNIBALIZING THEORY

THERE IS MORE to Paterno than the figure of the pompous buffoon. In tracing the obscured genealogy of Philippine studies, we need to see Paterno, first, in relation to how the Philippines had been represented by writers before him and, second, in the context of European scholarship in the cultural sciences. Reading Paterno thus—without erasing the specificity of his stance and style—renders his work less fantastic than it seems.

A historicized Paterno shows that the "objects" of European Orientalism were not just objects but subjects who actively assumed, negotiated, or subverted its premises. A mapping of this neglected intellectual terrain—Orientalism's margins, underside, other side—is necessary for clarifying Paterno's position and, in a wider context, the base and ambit of non-Western scholarship.

The career of Paterno sheds its own distinctive light on Philippine intellectual politics in the nineteenth and early twentieth centuries.

PATERNO CANNIBALIZED European knowledge. I say this not necessarily pejoratively, but to point to a nutritive ingestion of a foreign body of knowledge and, in another sense perhaps more germane in Paterno's case, an opportunistic disassembling and reassembling of parts of other thought systems. Both are ways of appropriating the power of the Other.

Paterno took what he could or needed from disparate, dissynchronic sources. He combines, without resolving contradictions, Biblical history and Darwinist science. His hermeneutics of verbal signs seems more sixteenth-century in its mystical interest in the primitive roots of words, rather than of a nineteenth-century when linguists were turning their attention to the structure and grammar of languages.

A body of knowledge Paterno drew from, whether directly or indirectly, was Spanish-American ethnology. Paterno studied at Universidad de Salamanca, one of the earliest seats of Orientalist scholarship in Europe. One of the founding events of Orientalism, Edward Said points out, was the establishment by the Catholic Church, through the Council of Vienne in 1312, of a series of chairs in Arabic, Greek, Hebrew, and Syriac at Paris, Oxford, Bologna, Avignon, and Salamanca.[144] Of more immediate import was the fact that, under the Dominicans and then the Jesuits, Salamanca built a venerable tradition in the theorizing of knowledge about the Spanish colonies and the World. Members of its law and theology faculties, led by the Dominican Francisco de Vitoria (1492–1546), laid the basis for comparative ethnology in Spain through their writings about the New World.[145] While nineteenth-century Spain was increasingly influenced by secular and liberal ideas, the conservative-Christian cast of Paterno's thought shows how he was steeped—to a degree Rizal was not—in a more traditional climate of ideas.

Of particular relevance was eighteenth-century Creole historiography in Spanish America.[146] By the end of the eighteenth century, Spanish-American *criollos* had developed a sense of belonging to a culture that was in many respects independent of the "mother country." Conflicts between creoles and peninsulars over precedence strengthened the creoles' attachment to the land and nourished claims that they were the "natural lords" of a distinct civilization. Creole revolts were fired by the vision that Mexico or Peru was not a colony but a tributary kingdom bound to the Spanish King on the basis of a "contract" between the local elite and the King. It was a quasi-autonomous "kingdom" within a larger cluster of kingdoms referred to as "Greater Spain," with its own identity, aristocracy, and government.

This mentality produced a Creole historiography that invested *criollos* with the double power of being lords of a distinct, separate and noble civilization as well as heirs to European culture. One of the earliest and most influential expressions of this view was made by the Mexican scholar and royal cosmographer Carlos de Siguenza y Gongora (1645–1700) who uses European models and categories to claim that ancient Mexico does not only have its own classical antiquity, like the ancient world of Greece and Rome, but that the two were connected in the remote past. Siguenza links ancient Mexicanos, ancient Greeks, and the sons of Noah by means of an interpretation of the name *Neptune*. Viewing all myths as garbled versions of real historical events, as did other seventeenth-century historians, he interpreted the maritime god Neptune as a real historical figure, Nephtium, the son of Misraim, son of Shem, who was the true progenitor of the New World. It was Neptune's return the Indians had been expecting in the guise of their creator-deity Quetzalcoatl, a belief that ties in with the tradition that Moctezuma had donated his empire to Cortes in the belief that he was Quetzalcoatl. Neptune and Quetzalcoatl are the same historical person, Siguenza argues. Hence the criollos are linked to the Greeks and Hebrews and, at a later point, the Egyptians.[147]

Similarly, the eighteenth-century historian Fray Servando Teresa de Mier claimed that Quetzalcoatl was, in fact, St. Thomas the Apostle. Hence the Indians already had a full understanding of the theological principles of Christianity even before the coming of the Spaniards. Mier also made the argument that an unwritten "magna carta" existed that derived from a pact made between the first conquistadors and the ancient Indian kings that guaranteed the rights of Indians (*indios*) and criollos.[148]

"Creole patriotism," Anthony Pagden has shown, was a bizarre combination of mythology and dynastic fantasy.[149] In creating a continuous, politically legitimating past, creole intellectuals wrote, painted, and constructed monuments of fabulous genealogies linking Indians and criollos to the Biblical world of Noah and the civilizations of the Hebrews, Greeks, and Romans. The fact that the colonial present appeared debased compared to this glorious past would later underwrite critiques of colonialism itself. Creole intellectual ambitions also led creoles to forge identifications with the Indians who were, as original owners of the land, indispensable (if subordinated) to their dynastic fantasy and had the numbers that could be mustered to back this fantasy, politically and militarily.

Affinities of motive, style, and content link Pedro Paterno to this tradition of New World scholarship. Paterno's source citations indicate some familiarity with this scholarship. He cites, in *Los Itas*, the Jesuit missionaries Joseph Francois Lafitau's *Moeurs de sauvages americains compares aux moeurs des premiers temps* (1724) and Martin Dobrizhoffer's mission history of Paraguay, *Historia de Abiponibus* (1784).[150] While his South American citations do not appear substantial, the influence may have taken the form not so much of direct borrowings as exposure to a given climate of thought. While this is a subject that has not been studied, the example of South America figured prominently in the formation of colonial intellectuals in the Philippines. Paterno is a fertile example of such influence.

Like early Spanish-American creole authors, Paterno was a baroque stylist, interested in arcane symbolic meanings and promiscuous in the use of classical analogies. Like them, he drew parallels between precolonial religion and Christianity, linked local places to places in the Bible, speculated on aboriginal inhabitants as Noah's descendants, and read indigenous scripts as though they were Egyptian hieroglyphs that stored deep symbolic meanings. Themes like the destruction by missionaries of indigenous "books" and a foundational "pact" binding Spaniards and Indians in relations of mutual respect were raised by Paterno (and other Filipinos) as well.

The affinities are not just textual but political. Jorge Cañizares-Esguerra says that the Spanish-American intellectuals' "patriotic epistemology" was the discourse of a patrician class.[151] These intellectuals argued that outsiders had a limited ability to comprehend America and its peoples but they also questioned histories written by "commoners" by privileging the social standing of authors and witnesses. Their historiography was "a reflection of aristocratic, racialized longings of members of *ancien regime* polities, not modern nation-states."[152] With Paterno's ambitions of *nobilitas* and dreams of *Luzonica* as an island kingdom in *magna hispaniae*, Cañizares-Esguerra's description of creole historians applies just as well to Paterno.

It is bizarre that in the Philippines the leading exemplar of South American "creole patriotism" and *ancien regime* intellectual politics is a

Chinese mestizo. While this seems perverse it has its own strange logic in the Philippine context. While Paterno did not hide his Chinese origins (he claimed double descent from the Chinese mandarin class and old Tagalog nobility), it was not something he chose to foreground. He is a good example (if extreme) of Edgar Wickberg's characterization of the nineteenth-century Chinese mestizo. For various reasons Wickberg takes up, the "Chinese mestizo" had declined as a distinct social, cultural, and political category in the late nineteenth century. Urban-bourgeois, culturally assimilated, and newly rich, "there seemed to be (among Chinese mestizos) no attachment to Chinese culture, and, instead, a very strong affinity for a Philippine version of Hispanic culture." Indeed, they "seemed almost more Spanish than the Spanish, more Catholic than the Catholics."[153] They were almost all Catholics, commonly took a Filipino surname and spoke the local language, and most did not speak Chinese. Given the almost complete absence of Chinese women and the consequent high rate of Chinese-indio intermarriage, the direction was toward the attenuation of the Chinese element. Thus Wickberg says: "Unlike the *baba* of Malaya or the *peranakan* of Java, the Chinese mestizo in the Philippines was not a special kind of local Chinese. He was a special kind of Filipino."[154]

There was a double-movement to their cultural-political evolution. Upwardly mobile, they identified with the "superior" Spanish culture rather than a "pure indio culture." Yet, given the obvious limits to their becoming Spaniards, the decline of the Chinese-mestizo category also meant a development towards "Filipinization"—at least, an urban, Hispanified, mixed-race version of Filipinization. The first move produced a Paterno. The other led mestizos like Gregorio Sanciangco and Rizal—even a belated and not quite reconstructed Paterno—to be the shapers of an autonomous national identity. In lifestyle, ideas, and politics, Chinese mestizos became leading catalysts of what being "Filipino" meant.

Paterno fed on the fantasies of an older colonial world. He was the most archaic of Filipino intellectuals.

PATERNO WROTE about the Philippines from within a European discursive formation. He drew not only from an earlier world of ideas but current European scholarship. How he used the intellectual resources available to him, for what purpose and to what effect, can be examined more closely by dealing with his treatment of language and religion.

There was high interest in comparative religion in nineteenth-century Europe. This interest was inspired by the revival of Western interest in classical mythology, expanding scholarship on the ancient Near East, and the "crisis of conscience" engendered by the clash of science and religion in the nineteenth century.[155] Filipino intellectuals were animated by these impulses but their interest in religion was driven by other motives as well. Religion was a site of struggle since colonialism, in its most visible and intimate forms, took the form of a hegemonic Christianization. The perceived lack of a native religion underwrote the project of evangelization; the need to maintain the Christianizing mission legitimized monastic influence; religious conversion lent moral justification to the violence of colonial conquest; and religious formation fostered an ethos of social submission.

Interrogations of colonial rule had to address the role of church and religion. Nationalist counter-constructions of religion interrogated the moral basis of colonialism, claimed priority in the values of civility and humanity, and created space for developing a national cultural identity. The recovery of an "ancient Filipino religion" was a major theme in early nationalist writings.

The use of religion as vehicle of early nationalism was not peculiar to the Philippines. Evoking an "ancient" religion was an important resource for building the moral power of the colonized. In the nineteenth century, interacting notions of religion, race, and nation were medium for ideas of a people's rebirth, the shaping of primordial bonds, resurrection of lost greatness, and creation of a "national" public sphere. In India, for instance, anti-colonial nationalists took the Aryan race theory over from Orientalism, but instead of accepting the view that Christianity was to redeem the "fallen state" of Hindu civilization, proposed a return to Vedic religion, which had preceded Christianity and was the very origin of all morality.[156]

In the Philippines, recovering precolonial religion was not as straightforward. At the time of Spanish contact, the spiritual geography of the islands was a loosely articulated, localistic composite characterized by an incipient Islam and a mix of animist, Hindu, and other religious influences from elsewhere in Asia. Without an indigenous corpus of written philosophical treatises, law books, and literary texts (as in India), Filipino nationalists (many of whom had the most superficial acquaintance with the country outside Manila and their localities of birth) had to construct a "Filipino religion" out of records produced by the colonizers themselves.

Paterno worked out of these records in claiming for indigenous beliefs the status of a "religion" (a modern category that privileges monotheistic, text-based, and coherent systems of ideas). In using these records, Paterno did three things: he selectively mined them for statements useful for his purposes; he recontextualized and reinterpreted these statements; and he freely elaborated on them, including fabricating data to fill gaps and build his arguments.

The ethnocentrism of colonial sources played into Paterno's effort to find resemblances between local culture and Western civilization. Early colonial writers wrote for European readers and worked with a determinate set of assumptions and categories. Missionary chroniclers like Pedro Chirino and Francisco Colin wrote in the grid of Biblical history, explained local phenomena against what was known of Roman, Greek, and Hebrew cultures, and located the Philippines in the European map of the world. Thus Colin began his *Labor evangelica* (1663) by speculating on the place of the archipelago in the cosmographies of Ptolemy, St. Isidore, Ortelius, and Mercator. It was a move made by missionary authors after him, like Gaspar de San Agustin and Juan Francisco de San Antonio. Colin further speculated that the archipelago was part of a great continent until it was separated in the Great Deluge and then settled by Noah's descendants, perhaps by "Tharsis, son of Javan, together with his brothers." In the same vein, Colin and other missionaries invoked the Tower of Babel in explaining the multiplicity of languages in the islands; drew parallels between local nature-worship and the religion of the Egyptians and Assyrians; and theorized on the existence in the islands of a primitive monotheism.[157]

By inserting the Philippines into the Judaeo-Christian history of the world, missionary sources allowed Paterno to claim these connections for his own purposes. In the same way, the Spanish writers' use of European categories to explain local realities (*templos, sacerdotes, infierno, paraiso, gobierno*) provided Paterno with openings to argue that precolonial

Filipinos had temples, priests, notions of Heaven and Hell, and a rational social and political system.

Spanish representation of local realities was not a simple reflex of language. Missionaries were intellectually primed to note both difference and similarity in the religions of the New World. Marking difference was embedded in assumptions of the priority and superiority of Spanish language and knowledge over heathen practices and beliefs. Thus the missionary anxieties over the danger of conflating "pagan" beliefs with Catholic ones by translating key theological concepts like *Dios, Virgen,* or *Espiritu Santo* in local terms. On the other hand, the anticipation of similitude drew from the premise that the universality of the Catholic faith meant that God was present even in the "barbarous" nations in which Europeans missionized. A common explanation for the similarities they found between Christianity and pagan faiths was that the Devil had arrogated to himself God's power and had fabricated counterfeits of holy things. Another was the theory that these were "survivals" or degenerate traces of an earlier and purer faith, usually assumed to be that of the Hebrews, the ancestral matrix of Christianity.[158]

There was a practical reason as well for missionary interest in Christian-Tagalog resemblances. In the task of conversion, missionaries were interested in local ideas and practices that suggested a predisposition for conversion and could be retained as vehicles for new messages. In this spirit, the Jesuit Mateo Gisbert reported in 1880 that the Bagobos had some notion of the Blessed Virgin and the Trinity in their belief in "a perpetual virgin" named Todlibon and "a divinity residing in three subjects or persons whom they call Tigiama, Manama, and Todlai."[159] Jesuit Pablo Pastells wrote that the first missionaries retained the use of *Bathala* because, containing as it does (he says) the notion of *Bata + Ala* or "Son-God" or "Son of God," it was useful for conveying the mysteries of Trinity, Incarnation, and Redemption. Pastells also noted that the Mandaya belief in the deity Mansilatan and his son Batla could be interpreted as a "degenerate" expression of the Christian Trinity.[160] Paterno appropriated this kind of analysis to "prove" the existence of primitive Christianity in the islands.

Paterno selectively mined and freely elaborated on his sources. He borrowed, for instance, the Franciscan Juan de Plasencia's description of twelve kinds of "infernal ministers" among the Tagalog but edited out what was inconvenient for his own argument. He chose instead to high-

76

light Plasencia's mention of the *Sonat* ("a sort of bishop who ordained priestesses") to convey the notion of a developed Tagalog system of priesthood that paralleled Christian practice.[161] He ignored contrary statements by other authors that the natives had no religions, priests, or temples.[162]

He fabricated evidence. An illustration is his argument that the Holy Eucharist has its Tagalog analogue in the practice in which participants in the rite called *pandot* partake of the *calantipas* ("thin, white *hostias* or hosts") and *gayoma* (vegetable juice converted to "divine essence" by pronouncing the magical formula called *mandala*). I suspect that Paterno, forcing an equivalence with the Christian Eucharist, improvised on the basis of fugitive references in Spanish lexicons to *pandot* (a Tagalog sacrificial rite), *mandala* (verbal spell or formula), *gayoma* (commonly, a love philter made out of the sap of vines and roots), and *calantipas* (or *calantipay*, defined in the Noceda-Sanlucar *Vocabulario* [1860] as "white and thin *hostias*"). However, an entry for *calantipay* in Franciscan Pedro de San Buenaventura's *Vocabulario de Lengua Tagala* (1613) makes clear that the word does not refer to an ecclesiastical or religious object but the thin, crystalline chip made out of mother-of-pearl (*tipas, tipay, kapis*) used for making lanterns.[163] (*Hostia*, in Spanish, can either mean the eucharistic Host or a wafer-like object or chip.) This is an instance of Paterno willfully building out of discrete words an elaborate, fanciful structure of meaning.

Paterno repositioned available data and filled the lacunae with his own inventions to construct a grand narrative of Tagalog civilization. What the missionaries recorded as degenerate remains or the Devil's counterfeits he took as evidence of high religion in precolonial times. His own contemporaries were put off by his exaggerations, willfulness, and vanity (and today's reader will find him archaic and eccentric); yet his works can be profitably studied as moves in the colonial's appropriation of Western knowledge.

ASSUMING THE PREMISE that religion—in particular, Monotheism and Christianity—was the highest possible expression of man's creative reason, Paterno mined European scholarship in comparative religion, cannibalized its evolutionary typologies, and used these to drive his argument about the existence of a "high" Tagalog religion.

Improvising on the stages of religious evolution theorized by scholars like John Lubbock and Max Muller, Paterno says that Philippine aboriginal society developed from atheism to the stages of fetishism, animism, polytheism, and then idolatry.[164] In characteristic fashion, he speculates that the Itas of Luzon—like people "in the kingdom of Peru and among some tribes in the region of Mississipi . . . and certain nomadic families of Asia"—have beliefs corresponding to *sabeismo* (the worship of the sun and celestial bodies among the Sabaeans of Arabia, in what is now Yemen).[165] Extending the argument to the case of Tagalog society, he plays with historical scales by claiming that the Tagalog progressed from the cult of sun and moon to the cult of birds and other animals to a belief in minor deities, and then the religion of a "Supreme Being." Enamored with European categories, he blurs local contexts and temporal sequence by his eclectic mixing of categories. Such was the patchwork character of Paterno's thought that inconsistencies in his theory were left unresolved. It sufficed for Paterno to indicate that the Tagalog, like others in the world, progressed from rudimentary beliefs to a complex, monotheistic religion.

Paterno does not speculate at length on the origins of religion. He states that shared or similar traits may be the result of diffusion since Tagalog civilization is a product of many influences. At times, he even asserts a crude, speculative diffusionism, saying that the *Tinguianes* may have descended from Persia, their ancestors coming from the Red Sea "before the time of Mohamed."[166] Mostly, he points to a psychic matrix common to all religions, one based on the human need for a transcendent power that orders the world. In the manner of European "progressionists," he argues that primitive peoples have elevated theological ideas, a fact that conduces them to even higher conceptions. His basic assumption about religion— one expressed by such ethnologists as Theodor Waitz—is that humanity is one, native capacity is roughly the same among peoples, and that differences are accounted for as differences in the rates of historical growth and the influence of physiology, environment, and inheritance of customs.

Taking the "intellectualist" position, Paterno speculates that religious ideas begin with the experience of hallucinations, apparitions, and dreams about dead persons, which leads to ancestor worship and the notion of soul (the "ghost" and "soul" theories of Herbert Spencer and Edward Tylor), as well as the perception of the infinite and powerful in nature, which leads to the deification of sun, moon, thunder, and other natural phenomena (as Max Muller, for instance, argues). His intellectualist position is shown in what the anthropologist E.E. Evans-Pritchard calls the "if I were a horse" fallacy, in which the observer puts himself in the mind of the "primitive" and presumes to recreate how the primitive makes sense of his experiences. In illustrating how religious ideas evolve, Paterno deploys the hypothetical Ita reflecting, asking questions, and making judgments about his sensations and experiences.

As with religion, so did Paterno approach language. Language was a major preoccupation among early Filipino intellectuals. It was an indigenous "archive" of knowledge particularly precious because of the lack of precolonial written texts or pictorial artifacts. It was a ready resource because of the numerous Philippine lexicons produced by Spanish missionaries. While Filipino intellectuals could (and did) claim privileged "native" knowledge of local languages they relied heavily in fact (and this is particularly true of Paterno) on what the Spaniards had studied, compiled, and preserved.

Stimulation came from European ideas on language. Eighteenth- and nineteenth-century philological theories were usable for Filipino arguments. Theories on the filiations of the world's languages (and the wealth of comparative data that had been made available) could be used to prove that Philippine languages were not isolated and barbarous. Hierarchies of languages could be manipulated to claim for Tagalog or Cebuano a higher level of development than others had assigned to it. The existence of a writing system was proof of "civilization"; the richness of local lexis demonstrated the people's elevated mental and moral state.

These moves are made by Paterno. He assumes classificatory, hierarchic, and evolutionary European views on language.[167] Citing the French Orientalist Abel de Remusat's statement that a people's language is an accurate mirror (*espejo mas fiel*) of their civilization, he points to the semantic plenitude of Tagalog to show the advanced character of the people. He connects Tagalog and other Philippine languages diachronically to ancient sacred languages (Aramaic, Sanskrit, Hebrew) and synchronically to widely distributed languages in the world. What Paterno does is to claim for Tagalogs parity with other peoples in the dynamic of their development at the same time that he marks difference in terms of level reached.

His debt to European philology is shown in his exercises in the etymological unpacking of local terms. Eighteenth- and nineteenth-century philologists believed that the underlying structure of language is common to all men, that diversities of language could be traced back to a limited set of ancient root-words. This *Ursprache* behind all languages is perfectly congruent with reality as shown in the correspondence between word-sounds and ideas or things. Onomatopoeic patterns, consonants, and sibilants were interpreted as universal ways of "sounding the world." Comparing etymologies across historical time (a practice that goes back to Plato's conjectural etymologies) was a favorite game of philologists. Similarities were documented and when resemblances were found, as they almost always were, a genetic cultural relationship was inferred. An influential example of this kind of analysis was the theory of the German philologist Max Muller (1823–1900) that the natural phenomena that were objects of awe were gradually obscured behind a tissue of linguistic and metaphorical usage, leading to a situation (a "disease of language," Muller calls it) in which many names for one object or the same name for several objects resulted in a confusion of several gods being combined into one or one god separated into many. Muller thus holds that the only way to discover the meaning of early religion is by an etymological analysis that restores to the names of gods and the stories told about them their original sense.[168]

Paterno was taken by this kind of philological play. While he cites Muller as one of his sources, inspiration also came from Christian and Kabbalistic exegetical writings that attributed an intrinsic symbolic value to numerals and letters of the alphabet. Paterno cites among his sources *Los nombres de Cristo* (1583–1585), by the great Spanish poet and mystic Luis de Leon (1527–1591). This dialogue in the Platonic manner expounds on the doctrinal, moral, and devotional aspects of the various names applied to Christ in the Old and New Testaments on the basis of the belief that words and vocables are acoustic images of things as these are reflected in the soul or mind.[169]

Asserting that Tagalog religion has its origin in solar myth, Paterno says that the Tagalog God before Bathala was *Arao* (sun) and that *Ra* in *Arao* corresponds to the Egyptian sun-god *Ra*. The *La* in *Bathala*, Paterno says, corresponds to the Egyptian *Ra*, which comes in turn from *Er*, the "divine onomatopoeia" for universal heat, breath of life, spirit of the Creator. In a play of "primitive onomatopoeias," therefore, *Bathala* is the "divine breath" of creative energy.[170]

Heedless of inconsistencies, Paterno piles on other etymologies. *Bathala*, he says, comes from *bahala*, which means *cuidado* ("being careful, concerned"). The insertion of the *T* (*BaThala*) heightens the idea to mean "the Supreme, the premier excellency 'One-Who-Takes-Care-of-All'" (*el Sumo, el excelencia primer Cuidado*); hence the concept of "Providence." Reversing the syllables, *Lahatba*, conveys the idea "All" (*Lahat*). The addition of *Ba* (◯), which is the sign of Woman and generation, amplifies the concept of God as "Creator of All." Elsewhere, Paterno also says that *BHL* is the equivalent of *IHV* (Jehova). The accent that gives form to both is the aspirated *H*, which expresses the invisible and the spiritual. The Tagalog ᜒ is pictogram for the "zig-zag of the heavenly ray that illumines the obscurity of Earth." It is "Light" and "the first name of God." The Tagalog ᜎ is symbol for Man, the sign of potency. Hence, the signs ◯ᜒᜎ mean the uniting of Man and Woman by the "light or spirit" of God.[171]

Claiming for Tagalogs an advanced state of mental development, Paterno illustrates by pointing to the depth and richness of Tagalog vocabulary. As example, he lists the highly differentiated sets of local terms for the Spanish *mirar*, "to look" (29 Tagalog words), *menear*, "to shake or stir" (83), *pensar*, "to think" (17), *abrir*, "to open" (37), and *amigo*, "friend" (17), with variants determined by the actions, circumstances, attitudes, and relations involved.[172] In *Familia Tagalog*, he uses the same strategy of deploying a wealth of lexical items for personhood, nuptial customs, and kin relations as proof of the highly developed nature of the Tagalog personality and kinship systems.[173]

Paterno's linguistic investigations vacillate between a mystical view that assigns to language divine origins and an intellectualist approach that takes it as index of social development. Hence he constructs a sequence that begins with a characterization of Ita language as "stagnant," gesture-dependent, and rudimentary in its abundance of mono- and disyllabic words, then shifts to a view of Tagalog as a language grown in richness and refinement in adaptation to changing material and mental conditions. He approvingly cites in this regard Francisco Colin's remark that Tagalog has the qualities of "the four finest languages in the world, namely Hebrew, Greek, Latin and Spanish."[174]

While Paterno does not systematically explain his theory of language, his arguments are grounded in the nineteenth-century Herderian view

81

that language expressed the level of a people's culture and the sophisti-cation of their thought, an idea that harks back, in Spain, to the view of the Salamanca theologians: "The poverty or wealth of a language, its ability to provide terms for the things, concrete and abstract, which were thought to exist 'in nature', was seen as a precise indication of its users' intellectual understanding of the world in which they lived."[175] Paterno himself says that one finds in language:

> . . . the true image of a people, wherein the past and the present can be seen, their beliefs, their traditions, their customs, in short, their history; with such a close correlation between ideas and words and in such a degree that perfection of the vocabulary argues necessarily for perfection of ideas.[176]

He approvingly quotes from a speech of Antonio Canovas del Castillo in 1887: "[Language] is the most complete tradition of the entire race, of the entire people at any time. This ought not to be disputed because all moral sentiments are involved in language; all spiritual elements are involved. Language is the soul exposed."[177]

As with religion, language provided evidence of the high grade of Tagalog culture. Unlike Herder or Wilhelm von Humboldt, who calls language "the mental exhalation of nationally individual life" and "the work of *nations*"—or, for that matter, Jose Rizal—Paterno was not too interested in pushing language as counter in building a case for nation-alism.[178] He was more interested (as many nineteenth-century European scholars were) in monogenetic speculation on a common source for all languages. He used the proof of language to universalize the Tagalog.

For the most part the early theories on language and religion are now (as Evans-Pritchard puts it) "as dead as mutton."[179] Muller and his fellow mythologists pushed their exercises in "linguistic palaeontology" to the point of absurdity. Paterno's etymological exercises have been dis-credited by a better understanding of phonetic laws and the arbitrary (versus "natural") relation between a form and its meaning. Scholars are no longer interested in the reductive and simplifying quest for origins and universals. Culture is too complex to be reduced to simple chrono-logical formulae and establishing chronologies from circumstantial evidence is no longer fashionable or tenable. Anthropology has turned

away from the conjectural to the experimental, moving away from speculations on genesis to analyses of social practice.

It is important, however, to appreciate where Paterno was coming
from and what he was about. His pastiche of theories and melange of
comparisons should not be dismissed outright as the recklessness of a
vain amateur. It is curious that he did not seem to feel the need to smoothen
the inconsistencies or resolve the contradictions in his work. He seemed to
relish the hybridity of his data, working by a method of piling up "evidence" instead of working toward a coherent synthesis. He cannibalized
European theories. Did he feel it sufficed to display a whole panoply of
distant and archaic connections to create a semblance of the "universality" of Filipino culture? Did he desire—by drawing connections between
the Tagalogs and the Sabaeans of Arabia or the Turanians of the Urals—
to explode the isolation and invisibility into which colonialism had
consigned his people?

IN THEORIZING a Philippine civilization, Paterno delved into the literature of the emerging discipline of anthropology. An *ethnologist* rather
than an *ethnographer*, he engaged in second-order interpretation rather
than primary investigation. As he said in his introduction to *Antigua
Civilizacion*, he was interested in reviewing what had been written about
the Philippines, correcting errors, and setting the accounts straight in
the light of modern, "scientific" knowledge. What he was about was the
construction of a "theory" of Philippine civilization.

Anthropology provided him with the tools to study the genesis of a
people's institutions, morality, and racial characteristics. Among the
sources he cites are Paul Topinard's *L'Anthropologie* (1876) and, more
important, Theodor Waitz's six-volume *Anthropologie der Naturvolker*
(1859–1871), a landmark in the history of anthropology as a discipline.
Waitz was an influence on Filipino propagandists, particularly Rizal who
embarked on the unfinished project of translating one of Waitz's works,
possibly the first volume of *Anthropologie* which the Anthropological
Society of London chose in 1863 as the most adequate presentation of
contemporary knowledge in the discipline. The fifth volume of
Anthropologie (posthumously completed and published by Waitz's disciple G. Gerland) dealt with the peoples of the Malay archipelago,
Micronesia, and Polynesia. Waitz must have attracted Filipino intellec-

tuals not only for his useful introduction to the discipline and Malay and Polynesian cultures but because of his liberal ideas. Following the "unity of mankind" thesis, Waitz argued that the mental potential of all races is the same, that mixed races are just as viable as "pure" types, that history is driven by an evolutionary progression, and differences in societies and cultures are to be explained by factors of environment and history.

Paterno cites such forerunners of anthropological theory as J.F. Blumenbach, James Cowles Prichard, and Armand de Quatrefages on race classification; William Jones and Max Muller in philology; J.J. Bachofen, Charles Letourneau, and John Ferguson McLennan on kinship and marriage; Lord Kames, Charles Francois Dupuis, and Ernest Renan on religion; Alexander Bain in psychology, and Georges Cuvier and John Lubbock on evolution. He was apparently familiar with the work of the most important scholars in anthropology at the time, Herbert Spencer, Edward Tylor, and (to a lesser extent) Charles Darwin.

Paterno used some of the earliest European anthropological investigations on the Philippines, citing among his sources Blumentritt, French ethnologist Joseph Montano, Rudolf Virchow, and Hendrik Kern. He does not, however, make extensive or systematic use of this class of sources either because of lack of access or the desire to appear "original." Pardo, for instance, complains that Paterno reproduced in *El Barangay* (1892) the Plasencia text Pardo published in *Revista Contemporanea* (1892) without acknowledgment, claiming that it was sourced from a "manuscript" in his personal possession.[180]

Paterno was a self-taught anthropologist at a time when the discipline's boundaries and methods were inchoate. Olympian in his habits, he worked alone and did not seem to have actively communicated (as Rizal did) with Filipino or foreign scholars. It is difficult to determine in all cases in what form and how well he used his sources. The protocols of scholarly and bibliographic practice in Paterno's time are not always the same as ours. Paterno was prone to parading his erudition, citing works he may have extracted from secondary sources and encyclopedias popular at the time. We are not sure what languages Paterno read (he footnotes works in Spanish, French, German, and English). Though he has not integrated his readings in a discriminating and coherent fashion, he nevertheless surveyed a vast amount of literature.

Paterno practiced "conjectural anthropology." He starts with a thesis or formula and proceeds to ransack missionary chronicles, travel accounts, and ethnological compendia for bits of evidence favorable to his theory. He cites authorities, from Aristotle and Herodotus to Vico and Lubbock, without locating them in time. He is mostly indifferent to the historical parameters of statements made in, say, a seventeenth-century missionary chronicle or a nineteenth-century French travelogue. It would seem that for Paterno world-knowledge formed a simultaneous order in which one could freely draw useful evidence from the most diverse and widely separated sources. This results in a synchronic patchwork in which the topoi of medieval Christian histories (such as the origin of the races in Noah's sons, Ham, Japhet, and Shem) are deployed as "evidence" together with statistics from nineteenth-century anthropometric science.

His basic approach involved the grouping of culture traits according to an evolutionary framework. Inspired by the classificatory approaches of the natural sciences, this interest in culture trait distributions relied on oversimplified equivalences and slighted the actual dynamics of human societies. Facts were wrenched from their social contexts and dealt with atomistically. It was a method already criticized in Paterno's time for producing overgeneralized, patchwork histories of traits rather than specific histories of societies as experienced and created by their members. It was, however, a dominant mode of doing cultural description at the time. Such leading ethnologists as Tylor and Spencer were aware of the pitfalls in relying on inadequate data gathered by "amateurs" but they still felt that this could be redressed by amassing large numbers of cases, that errors can be balanced out when large samples are employed.[181]

Paterno's comparatism is reckless and uninhibited. He says that the Ophir mentioned in the Bible may be the Philippines because the rare scented wood Solomon obtained there exists in the Philippines. He finds echoes of ancient Tagalog concepts in an Armenian song and executes quick shifts from Bagobo mythology to the Rig Veda and Zend-Avesta to the Holy Bible. He pushes philological analysis to absurd limits in excavating a whole theology from an etymological decoding of names of local deities. He mines old Philippine dictionaries for what suits his purposes and then, claiming "inside" knowledge, freely elaborates on the semantic nuances "outsiders" cannot grasp. He extracts from Spanish-colonial lexicons words like *lohaya* ("to ask for something with great earnestness"), *labusaquit* ("to be tenacious in an undertaking"), and *tagalasic* ("a free, unbridled person"), and proceeds to construct, out of nothing but isolated lexical items, a whole theory of Tagalog ethics and personality.

He claims the "native's point of view" when it suits his purposes. He simulates local data by referring to a trip he made to the province of Bay (Laguna) in 1882 during which he heard of "admirable traditions of the remote age."[182] He deploys literary devices, creating the hypothetical Tagalog sage speaking oracles or contemplating choices. He throws in such a welter of data, contradictions are unreconciled, conclusions loosely argued, and arguments broken and discontinuous.

Paterno was not his own perverse, esoteric creation. His assumptions and methods drew from the fund of Orientalist scholarship at the time: an interest in genetic explanations (tracing the origins of races, religions, laws and customs), the construction of synthetic, classificatory systems (with their bias for similitude and resemblance rather than discontinuity and difference); a classical evolutionism (with its sequential, hierarchic ordering of races and religions); a belief in the uniformity of human nature (which predisposed the observer to judge peoples according to a Eurocentric view of what was "civilized"); and a racial and social determinism (which simplified and exaggerated the influence of such factors as heredity, diet, and climate).

Paterno's works were not a freestanding performance. Reviewing the work of anthropology's pioneers, Evans-Pritchard writes:

> Indeed, looking backwards, it is sometimes difficult to understand how many of the theories put forward to account for primitive man's beliefs and for the origin and development of religion could ever have been propounded . . . even on the facts available to them it is astounding that so much could have been written which appears to be contrary to common sense. Yet, these men were scholars and of great learning and ability. To comprehend what now seem to be obviously faulty interpretations and explanations, we would have to

86

write a treatise on the climate of thought of their time, the intellectual circumstances which set bounds to their thought, a curious mixture of positivism, evolutionism, and the remains of a sentimental religiosity.[183]

Anthropology was in its infancy and, well into the early twentieth century, the leading practitioners were men of letters who wrote in a speculative mode. The pioneer theorists on primitive society were armchair intellectuals. Lubbock was a banker, Tylor a foreign languages clerk, and McLennan, Bachofen, and Lewis Henry Morgan were, like Paterno, lawyers. Fieldwork was not the privileged method it became in the twentieth century. The early ethnologists relied for their information on what European explorers, missionaries, administrators, and traders narrated.

Nineteenth-century comparatism allowed scholars to classify and control the variety and difference that threatened to overwhelm European consciousness with the surge of new knowledge about other lands and times. Classificatory systems, however, determined what was selected for description. They also implied a linear directionality, the assumption that things, ideas, and institutions could be seen as progressing through stages to some higher, Eurocentric goal. The spell of scientism masked the fact that the foundations of theoretical systems were period- and culture-dependent.

Comparatism occasioned its own favored genres and styles of mapping the world. Evans-Pritchard's comment on the comparative method in early anthropology applies to Paterno. It was a "scrap-book" treatment with little analytical comparison, the building of "preliminary classifications in which vast numbers of observations could be placed under a limited number of rubrics."

> This consisted . . . of taking from the first-hand records about primitive peoples, and willy-nilly from all over the world, wrenching the facts yet further from their contexts, only what referred to the strange, weird, mystical, superstitious . . . and piecing the bits together in a monstrous mosaic, which was supposed to portray the mind of primitive man.[184]

Paterno's style reflected the temper of European ethnological writing at the time. The form of the medieval encyclopedia, with its universal parade of illustrative cases, remained influential in the eighteenth and nineteenth centuries as model for documenting cultures. Its style is illustrated by works from Charles Francois Dupuis's *Origine de tous les cultes* (1795) to John Lubbock's *Origin of Civilization and the Primitive Condition of Man* (1870), works Paterno consulted.[185] Thus James Frazer, author of the classic *Golden Bough* (1890), has been criticized for a "butterfly collecting" methodology that "juxtaposes information, often of very dubious provenance, totally out of context, [and] allows the author to 'prove' almost any point he cares to make."[186] In the same vein, Evans-Pritchard comments on *Introduction to the History of Religion* (1896) by F.B. Jevons, a popular book written by a teacher of philosophy at the University of Durham: "It is a collection of absurd reconstructions, unsupportable hypotheses and conjectures, wild speculations, suppositions and assumptions, inappropriate analogies, misunderstandings and misinterpretations, and, especially in what he wrote about totemism, just plain nonsense."[187]

In historical context, Paterno's assertions are not entirely grotesque. Speculation on references to the Philippines in Diodorus Siculus's *Bibliotheca historica* (first century B.C.) and Ptolemy's *Geographia* (first century A.D.) and the introduction of Christianity to Asia by St. Thomas the Apostle were standard topoi in early Spanish-colonial chronicles. Early European missionaries also fancied seeing a wonderful harmony between many passages in Lao Tzu's *Tao Te Ching* (sixth century B.C.) and the Holy Bible. Sinologist Abel de Remusat (1788–1832) and other scholars argued that the Hebrew name Yahweh and the mystery of the Holy Trinity are to be found inscribed in *Tao Te Ching*. (Paterno, it may be noted, cites Lao Tzu and Remusat among his sources.) The geologist Georges Cuvier (1769–1832) "confirmed" the historicity of Noah's Flood. Franz Bopp (1791–1867) speculated on the relationship between Malayo-Polynesian and Indo-German languages. As late as the 1920s, there were scholars who drew connections between Malay languages and the Inca, Ful (Central Africa), and American Indian languages.[188]

On the question of Egypt, seventeenth-century Jesuit Francisco Colin drew parallels between Tagalog and Egyptian veneration of animals.[189] Nineteenth-century American naturalist Charles Pickering speculated on the possibility of a great ancient diaspora emanating from the Nile

River after hearing of the veneration of crocodiles in Samoa.[190] British philologist James Cowles Prichard (1786–1848) explained linguistic diversity according to the Biblical account of the Deluge and the tower of Babel and on this basis drew relationships between Egyptian and Chinese and a host of other languages.[191] Egyptomania persisted after Paterno, expressed most absurdly in the pan-Egyptian theory of Elliot Smith (1871–1937) who, in pushing the idea that Egypt was the source of higher cultures in the world, drew such farflung connections as the derivation of Cambodian and Javanese temple complexes from the Egyptian pyramids.[192]

Paterno's scholarship was not his own sole invention. He took from Spanish and other European texts much of the Philippine material he weaves into his writings. Stripped of exaggeration and conceit, he expressed ethnological ideas respectable in his place and time, many of which persisted as key ideas in Philippine history and anthropology after him. These include ideas on the archipelago's origin as part of the Asian continent, prehistoric stages of development based on the European model of tool types, the genetic descent of Negritos from the "Ethiopic Negroes" of Greater India, the race-based, diffusionist theory of "migration waves," the three-class organization of precolonial society into chiefs, freemen, and slaves, and the three-strata division of the population into what Colin calls *naciones barbaras* (Negritos or *Negrillos*), *naciones politicas* (groups like the Tagalog, Pampango, and Visayan), and *naciones medias* (intermediate, racially-mixed groups).[193]

The most respected "Philippinist" in Paterno's time, Ferdinand Blumentritt, relying on published sources, produced in 1882 a survey of the Philippine aboriginal population which also described a precolonial system of petty "states" and classes and such practices as sexual promiscuity, bride-capture, polygamy, the worship of crocodiles and celestial bodies, and the primitive belief in a Supreme Being.[194] Like Paterno, Blumentritt worked with a racialist, evolutionist view of Philippine inhabitants that ranged from "stationary" Itas doomed to extinction to hybrid, dynamic Malays. Dean Worcester, the American zoologist-turned-colonial official, would make similar remarks in 1900, characterizing Negritos as "at or near the bottom of the human series" in the matter of intelligence, "incapable of any considerable degree of civilization or advancement."[195]

If Paterno's classification of Philippine indigenes strikes us as underspecified and confused, we must remember that the problem of nomination and classification was to remain for a long time what Blumentritt calls "this labyrinth of nomenclature." Mixing biological, linguistic, political, and geographic principles of classification, Blumentritt estimated there were 82 "non-Christian" or "wild tribes" in the Philippines. Other scholars and sources after him would raise figures ranging from 27 to 116. As Karl Hutterer remarks: "Even today, there is no single, universally accepted system of ethnic classification for the Philippines."[196]

The theory of "migration waves"—elaborated and popularized by H. Otley Beyer to become a ruling paradigm in Philippine scholarship for decades after—was an idea already current in the nineteenth century (and even earlier), theorized by Spanish missionary authors and taken up by Paterno, Blumentritt, Rudolf Virchow, and the zoologist Armand de Quatrefages in his *Histoire generale des races humaines* (1889).[197] Speculation that Tinguians may have descended from Japanese shipwrecked in Luzon and that the Igorots may have mixed with the remains of Limahong's Chinese army was already in the literature in Paterno's time.[198] Beyer, hailed as "father" of Philippine anthropology, would even speculate that there may have been "a few settlements of Sabaean and Persian merchants in the southern Philippines."[199]

If Paterno did not get the respect other writers had, an explanation can be found in the framing of his ethnological statements. While other writers assumed a pseudo-objective scientific voice, he was polemical and hyperbolic.

Having said all this, we cannot gloss over Paterno's errors and excesses (which even his own contemporaries recognized). He deployed theories in crude, exaggerated terms. More important, Paterno accepted the basic assumptions of Orientalism. While he gloried in the resemblances that connected distant and diverse cultures and worried about the grade of culture given to his people, he accepted the conceptions of difference and hierarchy (high/low, black/white, savage/civilized) that legitimated such structures of power as aristocracies and empires.

Yet, his scholarship is not to be dismissed as merely idiosyncratic. It is important to understand what drives his work, to situate it not only as a venture in scholarship but a project in politics.

PEDRO PATERNO was not an untalented man. He is the first Filipino anthropologist. To a greater degree than did Rizal, Pardo, and de los Reyes, Paterno self-consciously attempted the systematic application of ethnological science to Philippine culture. Paterno's main interest for us today lies in his positioning within the discipline and its object. To study the position he took is to learn something about the disciplinary power of Western knowledge as well as the possibilities in testing its limits or opening up autonomous spaces within it.

No Filipino exemplified in such flamboyant fashion the appetite of the colonized for learning in a century that saw an unprecedented expansion of scientific knowledge in Europe. Rizal and Pardo were themselves remarkable Renaissance intellectuals, steeped in the sciences and humanities. Rizal, however, carried with him something of his roots in provincial gentry, his was an earnest and prudent intelligence. The Hispanic patrician, Pardo, a physician like Rizal, was the detached scientist suspicious of the political and the speculative. Trained in the scholastic arts of theology and law, Paterno—the merchant's son who aspired to be a prince—was a theorizer and a dilletante.

Paterno was well-read, an attainment he ostentatiously displays in his bibliographic citations and annotations. A student of philosophy and letters in Spain, he was introduced to the classical authors, from Tacitus and Virgil to Aristotle and St. Augustine, and was versed in the works of Spanish Catholic writers, in particular the mystic Fray Luis de Leon (1527–1591) and the philosopher Jaime Balmes (1810–1848). While Pardo and Rizal drifted away from Catholicism, Paterno remained loyal to the orthodoxies of the Faith.

Claiming the Olympian view, he chastised European observers of the Philippines for their failure to see local culture in the context of universal evolution. "To assess well a civilization," he says, "it is necessary to study first the civilizations which have preceded it in the world."[200] In assuming this perspective, he surveyed a most diverse range of travel, missionary, and ethnological accounts, such as the works of Joseph Francois Lafitau and Martin Dobrizhoffer on America, Verney Lovett Cameron on Africa, the Abbe Dubois and S.C. Bose on India, and Cesar Dumont d'Urville, John Forrest, and George Turner on Australia and the Pacific. His eclectic readings included works on Hindu astronomy by Jean-Sylvain Bailly, the Chinese language by Abel de Remusat, and Arabian kinship systems by W. Robertson Smith. Like many Europeans of the time, he was fascinated by Egyptology, reading expedition reports and compendias of Egyptian art and antiquities by John Wilkinson, C.-F. Volney, Gustave Le Bon, Heinrich Brugsch, Gaston Maspero, and even the historical romances of Theophile Gautier and Georg Ebers.

Rizal was the more purposive reader. In locating the Philippines in a wider cultural and geographic sphere, Rizal diligently tracked down all he could find on Asia and, in particular, the Malay world. Paterno was not unfamiliar with the Malay studies of William Marsden and John Crawfurd but he was "global" in his ambitions and consequently more superficial in his command of a particular culture-area. He was less interested in the nationalist pragmatics that guided Rizal's scholarship.

Paterno's scholarship was produced in the epistemic space of the nineteenth-century Filipino diaspora. Paterno was one of the earliest Filipinos to be educated in Europe, at a time when the idea of a *Filipino* nationality was, at best, inchoate. He arrived in Spain at the age of fourteen without the load of memories Rizal carried with him when Rizal left the Philippines eleven years later. The events of 1872 touched the Paterno family in a very direct way but affected Pedro Paterno differently. If the memory of 1872 stoked in Rizal a sense of separateness and difference, it apparently whetted in the young Paterno—more the immigrant than the sojourner Rizal was—a desire for acceptance, a recognition of sameness.

More than any of his contemporaries, Paterno worked out of the premises of the Orientalist renaissance in Europe. He had spent less time in his own country than Pardo and Rizal did at the time he wrote his defining works. Paterno admired Western science, believed in Christianity, and deeply desired to be regarded a full citizen of Spain. He demonstrated this in his *Influencia social del cristianismo*, in which, looking out from the vantage point of metropolitan and Catholic Spain, he delivers a fervent panegyric in the spirit of Francois Rene de Chateaubriand's shallow but seductive *Genie du christianisme* (1802).

He worked out of a specific site in Europe. He was trained in the conservative academic bastion of Salamanca and schooled in Spanish Romanticism, with its strong Catholic accent, vague humanitarianism, subjectivism, and medievalism. He was not intellectually connected to the French Revolution (a connection historians cite for Rizal and Andres

Bonifacio), but to the conservative European reaction to its dangers and excesses, as shown in Jacobin violence and Napoleon's imperial aggressions. The nineteenth century, it must be remembered, was not just an age of triumphant liberalism but a period that witnessed vigorous efforts by the ruling classes to counter and coopt such signs of social upheaval as the Napoleonic wars, the French Revolution, the Paris Commune of 1871, and, in Spain, the rise of Proudhonist anarchism. The conservative reaction was expressed in the works of Chateaubriand and French statesman-historian Francois Guizot (1787–1874), writers Paterno admired, as well as the nineteenth-century resurgence of Biblical interpretations of history, as shown in the works of Blumenbach, Cuvier, and Prichard, and the Italian Catholic historian Cesare Cantu's *Storia universale* (1838–1846), a widely influential book that plots human history as the work of Divine Providence. Closer to "home," Paterno imbibed the spirit of men like Jaime Balmes and aristocrat-philosopher Juan Donoso Cortes (1809–1853), both of whom responded to the anxieties of the age by seeking a synthesis of bourgeois liberalism and scientific progress with a traditional belief in the primacy of the monarchy and the Church. Spain's most influential conservative thinker, Cortes wrote against the dangers of socialism and atheism and exalted the directive role of tradition, religion, and an "aristocracy of intellect."[201]

Reading in the British Museum, Rizal embarked on interrogating the European construction of the Philippines. Studying in Salamanca, Paterno dreamed of locating himself and his country in Europe's map of the world.

Desiring entrée into Spanish metropolitan society, Paterno worked on both sides of his halfway location, an insider and outsider in both Spain and his home country. He used the idiom of Spanish privilege (a noble title and its appurtenances) and decorated it with local content. He dedicated his books to high Spanish officials and took pride in his having married into Spanish nobility. He demonstrated his fluency in Spain's intellectual conversation about the world, speaking in Spanish to Spaniards, quoting Campoamor and Balmes, discoursing on the role of Spain and Christianity in the world. He played the role of European world traveler, showing off his hoard of Orientalia in public exhibitions in Madrid. He parlayed his accomplishments and connections in the *metropoli* for status and influence in the colony.

Paterno's starting point was the center, its view of how races and nations are ranked and organized, how mankind has changed through the centuries and in what direction. A derivative thinker, he adopted European classificatory systems and then proceeded to locate himself and *his* people within these categories. The themes he dealt with were those Western science defined as the standards that characterized "civilized man": type of religion, complexity of language, and the ability to control nature and form civil societies. Where Rizal adopted the quick, interrogatory forms of the annotation and polemical essay, Paterno mimed the Orientalist scrapbook and encyclopedia.

His work, however, cannot be dismissed as a simple miming of Western scholarship. Scholarship is refracted, bent and shaped by the borders an author and his words have to cross. In Paterno's case, his status as a colonial, non-European subject necessarily shaped his writing. Despite his complacent view of power, Paterno could not quite escape his being classed part of an "inferior and colonized race." No matter how closely he identified himself with the metropolis—speaking its speech, affecting its manners, vicariously participating in its power, believing in its essential rightness— he could not (as he reportedly wished) erase his "color." The conditions of his enunciation were such that he had to engage in a series of repositionings: locating himself in a place and tradition to which he was not born, attempting the double vision of seeing Europe and, conversely, the Philippines from another place, using a language and mode of writing not his own, speaking to an audience "abroad" and at "home," negotiating the tension of being both subject and object of what he writes.

Though he kept his distance from the political activities of the Propaganda Movement, he was not disconnected from early nationalist thought. Locating himself "in-between" indigenous society and modern science, he appropriated the concepts and themes of Western scientific discourse to stake out a claim for the knowledge-object he called *nacion Tagala*. His act of subversion was to wrest for his people a higher grade of culture than what the colonizers had assigned them. Deploying the word *civilizacion*, he claimed for a people "without history" not just a "culture" but something deeper and grander. Using the word, he appropriated the meanings Europeans attached to it: the value of a forward, upward-moving historical process, the sense of a "condition of refinement and order" already achieved.[202]

94

In advancing the idea of a nation confirmed by long history and high culture, Paterno was making the same arguments other nationalists were making. Though Paterno's compass of the nation (*nacion tagala, Luzonica*) now strikes us as restricted, we must remember that he was writing at a time when nation-formation was inchoate. Rizal and de los Reyes, among others, also imagined the nation out of their own particular locations in it and in the image of that proto-national community colonialism itself had rendered visible.[203] Equally important, we must pay attention to the context of the argument of nationality. Spanish (and, later, American) colonizers denied the existence of the "nation" and what this implies of integrality, unity, and agency. Hence the characteristic portrait they drew of the conquered was that of a series of tribes, centerless and fragmented, without awareness of itself as a collectivity. Thus, as elsewhere, the anti-colonial movement began with the assertion of the nationhood colonialism denied.

It is in negotiating the colonial divide that Paterno constructed the image of a unitary nation and pointed to the epistemics of language and religion as sites from which the dominant Western characterizations of the country could be interrogated. This is shown in his ideas of *Bathalismo* and *Sangdugo*. Though he would retrospectively claim that, in developing these ideas, he laid the ideological basis of the Katipunan, these were part of late nineteenth-century Filipino discourse on the nation, as shown in the use of these ideas by Rizal, M.H. del Pilar, Juan Luna, and Andres Bonifacio.[204] In this discourse, *Bathalismo* functioned as sign for evoking a "civilization" integral and apart from colonialism. The symbolism of *Sangdugo* reinterpreted colonialism (or denied it) by tracing its beginning to a foundational compact between two autonomous nations instead of an act of possession, a planting of Flag and Cross. Paterno diverged in the political thrust of his arguments. Such men as Rizal and del Pilar moved beyond the mendicant desire for recognition and assimilation towards an assertion of autonomy and difference. Paterno undermined the possibilities of what he attempted by assuming a tributary position in relation to the West and by ultimately denying difference.

Paterno made the radical move of disengaging the Philippines from the colonialist view that what it amounted to as a culture is a Spanish creation. He exposed himself to ridicule because of his flamboyance in connecting the Philippines to the earliest civilizations of the Mediterranean and Ancient Near East and the roots of Christianity in Biblical times, but he was raising the same fundamental arguments of "long history" and "high culture" advanced by Rizal (who also invoked the flawed authority of Diodorus Siculus and Ptolemy). The key political difference is that while Rizal harnessed his arguments for what would be increasingly nationalist aims, Paterno deployed his theories for assimilationist purposes. He steered clear of direct criticism of Spanish colonialism. He pointed to Spanish misinterpretations of Tagalog cultural inheritance but discreetly blames this on a "loss of clarity" and a deficient knowledge of Philippine culture. He dedicates this ancient legacy to the enrichment of an imperial and universal history.

His was an essentially mendicant view. He accepted the premises and criteria by which Europe had divided and classified mankind. He conjured a unitary *nacion tagala* and invested it with a historical dynamic that placed it under the order of Reason and Progress; he did not, however, claim for it the status (or future) of being autonomous and sovereign. While he discreetly blamed colonialism for having obscured an ancient Tagalog legacy and called for its recovery (as Rizal did), he did so not to establish a claim for separateness and autonomy but to propose a more vital assimilation of colony to empire. In both his political and intellectual careers, he accepted the country's incorporation into more powerful worlds. Paterno remained the vassal who desired a place at the royal table.

In carving out tributary space for the "Tagalog nation" in a Spanish/ Western world order, Paterno was fashioning space for himself. It is easy to surmise why Paterno found the theory of Malay migrations congenial or why, despite the fact that anthropologists like Spencer and Morgan believed in the degenerative effects of racial mixture, Paterno the *mestizo* chose to argue—following Michelet and Renan—that it was in the mixing of races that society became robust and dynamic. Such ideas created the conceptual space in which he could present himself at the most advanced stage in the evolution of Philippine society. Unable to prove descent from "ancient kings," Paterno (and others as well) can claim to being at the forefront of the most progressive migratory wave. Unable to claim "purity of blood," he can assert the superior value of being a racial hybrid. This said, however, it is interesting that Paterno never really announced himself a Chinese mestizo, preferring the aesthetics and politics of having descended from Tagalog "blue blood" to the prosaic realities of his merchant origins.

Paterno's *nacion tagala* is objectified through a series of subordinations and exclusions. He distances it from the country's aboriginal and "backward" tribes by drawing racialist hierarchies that consign them to the past. He excludes Muslims by privileging the Christianizing process. He carves out privileged sociotemporal space for "Tagalogs" in developing the genealogical themes of Malay migrations, racial mixture, and culture contact. He centers the *nacion* in Manila and imagines a polity ruled by a virtuous and enlightened aristocracy. Paterno created a nation in which he was exemplar.

Paterno was the *asimilacionista* who imagined the Philippines as an exotic province of Spain. He was stranded in that early phase of the Propaganda Movement when Filipinos, desiring recognition, lamented that the colony did not receive the kind of attention the imperial metropolis gave to other Spanish possessions. He remained committed to the goal of political assimilation even when the Revolution broke out in 1896 and long after others had despaired of the reformist goals of the Propaganda Movement and had turned to a militant, separatist nationalism. He remained a votary of Spain long after Rizal began to shift his loyalties elsewhere.

Materially privileged and politically conservative, Paterno did not imagine, as Rizal did, the possibilities of a Philippines separate from Spain. He aligned himself with Spain when the revolution broke out in 1896, initiated the move to have the Philippines declared an autonomous Spanish province during the Spanish-American War, cast himself with the Republic when the United States seized Manila, positioned himself at the head of a campaign for U.S. protectorate status, and then tried once again to insinuate himself into a leadership position in the new political order under the Americans. Even when he issued his stirring calls for a war of independence in 1898–1899, he was the reluctant revolutionary. Circumstance rather than conviction forced the *hispanista* and *asimilacionista* to wear the ill-fitting cloak of a nationalist.

His ambitions were colonial and feudal. His sketch of the country in *Ninay* showcases the prosperous *arrabal* of Santa Cruz (his home district), the exploitable wealth of the islands, the delicacies of sentiment and unimpeachable virtues of the local aristocracy. He romanticizes *costumbres*

Filipinas to claim recognition not so much for his people as his own class. He constructs the nation out of his own imagined location in it. His "nation" is the *nacion tagala* or *islas Luzonicas* (encompassing by this phrase Luzon and—though he makes scant reference to it—Visayas). Though he frequently cites the indigenous peoples of Mindanao, his imaginary consigns this island to the outer margins or baser matrix out of which *civilizacion tagala* evolved as the most advanced stage. He centers his imagined nation in the Pasig River, "the cradle of Tagalog civilization." In one of his more exuberant musings on the superiority of Tagalog religious conceptions, he says that "on the banks of the Pasig have been spiritualized the religious ideas of the Nile and Euphrates," and even to some measure "the luminous ideas reflected in the crystalline waters of Jordan."[205]

The self-styled *maguinoo* born in the banks of the Pasig, Paterno fancied himself one of the most evolved beings of the Tagalog nation. Elitist (like other *ilustrados* though he exceeded them in a showiness almost naïve), he surrounded himself with bookish learning and had little personal knowledge of the country. He was thirty-six when he decided to settle down in the home country. He could not speak or write Tagalog passably. He published in Spain for Spaniards and it does not seem that his scholarly texts were widely read in the Philippines. Except for the peregrinations in Luzon forced on him by war and politics, he lived out the rest of his life in Manila. The story of his being carried in a hammock by a relay of twenty men to his mountain rendezvous with Aguinaldo in Biyak-na-Bato is wonderfully apt. Writing about this experience in 1910 (the year before he died), he was aware of the controversies surrounding his role in the forging of the pact, yet does not quite engage these directly. Instead, he creates out of history a theater of the self in which, at various turns, he engages in lyric ejaculations in which patriotism is rendered in tropes of sensuous feeling for the land's mountains, rivers, moon, and air. Traveling through the Tagalog countryside during the war, the images he saw (or imagined seeing) in the landscape across which he moved were not those of a war-stricken people but characters out of the pages of *Ninay*, ancient Bathala descending in a "carriage of thunder and lightning," and caves echoing secret, orgiastic rites harking back to "Egyptian-Babylonian liturgies."[206]

He was lord of a country that was largely a creation in his own mind.

NICK JOAQUIN has written eloquently about the turn of the century and the men who, grown old before their time, did not quite cross the divide.[207] Stranded in the nineteenth century, they were as ghosts in the interstices of the present, dreaming vanished glory, miming the grand gestures of the past, delivering unintelligible speeches. One of these men—perhaps the grandest relic of them all—was Pedro Paterno.

In a Joaquinesque coda to this story, the grand Paterno residence in Santa Cruz has gone to seed. The once-genteel borough has become a blighted urban district choked in humanity and concrete, and Pasig is a river no longer hospitable to dreaming. Today, the only street in Manila named after Paterno is a short, shabby street (formerly called Noria) in the old Paterno neighborhood, a street known to today's Manilans as "the hangout of itinerant rubber-stamp carvers, locksmiths, bootblacks, streetwalkers and pickpockets."[208]

The problem with Paterno's almost unlimited capacity for self-delusion is that it has defamiliarized him. Dismissed as travesties of Western scholarship, his works have been excluded from serious consideration. Insufficient attention has been given to what is more important than his perceived exoticism, the intellectual position he staked out. It is a position that offers an interesting perspective on how the "Third World" engaged Orientalism.

For all his errors and excesses, Pedro Paterno represented a significant tendency in Philippine intellectual life. Working within the dominant discourse on sameness and difference, he parlayed his halfway location between colony and metropole into a space of power. We cannot closely chart how his intellectual position was formed. (For a man who thought highly of himself, Paterno left behind few autobiographical records in the way of memoirs, letters or diaries.) His position can be appreciated by comparison with the stance taken by other Filipino émigrés. Impecunious and ambitious, Graciano Lopez Jaena tried to build for himself a career as a politician in the peninsula. There he died embittered and obscure. M.H. del Pilar, forced to flee to Spain because of persecution at home, was the sojourner who saw Spain as arena for a struggle that, he knew, would eventually shift home. He died impoverished in Barcelona waiting for a boat to bring him home. Rizal kept his distance from Spain, roamed through a wider Europe than Paterno knew, and refused the easy loyalties to an idea or place. He testified to a final faith by bravely facing a firing squad in Manila. The wealthy Paterno invented himself as the erudite Tagalog nobleman come to the court of Spain. Though he returned to the homeland and enjoyed a brief season of glory, events consigned him to the role of proconsul without a realm.

In inventing himself Paterno invented a country. The nineteenth century was fertile ground for such a project. European Orientalist scholarship generated popular interest in the description, ranking, and classification of cultures and nations. A nascent nationalism stirred great interest among Filipinos in discovering for themselves a history and tradition apart from coloniality. Paterno swam in these streams. Adopting the European narrative of evolution, manipulating ideas like monogenesis and diffusionism, plotting his material in Victorian taxonomies, assuming the encyclopedic authority of the Orientalist—he declared that the Philippines was home of a high civilization.

In the failure to imagine a future of the nation as sovereign, Paterno does not push the autonomous possibilities in the concepts of language and philosophy that he takes up; he does not fully ground the *nacion* in the Malay civilizational base he invokes; and he does not question the European categories of knowledge he employs.

Paterno turned such ideas as *Bathalismo* and *Sangdugo* into idealized signs of ancient heritage and universal brotherhood. In Rizal and del Pilar, these were politicized signs of a sovereign culture and a Rousseauan social contract the violation of which maimed colonialism's claim to legitimacy. In the revolutionary Katipunan, *Sangdugo* would become an organizing symbol, not only of a violated contract of mutuality that gave the revolution its moral justification but a compact of brotherhood entered into among Filipinos themselves. Similarly, Isabelo de los Reyes would write about *Bathalismo* some years after Paterno did. Envisioning a "Philippine Theodicy" (*Teodicea Filipina*) that combined religion and science, de los Reyes proposed *Bathalismo* as an ideology for the Katipunan and subsequently introduced it into the founding theological documents of the Philippine Independent Church.[209]

Serendipities have played a role in the advance of human knowledge. As Umberto Eco points out, the world has been changed (for better or for worse) and new truths have emerged from "ideas, projects, beliefs that exist in a twilight zone between common sense and lunacy, truth and error, visionary intelligence and what now seem to us as stupidity, though it was not stupid in its day and we must therefore consider it with great respect." This is a judgment one can make in Paterno's case as well.[210]

Discontinuities and dispersions in the history of thought are such that despite what may have been Paterno's original intentions, his ideas on *Bathalismo* and *Sangdugo* were appropriated for other purposes by more radical nationalists like de los Reyes (who credits Rizal and Paterno with having initiated the discussion on the subject) as well as Rizalist sects and nativist cults in the twentieth century.[211] Paterno's flamboyant claims about a precolonial civilization have persisted as part of a nativist, subcultural strain in Filipino thought. Themes of Philippine culture's ancient classical and Christian roots appeared in popular, vernacular histories written long after Paterno died. It is ironic that while Paterno imagined he was engaged in "high" scholarship, his theories have survived in the more subterranean realms of Philippine intellectual life.

The unfinished, hybrid character of Paterno's work has kept alive the possibilities he suppresses or excludes. His deployment of the themes of *Bathalismo* and *Sangdugo* stirred a current of anti-colonial impulses in his time. His philological musings on religious ideas and moral sentiments, though largely ignored, adumbrate today's interest in "indigenous psychology" and the epistemics of Philippine languages. While he does not fully exploit indigenous language and philosophy as sites out of which colonial power can be interrogated or subverted (reducing them instead to footnotes to imperial histories), he opens them up for other investigations. While he claims a "correct" understanding of Philippine culture for personal and conservative ends, he points to the emergence of Filipino "authority," the power of Filipinos to speak for themselves.

In the discourse of twentieth-century Filipino scholarship, his pioneering efforts have gone virtually unacknowledged. In 1915–1917, Colegio de Santo Tomas reprinted such Paterno works as *Antigua Civilizacion* and *Los Itas*. With a small book-reading public, limited access to Spanish, disinterest in the Spanish past, and the spell of America in education—it does not appear that these works were widely distributed and read. His writings are now largely of antiquarian interest. His ethnological treatises used secondary data in a loosely integrated fash-

101

ion; he employed discredited theories (unilinear evolutionism, palaeontological linguistics, primitive promiscuity, aboriginal uninventiveness); and he was given to grandiose exaggeration. He interests us for exemplifying the more exotic substance and style of nineteenth-century ethnology. Yet, beyond antiquarianism, he is important for providing us with a rich sense of the politics of national identity formation, particularly with respect to how Filipino intellectuals relate, on one hand, to the ground of local realities and their own social formation and, on the other, the seductive and everpresent claims of Western knowledge.

Today, the project of tracing a history apart from coloniality remains as does the problem of how the Filipino intellectual should locate himself in the country and the world. The refigurations of Orientalism in the twentieth century remain a matter of intense debate.

In a Borgesian play of resemblances and repetitions, Pedro Paterno (though we may no longer recognize his face or know him by name) still speaks to us today.

NOTES

1. I have since come across Portia L. Reyes, "Isang Kabanata sa Kasaysayang Intelektwal ng Pilipinas: Panahon at Kaisipang Pangkasaysayan ni Pedro Paterno, 1858–1911" (M.A. thesis, University of the Philippines, 1996). I thank the author for sharing with me a revised version of the thesis.

2. Leon Ma. Guerrero, *The First Filipino: A Biography of Jose Rizal* (Manila: National Historical Commission, 1974; first ed., 1963), 198.

3. On the Paterno family: E. Arsenio Manuel, *Dictionary of Philippine Biography* (Quezon City: Filipiniana Publications, 1955–1986), I:117, 214, 281; III:457; Santiago Albano Pilar, *Handbook of Painters, Sculptors, Architects, Printmakers, Photographers and Craftsmen Active in the Philippines, 1571–1941* (Typescript, n.d.); *CCP Encyclopedia of Philippine Art* (Manila: Cultural Center of the Philippines, 1994), IV:313–14, 3842–84; Miguel R. Paterno and Jean Marie Y. Paterno, *The Paternos* [Metro Manila, 2005], prepared for the First Paterno Family Reunion, March 5, 2005, Mandaluyong, Metro Manila.

4. John Foreman, *The Philippine Islands: A Political, Geographical, Ethnographical, Social and Commercial History of the Philippine Archipelago* (New York: Charles Scribner's Sons, 1906), 411. Foreman says that his biographical information was furnished by Paterno but does not indicate what statements are a direct quote or his own gloss.

5. Foreman, *Philippine Islands*, 411.

6. Edgar Wickberg, "The Chinese Mestizo in Philippine History," *Journal of Southeast Asian History*, 5:1 (1964), 79–80.

7. Regalado Trota Jose, "Felix Rojas and the Gothicizing of Earthquake Baroque," *1030 R. Hidalgo*, ed. A.S. Araneta (Metro Manila: MARA, 1986), II:20–21; Fernando N. Zialcita and Martin I. Tinio, Jr., *Philippine Ancestral Houses (1810–1930)* (Quezon City: GCF Books, 1980), 206–7.

8. Nick Joaquin, *Almanac for Manileños* (Manila: Mr & Ms Publications, 1979),

270; also Luning B. Ira and Isagani R. Medina, *Streets of Manila* (Quezon City: GCF Books, 1977), 82–83, 99–119.

9. See *Larawan: Immortality and Identity in Filipino Portraiture* (Makati: Ayala Museum, 1988), 5–7, 17–18, 22, 29; [Santiago Albano Pilar], "Portrait of Teodora Devera Ygnacio," *A Portfolio of 60 Philippine Art Masterpieces* (Quezon City: Instructional Materials Corporation, 1986), 41–44; *Idem.*, "A Loving Eye for Detail," *Archipelago* II:18 (1975), 19–25; "The Emerging Masters," *Archipelago* 3:A25 (1976), 24–25.

On the artistic achievements of the Paterno women: Eric S. Giron, "La Flor de Manila," *Mirror* (September 19, 1970), 6–7; Eloisa May P. Hernandez, *Homebound: Women Visual Artists in Nineteenth Century Philippines* (Quezon City: University of the Philippines Press, 2004).

10. Gabriel F. Fabella, "Pedro A. Paterno: Peacemaker," *Rizal the Historian and Other Historical Essays* (Manila: Philippine Historical Association, 1960), 152. On the education of the Paterno brothers: Luciano P. R. Santiago, "The First Filipino Doctors of Medicine and Surgery (1878–97)," *Philippine Quarterly of Culture & Society* [hereinafter cited as *PQCS*], 22 (1994), 117; *Idem.*, "The First Filipino Doctoral Law Graduates in Spain (1860–1890)," *PQCS,* 27 (1999), 111.

Other sources on Pedro Paterno: P. Reyes, et al., eds., *Directorio Biografico Filipino* (Manila: Imp. y Litografia "Germania" Alix, 1908), 40; Joaquin Pellicena Camacho (pseud., Antonio Medrano), "Pedro A. Paterno," *Cultura Filipina,* 1:12 (March 1911), 546–70; Manuel Artigas (pseud., Sagitra), "Filipinos Ilustres: Pedro A. Paterno," *Renacimiento Filipino,* 1:37, 39, 41 and 43 (April 7 and 21, May 7 and 21, 1911); *Enciclopedia Universal Ilustrada Europeo-Americana* (Bilbao: Espasa-Calpe, S.A., 1920), XLII:758–59; Zoilo M. Galang, ed., *Encyclopedia of the Philippines* (Manila: Exequiel Floro, 1951), III:393–96; Corona Salcedo Romero, "The Enigma That Was Pedro Alejandro Paterno: A Preliminary Study," *Unitas,* 40:3 (1967), 448–63; Gregorio F. Zaide, *Great Filipinos in History* (Manila: Verde Book Store, 1970), 383–93.

11. On these events: Manuel Artigas, *The Events of 1872: A Historico-Bio-Bibliographical Account,* trans. O. D. Corpuz (Quezon City: University of the Philippines Press, 1996). An excellent introduction to nineteenth-century Filipino nationalism is John N. Schumacher, *The Propaganda Movement: 1880–1895* (Manila: Solidaridad Publishing House, 1973; revised ed. Ateneo de Manila University [ADMU] Press, 1997).

12. Artigas, *Events of 1872,* 167, 169; W. E. Retana, *Vida y Escritos del Dr. Jose Rizal* (Madrid: Libreria General de Victoriano Suarez, 1907), 111; *Idem.*, *Aparato Bibliografico de la Historia General de Filipinas* (Madrid: Imprenta de la Sucesora de M. Minuesa de los Rios, 1906), II, no. 1384.

13. Ruby R. Paredes, "Ilustrado Legacy: The Pardo de Taveras of Manila," *An Anarchy of Families: State and Family in the Philippines*, ed. A. W. McCoy (Madison: University of Wisconsin, Center for Southeast Asian Studies, 1993), 367–68; ADMU Press ed., 1994. The Artigas version of these events (*Events of 1872*, 159–60) says that Paterno fled with other exiles to Hong Kong in May 1874 before the grant of amnesty.

14. Benito J. Legarda, Jr., *After the Galleons: Foreign Trade, Economic Change and Entrepreneurship in the Nineteenth-Century Philippines* (Madison: University of Wisconsin, Center for Southeast Asian Studies, 1999), 330; ADMU Press ed., 1999.

15. Miguel Zaragoza (pseud., Mario), *La Ilustracion Filipina,* IV:108 (January 28, 1894). Quoted in Alfredo Roces, *Felix Resurreccion Hidalgo and the Generation of 1872* (Metro Manila: Eugenio Lopez Foundation, 1995), 120–22.

16. Pedro A. Paterno, *Influencia Social del Cristianismo* (Manila: Tip. Linotype del Col. de Sto. Tomas, 1917; first published in 1876), 5.

17. Pedro A. Paterno, *Sampaguitas* (Madrid: Imprenta de F. Cao y D. de Val, 1881); F. Licsi Espino, Jr., "Pedro A. Paterno: The Neglected Poet," *Archipelago,* 4:A39 (1977), 13–15.

18. Retana, *Aparato Bibliografico,* II, no. 1749. See Pedro A. Paterno, *Poesias Liricas y Dramaticas* (Madrid: Establecimientos Tipograficos de M. Minuesa, 1880).

19. Schumacher, *Propaganda Movement,* 22; *Idem.,* "The Propaganda Movement, Literature and the Arts," *Solidarity,* 9:4 (1975), 18.

20. Retana, *Vida y Escritos,* 59; *Aparato Bibliografico,* II, no. 1534. Other comments on Paterno: *Reminiscences and Travels of Jose Rizal* (Manila: Jose Rizal National Centennial Commission, 1961), 84, 88.

21. Evaristo Aguirre to Rizal, Madrid, June 14, 1887. In *Rizal's Correspondence with Fellow Reformists* (Manila: National Heroes Commission, 1963), 131.

22. Retana, *Vida y Escritos,* 59.

23. Eduardo de Lete to Rizal, Madrid, June 20, 1887. In *Rizal's Correspondence with Fellow Reformists,* 136. Also see *The World of Felix Roxas* (Manila: Filipiniana Book Guild, 1970), 47, 50.

24. See Jose A. Valero, "Intellectuals, the State, and the Public Sphere in Spain, 1700–1840," *Culture and State in Spain: 1550–1850,* ed. T. Lewis and F. J. Sanchez (New York: Garland, 1999), 196–224.

25. Foreman, *Philippine Islands,* 412.

26. Pedro Paterno to Rizal, Ranoa, October 15, 1890. In *Cartas Entre Rizal y Otras Personas* (Manila: Comision Nacional del Centenario de Jose Rizal, 1961), 154.

27. Roces, *Felix Resurreccion Hidalgo,* 106.

28. E. Aguilar Cruz, *Luna* (Manila: Department of Public Information, 1975), 46–47; *Discovering Philippine Art in Spain* (Manila: Department of Foreign Affairs and National Centennial Commission, 1998), 227.

29. For a Madrid newspaper account (January 22, 1884) of Paterno's museum: Retana, *Vida y Escritos*, 77–79. On the exhibitions: *Catalogo de la Exposicion General de las Islas Filipinas* (Madrid: Est. Tipografico de Ricardo Fe, 1887); *La Solidaridad*, trans. G. F. Ganzon and L. Mañeru (Metro Manila: Fundacion Santiago, 1996), V:96 (January 31, 1893), 41; V:97 (February 15, 1893), 71, 73; V:99 (March 15, 1893), 123, 125; V:109 (August 15, 1893), 383, 385.

30. For the official Spanish view: Victor Balaguer, *Islas Filipinas (Memorias)* (Madrid: R. Angles, 1895). Balaguer cites the founding of Museo-Biblioteca de Ultramar as one of the results of the exposition and names Paterno among the notables who used the resources of Museo-Biblioteca.

31. Raymond Carr, *Spain, 1808–1939* (Oxford: Clarendon Press, 1966), 257–388.

32. Quoted in Stanley J. Kunitz and Vineta Colby, eds., *European Authors, 1000–1900* (New York: H. W. Wilson Company, 1967), 154. Also Carr, *Spain,* 293; E. Allison Peers, *A History of the Romantic Movement in Spain* (New York: Hafner Publishing, 1964), II:370. On Castelar and Pi y Margall: C. A. M. Hennessy, *The Federal Republic in Spain: Pi y Margall and the Federal Republican Movement, 1868–74* (Oxford: Clarendon Press, 1962).

33. Jose Rizal, *Political and Historical Writings* (Manila: National Historical Commission, 1972), 7.

34. *The Rizal-Blumentritt Correspondence* (Manila: Jose Rizal National Centennial Commission, 1961), I:70.

35. *Rizal's Correspondence with Fellow Reformists,* 494.

36. T. H. Pardo de Tavera, *Biblioteca Filipina,* in: *Bibliography of the Philippine Islands* (Washington: Government Printing Office, 1903), 1–439. See nos. 310, 431, 1938–1944.

37. Isabelo de los Reyes, *El Folk-Lore Filipino,* trans. S. C. Dizon and M. E. Imson (Quezon City: University of the Philippines Press, 1994; first published in 1889), 286.

38. Retana, *Aparato Bibliografico,* II, no. 2247; III, nos. 2518, 2902, 3206.

39. Pedro A. Paterno, *Regimen Municipal en las Islas Filipinas* (Madrid: Tipografia de los Sucesores de Cuesta, 1893), 278.

40. Paterno, *Regimen Municipal,* 279, 280.

41. See Foreman, *Philippine Islands,* facing 396; *Kasaysayan: The Story of the Filipino People* (Manila: Asia Publishing Company, 1998), V:202.

42. Retana, *Aparato Bibliografico,* III: no. 4556; Manuel, *Dictionary of Philip-*

pine Biography, I:71; Vicente S. Hernandez, *History of Books and Libraries in the Philippines, 1521–1900* (Manila: National Commission for Culture and the Arts, 1996), 63, 68–74.

43. Pedro A. Paterno, "A Reply" (April 15, 1895), in *Solidaridad*, VII:149, pp. 179, 181. On the Museo-Biblioteca: *Solidaridad*, VII:147 (March 15, 1895), 131. Also see *Solidaridad*, VI:37 (January 31, 1894), 37; VII:147 (March 15, 1895), 119; *Guia Oficial de Filipinas, 1897* (Manila: Imp. y Lit. de Chofre y Comp., 1897), 522.

44. Paterno, "Reply,"181.

45. Teodoro M. Kalaw, *History of Philippine Masonry*, trans. F. H. Stevens and A. Amechazurra (Manila: McCullough Printing Company, 1956; Spanish ed., 1920), 229.

46. See *La Situacion del Pais: Coleccion de articulos publicados por "La Voz Espanola"* (Manila: Imprenta de "Amigos del Pais," 1897), 27–29.

47. H. de la Costa, S.J., *The Trial of Rizal* (Manila: ADMU Press, 1961), 116–17; W. E. Retana, *Archivo del Bibliofilo Filipino* (Madrid: Viuda de M. Minuesa de los Rios, 1896), IV:275; *Idem., Vida y Escritos*, 390.

48. Jose M. del Castillo, *El Katipunan o el Filibusterismo en Filipinas* (Madrid: Imp. del Asilo de Huerfanos del S.C. de Jesus, 1897), 37; also Juan Alvarez Guerra, *The Origins and Causes of the Philippine Revolution*, trans. T. Alcantara, in *Views on Philippine Revolution* (Quezon City: Toyota Foundation/UP Press, 2002), I:185.

49. Francis St. Clair, *The Katipunan or the Rise and Fall of the Filipino Commune* (Manila: Tip. "Amigos del Pais," 1902; reprint ed., 1991), 55, 84–85, 151.

See Emilio Reverter Delmas, *La Insurreccion de Filipinas en 1896 y 1897* (Barcelona: Centro Editorial del Alberto Martin, 1899), 419, 529; del Castillo, *Katipunan*, 183. Reverter and del Castillo cite among those arrested in September 1896 "Maximo Paterno, *medico*," while Teodoro Kalaw says that it was Don Maximo, Paterno's father. See Teodoro M. Kalaw, *The Philippine Revolution* (Mandaluyong, Rizal: Jorge B. Vargas Filipiniana Foundation, 1969; first published in 1924), 29.

I surmise it was Maximino Paterno, a physician, who was arrested. See Retana, *Archivo Bibliofilo*, III:425, IV:323.

50. See Javier Bores, *The Philippine Insurrection: The Four Truths*, trans. R.M. Icagasi, in *Views on Philippine Revolution*, I:131–33. First published in 1896; Bores was director of administration under Primo de Rivera, his uncle.

51. For Paterno's embellished narrative of the negotiations, see *El Pacto de Biyak-na-Bato* (Manila: Imprenta "La Republica," 1910). Also Teodoro A. Agoncillo, *Malolos: The Crisis of the Republic* (Quezon City: University of the Philippines Press, 1997; first ed., 1960), 20–39; John R.M Taylor, *The Philippine Insurrection Against the United*

States (Pasay: Eugenio Lopez Foundation, 1971), I:79–89, 337–66, et passim; Pedro S. de Achutegui, S.J., and Miguel A. Bernad, S.J., *Aguinaldo and the Revolution of 1896: A Documentary History* (Quezon City: Ateneo de Manila, 1972), 478–555.

52. *Memoirs of General Artemio Ricarte* (Manila: National Heroes Commission, 1963), 60.

53. *La Paz y el Ayuntamiento de Manila (Relacion de los Festejos Realizados con motivo de la terminacion de la Guerra en Filipinas* (Manila: Tipo-Litografia de Chofre y Comp., 1898).

54. Paterno, *Pacto de Biyak-na-Bato*, 77.

55. Fernando Primo de Rivera, *Memoria Dirigida al Senado* (Madrid: Imprenta y Litografia del Deposito de la Guerra, 1898), 122.

56. The text of the letter appeared in Primo de Rivera, *Memoria Dirigida*, 155–58. It was translated into English in Foreman, *Philippine Islands*, 557–60. The letter was subsequently referred to by other authors. See, for instance, Edwin Wildman, *Aguinaldo: A Narrative of Filipino Ambitions* (Boston: Lothrop Publishing Company, 1901), 49–50; Mrs. William Howard Taft [Helen Herron Taft], *Recollections of Full Years* (New York: Dodd, Mead & Company, 1914), 85.

57. Foreman, *Philippine Islands*, 559.

58. Luciano P. R. Santiago, "Philippine Titles of the Spanish Nobility (1761–1897)," *PQCS,* 19 (1991), 281–87. See Taylor, *Philippine Insurrection*, I:492–500.

59. See Pardo de Tavera's statement before the U.S. Philippine Commission on August 22, 1899: *Report of the Philippine Commission* [hereinafter cited as *RPC*] (Washington: Government Printing Office, 1900), II: 388–400.

60. For the text of the manifesto: Foreman, *Philippine Islands*, 590–92. See Retana, *Aparato Bibliografico*, III, nos. 4034–38, 4054; Taylor, *Philippine Insurrection*, II:22–23; Agoncillo, *Malolos*, 115–17; Felipe G. Calderon, *Mis Memorias Sobre la Revolucion Filipina. Segunda Etapa (1898 a 1901)* (Manila: Imp. de El Renacimiento, 1907), 63–73.

61. Taylor, *Philippine Insurrection*, II:19.

62. For the text of the response: Foreman, *Philippine Islands*, 592–97.

63. Joaquin, *Almanac for Manileños*, 288–89.

64. Medrano, "Pedro A. Paterno," 550.

65. Kalaw, *Philippine Revolution*, 123. See Calderon, *Mis Memorias*, 126–28, 130–36.

66. *The Letters of Apolinario Mabini* (Manila: National Heroes Commission, 1965), 65, 257.

67. *RPC*, 1900, I:93–97. For a copy of the Autonomy Plan: facing p. 228.

68. Taylor, *Philippine Insurrection*, IV:82–83.

69. Vivencio R. Jose, *The Rise and Fall of Antonio Luna* (Quezon City: University of the Philippines, 1972), 336–48, 350–54, 373–74; Taylor, *Philippine Insurrection*, IV:99–100, 108–9, 113–14.

70. Correspondence ("Cartas Varias"), T. H. Pardo de Tavera to Antonio Regidor, October 3, 1899, Manila. In Pardo de Tavera Special Collections Archives, Rizal Library, Ateneo de Manila University, Quezon City.

71. Wildman, *Aguinaldo*, 97; William Henry Scott, *Ilocano Responses to American Aggression, 1900–1901* (Quezon City: New Day Publishers, 1986), 54, 82, 83, 124, 161, 162, 169, 186, 188; Howard T. Fry, *A History of the Mountain Province* (Quezon City: New Day Publishers, 1983), 6, 234n.

72. The testament is in John Bancroft Devins, *An Observer in the Philippines* (Boston: American Tract Society, 1905), 226–32.

73. Devins, *Observer in the Philippines*, 226.

74. *Facts About the Filipinos,* 1:9 (August 1, 1901), 29–49. This includes an Associated Press report on Paterno's activities in *New York Tribune* (August 26, 1900).

Also see *Affairs in the Philippine Islands. Hearings before the Committee on the Philippines by the United States Senate* (Washington: Government Printing Office, 1902), II:1923–26; James A. LeRoy, *The Americans in the Philippines* (Boston: Houghton Mifflin Company, 1914), II:248–53.

75. *Facts About the Filipinos*, 33.

76. Pedro A. Paterno, *El Problema Politico de Filipinas* (Manila: Imp. y Estereotipia de J. Alemany, 1900).

77. LeRoy, *Americans in the Philippines*, II:254.

78. *Affairs in the Philippine Islands*, II:1966.

79. For the text of these letters: Maximo M. Kalaw, *The Development of Philippine Politics (1872–1920)* (Manila: Oriental Commercial Co., 1926), 267–68.

80. Mrs. Taft, *Recollections of Full Years*, 87; Medrano, "Pedro A. Paterno," 546–70; St. Clair, *Katipunan*, 114; Kalaw, *Philippine Revolution*, 233–45; *Affairs in the Philippine Islands*, II:1965–68; Kalaw, *Development of Philippine Politics*, 266–69. For American opinion at the time: Edith Moses, *Unofficial Letters of an Official's Wife* (New York: Appleton and Company, 1908), 45–50; Daniel R. Williams, *The Odyssey of the Philippine Commission* (Chicago: A. C. McClurg, 1913), 66–69.

81. For the text of the speech: Medrano, "Pedro A. Paterno"; *Affairs in the Philippine Islands*, II:1966–68; *Facts About the Filipinos*, 45–47; Kalaw, *Development of Philippine Politics*, 268–69.

82. Mrs. Taft, *Recollections of Full Years*, 85.

83. Quoted in Peter W. Stanley, *A Nation in the Making: The Philippines and the United States, 1899–1921* (Cambridge: Harvard University Press, 1974), 67.

84. Charles Burke Elliott, *The Philippines to the End of the Military Regime* (Indianapolis: Bobbs-Merrill, 1917), 199.

An impoverished nobleman, Godoy (1767–1851) rose to power after he insinuated himself into the position of royal favorite of Charles III and the Queen (whose lover he was reputed to be). A master intriguer who fabricated lies about himself, he was named "Prince of the Peace" after he made peace with France in a war his own disastrous policies caused.

85. Kalaw, *Philippine Revolution*, 243, 245; Encarnacion Alzona, *Galicano Apacible: Profile of a Filipino Patriot* (Manila: National Historical Institute, 1971), 105–8.

86. Apolinario Mabini, *Memorias de la Revolucion Filipina* (Manila: Buro de la Imprenta Republica, 1960), 119.

87. Agoncillo, *Malolos*, 41, 512. A similar view is expressed in LeRoy, *Americans in the Philippines*, II:249, and Foreman, *Philippine Islands*, 412.

88. Wildman, *Aguinaldo*, 97.

89. See Romeo V. Cruz, *America's Colonial Desk and the Philippines, 1898–1934* (Quezon City: University of the Philippines Press, 1974), 183.

90. *RPC*, 1903, 1:61–62.

91. Quoted in Ruby R. Paredes, "The Origin of National Politics: Taft and the Partido Federal," *Philippine Colonial Democracy*, ed. R. R. Paredes (New Haven: Yale University Southeast Asia Studies, 1988), 21, 67n.

92. Pedro A. Paterno, *Gobierno Civil de las Islas Filipinas o Manual del Ciudadano Filipino* (Manila: Imprenta "La Republica," 1911).

93. Pedro A. Paterno, *Synopsis de Historia de los Estados Unidos (Apuntes)* (Manila: Imprenta "La Republica," 1909).

94. Pedro A. Paterno, *The Dreamed Alliance: Philippine Opera in One Act*, trans. W. H. Loving (Manila: Imp. de la "R. Mercantil" de J. de Loyzaga y Ageo, 1902). See "First Filipino Opera," *This Week* 9:35 (August 29, 1954), 12.

95. Quoted in Manuel, *Dictionary of Philippine Biography*, II:60.

96. Paterno, *Dreamed Alliance*, 22.

97. Jack O'Lantern, "Gave Play for Wright Last Night—*Magdapio*, Queerest Operetta Ever Perpetuated, Presented at Zorilla," *The Manila Cablenews* (February 2, 1904), 5. Quoted in Amelia Lapeña-Bonifacio, *The "Seditious" Tagalog Playwrights: Early American Occupation* (Manila: Zarzuela Foundation of the Philippines, 1972), 47.

For the text of the play: Arthur Stanley Riggs, *The Filipino Drama (1905)* (Manila: Intramuros Administration, 1981), 334–48, 652–66. Riggs, who uniformly disparaged Filipino plays of the period, was particularly contemptuous of Paterno. Calling Paterno "a wildly ebullient half-caste farceur," he writes that *Magdapio* presents "the spectacle of the noble art of the drama fallen to its lowest ebb of meaningless words, banal effects, and total weakness, without a single feature to redeem it from utter flaccidness and intellectual senility" (8, 334).

See Cristina Laconico-Buenaventura, *The Theater in Manila, 1846–1946* (Manila: De La Salle University Press, 1994), 73, 74, 103, 210, 211.

98. A detailed account of politics in this period: Michael Cullinane, "Ilustrado Politics: The Response of the Filipino Educated Elite to American Colonial Rule, 1898–1907" (Ph.D. diss., University of Michigan, 1989). Published by ADMU Press, 2003.

99. Rafael Palma, *My Autobiography*, trans. A. P. Bautista (Manila: Capitol Publishing House, 1953), 64.

100. "*Banqueros* are Heroes—New Musical Play by Sr. Pedro Paterno Honors the Arrival of Taft," *The Manila Cablenews* (August 6, 1905), 12. Quoted in Lapeña-Bonifacio, *"Seditious" Tagalog Playwrights*, 49–50.

101. Jaime C. de Veyra, "Un Poligrafo Filipino," *Efemerides Filipinas*, by Jaime C. de Veyra and Mariano Ponce (Manila: Imprenta y Libreria de I. R. Morales, 1914), 210–11. First published in *El Ideal* (February 27, 1912).

For a list of books Paterno planned to produce, see the backcover of the English edition of his *Ninay* (Manila: Imprenta "La Republica," 1907).

102. De Veyra, "Poligrafo Filipino," 209–12.

103. Artigas, "Filipinos Ilustres " (April 7, 1911), 3; "Los funerales del Sr. Pedro A. Paterno," *Renacimiento Filipino* 1:39 (April 21, 1911), 11.

104. Schumacher, *Propaganda Movement*, 204; *Idem.*, *The Making of a Nation: Essays on Nineteenth-Century Filipino Nationalism* (Quezon City: ADMU Press, 1991), 12–13; also 106–8.

105. Pedro A. Paterno, *Ninay (Costumbres Filipinas)* (Manila: Tip. Linotype del Col. de Sto. Tomas, 1917), 44–45, 54, 61, 132, 171–74.

106. Pedro A. Paterno, *La Antigua Civilizacion Tagalog* (Madrid: Tipografia de Manuel G. Hernandez, 1887).

107. Pedro A. Paterno, *El Cristianismo en la Antigua Civilizacion Tagalog* (Madrid: Imprenta Moderna, 1892); also serialized in *La Solidaridad*, IV:81–88 (June 15–September 30, 1892), 90–91 (October 31–November 15, 1892).

108. Paterno, *Antigua Civilizacion*, 2.

109. Paterno, *Antigua Civilizacion*, 4.

110. Paterno, *Antigua Civilizacion*, 35–40, 44–52; also 360–61.

111. Paterno, *Antigua Civilizacion*, 74, 77.

112. Paterno, *Antigua Civilizacion,* 268.

113. Paterno, *Antigua Civilizacion,* 225–62.

114. Paterno, *Antigua Civilizacion,* 143–44.

115. Paterno, *Antigua Civilizacion,* 145.

116. Paterno, *Cristianismo en la Antigua Civilizacion,* in *Solidaridad,* IV, 273.

117. *Solidaridad,* IV, 307, 407–11, 441–45.

118. *Solidaridad,* IV, 515.

119. *Solidaridad,* IV, 513–19.

120. *Solidaridad,* IV, 385.

121. *Solidaridad,* IV, 517.

122. Juan de Noceda & Pedro de Sanlucar, *Vocabulario de la Lengua Tagala* (Manila: Imprenta de Ramirez y Giraudier, 1860).

123. *Solidaridad,* IV, 379–85; Noceda and Sanlucar, *Vocabulario.* See Paterno's *Barangay* (fn. 131), 54–56, for Pitho, and *Antigua Civilizacion,* 154–55, for a fanciful version of human creation that Paterno attributes to "an elderly Tagalog."

124. *Solidaridad,* IV, 549.

125. *Solidaridad,* IV, 549.

126. *Solidaridad,* IV, 549.

127. Pedro A. Paterno, *Los Itas* (Manila: Tip. Linotype de Colegio de Sto. Tomas, 1915; first ed., 1890), 3.

128. Paterno, *Los Itas,* 1.

129. Paterno, *Los Itas,* 9–20.

130. Paterno, *Antigua Civilizacion,* 77–78.

131. Pedro A. Paterno, *El Barangay con la Relacion de Fr. Juan de Plasencia Escrita en 1589 de como se Gobernaban los Tagalos en la Antiguedad y una Carta de D. Miguel Villalba Hervas* (Madrid: Imprenta de los Sucesores de Cuesta, 1892).

See Rodrigo de Aganduru Moriz, *Historia General de las Islas Occidentales a la Asia Adyacentes, llamadas Philipinas* (Madrid, 1882). On the dating of the earth: Stephen Baxter, *Revolutions in the Earth: James Hutton and the True Age of the World* (London: Phoenix, 2004).

132. Pedro A. Paterno, *La Familia Tagalog en la Historia Universal* (Madrid: Imprenta de los Sucesores de Cuesta, 1892).

133. Paterno, *Familia Tagalog,* 108, 133.

134. Pedro Paterno, *El Individuo Tagalog y su Arte en la Exposicion Historico-Americana* (Madrid: Imprenta de los Sucesores de Cuesta, 1893).

135. Paterno, *Individuo Tagalog,* 25.

136. P. A. Paterno, "Philippine Art," *Solidaridad,* VII (March 15, 1895), 119–21.

137. Pedro A. Paterno, *Synopsis de Historia de Filipinas* (Manila: Imprenta "La Republica," 1911), 5–6.

138. Paterno, *Synopsis*, 1–9.

139. Paterno, *Synopsis*, 7.

140. Paterno, *Synopsis*, [36–46]. On Paterno's assistance to Luna, Hidalgo, and Zaragoza: Artigas, "Filipino Ilustres" (May 7, 1911), 12; Roces, *Felix Resurreccion Hidalgo*, 106.

No corroboration exists for Paterno's having financed Rizal's trip to Spain except that on the eve of his departure from the Philippines in 1882, Rizal paid a visit to Paterno who asked him to take family photographs and tins of tea to his brothers in Spain. On his return to Spain from the Philippines in 1883, Paterno also carried for Rizal some things from his family: noodles, fruit jelly and *bagoong*. See *Reminiscences and Travels of Jose Rizal* (Manila: Jose Rizal National Centennial Commission, 1961), 42–43; *One Hundred Letters of Jose Rizal* (Manila: Philippine National Historical Society, 1959), 178, 181–82.

141. Paterno, *Synopsis*, [39–46]. Also see the Paterno testament in Devins, *Observer in the Philippines*, 226–32.

142. *Reminiscences and Travels*, 36–37.

143. Graciano Lopez Jaena, *Speeches, Articles and Letters*, trans. E. Alzona (Manila: National Historical Commission, 1974), 6–10, 143–44, 146–56.

144. Edward W. Said, *Orientalism* (New York: Vintage Books, 1979), 49–50.

145. On the "School of Salamanca" and its role in the formation of anthropology in Spain: Anthony Pagden, *The Fall of Natural Man: The American Indian and the Origins of Comparative Ethnology* (Cambridge: Cambridge University Press, 1982).

146. See Anthony Pagden, "Identity Formation in Spanish America," *Colonial Identity in the Atlantic World, 1500–1800*, ed. N. Canny and A. Pagden (Princeton: Princeton University Press, 1987), 51–93.

147. Pagden, "Identity Formation," 73.

148. Pagden, "Identity Formation," 73n, 77–78.

149. Also Anthony Pagden, "Fabricating Identity in Spanish America," *History Today*, 42 (May 1992), 44–49.

150. Lafitau's *Moeurs de sauvages americains* was, according to Pagden, "perhaps the first text to attempt to combine a substantial collection of data which the author himself had collected 'in the field' with significant measure of 'universal speculation' as to its meaning." See Anthony Pagden, "Eighteenth-Century Anthropology and the 'History of Mankind,'" *History and the Disciplines: The Reclassification of Knowledge in Early Modern Europe*, ed. D. R. Kelley (New York: University of Rochester Press, 1997), 223–35.

Dobrizhoffer's book was published in Latin in Vienna but translated into German and in 1822 into English (it is the English title Paterno cites).

151. Jorge Cañizares-Esguerra, *How to Write the History of the New World: Histories, Epistemologies, and Identities in the Eighteenth-Century Atlantic World* (Stanford: Stanford University Press, 2001).

152. Cañizares-Esguerra, *How to Write the History of the New World*, 209.

153. Wickberg, "Chinese Mestizo," 89, 99. Also *Idem.*, *The Chinese in Philippine Life, 1850–1898* (New Haven: Yale University Press, 1965); Daniel F. Doeppers, "Tracing the Decline of the Mestizo Categories in Philippine Life in the Late 19th Century," *PQCS*, 22 (1994), 80–89.

154. Wickberg, *Chinese in Philippine Life*, 31.

155. E. E. Evans-Pritchard, *Theories of Primitive Religion* (Oxford: Clarendon Press, 1965), 100–1.

156. Peter van der Veer, "The Moral State: Religion, Nation, and Empire in Victorian Britain and British India," *Nation and Religion: Perspectives on Europe and Asia*, ed. P.v.d. Veer and H. Lehmann (Princeton: Princeton University Press, 1999), 15–43; *Idem.*, *Imperial Encounters: Religion and Modernity in India and Britain* (Princeton: Princeton University Press, 2001).

157. Francisco Colin, S.J., *Labor Evangelica de los Obreros de la Compania de Jesus en las Islas Filipinas* (Barcelona: Imprenta y Litografia de Heinrich y Compania, 1900–1902; first published in 1663), I:6–11, 15–18, 70; Pedro Chirino, S.J., *Relacion de las Islas Filipinas*, trans. R. Echevarria (Manila: Historical Conservation Society, 1969), 296–98, 329; Marcelo de Ribadeneira, O.F.M., *Historia del Archipielago y Otros Reynos* (Manila: Historical Conservation Society, 1970), 343; Gaspar de San Agustin, O.S.A., *Conquistas de las Islas Filipinas, 1565–1615*, trans. L.A. Mañeru (Manila: San Agustin Museum, 1998; first published in 1698), 47–49, 97; *The Philippine Chronicles of Fray San Antonio*, trans. P. Picornell (Manila: Historical Conservation Society, 1977; first published in 1738–44), 4, 149; "Native Races and their Customs," in Emma H. Blair and James A. Robertson, eds., *The Philippine Islands, 1493–1898* (Cleveland: Arthur H. Clark Company, 1907), 40:38, 56.

On Spanish writings on precolonial Philippines, the best guide is William Henry Scott, *Barangay: Sixteenth-Century Philippine Culture and Society* (Quezon City: ADMU Press, 1994); also his *Prehispanic Source Materials for the Study of Philippine History* (Quezon City: New Day Publishers, 1984; rev. ed.).

158. Margaret T. Hodgen, *Early Anthropology in the Sixteenth and Seventeenth Centuries* (Philadelphia: University of Pennsylvania Press, 1964), 301–3.

159. Mateo Gisbert to the Mission Superior, Davao, October 19, 1880. In Jose S. Arcilla, S.J., ed., *Jesuit Missionary Letters from Mindanao* (Quezon City: University of the Philippines Center for Integrative and Development Studies, 1998), 30. See Paterno, *Los Itas*, 149.

160. Pastells' annotation in *Labor Evangelica*, I:64; "Native Races and their Customs," 69–70.

161. Juan de Plasencia, O.S.F., "Customs of the Tagalogs," in Blair and Robertson, *Philippine Islands*, 7:194–96. Also Chirino, *Relacion*, 300; *Philippine Chronicles of Fray San Antonio*, 155.

162. See Chirino, *Relacion*, 299–300; Morga, *Sucesos*, 278–79; Ribadeneira, *Historia*, 342.

163. See entries for *calantipay* and *ostias* in Pedro de San Buenaventura, *Vocabulario de Lengua Tagala* (Pila: Thomas Pinpin y Domingo Loag, 1613). On *kapis* (*kulintipay* and *kalansipay* in Ilocano and Pangasinan, respectively): Jose Villa Panganiban, *Diksyunaryo-Tesauro Pilipino-Ingles* (Quezon City: Manlapaz Publishing, 1972).

164. See, for instance, John Lubbock [Lord Avebury], *Origin of Civilisation and the Primitive Condition of Man* (London: Longmans, Green, & Co., 1882; 4th ed.), 203–6; *Idem.*, *Marriage, Totemism and Religion: An Answer to Critics* (London: Longmans, Green & Co., 1911); W. Schmidt, *The Origin and Growth of Religion*, trans. H. J. Rose (New York: Dial Press, 1935).

165. Paterno, *Los Itas*, 197–99.

166. Paterno, *Antigua Civilizacion*, 122–23.

167. For Paterno's discussion of language: *Antigua Civilizacion*, 257–72; *Los Itas*, 117–47.

168. Evans-Pritchard, *Theories of Primitive Religion*, 21–22. On nineteenth-century linguistics: Holger Pedersen, *The Discovery of Language: Linguistic Science in the 19th Century*, trans. J. W. Spargo (Bloomington: Indiana University Press, 1931); Stephen G. Alter, *Darwinism and the Linguistic Image* (Baltimore: Johns Hopkins University Press, 1999).

169. Louis of Leon, O.S.A., *The Names of Christ*, trans. E. J. Schuster (St. Louis.: B. Herder, 1955; a translation of the 1595 Spanish edition), esp. 7–19, 295–315. On Kabbalism: Umberto Eco, *The Search for the Perfect Language* (London: Fontana, 1997), 25–33, 117–43.

170. Paterno, *Antigua Civilizacion*, 50–51.

171. *Solidaridad*, IV, 513–19.

172. Paterno, *Los Itas*, 133–37. Also Paterno, *Individuo Tagalog*, 8–12.

173. Paterno, *Familia Tagalog*, 10–16, 112–16.

174. Paterno, *Los Itas*, 118–19; Colin, *Labor Evangelica*, I:56; Chirino, *Relacion*, 275.

175. Pagden, *Fall of Natural Man*, 180.

176. *Solidaridad*, IV, 305.

177. *Solidaridad*, IV, 309.

178. Wilhelm von Humboldt, *On Language: On the Diversity of Human Language Construction and its Influence on the Mental Development of the Human Species*, ed. M. Losonsky (Cambridge: Cambridge University Press, 1999), xxiii, 51.

179. Evans-Pritchard, *Theories of Primitive Religion*, 100.

180. Pardo de Tavera, *Biblioteca Filipina*, no. 1941. See T. H. Pardo de Tavera, *Los Costumbres de los Tagalos en Filipinas segun el Padre Plasencia* (Madrid: Tipografia de Manuel Gines Hernandez, 1892).

181. See Marvin Harris, *The Rise of Anthropological Theory* (New York: Harper & Row, 1968), 156–62.

182. *Solidaridad*, IV, 303.

183. Evans-Pritchard, *Theories of Primitive Religion*, 4–5.

184. Evans-Pritchard, *Theories of Primitive Religion*, 10. Also E. E. Evans-Pritchard, *Social Anthropology* (Glencoe, Illinois: Free Press, 1951), 24–25.

185. Lubbock includes in his survey of primitive cultures such Philippine cases as the worship of alligators and trees and the curious practice of "groom capture" among the *Ahitas* (*Origin of Civilisation*, 121, 275, 292). A good introduction to anthropological tradition in Paterno's time is George W. Stocking, Jr., *Victorian Anthropology* (New York: Free Press, 1987).

186. Fiona Bowie, *The Anthropology of Religion* (Oxford: Blackwell, 2000), 15.

187. Evans-Pritchard, *Theories of Primitive Religion*, 5. See F. B. Jevons, *An Introduction to the History of Religion* (London: Methuen, 1902; 4th ed.).

188. A. Teeuw, *A Critical Survey of Studies on Malay and Bahasa Indonesia* (Hague: Martinus Nijhoff, 1961), 53–54.

189. Colin, *Labor Evangelica*, I:70. This was echoed by Juan Francisco de San Antonio in *Cronicas de la Provincia de San Gregorio Magno (1738–44): Philippine Chronicles of Fray San Antonio*, 149.

190. Barry Alan Joyce, *The Shaping of American Ethnography: The Wilkes Exploring Expedition, 1838–1842* (Lincoln: University of Nebraska Press, 2001), 66.

191. Hannah Franziska Augstein, "Linguistics and Politics in the Early 19th Century: James Cowles Prichard's Moral Philology," *History of European Ideas*, 23:1 (1997), 1–18.

192. See Robert H. Lowie, *The History of Ethnological Theory* (New York: Holt, Rinehart and Winston, 1937).

193. See, for example, Colin, *Labor Evangelica*.

194. Ferdinand Blumentritt, *An Attempt at Writing a Philippine Ethnography*, trans. M. N. Maceda (Marawi City: Mindanao State University, University Research Center, 1980), 27–28, 53, 58, 60, 116, 126, 131, et passim. Also *Idem.*, *The Philippines: Their People and Political Conditions*, trans. D. J. Doherty (Chicago: Donohue Brothers, 1900); Daniel G. Brinton, "Professor Blumentritt's Studies of the Philippines," *American Anthropologist*, I:1 (N.S.) (1899), 122–25.

195. *RPC*, 1900, I:11.

196. Hutterer, "Dean C. Worcester," 138. See Ferdinand Blumentritt, "List of the Native Tribes of the Philippines and of the Languages Spoken by Them," *Readings in Philippine Linguistics*, 19–39. From *Annual Report of the Board of Regents of the Smithsonian Institution (1899)* (Washington, D.C.: 1901); translated by O. T. Mason from *Zeitschrift der Gesellschaft fur Erdkunde zu Berlin*, 25 (Berlin, 1890), 127–46.

197. Rudolf Virchow, "The Peopling of the Philippines," *The Former Philippines Through Foreign Eyes*, ed. A. Craig (Manila: Philippine Education Company, 1916), 536–50. Reprint of O. T. Mason's translation in the 1899 Smithsonian *Annual Report*. See A. de Quatrefages, *The Human Species* (New York: D. Appleton and Company, 1881), 185–98.

198. See *Philippine Chronicles of Fray San Antonio*, 137–38; Paul P. de la Gironiere, *Twenty Years in the Philippines* (New York: Harper & Brothers, 1854), 137–38n.

199. H. Otley Beyer, "Early History of Philippine Relations with Foreign Countries, Especially China," in E. Arsenio Manuel, *Chinese Elements in the Tagalog Language* (Manila: Filipiniana Publications, 1948), xviii.

200. Paterno, *Antigua Civilizacion*, 173.

201. Paterno cites among his readings Balmes's *El protestantismo comparado con el catolicismo en sus relaciones con la civilizacion europea* (Barcelona, 1842–44) and Donoso Cortes's *Ensayo sobre el catolicismo, el liberalismo, y el socialismo* (Barcelona, 1851).

On Cortes and conservatism: Peter Viereck, *Conservatism* (Princeton: D. Van Nostrand, 1956), 63–69, 153–58.

202. On the history of the word, see Raymond Williams, *Keywords* (New York: Oxford University Press, 1985), 57–60.

203. In *Synopsis*, Paterno tries to expand his racially based definition of the nation to include "all the varieties of the Malay race" in the archipelago, to which he continues to give the name *Tagalog*. As late as 1914, Dean Worcester reserved the

name *Filipino* for the Christianized population (i.e., excluding non-Christians). See Dean C. Worcester, *The Philippines Past and Present* (New York: Macmillan Company, 1914), II:533.

204. Schumacher, *Propaganda Movement*, 134n, 137, 206–8; Cesar Adib Majul, *Mabini and the Philippine Revolution* (Quezon City: University of the Philippines Press, 1996; first published in 1960), 262–65. See *Rizal-Blumentritt Correspondence*, II:1, 215; Marcelo H. del Pilar, *Monastic Supremacy in the Philippines* (Quezon City: Philippine Historical Association, 1958; first published in 1889), 11–12; *Idem.*, "The Assimilation of the Philippines," *Solidaridad*, I:16 (September 30, 1889), 379–81; and Rizal's annotation to Antonio de Morga, *Sucesos de las Islas Filipinas* (Manila: Comision Nacional del Centenario de Jose Rizal, 1961; first published in 1890), xxxiiin, 304n.

On Juan Luna's *Pacto de Sangre* (1878): *Portfolio of 60 Philippine Art Masterpieces*, 53–56.

205. Paterno, *Antigua Civilizacion*, 210.

206. Paterno, *Pacto de Biyak-na-Bato*, 8–9, 101.

207. See, for instance, Nick Joaquin, *Prose and Poems* (Manila: Graphic House, 1952) and *The Woman Who Had Two Navels* (Manila: Regal Publishing, 1961).

208. Ira and Medina, *Streets of Manila*, 93.

209. Reynaldo C. Ileto, *Pasyon and Revolution: Popular Movements in the Philippines, 1840–1910* (Quezon City: Ateneo de Manila University Press, 1979), 102–5; Isabelo de los Reyes, *Apuntes para un ensayo de Teodicea Filipina: La Religion del Katipunan* (Madrid: Tipolit. de J. Corrales, 1900); *Idem.*, *La Religion Antigua de los Filipinos* (Manila: Imprenta de El Renacimiento, 1909).

210. Umberto Eco, *Serendipities: Language and Lunacy*, trans. W. Weaver (New York: Harcourt Brace, 1999), ix.

211. Frank Laubach, *The People of the Philippines* (New York: George H. Doran, 1925), 46. An early twentieth-century Rizalist sect, the Nueva Ecija-based *Bathalismo (Inang Mahiwaga)*, credits the writings of Paterno as one of the primary sources of its religious beliefs. See Marcelino A. Foronda, Jr., *Cults Honoring Rizal* (Manila: no pub., 1961), 8.

T.H. Pardo
de Tavera

A MAN APART

HE WAS THE QUINTESSENTIAL *ILUSTRADO*. Highly educated, of Spanish descent and a family of considerable wealth, T.H. Pardo de Tavera was marked for a position of prominence in Spanish colonial society. He did not quite live up to the promise.

An independent-minded creole, he spent years as an expatriate in Paris and had an uneasy relationship with power. The relationship remained testy even when, after the fall of Spain, he became the most highly placed Filipino in the land as the senior Filipino member of the U.S. Philippine Commission, the country's law-making body. Discarded by the Americans and maligned by Filipinos, his political career was brief. In nationalist constructions of the nation's birth, he is usually cast in a villain's role. In the strongest statement of this historiography, Teodoro Agoncillo remarks: "Pardo de Tavera should have been shot for his betrayal of the Revolution."[1]

His role in the nationalist narrative has obscured his other accomplishments. He was, at the turn of the twentieth century, the country's most eminent man of science, its most ardent apostle of modernity. While Pardo's stature as an intellectual is ritually conceded, he is, by and large,

121

unread and unstudied. Even in his own time, he was a figure rather distant and cold. He remains so to Filipinos today.

TRINIDAD HERMENEGILDO PARDO DE TAVERA was born in Escolta, Manila, on April 13, 1857, the oldest of the three children of Felix Pardo de Tavera and Juliana Gorricho.[2]

His family had a long and illustrious history. On his father's side, he descended from an aristocratic family that traced its roots to the town of Tavira (or Tabeira), a seaport in southern Portugal close to the present Spanish border. The Pardos added *de Tavera* to their name in the 1640s when it was customary to identify an aristocrat by the family's place of origin. Illustrious ascendants included Don Gonzalo Paez de Tabeira, who fought under Alfonso VIII in the war against the Almohad ruler in the thirteenth century; Don Juan Pardo de Tavera, who carried the title Marques de Magahon; and, the most famous of them all, Don Juan Pardo de Tavera, cardinal of Toledo, inquisitor general and regent of Spain in the reign of Charles I. *El Gran Cardenal* had such eminence his remains were interred in the Escorial, the palace-mausoleum of Philip II.[3]

Trinidad's grandfather was Julian Pardo de Tavera, a direct descendant of the Marques de Magahon. The founder of the family's Philippine branch, Julian was born in Toledo in 1795 and set sail for Manila on December 1, 1825, shortly after he married a Spanish woman, Juana Maria Gomez. (Beyond the common assumption that he went overseas to seek his fortune, the reasons for his move to the Philippines are not clear.) Arriving in the colony with his wife, he took up a post as a lieutenant in the Spanish Army. Within four years after arriving in Manila, the couple had two sons, Felix and Joaquin, and a daughter named Carmen.

Felix and Joaquin studied law at Universidad de Santo Tomas and had successful careers as lawyers. Felix, the elder brother, served as an inspector of *escuelas de latinidad* (secondary-level private schools) and was a member of the governor-general's advisory council, *Consejo de Administracion*. The latter, though a largely honorary post, attested to his prominence since the council was composed of the colony's leading officials and citizens.

The two brothers were admired in the capital as brilliant lawyers. They were tied even more closely since they married sisters, Juliana and

Gertrudis Gorricho. The sisters were heiresses to a wealthy Eurasian family of Manila and Cavite. Their father, Jose Damaso Gorricho was a rich, Paris-educated landowner credited with having established one of the earliest money-lending houses in the country.[4] He was born in the Philippines, the son of Miguel Ignacio Gorricho, a Basque from Pamplona who came to the Philippines and served as *alcalde mayor* of the Visayan province of Capiz. His mother, Rafaela Doyle, was the daughter of an Irishman named Jose Doyle, who arrived in Manila in 1750 in the entourage of governor-general Francisco de Obando, and Maria Apostol, the daughter of a Greek father and a Tagalog mother.

The sisters' mother, Ciriaca de los Santos, a *Tagala* from Cavite, had humbler origins but she appears to have been mainly responsible for the Pardos' family wealth. She was an enterprising woman who built the family fortune supplying hay (*zacate*) to the Spanish cavalry and acquiring tracts of land, including much of the land along what came to be the country's premier business street, the Escolta.[5]

The Pardos lived in Intramuros. The family residence on Cabildo Street stood in what was the colony's politico-religious nerve center, occupying a corner of the central square (*plaza mayor*) around which stood the Manila Cathedral, the governor's palace, and city hall (*Cabildo*). (In the 1870s, part of the Pardo building housed the *Academia de Dibujo y Pintura*, the country's first state-supported art school.) Trinidad spent his early years in the navel of Spanish colonial power.

IN 1864, when Pardo was only seven years old, his father died at the young age of thirty-five. With brother Felix Jr. and sister Pacita, he was placed under the guardianship of his uncle, Joaquin.

Joaquin Pardo de Tavera (1829–1884) was a major influence in his life. Among the most prominent in his generation of Philippine-born Spaniards, Joaquin received his first law degree at twenty-three. He declined an offer of appointment as law reporter (*relator*) in the Real Audiencia, the colony's highest court, but briefly served as lieutenant governor of the Batanes Islands. He worked under the famous Manila lawyers Jose Jugo and Juan Francisco Lecaros, the latter an associate of his brother Felix. He subsequently set up his own law firm, filled appointments as *promotor fiscal* of Manila (1861) and *teniente fiscal* of the Real Audiencia (1864), and was in the board of directors of Obras

Pias, Colegio de Santa Isabel, Real Hospicio de San Jose, and Sociedad Economica de Amigos del Pais. When Felix died in 1864, Joaquin was appointed to his brother's position in the Consejo de Administracion. For his civic contributions, he was conferred a knighthood in the Order of Isabel the Catholic.

In 1868, Joaquin received the title of Doctor of Jurisprudence and was named to the law faculty of Santo Tomas. As a professor, he influenced a generation of students who would become persons of influence themselves, like Antonio Regidor, Florentino Torres, and Felipe Buencamino. He was described as a principled man who did not balk at "expressing his views, no matter where, or who he was talking to, or how his opinions would be received by the authorities."[6] Pardo admiringly spoke of his uncle:

> A man of principle, he defended issues of justice with tenacity, courage and a characteristically passionate commitment to democratic ideals. He gave himself to the study of matters Philippine, for which he professed a deep and abiding love. He was highly esteemed for his liberalism and gracious personality, and he was so popular that he was often found, following his lectures at the Universidad de Santo Tomas, surrounded by large groups of students at the university gates eager for his attention and inspiring ideas.[7]

After the "Glorious Revolution" that deposed Queen Isabella II in 1868, the new republican government formed a *Junta General de Reformas* to propose reforms in the Philippines. Joaquin was named to the assembly together with four other creoles, eleven peninsulars, and five Spanish friars.[8] In the wave of reformism that swept Manila in the late 1860s, he emerged as a principal figure in the reform movement. He inspired the liberal activism of university students and took up the cause of Filipino secular priests in their conflict with the religious orders over the control of parishes. In 1869, Joaquin and the *reformadores* brought their cause to the public arena in a series of manifestations addressed to the new and reputedly liberal governor-general Carlos Maria de la Torre. Among the reforms they urged on de la Torre were changes in education and civil service policies, the abolition of the tobacco monopoly, and, most important, Filipino representation in the Cortes.

The outspokenness of the *creoles* and *mestizos* outraged conservative *peninsulares*. The authorities secretly surveilled the reformadores' activities, anxious about the kind of separatist movements that had caused trouble for the empire in the Americas. After a new governor general, Rafael Izquierdo, assumed office in 1871, a policy of suppression was carried out. The Cavite mutiny on January 20, 1872, gave government the excuse for a massive crackdown. Arguing that it was part of a wide-ranging conspiracy to take over the government, the authorities ordered the execution of a number of "rebels," most prominently the priests Jose Burgos, Jacinto Zamora, and Mariano Gomez, on February 17.

On January 21, the day after the mutiny, Joaquin and other prominent Filipinos were arrested and charged with "complicity in the crime of proclaiming the establishment of the republic." Joaquin was imprisoned in Fort Santiago, his house searched, and his correspondence intercepted. He was also suspended from the practice of law. In the court-martial proceedings, he declared that he was a reputable citizen who had contributed much to the state and that the governor-general himself could confirm this fact. Izquierdo, however, washed his hands off Joaquin, attesting instead that Joaquin had for some time been under surveillance as suspected member of a "junta" that conducted secret antigovernment meetings. Documents of the trial, however, make clear that the government had embarked on a program of indiscriminate vendetta.[9]

On February 15, Joaquin was sentenced to four years of exile and on March 14 shipped off to the Marianas. He spent almost four years in the Marianas (1872–1875) in the company of his wife Gertrudis (*Tula*), a remarkable woman who chose to join her husband to exile.

The imprisonment and exile of Joaquin must have exposed members of the Pardo family to harassment and humiliation as political outcasts. In later years, Trinidad would write that for the deportees' families, the events of 1872 were an "open wound" (*heridas abiertas*) that rankled for a long time.[10] As late as 1891 the Madrid press criticized the appointment of Cristobal Cerquella as president of the Court of Manila and temporary justice of the Supreme Court simply because he was married to Carmen Pardo de Tavera, "a sister of the one accused in the Cavite revolt of aspiring to be the head of the new Filipino state-to-be."[11]

Trinidad was a student at the time of the deportations. He had studied at Ateneo de Manila, moved to San Juan de Letran, earned a baccalaureate in 1873, and enrolled in the new school of medicine at Santo Tomas. Years later, he spoke of himself as a "non-conformist" under the colonial system of education but we have no record of what his thoughts or actions were at this time.[12]

Pardoned together with other exiles, Joaquin sailed out of Agana in January 1875. Prohibited from returning to the Philippines, Joaquin and Gertrudis chose to reside in Paris. Here, it is said, Joaquin's aristocratic and liberal credentials "opened the doors of the highest Parisian society." He was solicitously received by the exiled Spanish politician Manuel Ruiz Zorilla and gained the friendship of such notables as the statesman Leon Gambetta and French presidents Maurice de MacMahon and Francois Grevy.[13]

As soon as they were settled in Paris, Joaquin sent for his brother's family to join them in that city. Thus, in 1875, after less than two years of medical studies at Santo Tomas, the eighteen-year-old Trinidad left for Paris with members of his family. Reunited, the Pardos made Paris their home, supported by income from their real properties in the Philippines.

PARIS WAS A TIME of quiet domesticity for the family, sheltered from the stresses of politics in colonial Manila.

To live in Paris in the 1870s was to live in heady times.[14] It was the first decade of the Third Republic and France was struggling to forge a parliamentary democracy out of contentious traditions in French political life. In 1870, the German invasion of France's northern provinces led to the capitulation of Napoleon III and the overthrow of the Second French Empire. With society shaken by the war, suppressed energies harking back to the French Revolution of 1789 burst forth anew in the Paris Commune of 1871 and popular risings in other cities and towns. After the insurrection was quelled with much destruction and bloodshed, French democrats turned to the challenge of forging a non-extremist continuation of the revolutionary ideal of "sovereignty of the people" through the creation of a parliamentary democracy.

In 1875, when the young Pardo arrived in Paris, the city still bore the scars of the long German siege and the Communard uprising of 1871. Such signs of these events as the ruins of the palace of the Tuileries could still be seen (the ruins were cleared only in 1889 to make way for a public park). There was, however, a mood of earnest rebuilding. Paris had regained its spirit as a charivari of cafes, theaters, museums, and *grands magasins* (department stores), the center of Europe's intellectual and artistic life. This was the time of the authors Flaubert, Zola, and Hugo, the scientists Pasteur, Renan, and Taine, and the artists Manet, Degas, and Renoir.

It was a time of fierce contestation among republicans, monarchists, Bonapartists, and other political groups, but French Liberalism was ascendant with its bias for a representative government dominated by a bourgeoisie opposed to the monarchy, clericalism, and the extremists of Right and Left. The battle between science and religion was a major theme and there was enthusiasm for such projects as "universal" suffrage and the building of a secular, democratic, and science-based educational system.

The young Pardo was in "the capital of the nineteenth century."[15] For sure, he was not unaffected by the swirl of political ideas around him, the excitement of an era of expansion and experiment. It was a time and place that must have been exhilarating for his uncle Joaquin as well, recently emerged from exile for his libertarian beliefs, but we have no reference to what conversations on current events uncle and nephew may have had in Paris in the 1870s.

Paris exposed Pardo to the most radical ideas. He recounts, for instance, his friendship with two young Russians, Louise Ivanovna Krilof and Maria Michaelovna Lujine, who were introduced to him by his professor in medicine, Tarnier. (I assume the reference is to the surgeon Stephane Tarnier [1828–1897], a pioneer in the application of the ideas of Pasteur and Lister to obstetrics.[16]) Tarnier told Pardo and the Russians they should have a lot in common since they were political refugees in Paris and victims of religious and political tyranny at home. The Russians, it turned out, were dedicated Nihilists. In visits to the women's apartment Pardo met other Nihilists, learned about their struggle against the Tsar, and shared his own experience with repression in the Philippines. Pardo does not say anything about Nihilism itself but he was impressed by the women's idealism and Spartan lifestyle (and would later hold them up before Filipino women as examples of women's emancipation). The assassination of Russia's Alexander II by a bomb thrown by a Nihilist in 1881 did not dim Pardo's admiration for the Nihilists' "daring and enormous sense of responsibility."[17] Readers today would find the idea of Pardo consorting with "terrorists" weird. Yet there was much in Pardo—his positivism and intellectual seriousness—that would have appreciated the figure of the medical student Bazarov—the toughminded materialist to whom "nature is not a temple, but a workshop, and man's the workman in it"—in Ivan Turgenev's 1862 novel *Fathers and Sons*. (It was this novel that popularized the word *nihilism*).[18]

More important was Pardo's medical education in Paris. Pardo matriculated in the Paris *Faculte de Medecine* where he earned his licentiate around 1880 and his doctor of medicine degree in 1881. The *Faculte* was the leading medical school in the city that was a mecca for medical students and practitioners from various parts of the world. This was the time of Louis Pasteur and Robert Koch and revolutionary advances in clinical medicine and the basic sciences were transforming the knowledge, technology, and teaching of medicine.[19]

Nineteenth-century medicine was philosophically expansive and socially interventionist, claiming foundational knowledge not only in curing patients but understanding the problems of humankind. Seeing themselves vanguards of an embracive "science of man," physicians assumed social and political authority. Republican, Masonic, and materialist ideas pervaded French medical circles. The Paris Faculty of Medicine was dominated by atheistic professors, many of them involved in founding the *Societe d'anthropologie de Paris* in 1859 and *Societe d'autopsie mutuelle* in 1876. The latter, composed of leading anthropologists, scientists, and physicians, gained notoriety not only because of its purpose—members agree to autopsy and study each other's brains after death—but its aggressive public campaign to spread the gospel of a materialist science. Society of Mutual Autopsy included among its members the economist Yves Guyot, anthropologists Gabriel de Mortillet, Charles Letourneau, and Louis-Adolphe Bertillon, and, most prominent of them all, the surgeon Paul Broca, the "founder of French anthropology."[20]

Pardo wrote little about his experiences as a student, but the scientific climate of nineteenth-century Paris was crucial in his formation. In later years, attacked for his freethinking views, he would be called "disciple of the famous professor Dr. Fauvel [sic]," referring to Jean-Louis

Fauvelle, a physician-member of *Societe d'anthropologie* who had publicly dismissed the value of both philosophy and religion on materialist grounds.[21]

Pardo began to dedicate himself to scholarly pursuits. He enrolled in *Ecole nationale des langues orientales vivantes*, took courses under Pierre Etienne Lazare Favre, a French missionary and professor of Malay and Javanese, and earned his diploma in Malay in December 1885. He collected books and maps of the Philippines, tracking down rare items in bookshops and private collections in Paris and elsewhere. He contributed medical articles to various periodicals (what may be the earliest is a piece published in Madrid's *El Siglo Medico* in 1881, on Pott's disease, or tuberculosis of the vertebral column).[22] In 1884, he contributed an article to the Paris *Journal de Medecine* on the practices of healers and sorcerers in Luzon, relating these to modern medical knowledge, and in 1886 published his medical thesis, *Contribution a l'etude de la Periarthrite du Genou (Affections de la bourse sereuse de la patte d'oie)*.[23]

While still a student at *Ecole nationale des langues orientales vivantes*, he wrote *Contribucion para el estudio de los antiguos alfabetos Filipinos*, which was published in Lausanne, Switzerland, in 1884. Then in 1887, he published *El Sanscrito en la lengua Tagalog*, an investigation of Hindu influence in the Philippines through a study of Sanskrit-derived words in Tagalog. These early works appeared in French, Spanish, and German translations, and gained the attention of other scholars. *Contribucion para el estudio de los antiguos alfabetos Filipinos* was noted in such learned publications as *Journal of the Asiatic Society of Bengal* and *Journal of the Straits Branch of the Royal Asiatic Society* and received the following laudatory comment by Friedrich Muller in 1885: "The merit of Pardo de Tavera's interesting study consists in the way in which the author follows out the question, with special reference to the Philippines, more closely than his predecessors, and illustrates the question with several examples from the whole Philippine literature."[24] By 1886 he was a member of such societies as *Societe Academique Indo-Chinoise* (Paris), *Societe Espagnole d'Hygiene* (Madrid), and *Societe d'Anthropologie* (Berlin).

ON MARCH 19, 1884, Joaquin Pardo de Tavera died at the age of fifty-five, his remains interred in a family vault in the historic cemetery of

Pere-Lachaisse. He was survived by his wife Gertrudis and three children, Eloisa, Beatrice, and Joaquin, all born in Paris. With Joaquin's death his widow decided to return to Manila with her children. Trinidad, then twenty-seven, was left to look after his mother, brother Felix, and sister Paz.

They were living at the time in a well-appointed apartment at No. 14, Avenue de Wagram, a major thoroughfare that runs through the Arc de Triomphe. (In 1884, Pardo also indicates his address as 36 Boulevard Pereire.) Supported by income from the Philippines, the family lived in relative leisure. Pardo practiced medicine; worked for four years as secretary of the Paris legation of the Dominican Republic; and had the title of "official of public instruction" given him by the French government in 1890 (though we do not know what functions he discharged as such). His brother Felix also earned a medical degree in Paris in 1882 and served in hospitals in Paris and Bersur-Mer. (Trinidad and Felix were probably the first Filipinos to graduate as doctors in Paris.) Felix was beginning to earn a reputation as an excellent sculptor, winning prizes at European expositions, often in the company of Juan Luna and Felix Resurreccion Hidalgo.[25]

In 1887, Pardo sailed for Manila with a Spanish royal commission to study the medicinal properties of Philippine plants, a project authorized by the Spanish Crown but funded by Pardo himself. There was a personal reason for his return to the home country. A year earlier, Pardo met Concepcion (Concha) Cembrano when she visited Paris in the company of her grandmother, a friend of Doña Gertrudis. Concha was the daughter of Vicente Ker Cembrano and Carolina Gonzalez Calderon, and a cousin of the lawyer Felipe Calderon. Her grandfather, Ramon Gonzalez Calderon, was one of the founders of Manila's largest commercial bank, Banco Español-Filipino. Marrying Concha was apparently part of the occasion that brought Pardo back to the Philippines.

At this time, Pardo was already in contact with such Filipino émigrés as Jose Rizal, Juan Luna, and Felix Resurreccion Hidalgo. He first met Rizal in 1884 when, with his brother Felix, he went to Madrid for a vacation.[26] He had just published his book on precolonial alphabets and Rizal asked him for a copy and they corresponded thereafter. He was also in communication with the noted Austrian Filipinist Ferdinand Blumentritt. He obviously knew of the campaign by Filipinos in Europe for reforms in the colony but it appears that he kept his distance from their more overtly political activities.

How Pardo stood in relation to the Propaganda Movement at this time is indicated by a letter to Rizal written by Evaristo Aguirre in Madrid on March 10, 1887, conveying the news that "*le docteur* T.H. Pardo de Tavera" was leaving for Manila from Marseille on the thirteenth of the month. Aguirre averred it was doubtful whether they could ask him to carry copies of the recently published *Noli me tangere* to Manila. Aguirre writes that "it is doubtful (I doubt it, unless I'm refuted) that he will consent to undertake the double mission of importing books and performing the scientific work that the government has entrusted to him." "In view of what I have heard, he wants to be absolutely free of any embarrassment, for it is said that he decided to spend a couple of quiet years in political trimming (*pasteleando*) and then return to his Paris and enjoy, study, and write."[27] There were reasons for Pardo's diffidence: he carried the name of a *filibustero* and must have known that Manila in 1887 was astir with rumors of anti-Spanish activities.

Returning to Manila, Pardo sailed back into the teeth of civil agitation. He must have been struck by how little had changed from the Manila that had forced his family into exile twelve years earlier. Under governor-general Emilio Terrero, a new wave of civil reformism agitated the capital and its surrounding areas. Liberal-minded civil officials feuded with the friars over matters of jurisdiction and prerogatives. Local officials in Malolos and Binondo openly complained about the friars to higher authorities over personal tax-lists. Sectors of the Manila press opposed Augustinian control over a proposed government trade school. Controversy swirled around Jose Rizal—who arrived in Manila four months after Pardo got there—over the publication of *Noli me tangere*, a book the board of censors banned as "pernicious" on December 29, 1887. In nearby Calamba, tenants were locked in a struggle with the Dominican order over land rights. Tensions between church and state and the increasing boldness of citizens created a state of restiveness that climaxed on March 1, 1888, when hundreds of people, including many *gobernadorcillos*, marched to Manila's *Ayuntamiento* and presented to Manila's civil governor a manifesto addressed to Queen Regent Maria Cristina in which they denounced Archbishop Pedro Payo and asked for the friars' expulsion.

Pardo kept his distance from these events. He married Concha soon after he arrived in Manila and, a year after, had a son, Carlos. The botanical project kept him busy collecting plants in Manila and nearby towns, interviewing *curanderos* ("herb-doctors"), and conducting laboratory experiments. He also took time to publish *Consideraciones sobre el origen del nombre de los numeros en Tagalog* (Manila, 1889), which traced the Tagalog names of numerals to indigenous and other origins. An ardent bibliophile, he busied himself acquiring all sorts of materials about the Philippines. A precious item he found in the Franciscan convent in Manila was Fr. Juan de Plasencia's 1589 manuscript on Tagalog culture, which Pardo copied, edited, and published with the title *Las costumbres de los Tagalos, segun el Padre Plasencia* (Madrid, 1892).

His stay in the Philippines was not untroubled. Authorities regarded him with suspicion, ostensibly because of his name, status as a French-educated intellectual, and known association with Rizal and the reformists. Pedro Serrano Laktaw, writing to Rizal from Manila in 1888 on the arrest of gobernadorcillos after the March 1 demonstration, said that "Pardo (Trinidad) no longer makes visits and I believe he will soon leave the *Subdelegacion de Medicina*. They have demanded of him I don't know what things, not to say he is persecuted."[28] Rizal was not surprised that Pardo would be harassed. Writing to Blumentritt from Paris on September 4, 1888, he said that the Pardo family had received a letter from their daughter-in-law Concha in Manila "informing them that Trinidad Pardo de Tavera has been forbidden to treat patients." "Beware! Is this the first blow against Pardo? Pardo de Tavera has many enemies among the Peninsular Spaniards in Manila. Of that I am sure, but I thought that they would behave with more prudence."[29] In a subsequent letter to Blumentritt on May 8, 1889, Rizal said that Pardo had just returned to Paris. "He says that life in the Philippines is becoming impossible. They wanted to search his home and confiscate his books, if he had not left immediately. He believes that if conditions do not improve, before the lapse of ten years, a great revolution will break out."[30]

Rizal must have appreciated the irony in the vexations visited upon Pardo. He knew that the fastidious Spanish mestizo had studiously kept himself aloof from political involvement. When Rizal visited the Philippines in 1887 he decided (he wrote to Blumentritt on October 19,

1887) not to call on Pardo as "many in Manila are afraid of my calls." Of Pardo Rizal wrote: "He holds government commissions and I would not wish to soil his white gloves with my hands that are stained for writing novels. These things happen in my country, but at heart we remain friends, at least so far as I am concerned."[31] Later, however, Rizal, in the company of Maximo Viola, did call on Pardo "on your [Blumentritt's] behalf and we talked a great deal about you."[32] Pardo himself would mention another visit, saying that Rizal came to his house in Manila in the company of M.H. del Pilar and Antonio Vergel de Dios.[33]

What Rizal may have felt about his friend, del Pilar expressed bluntly. Del Pilar was still in the Philippines at the time of Pardo's visit and was active in the agitation that led to the popular manifestation of March 1, 1888. In a letter to Rizal attributed to del Pilar, written in Barcelona on May 18, 1889, del Pilar writes that when Rizal attended one town fiesta outside Manila, "Trinidad" (presumed to be Pardo; this was how he was referred to by friends) saw Rizal looking out a window of a house "and he passed along, but contented himself with greeting you with his hand, in spite of his great desire to embrace you." He reports that Trinidad goes around with a sergeant of the Civil Guards so he will have a ready witness that he had not met Rizal. Saying that he knew Trinidad "since I was a child," del Pilar called him "a person with a rather lively imagi-nation." He wrote in Tagalog: *Iyan ay isa roon sa manga kinakargahan pa lamang ang berso ay bali na ang daliri sa pagtatakip nang tainga.* ("He is one of those who break their fingers to cover their ears when the small culverin is just being loaded.")[34]

PARDO'S PHILIPPINE SOJOURN ended in 1889 after Manila's chamber of commerce named him its delegate to represent the Philippines and help organize the chamber's exhibits at the Universal Exposition of 1889 in Paris. With his wife and son, he sailed for Marseille around the end of March 1889.

Back in Paris, he published a catalogue of the exhibits, *Catalogo Memoria de la Exposicion de Productos de las Islas Filipinas* (1889), which carried a list of exhibitors and information about Philippine agriculture, commerce, and industry. The Philippine exhibit consisted of agricul-tural and industrial items—including perfumes, pharmacological products, Paete woodcraft, and 147 varieties of rice—crammed into a space of twelve square meters. It paled in comparison with exhibits from French colonies in Asia and Africa. *Solidaridad* blamed the "miserable exhibit" on such bureaucratic snags as inadequate preparation, lack of participation, and funding problems. *Solidaridad*, however, praised Pardo for his efforts and the honor he had as the only Filipino in the Philippine exposition committee and "the only Spaniard" in the international board of judges for the exhibition's Section of Hygiene and Mineral Waters.[35]

The exposition attracted Filipinos to Paris, including Rizal. While Rizal's planned international conference on the Philippines did not materialize, Filipinos used the occasion to organize a club called *Kidlat* for social and intellectual fellowship. It does not seem that Pardo was prominently involved in these gatherings, if at all. Pardo was busy with his medical botany project, which was delayed by problems in the transport of specimens from Manila. He had shipped plants to Paris for chemical analysis but, due to inexpert packing and the rigors of overseas shipment, these arrived decomposed or spoiled. In 1892, however, his *Plantas medicinales de Filipinas* came out. It established the standard for works on the subject.

He was busy with other research interests, publishing in 1893 *Noticias sobre la imprenta y el grabado en Filipinas*, a historical sketch of the development of printing in the Philippines. At this time, too, Pardo became involved in Freemasonry. In 1890, he joined Antonio Luna and Ariston Bautista in forming a Masonic triangle under the auspices of the Madrid-based Lodge Solidaridad, in which Luna was active together with M.H. del Pilar and other Filipino propagandists. With the addition of Felix Pardo de Tavera, Juan Luna, Valentin Ventura, and Antonio Vergel de Dios, the triangle expanded into the lodge called *Temple de L'Honneur et de L'Union*, under the auspices of the Gran Oriente de Francia. Rizal himself was affiliated with this lodge when he visited Paris in 1892.[36]

There were changes in the Pardo de Tavera family. On December 7, 1886, before Pardo made his trip to the Philippines, his sister Paz married Juan Luna, who was at the time lionized by Filipinos for his artistic accomplishments. On October 22, 1889, Pardo's younger brother Felix married an Argentine woman, Agustina Manigot. And in 1890, Pardo and Concha had a second son, Alfredo.

The Pardos frequently hosted Filipino émigrés in their home. The Pardo brothers were not above joining other Filipinos in diversions one of them called "healthy, historical humor" (*sano e historico humorismo*). A photograph taken in Juan Luna's studio in Paris in 1885 shows the Filipinos staging a *tableau vivant* of the death of Cleopatra, complete with costumes and props, with Juan Luna as Cleopatra, Rizal as scribe, Trinidad as priest, and Felix as Marc Anthony.[37] Gatherings at the Pardo home were so convivial there is even the suggestion a relationship may have been brewing between Rizal and Trinidad's cousin Eloisa. In a letter to Rizal from Paris on February 5, 1890, Valentin Ventura wrote that Doña Tula and the Pardos were disappointed Rizal left Paris early despite their wish that he stayed longer, at least for Eloisa's birthday. "Eloisa is so resentful; truly the commitment is strong, worse than..." Ventura alludes to Rizal's having said something about "having left on time," suggesting that Rizal barely escaped being ensnared in a relationship.[38] All this may have just been male byplay about romantic adventures, real or imagined, but the intimate gatherings at the Pardo home would have one dramatic and unfortunate result.

It must have been at these gatherings that the affair between the twenty-four year-old Paz and Juan Luna developed. The Pardos had reservations about the relationship between the tall, wan, and fragile Paz and the short, swarthy, and temperamental Ilocano. After the two were married, Doña Juliana financially supported the couple and moved in with them in their home at Villa Dupont on 28 rue Pergolese. It was a troubled marriage. Luna was a jealous and abusive husband, a situation aggravated by the fact that he did not quite fit into the Pardo household.

Tragedy struck on September 22, 1892. In a fit of depression and rage, triggered by suspicions about the infidelity of his wife, Luna murdered his wife and mother-in-law in their home at Villa Dupont.[39] Trinidad and Felix were caught in the middle of the tragedy as they tried, before the actual shooting, to placate Luna and extricate the women from what was developing into an extremely dangerous situation. Felix was wounded by a shot fired by Luna and Trinidad was deeply shaken, finding himself powerless to control the situation.

What compounded the family's grief was that, in the trial that followed, Luna was acquitted of the charges of murder and attempted murder after the defense successfully depicted him as victim rather than aggressor. In the trial, Luna's lawyer presented testimonials of support from Luna's highly placed patrons and friends and read ardent letters written by Luna (who signed himself *Lulu*) to his wife (*Chiching*) to show Luna's "loftiness and delicacy" of character. On the other hand, the lawyer slyly suggested that "racial differences" brought difficulties to the marriage and depicted Trinidad and Felix (who testified against Luna) as ungrateful and meanspirited. The lawyer remarked: "D. Trinidad himself should not forget that the honors he now enjoys and proudly shows have been obtained through the recommendations of Luna."

Arguing that Luna was driven by jealousy over his wife's infidelity, imagined or real, the defense pushed the race issue by bringing in a doctor-witness and citing "medical opinions according to which the natives live subject to certain irresistible impulses" and that Luna was governed by these impulses and, being "a native," he "should be judged as such." The French lawyer concluded: "You have before you a man who is not moved by the same impulses like we are. God has made him so. We have to pry into his nature, his soul, and inquire if he should be judged like a Frenchman."[40] It was high irony that Luna, who was held up by his compatriots as preeminent example of how the Filipino could "out-European" the European, now won his freedom for being a "native."

The tragedy devastated the Pardos. Pardo never spoke of Luna again and would not allow mention of his name. He destroyed the Luna paintings his family had in their possession. On January 19, 1897, Juan Luna wrote Trinidad a formal letter of apology for the Paris tragedy, asking for a reconciliation, but the apology was not accepted. In Manila, the private tragedy became the stuff of gossip. When Luna died of a heart attack in Hong Kong on December 7, 1899, there was a malicious rumor in Manila that he was poisoned by an assassin hired by Trinidad.[41]

The tragedy led to the breakup of the surviving members of the family. In 1894, Felix moved with his wife to Buenos Aires. He established a medical practice in that city, continued to devote himself to sculpture, became a naturalized Argentine, and never returned to the Philippines. In the same year, Trinidad decided to leave Paris and, with his own family, returned to Manila.

IN MANILA, T.H. Pardo de Tavera found refuge in scholarly work. In 1894, he joined the Santo Tomas faculty of medicine and remained active in the years that followed, handling subjects like descriptive anatomy, anatomic techniques, and embryology. He and Concha also had another child, Carmen. He practiced medicine and pursued his scholarly interests. In 1894, he published *El mapa de Filipinas del P. Murillo Velarde*, an essay on the Philippine map engraved by Nicolas de la Cruz Bagay in 1734. It brought to public attention a landmark map in Philippine cartography and provided historical data on its production and circulation.

He promoted medical science and its public benefits, writing in 1895 *Arte de cuidar enfermos*, a popular manual meant to promote modern health practices. It was issued in a Tagalog translation in the same year. He contributed articles to *La Correspondencia Medica de Filipinas* (1893–1897). On June 8, 1899, with Dr. Mariano V. del Rosario, he founded *Colegio Medico-Farmaceutico de Filipinas* and served as its first president (1899–1900). The professional association was active in organizing conferences in which scientific papers were read.[42]

Immersed in scientific studies, Pardo evinced little interest in politics. When the Revolution broke out in August 1896, he was not implicated in the events as other prominent Filipinos were. He was in fact commissioned *segunda jefe de la Guerrilla de San Miguel* as colonial authorities mobilized Spanish residents to defend the Crown. Pardo resigned from his commission for reasons of health and other professional commitments in April 1897.[43] We have no reference to his having participated in any of the actions although his enemies would later remind the public that Pardo commanded a company of Spanish-loyalist *voluntarios* in 1896.

In December 1896, Pardo and his young sons watched from a window in their house in Intramuros as Jose Rizal was escorted from Fort Santiago to his execution in Bagumbayan. We have no record of what thoughts Pardo had as he watched his friend being marched to his death. There is reference to letters preserved in the old Philippine Library and Museum indicating that at the time of Rizal's trial, Pardo presented himself to the Spanish authorities as opposed to both Rizal and the revolution.[44]

At the outbreak of the Spanish-American War, Pardo was among the select citizens named to the *Asamblea Consultiva* organized on May 28, 1898, by governor-general Basilio Augustin to rally support for the colony's defense against the United States. In a letter to Fr. Evaristo F. Arias on September 26, 1898, Pardo said that Augustin's assembly, headed by Pedro Paterno, was "born dead" (*nacida muerta*).[45] There was no way for Spain to save the situation but grant autonomy, Pardo wrote. He bore the friars no malice, despite the calumnies heaped against him, and that he had always acted with "reason," guided by the desire for "my country, *Filipinas*, peace, progress, well-being" (*mi pais, Filipinas, la paz, el progreso, el bienestar*).

By Pardo's own admission, he made contact with the Americans even before the U.S. takeover of Manila on August 13, 1898. In a letter he sent to President McKinley on July 30, 1899, he narrated that a few days before August 13 he sought out Major Frank S. Bourns after he learned that Bourns spoke Spanish and had been previously in the Philippines. A medical doctor and long-time friend of Dean Worcester, Bourns was active in liaising between American officials and members of the Manila elite. Convinced of "the immense good the Philippines would receive from America," Pardo said, he asked Bourns to introduce him to American authorities so he could offer his services. He was introduced to General F.V. Greene, with whom, Pardo said, he conversed in French. The encounter must have been so encouraging since Pardo wrote: "I have completely and most actively occupied myself in politics, employing all my energies for the establishment of American sovereignty in this country for the good of these ignorant and uncivilized people."[46]

We cannot tell how much of Pardo's declaration of personal belief is a gloss after the events for the U.S. president's benefit. It is clear, however, that early on Pardo was convinced that an independent Philippine state was not viable and that the most dignified option for Filipinos, in the face of superior American power, was to aspire to a protectorate status under the United States. An admirer of American political institutions, he genuinely felt that between a premature, dangerous, and "impossible" independent republic, on one hand, and a Spanish restoration or seizure by another foreign power, on the other, U.S. annexation was the more "progressive" option.

In the uncertain days of August 1898, however, Pardo "worked both sides." On the same day the Americans seized Manila, August 13, Pardo had his first meeting with Aguinaldo in Bacoor. Pardo later wrote that he wanted "to see what political system [Aguinaldo] had in mind; what ideas he had." In the same letter to Fr. Arias on September 26, 1898, referred to earlier, he said he wanted to hear what Aguinaldo and the other leaders had to say "in order to judge afterwards what ought to be done, what line of action should be followed, and if it was still possible [for me] to think of living in this land." He added that if he decides to cast his lot with the "Filipino flag," he would follow the same principles of "justice and humanity" that guided him while still a subject of Spain.[47]

Apparently, his meeting with Aguinaldo was not too productive. Pardo found that Aguinaldo, while goodhearted, appeared naïve and had a limited grasp of the developing situation. Aguinaldo referred him to Mabini but his meeting with the latter was not productive either. Pardo already knew Mabini ("I had attended to him as a physician for a sort of paralysis of the lower portion of the body which he had suffered from"). While conceding that he was "a man of talent," Pardo found him too legalistic and "a man who hated the Americans."[48]

Yet, despite his reservations, Pardo assumed a role in the Aguinaldo government when he joined the Malolos Congress, nominally representing Cebu. He was present when the congress was convened on September 15. He served as member of several congressional committees and was professor of medicine and surgery in the government's Universidad Literaria de Filipinas when this was created on October 19. Though this was a short-lived university, Pardo discharged his duties by giving lectures on *materia medica* and therapeutics in his home on Calle Raon in Santa Cruz. Pardo also contributed to the government's organ, *La Independencia*, launched on September 3, 1898.

On October 1, 1898, on Mabini's recommendation, he took his oath of office as the government's "director of diplomacy" and, shortly after, was named secretary of foreign relations, replacing Cayetano Arellano (who never assumed the post given to him). It was in this capacity that in October Aguinaldo sent him as head of a commission to confer with General E.S. Otis to iron out tensions arising from disagreements over the positions occupied by American and Filipino forces in Manila and its suburbs in the wake of the Spanish surrender of the city.[49] His stint as foreign affairs secretary, however, was brief since he resigned on October 30 on grounds of policy differences with the Aguinaldo government.

That Pardo assumed positions in the Aguinaldo government *after* he had apparently come to an understanding with the Americans raises serious questions about his good faith. Yet, it must be noted that the situation was fluid, both in terms of U.S. intentions and Aguinaldo's goals. Pardo would later write that he went over to Aguinaldo to "use my abilities in the reestablishment of order and the establishment of a stable and responsible government."[50] It appears that he judged at the time that there was still room to influence Aguinaldo to enter into a political settlement with the Americans. Four days before he took his place in the Malolos Congress on September 15, he expressed his concerns in a letter to Raymundo Melliza in which "he worried that a declaration of independence was insufficient for the establishment of a viable republic." "He did not believe that there was a nation in the world favorably disposed toward recognizing independence and thus transform it from *de facto* to *de jure* status. He believed that the ideal arrangement would be for American protection in the conduct of Philippine international affairs leaving internal administration in Filipino hands."[51] He was wary of the Aguinaldo government's dictatorial tendencies and he did not believe that the people were ready. Pardo, it is said, accepted the post of Director of Diplomacy believing he could take a direct hand in negotiating with the Americans.

For Filipino intellectuals, the situation, particularly from May 1898 to February 1899, was confusing, fast-moving, and uncertain. Between outright, unqualified support for U.S. annexation and an independent republic was a gradient of positions expressed in proposals for various forms of *autonomy, home rule, protectorate status, statehood,* and *independence*. Actors shifted positions according to the pressure of events and calculations of what was realizable or desirable in the short or long term.

American intentions were obscure in the beginning and there was no clear consensus among Filipino leaders themselves. When the newly returned Aguinaldo raised the ante by organizing a revolutionary Filipino government and declaring independence on June 12, 1898, a significant section of the local intelligentsia moved toward the Aguinaldo government. Relations with the U.S. had not yet turned openly adversarial and pledging support for the idea of independence did not court American reprisal. There were mixed signals from Filipino leaders, including Aguinaldo, on what relations should be established with the Americans. Many ilustrados believed it was Aguinaldo's policy to call for independence but, if this was not possible, to accept annexation. They may have viewed the Republic as a necessary means for Filipinos to establish a personality and negotiating position vis-à-vis the Americans or "a temporary expedient for bridging a period which would be followed by some form of government under American control."[52]

While Pardo would be maligned for "political 'acrobatism'" (Mabini's words) it is reductive to characterize his actions (as later nationalist historians would) as a simple case of "defection" and "treachery." Pardo did not assess the intentions of the Aguinaldo government on the basis of its militant manifestoes but what its leaders were saying in private. He found Aguinaldo less than categorical on his government's political strategy and he was not impressed by Mabini's legalistic defense of the Republic. Until the shooting started on February 4, 1899, official and nonofficial diplomatic contact was taking place between Americans and leaders of the Aguinaldo government. Hence it is not strange that in the critical last half of 1898 we find Pardo talking to both the leaders of the Republic and the Americans.

Within the Aguinaldo government, Pardo and Arellano openly advocated "a republican constitution in the Philippines under an American protectorate," an idea that, Pardo claims, was supported by members of Congress. On September 21, 1898, a week after Congress convened, Pardo wrote a letter to General Otis, saying: "The number of partisans to the idea of a Philippine Republic under a protectorate of the United States is daily increasing here. I am the most ardent upholder of that idea as its principal propagandist." He added: "*Señor* Emilio Aguinaldo and the principal Filipinos surrounding him are today very favorably disposed towards the United States, but they would like to know what the intentions of the Washington Government are with regard to the Philippines." He asked the "government of occupation" (United States) to organize "the Administration of Justice, Registration of Property, the University of Manila as well as a system of Municipal Elementary Education," saying that Aguinaldo would cooperate in this regard and that if the U.S. eventually decides to abandon the archipelago the country would be grateful for the civil order established.[53]

Elsewhere, Pardo reports that Aguinaldo was open to the idea of a protectorate though he adds that it was "very difficult to say what this man wanted." He identified those opposed to the protectorate idea as Pedro Paterno (who, Pardo says, wanted a Spanish restoration), Mabini,

141

and the "military elements."[54] Felipe Buencamino affirmed that the protectorate plan was accepted by Aguinaldo at a Cabinet meeting but that Aguinaldo changed his mind, purportedly because he had been encouraged by reports that the Japanese would support Filipino independence and that majority of the American people favored Philippine independence as well.[55]

With Arellano and Benito Legarda, Pardo was one of the leading *autonomistas* or advocates of "autonomy" under the Americans. When he took his oath as director of diplomacy on October 1, he had already accepted the invitation of military governor Elwell Otis, on September 29, to be an honorary member in Manila's board of health, which was headed by Frank Bourns and later became the Board of Health of the Philippine Islands. That Pardo "played both sides" was both a matter of personal conviction and a product of vacillations within the Aguinaldo government.

Pardo's relation with the Aguinaldo government ended when he formally resigned on October 30, 1898. On November 13, he notified Otis that "since the 28th of October, I have had nothing whatever to do with the Philippine Government." He quoted from the resignation letter he sent to Aguinaldo on October 30:

> Honorable President: My opinion as to the proper course to pursue in matters of foreign policy being at variance with the views held by you, by reason whereof my actions, if made to conform to your worthy judgment, must necessarily be contrary to my own ideas, or contrary to yours if my judgment prevails, I find myself under the necessity of definitively resigning the office of Director of Diplomacy to which I had the honor of being appointed by you.[56]

In explaining his relations to the Aguinaldo government and his own political position, Pardo recounted to the Schurman Commission on August 22, 1899:

> I made a second visit to Aguinaldo [i.e., after their first meeting in Bacoor on August 13, 1898] when he was established in Malolos, but was unable to talk to him at length on the question of a foreign policy. I told him it would be very desirable for us to make some

142

immediate determination in regard to our position with America. At this time they were about to discuss the future of the Philippines in Paris, and I told him that I feared America would abandon this country, for it would not be to their advantage to retain it. I made it plain to him that it was not enough for us to desire America to stay here, but that it would be desirable for us to show America that it would be to her interest to keep the country. I told him that it would be a very good thing to end this separation and to bring the two peoples together in order that the Filipinos might understand what the Americans desired, and that the Americans would also become familiar with the Philippine people . . . I advised him and all his government to write to President McKinley and ask him not to abandon the Philippines. . . . At another visit which I made to Aguinaldo he told me that the ideas which I had expressed to him pleased him, and he appointed me director of foreign affairs in order that I might further develop my policy. What I told Aguinaldo was that he should write to President McKinley asking him under no circumstances to abandon the Philippines, no matter what kind of government should be established, whether a republic or a protectorate, or whatever form, leaving that as a matter for future discussion. Aguinaldo pretended to accept my policy, but he only intended to go on with his own ideas, and in order to keep me from forming a party he called me to him. When I recognized this attitude of Aguinaldo I wished to present my resignation, but I feared one thing in particular, that is, the revolutionary forces which occupied certain important points in Manila. In fact, after I had succeeded in getting these forces out of Manila, three days afterwards, I presented my resignation and separated myself completely from the Malolos government, and have never had anything to do with them since.[57]

Their last meeting took place on January 31, 1899. When hostilities between Filipino and American forces began on February 4, Pardo was already firmly on the American side.

AFTER HOSTILITIES BEGAN, Pardo worked for the early settlement of the war. He considered the formation of a party with other leaders who believed winning independence through war "impossible"; feared popu-

143

lar anarchy and the ambitions of other foreign powers; and were impressed by the democratic traditions of the U.S. The time, however, was not propitious. As Pardo said, "a sort of delirium possessed all minds." People misjudged the Americans, he said, and were agitated by the belief that independence was at hand.

The arrival of the Schurman Commission in March 1899 and the capture of Malolos in April emboldened the "autonomists." On April 21, Pardo appeared before the Commission with Florentino Torres, Luis Yangco, F.R. Yangco, Tomas del Rosario, and Aurelio Tolentino. They came as "influential citizens" who had just formed a "peace commission" to find a way to bring about peace by determining what U.S. intentions were and communicating these to the Aguinaldo government. They came with an autonomy plan that envisioned a Filipino government under "the direction or intervention of the United States," with the following features: a Filipino governor appointed by the U.S. president; an all-Filipino Cabinet; a popularly elected national legislature; and American control of military and foreign affairs. The Schurman Commission, however, was noncommittal beyond encouraging Pardo's group to develop its ideas in furtherance of peace.[58]

Even before his appearance before the Schurman Commission, Pardo had sent personal letters to the generals of the Republic in which he appealed for an end to the war, saying that "absolute independence" was impossible and war would only bring ruin to the people. He was assessing the situation dispassionately and with no ulterior motive, he said, urging the generals to intervene with Aguinaldo who has not been getting "good advice." Explaining himself against the charge that he was a coward and traitor, he wrote that from the first time he talked to Aguinaldo he had declared to him "clearly and candidly my politics," telling Aguinaldo that they could not allow the situation to degenerate into a war they could not win and that they should use diplomacy to get what they could before final terms were made in Paris (where the decision on the status of the Philippines was being made by the U.S. and Spain). Aguinaldo made him understand that he accepted his "politics" but it soon became clear that neither Aguinaldo nor Mabini supported the line he was taking. Thus he resigned. Lamenting the lives sacrificed in persisting in a struggle already lost, he bluntly told the generals: "It is inevitable: neither you, nor I, nor anyone, can prevent that which will happen tomorrow from happening, and our tomorrow will be the total sovereignty of America in the Philippines."[59]

On May 16, Pardo launched an afternoon daily, *La Democracia.* The paper expressed the views of Pardo at this time: the separation of church and state, the grant of Philippine autonomy, representation in the U.S. Congress, and eventual admission of the country into the American union. Its maiden editorial declared:

> The Commission assures the Filipino people of the good will and fraternal feelings which the President of the United States and the American people have toward them. The Commission also states that the American mission has the purpose of insuring the well-being, prosperity and happiness of the Filipino people as well as its aggrandizement, so that it may occupy an honorable position among the most civilized in the world. Such noble purposes and promises solemnly made should not make the people of these Islands indifferent at such a time as this in their history. The time is therefore come when the Filipino people should all be united so that under the promise of liberty and justice an end might be put to intolerance and distrust, and we may again have the laws of peace, that beautiful peace without which we can do nothing, expect nothing. We believe in the noble purposes of the American people and heed the call of the Commission. We propose in *La Democracia* to give them our cooperation so that the just aspirations of our country may be realized.[60]

Pardo was in close contact with Americans, appearing before the Schurman Commission, hosting meetings at his Calle Raon residence where Dean Worcester and Frank Bourns were frequent guests.[61] (These were not just social gatherings but occasions for the Americans to mine their friends for intelligence on what the "insurgents" were doing.)

On December 23, 1900, in a building in Quiapo that housed the printing press of *La Democracia,* around 125 prominent citizens gathered to organize *Partido Federal.* Among those present were Cayetano Arellano, Benito Legarda, Florentino Torres, Felipe Buencamino, Tomas del Rosario, and Teodoro Yangco. Pardo served as the party's first president. The first political organization to be recognized by the U.S. authorities, the Federal Party (with *La Democracia* as its organ) established Pardo as the dominant Filipino politician. In unequivocal terms, he stated the party's aims thus:

> . . . a steadily increasing autonomy, the separation of church and state, representation of the Philippines in the Federal Congress, and the adoption of the American Constitution, culminating at last in the admission of the Islands as one of the States of the Union.
>
> Peace being secured, all the efforts of the party will be directed toward the Americanization of the Filipinos and the spread of the English language, so that by this medium the American spirit may be infused, its principles, political usages, and grand civilization adopted, and the redemption of the Filipino people will be radical and complete.[62]

In a society where staged public events were important in the discourse on politics, the new party was launched in festivities marking George Washington's birth anniversary in 1901. On the night of February 21, the party honored members of the Philippine Commission with a dinner at a new hotel in Manila. A French chef prepared the menu and—an American guest wrote—"the speeches were all of the friendliest character and the 'dove of peace', verily, seemed to be hovering near." The following morning, thousands marched through flag-decked streets to a Federalista rally in Luneta where scores of bands provided music and American and Filipino speakers took turns extolling the spirit of cooperation.[63]

From February to May 1901, Pardo joined the Taft Commission in a tour of 24 provinces to look into local conditions and organize provincial governments. It was a grueling trip, particularly since Pardo could not abide rough seas, but he was "getting into the game" (an American in the party remarked) as part of a battery of speakers that included Taft and such Filipinos as Arellano and Calderon. Daniel Williams, a Commission staffer, wrote: "It is hard to estimate the good Dr. Tavera has done on this trip. His speeches have interpreted in terms of local understanding the purposes of the Commission, and his closer intimacy with the people has rendered the information he has been able to gather of tremendous value in the appointment of officers and the handling of local questions."[64]

Pardo "invariably says the right thing in the right way," Williams reported. With disingenuous wit, Pardo told provincial audiences "that for three centuries and a half Spain had been teaching the Filipinos the way to heaven and little else; that now the Americans would try to teach them as well how best to live on earth." He justified the reorganization of the government, saying that "Filipinos in material affairs, as in the construction of their houses, began at the top, putting the roof on first." Pardo declared that the Partido Federal was

. . . continuing the insurrection, but by legal rather than by forcible means; that they were contending for the same rights as those set out by the Malolos Congress—the liberty of the individual; he pointed out to them that independence did not mean liberty; that with independence the Filipinos would simply change the despotism of Spain for a domestic tyranny as bad or worse; that they could but follow the system with which they were familiar, and, being untrained, their mistake would be greater; that the great American nation would save them from themselves, and prevent their furnishing to the world the spectacle of the Central and South American republics, which, though independent, labored under a slavery worse than that of their former masters; he said they had lost nothing; that the sun pictured upon the Filipino flag was replaced by the sun of liberty which now shone over the islands; that the colors of their banner found a counterpart in those of America, and they could look forward to the day when another star, the star of the Philippines, would be added to those many on that azure field which represented States "free but not independent."[65]

Pardo was hailed as the "interpreter of American intentions towards the Philippines" and "right-hand man of Governor Taft in the establishment of civil government." As America's principal ally in the pacification campaign, the Federal Party expanded rapidly, organizing in less than a year, according to a party report, 296 provincial committees throughout the archipelago and effecting the surrender of 11 generals, 14 colonels, 14 lieutenant colonels, 20 majors, 6 chiefs of guerrillas, 46 captains, 106 lieutenants, 2,640 soldiers, and 4,440 guns.[66]

Such were the contributions of the Federalistas that on September 1, 1901 three of them, Pardo, Benito Legarda, and Jose de Luzuriaga, were appointed members of the Philippine Commission, the country's highest executive and legislative body. They thus became the highest-ranking Filipino officials of the land, "the first Southeast Asians to enjoy a voice and a vote within the highest ruling council of a colonial administration."[67] Speaking at his induction as commissioner on September 1, Pardo declared:

> We shall only act as members of the Commission to serve always the interests of our country, and shall be guided therein by what we believe to be the best, a policy which has long since been followed by us: namely, the adoption of American thought, retaining always, however, the Filipino mind.[68]

Dean Worcester called Pardo "one of the most brilliant of Filipinos," adding that the likes of Pardo, Arellano, and Legarda were not "real" Filipinos since they were so cosmopolitan and highly educated.[69] As the senior Filipino in the commission, Pardo wielded great influence. He headed the committees on local governments and health; went on inspection trips to the provinces; and conferred with local officials. The Americans, in turn, helped Pardo and his party. In 1903, for instance, the Commission appropriated $6,000 for the Federal Party's ailing newspaper, *La Democracia*, for advertising and the publication of a Tagalog edition.[70]

To the Americans, he was the premier authority on the Philippines. His *Plantas medicinales* was translated into English in 1901 by a U.S. Army surgeon for use by the American army in the Philippines. In 1901, Pardo published *Etimologia de los nombres de razas de Filipinas*, which he dedicated to Worcester. To help fill the Americans' need for knowledge about their new colony, Pardo was persuaded to make a catalogue of his extensive library. This resulted in *Biblioteca Filipina*, jointly published in 1903 by the Library of Congress and Bureau of Insular Affairs. Also commissioned by the Americans was Pardo's *Reseña Historica de Filipinas*, which appeared in the first volume of the 1903 *Census of the Philippine Islands*. He was appointed to the Philippine Committee on Geographical Names that Taft created in 1903 for the task of recommending a standard orthography for local place names.

In 1904, he was named to the honorary board of Filipino commissioners to the Louisiana Purchase Exposition in St. Louis. The five-month

U.S. tour (April 23–October 1, 1904) was a symbolic climax to the U.S. annexation of the Philippines.[71] The 44-member party was royally received as they toured some 20 American cities, traveling 9,182 miles by rail and steamer within continental United States, visiting military installations, industrial plants, universities, and historical sites. The itinerary included an audience with President Theodore Roosevelt in the White House on June 10, a symbolic trip to Canton, Ohio, on June 30 where the Filipino delegation laid a wreath upon the tomb of the martyred President McKinley, and such vignettes of Americana as a baseball game in Detroit on July 1 and an introduction to the game of golf at the Glen Echo Country Club in St. Louis on August 3.

It was such a grueling trip that the Filipinos suffered from blistered feet and some took ill and dropped out. The tour organizers had to arrange a week-long respite in a Chicago hotel to allow members of the party to recuperate. Pardo himself left the group in St. Louis on July 29, went to New York and from there embarked for the Philippines by way of Europe.

The tour was a personal triumph for T.H. Pardo de Tavera. More important, it was a triumph for U.S. colonial authorities. Executive Secretary A.W. Fergusson proudly wrote that the trip had given the Filipino delegation "personal acquaintance with those mighty forces that have wrought such peaceful conquests in the commercial and industrial world through the employment and utilization of human ingenuity and labor, the true elements of our national greatness."[72]

VISITING THE UNITED STATES, received by the American president in the White House, conferred an honorary Master of Arts degree at Yale University, Pardo was at the height of his public career. His political fortune, however, was changing.

The Federalistas lost their patron when Taft left the governorship in 1903 to assume the post of Secretary of War. His successor Luke Wright, less genial than his predecessor, did not give the Federalistas the special treatment they had under Taft. Pardo's relations with the Americans turned testy. More transparent than Taft in asserting American prerogatives, Wright snubbed the Filipino commissioners and, in Pardo's view, reversed Taft's principle of "the Philippines for the Filipinos." Pardo criticized expanded taxation under the Internal Revenue Law as a measure that would depress rather than stimulate the economy. He criticized Wright's executive order on January 13, 1905, suspending the writ of habeas corpus in Cavite and Batangas and urged the dismissal of abusive Philippine Constabulary officers. He opposed Worcester's moves to abolish the Provincial Boards of Health and replace them with an American-dominated system of District Sanitary Inspectors, saying it was "despotic" and undermined Filipino interests. Pardo also considered Wright, a Southerner married to a Catholic, soft on the anti-friar issue. He publicly aired his disenchantment and lobbied with Taft and authorities in Washington for Wright's dismissal. On May 19, 1905, Pardo tersely wrote to Taft: "I had not accepted American sovereignty for the pleasure of being under the dominion of a foreign nation, but because I thought that such a dominion was necessary to educate us in self-government."[73]

The Federal Party started to decline, buffeted by internal dissension and competition from other groups vying for access to the Americans. Many Federalistas, seeing that the party's statehood plank did not generate popular support, began to deemphasize the issue in favor of other concerns. In a convention in June 1904 (while Pardo was in the U.S.), the party decided to drop the call for statehood and switch to the goal of ultimate independence through gradual preparation and Filipino participation in government. Pardo spoke against the change but found himself alone in advocating statehood. He, too, eventually changed his goals though he did not go beyond saying that he now favored "eventual" independence when the time came when Filipinos wanted it.[74]

In their U.S. visit, Pardo and the Federalistas found that few Americans seriously considered annexing the Philippines into the Union. Looking back to this visit, Pardo wrote in 1922:

> From the minute we stepped on continental United States, we understood that the idea of uniting ourselves with that Great Republic, which was the aim of our party, was absolutely impossible to carry out. All the Americans spoke to us of our Independence not only as a just ideal, but one that is possible and natural. To form part of the Union was always considered with the greatest benevolence, but at the same time as a thing absolutely impossible.[75]

Pro-independence sentiment ran high after the ban against pro-independence political parties was lifted in July 1906. In the runup to the election of the First Philippine Assembly on July 30, 1907, the Federal Party changed its name to Partido Nacional Progresista. Pardo actively campaigned for the candidates of his party and continued to oppose "immediate" independence. He warned: "If the country were governed solely by Filipinos, our government would not be democratic but auto-cratic, and the people would be oppressed by those who would be in power."[76]

Yet Pardo knew the political tide had changed and he was fighting a losing battle. In Federalista campaign rallies the reception was either lukewarm or even hostile, with people heckling the Federalistas, "Hang them, kill them."[77] Despite the change in their name and goals, the Federalistas did poorly in the elections, electing only 16 members to the Assembly against 32 Nacionalistas, 20 independents, and 12 of other affiliations. The party quickly declined and eventually ceased to exist.

Pardo was no sycophant. He considered himself equal, if not supe-rior, to the Americans he dealt with. In 1899, when two issues of *La Democracia* were censored, he stopped the paper's publication in pro-test. He indignantly wrote Worcester on July 9, 1899, that he would not "suffer quietly persecution from those who have the duty to render me their assistance and to treat me with respect."[78] When Taft tried to get his support for American historian James Robertson's appointment to head a research project in Philippine history, Pardo declined, saying: "It seems to me that Mr. Robertson is a qualified man to do work of that kind, but in my opinion, *it would be just that a work of that nature should be done by a competent Filipino*" (Pardo's italics). Pardo recommended that Epifanio de los Santos be appointed instead.[79]

He conducted himself with dignity as a commissioner and insisted that Filipinos be treated with due courtesy. On one occasion, when he criticized the constabulary for using torture to extract confessions, the American assistant chief of the Bureau of Constabulary asked that Pardo be "called to account for his language." Pardo immediately questioned the propriety of an assistant chief, even though he were an American, in calling down a commissioner, even though he were a Filipino. He won his point and the American had to apologize to him in public.[80]

American detractors accused Pardo and Legarda of attacking the In-ternal Revenue Law to protect their investments in the tobacco and distillery industries. It was clear, however, that Pardo was not the type who would go along with whatever the Americans desired. It was not just a matter of personality differences or a contest over prerogatives. Pardo had begun to put some distance between himself and U.S. colonial officials as his own party drifted away from its original goal of statehood.

While Pardo succeeded in getting Wright recalled from the Philippines, his relations with the Americans had soured. Americans judged Pardo proud and difficult and his criticisms tantamount to insubordination. After Wright was relieved at the end of 1905, Taft diplomatically suggested that Pardo resign as commissioner and seek election in the national assembly. Pardo declined. His removal from the commission, however, was one of the conditions set by William Cameron Forbes, an ally of Wright, when Forbes assumed office as governor in 1909. On February 28, 1909, Pardo resigned.

Pardo had lost his influence. He found himself isolated as the Americans started to cultivate new, younger leaders more malleable and politically ambitious, such as they found in Sergio Osmeña and Manuel Quezon, who would dominate the elections for the assembly that replaced the commission as center of Filipino influence. The shift in political alliances is indicated by an incident during the assembly's inaugural ball in Malacañan on October 16, 1907. Taft had returned to the Philippines to represent the U.S. President at the assembly's inauguration. At the Malacañan ball, Taft "upset all arrangements by handing down his appointed partner for the opening rigodon, Mrs. Pardo de Tavera, and taking the startled Mrs. Osmeña off the arm of Cameron Forbes."[81]

Pardo never really had much appetite for politics, particularly the kind that began to emerge with the advent of popular elections. He was, historian Ruby Paredes writes, "temperamentally unsuited to developing either a Filipino clientele or an American patron."[82] Maligned by fellow Filipinos, shunted aside by the Americans, Pardo knew that a phase of his career was at an end. What pained him the most was the coldness and hostility with which he was regarded by many Filipinos. In letters to his friend Antonio Regidor he bitterly complained about the attacks against him in the press by Manila Spaniards (who lambasted him for being anti-Spanish), Filipinos (like Pascual Poblete and Dominador Gomez), and even old friends like Ferdinand Blumentritt. Expressing regret that he had sacrificed his professional and personal

152

interests for politics, he complained: "Spain's foreign domination has disappeared but has been replaced by domestic domination that is more durable and odious."[83]

At a farewell banquet given him in Manila by friends on April 17, 1909, he declared, with a mix of regret and relief, an end to his "short but strenuous political career." While thanking those who had shown him sympathy, he could not mask his disappointment at having been cast in the villain's role:

> Of all the bitterness which I have suffered, and the moments of pain which I have undergone in life, nothing has caused me greater mortification and deeper sorrow than to see certain Filipinos, whom I always admired and respected, observe towards me an attitude of personal hostility on account of my ideas and labours.[84]

He has never "done politics," he said, if politics means working for power so one can impose one's will on others. After all, he said—in apparent reference to the new, ambitious leaders who had come to the fore (some of whom, like Quezon, were at the banquet)—the reality is that it is America that "dominates." He has not been too concerned with electoral contests for offices, Pardo said. Whoever has "political power" is not too relevant since it is America that rules. "Convinced of this, I have seen that I ought not to bother my head very much over politics, and that the most urgent question was a social one, because the solution of our political problem necessarily, and as sure as fate, depends upon the solution we give to our social problem." Instead of politicians (*autoridades politicas*), we should look to leaders in the economy, in agriculture, manufacturing, finance, and the professions. Such men "constitute the social authorities (*autoridades sociales*), and it is by such men, and no others, that the power of a nation and the height of its civilization are measured."[85]

The question of sovereignty, he said, does not interest him as much as preparing the people so they cannot be oppressed by the authorities. "That is my ambition, an ambition for a transformation in our society without which any political change would be factitious and never capable of subserving the true interests of the people." The central task of the time, Pardo concluded, was the production of educated citizens steeped in the virtues of labor, civic responsibility, and racial tolerance.

Confidence in the virtue of politics and politicians is one of the most evident signs of an inferior type of society. Political independence does not make a people safe from slavery: the law cannot protect the individual of inferior capacity. That is the reason of the natural subjugation to which I have referred, and it is only a social transformation that can shield us from this danger.[86]

One imagines that Pardo's listeners were not exactly thrilled at being so lectured. His was not a popular voice at the time, or long after. With elections and "self-rule" under the Americans, the scramble for positions in the new order had begun.

HE WAS AGAIN a man apart. After leaving the commission, he moved to a house in the fashionable suburb of Santa Mesa. He had been, for reasons of "personality differences," estranged from his wife Concha. They maintained separate households until his death in 1925.

He remained active in the promotion of science and education. He led moves to organize *Colegio Medico-Farmaceutico de Filipinas* in 1899 in an effort to professionalize medical practice, reorganize medical education, and free it from sectarian influence. As president of *Colegio Medico-Farmaceutico*, he led efforts to divest University of Santo Tomas of its ownership of Colegio de San Jose, Manila's only medical school, and place it under the control of the state.[87] The Church managed to retain ownership but Pardo's efforts to "secularize" science bore fruit when the commission passed Act No. 1415 on December 1, 1905 authorizing the establishment of the Philippine Medical School. Pardo served as the only Filipino in the school's board. The school became the first unit and nucleus of the University of the Philippines when the state university was created in 1908. Pardo was a member of the university's board of regents (1908–1913) and reportedly declined an offer to be university president because of the political interference to which the position was prey.[88] When his term as regent expired in 1913, the university conferred on him a doctorate in law *honoris causa*.

As a private citizen, he organized and headed *Asociacion Economica de Filipinas* in 1911 to promote investments in the country's economic development.[89] He was sought after as a lecturer and continued to pursue his scholarly interests, publishing, after he left the commission, *Notas para una cartografía de Filipinas* (1910). He also took up farming, developing a 300-hectare estate called "Hacienda Carmencita" (after his daughter) in Floridablanca, Pampanga. He was enthusiastic about experimentally growing foreign and native fruit trees.[90]

In 1913, he left the country in a sojourn that lasted six years. He traveled to Paris via Siberia and was in Lausanne, Switzerland, when World War I broke out. He proceeded to Barcelona where he spent much of the war period taking up farming, particularly wheat and fruit growing. In 1914, he visited his brother Felix in Buenos Aires (during which he had an audience with President Roosevelt when the latter was on a visit to the city).[91] He later traveled to Hong Kong, Macao, Canton, and Taiwan. He was always the curious traveler, observant of what the Philippines could learn from the way social and economic life was organized in the countries he visited.

Back in Manila in 1918, he confessed to feeling depressed. When the editor of a journal asked him for a contribution, he said: "Every day I feel less like writing. What is the use? I am convinced that nobody is going to read it."[92] He kept on writing, however, contributed to *Boletín de la Sociedad Orientalista de Filipinas* (a journal founded by prominent Filipino authors in 1918), even contemplated writing a history of the Philippines.

He remained active in civic affairs. In 1920, he was named president of the Commission of the Fourth Centennial of the Discovery of the Philippines (1521–1921) when Isauro Gabaldon resigned upon the latter's appointment as resident commissioner in the U.S. On January 23, 1923, he was appointed director of the Philippine Library and Museum, a position he discharged with characteristic diligence until 1925. The owner of one of the best private collections of Filipiniana, he enriched the holdings of the national library. To promote librarianship in the country, he formed the Philippine Library Association in October 1923 and was elected its first president. Earlier, on June 16, 1923, he accepted an appointment as head of the newly created department of Oriental languages of the University of the Philippines, a position he held until October 31, 1924, when he resigned because of poor health.

Dyspeptic for much of his life, he had never been in perfect health. He is said to have remarked once, "I am so used to being sick that I miss it when I am well." Once, during a visit to Java to attend the Congress of the Far Eastern Association of Tropical Medicine (which was organized in Manila where it had its first scientific congress in 1909), he had a near-death experience when, returning to his room in Hotel des Indes in Wetevreden (a suburb of Batavia, now Djakarta) in the early morning of September 2, 1921, he fell into such agony he thought he was going to die. Coming out of a long stupor, he deplored with all his heart that he was destined "to die a second time."[93] Yet, traveling back to Manila by boat, via Singapore and Zamboanga, he still had the graciousness, though he was quite ill, to entertain an interview with a local reporter when the boat docked in Jolo on October 9. The reporter left impressed by the catholicity of his interests (that he spoke Malay, was interested in Chinese music). Comparing Java and Singapore with the Philippines, Pardo remarked that we are better in some of our health facilities but "their masses eat better."[94]

His last act of public service came when, upon his return from another trip to the United States in 1924, he was named to the Board of Educational Survey created by the Philippine Legislature in 1924 to study the situation of education in the Philippines.[95] He had just begun work with the board when, on March 26, 1925, T.H. Pardo de Tavera died. He passed away in his room unnoticed—his sons thought he was just taking an afternoon nap. He was sixty-eight years old. He left a testament saying there should be no wreath, cross, or candles, and that his body be cremated and his ashes interred beside his mother's grave in Paris.[96] At the necrological service in his honor on March 28, the only speakers were the two most prominent Filipinos of the time, Senate President Manuel Quezon and opposition leader Juan Sumulong.

HE WAS "a figure eminently Filipino," a contemporary writes, "whose Franciscan features and beard give him the appearance of a resurrected Quixote, but whose inexhaustible fountain of experience and learning makes him a gentleman like no other."[97] (Wenceslao Retana had written: "The head of Pardo is that of an emblazoned Spanish gentleman of the sixteenth century."[98]) The unwitting contradiction befits Pardo, who took his being a Filipino not as a matter of natural right, of color or birth, but a product of work.

Tall, slender, and slow in gait, he wore a goatee and pince-nez eyeglasses that accented his cerebral look. An American writer who met him remarked on the inner energy he conveyed: a "nervous, delicate figure which, in repose, has a sort of breathless, nervous organism." "Below a forehead sprinkled with grey are eyes which can become piercing, meditative, or kindly at will, and they are more often the latter, with an expression of roguishness which is the charm of what might be else too severe a face."[99]

Private and reticent, he did not, as the flamboyant Paterno did, announce himself. One has to imagine how the private person was made: orphaned of a father at seven; scarred by the tragedy of witnessing the murder of his mother and sister; separated from his only brother and then, later, from his own wife. Sojourning in many lands, standing apart, for reasons of class and race, from a country he had elected as his own. He was, after all, a *Filipino* by an act of will rather than by simple natural right. He had the means to be somewhere else but he chose to be where he died.

He was fluent in Spanish, French, Italian, and English, and apparently took lessons in Russian, "a man not of one but of many countries, in the large sense, a man of the world."[100] Yet he staunchly considered himself a Filipino. It is narrated that he was invited by Spain's Council of Ministers to inherit his grandfather's title. He refused the invitation saying that he preferred to be simply T.H. Pardo de Tavera to being a marquis of Spain. In declining the title, he reportedly said: "I am a Filipino, not a Spaniard."[101]

Christian images decorated his house but he was an atheist. He did not embrace an established religion, saying that salvation was a personal affair. His creed was "to do good in the best way I can, in the form I honestly believe in, and to avoid evil." "Whether there is God or not, I do not know; nobody knows nor shall I take the trouble to find out. But supposing there were a God, I would do my duty; supposing there were not, I still would do my duty in the same manner."[102] Though he did not assume as high-profile a role in Freemasonry as other Filipinos, he remained dedicated to it, organizing Masonic lodges, including Lodge Rizal, which he organized in Manila on June 18, 1901, and headed as "Worshipful Master," apparently until its dissolution in 1909.[103]

He enjoyed farming and the quiet diversions of domesticity, tinkering in the kitchen, barbering for his grandchildren, serving them at the table before he himself began to eat. His house was a museum of Philippine and Asian religious and archaeological artifacts, works by his brother and Resurreccion Hidalgo, autographed photographs of Theodore Roosevelt, William Howard Taft, and Elwell Otis, and various items of cultural interest: embroidered piña, abaca wear, Mexican trunks, Chinese porcelain ware, coins, engravings, and other mementos.[104] He instilled in his family a respect for history and lineage, producing a carefully researched *Arbol genealogico de los Pardo de Tavera* for his children. In remembrance of the family past, Pardo sported on his watch fob the *escudo de armas* of his ancestor, the Marques de Magahon.

Rafael Palma wrote that he admired Pardo for his "varied and rich intellectuality" and cosmopolitan appetite for knowledge: "I always admire the Doctor for always having a new idea. As he grows in years his ideas always grow young." "He knew everything and wrote equally on numismatics, as well as on iconography, ceramics, cartography of the Philippines and could discuss obtuse problems on morals, religion, history, and language. No Filipino has written on such diverse materials with the same competence as a living encyclopedia." Colleagues considered him, with Cayetano Arellano, the most gifted conversationalist of the day. Eulogio Rodriguez wrote:

He is a master of the art of conversation. His conversation arouses greater interest as it proceeds because of its humour and the truths that it holds. His arguments are clear, limpid, convincing, and sound in logical analysis. They express his rational nature and his independent character. He has a way of saying things in the fewest possible words. He is never afraid to give his ideas, never afraid to talk . . . He possessed the charm of culture, of knowledge, and of an intense earnestness about the progress of the Philippines.[105]

Many respected his intelligence but felt no warmth for him. There were those who found him supercilious and arrogant. Teodoro Kalaw writes that Pardo was "one of those who can never let a joke pass at the expense of an adversary." Kalaw recalls an incident during the Philippine Commission's trip to Tayabas when an elderly man, seeking an audience, obsequiously approached the commission and, bowing and trembling, delivered a speech that opened with, "With your Excellency's kind permission," and "sounded like a legal thesis." Seated beside Kalaw,

Pardo nudged the journalist and whispered, "Kalaw, *there* is your Filipino Soul."[106] One object of his rapier-like wit was Tomas del Rosario, a colleague in the Malolos Congress whose oratorical flair had earned him the appellation "nightingale of the Philippine Parliament." Of him Pardo remarked: "Tomas, before delivering a speech, rehearses his postures and his gestures before a mirror. He is a shameless imitator, even worse than Paterno himself. His peroration before the Congress of Malolos on religious liberty is a plagiarism, a gross plagiarism of the prologue of *The Apostles* by Renan."[107]

There were times when his questioning of the prevailing orthodoxy seemed mere intellectual hauteur. Asked by a Cebu journalist in 1919 on a proposed bill in Congress that would reward parents with six children or more, Pardo replied: "I am very French in my ideas on this subject. Formerly I thought that in every family there should not be more than three children. Today, I believe that a civilized man should not have any children at all." Overpopulation, he said, has caused so much misery in the world. "Excessive breeding cannot benefit the human race; it detracts rather than adds to the sum of human happiness." Endorsing the use of contraceptives, he added that if people must have children they must have as few as possible and must see to it that they are better cared for and educated. "What we need," he concluded, "is not simply more men but more men who are physically, morally fit for civilized society." "The real heart of the problem then lies in the *quality* of the population. *Quantity* is nothing or far worse than nothing unless it be the *quantity* of *quality*."[108]

Pardo's comments raised a national storm of protest. Various quarters condemned his opinions as heretical and "subversive of our social order." *Philippines Free Press* lampooned the controversy, calling Pardo "that horrid man" who loves to drop "a Shavian bomb every once in a while." The magazine's editorial cartoon (December 6, 1919), captioned "Pity the Pickaninnies!," showed Pardo declaring, "The civilized man shouldn't have any children at all," and before him Isabelo de los Reyes, with his twenty-four children lined up on either side of him, saying, "Very well, Doctor! And what do you call me?" In a side box, Commissioner Gregorio Araneta and Sergio Osmeña, who had twelve and ten children, respectively, chorus, "And me?"[109] Interviewed for his reaction, de los Reyes admitted he had twenty-four children, adding he was "proud of it," but took a philosophical view, saying he did not believe Pardo wished to be taken literally, his point simply being that people should not have more children than they could properly care for.[110]

While his political enemies branded him a *Rasputin filipino*, others belied the view that he was meanspirited. Epifanio de los Santos praised him for a healthy humor that "refreshes and purifies."[111] Even Retana, an old adversary, was charmed by Pardo's gallantry when he first met him and rather surprised at Pardo's benevolent views on his critics, including Paterno and Retana himself.[112] Others found him generous with his ideas and gracious with subordinates. Rafael Palma, who did not share some of Pardo's views, rendered fair judgment. Praising Pardo for his erudition, he said: "He was rich and independent and did not embrace a cause for mere convenience, rather through conviction." "His one defect," Palma added, "was that his superior talent and education had withdrawn him from the masses so that he did not understand their ideas and aspirations."[113]

On attacks against him, Pardo said: "They cannot prevent me from speaking my mind with the greatest frankness if and when I am convinced that what I have to say will result in some good for the youth of my country."[114] He phrased the keynote of his life when he said, in that farewell banquet in his honor on April 17, 1909:

> The cultured Filipinos represent not only their own interests but those of the popular masses who look up to them for leadership. This trust places upon us a tremendous responsibility, and obliges us to always tell the truth and nothing but the truth. I shall be deeply sorry if, in complying with this obligation, I will incur the censure of the public; for I speak not to please people but to be useful to them even when I displease them.[115]

APOSTLE OF REASON

FROM THE TIME he published his first book in 1884 to his death in 1925, T.H. Pardo de Tavera tirelessly applied himself to the life of the mind. He published some sixteen books and pamphlets, delivered lectures, and wrote numerous articles on language, history, medicine, and current social issues.

Jose Rizal is reported to have remarked that, for his linguistic works, T.H. Pardo de Tavera deserved to appear ahead of him in encyclopedias of intellectual achievement.[116] When Pardo died, colleagues hailed him as "the chief Filipino Filipinista (*el primer filipinista filipino*)."[117] It is not entirely inflated praise.

Pardo is a precursor in the rise of the social and natural sciences in the Philippines. His writings can be divided into three roughly chronological groups: his pre-American scientific studies, his "U.S.-sponsored" projects, and his popular writings on social issues. Across shifts in interest, his work is always driven by an earnest passion for cultivating rationality as a way of understanding (and changing) a country and making it a part of the modern world.

161

HE WROTE on medicine while still a student in Paris. What may be his earliest published piece is "*Sobre el mal de Pott,*" in Madrid's *El Siglo Medico* (August 21, 1881), a short clinical observation on "Pott's disease" (tuberculosis of the cerebral column, named after English surgeon Percival Pott).[118]

In 1886, his medical thesis, *Contribution a l'etude de la Periarthrite du Genou (Affections de la bourse sereuse de la patte d'oie)* was issued in Paris.[119] (It was the requirement for students to publish a prescribed number of copies of their thesis at their own expense.) Dedicated to his mother and the memory of his father and uncle, the thesis is a standard treatise in clinical medicine that presents the candidate's observations as well as the relevant medical literature (in this case, German, British, and French sources, including the leading authority on the disease, Simon-Emmanuel Duplay, a professor of the Paris *Faculte de medecine* and member of Pardo's thesis committee).

In the succeeding years Pardo would occasionally publish on advances in Western medicine in popular Philippine periodicals.[120] Early on, however, he was drawn to medicine's sociocultural aspects, the problem posed by non-Western medical systems, and the need to promote "scientific" medical theory in societies like the Philippines. This is shown in "*La medecine a l'isle de Lucon (Archipel des Philippines),*" published in the Paris *Journal de Medecine* (March 31, 1884) and in Spanish translation in *Los Dos Mundos* (Madrid) in the same year.[121] Distinguishing *indios* of the Luzon lowlands from the less developed *aetas* or *negritos*, he surveys among the former beliefs and practices in the etiology and therapeutics of ailments. From the standpoint of Western medical science, he takes up such features of folk medicine as the belief in air (*aire*) as agent of sickness, notions of "hot" and "cold," and incipient understanding of a germ theory in the notion of *cagao*. (Now the local word for germ or microbe; in the seventeenth century, *cagao* meant plowman's mange or itch-causing mite.) Anthropologically minded, Pardo relates local practices to medical beliefs in China, Southeast Asia, and the Pacific Islands.

In the same vein, he published an article, "*Apuntes sobre la medicina en China,*" in Manila's *La Opinion* (1887) in which he discussed the organization of medical practice in China.[122] Privileging Western medical knowledge, Pardo worries about the spread of "false" ideas by popular healers (*mediquillos, medicos chinos*). In his introduction to Manuel Xerez's

La Eclampsia Infantil en Filipinas (1889), he praises the work for its attempt to "popularize useful knowledge," its scientific basis, and its being a local study that attends to particular conditions, thus raising awareness of the "dangerous practices and baneful methods of interlopers."[123]

While a practicing physician, it was ultimately medicine's cultural rather than clinical aspects that engaged him. An illustration of his lively, humane curiosity is a piece he contributes to *La Correspondencia Medica de Filipinas* in 1896 on the etymology of the word *beri-beri*.[124] He dwells on the common supposition, derived from such sources as Bontius (1642), that the word comes from the Malay word for sheep, *beri-beri*, because those stricken by the disease lift their legs like sheep. He says this is erroneous though sheep is indeed called *kambing beri-beri* in the Malay archipelago. The word, Pardo says, is Portuguese, originating from the Portuguese reference to sheep from Africa as *berebere* or *berbere* ("from the land of the Berbers").

Pardo's first long work is *Plantas medicinales de Filipinas*, published in Madrid in 1892.[125] Investigating how Filipinos use plants in the treatment of disease, Pardo approaches the subject with characteristic deliberation. Apart from specimen collection, interviews, and laboratory analysis, he examined the existing literature on the subject, reading scientific sources in Europe and works on Philippine botany by Manuel Blanco, Antonio Llanos, Celestino Fernandez del Villar, Andres Naves, Fernando Santa Maria, and Ignacio Mercado. Despite the constraints that attended his research, he produced what has been acknowledged as the most scientific and comprehensive treatment of the subject during the Spanish period, and long after.

Presenting 214 species of indigenous and foreign plants found in the Philippines, he organizes entries according to family and genus, and provides scientific and local names, botanical description, and data on chemical properties (where available), habitat, uses, and preparation. His zest for knowledge is shown not only in his medico-botanical observations but the cultural data he brings into the work. He notes the local use of the seeds of *pepita sa katbalogan* (S. philippensis) as talisman against evil spirits as well as the large amount of *tahu* (a decoction of ginger and brown sugar) consumed as morning beverage by the Chinese of Manila. He remarks on the anaphrodisiac effect of coffee, which led

Linnaeus to call it the "drink of the eunuchs," and tries to explain the inconsistency presented by "the fact that the Arabs, who are so much given to the abuse of the pleasures forbidden to eunuchs are most addicted to the use and abuse of coffee." On the *makahiya* (Oxalis sensitivum), Pardo notes that Hindus attribute to it mysterious virtues because of its peculiar property of closing its leaves when touched. "Symbolism has determined its therapeutic application and the Hindus pretend that it endows with delicacy and modesty women who lack these virtues and that it restores virginity."[126]

Plantas medicinales is not just a catalogue. In his preface, Pardo argues that more Philippine plants should be made official in the country's pharmacopoeia and used in therapeutics since they are fresh, cheap, and more acceptable to the people than foreign medicine. He defends the value of the "empirical" knowledge of *curanderos* since it is out of this kind of knowledge that "rational and scientific" remedies are developed.

Other preoccupations prevented Pardo from pursuing further work in medical botany. He remained, however, active in medical science. In 1895, he published a popular health pamphlet, *Arte de Cuidar Enfermos*, which was translated into Tagalog in the same year and distributed in Manila.[127] Its modest aim, Pardo says, is to popularize among readers, "particularly my clients," simple, practical guidelines to avoid or manage sickness. Saying it is not enough to prescribe medicines and cure patients but that one must help create a healthy environment, the manual includes tips on nutrition, sanitation, personal cleanliness, and maintaining a proper mental state. A member of societies like *Sociedad Espanola de Higiene*, Pardo contributed to *Correspondencia Medica de Filipinas* and *Revista Filipina de Medicina y Farmacia*, the organ of the Colegio Medico-Farmaceutico de Filipinas he helped organize in 1899. He gave lectures on medicine. One of these was a lecture at the scientific session of the *Colegio Medico-Farmaceutico de Filipinas* on December 23, 1922 in which he warned against the dangers of ignorance and spoke of the need for scientific medical knowledge.

Pardo was a rationalist convinced about the power of Western medical science and the benefits of spreading "modern knowledge." At the same time, however, he was interested in the phenomenon of medical pluralism and culturally specific health conditions. Despite his Sorbonne education he was cognizant of the value of folk knowledge, seeing it as an empirical base from which scientific theories can be developed. He distinguishes it from the false knowledge of charlatans, saying for instance (in a dig at the Spanish religious orders) that the exotic and erroneous household remedies used in the Philippines may have, in fact, originated from the popular health manuals of Spanish missionaries like Pablo Clain and Fernando de Santa Maria.[128]

INSPIRED BY HIS STUDIES at *Ecole nationale des langues orientales vivantes*, Pardo's first research interest, outside medicine, was language. Invoking (as did Paterno) French Orientalist Abel de Remusat's statement that a nation's language is a "faithful mirror of its civilization, the more complete picture of the social revolutions that have marked its existence," Pardo took to language as one who believed that this was important for reconstructing a people's history.[129]

His first book, *Contribucion para el estudio de los antiguos alfabetos Filipinos* (1884), is remarkable for the deliberate manner he approaches the subject of Philippine palaeography. In the words of American lexicographer Fletcher Gardner, Pardo "appears to have been almost the first person who brought an open and scientific mind to the investigation of this material."[130] Raising the motive behind the book, Pardo remarks on the irony that Filipino ethnography (*etnografia filipina*) has drawn the attention of Germans and Austrians but little interest from Spaniards. Spanish histories of the Philippines are filled with "marvelous events," "accounts of divine punishment," and "politico-religious" happenings but leave questions of ethnography lightly touched upon. A subject important for understanding history yet "much neglected and so little known" is palaeography.[131] *Filipinos* (a word he uses to refer to inhabitants of the islands) had their own precolonial writing system though this has been "abandoned and forgotten."

Finding the material on the subject sparse and contradictory, he proceeds to examine the available data by putting together, from European sources, twelve specimen sets (four Tagalog, two Visayan, two Ilocano, one each of Pangasinan and Pampango, and two of uncertain provenance).[132] He was the first to compile such a large number of specimens for comparative study, expanding on *Considerations sur les alphabets des Philippines* (1831), authored by the Brussels-born but Paris-based linguist Eugene Jacquet who examined a sample each of the Tagalog and

Ilocano alphabets. Pardo shows himself versed in philological method and source criticism, using internal and external evidence to determine the origin, descent, and integrity of the specimens. He does not only compare local specimens but looks at similarities and variations relative to other writing systems in Asia and Oceania.

Pardo addresses these problems: the form, order, and number of characters, the direction of writing, and the origin of the alphabets. He concludes that there are no fundamental differences among local syllabaries and what differences exist are in the matter of "tracing" (*trazar*), "as happens with the English, French or Spanish writing."[133] Other differences, he says, are accounted for either by the exigencies of recording and transmission or the phonetic character of the languages. Hence, the letters *w* and *h* are absent in the Ilocano alphabet because the language does not have the sounds (*sonido*) represented by these signs. For the same reason, Pampango lacks the aspirated *h*. On the other hand, *y* and *w* may be missing in the extant Pampango specimens because the characters corresponding to these sounds had been forgotten or left unrecorded.

Filipino alphabets, Pardo sums up, are syllabic and consist of three vowels and from eleven to fourteen consonants. Sounds confounded in local speech such as *e* and *i* or *o* and *u* are represented by just one vowel sign. The number of consonants depended on the "phonetic exigencies" of the particular language. On the *order* of characters, Pardo says that they are not (as some Spanish authors have argued) arranged in the Spanish manner but in the way of the Bugis alphabet which, in turn, conforms to the order of Sanskrit or Devanagari.

On the controversy over the direction of native writing (whether horizontal or vertical, top to bottom or vice versa), he weighs various opinions on the subject and concludes that Filipinos wrote from left to right in the manner of Indian-derived writings. He rejects the hypothesis of some Spanish observers that, at one stage, Filipinos adopted the Spanish direction in writing (left to right), saying that it is not likely that such a shift would occur uniformly across various language groups and that natives would change the direction of writing without changing the characters themselves.

On the question of provenance, he faults Spanish authors like Gaspar de San Agustin and Pedro Chirino for failing to establish the temporal parameters of their data, relying on hearsay, and assuming a misleading finality even if they have not closely examined the languages of which they speak. He criticizes these writers' loose assertion of the Malay origins of local scripts, saying *Malay* is "a word which is as vague as the name 'Moro' which many people use to refer to all the peoples who profess Islam." In drawing affinities between Filipino alphabets and early scripts of Asia and Oceania—such as Asoka, Gudjarati, Tegula, Tamil, Kawi, Toba, Pegu, and Djogja—Pardo closely analyzes the form of the characters. He concludes:

> The Filipino alphabets have a greater similarity with the characters of the Asoka inscriptions than with any alphabet of India or Oceania. We believe that they derive directly from the Asoka and have been faithfully preserved in their primitive form. The Hindu origin of these alphabets cannot be put in doubt.[134]

In approaching local palaeography, Pardo tries to understand it in its own terms and, in the process, interrogates European opinion. He concludes that Philippine languages were written with their own characters (*caracteres propios*) in their own style or direction (*direccion propia*). He corrects Jacquet's misimpression that the Tagalog word for alphabet, *baybayin*, was devised by the Spaniards, arguing that it is an indigenous word the root of which (*baybay*) means "a succession of things in a row," a line, series, or file (*alineacion, linea, fila*). He contests the observation that Filipino scripts are "easy to write but difficult to read" because of the omission of vowels. (Spanish authors had remarked that the inadequacy of local writing to fix exact sounds occasioned its displacement by romanized phonetic writing.) Pardo explains that this difficulty is occasioned by the loss or deletion of the *corlit* (*kudlit*, "mark, tilde"). Against the Spaniards' complaint that reading local characters was "pure guessing," he points to actual speech practice, the manner in which natives read written texts. Local reading partakes of decipherment or "divination" in which one arrives at a word, or sense of the word, by relating it to what precedes it. Hence, "missing vowels" are specified by what comes before them. This explains, he says, a reading style in which the Filipino prolongs the sounds of words, in a "monotonous" voice, until he comes upon the correct sound according to the sense of antecedent words or phrases. Pardo adds that while Filipinos have forgotten the old characters their ancestors used to inscribe poems and *cronicas* on banana and palm leaves, they have preserved the trace of the old alphabets in the drawn-out, nasal reading style they inherited from their ancestors.[135]

In sum, Pardo argues that, contrary to what Spanish accounts assume or suggest, Filipino writing was neither anomalous nor unintelligible but had its own "proper" and logical form. He acknowledges, however, that by the seventeenth century Filipinos had abandoned their old scripts since they recognized that the Latin alphabet was superior.

The same methodical temper marks *El Sanscrito en la lengua Tagalog* (1887).[136] The work consists of a forty-page *vocabulario* and a ten-page introductory essay. The lexicon lists 303 Tagalog words and indicates their Sanskrit equivalent, denotation, phonetic properties, and equivalent or analogous words in other Philippine languages as well as languages like Kawi, Batak, Dayak, Javanese, and Sundanese. Pardo started to compile Sanskrit terms in Tagalog in 1884 when Blumentritt referred him to a similar study published by the Leiden professor of Sanskrit Hendrik Kern. Urged by friends, he decided to publish his own study, integrating into his work Kern's observations but almost doubling Kern's wordlist. (The reference is to Kern's *Sanskritsche woorden in het Tagala*, published in *Bijdragen tot de taal-, land-en volkenkunde van Nederlandsch-Indie* [1881].)

He uses Eugene Burnouf's Sanskrit dictionary (1866) and the Noceda-Sanlucar Tagalog dictionary (1754) as basic reference but corrects the latter's Spanish orthography which, he says, disfigures the "physiognomy" of Tagalog words.[137] While some of Pardo's notes on meanings and derivations are speculative, he is generally restrained and meticulous. He prefaces the study by saying that there are two methods for establishing the filiation (*filiacion*) of languages. The old method, susceptible to errors, compares lexical items. The more scientific method investigates filiation by comparing grammatical forms, that is, the way a people present their thoughts by arranging and transforming words to form sentences. In this study, however, Pardo limits himself to the conventional approach of word comparisons although he tries to flesh out his analysis with observations on contexts and transformations of words.

From the evidence of Sanskrit and foreign-derived words in Tagalog, Pardo constructs a sketch of Philippine cultural history. He notes that while Chinese influence on Tagalog is apparent in the vocabulary of food and commerce, it is not evident in political, religious, and intellectual life. He posits that the Chinese who came to the Philippines were traders and adventurers of a lower class (*clase baja*) and carried little of the influence of high Chinese civilization. Arab influence, on the other hand, was limited because Spain's arrival aborted the spread of Islam. Hindu influence is not as evident in the Philippines as in Java with its rich Hinduized mythology, religion and architecture. It is remarkable, however, that the Sanskrit words adopted into Tagalog are those signifying "intellectual acts, moral operations, passions, superstitions, names of deities, planets, higher numerals, botany, war and its outcomes and vicissitudes."[138] Pardo's hypothesis is that Hindus did not only come as merchants but that they "dominated" parts of the archipelago. Proof are the "learned languages" spoken by the Tagalog, Bisaya, and other groups, with their Hindu-derived terms relating to political rank, fortifications, religious objects, sentiments, and beliefs.

Though little is known about the coming of the Hindus, Pardo assumes their "domination" was effected peacefully. He cites the peaceful Hindu occupation of Java as related in Malay chronicles that trace the descent of the sultans of Malacca from a son of Alexander the Great who lived in India, and of the first Hindu settlers from Telinga on the northeast coast of Decan. Hindu culture irradiated from Java to the Philippines, but gradually thinned out due to distance and survived only in its traces in local languages.

Extrapolating from linguistic evidence, Pardo sketches for the region four historical periods: (1) one in which people had their own civilization (*civilizacion propia*), and periods of (2) Hindu, (3) Mohammedan, and (4) Euro-Christian influence. The first of these cultural periods, he says, is illustrated by the Polynesian islands, the second by Java, the third by Malacca, and the fourth by the Philippines where Hindu and Mohammedan cultures are to be lightly observed because of Euro-Christian domination.

Pardo continues his philological investigation in *Consideraciones sobre el origen del nombre de los numeros en Tagalog* (1889) and *Etimologia de los nombres de razas de Filipinas* (1901).[139] An etymological investigation of the Tagalog names for numerals, *Consideraciones* is guided by the same method and purpose as the earlier works. He aims, Pardo says, not only to discover the "primitive" meaning of Tagalog terms for numbers but find what can be learned from such an analysis since measures of quantity are both a function and sign of a stage of civilization. He notes that Malayo-Polynesian languages share similarities of sound, vocabulary, and grammar, demonstrating a common origin, and that this language family is so immense he can only contribute a stone to the *edificio* of scholarship.

In this context, he observes a number of "facts" about the Tagalogs: they do not have written characters (*cifras*) for numbers; while they have a word for enumeration (*bilang*), they engage in arithmetical operations only with the aid of objects; and the local terminology for numbers is variable. The main text takes up numbers from *isa* (one) to *yota* ("hundred thousand"). After discussing etymologies and affinities with other Malayo-Polynesian languages, Pardo concludes that there are three sources of Tagalog numbers: (1) Polynesian, the earliest layer; (2) indigenous (*origen propio*); and (3) foreign sources like Hebrew, Arabic, and Sanskrit. He notes that Sanskrit-derived terms refer to high numbers (such as *yota*) but that these numbers were not used for practical, mathematical purposes but as figures in poetry and literature.

In the same vein, *Etimologia* takes up the naming and classification of population groups in the country. Racial classifications had vexed colonial scholars and administrators and, at the time Pardo wrote, there was a welter of opinions on the number and nomenclature of races (*razas*) and tribes (*tribus*) in the Philippines. While Pardo finds "race" a pompous appellation loosely applied to population groups, he accepts the theory that there are three races in the archipelago—*negritos, indonesianos,* and *malayos*—which have become so intermixed that one must turn to language to mark relations among population groups.

Pardo classifies into five groupings the various names given to "races" and "tribes" in the Philippines. These are names prefixed with TAGA (e.g., Tagalog, Tagabaloy, Tagacaolo, Tagabanua); those prefixed with I (Ifugaw, Ilongot, Ibanag, Ilokano); those prefixed with MA, MAY, or ME (Maguindanao, Malanaw, Manobo, Mamanua); those with the affix KA and suffix AN (Kagayan, Kalagan, Kalibugan); and other forms of nomination. He engages in interesting etymological speculation, as

170

in his discussion of *Tagalog*. He claims that *taga* means "man" (as it does, he says, in Samoa and Tahiti) but disagrees with the common explanation that here it is paired with *ilog* (river); hence "inhabitant of the river." This does not explain, he says, why the *i* in *taga-ilog* disappeared or why, if it did, the current word is accented on the last syllable instead of the second, *tagalóg* instead of *tagálog*, as would be phonetically proper. Pardo offers two alternative etymologies: that the word derives from *alog* (to wade, ford), hence "men of the ford," or that it comes from the archaic *alog*, meaning "low-lying land that fills with water when it rains," a denotation that survives in Pangasinan but has disappeared in Tagalog. Pardo prefers the latter explanation, saying it fits Manila's ecology at the time of the Spanish coming, "low-lying, flood-prone land."[140]

Etimologia is clearly meant as a preliminary sketch. Some of his etymological observations are speculative though he is better informed and more deliberate than Paterno. He restricts himself to a classificatory inventory of names and does not discuss historical and cultural relations among population groups. Pardo concludes that printing errors, the ignorance of some writers, and other factors have swollen the list of names, creating difficulties in etymological study. Each speech group should be designated by one name, he says. To establish ethnographic studies on a firm basis it is necessary that languages, their vocabulary and grammar, be closely studied.

THE NEED FOR AN ARCHIVE of knowledge engaged early Filipino scholars. To locate, preserve, and popularize knowledge about the Philippines, Pardo and his contemporaries collected *Filipiniana*, published lists and catalogues, and annotated and circulated primary documents.

In 1892, Pardo published Franciscan Juan de Plasencia's *Las costumbres de los tagalos*, a 1589 manuscript he found in the Franciscan convent in Manila in 1887. (This was subsequently translated and published in Dutch by Hendrik Kern and German by Ferdinand Blumentritt.) Pardo was the first to publish this key account of indigenous Tagalog social organization, religion, and customary laws.[141] He introduces the work with notes on Plasencia's life and the text's genealogy, and annotates the text by providing word etymologies and comparative data from Malay and Hindu cultures. (Years later, Pardo would augment this work by publishing a missing section of *Costumbres*, dealing with the Pampangos, that Clemente Zulueta obtained in Seville and gave to Pardo in 1904.)[142]

He published the Plasencia text, Pardo said, because it is "useful" for history and to pay tribute to a "good missionary." What must have attracted Pardo to the Plasencia account was not just its rarity but its motive and content. In the 1580s, rampant abuses committed by *encomenderos* against the local population had sparked local revolts. Dismayed at the conditions he found when he arrived in Manila in 1584, governor-general Santiago de Vera asked Plasencia for a report on Tagalog social and political organization since "to govern with justice one must know the practices and customs of the inhabitants of the country one has the mission to direct."[143]

Though Pardo's annotations are modest and not always accurate, his Plasencia edition enacts the same impulse behind Rizal's own edition of Antonio de Morga's *Sucesos de las Islas Filipinas* (1890): to create a record of the Filipino past and examine the integrity of this record from the standpoint of the present and a perspective free of racist and colonialist bias. While he does not quite engage in the polemics one finds in Rizal's Morga, it is clear where his sympathies lie. He corrects, for instance, Spanish scholar Vicente Barrantes for bibliographic errors and for mistakenly attributing to Plasencia the statement that *indios* are so immaturely formed that they have to be disciplined as children: "Where the *indio* is born there too the cane is found." Such a vulgar phrase, Pardo says, cannot possibly come from a missionary of "an observant, studious, and superior spirit" but "must have sprung from the benighted cranium of one of those encomenderos who know of no other literature than *Padre Nuestro*."[144]

The Plasencia edition was followed by *Noticias sobre la imprenta y el grabado en Filipinas* (1893) and *El mapa de Filipinas del P. Murillo Velarde* (1894), pioneering studies on printing and cartography in the Philippines.

Noticias sobre la imprenta y el grabado en Filipinas breaks fresh ground in the history of printing and engraving in the Philippines.[145] Pardo reviews previous work on the subject (such as those of Wenceslao Retana and Francisco Diaz Puertas) and proceeds to expand existing knowledge on the subject. He dates the beginning of printing with the introduction of the Gutenberg method in 1610 instead of the woodblock-printed *doctrinas* produced in Manila in 1593. He lists ninety-six printshops and printers, ranging from the "Imprenta de Bataan" (1610) of the Dominican Francisco de San Jose to the "Imprenta de la Oceania Filipina" (1878) of Jose Felipe del Pan. A short section includes a descriptive list of engravers.

The entries are mainly divided according to the religious orders that controlled the press through much of the colonial era. Pardo provides well-researched notes on printing presses, the earliest known books and periodicals they produced, and particulars like page sizes, kind of paper, editions, and condition of extant specimens. More important, he records what data he could find on early printers and engravers, many of them *indios* or *Filipinos* (such as Diego Talaghay, Tomas and Simon Pinpin, and Nicolas de la Cruz Bagay). He does not only mine published sources but draws from personal knowledge of late nineteenth-century Manila publishing and the examination of texts in his library, the collections of booksellers and scholars (such as his teacher Pierre Favre), and such libraries as the Bibliotheque Nationale and Maisonneuve library in Paris and the British Museum and William Marsden Collection at King's College in London.

In correcting gaps and errors in the colonial record, *Noticias* has a pronounced anti-colonial subtext. It is not just a catalogue but a critical note on intellectual conditions in the Philippines. Pardo says: "Printing in the Philippines has, in its material and moral aspects, features that give it its own physiognomy."[146] *Morally*, he says, it is "an instrument in the hands of the State and of religion." The printing press was used by the state to publish laws and decrees, and by the Church to produce institutional histories, pastoral works, grammars, and, to a limited extent, texts in the arts and sciences. With censorship in force, even works not directly produced by the state or church tended to conform to the aims of both. Due to censorship and "a kind of tacit convention," the press did not disseminate other than ideas that maintained "love and veneration for Spain and the unity of all races in the Catholic faith."[147]

Materially, he says, printing in the Philippines is limited in volume and quality. With rare exceptions, books are poorly crafted and of material that does not usually survive the harsh tropical environment. Recounting his travails as a book collector in Manila, Pardo laments the indifference of many to book preservation and the suspicion of those who thought him a government spy ferreting out prohibited books. He nevertheless pieces together an intriguing history of printing and the role played by obscure printers and engravers. While the Spaniard Jose Toribio Medina—whose *La imprenta en Manila desde sus origenes hasta 1810* (1896) would supersede Pardo's work—judged Pardo's work "far from completeness and thorough accuracy," he nevertheless found it "quite excellent" as a contribution to knowledge on the subject.[148]

Mapa de Filipinas is another notable contribution.[149] An ardent bibliophile, Pardo laments the loss of books and manuscripts due to humidity, termites, human neglect, and the flight of documents to repositories abroad. In this context he offers this bibliographic piece on the famous map of the Jesuit historian Pedro Murillo Velarde, which was commissioned by governor-general Fernando Valdes in 1733, engraved by the Tagalog Nicolas de la Cruz Bagay, and published in 1734. For over a century, it served as the basis for other maps by European geographers. Pardo gives a detailed description of the map's specifications, symbols and inscriptions, its various editions, and errors and inconsistencies in the map and previous references to it. Pardo says that in its detail, comprehensiveness, and excellence from both geographic and artistic considerations, the Murillo Velarde map deserved to be called "the first map of the Philippines."

Pardo was "probably the first collector of Philippine maps anywhere."[150] He maintained a life-long interest in the subject, publishing in 1910 "*Notas para una cartografia de Filipinas*," which historian Carlos Quirino (who missed out on Pardo's earlier work) calls "the first approach to the history of local cartography."[151] For some years Pardo had been preparing an inventory of Philippine maps and geographical charts but shelved the project when the Library of Congress came out with P. Lee Philipps's catalogue of Philippine maps and charts in 1903.[152] Hence it was not until 1910 that Pardo published his own descriptive list of some 60 maps (around 40 of which he had in his own collection), including a list of place names by which various Philippine islands were known to early cartographers.

Pardo locates Philippine cartography in the context of growing geographical knowledge in the wake of the European exploration of the Philippines. He reviews theories about the "Philippines" drawn from Ramusio, Mercator, and Ortelius, rejecting the notion (raised by Rizal and Paterno) that Ptolemy referred to the Philippines in the name *Maniolas*. Quirino says of his achievement: "His comments on the development of insular cartography are as valid today as they were half a century ago when they were penned, and we can consider his work as the first authoritative monograph on the subject."[153]

In 1899, Pardo published *Una memoria de Anda y Salazar*, governor-general Simon Anda's hitherto unpublished memorial to the Spanish King in 1768, which exposed the anomalies of friar rule in the Philippines.[154] Pardo provides the memorial (a copy of which he inherited from his uncle Joaquin) with copious notes and references. While he claims that his notes are not "opinions" but "facts" meant to clarify points in the memorial, it is clear that Pardo intended his Anda edition as a polemical contribution to the anti-friar campaign of the time. Reinforcing the "black legend" of friar rule, he elaborates on what had then become a familiar litany of charges against the religious communities. Pardo raises interesting points on what he calls the friars' suppression of the "diffusion of human knowledge" among Filipinos. On language, for instance, he cites how the friars, in studying local languages, reduced them to the grammatical grid of Latin and Spanish, creating an artificial language distinct from the language spoken by the people. The friars did not only misuse the local language, a gap developed between the language natives used in speaking to friars and that they used among themselves.

Pardo was not an antiquarian. He reproduced and annotated documents as interventions in the public discourse on the Philippines. He inquired into the production of books and maps, sensitive to local facts, and interpreted them as cultural artifacts of the evolution of Philippine society. A good illustration is the speech he gave in Manila in 1911 at the centenary of the history of printing in the Philippines in which he revisited his earlier work on the subject.[155] He stressed his belief that the work of Filipino printers was *sui generis* not only in the physiognomy of their types but their artistic and compositional particulars. While printers in Europe shared technology and innovations, Filipino printers were isolated and had to develop by themselves, using rudimentary molds and casings, hence developing "a distinct character, *filipino.*" He argued that until around the mid-nineteenth century, "the tradition of Philippine printing was not augmented by exotic [foreign] elements but made and constructed in the Philippines by Filipinos."[156]

175

Beyond this, Pardo saw in printers, engravers, and bookbinders the appearance of a new social type in the country, the pioneers of an industrial society (*sociedad industrial*). In a thesis he would reiterate and develop, Pardo argued that previously local society had been predatory (*depredatorio*) in type, one in which wealth and status were extracted through warfare and exploitation and passed on through inheritance (*herencia*) rather than individual merit and productivity. Early Spanish rule did not transform society's basic character since the Spanish population of priests, soldiers, and bureaucrats was parasitic and unproductive. Hence the appearance of skilled artisans and craftsmen signified the emergence of a new, more dynamic society.

IN THE "PRE-AMERICAN" PHASE of his intellectual career Pardo applied the instruments of Western science to Philippine realities. He stood at the margins of power, occupied an interstitial position, and (excepting *Plantas medicinales*) carried out independent work. Even at this time, he was conscious of negotiating a Western/non-Western divide, moved by the desire to represent the distinctness of the local, identify with the *pais*, and carve out space apart from Spanish colonialist discourse on the Philippines. Yet he was also convinced that progress lies with what the West represented. His diffident relations with the propagandists and restrained criticism of Spanish colonialism (which he does not openly question, limiting himself to interrogations of friars, encomenderos, and scholars) manifest his ambivalent position.

American rule revised the situation for Pardo. The Americans' need to *know* their new insular possessions primed the ground for intellectual projects aimed at organizing the country as an object of knowledge and control. Pardo was well-positioned to be the chief Filipino contributor to these state-sponsored projects.

He was involved in U.S. colonial work early. In September 1898, just weeks after the Americans seized Manila, he was named honorary member of the all-American Board of Health. In 1900, he was the only Filipino member of a "board of representative citizens" organized by the Department of Streets, Parks, Fire, and Sanitation to assist it in improvements at the Luneta. In particular, the board selected, from entries in a competition, the design for two Luneta band stands and the site for the statue of Legazpi and Urdaneta.[157] In 1900, he was named trustee of the American Circulating Library, a private library formed by a group of Americans and turned over to the government on March 6, 1901. It became the basis of the Philippine National Library.[158] In 1901, as member of the Philippine Commission, he was tasked, with Benito Legarda, to obtain designs from Filipino artists for the new Philippine coins and silver certificates that were to be issued and submit their recommendations to the Bureau of Insular Affairs. Eventually, the designs of Filipino engraver Melecio Figueroa (featuring the image of a Filipino worker at the anvil) were chosen for the silver, nickel, and copper coins because they conveyed the theme of "peaceful economic pursuit in order to learn the art of self-government" under U.S. guidance.[159] In 1903, Pardo was appointed to the Committee on Geographical Names created for the purpose of standardizing the spelling of Philippine geographic names. The committee's work went into the production of *Pronouncing Gazetteer and Geographical Dictionary of the Philippine Islands* (1902), prepared by the Bureau of Insular Affairs.[160] An impressive colonial undertaking, *Gazetteer* does not only inventory local place names, providing data on spelling, pronunciation, and etymology, it compiles in a huge volume basic data on the country's history, population, government, economy, and natural resources. With aids like maps and charts, it authoritatively "fixes" for the first time the territorial character and boundaries of a U.S.-owned "Philippines."

In 1901, Pardo was commissioned by the U.S. government to produce a catalogue of publications on the Philippines. At the time, the Library of Congress was listing Philippine-related materials in its extensive holdings in response to the surge of interest in the islands after the U.S. occupation. The U.S. War Department's Bureau of Insular Affairs was also doing a similar bibliography as part of its planned *Gazetteer*. Pursuant to a U.S. Senate Resolution (January 5, 1903), calling for the production of a Philippine bibliography for official use, the BIA and Library of Congress agreed on the joint publication of a single volume that would contain both the list prepared by the library and Pardo's own catalogue, *Biblioteca Filipina*. The volume appeared in 1903.[161]

Biblioteca Filipina contains 2850 entries in such fields as history, ethnography, linguistics, botany, and zoology. Selectively annotated, the book comes with an introduction in which Pardo sketches the history of publishing and bibliography in the Philippines. Wenceslao Retana criticized it harshly, saying it was mainly based on Pardo's own library and unacknowledged extracts from catalogues produced by others. An assiduous bibliographer himself, Retana was piqued that Pardo had put down his bibliographies as deficient in the field of linguistics. Pardo, he says, is not a "true bibliographer." Guided by an intent to influence readers interested in Philippine affairs, Retana says, Pardo omits otherwise important works and is biased in his annotations.[162]

Despite its lapses, *Biblioteca* demonstrates the admirable range of Pardo's erudition. Most of his annotations are mainly descriptive, useful particularly for the biographical notes he provides on authors. Pardo, however, had strong opinions which he vented on some of the works he lists. On Fr. Cipriano Marcilla's *Estudio de los antiguos alfabetos Filipinos* (1895), he says, "the author does not understand a word of matters palaeographic." On *Apuntes interesantes sobre las Islas Filipinas* (1869), which he attributes to Vicente Barrantes, he writes: "This is a book devoid of importance, whose object is to defend the religious communities of the Philippines." On Manuel Buzeta's *Gramatica de lengua Tagala* (1850): "It is not easy to find a plagiarism more shameless and foolish." On Fr. Casimiro Herrero's *Filipinas ante la razon del indio* (1874), he curtly notes: "This is absolute nonsense." Pardo did not reserve his contempt for Spanish authors since he makes his most scathing remarks on the works of Pedro Paterno.[163]

At this time, too, Pardo was asked by the director of the Census Bureau, General Joseph Sanger, to write a history of the Philippines for the 1903 *Census of the Philippine Islands*. Ever fastidious, Pardo requested and received Sanger's assurance that his work would not be censored except on points that may not be proper for an "official publication." *Reseña Historica de Filipinas* appeared in the 1903 *Census*. To correct errors in the translation of Pardo's original Spanish manuscript, the Philippine Commission authorized the printing of the original text as a separate volume in 1906.[164]

Reseña Historica is a concise survey of Philippine history until 1903. Attempting what may be the first "national" history of the Philippines, Pardo was conscious that he was breaking new ground. He begins by citing the limitations of Spanish colonial histories, saying they are not the history of the Filipinos themselves but religious-civic chronicles that recount the activities of the religious orders and colonial authorities.

They are not written in an impartial spirit but aim to glorify and enhance the prestige of the Spanish nation. Combining chronological and
thematic approaches, Pardo divides his history into six chapters under
the following headings: *Historia, Civilizacion, El Poder Monacal, Comercio
y Rentas, Gobierno*, and *La Emancipacion de España*. The first is a quick,
chronological sketch of events from the sixteenth-century Spanish voyages of exploration to the coming of the Americans in 1898. The second
describes the culture of the archipelago at Spanish contact and the social
and cultural changes under Spanish rule. The third focuses on the role
of the religious orders in colonial society. The fourth and fifth take up
the subject of commerce, taxation, and form of government from Spanish times to the American period. The final chapter traces the development
of Filipino nationalism, culminating in the revolution and U.S. annexation.

Pardo condenses as much information as he can in eighty pages and
tries to keep his editorial glosses to a minimum. Yet he plots his material
in a way that conveys how he views the "national history." His subject is
the predominantly Malay *Filipino* nation already possessed, more or less,
of a distinctive character at Spanish contact. He describes the sociopolitical
organization of indigenous petty states (*pequeños estados*), the barangay,
as the norm for the archipelago. He calls *anito* worship the "true religion
of the Filipinos" (*verdadera religion de los filipinos*). While he says that
indigenous syllabaries were "very imperfect," they constituted a "Filipino alphabet" (*un alfabeto que se puede llamar Filipino*) since their
differences were slight and they were universally used. He blames the
Spanish missionaries for destroying a precolonial legacy of palm-leaf
"books" in their zeal to destroy vestiges of ancient religion. He cites
native accomplishments and chastises Spanish chroniclers for exaggerated descriptions of native vices. While he mentions positive
transformations under Spanish rule, his account stresses the deleterious
effects of friar rule, to which he devotes a whole chapter. He blames the
monastic orders for creating among Filipinos a docile and weak character
by keeping them in a condition of "perpetual tutelage, an eternal adoles-
cence."[165]

While Pardo cites the folk revolts against Spanish abuses, he privileges the role of the educated and propertied Filipinos in the movement
for national emancipation. He sketches a narrative that proceeds from

the reform movement of the 1870s (citing Joaquin, his uncle, among the leading participants), its repression and the growing polarization between Filipinos and Spaniards, the Propaganda Movement, the incendiary effect of Rizal's novels, the formation of *Liga Filipina*, Rizal's execution, and the armed insurrection organized by Andres Bonifacio and the Katipunan. He says that the common people (*plebe*) did not participate in the reform movement until they were mobilized by the Katipunan, but locates the Katipunan as a phase in a single, linear narrative of Filipino self-assertion.

Given the time and circumstance of the writing, Pardo's treatment of U.S. rule is abbreviated. He endorses the U.S. presence as an opportunity for Filipinos to fulfill their aspirations for progress and credits the United States for the grant of civil liberties and separation of church and state, saying that the American nation "has bound itself in honor" to help Filipinos "reach the highest degree attainable of culture and civilization." He concludes that most Filipinos believe in the ideals of independence, but that the educated class is convinced that independence can be won through legal means and that an armed revolution does not serve the interests of the Filipino people.

Pardo did not singlehandedly invent the plot of the nation's history. In organizing the past and connecting it to the present, he deployed arguments other *ilustrados* were making. He may, however, be the first to put the material together in the form of a full and published narrative. Narrativizing the nation from where he stood in 1903, Pardo stresses the putative unity of precolonial culture, depicts the Spanish colonial period as a tragedy of friar misrule, sketches the formation of a national spirit in the dynamic of assimilation and resistance, assigns to the elite a leading role in the creation of nationhood, and assumes a benign view of U.S. rule as a way towards progress and freedom.

Though later authors would tone down its anti-Church content, Pardo's condensed, linear, evolutionary narrative would be reprised again and again in the decades that followed.

HE WAS the leading intellectual architect of a postrevolutionary Philippines. He articulated to the Americans the aspirations of the Filipino people and interpreted to Filipinos the designs of the United States. As statesman and scholar, he had a pivotal role in constructing, for both Americans and Filipinos, the nation as object of knowledge and as field in which they were to act as leaders and citizens.

Though Pardo's departure from the commission in 1909 diminished his official importance, he continued to exercise influence as a public intellectual. Publishing and lecturing, he stirred public debate in the early 1900s. He occasionally returned to his interests in medicine and historiography, writing on public health and publishing old documents like Plasencia's report on the Pampangos and a *relacion* on the history of Liliw, Laguna.[166] After 1909, however, he mainly devoted himself to responding to current social issues. Perhaps more than anyone at the time, he dealt with the challenges of nation building out of an explicitly formulated social philosophy.

This philosophy was not developed in a single work but elaborated and reiterated in lectures, articles, and interviews. Pardo's major theme was the need for the social transformation of the Philippines through the medium of modern, Western, and specifically "Anglo-Saxon" civilization. This is premised on a dichotomous divide he makes between past and present, tradition and modernity, religion and secularism, and Spanish and American colonialisms.

Undergirding his ideas on society is a view of history that he developed in more theoretical terms after *Reseña*. In "*Resultados del desarrollo economico de Filipinas*" (1912), he takes up the problem of "determining causes" in the evolution of Philippine society and, on this basis, offers a criterion which, he says, has been lacking in previous periodizations of Philippine history.[167] He briefly touches on the "primitive period" (which he describes as largely predatory and stagnant) and the "period of discovery and conquest" (which had been copiously dealt with in existing histories). (Elsewhere, he outlines precolonial history in evolutionary "stages" in which a primitive, subsistence-oriented aboriginal population of Negritos was displaced by a superior, essentially agricultural population of *indonesianos*, who were themselves displaced by "depredatory," martial Malays. Pardo constructs them as social types: the Negritos lived in what nature spontaneously provided; the "Indonesians" on what nature yielded through the medium of their labor; and the Malays on what the previous two produced and provided. Then came other influences: the "religious and military" Spaniards and the "industrial and commercial" Chinese.[168])

181

In *Resultados*, he focuses on the colonial era and the three periods of "tutelary sequestration" (*secuestracion tutelar*), "commercial liberty" (*libertad comercial*), and "national construction" (*construccion nacional*). His guiding thesis is that the determining cause in civilizational development must be sought in "natural" laws of human and social evolution rather than "artificial" phenomena. "Follow this method and you will see that political, religious, artistic, moral combinations all spring from the most essential phenomena of our own existence which pertain to nutrition. PRIMUM VIVERE."[169] Material conditions, or what he calls "the restriction or the development of economic combinations," determine social development.

On this basis, he sketches an early colonial period of crisis and stagnation characterized by a disturbed equilibrium between supply and demand and food scarcity caused by Spanish occupation. The Spaniards did not transform a "predatory" precolonial economy (characterized by warfare, slavery and exactions of tribute and personal services) but combined it with a parasitic, exploitative rentier system (*sistema rentistico*) that medieval religious indoctrination reinforced. "Material development was slow, odious, unjust, sterile."

> It was slow, because it was the product of cooperation resulting from coercion; it was odious, because it exploited the weak; it was unjust, because some performed the duties and others availed themselves of the advantages; it was sterile, because it did not form sentiments of a superior but of an inferior order such as deception, humiliation, passivity, discouragement and fatalism.[170]

Pardo calls this a period of "tutelary sequestration" because the colony was isolated and economic forces restricted. The colony was sequestered from contact with foreign countries, except for a limited trade with China, Japan, and other Asian countries; economic activity was focused on the Manila-Acapulco galleon trade; monopolies were exercised by State and Church; and population movements were curtailed. A "social constitution" in which a privileged few exploited the many fostered a "mentality of hunger" in which human action was driven by facts of scarcity. Restrictions on the freedom of production and exchange, "the foundation of all economic development," created a stagnant society, both materially and morally.

Such "tutelary sequestration" could not last as it was "contrary to the nature of the laws which rule human progress." Hence, it gradually gave way, by the operation of "purely natural causes," to a period of "commercial liberty." Early signs of this new order included the relaxing of restrictions on trade and capital with the establishment of *Real Compania de Filipinas* in 1733; the "opening up" of Manila during the British Occupation (1762–1764); the founding in 1781 of *Sociedad Economica de Amigos del Pais*, which promoted an ideology of improvement through "a society of select persons capable of useful thoughts;" the treaty with England in 1814 by which Spain opened colonial ports to foreign commerce and authorized therein the residence of foreigners; and the opening of the Suez Canal in 1869. A new commercial aristocracy emerged and though it could not respond right away to the challenge of the new, since it was educated in outdated ideas, it would gradually do so. It is the law elsewhere in the world, Pardo writes, that "man has ever marched from the conquest of material welfare to the conquest of intellectual and moral progress; from the acquisition of material necessities, beginning with the most essential, which is nutrition (*nutricion*), to those of a higher order, based one upon another, in a natural order determined by a concatenation of causes and effects which artificial means, voluntary or unconscious, placed to change its course, have only served to paralyze or retard."[171]

Capitalism primed the circulation of goods, ideas, and people and fostered prosperity and a growing confidence among the people, as demonstrated in the birth of *filibusterismo* in the late nineteenth century.

True economic life demanded *freedom of work and freedom of exchange*. Freedom of work hurt the social class which lived off its exploitation under the protection of the powers and the law: production escaped from their hands and the parasitical methods of the exploiters came to an end. The freedom of exchange also took commerce out of the hands of the same privileged class and placed it at the disposition of those better qualified for it. No change of more transcendental and beneficent results for the Filipino people could have been made. Commerce was to cease being a force for exploitation![172]

Those who had been maligned as "brutes loaded with gold" were the first "new persons" of an emerging order. With prosperity and leisure, they cultivated new values (tolerance, discretion, precision) that helped them increase status and wealth without coercion. They valued education; their appetite for material goods stimulated the economy; they demanded such necessities of commerce as roads, communications, and public safety. In this dynamic "monied Filipinos" were "the first of the discontented," eventually carrying along with them the poor in the colony. Their emancipation was occasioned by material progress rather than education. Colonial education was limited and reactionary: it fostered contempt for manual labor and inculcated the idea that "some men had been born to exploit and others to be exploited"; it formed a "directive class" incapable of giving the people good economic direction; it "served the purposes of fortifying the existing social type, making it more and more persistent in its error."[173]

The establishment of the Republic in 1898, Pardo says, marks the beginning of the period of "National Construction." The event "is and will always be the first page of the history of the Construction of Philippine Nationality."[174] He looks at the U.S. colonial order as an auspicious time for progress in the country.

Pardo holds that the "economic independence of the individual" is the "determining cause" of a society's moral and intellectual growth. Material progress creates in the person new desires and ambitions, sentiments of personal worth, autonomy and power. "Liberties relating to material interests are, by natural and historical order, anterior to and determinant of moral and intellectual liberties."[175] What holds for the individual is true of nations as well. Economic power lies at the foundation of a nation's military, political, and cultural power.

Thus he privileges the leading role of the *clase ilustrada* (the *burguesia* in other countries, he says). "Commerce, even on a small scale, is rather an intellectual occupation... it requires calculation, foresight, honesty, or trickery." It has two diametrically opposed moral aspects, depending on whether it operates under oppressive laws or under free institutions. In the first case, it exploits, deceives, oppresses, and abuses its privileged position. In the second, it wins by procedures of an elevated character, such as square dealing and free competition. As economies advance, Pardo believes, intellectual forces will acquire greater importance than the material in the rise of a modern civilization "essentially economic, essentially scientific and productive."[176]

184

The history he has sketched, Pardo writes, is not to be construed as a simple, linear succession of stages. From one stage to another, "we find phases gradually distinguishing themselves from one another in a continuous chain… It appears that at the end of the first period, phenomena began to appear which were related with those of the following one, and at the beginning of the latter we find characteristics of the last period which little by little became gradually dissipated until but vestiges of them remained."[177] He has, therefore, periodized history with a sense of what is dominant against what is merely residual or still emergent.

EDUCATION AND THE ECONOMY were Pardo's central concerns in his last years. So strongly did he feel about education that, a year before he died, he said: "In this stage of my life, when I am approaching its end, if I were asked to what activity I would wish to dedicate myself were I young again, I would answer without a moment's hesitation—to the *educative activity* in general."[178] On public education, he wrote:

> From whatever point of view we may study the state and problem of our society, whether political, social, or economic, we shall arrive always at the same conclusion, if we recognize the fact that public instruction, to which we should consecrate all our strength, is the principal factor of civilization.[179]

Pardo embraced the public school system as the most dramatic benefit introduced by the Americans. No one espoused as forcefully the need for a "complete assimilation of the American spirit," a future in which Filipinos will be "reading and thinking as Americans." As early as January 15, 1902, he wrote to Taft: "I want them [Pardo's sons] to be educated in America so that they may be Americans." He himself wished to spend, he said, some time in the U.S. to learn its social and political principles so that, returning to the Philippines, he will be more useful in advancing civilization in the country.[180] He acted on his words. Pardo authored Philippine Commission Act No. 854 (August 26, 1903), which sent Filipino students as government *pensionados* to the U.S. "for education, even complete Americanization." He chaired the selection committee on the program's first year.[181]

His lavish praise for American education was grounded in a manichaean view of the country's intellectual situation. On one hand, there was the intellectually benighted Spanish era; on the other, the promise of American enlightenment. Focused on producing pious Christians and docile colonials, Spanish education was narrow and medieval. It gave "inadequate instruction to a small minority," fostered passivity, made Filipinos despise manual labor, and discouraged intellectual growth. In a major essay entitled "*El Legado del Ignorantismo*," delivered before an assembly of teachers in 1920, he attacked church-dominated education as regressive and obscurantist. Based on a view of the native as immature and driven by the aim to dominate and control, colonial education stunted the growth of morality and mentality. It cultivated persons lacking in the capacity for rational, autonomous action and left a legacy of *ignorantismo*. Filipino colonial culture consisted of a medieval literature of devotional books (*novenas, pasyon*) and exotic romances (*awit, corrido*) as well as religious and social practices that fostered fanaticism and supernaturalism. The erosion of reason produced subjects prey to immorality, dependent on divine patronage, and infected by that "leprosy of superstition" which is "one of the strongest causes of criminality, of corruption, of formation of individuals who are useless and detrimental to society."[182]

What Filipinos needed was a "scientific" education that formed individual responsibility through the full exercise of reason and will. He calls this *logical mentality*, "the ability to know what we do and to plan a just route to follow, the *will*, that which enables us to exalt the dictates of reason above the impulses of our own desires." The U.S.-sponsored educational system, he says, lays the groundwork for forming an intellect free of religious, political, and philosophic restriction. It will produce rational, useful citizens and create the condition for progress, which is "the natural consequence of the regime of liberty, industry, work and logical mentality."[183]

Speaking before American and Filipino teachers in 1906, he underscored the importance of public education, quoting Montesquieu in saying that what a republic needs is personal and civic virtue. In fostering self-reliance, productive labor, and civic responsibility, Anglo-Saxon education creates the conditions for a progressive and democratic society.

Anglo-Saxon education cannot form subject nations: its destiny is to train individuals capable of independent thinking—of acting according to the impulses of their instructed conscience—and to create a community of individuals of an independent, strong, free, and cultured character. Anglo-Saxon education can never beget a mass of people that are slaves to foreign influences, but a people who are individually virile and strong in all ways.[184]

To this end, he staunchly advocated the use of English for government and instruction. He justified his stand on pragmatic grounds, saying that adopting English would be more practical and efficient since Tagalog, "the most perfect" of the local languages, does not have a "polished literature" and adequate dictionaries and grammars. He opposed the teaching of local dialects and dismissed as "utopian" proposals for creating a national language through a fusion of languages. He believed that national unity constitutes the "one great difficulty in the formation of a single country, a single nation," and that the plurality of languages was a problem since this "allows each group to retain a mentality distinct from that of the rest." English, he said, was the answer: "For the oneness of our rights, the singleness of our duties, the harmony of our aspirations, the unanimity of our ideals—all of which constitute our soul—we need a common language; and this common language we are beginning to acquire with the spread of Anglo-Saxon education."[185]

More important, he regarded English to be better suited as a medium for science and democracy. Arguing from the premise that languages are "essentially conductors of ideas, ideals, and knowledge," Pardo says that English is "the language of democracy and of liberty, in which is neither spoken nor written, any idea which may be utilized for oppression, or for the imposition of religious principles of any sort."[186]

In part, he saw his advocacy of English as "nationalist" since English, as vehicle of secularism and modernity, undermined Spanish-based education and the influence of the religious orders. On the other hand, he was impatient with the romancing of the native language. As chairman of the state university's Department of Oriental Languages, he opposed the use of a Philippine language as medium of teaching although he supported teaching it as a subject. "To teach our native dialects is not a necessity in the University but it is a necessity to teach its correct form, investigate its phonics, its lexicography, its syntax—in a word, to study [it] scientifically," Pardo wrote.[187]

Part of Pardo's "modernity" were his ideas on women's emancipation and individual self-determination. No male writer of his time was as vocal in championing women's rights. He called for greater educational opportunities for women, increased social participation, and the correction of discriminatory laws in matters like marriage and property rights. As in the issue of education, Pardo opposed modern feminism to feudal, Spanish-colonial *machismo*. To improve the status of women, he said, we must destroy the *mentalidad pueril* that idealizes the "effeminate" (*afeminado*) virtues of fragility and delicacy, feeds women's false vanity, makes her a mere object of male desire, and keeps her physically, intellectually, and morally inferior. A person's superiority is not a function of gender, he said, but the result of intellectual and moral achievement.[188]

Women's emancipation will not come from the actions of men but of women as they transform themselves into independent, productive, and modern persons. Addressing graduates of the Philippine General Hospital School of Nursing on April 3, 1920, he said that women do not have to be men, they exercise activity proper to their capacity for personal and social fulfillment. He praised nursing as "the quintessentially feminine profession," but added that it is "not a product of charity, it is not the offshoot of sentimentalism, but the creation of science in its continuing work of humanity's betterment."[189] For Pardo, women's emancipation was part of a general program of social amelioration founded on a Kantian belief in individual freedom and responsibility.

Pardo's liberal individualism is clearly set forth in what he calls an "empirical" rather than "sentimental" analysis of Rizal, *El Caracter de Rizal* (1918).[190] Turning Rizal into a Kantian hero, he stresses that Rizal perfected qualities—discretion, initiative, valor, nobility—that placed him high above the rest of his countrymen and belied the colonialist denigration of the moral and mental qualities of the "native." Rizal's exceptional qualities are the product of education, will, and the desire to know the truth. Contrary to the view of some that Rizal secretly desired revolution, Pardo argues that Rizal respected authority and worked within the framework of law. His significance lies in how, despite the odds, he molded himself as an individual others could emulate. He posed himself against the rule of ignorance by developing a rational, "scientific" mind.

Nobody had as yet had the scientific patriotism of Rizal: others who were dreaming of a fatherland did so with a bellicose patriotism of the old traditional type, of the warlike kind, based on hatred for the foreigner. Rizal reveals an independent character, as strangely unexpected as if a bamboo stalk were to bear roses.[191]

For Pardo, character comes from innate qualities, heredity, and the "ambient medium" formed by such factors as education and occupation. While he ascribes value to Rizal's European education, Pardo stresses will and reason in character formation. While factors of race and milieu kept the *indio* in a state of inertia, Rizal was the creation of his own will to perfection. Yet, Rizal's achievement—that "the Filipino race was able to give birth to individuals endowed with the highest attributes, who could be considered an honor to the human race"—also points to the innate potential of the race.

Pardo's individualism expressed a philosophical and political bias. Elsewhere he wrote: "A nation being only the sum of the individuals composing it, the higher the character of each individual, the greater the number of important units in education and productive capacity, the higher will be the type of the nation that these units make up."[192] Pardo defined the enemy as *ignorantismo*. Against such enemy he placed his trust in the individual's transformation through education. With a conservative's distrust of revolution, he repeatedly said:

We believed in the transformative force of the revolution, while in reality it does nothing but replace the persons governing the people by others who, imbued with the same principles and accustomed to the same methods, cannot but repeat that which has become the moral patrimony of the nation.[193]

Thus he valued Rizal and M.H. del Pilar higher than he did such men as Bonifacio, interpreting the former as exemplars of *civismo*, an enlightened civic consciousness, instruments of the force of "evolution" which history has shown to have more force and efficacy than "revolution" as a determinant of human progress.[194]

Pardo was responding both to the dangers of popular insurrection and the demagogic nationalism of political leaders in the early 1900s.

Independencia nacional, he said, is worthless if it does not guarantee at the same time *independencia individual*. He looked towards modern education for developing productive, self-reliant citizens who can create a "true democracy" and are responsible to themselves instead of a church, party, or political leader. Such an education "can redeem us from the double danger of domination by a theocratic minority or of a majority created by popular suffrage expanding before popular education has developed."[195] Impatient with the kind of politics that emerged in the American era, he declared that differences in parties were just a case of *personalismos*. What the country needed was *civismo*, "civil discipline," the formation of citizens on the basis of reason. "The great evil which afflicts us is the lack of really independent citizens!"[196]

Pardo believed in an "aristocracy of intellect" but balanced this with a faith in the democratizing power of education. Citing the experience of Prussia and France, he said that it is not enough to have a class of professionals of superior education, a democracy requires an educated population. Education must not be the patrimony of persons privileged by birth or fortune, it is everyone's right. This does not, however, abolish divisions of labor. Quoting Renan, Pardo said that the object of democratic education "is not that all should participate in the labor of science, but that all may participate in the results of scientific work."[197]

PARDO IS NOT VOLUNTARIST in his view of social change. He recognized that material progress determines a people's mental and spiritual development:

> Liberties relating to material interests are, by nature, determinant of moral and intellectual liberties. Whoever has no right to free work, whoever has no free disposition of the product of his labour, does not understand, nor seek, nor can avail himself, of other kinds of liberties.[198]

Analyzing the rise of Philippine nationalism, he stresses the agency of the bourgeoisie. Liberated by economic change, they were the leading element in the reform movement not because they were rich but because "a certain degree of material welfare" was a condition for intellectual and moral transformation. He writes: "Self-respect mistreated, vanity wounded, natural pride offended, first impelled the wealthy to make personal protests of an egoistic character, and these protests led to self-assertions of a general character,—first, for the individual, then for his race, for his countrymen."[199] It was as material conditions improved that the "poor" themselves became increasingly liberated in thought.

Pardo traces the stagnation of the Philippine economy to a mentality shaped by colonialism and environment: a distaste for work, inertia, and improvidence fostered by social and natural factors. Stating the matter in popular terms, he says: "The five obstacles to the progress of the Filipino people are constructions of nipa and bamboo, the coconut, the rooster, and the *Padre Nuestro*."[200] The perishable nipa hut does not constitute rational capital accumulation; it is a wasteful investment of money more suited to the profligate rather than the poor. The second does not require intelligent, productive work; it is "capital at rest" which does little to induce agricultural development. The third stands for cock-fighting and other pernicious, wasteful vices. The fourth signifies a religious formation that fosters passivity, fatalism, and otherworldliness.

As in his other arguments about Philippine life, Pardo blames Spanish colonialism for the lack of progress. Spanish rule was built on predatory and parasitic practices (tribute system, labor conscription, absentee landlordism) and a value system that discouraged initiative and work. He sets this against a dynamic Western industrialism that fuels production and consumption by raising living standards and aspirations for material and social well-being. In this binary view, he credits the U.S. government for organizing "an economic life whose skeleton, whose foundation did not formerly exist here" and inducing "economic activities making for the increase of wealth and hence, the material well-being which makes intellectual and moral progress possible in a nation."[201]

Pardo was a vocal supporter of foreign investments and the "association" of Filipino and American economic interests. He illustrated the contributions of foreign capital in the role of American and European merchant houses in introducing instruments of credit and exchange, the establishment of railroads and telegraphy, and the entry of banks. He dismissed the view that developing Philippine natural resources would bind the country more firmly to the United States, saying that, on the contrary, economic development would empower Filipinos and demonstrate their capacity for independence. Those suspicious of U.S. economic activities, he says, are still living under the old "religious and military" civilization, which looked towards the state and the Church for benefits of progress and did not fully understand the processes of an industrial society. He writes: "An ordained nation, with a responsible and stable government, ATTRACTS FOREIGNERS AND THEIR CAPITAL; in the same manner, a distrustful government in a backward nation repels and scares them away [Pardo's emphasis]."[202]

Industrialism, he says, is founded on individual initiative and free association. It releases the energies of production and consumption, fuels material and social progress and follows scientific methods. Its benefits redound to the individual irrespective of whether development takes place under "a foreign or domestic flag." Industrialism transforms agriculture by introducing new technologies and changing farm management. Thus Pardo calls for vocational and industrial education, lamenting that many Filipinos are still preoccupied with political, religious, and literary questions. "Dedicated to pursue literary careers, to exercise our understanding in Byzantine speculations, we have not perceived that the forces which impel humanity towards progress are neither philosophy nor rhetoric but, simply, CHEMISTRY (*QUIMICA*) and MECHANICS (*MAQUINISMO*)."[203]

> To establish schools is a necessity; to discuss political topics, a right; and to ask for independence, a just aspiration: but at the same time and parallel to these, we have the obligation to labour for the improvement of the material situation of the Filipino people."[204]

The need for productive labor was a theme Pardo repeatedly stressed. Work, he said, is "the foundation of the prosperity and greatness of nations." Outside intellectual work (he considered intellectuals *workers*, though he was partial to positivists), he underscored the contributions of industrialists, entrepreneurs, and skilled workers. In a speech at the public assembly organized by the *Comite de Defensa Social* in Manila's Grand Opera House on May 30, 1920, he extolled the cardinal importance of labor.[205] Labor, he said, is the medium through which God has given us the power to create an enlightened and progressive society. What is required, however, is not the labor of animals (which aims at survival

192

rather than progress) or the labor of "primitives" (subsistence-oriented, customary, repetitive), but labor that joins work and intelligence so that work is not just work but a means to accumulate capital, perfect methods, and build capacity and productivity.

A nineteenth-century utilitarian, Pardo underscores the need to educate the proletariat (*proletariado*) for building a democratic and progressive society. He speaks, however, not in terms of class but the emancipation of the individual.

> The nation in a democracy is composed of citizens free and responsible in their actions, and the first duty of these citizens is to work and produce to achieve their individual economic independence and obtain by the perfection of their manual or intellectual labor the highest possible level. Hence, from the sum of these men, thus educated, comes a democracy capable of directing its own destiny.[206]

Pardo looked toward the example of Japan and the role of the Philippine Chinese and, despite public opposition, supported the immigration of Chinese and Japanese workers on the grounds that the country needed productive manpower to prime its development.[207] He highlighted the role the Chinese played in Philippine history. The Chinese introduced the "industrial and commercial" type of social activity by pioneering in crafts and industries, filling such occupations as silversmiths, apothecaries, and printers, and demonstrating values of frugality, adaptability, hard work, and risk taking. Confessing that as a child he had shared colonial society's anti-Chinese bias, Pardo blamed the Spaniards for propagating the bias through policies of exclusion and ghettoization. In pre-Spanish times, Filipinos had no reason to dislike the Chinese since they performed a necessary role as traders and did not seek to enforce their laws or religion. Even Limahong's incursion was an "act of piracy, and nothing more," and "piracy was a profession, as it was in Europe," and practiced by Filipinos themselves as a mode of acquiring wealth.[208]

In his late years, Pardo was particularly drawn to the example of a resurgent Japan in the Meiji era. He greatly admired Japan's tradition of honor, discipline, and patriotism. Yet he believed that its development has been keyed by its appropriation of the sciences and institutions of the West and, as such, offers an example for the Philippines and other nations. (Among the authors he admiringly cites is Yukichi Fukuzawa [1835–1901], a Western-trained educator who advocated Japan's assimilation of Western technological and scientific achievements.) Pardo expressed optimism that Japan's role as "redeemer" (*redentor*) of Asian peoples can be exercised not by force but the example that an advanced civilization is not a matter of race or color.[209] Pardo did not quite stress the "Japanization" of European influence (instead of Japan's "Europeanization") and, as time would show, he did not fully appreciate the forces driving Japan to aggressive militarism.

For Pardo, the people's material welfare should be the focus of attention since the economy was the key to Filipino self-transformation. Citing the experience of Japan, France, and Germany, he approvingly quotes Herbert Spencer:

> What makes the relations of cause and effect existing between the industrial order and free institutions more comprehensible is the fact that the countries, where the greatest changes have been brought about in the sense of political liberty, have been industrial countries. Wherever industrial activity and structure are developed, the right of free private examination in religious matters is established little by little at the same time as political rights are established.[210]

For Pardo, democracy, national unity, and economic progress could be achieved if Filipinos, as individuals and nation, embraced the ideas and institutions of which the United States had become exemplar.

THE ESSAYS "The Filipino Soul" (1906), "The New Filipino Mentality" (1912), and "The Conservation of the National Type" (1921) are the fullest statement of Pardo's views on the question of Western influence and national identity. These were written as interventions in the early twentieth-century debate between so-called *americanistas* and *nacionalistas* over the erosion of the "Filipino Soul" because of rapid Anglo-Saxonization (*sajonismo*).[211]

Pardo was a vigorous critic of indigenism. Preserving what is truly "our own," he says, is tantamount to the *reductio ad absurdum* of modeling ourselves after the "primitive inhabitants of our Islands, who have taken refuge in the mountain fastnesses." In an interview in 1923, he says: "What belonged to our fathers is different from what was the patrimony of our grandfathers and more different still from that of our great grandfathers. What is 'our own' is the symposium of what has been that of generations gone, subject to the mutations imposed by progress and civilization." He criticizes *Filipinistas* for their failure to define what they mean by "nationality" and argues that what they point to as "Filipino" is in fact colonial Hispanic culture, the *mentalidad latina* Spaniards propagated in the country.[212]

He attacks those who hold back progress for sectarian reasons and laments the "political pressure" exerted by nativists and "sentimental patriots." He contests the position of those who proclaim "the doctrine that we must preserve our own, that our system of education and instruction should be shaped according to our peculiar nature, and that to adopt systems of thought and belief from foreign countries is simply to choose the wrong road and to take a course which will lead to the suppression of our national qualities."

I do not mean to oppose the development in the Philippines of a peculiar type of civilization. I cannot prevent it, however much I may want to, because it is purely a natural, spontaneous, involuntary, and fatal phenomenon. I have already affirmed that in the mass of the people there lies, in a dormant and latent state, the true Filipino soul. What I seek to do is to prevent the eventuality that, under the pretext of preserving and cultivating what we call our own that which is not our own, we effect only the sad and sure result of retarding our progress, of diverting the correct course of our youth, of vitiating Filipino intellect, and of subjecting it to control, prejudice, and false principles, which are so well known in the history of civilization to be potent factors of stagnancy and retrogression, and not of movement and progress.[213]

What the country needs, he argued, is not "sentimental" patriotism but a "scientific" patriotism. "A country that thinks, feels, and works accordingly; a country whose individuals, by reason of their education and instruction, know how to think for themselves—is a country capable of feeling and understanding patriotism."[214] An "aggressive patriotism" (*patriotismo agresivo*), expressed in the fear or hatred of foreigners, is a trait of backward societies, formed by the experience of slave-raiding and warfare. It is encouraged by overlords to disguise their oppressive powers, as illustrated by the Spanish persecution of the Chinese and other foreigners. History, however, shows that Philippine progress has been fueled by openness and contact, which brought with it capital, technology, and new values and opportunities. Promoting the ethic of "productive work" and economic development is the "constructive patriotism" (*patriotismo constructivo*) that is the hallmark of a modern society.[215]

In "The New Filipino Mentality"—an essay Salvador Lopez calls "the 'emancipation proclamation' of the Filipino mind"—Pardo situates these ideas in a discourse on the history of mentalities in the Philippines. Mentality, Pardo explains, is constituted of two kinds of representations, those that depend on intelligence, which may be termed "knowledge" (*conocimientos*), and those in the domain of sentiment, "beliefs" (*creencias*). Knowledge is formed with greater effort and difficulty; it is also more mutable, the result of experience and analysis, changing as new facts require rectification. Beliefs, on the other hand, are our first psychical acquisitions, formed by the observation of surrounding phenomena. They penetrate our conscience more easily and do not require great intellectual effort but are also the ones that become more firmly rooted. Beliefs come to be founded on faith; knowledge rests on reason. As in biology, where what is simple and primary tend to persist longer, a mentality ruled by beliefs changes little or slowly due to the force of tradition and inheritance. A mentality guided by knowledge or reason, on the other hand, is dynamic and progressive. Beliefs and knowledge belong to our psychic capacity, they both constitute what people call our "soul." They coexist such that man cannot be "absolutely rationalist," which explains why human error and suffering are not easily eradicated, if at all.

Mentality is not immutable. Its dynamic is always one of movement and change, a development of faculties from simpler, anterior forms, as *creencias*, the "hopes" that sustain us in our state of half-knowledge, are converted into *conocimientos* by the operations of science. Arguing out of the theory of evolutionary "determinism," Pardo imagines an inexorable evolutionary process in which man, through a long process of observation, labor, adaptation, and contact with more advanced cultures, develops and perfects—from such primitive inventions as the cane and the plow—the "machinery" of civilization. Employing analogies with biological growth, Pardo says that progress comes through "a process of new acquisition and rectification of errors, of change of forms."[216]

On this basis he sketches a history of mentalities in the Philippines. He does not dwell at length on the precolonial period, saying that our knowledge of this time is "rare, vague, dubious and obscure." He limits himself to observing that precolonial *barangays* tended to fission and did not constitute a *nacion* and that while people prized their independence their "patriotism" was localistic, inward-looking, and hostile to outsiders. He criticizes those who wrote on native psychology not in its own terms but according to other cultural standards, like those who judged local languages on the basis of Latin without distinguishing between two language types, one agglutinative and the other inflectional. (This knock on Eurocentrism does not prevent him from invoking the French philosopher Lucien Levy-Bruhl in characterizing indigenous mentality as one "mystical" and supernaturalist, governed by "a sentimental logic and emotive mentality."[217])

He dates the beginning of a "new Filipino mentality" with Spanish contact. Spanish conquest implanted "one flag, one law, one king, one religion and one language." In practice, this did not happen at the same pace, or spread far and evenly, or completely obliterate indigenous practices. Yet Spanish rule did bring about intended and unintended effects in the native mentality, such as an awareness of new, larger forms of collectivity (*solidaridad nacional*), religious values, notions of rights, duties, and relations between governors and governed. Gradually and inconsistently, a new mentality emerged, one that substituted a "logic of deeds" (*logica de hechos*) for "sentimental logic" (*logica sentimental*) and was characterized by critical discourse (*discussion*) instead of the passive, unquestioning repetition of custom and tradition. This paved the way for the ascendance of science and reason among those who would first claim for themselves the identity of *Filipino* and, in the same process, claim what comes with progress and civilization. Thus, modulating his earlier statements on Spanish rule, he would write: "the synthetic result of Spain's intervention in our archipelago was the *foundation of*

Filipino nationality and the *concept* translated into the desire and necessity of national independence" [Pardo's emphasis]."[218]

Thus the country began to evolve from a "military and religious"
type of society to one "scientific and productive," with a mentality characterized by a critical spirit, individual responsibility, values of labor
and productivity, and *discussion* as mode of arriving at truth. Pardo believed that humanity, in its long process of evolution, has reached "the
period of positive knowledge which is the true age of reason." The premium is on "positivist thinking" as basis for cooperation and progress.
To achieve this what the Philippines needed for national resurgence are
instruction, education, and faith in our own efforts.[219] The coming of
the Americans, Pardo believed, has powerfully hastened the evolution of
the new mentality.

Culture contact hastens evolution. The dynamic of civilization is
such that it is not a case of whether we like to adapt to the modern but
that we have to. Impatient with indigenists, Pardo argues that though a
"Filipino mentality" was formed out of Spanish influence, an identity
was not lost but gained as shown in the fact that the nationalist movement was formed not by the folk but ilustrados whose soul had been
"profoundly adulterated by European education."[220] As in the past Filipinos need not worry about "absolute assimilation" or loss of "soul."

IDEAS ON RACE and nation formation are part of Pardo's vision of modernity. Early on, Pardo adopts a racialist sketch of Philippine history in
which, in succession, indigenous Negritos were displaced by Indonesians, Malays, and then Spaniards, not to mention the Chinese, each
introducing into the country their distinctive ethos ("agricultural" Indonesians, "depredatory" Malays, "industrial-commercial" Chinese). He
goes on to stress, however, that racial inferiority is not an inherent or
natural condition but the result of conditions of physical isolation, political and religious dogmatism, and social heredity.

Pardo believes that in time racial boundaries have been blurred and
"race" has been subsumed under "nation." There is thus, he says, the
need to shift public discourse away from "race" to "nation."

We Filipinos should not continue our former error of speaking of our
race because there is no such Filipino race. Instead of that narrow,

false, and primitive conception, we should adopt a broader, more just, and more certain criterion of "people" or "nation." We are the result of the union and fusion of very different races; and although the Malay race enters in the combination to a great extent, yet the part played by the Chinese, the Japanese, and others, especially the Spanish race, is by no means small. We should not recall our origin because it will be of no avail in strengthening our union, which should be our objective. The idea of race has always been invoked among us in order to brand some men with inferiority and to attribute superiority to others. Our origin should not engage our attention, but rather our orientation, our future.[221]

Invoking Renan, he says that *nation* is a product of will, created by a "group of men who have the will to live together."

If we adopt, instead of the idea of race, the idea of "people and nation," which is more just and is more in harmony with reality, we place ourselves in a condition favorable to progress, because we shall always bear in mind that our interests should be to work in the domain of national convergence, not of divergence, which always results from the idea of race.

Pardo continues:

In order to live together, we must not unfurl the old flags of times past which were the emblems of tribes . . . we should not revive, but rather reject, the atavistic sentiments of divergence; and we should adopt national methods of convergence which would maintain our national solidarity and wipe out the elements of exclusivism and particularism.[222]

As Pardo subsumes race to nation so does he subordinate nation to "civilization." Pardo's view of historical process is of a unilinear, civilizational advance, with the Greek giving way to the Roman, and now to the Anglo-Saxon, which has become "the trustee and the dictator of the highest state of civilization."[223] Distinguishing between "civilization" and "state," Pardo says that the ascendancy of a civilization, like that of religion, need not translate into political or state domination. Political arrogance, in fact, causes a civilization's decline. To illustrate this point, Pardo recounts his encounter with the governor of Connecticut during his U.S. trip in 1904. Smarting at the governor's statement that the Anglo-Saxon race will rule the world, Pardo told the governor:

> I do not believe or hope that in the future the Anglo-Saxon race will dominate the world; my sentiments and convictions recoil at the notion of the absolute sway of any race over another. But I firmly believe that the Anglo-Saxon civilization will predominate in the world in the future, in the same way that the Latin civilization had its hour of ascendancy, as before this time, other civilizations had had their hour of world supremacy and splendor. The races that dominate others through the arbitrament of arms, stir up hate, protests, and antagonisms which pave the way for violence and continual use of force. I do not hope or desire the Anglo-Saxon race to provoke violent acts against itself by subjecting other nations: but I rather wish that it sow the seeds of its civilization among them,—that civilization which humanity, in its history, has commended into the hands of the Anglo-Saxon race as its trustee, so that the world may make use of it, without regard to race, as an object of the common weal—free as light, air, and water, to which all the world has a right.[224]

Reflecting Kant's vision of an evolution from barbarism to civil society to a "universal civic society" that transcends the rivalries of competing states, Pardo envisions a convergence of races, cultures, and nations in a "world civilization" under the rule of Reason. Imagining himself set above the ethnic and factional conflicts of the time, he states his personal conviction thus:

> I shall not, out of vanity, invoke the name of country in order to seek its support; but of something that is superior, is higher than country, which towers above all nations and which shall still live after countries shall have disappeared, when humanity as a unit shall reign supreme. That something is "reason."[225]

CONSTITUTING THE NATION

HE STOOD AT THE CENTER of Philippine political life at the beginning of the twentieth century. The foremost Filipino intellectual of the time, he was the leading interpreter of what the Philippines was and who the Filipinos were. Constructing the nation in a body of texts, he pioneered in the formation of a social science discourse on the Philippines.

When he died in 1925, colleagues and admirers paid tribute to his integrity and erudition. A Manila newspaper mourned his death as the passing of "an institution, a criterion, an epoch, in short, a man."[226] Yet, even in his most active years, he was a figure distanced and remote. He neither courted (as Pedro Paterno did) nor received (as did Rizal) public adulation. He was maligned or ignored for having embraced too openly a power many wished to avoid or hide.

PARDO WAS CAST in a certain "outsideness" by intersecting factors of race, class, education, personality, and politics. He defied easy classification. He was a *cuarteron*, three-fourths Spanish by blood, a *mestizo de español*, the offspring of a "fullblooded," Philippine-born Spaniard and a mestiza. Though Pardo referred to his mother as *Tagala*, Doña Juliana was part Tagalog, part European, and possibly part Chinese, since her own mother may have been a Chinese mestiza.[227] In status and appearance, he was more *español* than *mestizo* in the eyes of many. He was so European in his features, Juan Luna chose him as the model for the Spanish conquistador Miguel Lopez de Legazpi—counterpointing Rizal as Sikatuna—in *Pacto de Sangre*, Luna's recreation of one of the most symbolic scenes in Philippine history. As Rizal was the quintessential "Malay," Pardo was etched as the face of the white conqueror.

Yet, in race-conscious Manila, he was not quite a Spaniard either. Neither *limpios de sangre* ("of unblemished blood") nor Iberian-born (*peninsular*), he was a Spaniard born in the colony, a *criollo*, *hijo del país*, *insular*, or *español filipino*. While mestizos and creoles were not legally discriminated against in colonial Philippines (as shown in the professional success of the brothers Felix and Joaquin Pardo de Tavera), they did not quite have the political ascendancy and social cachet of peninsulares. This became an important distinction particularly after 1872 when matters of birth and race acquired distinct political overtones and many creoles became—in the eyes of the authorities and their own—*Filipinos*.

In the early nineteenth century, *Filipino* meant a Spaniard born in the Philippines. By the 1860s, however, the word was increasingly used by natives (*indios*), Chinese and Spanish mestizos, and creoles to identify themselves as members of an emerging, multiracial community politically set apart from Spanish peninsulares. The events of 1872 and their aftermath poisoned the atmosphere with suspicion, racism, and blatant acts of vindictiveness that polarized sectors in colonial society and sharpened the divide between *Filipinos* and Spaniards.

Yet, the Pardos were not quite of the country. In the eyes of indios, the *insular-peninsular* distinction was either not apparent or important. Both were *kastila*. It was not just a question of color. Spaniards and Spanish-mestizos constituted a thin overlay in local society. They never amounted to more than one percent of the population, set apart by status, lifestyle, and a history of racial and residential segregation. Even in Manila and its wards, populated by about 340,000 in 1896, Spaniards and Spanish mestizos constituted only three percent of the population.[228] The Pardos were of a professional, bureaucratic elite in the urban center. They led the sedentary existence of intellectuals isolated from the baser realities of common life. They were linked to the more "naturalized" and vigorously mercantile Gorricho family but it does not seem like they were deeply rooted in local social networks. They had the character of a small, closed family.

This aura of apartness was heightened by their émigré experience. Pardo lived in Paris from 1875 to 1894 (except for his two-year visit to the colony in 1887–1889) and again sojourned abroad in 1913–1918. European-educated, immersed in bookish knowledge, he wrote in Spanish and, later but sparsely, in English. It does not appear that he wrote anything in a local language. In the 1900s, his public reputation as an *americanista* and unapologetic advocate of *sajonismo* strengthened his image as someone not quite "one of us."

Neither was he considered "one of us" by either Spaniards or Americans. A Paris-educated creole, he dissociated himself from Spanish colonialist discourse on the Philippines, criticizing the works of Spanish authors like Vicente Barrantes and Wenceslao Retana for lapses in scientific method or clerical and racist bias. Retana responded in full measure by criticizing Pardo's *Biblioteca Filipina* "harshly, seemingly with a great deal of personal feeling" (James Robertson remarks). Retana called down Pardo for lapses in bibliographic practice and remarked that *Noticias sobre la imprenta* "does not contain one sure statement in regard to the origin of printing in the Philippines." Retana condescendingly calls him "a distinguished bibliophile," after distinguishing between a "bibliologist" (*bibliologo*, one who knows how to critically evaluate books), "bibliographer" (*bibliografo*, one who knows how to describe them), and "bibliophile" (*bibliofilo*, an "amateur or eccentric" who has some qualities of the preceding two).[229]

Pardo was tarred as an *hispanofobo*. In 1901, Pardo so incensed Manila Spaniards they gathered in a meeting in Casino Español to lambast him. Some reportedly threatened to kill him that, hearing about it, Pardo armed himself with a Colt revolver. Complaints lodged with the Spanish Consul called him a "traitor to Spain" and asked that he be stripped of his Spanish decorations. Harassed, he received in 1902, Pardo said, a communication from the Spanish Minister of State stripping him of civil and military honors he had received from Spain for having "insulted the Spanish Nation." Representations were also made by the

Spanish Consul with Taft not to have Pardo appointed to a government position as this would displease the Spanish King. In response, Pardo declared he was never anti-Spain, saying that while he had dissociated himself from being a Spaniard "politically," "my race and my surname" cannot be changed.[230]

Pardo was aware that Filipinos themselves did not quite embrace him as one of them. One notes Pardo addressing this difference when, in 1913, he lamented as pernicious the distinction made by some nationalists between so-called "Filipinos in face and at heart (*cara y corazon*)" and "Filipinos at heart alone."

> It is not within the power of man to change his race or his physical type; and nations should not be constituted according to the similarity of physical types, but by the community of sentiments, of aspirations, of ideals; . . . the sentiments, the aspirations, and the ideals of Filipinos, irrespective of the color of the skin and shape of the nose, or of the presence or absence of a beard, are identical: we all desire a Filipino nation, highly civilized, rich, independent, responsible and sovereign.[231]

Pardo appreciated his difference early. He was fifteen when Don Joaquin was exiled. He carried with him the unpleasant political realities of colonial life when he arrived in Paris in 1875. He could have turned away from the country and the past, practising a career in Europe (as the *deportado* Antonio Regidor did as a London-based solicitor, or, for that matter, the artists Juan Luna and Felix Resurreccion Hidalgo). He could have just stayed away, as his brother Felix did, who immigrated to Argentina and did not return to the Philippines. Felix became so disengaged from the country of his birth that, when the revolution broke out in 1896, he is reported to have expressed himself "opposed to emancipation."[232] And then there was the tragedy at Villa Dupont. What essentializing fantasies of the dark Other were released for the Pardos when Luna went amok?

Pardo's ties with the Philippines, however, remained firm. He married a Manileña and, more important, there was the largely unremarked influence of his mother, Doña Juliana, who, in Paris, remained, as Rizal noted, steadfastly "Filipina."

204

He also developed an abiding scholarly interest in the Philippines. In a time and place that gave great importance to the cultivation of the life of the mind, his turn to scholarship was not surprising. That, in the middle of his medical studies, he took up the study of language was not unusual. Physicians at the time (like other scientists) pursued diverse interests, like geology, anthropology, and linguistics. Yet, the fact that he chose to investigate ancient Filipino writing systems begs for an explanation. It is told that he was inspired to go into Philippine studies after being repeatedly asked by classmates about his home country, but this does not seem to be sufficient explanation. His uncle was obviously an influence. Joaquin was immersed in Philippine affairs and Trinidad inherited his uncle's library and interests.

Ferdinand Blumentritt was an influence as well. (A relatively obscure European scholar, Blumentritt, because of his personal qualities as much as his scholarship, was an important influence on the first generation of modern Filipino intellectuals.) Pardo began corresponding with Blumentritt at the end of 1882 when he was just starting out in his studies and in 1885 visited Blumentritt in Leitmeritz, Bohemia, spending ten days "completely dedicated to conversing with him on Philippine matters." They would from that time on exchange notes and publications, even collaborating, sometime in 1891–1893, on an unfinished project for a multivolume ethnographic dictionary of the Philippines.[233] Blumentritt may have been instrumental as well—as he was with Rizal—in introducing Pardo to European scholars like Rudolf Virchow and Fedor Jagor.

Embarked on his studies, Pardo came to be increasingly enmeshed in the *pais*.

HE IS A CURIOUS FIGURE in the Propaganda Movement, the "movement" considered the primary vehicle in creating Filipino national consciousness in the nineteenth century. Historians like John Schumacher place Pardo at the margins of the movement.

Pardo's work on ancient alphabets is credited by Rizal with having inspired his interest in developing an *escritura nacional* by reforming Tagalog spelling on the basis of Tagalog's phonetic character rather than Spanish orthography. Rizal adopted the letter *k* in his translation of *Wilhelm Tell* and wrote about the new orthography in *La Solidaridad* in

April 1890. Rizal's example was followed by others and sparked an acrimonious response from Manila's Spanish press charging that the new system was anti-Hispanic and its proponents were out to "Germanize Tagalog." That reforming orthography could be imagined as a subversive project reveals the heated political climate of the day.[234]

Schumacher notes that "curiously enough" Pardo did not practice his own views when he published a medical pamphlet in Tagalog translation in 1895 (even as Schumacher acknowledges that Pardo was not the translator). He concludes that, unlike Rizal, Pardo's advocacy was "purely philological" rather than "nationalist." Schumacher writes: "It may well be that Pardo de Tavera deliberately refrained from using his own orthographic system . . . because it had taken on a nationalist connotation, and Pardo was very careful not to be publicly associated with the Filipino nationalists up to 1896, though privately on friendly terms."[235]

In fact it was Pardo who stirred debate in the Philippines when (taking up a proposal he made in *Contribucion para el estudio de los antiguos alfabetos filipinos* in 1884) he contributed the articles "*Ortografía del Tagalog*," *Diario de Manila* (August 5, 1888), and "*Una opinion filologica*," *La España Oriental* (November 7, 1889), in which he called for changes in orthography—specifically, the use of *k* and *w* instead of *c* and *u*—to conform to the proper *fisonomia* of the language. He justified the changes on the grounds of simplicity, comprehensibility, and propriety. The proposals were endorsed by some but mostly sparked an adverse response from the Manila press, notably *Revista Catolica de Filipinas,* mocking the *filologo* and *Orientalista* for presumptuousness. Defenders of the old orthography presented themselves as the "true" Tagalogs and attacked the proposals of Pardo and the *Orientalistas* as "German"-inspired.[236]

The response must have surprised Pardo who clearly meant his piece on orthography to be a practical and scholarly contribution. Yet, Pardo was not isolated from Filipino reformist currents. He knew the leading propagandists, subscribed to *Solidaridad,* and read the works of Rizal, Paterno, and M.H. del Pilar. Filipino propagandists, in turn, were aware of his writings. He promised Rizal he would contribute scientific articles to *Solidaridad* though it appears that his only contribution was an article in the issue of March 31, 1891, under the pseudonym *Barbilampino,* which ridiculed the racism of Spaniards who are backward in their own country but take on superior airs in the Philippines.[237] The article does not seem characteristic of Pardo but the attribution is plausible since this was written after Pardo's difficult sojourn in Manila.

The Pardo home in Paris was a Filipino haven in a foreign land. Pardo's mother, Doña Juliana, carried the Philippines with her to Paris. She set a Filipino-Hispanic table, collected recipes from Filipino friends (even ordered foods from Manila), and hosted émigrés like Rizal, Paterno, and others.[238] Rizal wrote about these gatherings:

> The Pardo family who live here also invite me to eat at their home from time to time. Then Luna, Resurreccion and I go there. On such days we do nothing else but talk about our country—its likes, food, customs, etc. The family is very amiable. The mother (widow) is a sister of Gorricho and remains very Filipino in everything. Her sons Trinidad and Felix Pardo are both physicians; her daughter Paz speaks French and English and she is very amiable and also very Filipino. She dresses with much elegance and in her movements and manner of looking she . . . is beautiful and svelte.[239]

In later years, Pardo would speak with great admiration for Rizal. (It was Pardo's suggestion that led to the renaming of the combined districts of Manila and Morong as "Rizal Province" in 1901.[240]) Of his personal acquaintance with the hero, he said, "we were united by the ties of sincere friendship and affection."[241] Socially and politically, however, Pardo's relation to Rizal and the propagandists was reserved, if not distant.

In judging how Pardo located himself in relation to the nationalist movement, we need to look into his writings. E. Arsenio Manuel offers a sympathetic view:

> The value of his contributions to propaganda work has yet to be studied fully from other angles in order to appreciate the history of that movement. Besides, he was of a different temperament; he did not have a "political" mind. . . .
> Without posing as a Filipino, his studies threw much light on the culture of the early Filipinos which many Spanish ethnocentric

writers and colonialists at home and abroad tried in any way they could to mitigate or disparage. Pardo de Tavera therefore lent, though his contemporaries were scarcely aware of it, substance to the assertions of the propagandists and hence prestige even unto Rizal's political writings.[242]

On the contrary, Pardo's contemporaries were not unaware of his works and Pardo did position himself as a *Filipino*. He did not use the word in its early sense as *español Filipino* but the late-nineteenth-century sense of belonging to a community wider than just creoles. In *Contribucion para el estudio de los antiguos alfabetos Filipinos* (1884), he used the word *Filipino* to mean not just creoles and mestizos but the inhabitants of the archipelago. In the preface to *Plantas medicinales* (1892), he referred to the Philippines as *mi pais* ("my country").[243] Adopting an 'objective' tone and approach, he distanced himself from the views of Spanish authors. While he did not foreground his self-definition as Filipino this can be deduced from the stance he took.

Though he worked at the margins of the Propaganda Movement, Pardo enunciated ideas that coincided with arguments Filipino propagandists were making about the history and culture of the Philippines.

His early writings on language have the character of academic exercises in philology, based on his training in Sanskrit and Malayo-Polynesian languages. Aspiring to the status of empirically-based scientific investigations, they did not have the extravagant theorizing ambition of Paterno's works or the overtly political bent of Rizal's writings on language. Yet his works developed themes similar to those expressed by Paterno and Rizal. This is occasioned by how he defines his object and how he locates himself in relation to it. He objectifies the Philippines—albeit an underdefined *pais*—as an intellectually discrete field, one that can be bounded off from, say, Hindu or other Malayo-Polynesian cultures. Using the tools of European linguistic science, and writing from Paris, he nevertheless takes the stance (even if not quite explicit) of someone speaking from "inside" the *pais*.

In his study of precolonial syllabaries, which he groups under the name *alfabetos filipinos*, he laments how many writers about the archipelago have ignored or neglected the fact that the art of writing was practiced by its precolonial inhabitants. He dissociates himself from the misrepresentations of earlier, mostly Spanish missionary writers on local syllabaries. He argues for a basic unity in writing systems in the archipelago. By demonstrating that these systems have a "proper" and "logical" form, he shows the failure of earlier commentators to attend to indigenous scripts in their own terms. He contests judgments on the crudity of local syllabaries by showing that these are occasioned by the failure to account for phonological differences or the local mode of reading lexicographic signs. He gives native culture a deep and reputable history by embedding local practice in a web of filiations with Indian and Malayo-Polynesian culture-worlds.

The same themes underlie *Sanscrito en la lengua Tagalog* and *Consideraciones sobre el origen del nombre de los numeros* where he shows the affinities of Tagalog with other Asian languages, particularly Sanskrit, and corrects Spanish orthographic rendering of Tagalog where this violates what he calls the "physiognomy" (*fisonomia*) of local words. Invoking Remusat's dictum that language is a faithful mirror (*espejo mas fiel*) of a civilization, Pardo puts forth an argument expressed by the propagandists by constructing a Philippine cultural history that evolves from an indigenous base through successive periods of Hindu, Islamic, and Euro-Christian influences. Like Paterno, he posits a stage of Hinduization deeper than was conceded in colonial accounts.

However, Pardo tried to stay close to the ground of empirical evidence, arguing for a Hindu period in Philippine history through a close examination of similarities between Indian and Philippine scripts and detailed etymologies of local lexis. He was contemptuous of Paterno's extrapolations and lamented the deleterious influence of these exaggerations. Paterno, he said in 1899, made "the natives to believe that a civilization had existed here in former times, similar to the civilization which had once existed in India, and also similar to the civilization which existed in Mexico among the Aztecs and Incas before the Spaniards went there."[244]

While politically diffident, Pardo's scholarly studies impressed Rizal and the propagandists. On August 22, 1886, Rizal wrote to Blumentritt that "my learned and talented friend Dr. T.P. de Tavera (who) has excelled himself in his exposition and has given me a pleasant surprise."[245] Rizal found *Sanscrito en la lengua Tagalog* "very interesting," a "charming little book which interests me greatly." While he had reservations about

Pardo's knowledge of Tagalog, he expressed envy for Pardo's competence in Sanskrit. "If I knew as much Sanskrit as he does, I could perhaps discover more Sanskrit words in our language than he, because he does not know much Tagalog."[246] In particular, Rizal found Pardo's work useful support for his plan to develop a "national orthography" by reforming Castilian practice in writing the local languages.

While Pardo distanced himself from the political agenda of the Propaganda Movement, he had no sympathy for the metropolitan posturing of Paterno in Madrid. While Paterno devoutly wished to be a Spaniard, Pardo—for reasons of blood and memory—could not quite feel himself to be one. At the same time, his genealogical roots in the land of his birth were too shallow for him to be possessed by it, as Rizal was, or imagine possessing it, as Paterno did. Circumstance, intellection, and sentiment bound him to the Philippines but a sense of outsideness stayed with him to the end.

POSTREVOLUTIONARY FRANCE shaped Pardo's scholarly interests and political sympathies. In the years of the Third Republic an ascendant bourgeoisie rejected the *ancien regime*, professed belief in the democratic ideal of "sovereignty of the people," but stayed wary of the socialist and more radical strands of the French revolutionary tradition. As David Thomson writes of French democrats at the time:

> They were against monarchy, against clericalism, against Bonapartism, against too powerful an executive. They were for the ideals of 1789—for Liberty, Equality, Fraternity and the sovereignty of the People. But they remained puzzled as to how these great ideals might best be reduced to terms of practical politics and embodied in the actual machinery of government.[247]

Having experienced a profound upheaval, French intellectuals were challenged by the need to orient human life to a new environment, consolidate changes already effected, and carry them still further. A sense of experiment was anchored in a firm belief in the governing power of Reason and a confidence in French civilization as expressed in the national language, a national system of education, the generous extension of citizenship, and the national prestige accorded to scientists and artists. This highminded vision of the nation did not quite account for radical undercurrents in nineteenth-century France: its legacy of political violence, the discontent of a growing proletariat, and the specter of French imperialism in the world. But as Thomson remarks, "To identify nationalism with rationalism is characteristically French."[248]

Pardo imbibed this imperial rationalism. His introduction to the Enlightenment came early since his uncle was a well-read liberal and Santo Tomas in Manila, where he began his university studies, was not (as Pardo and Filipino liberals would later depict) entirely cocooned in the Middle Ages. (It had, for one, Sorbonne-educated doctors in its medical faculty). In Paris, however, Pardo was in the center of the Enlightenment. The Paris Faculty of Medicine, where he studied, was at the cutting edge of medical science, innovating in the practice of dissection and hospital-based methods of instruction. Beyond this, the physicians in the faculty were active public figures in promoting science as a way to solving society's problems.

Paris was also a nexus of Orientalist scholarship that attracted students from elsewhere in Europe and the world. *Ecole nationale des langues orientales vivantes*, where Pardo studied Malay and Sanskrit, was formally established in 1795 (though it apparently already existed as of 1769) in response to the interest in the study of such languages as Arabic, Turkish, and Persian, particularly in the wake of Napoleon's Oriental expedition. The French philologist Silvestre de Sacy, the school's first teacher of Arabic and director in 1824, was the first president of the *Societe asiatique* when it was founded in 1822. Author of *Principes de grammaire generale* (1799), he was indefatigable in knowledge-building through translation, annotation, codification, and archiving. With Ernest Renan, he was a key figure in the formation of Orientalism as a scholarly discipline.[249]

At *Ecole* the course in Malay (initially also Javanese) existed uninterruptedly since 1841 and became official in 1844.[250] Pardo's teacher, Pierre Favre, was a pioneering scholar of Malay languages, author of *Dictionnaire Malais-Francais* (1875), *Grammaire de langue malaise* (1876), and *Dictionnaire Francais-Malais* (1880). A French missionary who had spent time in Indochina and the Malay archipelago (including a visit to Manila), he taught Malay and Javanese at *Ecole*. Filipino expatriates were not isolated from the currents of French Orientalist scholarship. Around 1890, upon Pardo's invitation, Rizal attended the lectures of the linguist Aristide Marre at *Ecole.*

In Paris, the Pardo brothers, Juan Luna, and Rizal also had contact with such scholars on the Philippines as Jean Mallat and Fedor Jagor (a guest at a dinner hosted by the Pardos).[251]

Pardo's turn to the study of languages was in the spirit of the times. Called philology, it was a veritable science of humanity, a way towards understanding human history through a method of establishing origins, families, and hierarchies of cultures and societies. (It was so expansive in scope, Renan and Nietzche considered themselves philologists.) In Paris and elsewhere, there was much interest in Oriental languages, particularly Sanskrit, which many believed superior to Greek and Latin and a key to understanding older civilizations. It was in this context that Pardo turned to the study of language, producing his monographs on indigenous alphabets, etymology, and Sanskrit influence.

Pardo, however, did not aim to be a professional linguist; he also wrote on medicine, botany (a standard subject in medical education until about 1900), cartography, history, and politics. It was society and culture that interested him. He did not publish much on medicine, but when he did he was more interested in its "anthropological" rather than clinical aspects. Like Rizal, he was a believer in the great human and social benefit of modern medicine and, again like Rizal, much of the "medical authority" that came from this knowledge permeated his thinking about society itself.

The "medical authority" exercised by Pardo and Rizal is not to be conflated with the arrogant triumphalism of, say, Victor Heiser (the American chief of the Bureau of Health in 1905–1915) who said upon arriving in the Philippines, "I set myself the goal of trying to save fifty thousand lives a year," and declared that the goal of the U.S. health program was "to transform the Filipinos from the weak and feeble race they were into the strong, healthy, and enduring people that they might become."[252] The stance taken by Pardo and Rizal is better described by Terry Eagleton who, in explaining the prominent role played by physicians in Irish nationalism, wrote that medicine was "the most humane and socially minded of the hard sciences, a link between scholarly research and human welfare, and thus peculiarly suited to an intelligentsia which had brains and a social conscience in equal measure." "Like antiquarianism," he added, "medicine forms a connection between science and society, as the physician combines erudition with worldliness."[253]

While Pardo criticized superstitions and quackery (as did Rizal), he was not insensitive to pluralist, culturally specific, folk-based views of medicine. He staunchly advocated the regulation and professionalization of medicine yet was cognizant of the value of "pre-scientific" knowledge and practices (as in his comments on herbalists, *cagao*, and the virtues of traditional massage or *hilot*). He distinguished between folk knowledge and popular quackery, blaming some of the latter on Spanish authors of popular medicine (as did Isabelo de los Reyes in his work on Philippine superstitions). Pardo, however, wrote little on this subject and did not develop his ideas on the relationship between modern and folk medicine at length.

This is true as well of his studies on language. In his "pre-American" studies, he began to trace the beginnings of a "national philology" by pointing to a definably integral body of *Filipino* writing and languages and locating it in relation to other language and writing systems. Citing the Spanish-colonial misuse and misrepresentation of local languages, he initiated the debate on orthographic reform though he left it to others to carry this forward. His interest was more academic than political. After 1900, he would urge the study of local languages as an *object* of science, but advocate the use of English as medium of government and education for pragmatic and ideological reasons.

Though Pardo enjoyed faculty appointments in medicine and linguistics, he was a "free-floating" intellectual rather than an academic. Some of his works were commissioned but, mostly, he wrote on subjects according to the occasion and his personal interests. He was, in the end, interested in a country rather than a discipline.

PARDO VIEWED the Philippines from the vantage point of Western science. Like Rizal and Paterno, he moved easily in the world of European scholarship. He was a member or delegate of learned societies, such as Berlin's Anthropological Society, the Hague's Royal Institute of the Netherlands Indies, and Spanish royal academies of History, Languages, Science, Hygiene, and Economics. He received honors from *Real Academica de Medicina de Madrid* and the *Real Orden Militar de Carlos III* and *Cristo de Portugal*. He was a correspondent of the French *Societe*

Academique Indo-Chinoise, a society inspired in the 1870s by Anglo-French imperial rivalry and France's desire to turn Indochina into its own "India."[254]

As a student of languages, Pardo read works by such seminal figures as Wilhelm von Humboldt (1767–1835), Abel de Remusat (1788–1832), and Eugene Burnouf (1801–1852). Professors at College de France, Remusat and Burnouf published on Oriental languages and influenced the rise of linguistic science. Pardo worked at the British Museum in 1879 and 1891 when he attended a "Congress of Orientalists" in London. He communicated with the Dutch scholars Hendrik Kern and J.L.A. Brandes and the Germans Rudolf Virchow and Fedor Jagor. He corresponded with Blumentritt, to whom he dedicated his first book, *Contribucion para el estudio de los antiguos alfabetos Filipinos* (1884), and who in turn dedicated his *Vocabular* (1885) to Pardo. He appraised Blumentritt of Rizal as "a man of extraordinary talent" before the Austrian came to know Rizal personally.[255]

Pardo immersed himself in primary sources on the Philippines, meticulously examining *vocabularios* produced by Spanish missionaries, like Diego Bergano, Domingo de los Santos, and Andres Carro, as well as texts on subjects like botany and medicine. Like Rizal, he read comparatively, exploring sources on Malay and other Asian cultures, such as the works of von Humboldt, Theodor Waitz, H.N. van der Tuuk, William Marsden, John Crawfurd, and John Leyden. Among the projects he pursued in Paris upon his return from Manila in 1889 was a Spanish translation of the famous Malay chronicle, *Makota Radja-radja*, and on his trip to London in 1891 he took time to study Malay chronicles in the British Museum. Blumentritt is reported to have said that Rizal and Pardo were "the only learned scholars of *Malaysia* produced by Spain."[256]

His intellectual interests are indicated by his extant personal library, with its eclectic collection of Spanish, French, and English titles, not to mention works in Philippine languages.[257] Literary titles include works by Spanish (Benito Perez Galdos, Pio Baroja, Vicente Blasco Ibañez), French (Balzac, Anatole France, Edmond de Goncourt), Russian (Dostoevski, Chekhov, Gorki), and Anglo-American authors (Ralph Waldo Emerson, O. Henry). The library is heavy in the sciences, from classic Orientalist texts like Jean Francois Champollion's *Precis du systeme hieroglyphique* (1827) and Emile Burnouf's *Methode pour etudier la langue sanscrite* (1885) to works by Armand de Quatrefages, Gabriel de Mortillet, and Gustave Le Bon. Volumes of Renan, Montesquieu, Taine, Marx, and Nietzsche formed part of his library.

Pardo was immersed in evolutionist theories. His personal library does not only include French editions of Darwin's *Origin of the Species* (1859) and *Descent of Man* (1871) but such texts as British economist Walter Bagehot's *Lois scientifiques du developpement des nations* (possibly a translation of *Physics and Politics*, 1869) and the American scientist John William Draper's *History of the Intellectual Development of Europe* (1862).

Immanuel Kant, Auguste Comte, and Ernest Renan, whose ideas dominated French intellectual life when Pardo was in Paris, stimulated Pardo with the possibilities of rebuilding society and culture on a scientific basis. They inspired Pardo's earnest rationalism, political elitism, and individualistic liberalism. Renan, in stressing the ascendancy of science and reason, accepted the pragmatics of the rule of advanced nations over the less developed ones and favored an aristocracy of intelligence that protects and guides the masses. In Kant as in Pardo one finds the conviction that individual self-mastery is the essence of man, reason is the source of morality, morality is the work of freedom, and republicanism increases the scope of this freedom. Pardo's hatred of all exclusiveness and privilege based on mere tradition as well as antipathy to disordered enthusiasm and emotionalism are Kantian. Kant warned that unless ways of thinking are reformed a revolution will only replace an old despotism with a new one by feeding on "the great unthinking masses." Kant's famous declaration of Enlightenment faith might as well be Pardo's:

> Enlightenment is man's release from his self-incurred tutelage. Tutelage is man's inability to make use of his understanding without direction from another. Self-incurred is this tutelage when its cause lies not in lack of reason but in lack of resolution and courage to use it without direction from another. *Sapere aude*! "Have courage to use your own reason!"—that is the motto of enlightenment.[258]

Nineteenth-century positivism influenced Pardo's intellectual formation. Writing on Philippine society, he works out of the sociological tradition of Henri de Saint-Simon, Auguste Comte, and Herbert Spencer, with its positivism (belief in scientific explanations and invariant laws in the social and natural world); "organismic" view of society (that social change everywhere goes through the same sequence and that all the elements of society change together); and conviction that industrialism and *laissez-faire* economics herald a new era in which humanity would advance under the guidance of science and reason. Like Saint-Simon, Pardo preaches the gospel of productivity and privileges such types as industrialists and bankers as the natural leaders of society. His theory of Philippine history adopts Comte's ideas on society's evolution from a "theological-military" to a "positivistic-industrial" stage, as well as Spencer's two main types of society, the "militant" (coercive, warlike, autocratic, theocratic) and the "industrial" (voluntaristic, meritocratic, market-oriented, democratic).

Theodor Adorno has remarked that "late-comers and newcomers have an alarming affinity for positivism," exhibiting an "unimaginative, indolent taste for everything proven, and for the successes of the West." Warning against the appetite of "late-coming" non-Western intellectuals for the new, radical theories of the West, he says: "One must have tradition in oneself, to hate it properly."[259] Though meant to provoke, the remarks are distinctly condescending nevertheless.

While the lines of influence in Pardo's case are clear it is misleading and reductive to dismiss his discourse as simply "derivative." To do so is to suggest that there was a meaningful choice (in terms of an alternative, indigenous intellectual archive) or that a creole like Pardo considered himself other than a natural heir to the ideas he harnessed. It is more important to consider why or how these ideas were selected, interpreted, and applied. "Influence" is a tricky problem: it is best looked at from the point of reception rather than the point of origin. It is from this vantage point that monoliths like "Enlightenment" or "Social Darwinism" are broken down and pluralized and their temporal order rearranged such that distinctions between, say, "Enlightenment" and "Post-Enlightenment" are blurred and what are not synchronic in the chronologies of their origin, occupy, at the point of reception, simultaneous existence.

British social philosopher Herbert Spencer (1820–1903) was a major influence.[260] (Pardo had seven volumes of Spencer's works in his library, including the four-volume *Principles of Sociology* [1873–1885].) Now little regarded, Spencer was popular among intellectuals in Asia and Latin America for his synthesis of the scientific movement sweeping the late nineteenth century. His vision of competition and progress appealed to a newly self-conscious bourgeoisie empowered in its role of "directing element" in society as well as distrustful of an interventionist state. For those besieged and perplexed by dramatic social and economic changes, Spencerian philosophy gave the reassurance of a stable, underlying explanation. In a case like the Philippines, where colonial intellectuals saw monastic obscurantism as the primary obstacle to progress, positivism was a powerful weapon.

Speaking of Mexico's experience, Octavio Paz attacked positivism as a philosophy destined to justify the prevailing social order, embraced not, as in Europe, by industrialists and businessmen but by heirs to colonial feudalism. "Positivism offered the social hierarchies a new justification. Inequalities were now explained, not by race or inheritance or religion, but by science." Furthermore, by ignoring that part of human nature expressed in myths, festivals, and dreams, Mexican intellectuals embraced "a philosophy whose beauty was exact, sterile and, in the long run, empty." In negating what was represented by myth and religion, the positivists founded Mexico on "a general notion of man, rather than on the actual situation of our people, sacrificed reality to words and delivered us up to the ravenous appetites of the strong." "In breaking its ties with the past, it also broke its ties with Mexican realities."[261] Much of this rings true of Pardo's advocacies as well.

Yet, theories are multivalent and can be adapted to a wide range of ideological stances. Spencerian philosophy had to find (or lose) its way in specific national contexts. Kant, though he remained an individualist, can be "unfamiliar source of nationalism" (Isaiah Berlin points out) since his notion of the individual's moral autonomy can be transformed into "the notion of the moral autonomy of the nation."[262] Thinking in a *national* context, Pardo tried to apply Kantian principles to the needs of his country's social transformation, placed more trust in the emancipative value of education than did Spencer, and had late doubts whether, indeed, as Comte believed, the outcomes of social change are inevitable and benevolent. Theory biased Pardo's understanding of Philippine realities. In his views on education, the economy, and U.S. rule, he glossed over inequalities of opportunity and power and was naively optimistic about the liberating effects of industrialism, a free-enterprise market economy, and American altruism. Yet, he revealed as well the serious intellectual's readiness to think things through.

THE U.S. OCCUPATION marked an important qualitative change in Pardo's writings. The inhibited, covert critic of Spanish colonialism became "legislator" of a new order. American rule opened space for Pardo to move from the margin to the center of Philippine intellectual life. With Rizal's death and Paterno's fall from grace, he was the country's leading public intellectual. As participant in the American project of objectifying the Philippines, he helped create for Filipinos a vision of their country and themselves.

He produced texts that investigated, classified, and "officialized" the names of "races" and places in the archipelago. He helped build an archive of knowledge on the Philippines and its inhabitants. He was the first Filipino to write an official "national" history of the Philippines. In *Reseña Historica de Filipinas*, he organizes the Filipino past into a coherent, evolutionary national narrative. Pardo projects a pre-Hispanic past with a distinct and definable character, freely using the word *Filipino* to refer to cultural complexes that made for a "national" religion, alphabet, and forms of social and political organization. He traces the disabling as well as enabling influence of Spanish colonialism in the formation of a "national" spirit that would result, in the late nineteenth century, in an elite-led independence movement. He frames U.S. colonial rule as a culmination of earlier developments and auspicious prelude to full modernity.

Other Filipino intellectuals—like Felipe Calderon, Rafael Palma, and Teodoro Kalaw—experienced the American period as a bracing time of experiment and possibility. Pardo expressed the sentiment of many that the U.S. order was an opportunity for Filipinos to break away from the stultifying "structures of the past" and create themselves anew. "We must construct," Pardo wrote, "a new national edifice," and "extricate ourselves from the limited circle in which our reason and mind have been confined."[263] In lectures, articles, and interviews, he devoted himself to the task of intellectually constituting a new nation. The central need, he said, was the transformation of Filipino mentality along the lines of Western science. This was the key to progress and its chief instruments were the educational and economic policies the Americans introduced.

No Filipino of his time spoke of the country—its past, present, and future—on the basis of a social philosophy as explicitly articulated. His position on politics, education, and international relations was always an *intellectual* position, arising out of systematic premises about human nature and social-historical process. While he assumes the universal laws of "Social Darwinism" (the phrase itself does not appear in Pardo), he was less interested in the ideas themselves as in their *practice*, deploying them in current debates on what was to be done in the Philippines. It was this engagement that led Epifanio de los Santos to call him "a practical artist" (*un artista practico*). Pardo himself is reported to have said on the day before he died: "Of all Filipinos I am the most Filipino. All my writings are for the interest, improvement and progress of the Filipino people. They are writings which could not be of any interest to the French, Germans, Japanese or any foreigners."[264]

The country's most ardent evangelist of modernity, he was the *bete noir* of the Catholic Church. He criticized the missionary legacy and opposed the teaching of religion in public schools, arguing that the state should not be partial to one religion and teaching religion interfered with the "scientific character" of education. Religion is a discipline "sentimental, essentially conservative and traditional" while science is "rational and purely innovative and progressive." If it is to be taught in the university at all it should be taught as a subject in the "history of religions."[265] His opposition to religious instruction drew a scathing attack from the U.S.-educated Cebuano priest Jose Ma. Cuenco who called him senile, intolerant, and more (*maquiavelo filipino, doctor federal, bolsevik*).[266] Cuenco accused Pardo of "a villainous assassination of History" for negating the positive contributions of Catholicism and suggesting that monastic domination occasioned immorality and that there was no difference between native superstition and Catholic beliefs.

Pardo's *Reseña Historica de Filipinas* was condemned in a series of articles attributed to the Dominican Serapio Tamayo, published in the Catholic periodical *Libertas* and as the book *Sobre una "Reseña Historica de Filipinas"* (1906).[267] Mixing sarcasm and ridicule, the reviewer calls Pardo a "mediocre intelligence" who surrounds himself with the *aureola de filipinologo* and makes "oracular" pronouncements on matters in which he lacks the competence. Pretending to be "encyclopedic" in his learning, Pardo is a pretender to all kinds of knowledge and a master of none:

Pardo de Tavera studied to be a physician; wrote of Botany, dabbled in Philology, meddled in Politics, metamorphosed as Solon, and finally presented himself to us in the guise of a Suetonius. What does it all amount to since the pretentious doctor is not a Suetonius in History, nor Solon in legislation, nor Bismarck in Politics, nor Max Muller in Philology, nor De Candolle in Botany, nor Pasteur in Medicine? In a word: *nihil in toto et totus in cunctis.*[268]

Pardo, the reviewer says, caricatures the friars as "enemies of Science" and colonial education as one that "condemns all modern ideas," while ignoring the Church's contribution in advancing science and progress in the world, as shown in the founding of universities, libraries, science laboratories, and natural history museums. Did not Pardo himself use these libraries and cite Dominican authors like Manuel Blanco and Antonio Llanos in his *Plantas medicinales*? Did not Universidad de Santo Tomas garner honors for its educational work in various international expositions?

While the reviewer raises valid criticism against Pardo's reductive treatment of the Church, he is inquisitorial in defining the root of Pardo's errors: French Encyclopedism and Freemasonry, "Luciferian" atheism, and misguided devotion to a dogmatic cult of Reason that rejects supernaturalism and divine revelation. Saying that this cult has raised up theories, "such as Darwinism," which have already been discarded by reputable scholars, he admonishes Pardo with a quote from Roger Bacon that "a little philosophy alienates a person from religion but much conduces one to it."[269]

Pardo's ideas were not generated in a vacuum but interventions in a public debate. Early twentieth-century nationalism was shaped by diverse impulses. While there was general acceptance of the reality of U.S. rule, there were unresolved tensions bred of the revolution and the anti-American war, as manifested in pockets of continuing, armed resistance. Rapid Westernization stoked anxieties over the loss of familiar frames of reference. Fears were expressed that the "Saxonization" of culture and education was eroding nationalism and native virtues. The Catholic Church criticized the secularization of education. Literary writers opposed the promotion of English and turned towards the "native tradition" as a medium of nationalism and defense against Americanization.

The question of how the nation should position itself vis-à-vis American rule was the subject of a running debate between the "pro-independence" *El Renacimiento* and Pardo's *La Democracia* in which the *americanistas* were attacked as "renegades" and "opportunists" and the *nacionalistas* were called "dreamers" and "foolish theorists."[270] "Nationalism" was powerful tender among politicians. While they actively collaborated with the Americans, they recognized the value of being *Filipinists*, of maintaining the appearance of autonomy and distance from the imperial power. Pardo did not play this game. He did not disguise his admiration for the United States and completely trusted in the American "sense of justice." Pardo's unapologetic defense of Americanization did not endear him to the nationalists of the time, or long after.

Pardo was impatient with the posturings of "nationalist" politicians and "sentimental" patriots. Their politics, he says, distracts people from resolutely attending to pressing social issues: "in our society there exists true tyranny, a dominating influence; namely, politics enthroned."[271] He attacks self-proclaimed patriots who call for a "policy of conservation" in the guise of preserving the "national soul." What they call the Filipino *soul* is not indigenous but "a completely foreign mentality" transmitted to a small portion of the population through Spanish education. Cultivating what we call our own that which is not our own, he says, will only result in stagnation and retrogression.

Pardo was not against the development of a "peculiar type of civilization." He was against nativism, interpreting it as a return to "primitivism." On the other hand, he validly questioned the claim to an ill-specified "Filipino" culture, arguing that what the nationalists sought to conserve was in fact an Hispanic-colonial culture that needed to be renovated if the country were to modernize. We should instead foster "another Filipino soul," latent in the Filipino, a "genuine Filipino soul which lives in our masses" and can be awakened through modern education and the promotion of civic virtues.[272] What is needed is a "scientific patriotism" guided by reason and the imperatives of progress.

Pardo is less than clear, however, on the problem of culture formation. On one hand, he believes in the emergence of a "true civilization" founded on reason, one that has "no racial, national, or artificial boundaries." On the other hand, he maintains that a "Filipino character" will persist and remain, by which he means a people's "moral nature," the "domain of sentiment" which, he says, is "so difficult to transform that it is considered sometimes immutable." Man's moral nature will remain though it manifests itself differently in history. He illustrates this by citing the people's desire for independence, which has remained though it has evolved in orientation from the "feudalistic" (when it was expressed through the people's loyalty to their barangays and local chiefs) to the "nationalistic" (with the emergence of Filipino nationality), and then the more modern and "universal" form of the present.

There is no such thing as absolute assimilation, he says. The "imitation" of other nations is part of the process by which a nation develops its own culture (*cultura propia, inteligencia agena*). A plant transferred to another environment "acquires peculiar traits that give it its peculiar, individual physiognomy without losing the features of its family type."[273] Progress, Pardo says, "does not consist in destruction: it is nothing but a process of acquiring new ideas, of rectifying errors, of changing forms."[274]

An interesting counterpoint to Pardo is the case of Teodoro Kalaw, an intellectual who came of age during the U.S. occupation. Called the "champion of an independent Filipinism," Kalaw argued that Filipinos cannot adopt an American "mentality" but must develop their own under a democracy.[275] He advocated the adoption of Tagalog as national language as early as 1907. He did not think that speaking many languages was a bar to national unity nor did he believe that such forms as the *corrido* or *moro-moro* were devoid of value. In the pages of *Renacimiento*, which he edited from 1907 to 1909, Kalaw tried to instill pride in local culture and, as a writer puts it, "succeeded in extracting from the very roots of tradition and the soul of the race valuable lessons of individual and national discipline."[276] Perhaps more than anyone, Kalaw was responsible for interpreting for the new generation the country's revolutionary past, writing its history, exalting its theories and spirit, creating the public significance of men like Bonifacio, Jacinto, and Mabini.

The difference between Pardo and Kalaw, however, was not as great as it seemed. Kalaw also actively participated in the U.S.-led government. Like cohorts Rafael Palma and Camilo Osias, Kalaw was not a nativist. He stressed the "prudent adaptation," "eclectic selection," and "intelligent assimilation of foreign ideas," saying: "our ambition is to conserve the best of our virtues and to get the best of foreign virtues, in order to create a nation more excellent, which is the aim and essence of true nationalism."[277] The difference is that Pardo, less "sentimental" about the past, sought to hurry the nation into the future, Kalaw wanted it grounded in the past—at least, in both cases, their visions of what this future or past was.

PARDO PICTURED the Philippine cultural situation in broad brushstrokes. His speeches and journalistic pieces were done in a polemical mode, sallies in a public debate where illocutionary force was often prized over scholarly refinement. Pardo confessed as much when he said, anticipating objections to his sympathetic view of Japan as a model for the Philippines, that if he is one-sided it is because "her defects do not interest me; these affect only the Japanese who should discover them in order to correct them."

> For the same reason, I have not wasted my time looking for the defects of the Americans; what interests me is to discover our own defects in order to correct them and to observe those qualities which have enabled other peoples to progress, which have formed free, rich, and powerful nations, because by following their courses and imitating their qualities and conduct, it seems to me evident that we will attain the same methods and virtues that they themselves have attained.[278]

He reduces the components of Philippine cultural history into such Orientalizing essentializations as the "agricultural" Indonesians, "depredatory" Malays, and "commercial-industrial" Chinese. He speaks of the "Arab mentality," "Japanese soul," and "Anglo-Saxon spirit." He poses Anglo-Saxon "logical mentality" to Spanish-colonial "ignorantism." He sententiously opposes the "military and religious" type of society produced by Spanish-colonial influence to the "scientific and productive" society promised by modern American education.

He is dismissive of folk and popular culture, interpreting such colonial forms as the *corrido* and *pasyon* in positivistic terms. Illustrating Pardo's puritanical approach to cultural forms is his 1917 analysis of the popular Spanish play *Don Juan Tenorio* (1844) by Jose Zorrilla.[279] He critiques the play by way of commenting on America's liberation of the

223

Filipino woman from Spanish *machismo*. He laments the play's glorification of Don Juan ("apotheosis of the triumphant *macho*") and sympathetic portrayal of Doña Ines ("the most deplorable example of the servile woman"). Zorrilla's play popularized a hero many regarded as symbol of the Latin race. For Pardo, however, the "ridiculous and absurd" play illustrated a benighted social psychology.

He usefully draws attention to the role of culture and education in the reproduction of a social order. Constructing binaries, however, he underestimates the capacity of individuals to reinterpret and remake received forms as well as overestimates the power of institutions. In a thoughtful criticism in 1913, Epifanio de los Santos questions Pardo's reductively negative judgments on precolonial culture and the role of the Church. Questioning Pardo's interpretation of the revolution, de los Santos argues for the decisive role played by the masses (*plebeyos analfabetos*) and popular culture, citing the importance of forms like the *awit* and "the small satirico-political gospels (*evangelios*), anonymous posters and revolutionary sheets in vernacular languages" in mobilizing patriotic sentiment. For de los Santos, the true heroes of the struggle were not the rich but "the proletarian class and the poets and *literatos* of the same class."[280]

In his early writings, Pardo attended to the values of internal coherence in native culture. Yet he also acknowledged the superiority of European technologies, such as the superiority of the Latin alphabet to the Tagalog *baybayin*. He appreciated the value of the *curandero*'s knowledge of the healing properties of plants but framed this in the need for the validation and refinement of folk knowledge by medical science. All this pointed to his later advocacy of English and Western science as vehicles of modernity. It would seem that his earlier ideas on the integrity and coherence of Filipino culture were subsumed under his rabid advocacy of "assimilation" into the American Union and its civilization. The two poles, he believed, were not necessarily contradictory.

There are problems, however, in Pardo's discourse on assimilation and autonomy. His rabid advocacy of Westernization is driven by a kind of impatience that derives from a philosophical bias, the style of turn-of-the-century cultural polemics, his involvement in the task of consolidating U.S. rule, and his political ostracism after 1909. There is a crudity to the binary categories he constructs and a stridency to his campaign for

Filipinos to free themselves from the confines of heredity and tradition. To a certain extent, the tendency towards dogmatism and arrogance was mitigated by his willingness not only to engage ideas but see them in practice. He was no "ivory-towerist." He read self-help manuals like Samuel Smiles's *Self-Help* (1859) and Peter Kropotkin's *Mutual Aid* (1902) for lessons that could be applied in the Philippines.[281] He publicly weighed in with his views on a wide variety of issues. When Hadji Gulamu Razul proposed in 1922 that the word *moro* be purged because of its derogatory connotation, Pardo endorsed the proposal, writing that in Spanish history, *arabe, sarraceno, mahometano,* and *moro* were used to disparage enemies considered inferior because of their religion. The bias was brought to the Philippines where Muslims were demonized as treacherous and persecuted on the basis of religion. Pardo urged that words and categories like *moro, infiel,* and *non-Christian* be purged since they expressed religious intolerance.[282]

He remained an engaged intellectual to the end. There are indications that the Great War and the social turmoil in its wake darkened Pardo's optimism in human progress.[283] He worried about the escalating "war" of Labor and Capital in Europe and the rise of workers' militancy in the Philippines. Pardo held on to an elitist rationalism in his view of these changes. There is a rising consciousness of social exploitation, he wrote, because realities of social inequality are no longer mystified as natural and divinely ordained. Political power is no longer based on divine natural rights but conceived as "popular will" expressed through suffrage. He credits this change to the "general altruism" of "the educated classes" who discovered that ignorance could be remedied by instruction and that men themselves could correct the inequality among them.

Pardo, however, stressed the distinction that should be made between workers who are productive and those who are not. He takes a dim view of the "ignorant" and "indolent" who live in a parasitic manner, feeding themselves on what nature offers, struggling against adversities in a "passive and instinctive" manner. They do not contribute to the movement for justice in the world. Workers in Europe and America, he said, arrived at a consciousness of class exploitation and social injustice "not through philosophies nor political disquisitions nor theories" but "productive work," of "what has been and will be the origin of all

moral and intellectual progress in humanity, to wit: WORK AND PRO-
DUCTION [Pardo's emphasis]."[284]

Pardo laments that the new awareness of social oppression has caused
"general confusion." It has occasioned in the oppressed reactions of "hatred" instead of "responsibility." Enthusiasm for equal rights has obscured
the corollary notion of obligation and duty. Popular suffrage has created
problems because it has given the masses (*masas*) a right for which they
are ill-prepared. Pardo continued to believe in the directive role of an
enlightened minority. Instead of using their advantages to abuse the
ignorant and the weak, the educated must help to think those who do
not think and encourage work among those who neither work nor produce. They must help capacitate the "ignorant" so that they can take an
active part in the advancement of humanity.

Eulogio Rodriguez wrote that Pardo, shortly before his death, was
very interested in Russia and wanted to visit the country and study its
government. He was excited by the dramatic changes in Russia where
the Bolsheviks had seized power and Lenin had declared the "New Economic Policy" to reconstruct the economy and transform Soviet life. Pardo
reportedly said: "I have anticipated long before this government was
established that this will be the kind of government which will be eventually adopted by the civilized world. Can there be any better rule
governing a society than, 'He who will not work shall not eat,' making
work the basis of existence?" Pardo reportedly declared that if such a
system is adopted in the Philippines, "I am willing to part with my
property and hand it to the government. I am willing to start from the
bottom as an ordinary citizen and work for my living."[285]

All this may have been hypothetical on the part of one who remained staunchly utilitarian in his philosophy. Yet there is no mistaking
the intellectual earnestness that had marked his career. Reviewing his
work, Pardo said: "I know not what others may think of my Filipinism,
although I am clear as to my opinion of myself. All I can say is that all
my strivings, studies, labours, writings, and other activities have been
consecrated to the Philippines and matters Philippine."[286]

HE WAS THE SOLITARY INTELLECTUAL after 1909. He did not head a
party, held no political office, and had no constituency. Such events as
the establishment of the Assembly in 1907 and passage of the Jones

Law made it clear that independence was an imminent or eventual reality. Nationalism had been domesticated and, in this form, became the legitimate, dominant idiom for the expression of Filipino aspirations.

Nationalism was a theme variously invoked. The anti-Spanish revolution and war against the Americans released currents of patriotic and libertarian sentiments that politicians mined by styling themselves as nationalists and democrats. Filipino leaders had given themselves over to the practice of accommodation to U.S. rule, staking out space that had opened up for them to gain and accumulate local power; yet saw the utility of the idea of nationalism for widening negotiating space with the Americans and legitimating themselves in the eyes of the people. Intellectuals worried about the erosion of familiar values by rapid Westernization and called for the preservation of "tradition" and the "national soul." Yet at no time as well did intellectuals have as much room to maneuver or as many privileges to gain.

Pardo worked against these currents. He did not balk at speaking aloud ideas many politicians privately shared but would rather disguise because these were politically inconvenient. He spoke with disdain of politicians and their arts of procrastination and dissimulation. He criticized traditionalists and nativists for romanticizing the past and keeping the people from forging ahead with the urgent, pragmatic tasks of modernization. He took a distant, academic view of the masses, believing that their emancipation lies in education and economic improvement, both of which shall be led by a modernizing elite. He was a non-believer in a country that remained, despite the revolution, staunchly Catholic.

National history consigned him to a peripheral role; his name usually mentioned as shorthand for the Filipino elite's collaboration with the Americans. He represented an awkward, guilt-ridden interregnum in history. Two intellectual problems confronted the new government: asserting its moral legitimacy by presenting itself as the bearers of the "new" revolution and, at the same time, disguising its capitulationist origins by mystifying U.S. rule as a partnership aimed at enlarging Filipino autonomy and achieving eventual independence. Pardo's *Federalista* background and unvarnished pro-American views made him an inconvenient figure in a narrative organized around the theme of political nationalism. It is not surprising that he had a bad press though he espoused what had in fact become ascendant tendencies: close alliance with America, the promotion of liberal education, and the spread of the English language. His "betrayal" of the revolution, closeness to the Americans, and aristocratic demeanor made him an easy target for nationalists.

The pious nationalism of twentieth-century Philippine historiography cast him as one of the procrastinators and collaborators in the "struggle for independence," the dominant theme in this historiography. In the nationalist imaginary, he is the bespectacled, austere-looking Spanish mestizo who may not have collaborated with the Americans for crass, power-seeking reasons but, nevertheless, missed out on history through his vain elitism and excess of mental diffidence. Like all caricatures, the image is not entirely incorrect, but it misses out on the vital complexities of both man and moment.

In the late 1940s and 1950s, in the context of the Huk rebellion and the influence of Marxism on Filipino intellectuals, class-based interpretations of the national history made Pardo even more unpopular. He was a convenient sign (together with men like Paterno and even Rizal) for a vacillating, opportunistic middle class that—fastidious in its concern for order, fearing the loss of its prerogatives, and failing to appreciate the power of the "masses"—betrayed the revolution. The most influential exponent of this view, Teodoro Agoncillo writes that "the middle-class has always rejected or opposed the position taken by the mass of the people." He concludes: "The Revolution, therefore, failed miserably in its aims and ideals of establishing an economic democracy; and its failure, if one is candid and honest enough to admit it, was caused by the betrayal of the intellectuals."[287]Agoncillo's instrumentalist analysis—in which historical actors are driven by class-determined calculations and "subconscious desire"—leaves categories like "middle class" and "masses" (or, in his words, "haves" and "have nots") underspecified, fails to fully account for the specific positions and choices of actors, and simplifies what Agoncillo himself calls the "multiform actuality" of history. A morality play about who was *for* and *against* the revolution foregrounds binaries and by intellectually keeping the two sides of the conflict apart, obscures what is temporal, intermediate, and provisional. To characterize Pardo's actions as class opportunism does not quite account for the kinds, circumstances, and consistency of the choices he made.

228

Forgotten were Pardo's contributions as a scholar. He pioneered in medicine, linguistics, sociology, and history. Perhaps more than anyone, Pardo could be said to have initiated a social science discourse on Philippine problems. Formally trained in medicine and linguistics, well read and theoretically informed, he was an Enlightenment intellectual who crossed intellectual boundaries and took the world of knowledge (rather than a profession) as his domain.

Yet, for all his cosmopolitanism, he was a colonial intellectual as well. He was not a Diderot or Locke who, born in the center of Europe as Western civilization's natural heirs, could survey the world from imaginary heights and confidently discourse on Man. For the colonial intellectual there is always the sense that he is coming to knowledge from the outside, and that his relations to it are illicit, dangerous, contentious. One recalls Rizal's mother's fears for her son's pursuit of higher knowledge. Given the circumstances of his birth, Pardo could embrace this knowledge as his patrimony but colonial realities showed him that he could be punished for it.

Pardo was a colonial intellectual in his choice of discursive location. He did not only write about the Philippines but located himself in it as one whose stake in the country was not just intellectual but existential. He did not cultivate the hermetic values of science nor fashioned himself a specialist; he took the intellectual disciplines as instruments for engaging other Filipinos in the debate over what the country's transformation required. Speaking out of where they had come from, Rizal and Pardo would interrogate European knowledge as something that did not quite explain them at the same time that they would claim its universalizing discourse of equality and freedom as one that includes them.

In the early 1900s, foreign and Filipino scholars (like the linguists Fletcher Gardner and Frank Blake and the critic Epifanio de los Santos) studied Pardo's contributions in linguistics and history.[288] Pardo's reputation as a scholar, however, went into eclipse with the twentieth-century changes in language, philosophical models, and scholarly orientations as the increasing division of intellectual labor encouraged not only the separation of the disciplines but of science and society.

Pardo was involved in education to a greater degree than were Rizal, Paterno, or Isabelo de los Reyes. He served in the medical faculty of Universidad de Santo Tomas and Universidad Literaria de Filipinas, was involved in the Philippine Commission's efforts to lay the basis for a national educational system, and served as regent of the University of the Philippines and chairman of its Department of Oriental Languages. In 1922, with Otto Scheerer and Epifanio de los Santos, he was part of the committee that studied the advisability of a department of languages in the state university. The committee, in its report to university president G.P. Benton, did not only endorse the need for the study of Austronesian and Philippine languages, it recommended the establishment of a department of "National Science," which would "have for its aim the deepening of national feeling by instilling knowledge of things Philippine to the students, whether in the branches of history, sociology, folklore, anthropology, or linguistics."[289] Pardo's role as advocate of what would be called "Philippine studies" has been forgotten.

WRITING IN 1927, Teodoro Kalaw called Pardo "the greatest, the most avid, and the most respected champion of Americanism," but conceded that his was a "healthy Americanism" since it sought to import what was "good in American civilization." However, Kalaw added, Americanization "as an ideology" was dead. It died twice, first with the political death of Pardo in 1907 (with the defeat of the Federal Party) and then with the natural death of Pardo in 1925.[290]

It is a clever but misleading epitaph for a period, and the man.

NOTES

1. Teodoro A. Agoncillo, *Malolos: The Crisis of the Republic* (Quezon City: University of the Philippines Press, 1997; first ed., 1960), 551.

2. Biographical sources: *Enciclopedia Universal Ilustrada Europeo-Americana* (Madrid: Espasa-Calpe, S.A., 1920), 41:1447–48; Epifanio de los Santos, *Trinidad H. Pardo de Tavera* (Manila: Imprenta "Cultura Filipina," 1913); M. M. Norton, *Builders of a Nation* (Manila: [s.n.], 1914), 93–102; Encarnacion Alzona, "Doctor T. H. Pardo de Tavera and Philippine Historiography" (Typescript, n.d.); *Idem.*, "T. H. Pardo de Tavera, A Biographical Sketch," *The Character of Rizal and the Legacy of Ignorantism*, by Trinidad H. Pardo de Tavera (Quezon City: U.P. Publications Office, 1960), vii–xiii; Emiliano L. Laus, *Brief Biographies of the Ten Most Oustanding Filipino National Leaders* (Manila: National Printing, 1951), 25–30; *Dr. T. H. Pardo de Tavera* [Manila: National Historical Institute, 1982]; E. Arsenio Manuel, *Dictionary of Philippine Biography* (Quezon City: Filipiniana Publications, 1955–86), I:317–48; Ruby R. Paredes, "Ilustrado Legacy: The Pardo de Taveras of Manila," *An Anarchy of Families: State and Family in the Philippines*, ed. A. W. McCoy (Madison: University of Wisconsin, Center for Southeast Asian Studies, 1993), 347–427 (also published by Ateneo de Manila University [ADMU] Press, 1994).

On Joaquin Pardo de Tavera: *Enciclopedia Universal Ilustrada*, 41:1447; Manuel Artigas, *The Events of 1872*, trans. O. D. Corpuz (Quezon City: University of the Philippines Press, 1996; first published in 1913), 178–81; Clarita T. Nolasco, "The Creoles in Spanish Philippines" (M.A. thesis, Far Eastern University, 1969), 351–54; Manuel, *Dictionary of Philippine Biography*, I:313–17.

On Felix Pardo de Tavera: *Enciclopedia Universal Ilustrada*, 41:1446–47.

3. Another source states that the cardinal's remains were interred in a mausoleum in Hospital de Tavera, in Toledo, which the cardinal founded. See Artigas, *Events of 1872*, 178.

4. Antonio M. Regidor and J. Warren T. Mason, *Commercial Progress in the Philippine Islands* (Manila: American Chamber of Commerce of the Philippine Islands, n.d.; first published in 1905), 23, 28; Nolasco, "Creoles in Spanish Philippines," 169–70.

5. The Gorrichos "opened" Escolta Street, it is claimed. When Juliana Pardo de Tavera died in 1892, her Escolta property alone was valued at P138,258.56 and the inventory of her liquid assets showed P204,953.33. See [National Historical Institute], *Dr. T. H. Pardo de Tavera*, 29.

6. Artigas, *Events of 1872*, 179.

7. Quoted in Paredes, "Pardo de Taveras of Manila," 357.

8. John Foreman, *The Philippine Islands* (New York: Charles Scribner's Sons, 1906; 3rd ed.), 362–63.

9. Artigas, *Events of 1872*, 153–55, 167–77; W. E. Retana, *Aparato Bibliografico de la Historia General de Filipinas* (Madrid: Imprenta de la Sucesora de M. Minuesa de los Rios, 1906), II, no. 1400; Jose Montero, "Spanish version of the Cavite Mutiny of 1872," *Documentary Sources of Philippine History*, ed. G. F. Zaide (Metro Manila: National Book Store, 1990), VII:269–73.

10. T. H. Pardo de Tavera, *Reseña Historica de Filipinas Desde su Descubrimiento Hasta 1903* (Manila: Bureau of Printing, 1906), 71.

11. Cited in Ferdinand Blumentritt, "The Punishment of Cavite," *La Solidaridad*, trans. G. F. Ganzon and L. Mañeru (Metro Manila: Fundacion Santiago, 1996), III:62 (August 31, 1891), 411. See Nolasco, "Creoles in Spanish Philippines," 352n.

12. T. H. Pardo de Tavera, "The Conservation of the National Type," *Thinking for Ourselves*, ed. E. Quirino and V. M. Hilario (Manila: Oriental Commercial Company, 1924), 270.

13. Artigas, *Events of 1872*, 181.

14. See David Thomson, *Democracy in France: The Third and Fourth Republics* (London: Oxford University Press, 1958); Rupert Christiansen, *Tales of the New Babylon: Paris in the Mid-19th Century* (London: Minerva, 1995).

15. Walter Benjamin, *Reflections: Essays, Aphorisms, Autobiographical Writings*, trans. E. Jephcott (New York: Schocken Books, 1978), 146–62.

16. See *World Who's Who in Science* (Chicago: A. N. Marquis, 1968), 1649; Patrice Debre, *Louis Pasteur*, trans. E. Forster (Baltimore: Johns Hopkins University Press, 2000), 261, 262, 337.

17. T. H. Pardo de Tavera, "Las Nihilistas," *The Woman's Outlook* (November 10, 1922).

18. Nihilism was loosely applied to radicals in the Russian intelligentsia from the 1860s to 1880s who called for the destruction of established institutions, exalted positivism and scientism, envisioned a society of independent, critically thinking individuals, but never developed a coherent program for political change. See Avrahm Yarmolinsky, *Road to Revolution: A Century of Russian Radicalism* (London: Cassell & Company, 1957), 122–24; Ivan Turgenev, *Fathers and Sons*, trans. R. Edmonds (London: Penguin Books, 1975), 116.

19. Universite de Paris (familiarly called Sorbonne) disappeared after 1784 because of the revolutionary upheaval when it was divided into autonomous "faculties" and academies. It was recreated only in 1896.

On the education of Trinidad and Felix Pardo de Tavera: Luciano P. R. Santiago, "The First Filipino Doctors of Medicine and Surgery (1878–1897)," *Philippine Quarterly of Culture and Society* [hereinafter cited as *PQCS*], 22 (1994), 112–14, 115–17.

On medical education in Pardo's time: Erwin H. Ackerknecht, *A Short History of Medicine* (Baltimore: Johns Hopkins University Press, 1982); Thomas Neville Bonner, *Becoming a Physician: Medical Education in Britain, France, Germany, and the United States, 1750–1945* (New York: Oxford University Press, 1995). On the menacing features of medical modernity: Michel Foucault, *The Birth of the Clinic: An Archaeology of Medical Perception* (New York: Vintage Books, 1994).

20. See Joy Harvey, "Evolutionism Transformed: Positivists and Materialists in the *Societe d'Anthropologie de Paris* from Second Empire to Third Republic," *The Wider Domain of Evolutionary Thought*, ed. D. Oldroyd and I. Langham (London: D. Reidel, 1983), 289–310; Elizabeth A. Williams, "The French Revolution, Anthropological Medicine, and the Creation of Medical Authority," *Re-creating Authority in Revolutionary France*, ed. B. T. Ragan, Jr. and E. A. Williams (New Brunswick, N.J.: Rutgers University Press, 1992), 79–99; Jennifer Michael Hecht, *The End of the Soul: Scientific Modernity, Atheism, and Anthropology in France* (New York: Columbia University Press, 2003), 56–57, et passim.

21. For references to Fauvelle: Hecht, *End of the Soul*, 73, 78, 79.

22. T. H. Pardo de Tavera, "Sobre el Mal de Pott," *El Siglo Medico* (Madrid) (August 21, 1881), 534.

23. T. H. Pardo de Tavera, "La Medecine a l'Isle de Lucon (Archipel des Philippines)," *Journal de Medecine* (Paris), 6:2231 (1884); *Idem., Contribution a l'etude de la Periarthrite du Genou* (Paris: A. Parent, Imprimeur de la Faculte de Medecine, 1886).

Listed as his thesis committee are Simon-Emmanuel Duplay and Charles Fernet (professors of the Faculty of Medicine), F. Siredey (member, *Academie de medecine*), and Le D'Ozenne (chief of clinic, Faculty of Medicine).

24. "The Alphabets of the Philippine Group," *Journal of the Straits Branch of the Royal Asiatic Society*, 17 (1886), 158.

25. "It's Me," and "El ilustre hermano de un hombre ilustre," *Philippines Free Press* (May 24, 1913), 4, 28–29. See *Solidaridad*, I (March 28, 1889), 83–85, (July 31, 1889), 273–75; II (May 15, 1890), 216–17; III (July 31, 1891), 373; IV (December 30, 1892), 633–35.

26. Cornelio de los Reyes, "Dr. Tavera's Reminiscences of the Filipino Patriot," *Philippines Herald* (December 30, 1924).

27. *Rizal's Correspondence with Fellow Reformists* (Manila: National Heroes Commission, 1963), 88.

28. *Rizal's Correspondence with Fellow Reformists*, 192.

29. *The Rizal-Blumentritt Correspondence* (Manila: Jose Rizal National Centennial Commission, 1961), 198.

30. *Rizal-Blumentritt Correspondence*, 255.

31. *Rizal-Blumentritt Correspondence*, 144.

32. Rizal to Blumentritt, Kalamba, December 3, 1887. In: *Rizal-Blumentritt Correspondence*, 157.

33. T. H. Pardo de Tavera, "La Independencia Individual," *Philippines Free Press* (January 8, 1921), 35.

Pardo said that del Pilar and de Dios left for Europe the day after the visit. There is some confusion in this claim since Rizal had already left the Philippines, on February 3, 1888, at the time of this purported visit.

34. *Epistolario de Marcelo H. del Pilar* (Manila: Imprenta del Gobierno, 1955), I:126–27. Also in *Rizal's Correspondence with Fellow Reformists*, 331.

We have no information on del Pilar's personal acquaintance with Pardo, who was seven years younger, except that both were students at Santo Tomas in 1873–1875. Del Pilar left the Philippines for Spain on October 28, 1889 when Pardo was still in Manila.

35. *Solidaridad*, I (August 15, 1889), 313–15, 317–19; T. H. Pardo de Tavera, [Letter to the Editor], *Diario de Manila* (November 13, 1889).

36. Teodoro M. Kalaw, *History of Philippine Masonry*, trans. F. H. Stevens and A. Amechazurra (Manila: McCullough Printing Company, 1956; a translation of *La Masoneria Filipina* [1920]), 21, 137–38, 203; Reynold S. Fajardo, *The Brethren: Masons in the Struggle for Philippine Independence* ([Manila]: Enrique L. Locsin/Grand Lodge of Free and Accepted Masons of the Philippines, 1998), 89–90, 108.

37. "Rizal en un simulacro de la muerte de Cleopatra," *Philippines Free Press* (December 30, 1922). Other references to Filipino gatherings in the Pardo home: *Rizal's Correspondence with Fellow Reformists*, 375; *Rizal-Blumentritt Correspondence*, 200; *Epistolario de Marcelo H. del Pilar*, II:200–6.

38. *Rizal's Correspondence with Fellow Reformists*, 426–27. It is said that the alcohol lamp Rizal used to smuggle out the manuscript of his *Ultimo Adios* from his cell on the eve of his execution was a gift from Doña Juliana when Rizal was in Paris. See "Una Amiga y Protectora del Dr. Rizal," *Philippines Free Press* (December 29, 1923).

39. For a detailed account of the tragedy: Paredes, "Pardo de Taveras of Manila," 374–94.

40. "The Defense of Don Juan Luna Novicio Before the Paris Jury by Attorney Danet," *Solidaridad*, V (April 15, 1893), 170–77. Excerpts from *Gazette des Tribunaux* (February 9, 1893).

41. Juan Luna to T. H. Pardo de Tavera, Manila, January 19, 1897. (The original of the letter is in the Lopez Memorial Museum.) Also in Santiago Albano Pilar, *Juan Luna: The Filipino as Painter* (Metro Manila: Eugenio Lopez Foundation, 1980), 190–91.

42. See Manuel Artigas, *Bibliografia Medico-Farmaceutica de Filipinas* (Manila: Imprenta de I.R. Morales, 1915), 236–38.

43. The notice of his resignation appeared in *Diario de Manila* (April 22, 1897) and in *El Comercio* and *La Voz Española* on the same day.

44. Maximo M. Kalaw, *The Development of Philippine Politics (1872–1920)* (Manila: Oriental Commercial Co., 1926), 274n.

45. T. H. Pardo de Tavera to Fr. Evaristo F. Arias, Manila, September 26, 1898, in: Correspondence ("Cartas Curiosas, 1885–1905"), Pardo de Tavera Collection [hereinafter cited as *PTC*], Pardo de Tavera Special Collections Archives, Rizal Library, Ateneo de Manila University, Quezon City.

46. Quoted in Agoncillo, *Malolos*, 306–7, from a document in the William McKinley Papers, Manuscripts Division, Library of Congress, Washington, D.C., USA.

47. Pardo de Tavera to Fr. Arias, September 26, 1898, [3–4].

48. *Report of the Philippine Commission* [hereinafter cited as *RPC*] (Washington: Government Printing Office, 1900), II:390. Appearing before the Commission, Mabini also left the impression of "a student philosopher dealing with abstract and purely theoretical problems." See Daniel R. Williams, *The Odyssey of the Philippine Commission* (Chicago: A.C. McClurg & Co., 1913), 69–71.

Mabini was struck by paraplegia when he was thirty-one, a condition that gave rise to scurrilous talk that this was due to syphilis. It was medically ascertained in 1982 that he had polio. See *The Letters of Apolinario Mabini* (Manila: National Heroes Commission, 1965), 37; Jose M. Pujalte, et al., *Philippine Orthopaedics: A Historical Perspective* (Metro Manila: [The Authors], 1999), 59–66.

49. Agoncillo, *Malolos*, 340–41; *PTC*, Correspondence ("Cartas Varias"), T. H. Pardo de Tavera to Gov. Otis, October 18, 1898, Manila.

50. T. H. Pardo de Tavera, "Documentos Historicos de Filipinas: Pardo no es Anti-Español," *The Independent* (February 28, 1920), 23.

51. [National Historical Institute], *Dr. T. H. Pardo de Tavera*, 12–13.

52. Charles Burke Elliott, *The Philippines to the End of the Military Regime* (Indianapolis: Bobbs-Merrill, 1917), 475; also 416–77.

53. *PTC*, Correspondence ("Cartas Varias"), T. H. Pardo de Tavera to Gov. Otis, September 21, 1898, Manila ; Kalaw, *Development of Philippine Politics*, 258; *Cartas Politicas de Apolinario Mabini* (1930), 76.

54. *RPC*, 1900, II:391.

55. See *Annual Reports of the War Department* [hereinafter cited as *ARWD*] (Washington: Government Printing Office, 1901), IV:117–18.

56. *PTC*, Correspondence ("Cartas Varias"), T. H. Pardo de Tavera to Maj. Gen. E.S. Otis, November 13, 1898, Manila.

57. *RPC*, 1900, II:390–91.

58. *RPC*, 1900, II:60–67.

59. *PTC*, Correspondence ("Cartas Curiosas, 1885–1905"), T. H. Pardo de Tavera to Gen. Mariano Trias, April 11, 1899, Manila; T. H. Pardo de Tavera to Gen. Makabulos-Soliman, April 11, 1899, Manila; T. H. Pardo de Tavera to Gen. Pio del Pilar, April 12 and April 27 1899, Manila; and other letters in the file.

60. Quoted in Kalaw, *Development of Philippine Politics*, 258–59. See Jesus Z. Valenzuela, *History of Journalism in the Philippine Islands* (Manila: The Author, 1933), 124–26.

61. *RPC*, 1900, II:388–400; [Felix M. Roxas], *The World of Felix Roxas* (Manila: Filipiniana Book Guild, 1970), 206; Rodney J. Sullivan, *Exemplar of Americanism: The Philippine Career of Dean C. Worcester* (Ann Arbor: University of Michigan, Center for South and Southeast Asian Studies, 1991), 71–72.

62. *ARWD*, 1901, IV:116; *RPC*, 1901, I:Appendix A. For the text of the Federal Party platform and accounts of the party's formation: *ARWD*, 1901, IV:114–23; Taylor, *Philippine Insurrection*, V:383–88; Kalaw, *Development of Philippine Politics*, 270–71.

63. Mrs. William Howard Taft, *Recollections of Full Years* (New York: Dodd, Mead & Company, 1914), 148–50.

64. Williams, *Odyssey of the Philippine Commission*, 237–38.

65. Williams, *Odyssey of the Philippine Commission*, 237.

66. Kalaw, *Development of Philippine Politics*, 278.

67. Michael Cullinane, "Ilustrado Politics: The Response of the Filipino Educated Elite to American Colonial Rule, 1898–1907" (Ph.D. diss., University of Michigan, 1989), 90; published by ADMU Press, 2003.

68. Quoted in Teodoro M. Kalaw, *The Philippine Revolution* (Mandaluyong, Rizal: Jorge B. Vargas Filipiniana Foundation, 1969), 294–95.

69. Worcester, *Philippines Past and Present* (1930), 123n; Sullivan, *Exemplar of Americanism*, 71–72.

70. Elliott, *Philippines to the End of the Military Regime*, 73.

71. For a chronicle of the trip: *RPC*, 1904, I:325–37.

72. *RPC*, 1904, I:336.

73. *PTC*, Correspondence ("Cartas Varias"), T. H. Pardo de Tavera to Luke Wright, March 25, 1904, Manila, and related letters in this file. Quoted in Ruby R. Paredes, "The Origin of National Politics: Taft and the Partido Federal," *Philippine Colonial Democracy*, ed. R. R. Paredes (New Haven: Yale University Southeast Asia Studies, 1988), 57. On Pardo's conflict with Wright: Elliott, *Philippines to the End of the Military Regime*, 117–23.

74. *La Democracia* (May 31, 1905). See Kalaw, *Development of Philippine Politics*, 292–93; Cullinane, "Ilustrado Politics," 151–52, 158–60, 162–63.

75. "Lest We Forget," *Philippines Herald* (September 24, 1922), quoted in Salvador P. Lopez, "The Social Philosophy of Dr. Trinidad H. Pardo de Tavera," *Philippine Social Science Review*, 5:3 (July 1933), 157.

76. *La Democracia* (February 11, 1907), in Kalaw, *Development of Philippine Politics*, 309. Also "Discurso del Dr. Pardo de Tavera," *La Democracia* (November 7, 1904); "Tavera Does Not Want Independence Now," *The Manila American* (February 26, 1907).

77. See *The Manila American* (June 7, 1907), *PTC* clipping.

78. Quoted in Ruby R. Paredes, "Introduction: The Paradox of Philippine Colonial Democracy," *Philippine Colonial Democracy*, 9.

79. [National Historical Institute], *Dr. T. H. Pardo de Tavera*, 20–22.

80. *PTC*, Correspondence ("Cartas Varias"), Col. W. S. Scott to Chief of Constabulary, June 3, 1904, Manila; T. H. Pardo de Tavera to Luke E. Wright, December 12, 1904, Manila. Also Kalaw, *Development of Philippine Politics*, 277.

81. Elliott, *Philippines to the End of the Military Regime*, 133.

82. Paredes, "Origin of National Politics," 45, 46.

83. *PTC*, Correspondence ("Cartas Varias"), T. H. Pardo de Tavera to Antonio Regidor, October 22, 1899, Manila; also letters to the same addressee on October 3, 1899, October 2, 1901, and October 20, 1905.

84. *Address of Dr. T. H. Pardo de Tavera at the Farewell Banquet Given Him by his Friends on the Night of the 17th of April, 1909* (Manila: Bureau of Printing, 1909). Published as "Autoridades Sociales," in De los Santos, *Trinidad H. Pardo de Tavera*, 67.

85. *Address*, 5–7; "Autoridades Sociales," 70–71.

86. *Address*, 7–8; "Autoridades Sociales," 73.

87. *PTC*, Correspondence ("Cartas Varias"), T. H. Pardo de Tavera to Gov. Otis, June 15, 1899, Manila, and related letters in this file. Also Alzona, *Education in the Philippines*, 137–39.

88. Alzona, "Doctor T. H. Pardo de Tavera," 13–14.

89. "The Economic Association," *The Manila Times* (September 30, 1911); "Filipinos Form an Economic Society," *The Cablenews-American* (October 1, 1911); "La Asociacion Economica en accion," *La Democracia* (October 5, 1911); "La Asociacion Economica de Filipinas," *Boletin de la Camara de Comercio Filipina*, 8:98 (October 1911), 1.

90. "Farming Engages Tavera," *The Manila Cablenews* (June 7, 1910).

91. His visit was noted in the local press: "Doctor T. H. Pardo de Tavera; De Paso en esta Capital," *La Prensa* (Buenos Aires) (October 21, 1914); "T. H. Pardo de Tavera," *La Razon* (Buenos Aires) (October 21, 1914).

92. Pardo, "Recollections of Hongkong," 765.

93. Quoted in Lopez, "Social Philosophy" (July 1933), 174–75; "An Hour with Dr. Pardo de Tavera," *The Philippines Herald* (July 1, 1923); Jaime C. de Veyra, et al., *Filipino Civic Code* (Manila: Philippine Historical Association, 1958), 68.

94. "An Interview with Dr. Tavera," *The Sulu Courier* (Jolo) (October 15, 1921).

95. *A Survey of the Educational System of the Philippine Islands* (Manila: Bureau of Printing, 1925), 4.

96. "Huwag akong lagyan ng krus ni kandila—Tavera," *Taliba* (March 27, 1925), 1, 4; "Philippines' Foremost Scholar," *Philippines Free Press* (April 4, 1925), 2, 7, 8; "Dr. T. H. Pardo de Tavera," *Philippine Agricultural Review*, 18:2 (1925), 181–82.

97. "Galeria Filipina," *La Vanguardia* (June 10, 1923), quoted in Lopez, "Social Philosophy" (July 1933), 165.

98. W. E. Retana, "Pardo de Tavera en Madrid," *El Renacimiento* (November 5, 1909).

99. Norton, *Builders of a Nation*, 95.

100. "Philippines' Foremost Scholar," *Philippines Free Press* (April 4, 1925), 7.

101. Anastacio Teodoro, "Pardo de Tavera en la Intimidad," *La Vanguardia* (April 4, 1925), quoted in Lopez, "Social Philosophy" (July 1933), 166; *Filipino Civic Code*, 49–50.

102. Teodoro, "Pardo de Tavera en la Intimidad"; Eulogio B. Rodriguez, "Trinidad H. Pardo de Tavera as a Scholar and as a Man—His Conversations and Utterances," *La Vanguardia* (April 18, 1925). On Pardo's views on religion: T. H. Pardo de Tavera, "Moral Laica," *Acacia* (November 30, 1920).

103. Kalaw, *History of Philippine Masonry*, 137–38, 203.

104. Amando Calleja, "De Silla a Silla," *The Independent* (September 20, 1919), 29; De los Santos, *Trinidad H. Pardo de Tavera*, 46–47; Norton, *Builders of a Nation*, 99–102; Manuel, *Dictionary of Philippine Biography*, I:339–40. The government acquired the Pardo de Tavera Filipiniana collection for twenty-five thousand pesos in 1914. It was lost when the National Library was destroyed in World War II.

105. Rodriguez, "Trinidad H. Pardo de Tavera," 3, 8. Also Rafael Palma, *My Autobiography*, trans. A. P. Bautista (Manila: Capitol Publishing House, 1953), 84; De los Santos, *Trinidad H. Pardo de Tavera*, 46, 48.

106. Teodoro M. Kalaw, *Aide-de-Camp to Freedom*, trans. M. K. Katigbak (Manila: Teodoro M. Kalaw Society, 1965), 44.

107. Kalaw, *Aide-de-Camp to Freedom*, 89. Felipe Calderon shared this view of Tomas del Rosario, narrating that in the constitutional debate on religion in the Malolos Congress, del Rosario delivered a five-hour speech that "began with a disquisition on Tacitus' approach to history; then he proceeded to a discussion of the early Christian epoch, the Middle Ages, the Crusades; and of the papal bulls and papal politics in Europe; followed by a survey of the Reformation and the Protestant-Catholic wars; and then of the achievements of Richelieu and Mazarin, and the epoch of the Treaty of Westphalia." See Corpuz, *Roots of the Filipino Nation*, II:323–24.

108. "Dr. T. H. Pardo de Tavera's Message to the Youth of Cebu and His Ideas on Birth-limitation and Immigration," *The Freeman* (Cebu), I:28 (November 16, 1919), 1, 3.

109. "Pity the Pickaninnies!," *Philippines Free Press* (December 6, 1919), 1. For other reactions: "A Dangerous Theory," *Philippines National Weekly* (*PTC*, undated clipping); Luis Rivera, "Individualism vs. Procreation," *The Citizen* (January 8, 1920),

3, 15. Pardo emphasized his views in "Dr. Pardo de Tavera Reiterates Procreation Theory," *The Freeman*, I:32 (December 14, 1919), 1–2.

110. "The 'Tribune of Tondo,' the father of 24, replies to Dr. Pardo de Tavera," *Philippines Free Press* (December 6, 1919).

111. De los Santos, *Trinidad H. Pardo de Tavera*, 47.

William Cameron Forbes blamed him as head of the "insidious cabal" that maneuvered to have Wright removed as governor. Citing Wright's removal, historian Peter Stanley unfairly says of Pardo: "It is all true: he was vain, backbiting, and Europeanized; and he despised the Filipino people, because he considers them indolent." See Peter W. Stanley, *A Nation in the Making: The Philippines and the United States, 1899–1921* (Cambridge: Harvard University Press, 1974), 70.

112. Retana, "Pardo de Tavera en Madrid."

113. Palma, *Autobiography*, 84.

114. T. H. Pardo de Tavera, "Porque Debemos Aprender Bien el Idioma Ingles," *El Ciudadano* (December 24, 1920), 2.

115. Pardo, "Autoridades Sociales," 76.

116. Jose Alejandrino, *The Price of Freedom* (Manila: M. Colcol & Company, 1949; Spanish ed., 1933), 6.

117. De los Santos, *Trinidad H. Pardo de Tavera*, 48.

118. Pardo, "Sobre el Mal de Pott," 534.

119. Pardo, *Contribution a l'etude de la Periarthrite du Genou.*

120. Examples are his "Correspondencia medica," *El Comercio* (April 9, 1892) and (June 7, 1892), on recent knowledge in bacteriology and the treatment of neurasthenia.

121. Pardo, "Medecine a l'Isle de Lucon"; *Idem.*, "La medicina en la isla Luzon," *Los Dos Mundos* (Madrid) (September 28, 1884) and (October 8, 1884).

122. T. H. Pardo de Tavera, "Apuntes sobre la Medicina en China," *La Opinion* (October 9, 1887; and succeeding issues).

123. T. H. Pardo de Tavera, "Prologo," *La Eclampsia infantil en Filipinas y Medios para Reducir la Excesiva Mortalidad de los Niños*, by Manuel Xerez (Manila: Tipo-Litografia de Chofre y Comp.a, 1889), xv–xviii. Further illustration of Pardo's medical views: T. H. Pardo de Tavera, "Correspondencia Medica," *El Comercio* (May 11, 1892), on the therapeutic massage or *hilot*, and "Algo sobre el Colera," *El Comercio* (July 7, 1895), on measures to prevent the spread of cholera.

124. T. H. Pardo de Tavera, "El Beri-Beri: su etimologia," *La Correspondencia Medica de Filipinas*, IV:32 (May 1896), 71–73; reprinted in *Revista Filipina de Medicina y Farmacia* (June 19, 1923).

"Bontius" is a reference to Jacobus Bontius (1591–1631), a Dutch pioneer of tropical medicine who was in Java in the seventeenth century.

125. T. H. Pardo de Tavera, *Plantas Medicinales de Filipinas* (Makati: Ayala Foundation/Filipinas Heritage Library, 2000).

See Leon Ma. Guerrero, "Medicinal Plants," *Census of the Philippine Islands*, 1918, III:759; Jose P. Bantug, "The Beginnings of Medicine in the Philippines," National Research Council of the Philippine Islands, Report No. 1 (1935), 240; *Idem.*, *A Short History of Medicine in the Philippines During the Spanish Regime, 1565–1898* (Manila: Colegio Medico-Farmaceutico de Filipinas, 1953), 13–16; Daniel de la Paz, "Development of Pharmacology in the Philippines," National Research Council of the Philippine Islands, Report No. 1 (1935), 317–318.

126. Pardo, *Plantas Medicinales*, 43, 110, 130, 175.

127. T. H. Pardo de Tavera, *Arte de Cuidar Enfermos* (Manila: Tipo-Litografia de Chofre y Comp., 1895).

128. T. H. Pardo de Tavera, "La Medicina Casera y sus Peligros," *Revista Filipina de Medicina y Farmacia* (June 1923). The reference is to Pablo Clain, S.J., *Remedios Faciles para Diferentes Enfermedades* (Manila, 1712); Fernando de Santa Maria, *Manual de Medicinas Caseras para Consuelo de los Pobres Indios* (Manila, 1815).

129. T. H. Pardo de Tavera, *El Sanscrito en la Lengua Tagalog* (Paris: Imprimerie de la Faculte de Medecine, A. Davy, 1887), 9.

130. Fletcher Gardner, *Philippine Indic Studies* (San Antonio, Texas: Witte Memorial Museum, 1943), 2.

131. T. H. Pardo de Tavera, *Contribucion para el Estudio de los Antiguos Alfabetos Filipinos* (Losana: Imprenta de Jaunin Hermanos, 1884).

132. His sources are Pedro Chirino's *Relacion de las Islas Philipinas* (1604), San Jose's *Arte y Reglas de la Lengua Tagala* (1610), Melchisedec Thevenot's *Relations de Divers Voyages Curieux* (1696), Gaspar de San Agustin's *Compendio de la Arte de la Lengua Tagala* (1787), Ezguerra's *Arte de la Lengua Bisaya* (1747), Mentrida's *Arte de la Lengua Bisaya* (1818), Jacquet's *Considerations sur les Alphabets des Philippines* (1831), Sinibaldo de Mas's *Informe sobre las Islas Filipinas* (1843), Jean Mallat's *Les iles Philippines* (1846), Pierre Favre's *Dictionnaire Malais-Francais* (1875), and K.F. Holle's *Tabel van oud-en Nieuw-Indische Alphabetten* (1882).

133. Pardo, *Contribucion*, 12.

134. Pardo, *Contribucion*, 18.

135. On the *baybayin*, see Vicente L. Rafael, *Contracting Colonialism: Translation and Christian Conversion in Tagalog Society Under Early Spanish Rule* (Ithaca: Cornell University Press, 1988), 44–54; also published by ADMU Press, 1988.

Rafael, who does not cite Pardo, argues for the values of multivocality and tonal sensuousness in the indigenous "reading" of the baybayin. For Rafael, *baybayin* means "coasting along a river," hence randomness as "one floats, as it were, over a stream of sounds elicited by the characters" and "suspend(s) sense in favor of sensation." (49, 54).

More precisely, *baybayin* means "coasting, staying close to the land," and may as well signify (though this is as much an extrapolation as Rafael's) the idea of "shadowing, approximating" meaning as against actually possessing or inhabiting it.

Pardo's explanation, of course, is much more straightforward.

136. Pardo, *Sanscrito en la Lengua Tagalog*.

137. Juan de Noceda and Pedro San Lucar, *Vocabulario de la Lengua Tagala* (Valladolid, 1832; first published in 1754); Eugene Burnouf, *Dictionnaire Classique Sanscrit-Francais* (Paris, 1866).

138. Pardo, *Sanscrito en la Lengua Tagalog*, 9.

139. T. H. Pardo de Tavera, *Consideraciones sobre el Origen del Nombre de los Numeros en Tagalog* (Manila: Tipo-Litografia de Chofre y Cia., 1889); *Idem.*, *Etimologia de los Nombres de Razas de Filipinas* (Manila: Establecimiento Tipografico de Modesto Reyes y C.a, 1901).

140. Pardo, *Etimologia*, 6–7.

141. T. H. Pardo de Tavera, *Las Costumbres de los Tagalos en Filipinas segun el Padre Plasencia* (Madrid: Tipografia de Manuel Gines Hernandez, 1892). See Blair and Robertson, VII:173–96; James Alexander Robertson, *Bibliography of the Philippine Islands* (Cleveland: Arthur H. Clark Company, 1908), 107.

142. T. H. Pardo de Tavera, "Antiguas costumbres de los Pampangos," *El Ideal* (July 18, 1919) *(PTC)*. See Blair and Robertson, *Philippine Islands*, XVI:321–29.

143. Pardo, *Costumbres de los Tagalos*, 3.

144. Pardo, *Costumbres de los Tagalos*, 9. The expression, "the rattan grows where the Indian is born," comes from Gaspar de San Agustin who claims it is a saying among the "Indians" themselves. See Gaspar de San Agustin, O.S.A., "Letter on the Filipinos" (1720), in Blair and Robertson, *Philippine Islands*, 40:226, 228.

145. T. H. Pardo de Tavera, *Noticias sobre la Imprenta y el Grabado en Filipinas* (Madrid: Tipografia de los Hijos de M. G. Hernandez, 1893). Also his "Adiciones y Rectificaciones," in: W. E. Retana, *El Periodismo Filipino: Noticias para su Historia (1811–1894)* (Madrid: Imprenta de la Viuda de M. Minuesa de los Rios, 1895), App. II, 561–64. See W. E. Retana, *Origenes de la Imprenta Filipina* (Madrid: Libreria General de Victoriano Suarez, 1911), 22–23.

146. Pardo, *Noticias sobre la imprenta*, 5.

147. Pardo, *Noticias sobre la imprenta*, 6.

148. Quoted in Robertson, *Bibliography of the Philippine Islands*, 91.

149. T. H. Pardo de Tavera, *El Mapa de Filipinas del P. Murillo Velarde* (Manila: Tipo-Litografia de Chofre y Comp., 1894).

150. Carlos Quirino, *Philippine Cartography (1320–1899)* (Amsterdam: N. Israel, 1963), 134.

151. Quirino, *Philippine Cartography*, vii; T. H. Pardo de Tavera, "*Notas para una Cartografia de Filipinas*," *Cultura Filipina*, I:8 (November 1910), 102–76. Quirino does not cite Pardo's earlier *Mapa de Filipinas*.

152. P. Lee Phillips, *List of Maps, Charts, and Views of the Philippines in the Library of Congress* (Washington, 1903).

153. Quirino, *Philippine Cartography*, 134.

154. T. H. Pardo de Tavera, *Una Memoria de Anda y Salazar* (Manila: Imprenta "La Democracia," 1899). See T. H. Pardo de Tavera, *Los Frailes en Filipinas* (Manila: Estab. Tip. de Modesto Reyes y Cia., 1901); Robertson, *Bibliography of the Philippine Islands*, 128–29.

155. T. H. Pardo de Tavera, "La Imprenta en Filipinas," *La Vanguardia* (June 20, 1911), in: De los Santos, *Trinidad H. Pardo de Tavera*, 77–92.

156. Pardo de Tavera, "Imprenta en Filipinas," 84–85.

157. *ARWD*, 1901, IV:439, 451.

158. Adoracion B. Mendoza and Manuel F. Martinez, *Public Libraries in the Philippines* (Manila: National Library, 2000), 24–26.

159. Romeo V. Cruz, *America's Colonial Desk and the Philippines, 1898–1934* (Quezon City: University of the Philippines Press, 1974), 76–77.

160. *A Pronouncing Gazetteer and Geographical Dictionary of the Philippine Islands* (Washington: Government Printing Office, 1902).

161. *Bibliography of the Philippine Islands* (Washington: Government Printing Office, 1903). Contains Pardo's *Biblioteca Filipina* and a list of books, maps, and other materials in the Library of Congress prepared by A. P. C. Griffin and P. Lee Phillips.

162. Retana, *Aparato Bibliografico*, I:vii–viii, xxxvi, xxxix; III, no. 4391.

163. On these remarks, see Pardo de Tavera, *Biblioteca Filipina*, nos. 91, 431, 501, 1616, 1938–44.

164. *Census of the Philippine Islands, 1903: Geography, History and Population* (Washington: U.S. Government Printing Office, 1905), I:309–410; Pardo, *Reseña Historica de Filipinas*.

On the politics of the census: Vicente L. Rafael, "White Love: Census and Melodrama in the U.S. Colonization of the Philippines," *White Love and Other Events in Filipino History* (Durham: Duke University Press, 2000), 19–51, 233–37; also published by ADMU Press, 2000.

165.Pardo, *Reseña Historica*, 21, 23, 24, 29–30.

166. T. H. Pardo de Tavera, "La Tuberculosis y su Significacion Economica en la Nacion," *The Citizen* (November 11, 1922); "Medicina Casera y sus Peligros"; "Antigua Costumbres de los Pampangos"; *Liliw, Laguna* (Manila: Times Press, [1920].

167. T. H. Pardo de Tavera, "Resultados del Desarrollo Economico de Filipinas," in De los Santos, *Trinidad H. Pardo de Tavera*, 138–37. First published in Spanish in *Revista Economica* (November 1912).

Translated into English: "Results of the Economic Development of the Philippines," *Philippine Agricultural Review*, 18:2 (1925), 151–78; also in *Philippines Free Press* (March 29, April 5, 12, 19 and 26, 1913) under the title "The Economic History of the Philippines."

168. Pardo, "Conferencia Pronunciada," 13–14.

169. Pardo, "Resultados," 145; "Results of the Economic Development," 156.

170. Pardo, "Resultados," 144; "Results of the Economic Development," 155.

171. Pardo, "Resultados," 161; "Results of the Economic Development," 169.

172. Pardo, "Resultados," 159; "Results of the Economic Development," 168.

173. Pardo, "Resultados," 145; "Results of the Economic Development," 155.

174. Pardo, "Resultados," 167; "Results of the Economic Development," 174.

175. Pardo, "Resultados," 162; "Results of the Economic Development," 170.

176. Pardo, "Resultados," 162; "Results of the Economic Development," 170.

177. Pardo, "Resultados," 150; "Results of the Economic Development," 160.

178. T. H. Pardo de Tavera, "Deberes Sociales," 1 (*PTC*, Typescript, 1924). Published in *La Vanguardia* (March 22, 1924), 6.

179. T. H. Pardo de Tavera, "El Alma Filipina," in De los Santos, *Trinidad H. Pardo de Tavera*, 50. English translation: "The Filipino Soul," *Thinking for Ourselves*, 138–55. First published in Spanish in *El Renacimiento* (May 17, 1906).

180. Quoted in Stanley, *Nation in the Making*, 72.

181. *RPC*, 1904, III:919–30; Cruz, *America's Colonial Desk*, 86–87.

182. T. H. Pardo de Tavera, *The Legacy of Ignorantism* (Manila: Bureau of Printing, 1921), 35.

183. Pardo, *Legacy of Ignorantism*, 13, 41; T. H. Pardo de Tavera, "El 'Desideratum' de la Pedagogia Moderna," *Philippines Free Press* (February 4, 1922).

184. Pardo, "Alma Filipina," 53, 57; "Filipino Soul," [146].

185. Pardo, "Alma Filipina," 65; "Filipino Soul," [189]. Also "Dialects Great Danger to P.I.," *Manila Daily Bulletin* (March 3, 1925), 4, quoted in Lopez, "Social Philosophy" (July 1933), 185; "One Language Here Utopian, says P. Tavera," *Philippines Herald* (October 4, 1924); "Saleeby is a Chiropractor in Linguistics Compared with Tavera, says Craig," *Philippines Herald* (March 15, 1925).

186. "Porque Debemos Aprender Bien el Idioma Ingles," *El Ciudadano* (December 24, 1920), 25–27.

187. "University of the Philippines will teach P.I. languages in 1923," *The Philippines Herald* (August 29, 1922). See Barbara S. Gaerlan, "The Pursuit of Modernity: Trinidad H. Pardo de Tavera and the Educational Legacy of the Philippine Revolution," *Amerasia Journal*, 24:2 (1998), 87–108.

188. T. H. Pardo de Tavera, "Mentalidad Pueril," *The Rising Filipina* (October 15, 1920); also in *The Independent* (October 30, 1920). Also *Idem.*, "Peor es el Otro," *The Woman's Outlook*, 1:1 (October 1922); "Deberes Sociales," *PTC*, Ts., 7–11, published in *La Vanguardia* (March 22, 1924); "La 'Rising Generation,'" *La Vanguardia* (February 21, 1925).

189. T. H. Pardo de Tavera, "Las Nurses." Address at the Commencement Exercises of Philippine General Hospital School of Nursing, Manila, April 3, 1920 (Typescript in *PTC*.)

190. T. H. Pardo de Tavera, *El Caracter de Rizal* (Manila: Imprenta Manila Filatelica, 1918), 39 [83pp.]. First published in *The Philippine Review* (May 1917). See also Pardo's statement on Rizal in *RPC*, 1900, II:400–01.

191. Pardo, *Caracter de Rizal*, 19.

192. Pardo, "Filipino Youth," 32.

193. Pardo, "Obra de America," 65.

194. Pardo, "Independencia Individual," 35, 38.

195. Pardo, "Independencia Individual," 46.

196. T. H. Pardo de Tavera, "Las Tres Fuerzas Empleadas por el Ignorantismo," *El Ciudadano* (February 4, 1921), 26.

197. Pardo, "Filipino Youth," 24.

198. Pardo, "Resultados," 162; "Economic History of the Philippines" (March 29), 5.

199. Pardo, "Resultados," 166; "Results of the Economic Development," 174; "The Consequence of Economic Progress," *Thinking for Ourselves*, 339.

200. Pardo, "Resultados," 157; "Results of the Economic Development," 165–66. Also: T. H. Pardo de Tavera, "Conferencia Pronunciada por el . . . en el 'Rizal Hall'

de la Universidad de Filipinas el 25 de Febrero de 1924, ante los estudiantes de Economia Politica de dicha Universidad." Manila, 1924. (Typescript in *PTC*).

201. "Filipino Views of American rule," *The North American Review* (January 1902), 73–79; "La Bandera Filipina," *Philippine National Weekly* (November 8, 1919), 17.

202. T. H. Pardo de Tavera, "Patriotismo Constructivo. Articulo Escrito para la Camara de Comercio de las Islas Filipinas" (Manila, January 14, 1920). (Typescript in *PTC*).

203. T. H. Pardo de Tavera, "Desarrollo Industrial," *Merchants' Association Review*, I:4 (August 1911), 8; in de los Santos, *Trinidad H. Pardo de Tavera*, 174.

204. Pardo de Tavera, "Desarrollo Industrial," 9; in de los Santos, *Trinidad H. Pardo de Tavera*, 177.

205. T. H. Pardo de Tavera, "El Trabajo mas Util," *El Ciudadano*, 3:6 (June 11, 1920), 25–27.

206. Pardo, "Trabajo mas Util," 27.

207. See T. H. Pardo de Tavera, "La Agricultura y la Inmigracion," *Revista Economica*, 8 (September 1912); "Discurso sobre Inmigracion en el Junior Philippine Senate (University of the Philippines)" (September 25, 1920); notes for a speech in *PTC*.

208. T. H. Pardo de Tavera, "Los Chinos de mis Memorias," *El Ciudadano*, 3:20 (September 17, 1920), 18–20, 30.

209. Pardo's "El Japon Moderno," in de los Santos. *Trinidad H. Pardo de Tavera*, 93–111; T. H. Pardo de Tavera, "Japan Redentor," *Boletin de la Sociedad Orientalista de Filipinas*, I:7 (July 1918), 13–15. Also see Pardo, "Alma Filipina," 60–61; "Porque se Suicido el General Nogi," in de los Santos, *Trinidad H. Pardo de Tavera*, 112–16.

210. Quoted in Pardo, "Resultados," 169; "Consequence of Economic Progress," 342; "Results of the Economic Development," 176.

211. T. H. Pardo de Tavera, "La Nueva Mentalidad Filipina," *El Comercio* (November 14, 1912), in de los Santos, *Trinidad H. Pardo de Tavera*, 116–38.

On the "Filipino Soul," see Kalaw, *Aide-de-Camp to Freedom*, 43–44; Felipe Buencamino, "El Alma Filipino," *El Renacimiento*, 1:7 (August 21, 1910), 6–7.

212. Pardo, "Alma Filipina," 56; *Idem.*, "Conservation of the National Type," 345–46.

213. Pardo, "Conservation of the National Type," 350–51.

214. Pardo, "Conservation of the National Type," 282.

215. T. H. Pardo de Tavera, "Patriotismo Constructivo," *PTC*, Ts., January 14, 1920.

216. T. H. Pardo de Tavera, "The New Filipino Mentality," *The Independent*, 8:405 (December 9, 1922), 8.

217. Pardo, "Nueva Mentalidad," 122.

218. Pardo, "Nueva Mentalidad," 135.

219. T. H. Pardo de Tavera, "Lo que Necesitan los Filipinos," *The Independent*, 10:467 (March 15, 1924), 24; *Idem.*, "Los Filipinos Necesitamos de Tres Cosas Esenciales: Instruccion, Educacion y Fe en Nuestro Propio Esfuerzo," *El Debate* (June 17, 1923).

220. Pardo, "Alma Filipina," 57.

221. Pardo, "Conservation of the National Type," 282–83; "Conferencia pronunciada" (1924), 23–24.

222. Pardo, "Conservation of the National Type," 283, 287.

223. Pardo, "Alma Filipina," 57; "Filipino Soul," 146.

224. Pardo, "Alma Filipina," 58; "Filipino Soul," 147.

225. Pardo, "Conservation of the National Type," 281. On the idea of a "league of nations": Immanuel Kant, "Idea for a Universal History from a Cosmopolitan Point of View," *On History*, ed. L.W. Beck (Upper Saddle River, N.J.: Prentice Hall, 2001), 11–26.

226. *La Vanguardia* (March 27, 1925), quoted in Lopez, "Social Philosophy" (July 1933), 176.

227. Lopez, "Social Philosophy" (July 1933), 166. On race categories in Spanish Philippines, see Domingo Abella, *From Indio to Filipino and Some Historical Works* [Manila: Milagros Romualdez-Abella, 1978], 1–40.

228. Foreman, *Philippine Islands*, 410.

229. Retana, *Aparato Bibliografico*, I:v, vii–viii, xxxvi, xxxix; III: no. 3381, 4391. Also: Retana, *Periodismo Filipino*, 165n; *Idem. Origenes de la Imprenta Filipina*, 22–23; Robertson, *Bibliography of the Philippine Islands*, 62, 91.

230. *PTC*, Correspondence ("Cartas Varias"), T. H. Pardo de Tavera to Antonio Regidor, October 2, 1901, Manila; [T. H. Pardo de Tavera to General Licerio Geronimo, Dumaguete, April 9, 1901], *La Democracia* (April 17, 1901), *PTC* clipping; T. H. Pardo de Tavera, "Documentos Historicos de Filipinas: Pardo no es Anti-Español," *The Independent* (February 28, 1920), 23–25.

231. Pardo, "Autoridades Sociales," 74.

232. *Rizal's Correspondence with Fellow Reformists*, 732.

233. *PTC*, "Cartas del Prof. Ferdinand Blumentritt al Dr. T. H. Pardo de Tavera," various letters; see the cover page dated May 7, 1924. An early version of this project may have been Blumentritt's *Versuch Einer Ethnographie der Philippinen* (Gotha: Justus Perthes, 1882); English edition: *An Attempt at Writing a Philippine Ethnography*, trans. M.N. Maceda (Marawi City: Mindanao State University, University Research Center, 1980).

234. John N. Schumacher, *The Propaganda Movement: 1880–1895* (Manila: Solidaridad Publishing House, 1973), 211–12 (revised ed., ADMU Press, 1997); Jose Rizal, "On the New Orthography of the Tagalog Language," *Solidaridad*, II (April 15, 1890), 180–89; also in *Philippine Social Science Review*, 7 (1935), 193–208; Jaime C. de Veyra, *Sobre la "K" y "W"* (Publications of the Institute of National Language, 4:18 [September 1939]). Also Ferdinand Blumentritt, "Cui Bono?," *Solidaridad*, I (November 15, 1889), 451–57.

On this issue see Megan C. Thomas, "Orientalist Enlightenment: The Emergence of Nationalist Thought in the Philippines, 1880–1898" (Ph.D. diss., Cornell University, 2002).

235. Schumacher, *Propaganda Movement*, 212n.

236. T. H. Pardo de Tavera, "Ortografia del Tagalog," *Diario de Manila* (August 5, 1888); *Idem.*, "Una Opinion Filologica," *La España Oriental* (November 7, 1889). See "Ortografia del Tagalog," *La España Oriental* (July 18, 1889) and *Revista Catolica de Filipinas*, II:58 (November 17, 1889), for a series of anonymous satiric verses: Sant., "Sa mabunying filologo"; Odalager, "Sa Orientalista"; Franc., "Sa cay Pardo de Tavera"; and Aba Muc-hang, "Sa Señor Doctor." For a positive response: Xerez, *Eclampsia infantil.*

237. See *Rizal's Correspondence with Fellow Reformists*, 346–47, 350, 393, 403, 601; Barbilampino [*pseud.*], "La Tierra de Quioquiap," *Solidaridad*, III:52 (March 31, 1891), 142–47.

238. Doreen G. Fernandez, "Juliana's Notebook: The 19th Century Filipino Table," *The World of 1896* (Makati: Bookmark / Ateneo de Manila University, 1998), 82–87.

239. *Letters Between Rizal and Family Members*, II:204.

240. Act No. 137 of the Philippine Commission on June 11, 1901.

241. Pardo, *Caracter de Rizal*, 41; T. H. Pardo de Tavera, "Recuerdos Personales de Rizal," *El Espectador* (Cebu) (February 9, 1920).

242. Manuel, *Dictionary of Philippine Biography*, I:322.

243. Pardo, *Plantas Medicinales*, 5.

244. *RPC*, 1900, II:394–95.

245. *Rizal-Blumentritt Correspondence*, 11.

246. *Rizal-Blumentritt Correspondence*, 41, 43.

247. Thomson, *Democracy in France*, 16.

248. Thomson, *Democracy in France*, 124, 126.

249. Edward W. Said, *Orientalism* (New York: Vintage Books, 1979), 83, 123–30; A. L. Macfie, *Orientalism* (London: Longman, 2002), 33–34, 46.

250. C. O. Blagden, "Curriculum of a Course in Malay in Paris," *Journal of the Straits Branch of the Royal Asiatic Society*, 50 (September 1908), 81–83; Vera Sokoloff, *Le Malais a l'Ecole Nationale des Langues Orientales Vivantes* (Paris: Imprimerie Nationale de France, 1948), 164–66; A. Teeuw, *A Critical Survey of Studies on Malay and Bahasa Indonesia* (Hague: Martinus Nijhoff, 1961), 19.

Favre's travels and observations in Southeast Asia: Rd Favre, *An Account of the Wild Tribes Inhabiting the Malayan Peninsula, Sumatra, and a Few Neighboring Islands* (Paris: Imperial Printing Office, 1865). There is an interesting inventory of Favre's library: *Bibliotheque de M. l'abbe Favre. Linguistique et Histoire de l'Oceanie (Malaisie, Philippines, Australie et Polynesie en vente chez Maisonneuve & Ch. Leclerc* (Paris: Maisonneuve et Ch. Leclerc, 1888).

251. Francisco Villanueva, Jr., *Reminiscences of Rizal's Stay in Europe* [Manila: no pub., 1936], 8–11; Jose P. Bantug, *Epistolario del Pintor Juan Luna* (Madrid: Circulo Filipino, 1955), 38; Denis Nardin, *France and the Philippines*, trans. M.J. Cruz (Manila: National Historical Institute, 1989), 112.

252. A more extended study of Filipino physicians is important as corrective to Foucauldian studies on imperial medicine focused on Western/non-Western, colonizer/colonized binaries.

Pardo's views on the relationship between folk and modern medicine can be compared with Rizal's unpublished *"La Curacion de los Hechizados. Apuntes Hechos para el Estudio de la Medicina Filipina"* (1895). Influenced by such scientists as French psychiatrist Hippolyte-Marie Bernheim (1840–1919), Rizal privileges "the enlightened physician" but endorses at the same time learning from indigenous knowledge in psychotherapy.

See Luciano P. R. Santiago, "Centennial: The First Psychiatric Article in the Philippines (1895)," *PQCS*, 23 (1995), 62–75; Victor Heiser, *An American Doctor's Odyssey* (New York: W.W. Norton, 1936), 38, 39. On "imperial medicine": David Arnold, ed., *Imperial Medicine and Indigenous Societies* (Manchester: Manchester University Press, 1988); Roy MacLeod and Milton Lewis, eds., *Disease, Medicine, and Empire: Perspectives on Western Medicine and the Experience of European Expansion* (London: Routledge, 1988).

253. Terry Eagleton, *Scholars and Rebels in Nineteenth-Century Ireland* (Oxford: Blackwell, 1999), 77.

254. Said, *Orientalism*, 218.

255. *Rizal-Blumentritt Correspondence*, 63; Ferdinand Blumentritt, *Vocabular einzelner Ausdrucke und Redensarten, welche dem Spanischen der philippinischen Inseln eigenthumlich sind* (Leitmeritz, 1885). See Pardo, *Biblioteca Filipina*, no. 363.

256. *Solidaridad*, I (April 30, 1889), 133; III (August 15, 1891), 407; (November 15, 1891), 565. The reference is to Bokhari de Djohor, *Makota radja-radja ou la Couronne des rois, traduit du malais et annote par A. Marre* (Paris, 1878).

257. *T. H. Pardo de Tavera Collection* (Quezon City: Rizal Library, Ateneo de Manila University, 1996). Mimeographed; various pagings.

258. Immanuel Kant, "What is Enlightenment?," *On History*, 3.

259. Theodor Adorno, *Minima Moralia*, trans. E.F.N. Jephcott (London: Verso, 1978), 52–53.

260. On Spencer and the positivists: Herbert Spencer, *Political Writings*, ed. J. Offer (Cambridge: Cambridge University Press, 1994); David Wiltshire, *The Social and Political Thought of Herbert Spencer* (Oxford: Oxford University Press, 1978); Mike Hawkins, *Social Darwinism in European and American Thought, 1860–1945* (Cambridge: Cambridge University Press, 1997).

261. Octavio Paz, *The Labyrinth of Solitude* (New York: Grove Press, 1985), 128–33.

262. Isaiah Berlin, "Kant as an Unfamiliar Source of Nationalism," *The Sense of Reality: Studies in Ideas and their History* (New York: Farrar, Straus and Giroux, 1996), 232–48.

263. Pardo, "Conservation of the National Type," 358–59.

264. Rodriguez, "Trinidad H. Pardo de Tavera," 1, 2; De los Santos, *Trinidad H. Pardo de Tavera*, 47.

265. T. H. Pardo de Tavera, "La Enseñanza de la Religion," *The Independent*, VIII:390 (September 23, 1922), 22; *Idem.*, "La Enseñanza de la Religion en la Universidad de Filipinas" (*PTC*, ms., written for *The Alumni News*, July 28, 1922).

266. Jose Ma. Cuenco, *Una Refutacion de la Conferencia Pronunciada por el Dr. T. H. Pardo de Tavera* (Cebu: Imprenta Rosario, 1920). Also "Tavera's talk disgusts *Boletin Catolico*," *The Freeman* (Cebu) (December 30, 1920).

267. *Sobre una "Reseña Historica de Filipinas"* (Manila: Imprenta de Santo Tomas, 1906).

268. *Sobre una Reseña*, 1–2. The references are to Greek statesman Solon, Roman historian Suetonius, Swiss botanist Augustin de Candolle (1778–1841), German chancellor Otto von Bismarck (1815–1898), French scientist Louis Pasteur (1822–1895), and German philologist Max Muller (1823–1900).

269. *Sobre una Reseña*, 161.

270. See Palma, *My Autobiography*, 40–41.

271. Pardo, "Conservation of the National Type," 274.

272. Pardo, "Conservation of the National Type," 279–80.

273. T. H. Pardo de Tavera, "Hay que Empezar Imitando" (*PTC*, ms., October 14, 1922).

274. Pardo, "Filipino Soul," [21].

275. The *"El Renacimiento" Libel Suit* (Manila: [Pura Villanueva Kalaw], 1950), 33.

276. *"El Renacimiento" Libel Suit*, 33.

277. Teodoro M. Kalaw, *Spiritual Register*, trans. N. Joaquin (Metro Manila: Anvil Publishing, 2001), 164. From *Dietario Espiritual, 1926–1927* (1930), a selection of columns from *La Vanguardia*.

278. Pardo, "Japon Moderno," 111.

279. T. H. Pardo de Tavera, "Don Juan Tenorio," *The Philippine Review*, II:3 (March 1917), 14–18. See Susan Kirkpatrick, "Constituting the Subject: Race, Gender, and Nation in the Early Nineteenth Century," *Culture and the State in Spain: 1550–1850*, ed. T. Lewis and F. J. Sanchez (New York: Garland Publishing, 1999), 225–51.

280. De los Santos, *Trinidad H. Pardo de Tavera*, 27–30, 36–37.

281. See Asa Briggs, "Samuel Smiles: The Gospel of Self-Help," *Victorian Values: Personalities and Perspectives in Nineteenth-Century Society*, ed. G. Marsden (London: Longman, 1990), 103–13.

282. T. H. Pardo de Tavera, "Moros y Cristianos" (*PTC*, ms., November 14, 1922); submitted to *Philippines Herald* for publication.

283. T. H. Pardo de Tavera, "La Guerra Europea," *El Comercio* (July 7, 1915), 2–4; *Idem.*, "España y la Gran Guerra," *La Vanguardia* (February 14, 1918), a translation of Pardo's article in *The Century* (New York) (January 1918); *Idem.*, "Philippine Loyalty Example to Orient," *The Manila Times* (June 5, 1918); *Idem.*, "Two Battles for Democracy," *Philippines Free Press* (June 8, 1918).

284. Pardo, "Deberes Sociales," 3.

285. Rodriguez, "Trinidad H. Pardo de Tavera," 8.

286. "El Dr. Pardo como Escritor," *La Vanguardia* (March 27, 1925), quoted in Lopez, "Social Philosophy" (July 1933), 168.

287. Teodoro A. Agoncillo, "The Filipino Intellectuals and the Revolution," *Philippine Social Sciences and Humanities Review*, 18:2 (June 1953), 140. Also Agoncillo, *Malolos*, x, 510–33.

288. See Frank R. Blake, "Sanskrit Loan-Words in Tagalog," *Johns Hopkins University Circular* (June 1903), 2–3, 13–14; Fletcher Gardner, *Philippine Indic Studies*. More recent studies: Juan Francisco, "Further Notes on Pardo de Tavera's 'El Sanscrito en la lengua Tagalog,'" *Asian Studies*, VI:2 (1968), 223–34; Zeus A. Salazar, "A Passage from India: Dr. Francisco's 'Notes' on Tavera," *The Malayan Connection* (Quezon City: Palimbagan ng Lahi, 1998), 43–58.

289. C. P. Gloria, "The Class in Linguistics," *Philippine Collegian* (October 15, 1923), quoted in Frei, *Historical Development of the Philippine National Language*, 67.

290. Teodoro M. Kalaw, "Americanization," *Rediscovery*, ed. C. N. Lumbera and T. G. Maceda (Metro Manila: National Book Store, 1981), 155–57. From *Dietario Espiritual* (September 9, 1927), translation by N. Tiongson.

ISABELO DE LOS REYES

BROTHER OF THE WILD

HE WAS the country's most unorthodox intellectual. Energetic and erratic, Isabelo de los Reyes waged a campaign against Spanish and American rule; was incarcerated in Manila's central prison and Barcelona's infamous Montjuich Castle; consorted with anarchists and socialists; established a rebel church; and founded the Philippine labor movement. A prodigious pamphleteer, he wrote on diverse topics in history, folklore, language, politics, and religion.

He was as fecund in his private life. He married thrice (a *Tagala*, a Spaniard, a Chinese mestiza) and sired twenty-seven children. He is reported to have said: "There is enough chaos in me for God to create another world."[1]

ECONOMIC CHANGES in the nineteenth century primed the rise of regional trading centers in the archipelago. One such center was the town of Vigan in the northwestern Luzon coast between the Gran Cordillera Central mountains and the South China Sea. A precolonial trading post, Vigan appeared in the Spanish colonial map when Juan de Salcedo "conquered" the Ilocos in 1572 and founded near Vigan the first Spanish

255

town in northern Philippines, *Villa Fernandina*. In the centuries that followed, Vigan grew as an administrative, military, and religious center in the Ilocos region. By the late nineteenth century, it was a thriving community with a population of around 15,000 and a merchant class of mostly mestizo families who prospered through the cultivation and trade of such commodities as rice, indigo, and tobacco.

In the heart of Vigan, in the house of his grandfather, Isabelo de los Reyes was born on July 7, 1864, the son of Leona Florentino and Elias de los Reyes.[2] Of the local elite, his mother was a remarkable woman who wrote *comedias* and verses that earned her some renown beyond the Ilocos region and, years later, the honor of being called "the first poetess of the Philippines."[3] On his father's side he may have been distantly related to the Vigan-born creole merchant Ventura de los Reyes who was the first Philippine delegate to the Spanish Cortes in 1810–1813 and the only "Filipino" signatory to the historic Spanish Constitution of 1812.[4] A claim has also been made that Isabelo (called *Beluco* in his youth, *Don Belong* in his late years) was a "distant cousin" of Jose Rizal, linked through a Chinese tax collector married to both Rizal's grandmother and Isabelo's grand-aunt.[5]

His parents had a troubled marriage and when he was six Isabelo was placed in the care of his uncle Mena Crisologo (1844–1927).[6] A lawyer educated at Universidad de Santo Tomas, Crisologo was one of Vigan's notables, a status signified by his imposing residence fronting the town's plaza. Regarded as one of Ilocos's leading poet-playwrights, Crisologo was an early influence on the young Isabelo. As a lawyer, Crisologo took up such causes as championing a petition by Tinguians for the establishment of the township of Salcedo in 1872. As ecclesiastical notary of the diocese of Nueva Segovia, he feuded with the Augustinians, who controlled the Ilocos parishes, when he aligned himself with the non-Augustinian bishop and the seculars who controlled Vigan's Cathedral parish. In this feud, he wrote notarial pronouncements that led to the excommunication of two Augustinians. Isabelo worked for him as a copyist, an experience that must have introduced the young man to the possibility that there were spaces and means for critically engaging colonial power.

Isabelo attended the Seminary of Vigan, an institution established in 1822. At the time Isabelo was there, it was run by the Augustinians according to a regimen that inculcated in students Latin, Spanish Grammar, Arithmetic, and a program of moral and religious discipline.[7] A free spirit, Isabelo chafed against seminary life, played truant, and was interested in girls. Legend has it that he learned to dislike the Spanish friars and one day led a student strike to protest the maltreatment of students. The maverick churchman Gregorio Aglipay, who studied in the Vigan seminary, writes of Isabelo the student:

> He was avid at the Bible but he found that the keepers of the souls at the Villa Fernandina were not in accord with it in practice, nor was the behavior of the laymen of that tiny feudal-like city of fanatics. Belong, even at that time, began manifesting his hatred of hoaxes.[8]

In 1880, his parents finally separated and, without his uncle's consent, Isabelo struck out for Manila on his own. He was sixteen. He matriculated in Colegio de San Juan de Letran where he finished the bachelor's program with honors in 1883. To supplement an allowance he was getting from his mother (his father died on July 7, 1882), he took to journalism, setting type for *La Oceania Española* as well as writing for it and such periodicals as *Diario de Manila*, *El Comercio*, *La Revista Popular*, and *La Opinion*. His *"La expedicion de Li-Ma-Hong contra Filipinas,"* published in *Diario de Manila* in November 1882, won for him a prize.

In 1886, he worked as Manila correspondent for *El Eco de Panay*, a newspaper in Iloilo, but was replaced by a peninsular Spaniard, Wenceslao Retana, when his reports began to appear too liberal to the paper's editors. He was beginning to earn a reputation as an independent-minded writer such that *La Opinion*, which began publication as a political daily in 1887, hired Isabelo as foil to an ultra-conservative staff member, the Spaniard Camilo Millan, to create for the paper the appearance of a "balanced" publication.[9] Isabelo loved to flirt with danger. In 1887, while working as a part-time typesetter for *Oceania Española*, he attended a banquet of the Sculptors Guild in honor of Liberal Overseas Minister Victor Balaguer. The *Oceania Española* editor had refrained from sending a representative because of the meeting's political implications. Isabelo, however, spoke at the meeting in the paper's name. For his brashness the paper had him publish a retraction the next day.[10]

Isabelo came into his own in other ways. On June 14, 1884, only nineteen, he married Josefa Hizon Sevilla, daughter of Gregorio Sevilla, the *capitan* of the Manila suburb of Malabon. He was at this time enrolled in law at Santo Tomas. Though he graduated in 1887, he could not practice as a notary because he did not meet the age requirement of 25. Isabelo had to scramble to support his family. (He and Josefa would eventually have ten children). His mother (who opposed his marriage and passed away less than four months later) had given the young couple a thousand pesos, which they used to start a pawnshop. The business failed, and so did a bookstore the couple opened because "he refused to sell the good ones." The couple's fortunes started to change only after Isabelo inherited some of his mother's properties. He proved to be quite enterprising and proceeded to build a modest fortune as a commercial agent (*consignatorio*) of rice, tobacco, indigo, and other products.

This was the time of *La Propaganda*, the Filipino movement for reforms that simmered after the execution of the Filipino priests Jose Burgos, Mariano Gomez, and Jacinto Zamora in 1872 (when Isabelo was still a child in Vigan) and surged in the 1888 anti-friar demonstration in Manila (when Isabelo had just finished his studies and was well-embarked on a journalistic career). There is no information that Isabelo was involved in the 1888 demonstration. He missed out on another opportunity as well. Jose Rizal, who visited the Philippines shortly before the outbreak of the demonstration, called on Isabelo with letters from Ferdinand Blumentritt but Isabelo was out of the house and they did not meet.[11]

The post-1888 crackdown on liberals scattered the *reformadores* as the focus of *La Propaganda* shifted to Spain where Filipino émigrés pushed the campaign for reforms. Ironically, it was this period that saw Isabelo most active as a writer and intellectual. In rapid succession, he published *Ilocanadas* (1887), *Articulos Varios* (1887), *Las Islas Visayas en la epoca de la conquista* (1889), *Historia de Filipinas* (1889), and the two-volume *Historia de Ilocos* (1890). These and other works won him a measure of recognition as a scholar. In 1887, his journalistic articles and *Folklore Filipina* were among the exhibits at the *Exposicion General de las Islas Filipinas* in Madrid.[12] His ethnological articles found their way to Europe and appeared in German translation in such scientific reviews as *Globus* and *Ausland*. By 1889, he already had the honor of being listed as corresponding or honorary member of such societies as the *Imperial y Real Sociedad Geografica de Vienna, Academia Indo-China de Francia*, and *Sociedad Española de Geografia Comercial.*[13]

Audaciously, in June 1889, he founded the fortnightly Spanish-Iloko newspaper *El Ilocano* (1889–1896). Isabelo became "the only *indio* ever licensed to own and operate a paper in the colony" and his paper "the first genuinely Filipino periodical."[14] (The first vernacular newspaper in the Philippines, *Diariong Tagalog*, preceded it by seven years but lasted only five months.) In a statement of the paper's policy, Isabelo declared that he "founded *El Ilocano* with no other object than to serve our beloved *pueblo* Ilocos by contributing to the enlightenment of her children, defending their interests."

By 1893, it had a run of 600 copies, mostly circulated in northern Luzon. By establishing a relationship with a specific audience (*indio*, Ilocano), the venture proved so successful that Isabelo was able to acquire his own printing press on the paper's third year. With the machine and types imported from Europe and parts manufactured by Vigan artisans, *"Imprenta de Isabelo de los Reyes"* was set up in the basement of Isabelo's house on Lara Street in Binondo. Declaring pride in his provincial origins, he did not only boast that press parts were fabricated by Vigan artisans but that his printshop personnel were Ilocanos. He did not see regionalism incompatible with *patriotismo*. "All our aspirations are directed towards the intellectual, moral, and material aggrandizement of the Philippines in general, and the Ilocanos in particular; and all our efforts are exerted to this end."[15]

Established as a merchant-entrepreneur, he also published the periodicals *La Lectura Popular* (1890–1892) and *El Municipio Filipino* (1894). *Lectura Popular*, a Tagalog biweekly, was a joint venture of Jose de Jesus, owner of Imprenta de Santa Cruz, and Isabelo who did not only edit the paper but wrote most of its contents. *Municipio Filipino* was a short-lived Spanish-Tagalog magazine devoted to colonial jurisprudence. From his growing income, Isabelo purchased and built houses in Binondo and Tondo and acquired farmland in Tarlac and Pangasinan. His economic independence allowed him to participate actively in the public life. He was a member of a musical society called *La Euterpe* in 1891 and, in 1893, sought but failed to get government authorization to form *La Hormiga de Filipinas* ("Ants of the Philippines"), a society that aimed to promote agriculture by developing uncultivated lands in Tarlac and Pangasinan.[16]

ISABELO DE LOS REYES was no gentleman-scholar in the mold of Pedro Paterno and T.H. Pardo de Tavera. Neither was he an intellectual of the type of Jose Rizal, who was monastic in his habits and exilic in temperament. Denizen of an urban, mercantile environment, Isabelo combined commerce, the letters, and politics. He did it as an *indio* and *provinciano* working in race-conscious, socially conservative, and politically repressive Manila. His performance is not always coherent but it is a remarkable performance nevertheless.

Of Manila in the 1880s Isabelo wrote: "Here the only things that grow luxuriantly are cogon-grass and molave—two tenacious local weeds."[17] This is not entirely true. Late-nineteenth-century Manila was an expansive, if dangerous, time for Filipino intellectuals. Converging factors primed this expansiveness: a new prosperity and cosmopolitanism in the urban centers and closer contact between the Philippines and Europe. In 1869, the Suez Canal was opened and, by 1870, there was a direct steamship link between Barcelona and Manila and regular mail steamer service between Manila and Hong Kong. Manila was astir with literary and artistic activities. There were theaters, bookstores, and newspapers (more than a dozen newspapers appeared in Manila in the 1890s).[18] By the second half of the nineteenth century, the printing press ceased to be a monastic monopoly and privately owned printshops began to appear. Trade guilds were being established. Literary, artistic, and scientific periodicals—*Ilustracion Filipina* (1859), *Trovador Filipino* (1874), *Revista del Liceo Artistico y Literario* (1879)— appeared and while they were characteristically short-lived, they manifested a growing self-consciousness and appetite for urbanity. There was a living to be made (not lucrative but sufficient) for enterprising *literatos* like Isabelo.

The Glorious Revolution of 1868 in the peninsula had sired liberals in the colony who were interested in a secular ideology of "improvement." This is shown in the career of Jose Felipe del Pan (1821–1891), the colony's foremost journalist.[19] It was del Pan who encouraged and supported Isabelo when he began work as a journalist. Although a peninsular (he was born in Coruña, Spain), he lived and worked in the Philippines for forty years and served as secretary to the governor-general. Politically conservative but a liberal by Manila's standards, he espoused such causes as economic self-sufficiency, women's education, and the eradication of such ills as racism. His writings were secular and utilitarian: *Diccionario de la Administracion, del Comercio y de la Vida Practica en Filipinas* (1879), an unfinished series he started with Jose de la Rosa; *La Poblacion de Filipinas* (1883), a book of statistics, a major interest of del Pan; *Los Chinos en Filipinas* (1886), an anti-Chinese immigration tract; and *Los Ferrocarriles en General y el de Manila a Dagupan* (1887). Interested in Philippine history, he annotated and published Tomas de Comyn's *Estado de las Islas Filipinas en 1810* (1820) in 1877 and in an amplified version in 1878, and a Spanish edition of John Bowring's *A Visit to the Philippine Islands* (1859) in 1876. The prolific del Pan also wrote articles and novels in the *costumbrista* tradition. His novels expressed the same impulses behind his journalism: a peninsular patriotism combined with a didactic zeal for "modern" causes like social equality and productive work.[20]

Del Pan edited *Diario de Manila* until 1877 when he left it to run *La Oceania Española*. At this time he was also editor of *Revista de Filipinas* (1875–1877), founded to spread "scientific-literary" knowledge about the Philippines. While it lasted only two years—because, it was said, of the country's lack of "well-nourished brains and souls anxious for learning"—the review demonstrated del Pan's crusading spirit. It published such works as his annotations of Comyn and Bowring and his *Diccionario de la Vida Practica en Filipinas*.[21] Though Retana took a condescending view of his scholarship, del Pan was influential in promoting a scholarly interest in the Philippines not only through his writings but his encouragement of young writers like Isabelo de los Reyes. Stressing social utility over art for art's sake, he urged Filipino writers like Isabelo and Mariano Ponce to write on topics like folklore instead of the florid romantic verses they contributed to his newspapers.[22]

A product of the Enlightenment (*Ilustracion*), the ideology of "improvement" expressed the ambitions of a "benevolent" imperialism.[23] Mediated by liberals like del Pan, the ideology inspired Isabelo's own journalistic efforts but it would be inflected and carried forward differently. Del Pan wrote as the enlightened Spaniard, Isabelo was the enlightened *indio*. The difference was consequential. Thus, of Isabelo's editorship of *Lectura Popular*, Retana wrote: "He wasn't slow in making it a seedbed and propagator of 'useful information,' among which his writers, almost all native Filipinos, inserted plenty of little items of questionable intent."[24] *Municipio Filipino* served a worthy purpose by publicizing colonial laws but the texts of these laws were presented as "annotated, verified and commented upon" by an *indio*. While the annotations were not attributed it was clear it was Isabelo who was doing the annotating since there does not seem to be anyone else involved in the periodical that was published by *Imprenta de Isabelo de los Reyes*.[25]

From "useful" knowledge Isabelo moved to matters more overtly political. He aligned himself with such liberal causes as the call for press freedom and Philippine representation in the Spanish Cortes. He questioned the undue influence enjoyed by the friars and criticized them and their allies for blocking the extension to the colony of the Madrid government's liberal policies by raising alarmist arguments that "simulated revolts and imaginary conspiracies" that imperil "national integrity." Positioning himself as one of the "sons" addressing the "Mother Country," he called for equality of rights for Filipinos under the Constitution of 1812, freedom of religion, and strengthening the civil state by, among others, implementing a system of civil registration and giving it priority over the Catholic parish registration of births, marriages, and burials.[26]

He used indirection and restraint in handling political issues given the conditions he had to work under in Manila. Yet his work gained admiring notice abroad, particularly in *Solidaridad*, to which he contributed articles he felt he could not publish in Manila. In Manila, however, he was beginning to be unpopular with Spanish conservatives. An article of his on Filipino representation in the Cortes in *La España Oriental* in 1889 subjected him to a mocking attack from *La Opinion* and the conservative papers in the capital.[27] Columns of *La Opinion* and *La Voz de España* ridiculed him as a hick by pointedly referring to his being an *Ilocano*. Retana, Vicente Barrantes, and the scurrilous Pablo Feced (*Quioquiap*) mocked his scholarship, saying he was merely echoing the Germanic ideas of Blumentritt. Barrantes dismissed his folklore studies as "real *romantic* works." Feced was typically uninhibited, calling *Historia de Ilocos* a "monstrosity" and de los Reyes "a remarkable simpleton, a fool."[28]

Isabelo responded by saying that a historian is not an acolyte (*sacristan*) and that he had only tried to convey what was objective and true.[29]

In his defense, Blumentritt wrote that de los Reyes was the target of malicious accusations because he worked in a place intolerant of free thought and some Spaniards simply could not abide with the idea of an *educated* indio who dared to think for himself.[30]

Isabelo was in contact with personalities of the Propaganda Movement in Europe. Blumentritt encouraged his work and brought it to the attention of other scholars by translating and publishing his writings in Europe. Isabelo reciprocated by initiating a project in 1890 to sell photographs of Blumentritt at a peso each to raise funds to be given to the Austrian scholar in appreciation for his contributions to the Filipino campaign for reforms. Blumentritt appreciated the gesture but was concerned that Isabelo, "for being so little prudent, may expose himself to great danger for his propaganda in my favor."[31]

Isabelo charted his own course, however, and does not seem to have been directly involved in the groups agitating for state and church reforms at this time.

THE OUTBREAK of the revolution on August 26, 1896, unleashed terror as the authorities carried out a frenzied campaign to root out the revolutionary society *Katipunan* and "secret conspiracies" in Manila and the provinces. The "terror" spread to Ilocos where friars, with the help of local officials, went after suspected enemies, arresting people and extracting "confessions" through torture. One of those arrested, in November 1896, was Isabelo's uncle Mena Crisologo, who was accused, together with other Vigan *principales*, of being part of a "Masonic cabal" although it does not seem that he was actually involved in the rebellion.[32]

Later, romanticized accounts say Isabelo wanted to go North to join the rebels but was dissuaded by Crisologo who said, "in a revolution, each one of us has his functions and we must do what we are best suited for." Isabelo's fire was undimmed, it is said. "His defiance was open. In cafes and restaurants, in public as well as in secret gatherings in Intramuros, the young patriot advocated reforms. And 'if reforms are impossible,' he said, it would be necessary 'to take up arms against the tyrants.'"[33]

On February 12, 1897, while his wife Josefa was sick in bed, Isabelo was arrested by the Guardia Civil and taken to the Bilibid where he was chained to a pillar in the prison basement. Many reasons have been cited for his arrest. It is said he was suspected of being a member of the highest council of the Katipunan; that, sporting the *nom de guerre* "*Ciclon*," he was head of the "Ilocano conspiracy" and (as *consignatorio* in Manila of Ilocos merchants) the link between Tagalogs in the capital and Ilocanos in the North; that he founded a "Masonic cabal" in Vigan; and that he was involved in a plot to kill Spaniards in the Ilocos on September 10, 1896.[34] In Vigan, a 60-year-old Filipino priest was beaten into testifying that he had been inducted into Masonry by Isabelo. Mena Crisologo, Isabelo's cousin Estanislao de los Reyes, and other family members were implicated in the insurrection. Crisologo later claimed, self-interestedly, that it was because of Isabelo's association with him that the governor-general decided against granting Isabelo a reprieve from the Bilibid.[35]

There was, of course, the fact of Isabelo's writings for which, it is said, he was once threatened with excommunication. Yet, Isabelo does not seem to have been part of any of the political groups of the time. An attempt was made in 1884 to recruit him to Freemasonry by Jose A. Ramos, the British-trained owner of *La Gran Bretana* in Manila (a bazaar frequented by Filipino liberals) and one of the earliest Masons in the country. A printshop owner, Ramos published Isabelo's *Articulos Varios* (1887). The two had worked for *La Oceania Española* and once planned to jointly put out a paper. Isabelo later recounted that Ramos and Doroteo Cortes approached him in 1888, asking him to sign a petition and join the popular demonstration of March 1 for the expulsion of the friars. Isabelo said he declined because he did not agree with the petition's demand for the exile of the Archbishop. It does not seem that Isabelo became a Mason.[36]

He denied membership in *Liga Filipina*, the political association organized by Rizal in Manila on July 3, 1892, and disclaimed knowledge of the existence of the Katipunan. Yet, he sold types from his shop to Emilio Jacinto for the small printing press the Katipunan set up to publish the revolutionary organ, *Kalayaan*, and later claimed that he made a financial contribution to *Liga*.[37] Subsequently, he was asked by Julio Nakpil to join *Liga,* but he declined saying he had a large family to attend to and could not abide with the discipline of being part of an organization. Yet he also claimed that he offered to give Nakpil, shortly before his arrest, a thousand pesos to purchase revolvers from someone on board the steamer *Salvadora*, and that he offered his services to the revolution as a simple soldier.[38]

In Bilibid, Isabelo was thrown into the company of "three hundred" prisoners, Katipunan rebels, assorted liberals, and innocents. Ever the researcher, he interviewed prison mates and tried to learn all he could about the Katipunan society that organized the insurrection. While in prison, he started work on his *Memoria sobre la revolucion*, encouraged by the change of command when the more conciliatory governor-general Fernando Primo de Rivera took over. Initially, the document took the form of a *Memoria de agravios de los Filipinos*, a list of complaints addressed to Primo de Rivera and meant to gain sympathy for the rebels by exposing the abuses of the friars that had caused the rebellion. In it Isabelo offered his services to go to the field and represent the governor-general in effecting peace if the government was willing to make some political concessions. He offered to leave his six children as hostage to guarantee his return. Many prisoners wanted to sign the *memoria* but Isabelo decided to take sole responsibility. Several copies were made in prison (one of which was given to Luis Viza, S.J., Bilibid chaplain, and eventually wound up in the Jesuit Archives in San Cugat, Barcelona). The original was smuggled out of Bilibid in the shoe of Isabelo's ten-year-old son Jose and sent to the governor-general on April 25, 1897.

Isabelo's wife Josefa died and was interred on February 13, 1897. When his son Jose broke the news to him in prison, Isabelo wept unashamedly. The story is told (and here the sequence of events gets confused) that when Pedro Paterno, in the company of Isabelo's son Jose, saw the governor-general in Malacañang to ask for Isabelo's temporary release to visit his dying wife, the governor-general told Paterno that Isabelo had put the Spanish government in a bad light with his memorial. "The peace and the security of the country demand that a man of such a character, a dangerous rebel, should be kept behind prison bars."[39]

Whatever may be the truth in the Paterno story, Isabelo was amnestied together with other prisoners on May 17, the King's birthday. He took his six small children to his father-in-law's house in Malabon and there rewrote parts of the *Memoria*. One item he wrote at this time was a document in Tagalog urging the revolutionary forces to shift tactics to "the Cuban system of ambuscades and guerrilla warfare" to prolong the

265

war and wear out Spain's resources. This document assumed many forms. It was clandestinely circulated (with or without Isabelo's knowledge, it is not clear) as a manifesto, dated September 6, 1897, addressed to "The Brave Sons of the Philippines," signed by "Malabar." It appeared under Emilio Aguinaldo's name in an English version published in the Yokohama paper *Anunciador diario del Japon* on August 10, 1897. This version was picked up by newspapers in Spain.[40]

Isabelo also reworked a series of items he had written in Bilibid with the hopes of publishing them in Spain. These were personally delivered to Primo de Rivera as the "second part" of the *Memoria* when Isabelo went to Malacañang on May 26 as part of a commission of amnestied prisoners that had an audience with the governor-general to thank him for their release. Brashly (it is reported), Isabelo used the occasion to complain about the injustice of his arrest and remind the governor-general of the *Memoria* he sent him (which the governor denied receiving). At these remarks (one of those present said) the governor "abruptly stood up from his chair as though struck by a snake and said it was a great crime to have such political ideas in the Philippines."[41]

For his impudence Isabelo was rearrested the following day. In prison, he was held incommunicado, had to sleep on the ground, and was denied food, clothes, and medical attention. Stories that came out of the prison depicted Isabelo so wrought with emotion, shouting and cursing the injustice of his imprisonment, many thought he had become unhinged.[42]

Without benefit of a trial, Isabelo was deported from the Philippines on board the *SS Alicante* in June 1897. Pedro Paterno would claim that Primo de Rivera's action was taken to save de los Reyes from the firing squad.[43] "In transit he was treated like a pig with his feet encased in an iron bar during the long voyage of more than thirty days," his son Jose later wrote.[44] While in transit in Singapore, on June 18, 1897, Isabelo wrote a letter to Bilibid chaplain Luis Viza, S.J., asking him for help in getting the order for the forfeiture of his properties canceled and for these properties to be delivered instead to Mena Crisologo "in order that my children may have something to eat." He also asked that if he is brought to Barcelona, instead of being dumped in Africa (as he feared), he would be grateful if the good father could recommend him to the Jesuits in Barcelona where he hoped to dedicate himself to commerce.[45]

He was held in the national prison in Barcelona for 23 days, then transferred to Montjuich Castle on August 7 where he remained incarcerated for six months. Well-known Spanish politicians had spent time in this medieval, mountaintop prison overlooking Barcelona. Ten months earlier Rizal himself was briefly held in Montjuich before he was shipped back to face execution in Manila. Isabelo thought—he later said—he had to "prove himself worthy of the honor of having been brought in there if he would come out alive."[46]

At Montjuich, Isabelo was kept in a windowless cell, allowed only two hours of daily exercise in the open air, and fed twice a day a meager meal of peas and potatoes. In poor health, he battled despair. In prison, he wrote a letter to Wenceslao Retana on September 14, 1897—responding to Retana's offer of help if Isabelo retracted his "political errors" —in which he expressed his disillusionment with politics (which he calls *maquiavelico*), his lament over how his fellow Filipinos had abandoned him, and his pain at being separated from his children.[47] He declared he had written *Memoria* out of bitterness and desperation, "to save my head and the future of my children," and that he was not responsible for its circulation in Spain and Manila. He had written it, he said, thinking that the Augustinians in Vigan had caused his arrest. He has realized, he said, he was mistaken and had been unjust to the friars and that he now wished to take back the harsh things he said against them.

He pictured himself as an idealistic, well-intentioned young man devoted to his country's progress. He wrote to Retana: "We were young (hardly twenty years old) and consequently partisans of progress and liberty. Nothing could overcome nature and the impulses that came with our age." Though he advocated Filipino representation in the Cortes, a free press, and other reforms, he had always expressed himself with respect and moderation. He recalled what Retana and others had said about him, that *Isabelito* was "the height of boldness," that neither Rizal nor anyone in *Solidaridad* was "daring enough to take on this question" (Cortes representation), but that he was "a small child" (*chiquillo*) who did not deserve the persecution to which he had been subjected.[48] Treading the line, he tried to exculpate himself even as he labored to maintain the dignity of his motives and purpose.

While prison chastened him it had its radicalizing influences as well. Isabelo left a revolution in the Philippines only to find himself in a

Spain rocked by its own political troubles. On August 7, 1897 (the day Isabelo was moved from Barcelona's national prison to Montjuich), Prime Minister Antonio Canovas del Castillo was assassinated by an Italian anarchist. While in the national prison, Isabelo was visited by Ignacio Bo' y Singla, a radical Catalan journalist serving a six-year term for having distributed leaflets calling for the immediate independence of Cuba. Finding in the Filipino an ally in the anti-government campaign, Bo smuggled out Isabelo's articles into print in the Spanish radical press. Versions of Isabelo's *Memoria* appeared in *El Republicano* (Barcelona), *El Nuevo Regimen* (Madrid), *La Republica* (Cadiz), *La Marsellesa* (Huelva), *El Francoli* (Tarragona), and *La Democracia* (Segovia).

The wave of political violence in Spain filled Montjuich with anarchists, syndicalists, and other extremists who gave Isabelo his first lessons in anarchism, socialism, and the class struggle. At Montjuich, a sympathetic guard supplied him with anarchist books and newspapers. In September he had as cellmate Ramon Sempau, accused of having attempted the assassination of a notorious military official responsible for tortures in Montjuich. A poet-journalist who had experienced persecution and exile, and narrowly escaped execution, Sempau impressed Isabelo who would write thirty years later:

> This Sempau was very well-educated: he knew the scientific names of the plants of the Philippines by heart, and later he translated Rizal's *Noli me tangere* into French. In his fight with some hundred police agents, he showed an absolute lack of fear. His very name caused terror in Europe. Yet in reality he was like an honest and good-natured child—yes, even a true Christ by nature . . . I repeat, on my word of honor, that the so-called anarchists, Nihilists or, as they say nowadays, Bolsheviks, are the true saviors and disinterested defenders of justice and universal brotherhood. When the prejudices of these days of moribund imperialism have disappeared, they will rightfully occupy our altars.[49]

After seven months of confinement, Isabelo was released on January 9, 1898, as a result of the general amnesty under the Pact of Biyak-na-Bato of 1897. Barred from leaving Spain, he drifted a stranger in Barcelona. Sempau's cousin Amparo provided help; Isabelo also found lodging in cheap "anarchists' clubs." It was not just cheap lodging that he found in these clubs.

Located in Spain's industrial region, Barcelona had been a hotbed of Anarchist and Anarcho-Syndicalist activity after Mikhail Bakunin's emissary, the Italian engineer Giuseppe Fanelli, visited Spain in 1868 and planted the seeds of the Socialist International in the Iberian peninsula.[50] In the years that followed trade unions and clandestine clubs proliferated and Catalonia witnessed a spiral of insurrection and repression. It was at this moment in time that Isabelo wandered into the scene. Aside from Sempau and Bo, he came to know a remarkable cast of radicals. These included Francisco Ferrer, Alejandro Lerroux, Federico Urales, and Fernando Tarrida del Marmol. We have no information, however, about the exact nature of his association with these men. Ferrer was an anti-clerical reformer who founded the famous "Modern School" movement that sought to establish schools on a strict modernist and scientific basis. Lerroux, editor of Barcelona's *La Publicidad*, was a vigorous polemicist of pro-Labor and republican sympathies. He later founded the *Union Republicana* party and became a deputy in the Cortes. Editor of the atheistic *La Revista Blanca*, Urales (whose real name was Joan Montseny) waged such an unrelenting campaign against the authorities that he spent a great part of his life in and out of exile and prison. Tarrida del Marmol was a Cuban anarchist who had spent time in Montjuich and won renown waging a campaign in Europe to expose police brutality and the new "Inquisition" in Spain.

In this heady milieu, Isabelo read Pierre-Joseph Proudhon, Mikhail Bakunin, and other socialist thinkers. He joined protest actions, carried a revolver, and once got his nose bloodied in a street demonstration. When some public buildings in the heart of Barcelona were bombed in the wake of a socialist demonstration, Isabelo was arrested and imprisoned in the company of socialists and anarchists. He was later released but the police crackdown on radicals forced him to move from Barcelona to Madrid.

In Madrid, he was taken in by Justa Jugo Vidal—daughter of the prominent Manila lawyer Jose Maria Jugo—who was *Nanay* ("mother") to Filipinos in Madrid. He linked up with other Filipinos who, in early 1898, met regularly in the residence of Miguel Morayta or the house of Doña Justa to socialize and discuss the Philippine situation. He was one of thirteen Filipinos who presented themselves as *la Colonia Filipina Reformista* in Madrid and addressed a petition to the "Spanish Nation" on February 10, 1898, that, while disavowing any separatist ambitions called for political and economic reforms in the Philippines.[51] In May 1898, Isabelo also joined Tomas Arejola in forming *Agencia de Asuntos Filipinos,* a business venture that offered representation services to Filipinos in the Philippines who had business with the Madrid government in the form of complaints, licenses, appointments and such.

Through Doña Justa, Isabelo met Maria Angeles Lopez Montero (nicknamed *Geluz* or *Gelinos*), the eighteen-year-old daughter of a retired Spanish Infantry colonel. With characteristic ardor, Isabelo wooed her through passionate letters and marginal scribblings in a book of poetry the lovers shared, Alphonse de Lamartine's *La Caida de un Angel* (*Chute d'un ange*). Isabelo and Geluz were married on Christmas Eve of 1898.

Isabelo was busy with projects. On October 18, 1898, he was approached by R.O. Walker, the British and Foreign Bible Society representative in Spain, and commissioned to translate the Bible to Iloko.[52] He began work in December 1898, translating to Iloko from C. de Balera's Spanish version of the Bible, with Walker correcting it against the Greek text and modern Spanish translations. (He continued to do this kind of work in the years that followed. It was, he later said, "one way by which I could contribute to the liberalization of dogmatic religion.")

DRAMATIC EVENTS were taking place in the Philippines. The Revolution had entered its "second phase" with the outbreak of the Spanish-American War. Against the background of this war, Isabelo was employed as publications consultant by Overseas Minister Segismundo Moret to help rally Filipino support for the anti-American effort. The appointment of a known radical was sharply criticized by the Spanish and Philippine press. Isabelo judged at this time that taking the Spanish side in the war would create conditions favorable to the Philippines. A Filipino-Spanish united front would repel the Americans, Filipinos would be granted autonomy in exchange for their show of loyalty, and if Spain reneged on autonomy, an already armed Filipino force can take matters into their own hands. Isabelo reportedly received assurances from the newly appointed governor-general Basilio Augustin on the matter of autonomy and, together with other Filipinos in Spain, he offered to return to the Philippines to organize militias in their home provinces to fight the Americans.

Isabelo launched into propaganda work, writing anti-American articles for *La Correspondencia de España* and other papers. On November 10, 1898, as Spain's loss of the Philippines became imminent, he launched, with the collaboration of Dominador Gomez, the fortnightly newspaper *Filipinas ante Europa* (1899–1901) as mouthpiece of the Philippine Republic. The periodical had two purposes: win Spanish support for the Filipino struggle against U.S. aggression and raise Filipino morale.

Events moved quickly. On December 10, 1898, in the Treaty of Paris, Spain ceded the Philippines to the United States. Isabelo's campaign now shifted from the Filipino-Spanish alliance against the U.S. to the Filipino push for independence in the face of U.S. expansionism. He was at this time part of *Comite Filipino de Madrid*, together with Dominador Gomez, Rafael del Pan, Tomas Arejola, and Vicente Ilustre. This committee was part of a coordinated effort by the Aguinaldo government to win international recognition for an independent Filipino state. On a trip to London to visit the Bible House in that city, Isabelo proceeded to Paris where he met with Felipe Agoncillo, Aguinaldo's "minister plenipotentiary," to convey to him the readiness of the Filipinos in Madrid to go back to the Philippines to fight the Yankees even as "common ordinary soldiers."[53]

Isabelo waged a vigorous campaign against the U.S. invasion of the Philippines. *Filipinas ante Europa* published news smuggled out of the Philippines through Hong Kong; articles on Aguinaldo and Filipino heroes; attacks against the friars and pro-American Filipinos; fervid diatribes against the U.S.; and propaganda on Filipino "victories" in the field. Choice pieces from the periodical were collected into *Filipinas: Independencia y Revolucion!*, published in Madrid in 1900 with a covering letter to president William McKinley that ended with the words: *Cesar, morituri te salutant* ("Caesar, we who are about to die, salute you").[54]

Copies of the paper were clandestinely circulated in the Philippines; it was the underground's most "subversive" item, possession of which meant imprisonment. Retana writes, "The American authorities persecuted this biweekly even more than the Spaniards had persecuted *La Solidaridad*."[55] In Manila, U.S. authorities seized Isabelo's correspondence, penalized possession of his works, and confiscated his properties, including his house in Tondo. The house escaped seizure by the Spanish authorities in 1896 and, at the time the Filipino-American War broke out, Mena Crisologo occupied the house which also contained P25,000 worth of indigo and the idle *El Ilocano* press. Alleging that shots had been fired from the house at American soldiers on February 22, 1899, the Americans seized the house, sold its contents at public auction, and jailed Crisologo for two months.[56] Crisologo, who had served as member of the Malolos Congress, retired to Vigan and shortly became an active *americanista*, and governor of Ilocos Sur under the Americans.

The confiscation of his properties caused Isabelo great anxiety about his family. In a letter to T.H. Pardo de Tavera on November 30, 1899, he asked for Pardo's help for his family.[57] The two were not close and belonged to opposing camps but Pardo, Isabelo knew, had great influence with U.S. authorities. In the letter, Isabelo said that he respected Pardo and liked him better than he did Antonio Luna, that they differed in their view of the U.S. occupation, but there was still room for them to share a common cause despite their differences. He was pained by the attacks against him in Pardo's *La Democracia* since his own *Filipinas ante Europa*, he said, never attacked the collaborationists directly. Isabelo was not entirely dishonest. He was, despite his contrariousness, not one to vent personal malice against those who did not agree with him.

As part of the pro-independence campaign, Isabelo published in 1899 *La Religion del Katipunan* under the imprint of the "Philippine delegation in Europe" (the Aguinaldo government's arm in Europe). An expanded edition was issued in 1900. Presented as "notes" on "the religion of the ancient Filipinos now being revived by the Association of the 'Sons of the Country' (KATIPUNAN), the agitator of Philippine Revolucion," the short treatise aimed to boost the reputation of the Aguinaldo government by explaining something of its ideological basis.

In 1899, Isabelo also took time to publish a full edition of his *Memoria*, parts of which had been serialized by Spanish newspapers under the title *Sensacional memoria sobre la revolucion filipina*. Published un-

der the imprint of the "Filipino delegation in Europe," it carried a prologue by Miguel Morayta who praised Isabelo as one in the "pleiad of
enlightened Filipinos" and one who demonstrated "admirable virility
and patriotic nobility" in writing the document under most adverse circumstances. Morayta recommended the book as an important document
for those who wanted to know why Spain lost the Philippines.[58] The new
Memoria was a palimpsest, with revisions and additions laid over the
original memorial Isabelo addressed to Fernando Primo de Rivera on
April 25, 1897. It even included the text of Rizal's *Mi ultimo adios*,
copies of which were said to have been circulated inside Bilibid Prison a
week after the poem was written. The roughness of *Memoria*, however,
with its patchwork of first-hand information, hearsay, and speculation,
gave it immediacy and did not diminish the audacity of its revelations.

As though he did not have enough on his hands, Isabelo was also
involved in efforts of the revolutionary Filipino clergy to enter into direct negotiations with the Holy See. Members of the Filipino clergy had
played an active role in the revolution and there was talk of expelling the
Spanish friars and reorganizing the Catholic Church under Filipino leadership. As early as January 22, 1899, Isabelo, representing the
"Committee of Paris" (the Filipino delegation in Europe), visited Papal
Nuncio Nava di Bontife in Madrid to convey the Aguinaldo government's
desire for the Holy See to send an apostolic delegate to look into conditions in the Philippines. While he was graciously received, the Nuncio
chided him for cheek after Isabelo rashly threatened that the imprisoned
friars will not be released until Vatican institutes reforms by appointing
Filipinos to head the Church in the Philippines.[59]

Back in the Philippines, a "religious coup d'etat" took place on Oc-
tober 23, 1899 when, at an assembly of the Filipino clergy in Paniqui,
Tarlac, Filipino priests headed by Gregorio Aglipay (the Aguinaldo
government's military vicar general) declared their independence of the
Spanish ecclesiastical hierarchy even as they affirmed their allegiance to
Rome.

Aglipay, it appears, had written Isabelo, as early as July 7, 1899,
asking him to represent the Filipino clergy before the Holy See.[60] Aglipay
was a fellow Ilocano and Isabelo's schoolmate in Letran. After October, the Paniqui assembly also authorized Isabelo to negotiate for
the revolutionary government with the Spanish Papal Nuncio for the

release of friar prisoners in exchange for Rome's *de jure* recognition of the Malolos government and the rights of the native clergy.[61] Thus, on March 29, 1900, Isabelo wrote a letter to the Filipino Clergy asking for letters from Filipino priests authorizing him to represent them in Rome. Citing his record in defending "the rights of the clergy and all the Filipinos in general," he promised to work so that all parishes will be "exclusively" occupied by Filipinos.[62] Isabelo was unable to go to Rome but, on June 29, 1901, he sent a memorial to Pope Leo XIII in which he sought the Pope's intercession and asked that Filipinos be appointed bishops and archbishops in the Philippines. Together with Tomas Arejola, Felix de Leon, and others, Isabelo signed the memorial as *presidente* of the "Europeo-American lay commission for the Filipino Clergy."[63]

After Aguinaldo's surrender proclamation of April 19, 1901, the Madrid *Comite Filipino* disbanded and Isabelo published the last issue of *Filipinas ante Europa*. (The newspaper ran for 86 issues from October 25, 1899 to June 10, 1901.) Shortly after, on July 1, he started the short-lived *El Defensor de Filipinas* as Filipino republicans abroad tried to regroup. Correspondents of the "Hong Kong Junta" tried to form a "government in exile" in a meeting in London on September 20, 1901, to continue the campaign for independence. De los Reyes was named "Secretary of Interior" of what appears to be a stillborn government under the presidency of Eduardo Lete.[64]

Isabelo, however, was already on his way back to the Philippines on board the steamer *Montevideo*. According to his son Jose, Isabelo was repatriated to Manila on July 1, 1901 "with the strong guarantee of the American Consul in Barcelona that he would not at all be molested in the Philippines, the Americans being good democrats."[65] It is likely he may have taken the required oath of allegiance to the U.S. at this time. Practically penniless, Isabelo left Spain on September 14. In letters to family and friends on the eve of his departure, he said he had sent advance notice of his return to William Howard Taft and the Manila Provost Marshall but expressed anxiety over the prospect of being arrested upon arrival.[66]

HE WAS BACK in Manila on October 15, 1901. The return of a known "agitator and anarchist" created a stir in the Manila press. Yet, hardly taking pause, the irrepressible Isabelo waded right back into Manila's political life. In a remarkable and frenetic display of energy, he simultaneously forged ahead on several initiatives he clearly already had in mind while he was still in Spain.

On October 25, he sought authority from the Philippine Commission to publish and circulate *Defensor de Filipinas*, the paper he started a few months earlier in Spain. He was refused. At a time when the Commission was discussing the Sedition Bill (Isabelo also appeared before the Commission on November 1 to register his opposition to the bill; the bill was enacted a few days later), there was a boldness to Isabelo's moves to engage the authorities directly.

On October 31, he appeared before the Commission, with Pedro Paterno and Pascual Poblete, to seek permission to form a legal political party, *Partido Nacionalista*. Writing in his diary, commissioner Bernard Moses scoffed:

> Paterno, Poblete and Reyes . . . fancy they have a large part of the population ready to follow after them in their several careers of political leadership. As thinkers on practical questions they are simply pitiable, and are significant only by the fact that in the presence of an ignorant and benighted people they are still capable of doing much harm.
>
> They have been thrown to the surface under a system that . . . laid stress on shallow egotism and gave great credit *for self-assertion.*[67]

Despite Moses's smug dismissal, there was a clear logic to Isabelo's actions. While in Madrid, Isabelo had discussed with Dominador Gomez and Eduardo Lete plans to form a party that would work for independence within the framework of the U.S. occupation. Upon returning to Manila, he published on October 26 a "Political Program" for a new political party, nationalistic in character, and advocating a separation of Church and State.[68]

There were other, probably independent moves to found a "nationalist party" prior to Isabelo's return. Pascual Poblete, editor of *Grito del Pueblo*, founded a *Partido Nacionalista* in July 1901 and, in late August, submitted its political program and list of officers to Taft. Staking a role as alternative to the pro-U.S. Partido Federal, "its members came from the middle and lower strata of the urban society." Its organizers (co-presidents were Poblete and former revolutionary Santiago Alvarez) declared they desired an end to the war and "will actively work within the law to secure for the Filipinos at the earliest possible date a most ample autonomy and in opportune time independence under the pro-tectorate of the United States of America." Authorities, however, suspected it was linked to efforts to revive the Katipunan and feared its inflamma-tory rhetoric was feeding a state of agitation in the city and countryside. They had reasons to be suspicious since the party's roster of leaders included "ex-revolutionaries" like Macario Sakay, Aurelio Tolentino, and Jose Palma.[69]

Upon arriving from Spain, Isabelo became the party's most aggres-sive spokesman and virtually took the party over. (For a time, Isabelo and Poblete were also associated with Paterno's *Asociacion de la Paz*, or-ganized in November 1901 in an aborted attempt to form a party.) The triumvirate of de los Reyes, Poblete, and Dominador Gomez—who were together in Madrid in 1898–1899—was a disturbing combination for the Americans. All three had "revolutionary" backgrounds and consider-able influence in the press, the labor movement, and the schismatic Filipino clergy. They were a colorful trio. A nephew of the martyred Fr. Mariano Gomez, Dominador Gomez (1866–1930) was educated as a physician in Spain, volunteered his service in the Spanish Army Medical Corps in Cuba in the Spanish-American War, and returned to the Phil-ippines in 1902. Poblete (1857–1921) was a tireless journalist who was deported to Spain and Africa after the revolution broke out in 1896 and returned to the Philippines in 1899. All three briefly worked in the Over-seas Ministry's propaganda arm when the Spanish-American War began.[70]

American authorities imagined a shadowy conspiracy that linked renegade party building, union organizing, schismatic theology, and the insurrectionary activities of a conglomeration of "Ricartistas" and as-sorted rebels and brigands. They took Isabelo de los Reyes to be the pivotal figure in this network. A government intelligence report said:

there was much more to the Reyes-Gomez labor movement than was believed at the time efforts were being made by the government to suppress it. For some reason the lenient and complacent authorities took Reyes for a mere fool without stopping to consider that peculiar Oriental trait of dissimulation that was one of his most marked characteristics.

Dismissing Gomez as "a conceited windbag" the government should not have taken seriously, the document went on:

it was Isabelo de los Reyes, the Roman Catholic-non-Catholic-Aglipayan-Methodist-Atheist, etc., etc., in religion, and the all-around little-of-everything in politics, who was secretly in league with the outlaws in the field, and the real power behind the bandit throne.[71]

With Isabelo's arrest in August 1902 (an episode we shall discuss shortly), leadership of the party passed to Gomez who took over as president on September 25, with Poblete as vice-president. Under Gomez, party-building escalated through such activities as public meetings and the staging of "seditious" vernacular plays, using the labor movement as base. The subsequent arrest of Gomez scattered these efforts.

In mid-December 1904, Isabelo and Gregorio Aglipay formed their own *Partido Republicano* with "independence under an American protectorate" as its plank and the *Iglesia Filipina Independiente* as its base.[72] Founded at the time of a U.S. congressional visit to assess Filipino competence for self-rule, the party sought to demonstrate that the Federal Party did not represent Filipino opinion. With Poblete's *Grito del Pueblo* as mouthpiece, the Republicans challenged the Federal Party to a show of numbers. The two parties would hold simultaneous public rallies at the Luneta to receive the U.S. delegation headed by Secretary of War William Howard Taft. The Federalistas refused to take up the challenge, scoffing that "superiority does not consist in numbers but quality, and the power of opinion does not rest on the insolence of an irresponsible mob but on the discreet direction" provided by enlightened leaders.

Undaunted, Isabelo and his associates did not allow the opportunity of Taft's visit to pass without making their presence felt. Even before Taft could step on dry land in Manila, they presented him with a manifesto of the Republican Party. Isabelo attended the receptions, pinning little medals on senators' lapels with slogans like "The Philippines asks America's help for immediate independence," and gifting Taft himself with an Ilocano fan which unfolded to display the forbidden Filipino flag.[73]

IN TANDEM with party building, Isabelo already considered, prior to his return from Spain, moving on other fronts: a pro-independence campaign in the press, the formation of an independent national church, and organizing a workers' movement.

On January 1, 1902, Isabelo was approached by a group of lithographers for help in forming a modest cooperative store of rice and other staples. Isabelo was no stranger to the fraternity of printers. As a printshop owner before the revolution, he was part of this fraternity when printers were leading elements in the craft guilds (*gremios*) that began to appear in the 1870s not only among printers, compositors, and bookbinders, but carpenters, sculptors, and shipyard and tobacco factory workers. Instead of a *sari-sari* store, Isabelo convinced his visitors to form a workers' federation. As a result, approximately 140 printers, lithographers, and other laborers formed *Union Democratica de Litografos, Impresores, Encuadernadores y Otros Obreros* at the Variedades Theater in Sampaloc on February 2, 1902. It came to be known as *Union Obrera Democratica* (UOD), the first Philippine labor federation, and Isabelo was its first president.[74]

Years later, Isabelo wrote: "I took advantage of the occasion to put into practice the good ideas I had learned from the anarchists of Barcelona who were imprisoned with me in the infamous Castle of Montjuich."[75] He had brought home with him from Europe works by Kropotkin, Proudhon, Marx, and the Italian anarchist Errico Malatesta, and these he shared with labor activists. Malatesta's *Propaganda socialista fra contadini* (Socialist propaganda between peasants, 1884), a popular exposition of class struggle (which was published in Tagalog translation years later), soon became familiar to union organizers. Workers' publications carried ideas from anarchists and socialists like the French geographer Elisee Reclus (1830–1905) and Spanish labor leader Pablo Iglesias (1850–1925).

In the first months of 1902, Isabelo filed labor protection petitions, mediated in capital-labor disputes, and staged such union-organizing activities as "educational-recreational soirees" (*veladas instructivo-recreativas*). From the original group of printers and lithographers, ideas of mutual protection spread to include barbers, tailors, mechanics, stevedores, and tobacco workers. A wave of militancy was generated not just by workers' issues but anti-U.S. sentiment and the campaign for the expulsion of friars. These themes dominated the so-called "seditious" plays in local languages that were a standard feature in union events.

In early April 1902 (while Isabelo was in Hong Kong, ostensibly to buy a printing press), a series of strikes crippled printing houses and other establishments. By June, hardly a day passed without a new strike breaking out somewhere and, in July, reaction came from businessmen with a six-week lockout by tobacco factories in the capital. In a show of force on July 4, 1902, Isabelo led a labor contingent at a U.S. Independence Day parade and, before the reviewing stand, the workers raised cheers for America and Isabelo delivered a brief address, before moving on. Fears were expressed by some quarters that, leavened with socialist ideas, the workers' movement had the makings of a revolution more threatening, "more formidable than the one Aguinaldo headed and Malvar is trying to continue." The press criticized Isabelo as "an arch rebel, a dishonest and dangerous agitator," compared him to Pablo Iglesias, a "Malay Lerroux," and called UOD a "Katipunan in new guise."[76]

Despite the show of unity, the workers' strikes of 1902 were not a "general strike" but uncoordinated actions staged by largely autonomous workers' groups. Isabelo himself had mixed, inchoate aims as a labor leader. He preached incendiary socialist principles at the same time that he invoked the alliance of Labor and Capital and devoted himself to educational-recreational activities for workers. He had an anarchist's belief in spontaneity rather than long-term organization and it may be that he was more interested at this time in mobilizing workers for political party building rather than unionism itself. Authorities, however, were alarmed at the prospect of civil disorder and Constabulary officials and business leaders (such as the American and Spanish chambers of commerce) believed that Isabelo was the main conspirator who had to be eliminated.

On the night of August 16, 1902, an American-led unit of the Philippine Constabulary entered Isabelo's home on Padre Rada St. and hauled him to the Parian police station. The ostensible reason for the arrest was the trumped-up charge that he gave orders to assassinate scabs in a protracted strike at the German-owned Commercial Tobacco Factory in Tambobong (Malabon). On August 25, he was arraigned before the

Tambobong Justice of the Peace, charged under Article 543 of the antiquated Spanish penal code for conspiring "to increase or decrease the price of labor or regulate its condition *abusively*." Isabelo declined a union offer of counsel and presented his own defense. A hasty trial convicted him on August 29, sentencing him to four months and a day in prison, but released him on bail pending appeal.

On December 12, Isabelo's appeal was heard by Judge Felix Roxas in Parañaque.[77] By this time, Isabelo's supposed goons had withdrawn the false declarations allegedly coerced by members of the Constabulary. On December 29, however, Judge Roxas upheld the lower-court verdict on "abusive" labor conspiracy and sentenced him to two months in prison. But instead of the Bilibid he was committed to Malabon where Rizal Governor Arturo Dancel, a former revolutionary leader, had him housed in a salon of the *presidencia* instead of the town jail. Here Isabelo held court as visitors came with food and blankets to make his stay comfortable.

While in detention, his speech was read at a Rizal Day rally in Malabon on December 30, in which he urged the audience to honor Rizal by their collective unity in achieving what Rizal died for, "the liberation, progress, and well-being of our land." He exhorted: "Cowardice is our greatest stumbling block. What are you afraid of if you are innocent? Ah, my brothers, Montesquieu said that the reason we are slaves is that we refuse to say *No* to unjustified and illegitimate claims and desires."[78] Hailed as a martyr, *insurrectos* holding out in the field offered to raid Malabon, liberate him by force, and install him president of the *Republica Universal Democrata Centro* (a "republic" led by a shadowy anarchist named Manuel "Prin" Ruiz).[79] Appeals for pardon or retrial were made by his lawyers Rafael Palma and Juan Sumulong. On January 30, 1903, Taft pardoned the unexpired portion of Isabelo's sentence.

While in prison, Isabelo tendered his resignation as UOD president and was replaced by Dominador Gomez on September 14, 1902. State harassment, organizational problems, and the political adventurism of its leaders forced it out of existence on May 29, 1903. Out of prison, Isabelo tried to patch up internal rivalries but on October 11, 1903, UOD was superseded by another federation, *Union del Trabajo de Filipinas*.

William Henry Scott writes that de los Reyes was "an impractical socialist visionary," but concludes that it is incorrect to say that UOD "failed."

The *Union Obrera Democratica* was certainly successful in its immediate goals. It raised the wages of some 6,000 workers between 25 and 100 percent by direct action, and probably of many thousands of others by making the strike a potent force in labor relations. It can also be argued that the Union was successful in its longer-range goals. Although there had long been a peasant tradition of millennial salvation . . . the concept of "redemption" through self-determination on the part of the working class itself seems to have been articulated for the first time in UOD meetings in 1902 . . . It was there that the printers' background of confrontation with employers proved to be the dry tinder into which Isabelo de los Reyes dropped the sparks of class consciousness, and if they did not produce a general conflagration, they at least set fires which are still burning in the Philippine labor movement.[80]

Isabelo relinquished leadership in the movement but the issue of labor remained one of his main concerns. *Redencion del Obrero*, the labor organ that he launched on October 8, 1903, continued "to report labor conditions at home and abroad, propose socialist legislation, and expound anarchist dreams of universal brotherhood" until it folded up on February 18, 1904.[81] Isabelo kept a high profile in the press, contributing to *El Comercio*, *Grito del Pueblo*, and other papers, taking up such causes as labor rights, universal suffrage, the exclusion of Chinese immigrant labor, and parity of Filipinos and Americans in the civil service.

ISABELO DE LOS REYES confronted power on another front. The Philippine revolution was not just political but "religious" as well. In the Paniqui assembly of 1899 the Filipino clergy broke away from the Spanish religious hierarchy and sought control of parishes and a direct concordat with the Holy See. The entry of American Protestant missionaries in the wake of the U.S. occupation made the situation even more unstable.

Upon his arrival from Spain in October 1901, Isabelo went into consultations with Gregorio Aglipay on the status of the Filipino clergy. On November 15, with Aglipay, Isabelo met with Protestant missionaries in the Intramuros office of the American Bible Society to discuss plans for establishing an independent Filipino church. (Isabelo had contact with Protestants in Spain because of the Bible translation project which the American Bible Society commissioned him to continue when he returned to Manila.) Nothing much came out of the Intramuros meeting because of the seeming hostility of the Protestants who demanded as condition for their cooperation agreement on such issues as making the Bible the sole rule of faith, ending the celibacy of the clergy, and abolishing Mariolatry.[82]

It was then that Isabelo decided to go his own way by proclaiming, even without Aglipay's consent, the establishment of *Iglesia Filipina Independiente.* He planned on making this proclamation at a public meeting organized by Pascual Poblete at Teatro Zorrilla to demand the expulsion of the friars. This meeting, however, was banned. Hence, Isabelo gathered *Union Obrera Democrata* members at *Centro de Bellas Artes* on Villalobos Street in Quiapo on August 3, 1902. At this meeting (attended by 42 people but inflated to "more than two thousand" in later accounts), he announced "without vacillation that from now on we definitely separate ourselves from the Vatican, forming a Filipino Independent Church." He branded the Pope the "*caudillo* of our eternal enemies, the friars," for refusing to name Filipino bishops. While it has been questioned whether he actually delivered the speech on this day, the text of the speech was published in Poblete's *Grito del Pueblo* on August 8.[83]

In this speech, Isabelo proposed an organizational structure for the new church that included a lay executive council (composed of Gomez, Poblete, and well-known nationalists) and a "dogmatic" council of sixteen priests from which the new bishops would be chosen. He named Aglipay *Obispo Maximo* of the new church, and, as honorary presidents, Taft, Aguinaldo, and Pardo. Most of those he named had not been previously consulted and they (including Pardo, Poblete, and the priests he named) publicly dissociated themselves from Isabelo's declaration of schism in the days that followed.

Isabelo may have been motivated by the desire to force the schism on those, including Aglipay, who were hesitant. In a letter responding to questions from the American historian James Robertson on May 3, 1908, six years after the event, he boasted he was the "true founder" of the independent church:

The Pope, bribed by the Spanish friars in the Philippines, turned over to them the most sacred rights of the Filipino clergy. I saw with my own eyes how they shot, hanged and tortured many poor Filipino priests in 1896–1897 despite their patent innocence. They had been imprisoned with me in the Manila jail with chains on their legs like criminals, merely because of the satanic egoism of the friars.

For this reason, availing myself of the popularity (patriotic, socialist and labor) which I then enjoyed in Manila, I proclaimed the nationalist schism on August 3, 1902, in a meeting of laborers held in the *Centro de Bellas Artes* in Manila. I founded the first labor union in the Philippines and I introduced Socialism into the country. I had obtained a raise in salary for all from 50 to 200 per cent, thanks to the strikes which I introduced in the country. You may therefore imagine my popularity heightened by my radicalism and independentism. As a result I was able to bring about the schism, against wind and waves, against the rooted Catholicism of the Filipinos, against conservative Filipinos and against Americans who looked with suspicion at any reforms as possibly leading to a political insurrection (which was an error on their part); and finally against the Filipino priests themselves, including Monsignor Aglipay, who on the 20th of that same August 1902 sent around a printed circular letter disapproving the schism.[84]

Though Aglipay initially dissociated himself from Isabelo's proclamation, he joined the movement on September 22 when, assuming the title of *Obispo Maximo* and naming Isabelo executive president, he issued the first of six Epistles that gave form and organization to *Iglesia Filipina Independiente*. With Isabelo among those in attendance, the new church was formally inaugurated on October 26 when Aglipay celebrated a pontifical Mass at a makeshift, open-air altar in Tondo, Manila.

Isabelo traveled to many parts of the country to rally people to the new church. He wrote devotional and doctrinal Aglipayan texts and directed the church publications *Boletin de la Iglesia Filipina Independiente* and *La Iglesia Filipina Independiente: Revista Catolica* (1903–1904). He turned his residence on Padre Rada St. into a temporary seminary where he himself taught aspiring Aglipayan priests. Aglipay later named him "Honorary Bishop" of the church.

Jesuit scholars Pedro Achutegui and Miguel Bernad call him "the final catalyst in the religious struggle." "Aglipay remained the rallying figure, but it was Isabelo de los Reyes who organized the movement into a schism and who gave to the new church its doctrinal direction by writing its liturgical and doctrinal books and formularies."[85]

IN FEBRUARY 1903, Isabelo left for Japan and China for a vacation and to continue his Iloko translation of the Bible and supervise its printing in Yokohama. Other sources suggest that his "real" purpose was to confer with revolutionary general Artemio Ricarte, a fellow Ilocano, in Hong Kong.

Hong Kong was a cooking pot for "conspiracies" to pursue the armed struggle for independence. The pot simmered when, at the end of February 1903, Filipinos in the Crown Colony were joined by revolutionary general Artemio Ricarte. Ricarte had served out exile in Guam and had been barred from landing in Manila because he refused to take the oath of allegiance to the U.S. It was around this time that Isabelo visited Hong Kong. Members of the "Hong Kong Junta" honored him with a banquet at which Isabelo boasted that during his detention in Malabon "insurgent leaders" daily visited him for consultations.[86]

It is not clear whether a meeting between Isabelo and Ricarte took place in Hong Kong but a meeting did take place in Manila on December 28, 1903. Ricarte had returned incognito to the Philippines on December 23 and conferred with various personalities, including Aguinaldo, Aglipay, and Gomez, on his plans for continued armed struggle. He had a long conference with Isabelo in the latter's house in Tondo, during which (Ricarte wrote) Isabelo "tried to dissuade me from my intentions, picturing the situation of the country to me, assuring me the people would not respond." Ricarte remained adamant and continued to work underground. He was captured on April 29, 1904.[87]

This did not end the career of the maverick general they called "the Viper." In 1910, after six years in Bilibid Prison, he still refused to swear allegiance to the U.S. and was again shipped to Hong Kong where he continued to plot the restoration of the Philippine Republic. Isabelo had a good reason for dissuading Ricarte from resuming hostilities when they met in December 1903. While popular sensibilities about the U.S. conquest remained raw, practically the entire Filipino leadership was more intent on reaching a peaceful accommodation with the U.S. than waging war.

In 1905, Isabelo left for Spain where he stayed until 1909. He may have gone back to mend relations with his wife Geluz. It was a tempestuous marriage; she had repeatedly urged him to stay away from politics. In Spain, he occupied himself by publishing such Aglipayan texts as *Gregorio Aglipay y otros prelados de la Iglesia Filipina Independiente* (1906) and *Biblia Filipina* (1908). He also published *La Religion Antigua de Filipinas* (1909), an elaboration of earlier studies he made on indigenous religion. He continued to comment on Philippine affairs, sending contributions to the Manila press. On the opening of the Philippine Assembly in 1907, he sarcastically wrote that Filipinos had no need for this joke to be foisted on them by the Americans— "for musical comedies, the opera *Magdapio* of composer Paterno is enough for us."[88]

It is interesting that he was in Spain when there was a resurgence of anarchist violence, particularly in Barcelona where Isabelo was.[89] A year before he arrived in that city a knife-wielding anarchist seriously wounded Prime Minister Antonio Maura as he was leaving the Barcelona Cathedral. Barcelona anarchists plotted two attempts on the life of King Alfonso XIII, the first on May 31, 1905, while the king was on a visit in Paris, the second in Madrid on May 31, 1906, during the king's royal wedding. From 1904 to 1909, a total of 66 randomly planted bombs went off or were found before they exploded in the streets of Barcelona. Suspected of being principal plotters of these terror attacks were Francisco Ferrer (who was executed in Montjuich on October 13, 1909), Alejandro Lerroux, and Federico Urales, men Isabelo knew when he was in Spain in 1897–1901. We know little of Isabelo's second Spanish sojourn but it appears that he kept his distance from an anarchism that had turned virulent. He never had, despite his reputation as a firebrand, much of a taste for violence.

On April 3, 1909, he returned to Manila with Geluz. She could not adjust to the climate and, after a few months, Isabelo brought her to Japan to recuperate. Geluz died in a Tokyo hospital on February 10, 1910, while giving birth to twin daughters doomed to die within a week. Her remains were interred in the Somei cemetery outside Tokyo.[90]

Back in the Philippines in 1911 it appears that the weight of his labors—private and public—had started to weigh him down. The situation had changed. Politics had been domesticated with the establishment of the Assembly in 1907; new leaders had taken over the labor movement; and public enthusiasm for the Philippine Independent Church, after the boom in membership in its first years, started to decline. He continued to be the gadfly, publishing almanacs in Spanish, Tagalog, and Iloko that were popular for their satirical comments on mores. In a series called *Kalendariong maanghang* (1911), for instance, he ridiculed assemblymen: "If you can't stand up to the Civil Commission, what are you wearing pants for? Better put on a skirt."[91] He was involved in ephemeral alliances the fragmented political opposition tried to mount against the dominant Nacionalista Party of Manuel Quezon and Sergio Osmeña. One of these groups was *Solidaridad Filipina*, a short-lived, "non-partisan" organization launched in 1911 to take up such causes as political and economic reforms, universal suffrage, and "immediate independence."[92]

From 1912 to 1919, Isabelo served two terms as councilor of Manila after running as a candidate for a labor-based group called *Union Reformista*. (One of the *Union Reformista* candidates was Crisanto Evangelista, a typesetter who became a labor leader and would organize in 1930 the Communist Party of the Philippines.) In the council, Isabelo worked on social welfare ordinances, pushed for the "Filipinization" of the civil service, and, to the amusement of Americans, filed resolutions urging immediate and absolute independence for the Philippines.

In 1912, he also entered into his third marriage when he wedded nineteen-year-old Maria Lim, a Chinese mestiza of Binondo, on November 12. (She died in childbirth—her ninth; his twenty-seventh child—on May 27, 1923.)[93]

In 1922, buoyed by his reputation and the huge Aglipayan vote in the North, Isabelo was elected senator, representing the senatorial district comprising Ilocos Sur, Ilocos Norte, Cagayan, Isabela, Abra, and Batanes. In this election, he defeated Quezon's candidate, Congressman Elpidio Quirino, who would year later become President of the Philippines. Like other legislators, Isabelo brokered projects, appointments, and other forms of patronage for his constituents. Yet his contrarian streak remained. He was quick in criticizing erring officials, calling down the Americans for political hypocrisy, and speaking his own mind on a variety of issues. He was known for crying out, "Enough of this nonsense!," whenever he was exasperated with debates on the Senate floor. His intent was often lost on those who took his actions as the antics of

an unregenerate and aging politician. A provocateur rather than an organizer, he was an irritant rather than a threat.

Isabelo retired from politics after a stroke left him paralyzed on June
5, 1929. Bedridden in the last decade of his life he busied himself compiling Aglipayan devotional texts and largely slipped out of public notice.

The general election for the Commonwealth government on September 17, 1935—the country's first presidential election—marked a
divide in time. It was viewed by many as a culminating affirmation of
the wisdom of a U.S.-guided democracy and, on a more local level, the
enthronement of the Quezon-Osmeña leadership. Yet, it did not quite
mask popular discontent over the unfulfilled promise of the revolution.
The election resurrected figures from the revolutionary past. Emilio
Aguinaldo, with his National Socialist Party, and Gregorio Aglipay, under his Republican Party (a revival of the defunct *Partido Republicano*
Isabelo and Aglipay founded in 1904), ran for president at the head of a
badly fragmented opposition that included such groups as "Socialist
Party of Manila," "Philippine Fascists," and "Cigar Makers' Civic League."
For reasons that are not clear, Isabelo de los Reyes also entered his name
as candidate for the National Assembly. The election saw a falling out
between Isabelo and Aglipay who resented the use of his name in Isabelo's
campaign and did not endorse his candidacy. Even Isabelo's own son
Jose called the candidacy of the paralytic septuagenarian a joke.[94]

The three old men lost badly.

"THERE IS enough chaos in me," Isabelo said, "for God to create another
world."

He had a life crammed with ideas, projects, and events. He has been
variously hailed as the "First Filipinologist" and the "father" of Philippine socialism, the Philippine labor movement, and Philippine folklore
studies. A man of capacious sympathies, he married thrice, wooed other
women, and sired a progeny that included an Aglipayan bishop, Roman
Catholic nuns, a Shintoist, and atheists.

He was an instigator, an anarchist who believed in spontaneity and
the power of ideas rather than the more pragmatic, long-term require-
ments of building institutions. Fiercely independent, he could not abide
with rigid structures of authority. There were many who found him
reckless, subject to "excessive fits of enthusiasm." Though he had a "good

heart," his indiscretions often caused pain and embarrassment to friends. When Taft pardoned Isabelo on January 30, 1903, he called Isabelo "a born agitator" and expressed doubt whether he could be controlled. One cannot restrain him, Taft said, as one cannot "prevent a torpedo from making a noise when it strikes the ground."[95]

Open-faced, with a stout figure that made him look shorter than he really was, he had the virtues of the hardy and frugal Ilocano peasant. He did not smoke, drink, or gamble, and he was a caring husband and father. "Educated but not elite, bourgeois but not aristocratic," he dealt as easily with stevedores and tobacco workers as with bishops and governors.[96]

Isabelo de los Reyes died in a Manila hospital on October 10, 1938. Controversy attended his last years as family members and associates feuded for control of his body.[97] It is debated whether he retracted his Aglipayan beliefs and died a Catholic. Efforts were exerted, particularly by his daughters who were Catholic nuns, to make him return to the Catholic faith, and, on September 14, 1936, he executed a document of retraction. Aglipayans and other family members assailed the document as spurious and, if authentic, one executed when de los Reyes no longer had full control of his faculties. A legal battle was fought for custody of the bedridden old man when one of Isabelo's sons, an Aglipayan bishop, filed a case against one of his sisters for the alleged abduction of their father. The struggle over his body continued after his death. It was blessed by Gregorio Aglipay at the Funeraria Nacional and then according to Roman Catholic rites at the San Sebastian Church in Manila. It was interred at Cementerio del Norte but, in 1944, transferred to the Aglipayan Cathedral in Tondo, Manila, on order of Supreme Bishop Isabelo de los Reyes, Jr.

He was a figure of hybrid meanings even after death.

DEPLOYING LOCAL KNOWLEDGE

THE CAREER of Isabelo de los Reyes reminds us that the Propaganda Movement was as much a local as a diasporic phenomenon. While attention has gravitated towards the work of Filipinos in Spain and elsewhere in Europe, the movement was shaped not only by realities in the colony but Filipinos working within the colony's political and intellectual confines.

While de los Reyes's forced exile in Spain was an important experience, he was more the "home-grown" intellectual than Rizal, Paterno, or Pardo were. He was proud of his provincial and ethnic origins, worked in the country, and deployed "local knowledge" as an important aspect of his authority. He illustrates, more than does Paterno or Pardo, that the "Enlightenment" was a locally produced, rather than merely imported, phenomenon.

BRASH AND PRECOCIOUS, Isabelo started writing for the Manila press at the age of sixteen. He made it clear where he was coming from, doing reportage on the Ilocos and using every opportunity to foreground the role of Ilocanos in history. In 1881, he published an article in *El Comercio*

289

(March 29, 1881), entitled *"La lealtad de los Ilocanos a España,"* on the successful defense of the islands against the Limahong incursion in the sixteenth century. Going beyond the standard tribute to Spain's glory, the article praised "the loyalty of the Ilocanos" in defending Manila against "the evil designs of Lima Hong," narrating how, under the Spaniard Juan Salcedo, "a multitude of valiant Ilocanos and a handful of Spaniards" set off from the Ilocos to Manila and drove out the Chinese invaders. In narrating this story, Isabelo chided Manila for not memorializing, whether by monument, hymn, or paintings, Salcedo's heroism as well as "the deeds of the loyal Ilocanos." Assigning agency to the "passive" natives of the provinces, the article was a jab at Manilans and the capital.[98]

He was the proud provincial. His articles praised Ilocano accomplishments, the opening of a *museo-biblioteca* in the Vigan seminary, the first prize won at the 1887 Madrid Exposition by the Vigan *calesa* (horse-drawn rig) invented by German Quiles, the successful exposition of commercial products (reported "exhibit by exhibit and medal by medal") that accompanied the 1892 fiesta of Candon in Ilocos.[99]

He addressed not only Manila but his fellow Ilocanos. He created a stir by proposing to rename two Ilocos towns after local heroes Lorenzo Peding and Pedro Lopez and when the alcalde-mayor of Ilocos raised a monument to the Spanish mestizo Miguel Vicos to honor his loyalty to Spain in assassinating the rebel Diego Silang, Isabelo asked that it be destroyed and one raised to Diego Silang instead. He wrote Ilocano almanacs with such features as "Dates Ilocanos Should Know," in which he entered not only such "useful" information as the introduction of the semaphore telegraph in 1797 but the dates of various Ilocos uprisings (1589, 1661, 1762, 1807, 1811, 1815, 1817). His *Ilocanism* was such that by 1887, Isabelo "had won the praise, bemusement, or scorn of his readers by his constant allusions to his home province."[100]

He was not parochial, however. Behind his *Ilocanism* was the will to broader native self-assertion. When Spain dispatched troops to the Caroline Islands in 1885 to put down an uprising, he published a report in *Eco de Panay*, a newspaper in Iloilo, in which he complained that Spanish soldiers were ferried in comfortable steam launches to the troopship anchored in Manila Bay while Filipino troops were delivered on lighters "like cargo" in the hot sun. The report turned out to be inaccurate (there were Spanish soldiers on the barges as well, the distinction being one of rank rather than race), but it created such consternation that the colonial government issued in 1887 a new censorship decree requiring all provincial releases to be cleared in Manila first.[101]

He was gaining a reputation as a gadfly. His treatment of Diego Silang in *Historia de Ilocos* (1890) drew the ire of the Spaniards Vicente Barrantes and Pablo Feced for suggesting the friars' complicity in Silang's assassination. Writing on the 1807 revolt in *La Ilustracion Filipina* (August 14, 1892), de los Reyes made such provocative statements as: "Revolutions are caused by concentrated grievances: when the atmosphere gets heavy enough, any little pretext can set off the explosion of the storm; but the pretext is not the real cause."[102] In various articles, he insinuated criticism of such practices as the use of torture by judicial authorities, the narrowness of colonial education, discrimination against the Filipino clergy, and the maltreatment of tenants by Spaniards and Filipinos alike. William Henry Scott says: "Indeed, it is hard to find an article of his which does not contain some subtle barb."[103]

Some of his articles of this period were issued in book form. *Filipinas: Articulos varios sobre etnografia, historia y costumbres del pais* (1887) contains four articles on historical and ethnological topics (the Tinguians, the Limahong invasion, the Dutch-Spanish wars, and the first rulers of Manila) and a miscellany of shorter pieces, called *Juguetes literarios sobre costumbres e historia* ("Literary-comic sketches on customs and history"), that show Isabelo's gift for witty, acerbic social commentary.[104]

A reprint of a study he did on the encouragement of Ferdinand Blumentritt (who generously praises it for "the erudition and competence of the author in ethnological matters"), "*El Tinguian*" expresses Isabelo's early interest in *ciencias* and nationalist counter-representation.[105] He says he has been motivated by the desire to rectify errors in what has been written about the Philippines and contribute what he can to the growth of science. Isabelo writes in the grid of a Western ethnological treatise, organizing his material under such topics as racial origins, geography and material culture, theogony, government, language, arts and customs. He speaks with the authority of one familiar with European scholarship, quoting Cicero in Latin, and invoking such authors as John Lubbock, Max Muller, and James Cowles Prichard. He reprises familiar topoi in ethnological science in locating the Tinguian in an evolutionary, hierarchic arrangement of races. He attributes to Philippine mountain tribes features of a rudimentary existence, using words like "glacial in-difference" (*glacial indiferentismo*), "indolence" (*desidia*), and "stupidity" (*frialdad*).

Within this discourse, however, he takes a critical stance, interrogat-ing what Europeans have said and claiming local, intimate knowledge of the subject. He has not only examined published sources, he has (he proudly states) been to the field (Abra province and other parts of Ilocos) collecting data. He speaks as one familiar with local places and lan-guages and at various turns refers to his having talked to locals and being an eyewitness to such events as a *baglan* (shaman) performance in the *rancheria* of Baric. The self-assurance of the young colonial is remark-able. He shows no consciousness that his was a subaltern voice, either in relation to Europeans or the "better-educated" Filipinos in Europe.

He dismisses speculative theories that the Tinguians originated from Malabar or Coromandel or China and proceeds to argue that they are of Malay descent on the basis of language, traditions, and other evidence. He distinguishes the Tinguians from the ruder tribes of the islands, say-ing that the Tinguian possesses intellectual aptitudes that can be developed and "polished" to bring him to a higher stage of civilization. Debunking static racial categories, he argues that differences are "insig-nificant" between "the partly civilized Ilocano, the Tinguian who wears pants and jacket, the pacified Igorot who though still naked has lost his unsociable and cruel nature, and the runaway fugitives with their savage customs." Differences are the effects of location and degree of civilizational exposure to lowland Ilocanos and Spaniards. He disputes the theory of John Lubbock and others that some mountain tribes have no religion, citing for support Gustav Roskoff's *Religion entre los pueblos salvajes* [*Das Religionswesen der rohesten Naturvolker* (Leipzig, 1880)]. Tinguians, he says, are "rational creatures" who recognize the existence of a "Supreme Being." Like Paterno, he argues that the Tinguians have notions of an after-life (citing the belief that the soul goes to a mountain, "as in Para-dise"), *sacerdotes* (*baglan* and other religious specialists), rites and temples (*templos*, of which he cites three kinds, *balaoa*, *cal-langan*, and another that, he says, he cannot recall).

While the Tinguians lack written laws, they have customary laws that are, Isabelo says, "law in an embryonic state." He corrects the Tinguian word list in Hans Meyer's *Vocabular des Guinaan u Tinguiano*, saying Meyer has confused some Iloko terms for Tinguian. He argues that the linguistic evidence proves that the Tinguian and the *indios* belong to the same race (*raza*). Whether claiming for the Tinguian the practices of monotheism and monogamy or their own distinct artistic forms, Isabelo locates them in the stream of history, evolving and endowed with a capacity for progressive change as well as features that make them part of a wider Malay community.

Isabelo's fascination with history is shown in his articles on the Limahong invasion, Spanish-Dutch wars, and early rulers of Manila. His narrative of the attack on the Philippines by the Chinese corsair Limahong in 1574 was praised by editor Jose Felipe del Pan as "without dispute the most extensive and thorough account to date" of the event.[106] His appetite for historical research is also shown in "*Los Regulos de Manila,*" the material for which also appeared in *La Oceania Española* (February 17, 1885) and was apparently spurred by his discovery of a notarial copy of a 1660 *expediente* that granted tax exemption to the descendants of Lacandola, "ruler of Tondo," in recognition of his services to the Royal Crown.[107] Written documents of this kind were rare since, despite the nationalist claim of widespread precolonial literacy, no precolonial documents of this kind survived, if in fact they existed. Isabelo mined the document for information on sixteenth-century Manila, interviewed Lacandola's descendants, and even tracked down a sword that Legazpi gave to Lacandola and which was still in the possession of the latter's descendants in 1834.

Isabelo recognized that source materials were scarce and riddled with bias and inconsistencies. He showed himself adept at source criticism as he tried to demonstrate how errors of interpretation were passed on from one Spanish author to another and how these authors confused the identities of historical persons because of carelessness and unfamiliarity with local usage. Marshalling available evidence, he corrected the characterization of Lacandola as a rebel, saying that he was in fact loyal to the Spanish Crown. Even as there are weaknesses in Isabelo's critique, his pursuit of "historical facts" is quite notable.

His "*Triunfos del Rosario o Los Holandeses en Filipinas*" first appeared in *Diario de Manila* and was issued as a chapbook in 1888. It is a brief history of Dutch incursions into the Philippines from the Olivier van Noort expedition of 1600 to the Spanish-Dutch encounters that continued until 1763.[108] Isabelo again displays an active intelligence in using not only published sources but primary documents he was able to examine in Manila. While his account presents itself as empirically minded—with dates, names, places, and such battle details as fleet formations—he repeats Spanish providential interpretations of events by referring to the "miraculous" intervention of the Virgin Mary (Manila's *Virgen del Santisimo Rosario*) in protecting Spain and "her children" (including, he points out, the Ilocanos who remained loyal to Spain despite Dutch agitation). He says (perhaps with an eye at Spanish publisher and censor) that his principal object is to describe "the triumphs of *Rosario*." Yet it is clear that his purpose is not mainly devotional. He speaks of the miracles with a degree of detachment, conscious of readers who may not quite believe them, he says, in "these days of incredulity." This "double-voicedness" did not escape Retana who writes that Isabelo does not believe in miracles but had the good sense to disguise his lack of faith to avoid being branded *sospechoso* ("suspect," euphemism for a subversive).[109]

Interpellating European discourse on the Philippines, Isabelo saw himself as a contributor to the fund of knowledge not only because of "local access" but because he knew what the Europeans knew. He dedicated *Triunfos del Rosario* to P.A. Tiele, the librarian of University of Utrecht (Holland), offering his text to the Dutch scholar to amplify (*ampliar*) the latter's *De Europeers in den Maleischen Archipel*. Apologizing for his work's shortcomings, Isabelo says that he has tried to be the "impartial" historian, taking his data from declarations properly subscribed before ecclesiastical authorities. He corrects, for instance, Blumentritt's *Hollandische angriffe auf die Philippinen im XVI, XVII, XVIII* (1880), saying that in some points Blumentritt may have been misled by that "famous Calvinist Baldaus" [chronicler Philippus Baldaeus] of the Dutch East Indies Company.[110]

He did not only correspond with European scholars but participated in local discourses. In the second part of *Filipinas*, Isabelo presents short satiric sketches of Philippine life dedicated to such friends as Pedro Paterno, T.H. Pardo de Tavera, and Wenceslao Retana. The miscellany displays Isabelo's comic gifts as he talks about Manila typesetters (*cajistas*) and hitchhikers, a festivity in Malabon, and love and courtship in the Ilocos, including a local parody of the European manual of courtly love ("*Il Libro dell'Amore*").

One of the most interesting of these sketches, "*El Diablo en Filipinas*" (which first appeared in *La Oceania Española* in 1885), irreverently sketches a "history of the devil in the Philippines."[111] It is framed as a dialogue of two friends attending a wake in Bulacan in which one of them defends his belief in ghosts and spirits by invoking the authority of Spanish missionary chronicles. Citing these chronicles—in the manner of a Biblical exegete, complete with volume and page numbers—he demonstrates that the friars themselves reported apparitions of the Devil. Isabelo wickedly concludes that it must have been the friars who introduced the Devil into the Philippines. Cleverly associating white foreigners with malevolent spirits, the piece (which Isabelo calls a *centon*, "crazy quilt") contains naughty observations like, "It is so that the crazies of my country assert that they have *Spanish* (*castilas*) friends visible only to them."[112]

ISABELO EMBARKED in 1889 on writing the history of the Philippines, serializing in *Revista Catolica de Filipinas* what he hoped would be a two-part account dealing with the *prehistorica* and *historica*, the precolonial and colonial phases, of Philippine history. He completed the "prehistorical" part but *Revista Catolica* discontinued the series (for lack of interest among readers, according to Retana). *Prehistoria de Filipinas* was published in 1889 as "first volume" of *Historia de Filipinas*. No second volume appeared.[113]

Much of the material of *Prehistoria* also appeared in Isabelo's *Las Islas Visayas en la epoca de la conquista*, issued as a chapbook by an Iloilo press in 1887 and reissued in an enlarged edition in 1889.[114] Focused on the Visayas (because Isabelo was writing for a Visayan paper and the Visayas is the best chronicled region in early Spanish accounts), *Islas Visayas* uses the region for what, in effect, is a brief, summative survey of precolonial Philippine culture. Isabelo also incorporates his material on "prehistory" into the more fully-developed, two-volume *Historia de Ilocos*, published in Manila in 1890.[115]

Reviewing Spanish missionary accounts, Isabelo points to limitations and contradictions occasioned by their aims (they were written as histories of the religious orders rather than the Filipinos), sources, and conditions of production. He confesses to the difficulty of writing the country's history because of the flaws and rarity of sources. Yet he privileges his own account by locating himself "after" and "above" these sources with references to his methodology and fidelity to truth (*verdad*). He states, for instance, that in resolving contradictions he will attend to "the antiquity (*antiguedad*) of the authors, their sources and degree of their respectability" and the "thoroughness" of their works.[116]

Isabelo's histories use a Western template for describing a culture, organizing the text around such topics as geography, material culture, race, cosmogony, social organization, arts and customs, and language. He draws from three kinds of sources. The most important of these are the colonial-missionary reports, dictionaries, and chronicles (Pedro Chirino, Francisco Colin, Gaspar de San Agustin, Joaquin Martinez de Zuñiga). The second are non-Spanish, European texts (A.B. Meyer, William Marsden, John Crawfurd, Joseph Montano), and works by Filipino contemporaries like Paterno and Pardo. The third is personal knowledge, drawn from experience or interviews with respondents, which he embroiders into the text. Only in his twenties, Isabelo impresses the reader with the range of his learning. He cites Cuvier and Prichard and mentions titles in German, French, and English. While it is not clear in what form or language he accessed these sources, his historical writings are nevertheless a remarkable performance.

He assumes that *Filipinas* constitutes a distinct, definable entity. He describes the Visayan islands, at Spanish contact, as places already endowed with population, natural resources, and rich cultural forms and practices (such as boats and dwellings, clothing and adornments, weapons, and the use of gold powder as currency), and linked by trade to lands like Borneo, China, and Japan. In describing local society, he repeats what at the time had become standard characterization of precolonial Philippines. It was a land divided into many *estados*, in which even small islands like Limasawa and Mactan had their own *regulos* or *dattos*, though there were large ones with "true kings" (*verdaderos reyes*), like Lacandola of Tondo, who ruled over an extensive territory. There was a well-articulated social structure in which inhabitants were divided into five *clases* of noblemen, freemen, and certain orders of serfs and slaves: *principales* ("a species of nobility"), *timauas*, *tomatabanes*, *tumarampoques*, and *ayueis* or *halon*.

He cites the barangay as the basic political unit, explaining the word as derived from the *barcadas* ("boat-load") of early Malay migrants, that later evolved into a *barrio* or *rancheria* of more or less a hundred families under a chief who acquired his title through force, wealth, bravery, moral excellence, and "in some cases by inheritance." The chief was called *agturay* in Ilocos and not, he says (demonstrating his interest in local distinctions) *rey* in the Spanish sense, *datto* among the Moros, or the Tagalog *maguinoo* or Arabic *rajah*. Prehispanic inhabitants, he continues, had customary laws governing chieftainship and succession, conflict settlement, inheritance, and family relations. They had their own system of weights and measures, mode of reckoning time, and a wealth of other cultural possessions. Like Paterno, he argues that pre-Hispanic Filipinos believed in a Supreme Being, together with a hierarchy of lesser deities, and that, contrary to Spanish missionary opinion, Filipinos had religious images (*idolos*) and a hierarchy of religious specialists that included "a kind (*especie*) of Bishop" called *Sonat*.

Isabelo is less ebullient than Paterno, of whom he had written: "I really regret the harm that can be caused to the strict sciences by the many invented traditions one reads in *La Antigua Civilizacion de Filipinas*."[117] For himself, he writes: "The history of the Philippines suffers from contradictions, and it is necessary to patiently compare one and the other, investigating the truth with a serene and impartial spirit."[118] Assuming a stance of objectivity, he says, for instance, that a nobility (*nobleza*) "in its proper sense" did not exist either in the Visayas or Ilocos.[119] What constituted the privileged class (*principalia*) were those who had wealth, physical prowess, or sagacity, a nonhereditary status from which *dattos* were drawn. He points out that "rights" (*derechos*) could not be properly spoken of in relation to precontact society since the notion of rights implies a collection of formally promulgated, written laws. He does not gloss over such practices as slave-raiding, saying that "the Visayan pirates were more terrible than the Mohammedans of Jolo and Mindanao."[120] His "objectivity" was such that Retana inaccurately writes of *Islas Visayas*: "Far from following the footsteps of Paterno, the author hardly concedes anything worthy of true praise to the ancient inhabitants."[121]

Like many writers of the time, he Orientalizes the native, saying that precontact society was "very young, almost infantile, in its customs," and ruled by force as is characteristic of "savagery" (*salvajismo*). Or that Visayans, "like all Orientals are somewhat lazy," fond of "foolery and fiestas" (*devaneos y fiestas*), and so improvident that "once they have a handful of rice in the house, they do not like to work."[122]

Like his contemporaries, he speculated on the origins of race and language. As he says: "There is no issue more debated in the History of the Philippines than the filiation (*filiacion*) of its inhabitants."[123] He reviews the most exotic hypotheses that had been advanced: that Filipinos were born *ex putre*, created by magic or an incubus, or sired by the sun or descended from Adam. Writers had theorized that the islands' inhabitants came from Malabar and Coromandel in Hindustan, from China, Japan, or America. Others surmised an Arab origin, such that even Blumentritt had commented on seeing Isabelo's photograph that he was of "Arabic type" (*tipo arabe*).[124] Isabelo mentions, with obvious amusement, that "the scholarly and elegant Filipino writer Doctor Paterno" has "fantasized"—in *Antigua Civilizacion de Filipinas*, which Isabelo slyly calls a *novela*—that one finds in the country's prehistory "no less than the vestiges of Egypt, Persia, America, China, Japan, India, Europe, etc."[125] In the same breath, he mentions the theory of the *darwinistas* and *haeckelistas* that the Negritos or Aetas are immediate descendants of Haeckel's "dumb, ape-like *Homo Pithecoides*" [referring to German zoologist Ernst Haeckel (1834–1919)].

Taking off from the work of French anthropologist Joseph Montano, Isabelo proceeds to examine the scholarship on the subject. He agrees that the *razas Filipinas* have been "profoundly altered by racial mixing" but finds Montano's three zones of settlement simplistic and arbitrary. Montano had classified the races into spatio-temporal zones of the "interior," into which the Negritos had been pushed by the Malays; an "intermediate" zone occupied by Malays, who had, in turn, been pushed back by the *indonesianos* who occupied the "exterior" or coastal zone.[126] Isabelo says that the reality is not as neat since races are found mixed across these spaces.

At the same time, Isabelo affirms Montano's thesis of three Malay "subraces" in the archipelago—*mestiza de negrito*, *mestiza de chino*, and *mestiza de indonesiano y arabe*. On the Chinese mix, however, he disagrees with Montano and other writers that such racial mixing already took place in pre-Hispanic times when, according to a theory advanced by writers like Colin and repeated by Cesare Cantu, the archipelago was part of the Chinese empire. The Chinese and Japanese did not settle in the islands in precolonial times but "traded out of their boats," Isabelo argues, citing an "unpublished official document" in his possession indicating that Lacandola, the ruler of Tondo, monopolized the trade in foreign goods in his territory. Lacandola received these goods on consignment and distributed them to his subjects who were barred from trading directly with either the Chinese or Japanese.

On the matter of "Indonesians," Isabelo asks: "But what does *indonesiano* mean? Where do they live? Is there a country called *Indonesia*? No: *indonesio* or *indonesiano* is a name recently invented to better classify the numerous branches of the Malay race, as with *germano*, *eslavo*, *latino*, etc." Most ethnographers, he says, do not adopt the Indonesian category, and even among its proponents there is no uniformity of views on the races that pertain to this category. He concludes: "Since this new ethnographic division is based, apparently, on very recent and not too well-clarified data, we shall not give it any importance."[127]

On the Aetas or Negritos, he concurs with the common opinion that there are to be found not just in the Philippines but other Malay lands (*paises malayos*) where they had been pushed into the hinterlands because of their "unsociable, misanthropic, and nomadic" nature. On their origins, he favors the view that they descended from the *raza negra* that appeared in the Malay archipelago in remote times. He rejects the opinion (made by Blumentritt and Carl Semper) that Negritos came from the *papuas* of Melanesia, citing as proof Rudolf Virchow's osteological studies of skeletons collected by Semper and Fedor Jagor showing that Negritos have physiognomic features different from those of the *papuas* and *australianos*. He does not agree with Alfred Russel Wallace, Hendrik Kern, and others who believe that Papuans, Negritos, and Malays belong to the same race.[128] The linguistic evidence used to support this theory does not convince de los Reyes. Linguistic affinities may be the result of borrowing (facilitated, he says, by the rudimentary character of these languages) and the linguistic evidence should not be confounded with racial filiation. Like "most European anthropologists," he says, he believes that there are no more than two distinct races in Oceania: Malay and Negro (the latter proceeding from one or two origins, *Papua* and *Africano*). Isabelo says that the more he has studied history, ethnography, and folklore, the more convinced he is that "the Malay origin of Filipinos, excepting Aetas, is INDUBITABLE [Isabelo's emphasis]."[129]

Isabelo attempts to untangle the welter of opinions on the place of origin of Malay Filipinos. He troubles the theory that Sumatra is the originary place by asking (anticipating today's knowledge): "But is it not possible that the direction of the Malay invasions may have been from East to West, that is, from the Philippines to Sumatra?"[130] While he believes there is no strong reason to dismiss this hypothesis, he is, however, inclined to follow general opinion, citing sources like Francisco Colin and William Marsden, that Filipinos descended from the *Battaks* of Toba lake (Sumatra) who may have come, "in remote times," from the territory of *Menang-kabau*.[131] What he cannot admit are arguments, raised by some Spanish chroniclers, that trace Philippine groups to specific places of origin, i.e., that Visayans came from Macassar, Pampangos from Sumatra, or Tagalogs from Malacca. This is too speculative and it should suffice to simply speak of a *Malay* origin.

He criticizes writers who devise facile racial distinctions among Ilocanos, Tagalogs, Bicolanos, Visayans, and others, saying that these groups share many racial and cultural characteristics and constitute a definable unity. Rejecting Cuvier's characterization of a plethora of races in the Philippines, Isabelo claims an integrity to the population of the islands. "In my insignificant opinion, Visayans, like Tagalogs, Ilocanos, Bicolanos, and other civilized peoples inhabiting the coast of Luzon, are Malay in origin, although perhaps with some dose of other blood types like Negritoid and Mongoloid (*tipo negritoide y mongoloide*)."[132]

Isabelo was also preoccupied with the problem of language. Like Paterno and Pardo, Isabelo takes up the question of precolonial syllabaries, devising his own *cuadros paleografico* in which he presents local scripts with samples from elsewhere in the Malay archipelago. Like the others, he weighs the opinions of authors like Martin de Rada, Sinibaldo de Mas, and William Marsden; discusses the number of characters and the use of the *corlit*; and tackles the controversy over the direction of local writing. He compliments Pardo, "distinguished Filipino linguist," mentioning that Pardo kindly shared with him a bamboo specimen of Tagbanua writing. While acknowledging the work of others, Isabelo always makes it a point to stake out his own position as an independent investigator.

Like other scholars of the time, he turned to language as a way to understand the genealogy of peoples. Citing such authorities as G. W.

Leibniz and Wilhelm Schlegel, Isabelo says it is not enough to compare words (*voces*) but must examine structure (*estructura*) and compare grammars. It is not enough to focus on terminologies since there are *vocablos* shared by many languages, correspondences that have been used to justify a common linguistic matrix lost from the time of the Tower of Babel. Hence, it is important to study language "conscientiously" as it is easy to fall into error. Isabelo, however, does not engage in grammatical analysis but, like Paterno and Pardo, focuses mostly on lexical data, supporting his arguments with word comparisons in Philippine and non-Philippine languages.

Isabelo concurs with other scholars on the descent of Visayan, Ilocano, and other local languages from Malay. As in the question of race, Isabelo, however, dismisses as speculative theories of the specific origin for Visayan or Ilocano (whether Celebes, Borneo, or Sumatra), saying it suffices to affirm the Malay base of Philippine languages. This does not deter him from speculating that Visayan and Ilocano are dialects of Sumatran Malay; that the Malays who came to the Philippines spoke one language which later divided into dialects because of difficulties of communication and factors like the natives' penchant for novelty and invention. He says: "The indigenes are natural corruptors of languages and inventors of thousand upon thousand of new terms." (He cites as example how the Spanish *tranvia*, "streetcar," was "Filipinized," *filipinizado*, by Manilans to refer to prostitutes, *muger publica*.) He asserts that Filipinos shared one language in the beginning but, following the law of "philological evolution," this divided into many languages and dialects "just as Latin decomposed into Spanish, Italian, French, Portuguese, etc."

While acknowledging the provisionality of current knowledge, he confesses to being partial to the theory of Malay's diffusion from a Sumatran "homeland," a process in which Malay was enriched by Persian, Sanskrit, and "primitive" dialects in the region. For this reason, Arab or Sanskrit elements in Philippine languages do not necessarily prove an Arab or Hindu presence since these were elements that may have already been part of the Malay language that entered the Philippines in precolonial times. Islam, for one, was not introduced to the Philippines by Arabs but Islamized Malays from places like Borneo and Sumatra.

Isabelo could be fanciful as when he suggests a historical link by playing with the correspondence between Francisco Colin's thesis of a

Malay originary home in the environs of Toba lake in Sumatra and the etymology of *Tagalog* (*taga* + *ilog*, "from a river or riverine area"). *Tagalos*, he adds, while commonly used to refer to the coastal people of Central Luzon, may be used to refer to all *malayos Filipinos*, encompassing Ilocanos, Bicolanos, Visayans, and others. It is a term more proper than *indios* (with its false reference, he says, to India), *indigenas* (which means *natural* and refers to whoever is born in a given place), or *filipinos* (which does not distinguish race, since it also means Europeans born in the Philippines).[133] (In his own practice, however, Isabelo uses the word *Filipino*.)

Isabelo's histories mainly take the form of a descriptive sketch that inventories culture items and historical facts, organized according to how European historico-ethnological accounts characterized cultures, drawn from published sources and the author's own personal experience, and supported by comparative data from other societies. He adopts Western scientific discourse, deploying racialist terms and categories, citing cranial shape, skin pigmentation, or hair type and using terms like "prognathic" and "dolicephalic."

He does not start out with autochthonous sources, categories, or methods. His claim to difference lies in his persona as a native writing about his own country, "independently" interrogating European texts. Responding to John Crawfurd's view that Malay is a branch of Polynesian, he wonders whether one can argue just as well that Polynesian dialects come from Malay instead of vice versa. He warns against facile analogies of customs and languages since these do not prove anything except the idea of a primordial unity of races and languages "as we are taught by the Bible." Chiding other authors for gratuitous conclusions made on the basis of weak and insufficient evidence, he says that if mere resemblances are taken as proof then the Filipino can be connected to anyone and everyone. In effect, he appreciates that filiations can be quite hidden and complex. In this, he counters (though he does not explicitly say so) Paterno's rampant comparisons and demonstrates (though he does not say it) that he is as versed in the philological scholarship of the day as the better-trained Pardo was. While positioning himself as a critical participant, he nevertheless operates within a Europe-dominated discursive domain. The contradiction between autonomy and subordination makes for the creative gaps and tensions in his work.

Isabelo is not a primitivist. He appreciates the historically contingent. Yet his interpretation of history is animated by the impulse to define an object (the *Filipino*) that is integral and distinctive. He asserts the shared racial and cultural origins of Ilocanos, Tagalogs, Bicolanos, and other *filipinos civilizados*, minimizes the differences between, say, the Ilocano and the Tinguian, and criticizes those who overstress the multiplicity of races and languages. He says that the country's inhabitants professed a "single religion" (*una sola religion*), animism, before the introduction of Islam and Christianity; their beliefs revealed the "Filipino Psychology" (*la Psicologia Filipina*); they had their own form of writing, which was more widely diffused than had been acknowledged and shows that they were not "so backward as commonly believed."

In *Historia de Ilocos* (1890), Isabelo attempts what may be the first comprehensive history of a region and—he claims— "the first time that a Filipino criterion (*criterio Filipino*) emerged independently in the history of the country."[134] It was planned as a three-volume work, the first to cover the pre-Spanish period, the second the span from 1572 to the division of Ilocos into two provinces in 1818, the third to carry the account from 1818 to the end of the nineteenth century. Only the first two volumes appeared. The first (*parte prehistorica*) repeats and develops material earlier contained in *Islas Visayas* (1888) and *Prehistoria de Filipinas* (1889). The second (*parte historica*) pieces together articles Isabelo published in Manila newspapers.

Volume II is a dry chronicle of the establishment of towns, successions of bishops, and events like disasters, raids, and revolts. Mostly annalistic, it is biased by the author's Spanish sources towards the chronicle of civic and religious events. It is relieved, however, by the author's alertness to opportunities to highlight the agency of Ilocanos. He accords attention to the Ilocano poet Pedro Bukaneg and the "Ilocano generals" Lorenzo Peding and Pedro Lopez who led Ilocanos in defending the province against rebels from Zambales in 1660. In a pointed aside, he proposes a monument to Peding and Lopez who are, he says, vastly more heroic than the "*traidor amigo* Vicos" to whom a monument was built in Ilocos.[135] The reference is to Miguel Vicos, the assassin of Diego Silang, the Ilocano hero to whom Isabelo devotes a substantial section of the book. Silang (1730–1763) led an Ilocos uprising at the time of the British invasion of Manila in 1762. Against the official view of Silang as a misguided, disloyal subject who allied himself with the British, de los Reyes depicts Silang as intelligent, brave, and fairly well-educated (he had worked in Manila and was literate in Spanish, Isabelo claims) whose "exploits seem to have been inspired by the theories of Voltaire, Rousseau, Diderot, and other philosophers that produced much later the events of the Paris Commune."[136] Isabelo says that Silang was not a British agent, his real goal was "the independence of Ilocos" and the liberation of the lower class (*kailianes, clase baja*) from the "odious tyranny of the *babaknang (principales indigenas).*"[137]

Isabelo was extemporizing out of limited evidence. His boldness drew a sharp response from Vicente Barrantes and Wenceslao Retana. *La Voz de España* denounced his book as "a book of propaganda against the Spaniards, a book consisting of scandalous infamies and calumnies."[138]

Unfinished, *Historia de Ilocos* did not measure up to Isabelo's ambitions. Material and intellectual conditions militated against the project of a "comprehensive" history. This is shown in the radical disjunction between *Historia*'s "prehistorical" and "historical" parts, between an ethnological treatise on an autonomous "Filipino" civilization and a colonial chronicle in which the "native element" appears only in the manner of a querulous, running footnote. I doubt that Isabelo intended the inconsistent, hybrid nature of his project to be read as a political comment but he must have been, as he wrote it, aware of the inherent difficulties in writing an autonomous history of a people under colonial domination.

THE CONTRADICTION in writing an autonomous history based on foreign sources may have occasioned *El Folk-Lore Filipino*. In writing the history of the Philippines, Isabelo laments that current knowledge does not allow greater certainty. He says that the question of determining races and origins cannot be seriously considered without a profound knowledge of *Antropologia* and *Folk-Lore*. With limited knowledge, nebulous hypotheses will be advanced today which will be refuted tomorrow. For this reason, he says, eminent scholars "like the Germans [Rudolf] Virchow and [Adolf] Bastian and the Frenchmen [E.T.] Hamy and Rosng [presumably, French ethnologist Leon Prunol de Rosny]" have completely left the "fantastic field of conjectures" to espouse the law of the "New School" (*Nueva Escuela*) which, he says, is *ciencia folk-lorica*, an all-inclusive science that aims "to recover customs, legends, traditions, superstitions, architecture, paintings, clothes, popular music, vocabularies, grammars of civilized and savage peoples, and other vestiges of past ages, to save them from progress, which tends to level with great speed all the races with their boats, railroads, telegraph, and commercial activity."[139]

This was a subject he pursued in what may be his most important contribution to Philippine studies, *El Folk-Lore Filipino*, which was published in two volumes in Manila in 1889.[140] Isabelo credits editor Jose Felipe del Pan for spurring him to embark on folklore studies. Del Pan had written an article in *La Oceania Filipina* (March 25, 1884) calling on readers to contribute folklore articles. Inspired by interest in the subject in the peninsula (just four years earlier, Spanish folkloristics was born when *Bases del Folk-Lore Español* was published in Seville), del Pan urged Isabelo, then only nineteen, to write on local folklore, giving him books on the subject to whet his interest. (It was del Pan who collected Isabelo's articles and sent them off to the Madrid *Exposicion General de las Islas Filipinas* in 1887 where they won a silver medal.)

Isabelo felt he was well positioned for folklore research. As he related in *Historia de Ilocos*, he was born in a province far from "the light of civilization," lived with household servants from the hinterland "where all is shadow and superstition," and was raised on nighttime stories "fabulous and superstitious." In a class assignment by his teacher in Vigan, he won in a contest of who could present the longest list of local superstitions. He narrated that traveling by boat to Manila in 1880, he joined other passengers in kneeling to pray, as they passed a furnace-like mountain crag on the Zambales coast that was reputed to be enchanted. He feared that if he did not comply with the obligation, he and his companions would be sick all the way to Manila. His head full of "absurd beliefs," he was a folklore resource.[141]

Isabelo received encouragement from folklorists in the peninsula, among them Antonio Machado, "founder of Spanish folklore," and Alejandro Guichot, editor of the journal *Folk-Lore Andaluz* (1883–1888). They encouraged him to organize a Philippine folklore society by giving him books on folklore published in Spain. Enthused, Isabelo collected materials, wrote for periodicals (including Madrid's *Boletin de la Ensenanza Libre*), and issued an open letter calling on readers to collect, publish, and organize regional branches of the proposed folklore society.[142] (While the society did not materialize it was a remarkable move nevertheless. The British Folk-Lore Society was established only seven years earlier, in 1878, and the American Folk-Lore Society only in 1888.) Jose de Lacalle (pseud., *Astoll*), an anatomy professor at Universidad de Santo Tomas, reacted to Isabelo's call with a sardonic piece in *El Comercio* (June 27, 1885) in which he expressed pessimism about the project because of the "lazy intellect" and cosmopolitan pretensions of colonial society. He nevertheless lauded Isabelo for his initiative.

Folk-Lore Filipino is an anthology of "curious" and hitherto unpublished documents, letters, reports, poems, and periodical articles authored by Isabelo and other contributors. It was what the French called a *bibliotheque*, a loosely ordered, open-ended compilation of items, some of them appended to the book already in press, meant not so much as a finished "book" as a ready, accessible archive. At one turn, Isabelo apologizes that he had some difficulty because he had to "write this book away from Ilocos"; at another, he said that he had originally planned a much longer work, with "seven chapters" just on Iloko folklore, but had to leave planned chapters unwritten because of pressing commitments as a journalist.[143]

He was not just writing a book but building an "archive" of his people's culture and history. Approaching the project with the excitement of the recently initiated, he saw it as a contribution to a new "school" (*escuela*) that would generate systematic and reliable data for "scientific" theories. He was conscious of folklore as a *ciencia nueva* ("new science"), noting that the word *folk-lore* was first used in the British newspaper *The Athenaeum* in 1846 by William J. Thoms and that the world's first folklore society was established in London only in 1878.[144] He alludes to European folklorists, including Paul Sebillot (1846–1918), the most active French folklorist at the close of the nineteenth century. Isabelo says it was the initial objective of *Folk-lore* to gather legends, fables, and superstitions, investigate and compare cultures, and deduce theories pertinent to prehistoric man. Its scope was expanded, however, to serve the needs of anthropology and other sciences and help create new ones, like Astronomy from Astrology or Chemistry from Alchemy. It is, in effect, "a general archive at the service of all sciences."[145]

He adopts an expansive definition of folklore that takes it as coextensive with all branches of human knowledge. He variously calls it "an arsenal of data useful to all the sciences" and "a universal museum where scholars can study the complete history of the past."[146] His own project, Isabelo says, aims to gather popular knowledge relevant to all sciences, to include such items as popular literary forms, ceremonies and games, folk speech, and names of places, plants, and animals. "In short, all the elements that constitute the temperament, knowledge, and languages contained in the oral tradition, in monuments and in writings, are considered indispensable materials in understanding and reconstructing scientifically the history and culture of a people."[147]

On whether *Folk-Lore* is a "science" and whether it should concentrate on "primitive man," he coyly suggests that such questions can be left to more learned scholars. He is not shy, however, in calling down some European authors for confusing Folklore with Mythology and Mythology with Theogony. He is explicit in claiming for his work the status of science. "[N]o nursemaid or peasant who has a wide repertoire of stories can be called a folklorist," he wrote, "because there are specific rules to follow." Neither the village storyteller nor the antiquarian who indiscriminately collects curiosities can be properly called a folklorist. He has, in his own work, been guided by "objectivity" (*imparcialidad*) such that his fellow Ilocanos have complained about his having publicized their unpleasant practices. Neither is Isabelo inclined to limit folklore to the study of "primitive man." He defines folklore thus: "The endeavor of human thought that has for its object to gather all the data that the unenlightened folk (*gente no ilustrada*) know and have, which have not yet been studied."[148]

Isabelo saw himself as a participant in a world community of scholars advancing the cause of modern knowledge. He drops the names of foreign authors, acknowledges the support given him by Spanish folklorists (to whom he dedicates his work), reproduces in his book the silver medal certificate awarded him at the Madrid Exposition of 1887, and cites his membership in Europe's learned societies. He stresses such methods as documentation of sources, faithfulness of transcription, and utilization of materials like musical scores and drawings. He takes a comparatist approach, making references to Spanish, Chinese, or Norse legends and myths. He says: "In order to distinguish genuine Philippine superstitious beliefs, it is necessary to have an exhaustive knowledge of *Folk-Lore Universal* and the country's prehistory."[149] Otherwise, we err in identifying as our own what may have come from elsewhere.

This went beyond simple vanity. Underscoring his intellectual links to the peninsula, he located himself at the vanguard of a "new science," boasted of unmediated access to the metropolis, and "provincialized" less enlightened Spaniards and creoles in the colony. Beyond the claims to cosmopolitanism, he saw his work as an act of *patriotismo* as well. He believed that the knowledge gained would not only be useful and practical, it would allow a "scientific reconstruction" of the history of Filipino culture. Against those who had criticized him for exposing what was unflattering to the Filipino, he claimed the privilege of speaking as an "indigene" (instead of an outsider) and argued that patriotism must be grounded in critical self-knowledge.[150]

Given his ambitions of a total archive, the contents of *Folk-Lore Filipino* are eclectic. Devising a system he does not quite sustain, he divides folklore into "Folk-Thought" (popular mentality) and "Folk-Wont" (popular customs and practices). Focused on Ilocano folklore, the first volume consists of sections on (1) "religion, mythology and psychology," (2) "types, customs and practices," and (3) "literature." In an appendix, he expresses regret he does not have the time to produce a more voluminous work. He outlines what remain to be written, including chapters on popular medicine, "folk-wit," and "folk-science." Brimming with projects, he speaks of a plan to publish a dictionary of Spanish words that had been Filipinized and Filipino words without Spanish equivalents. Still he does append to the volume a miscellany of pieces he had either written for the book, published in local papers, or submitted to the Madrid Exposition, including articles on Ilocano hero Diego Silang, millenarian revolts, and local miracles of the Virgin.[151] To justify the book's title, he includes articles on the folklore of Zambales and Malabon, the local history of Malabon, and a long, fictional narrative entitled "*Folk-Lore Administrativo?*"

In this loose and hybrid book, Isabelo offers descriptions of mythological creatures, origin myths, venerated objects, amulets and potions, meteorological and zoological beliefs, maritime lore, healers and seers, and local notions of the soul (under the heading *psicologia*). In random order, he throws in descriptions of local Catholic feasts, stories of crime occasioned by the use of amulets (which he calls *crimenes folk-loristicas*), and "Ilocano superstitions that are similarly found in Europe." In the chapter on *Folk-Wont*, he gives an ethnographic profile of the Ilocanos, their physical characteristics, social organization, material culture, verbal and artistic forms, and life-cycle rituals and practices.

For *Folk-Literature*, Isabelo gathers the articles he wrote on his mother Leona Florentino's poetry, which he had earlier sent to Andzia Wolska as a contribution to the *Bibliotheque International des Oeuvres de Femmes* in the Paris Universal Exposition of 1889. Here Isabelo puts together twenty-one of her unpublished poems in the original Iloko and his Spanish prose translation. He introduces the collection with a dedication to his mother and brief articles on "The Filipino Woman," "The Filipina in Ancient Times," "The Education of the Filipina Under the Spaniards," "The Filipina and Literature," and "Philippine Poetics." Leona's poems are presented under two headings: "congratulatory poems" and "erotic compositions." These are occasional poems, written for friends for such occasions as a betrothal, birthday, or (in the case of the "erotic" poems, which are more romantic than erotic) a declaration of love. Locally renowned, Leona wrote many of these verses without thought of preserving or publishing them.

Rendering fulsome tribute to the Filipino woman ("morally superior to the Filipino male," "more intelligent," artistically gifted), Isabelo claims that the precolonial woman did not only enjoy high symbolic and religious status (as attested, he says, by the belief in goddesses and women *babailan*), customs and laws on matters like marriage and work were "very generous" for women. While Spanish colonial education restricted women's education to the "practical arts," women have not been passive, as shown in their founding of sodalities and beguinages. Because of their superior qualities, he writes, they should be freed to play a more active civilizing role in society.[152]

Apologetic about how the poems may not appeal to Europeans, Isabelo strains to explain them, saying first that these were written "according to purely Filipino or Ilocano taste and style," and that these will be valuable to philologists in studying "Filipino poetics" (*poetica Filipina*) as a contribution to "an archive of tastes and styles" which is international and richer for having more variety. Isabelo's discussion of the verses reveals his ambivalent position vis-à-vis "native tradition." On one hand, claiming an ontological status for what he calls *poetica Filipina*, he claims for Florentino's poetry a distinctness of language and style the Spanish translation does not quite convey. Yet, he cannot explain these qualities beyond saying that they are peculiar and effective, that they express the native temperament and are loved by the people because they satisfy their "taste" (*gusto*). He says: "Her poems are interesting for their naturalness and originality; they are not composed in the European style. . . . They are written in the genuinely Filipino style."[153]

While he briefly points out distinctive sound patterns and facets of the poet's sensibility, he is impressionistic in his judgments and rather Eurocentric, as in his statement that the poems do not follow strict rules on rhyming and are lacking in "an art that would coordinate and polish." He does not examine the poems in relation to autochthonous poetic tradition or, for that matter, the Europeanization of literary forms already evident in Florentino's poetry. He confesses that he has himself studied European poetry and prefers it to Filipino poetry. Yet, he says that he is always moved when he hears a native song even "though subsequent analysis of its lyrics reveals them to be a bundle of nonsense (*cumulo de disparates*)."[154] Caught in this ambivalence, Isabelo falls back on arguments of nativist sentiment and folkloric value.

THE SECOND VOLUME of *Folk-Lore Filipino* presents the contributions of writers who responded to Isabelo's call for folklore articles.

Miguel Zaragoza's "*Al Rededor de un Cadaver*," published in the Iloilo newspaper *Porvenir de Bisayas* in 1885, is a first-person narrative written in the style of the *cuadro de costumbres*.[155] It relates, in an animated and comic style, the narrator's experience of finding himself in an incongruously festive wake for a dead woman. Isabelo, speaking as the initiated, comments that Zaragoza's contribution cannot be "properly" called folklore (which, he says, follows a higher "scientific" aim) since it is a piece of fiction that exaggerates the customs it depicts to amuse its readers. He will, however, allow "imaginative" works like this (acknowledging that he himself wrote in this genre) since it contains a "chain of truths" (*cadena de verdades*) in its account of local lifeways.

Mariano Ponce's "*El Folk-Lore Bulaqueño*," Pedro Serrano's "*Folk-Lore Pampango*," and Pio Mondragon's "*Folk-Lore Tayabeño*" are straightforward, documentary pieces on the folklore of Bulacan, Pampanga, and Tayabas, respectively.[156] Together, they form a rich grab bag of local lore. Legends, myths, and local personalities (like Bulacan folk hero Sarong-bayani and Tayabas rebel Hermano Pule) are paraded in loose taxonomic order, with little or no editorial commentary. The contributors are educated Filipinos who appear ambivalent about what they are describing (amused and parodic, in the case of Zaragoza, a noted painter; detached in the case of Ponce). Yet they appreciate the value of folklore-collecting as scholarship and expression of *patriotismo*. In Serrano's words, the project was a way of "tightening the bond that unites all Filipinos."[157]

Isabelo fills the remainder of the volume with his own contributions. Under the title "*Miscelanea Folk-Lorica*," he presents a series of "curious" documents he received from an unnamed old man. These purport to be properly notarized nineteenth-century wills and testaments that incorporate, among others, a *testamento* executed in San Carlos, Pangasinan, on March 25, 1539, by Fernando Malang Balagtas, a Christian convert. The documents set forth property inventories and genealogical data that trace the testators' descent back to Lacandola, "ruler of Tondo," and assorted nobility, including the rulers of Ternate and Borneo. Isabelo admits he did not have the time to diligently examine these documents in the "light of History" and would leave it to historians to ascertain their authenticity. He himself introduces some footnotes to point out anachronisms though one senses his desire for the manuscripts to be true. He judiciously says that he is not giving these documents more value than as "*material folk-lorico,*" "coarse material that the artist can polish" in writing Philippine history.[158]

Ending the second volume, Isabelo includes a piece on the folklore of Pandacan and, more important, "*Vida de Lam-ang (Antiguo Poema Popular de Ilocos),*" a version of an epic poem a copy of which Isabelo procured from Fr. Gerardo Blanco, Spanish parish priest of Bangar.[159] He presents Blanco's verse transcript (which, he says, he had changed to the "traditional" quatrain form from the six-line stanza of the copy), with intercalated prose translation in Spanish. Now regarded "the oldest recorded Philippine folk epic," *Lam-ang* was first serialized in *El Ilocano* (December 1889–February 1890).

Though *Folk-lore Filipino* seems like a print version of the "cabinet of curiosities," Isabelo was no mere collector of curiosities. He appreciated the grand ambitions of the "new science" and tried to learn all he could about its principles and methods. Moreover, he conceived his work as a "national" project. He publicized it in the local papers and called on the participation of other Filipinos. He was excited not only by the prospect of recovering what was obscured or misrepresented, but by folklore's promise of providing the basis for uncovering his people's origins and character. He gathers materials under the inclusive title of *Filipino* folklore. He writes: "The Filipinos of color (*filipinos de color*) are of the same family: the Malay. Thus, their features and customs, such as their theogonies and superstitions, are very similar."[160]

He places himself *within* this culture. In *Folk-Lore Filipino*, he proudly introduces himself as "*hermano de los selvaticos, aetas, igorrotes y tinguianes*" ("brother of the forest dwellers, Aetas, Igorots and Tinguians.")[161] On top of the published sources he mines (from Recollect Juan de la Concepcion's *Historia general de Philipinas* [1788-92] to Englishman George Forster's *A Voyage Round the World* [1777]), he interposes his personal recollections and experiences and names specific persons or places in a display of "local knowledge." While the work is mainly documentary in character, he freely offers his own opinions and analyses.

He has a historically dynamic view of folklore. Unlike some European folklorists who would limit the study to "primitive" man, Isabelo does not draw rigid distinctions between past and present, pure and hybrid, or autochthonous and foreign. He includes contemporary data on current history and economy, describes Spanish-colonial accretions, localized Christian rites, and linguistic mixes, and presents them in a variety of literary styles (inventories, fictional narratives, archival documents).

He uses folklore as medium for social and political criticism as well. His article on "Ilocano superstitions that are similarly found in Europe" subverts the colonialist's modern/primitive dichotomy by showing that superstitions in "pagan" Philippines do not only have analogues in "modern" Spain but may have been introduced into the islands by Spaniards. In "*Folk-Lore Administrativo?*," first published in *Diario de Manila* in 1890, he introduces his original take on what constitutes folklore by relating the story of a decent and hardworking Ilocano named Isio who is corrupted and impoverished by the experience of serving in the colonial bureaucracy. Expanding the boundaries of "folklore," Isabelo unsettles it from the plane of the exotic and remote by showing how the Kafkaesque workings of the colonial state can be just as perversely fantastic. Exposing Spanish pretensions to law and order as so much "folk-lore," the piece was (Isabelo would later boast) "pure *filibusterismo*."[162]

THE REVOLUTION created opportunities for Isabelo de los Reyes to push his intellectual initiatives forward. This is not always or easily apparent. Written "on the run," his works have a very complicated textuality. He repeats, elaborates, and repositions ideas in a variety of forms and contexts. Occasional and opportunistic rather than planned, his books characteristically take the form of compilations or palimpsestic writings-upon-writings. This makes it important to see his works always in relation to the particular forms they take and the particular sites and moments of their enunciation.

This is shown in two works he published in 1899: *La sensacional memoria sobre la Revolucion filipina de 1896–1897* and *Apuntes para un ensayo de teodicea filipina: la religion del Katipunan.* Published in Madrid under the auspices of the "Filipino delegation in Europe" during the Spanish-American interregnum, both recast earlier works as contributions to the Filipino campaign for independence.

Sensacional memoria was apparently meant to be the definitive edition of a work that appeared in many places and forms, the memorial Isabelo addressed to Fernando Primo de Rivera "in the name of the political prisoners in all of the provinces of the Philippines" on April 25, 1897. Spanish rule having ended, Isabelo freely elaborates on the original manifesto. In explaining the causes of the revolution, the original memorial focuses on the abuses of a "macchiavellian frailocracy," but also raises "the agrarian question" (*la cuestion agraria*) in the form of landgrabbing and onerous rents and other levies. To forestall revolution, it calls for the expulsion of the friars, return of usurped lands, Filipino participation in government, and the grant of the political and economic concessions given to the Antilles (Cuba and Puerto Rico).

The 1899 edition gave Isabelo the opportunity to proclaim and embellish his role in the revolution. He boasts that his reputation in the Philippines as a *progresista* won him the admiration of "radical elements" in the country. He was perhaps the only *ilustrado*, he says, who associated with the poor Katipuneros and sympathized with their aims. His reputation was such that in 1888 some liberal priests wanted him to head a pro-Church *progresista* party. Nothing came out of it because he set certain conditions on reforms the priests could not accept. He was also asked, he says, to translate the anti-Rizal pamphlets of Fr. Jose Rodriguez for popular distribution. He accepted with the intention of "subverting" the texts to make the friars look ridiculous but he was not given permission to publish. Because of his writings, he was threatened with exile and excommunication. The friars prevented him from being appointed to a public office and lobbied with newspaper owners to have him removed. Though he was not part of any revolutionary group, he was arrested when the revolution broke out. When he was released from prison in May 1897, Isabelo says, he was invited to be a chief in the insurrection but he declined because of his responsibility to his orphaned children.

In *Sensacional memoria* and *Apuntes para un ensayo de teodicea filipina* he offers an account of the origin, structure, and philosophy of the Katipunan. Of particular interest is Isabelo's interpretation of the class character and ideology of the Katipunan. While he situates the revolution (a "true and important revolution" and not just a "simple insurrection," he says) in the context of the "universal" human struggle against tyranny, Isabelo gives it a distinct class character. He says that the Katipunan was an "association of the poor" separate and distinct from Freemasonry and *Liga Filipina*, both of which were of the elite, conservative, and inclined to the defense of personal interests and the status quo.

He says of the Katipunan: "The moral aim was democratic education, urbanity and hygiene (*urbanidad e hygiene*), combating religious fanaticism, the effeminate character, and obscurantism the friars wanted to imbue in the Filipino."[163] Isabelo gives an interesting account of the early organization of the Katipunan, saying that its leaders used Masonic formulas but adapted them to the cultural grade of its mostly peasant and proletarian membership. He describes an initiation ritual in which the initiand is asked questions to which he gives the replies in which he had been instructed by his sponsor (*padrino*):

Q. In what state did the Spaniards find the Tagalog people in the time of the conquest?

A. On the Spaniards' arrival, the coastal Filipinos enjoyed a particular civilization, inasmuch as they had cannons and silk clothing, enjoyed political liberty, maintained diplomatic and commercial relations with neighboring Asian countries, had their own religion and writing system; in a word, they lived happy in their independence.

Q. What situation are they in now?

A. The missionary friars have done nothing to civilize the Filipinos inasmuch as they considered the civilization and enlightenment of the country incompatible with their interests; they did nothing but teach the formulas of Catholicism without deepening it, dazzling the Tagalogs with the spectacles of splendid religious feasts that they had to pay for to the benefit of the friars...

Q. What future can the Filipino hope for?

A. With faith, valor, and constancy, all these evils shall in the future be redressed.[164]

The revolution was not just separatist, it envisioned a new social and moral order. Isabelo states, "The highest (*summum*) of the aspirations of the Katipunan was a <u>Communist republic</u> [His emphasis]."[165] Isabelo's interpretation of the Katipunan ideology takes authority from interviews he had with leaders and common participants imprisoned in Bilibid. Yet it is determined as well by the circumstances of its writing. As a propagandist based in Spain in 1899–1900, he wanted to make "respectable" the beleaguered Philippine Republic by basing it on a coherent, modern philosophy. Moreover, his acquaintance with Catalonian radicals and readings in socialist literature at this time— combined with the populist sympathies he already had when he was in the Philippines—may have predisposed him to find "communist" ideas in the Katipunan movement.

However, in *Apuntes para un ensayo de teodicea filipina* (1899), he also claims an indigenous philosophical foundation to the Katipunan and the Revolution. (This small treatise was reissued in an expanded edition in 1900.) Its full title reads: "Notes in Order to Familiarize Myself with Philippine Theodicy. The Religion of the Katipunan which is the religion of the ancient Filipinos now being revived by the Association of the 'Sons of the Country' (*KATIPUNAN*), the agitator of Philippine Revolution."[166] Isabelo says he wrote the work in Bilibid Prison, aboard the ship that brought him to Spain, and in Montjuich on a "worm-eaten board placed on top of two earthen jars," the only furniture in his cell. He apologizes that, given these circumstances, he had to write what he calls "notes," "meditations," a series of "bas-reliefs," without the benefit of his library or papers.

He declares that it is his purpose to "reconstruct the foundations of that primitive religion of the Malay Filipinos." Isabelo's immediate aim, however, is to produce a piece of propaganda and a moral guide for the revolution. He dedicates the work to Emilio Aguinaldo ("most meritorious apostle of *Bathala*"); its second edition carries a brief sketch of Aguinaldo and is illustrated with photographs of Filipino reformers and revolutionaries. In sketching what he calls a "Filipino theodicy," he performs the double task of outlining the principles of the religion being "revived" and "practiced" by the Katipunan and explaining its potential as religion for the nation the revolution aimed to create. In aligning the religion to the needs of the moment and the future, he says:

> the philosopher of the Katipunan must study hard in order to bring this religious system back to its ancient purity, to purge and cleanse it of its historical inaccuracies and exotic superstitions, perfecting and finishing it with the modern accomplishments of progress and rejecting its childish and trifling fears. He should consult the philosophies of other well known religions.[167]

Citing "authoritative" religious and scientific texts, name-dropping Spinoza and Renan, Isabelo constructs a Filipino religion called *Bathalismo* to claim ideological legitimacy and coherence to the Katipunan struggle, claiming for it not only an indigenous basis but a universalist and progressivist essence.

HIS CONSTRUCTION of a "Filipino Religion" developed out of his earlier studies in Philippine mythology. He built on his work on precolonial mythology in such texts as "*Mitologia ilocana*" (1888), and the books *Las Islas Visayas*, *Historia de Ilocos*, and *Prehistoria de Filipinas. Apuntes para un ensayo de teodicea filipina* would in turn metamorphose as *La Religion Antigua de los Filipinos* in 1909 and adumbrate the doctrinal works he produced for the Philippine Independent Church.

In setting forth the principles of what he calls the "Filipino Theodicy," Isabelo begins with the idealist premise that all great religions are basically similar: "Basically all religions are the same, their only differences lie in the language and systems... religion and morality are Universal."[168] The creator of man and the universe is the "infinite Wisdom, limitless Love, and omnipotent Creator" that is called God, a notion that underlies all religions and makes all of them, including *Bathalismo*, worthy of respect.

Taking the evolutionist view, he explains differences by saying that God communicates to his creatures in "the form called for by their grade of culture." He idealizes indigenous religion as purer and holier since the people were "new-born" and without malice, as contrasted with a "too materialistic" Spanish-colonial Catholicism. The primitive Filipinos were as much God's children as the first Christians. "If God appeared to the Hebrews with the name Jehova, to the Jews with the name Jesus, to the Hindus with the name Brahma, and to the Mohammedans with the name Ala, etcetera, why can we not speak also of his appearing with the name Bathala to the Filipinos, if we are all equally His children?"[169]

Peeling away "errors" in European sources, Isabelo argues that "Malay Filipinos" (by which he excludes Muslims and Negritos) had the makings of a common and high religion. They professed one religion and believed in one Supreme Creator, *Bathala*. Plurality of nomenclature occasioned the foreigner's error in assuming Filipinos had many cults and deities. The representation of the sun or moon as the abode of Bathala was mistakenly taken as sun- or moon-worship, and *maykapal* ("powerful"), an attribute of Bathala, was confused with the name of a deity. He blames Spanish friars not only for misrepresenting indigenous beliefs—saying, for instance, that the Filipino deity was a crocodile, a crow, or the rainbow—but for having corrupted a "pure" religion with their own fanatical practices. Local beliefs in such mythological creatures as *patianak*, *cafre*, and *tigbalang* are Spanish accretions. Indigenous *aniteria* has been ridiculed by the friars, yet (Isabelo says) it is not too different from the frenzied dancing of Catholic worshippers in the church of Obando (Bulacan) petitioning St. Pascual Baylon to cure them of their maladies.

Isabelo proceeds to distill the elements of Filipino theology: ancient Filipinos believed that man is "composed of material forms and of the Spiritual Motor that animates them"; that man is endowed by the Creator with "Free Will" and Reason to guide him; and that ancient Filipino

Morality is a "Universal Morality" since it is made up of "natural laws" inscribed in the human "conscience." This morality, he says, can be reduced into the following precepts: "to love always and not to harm anybody," "to be just always and refrain from perpetrating abuses," and to have "zeal for one's own development and one's neighbor's development and perfection, which is nothing else than the Universal Law of Progress."[170]

Like Paterno, Isabelo highlights the similarities between *Bathalismo* and Christianity. The ancient Filipino, he says, had ideas of the soul (*kalolua, kararua, karkarma*) and Hell (*kasamaan, solad*) as well as his own rites of baptism and marriage (effected, he says, through the blood compact that, he adds, the Katipuneros practice). The ancient Filipino believed in secondary deities with specialized functions reminiscent of Greek religions and the saints of Catholicism. He had an idea about a Triune God but conceived the Trinity as attributes rather than persons, these attributes being "Eternal Love, Omnipotent Creator, and All-Knowing Providence."

Isabelo locates the most developed form of this ancient religion among "Malay Filipinos," marking a distinction between their religion and the beliefs of such aboriginal groups as the Gaddang, Ifugao, and Igorot. He writes: "As we leave the coastlines, center of the ancient Filipino civilization, and go to the hinterland, we will notice that the Filipino religion gradually loses its purity and becomes more barbarous, as more superstitions and uncivilized ideas get into it."[171] Thus he says: "The purity of the Filipino religion is obscured by superstitions of mountain dwellers and by inaccurate remarks made by the historians." He urges "the philosopher of the Katipunan" to study this problem thoroughly "in order to bring this religious system back to its pristine purity, by expurgating its historical inaccuracies and superstitions." He adds: "The Katipunan Philosopher must also explore and dig deeply into other religions and the sciences, to enable him to improve and perfect this religious system, by making it compatible with all possible human progress because it is for this that the Creator has given us the light of reason."[172]

This ancient religion was "more or less advanced," even if not quite elaborated, and "purer and more rational than those religions which today claim to be true and philosophically correct, such as certain mysticisms of Christianity and Brahmanism." It partakes of "Pantheism,

Philosophic Spiritism, Darwinism, Greek Mythology and all other systems, without excluding scientific progress." Such an advanced theodicy presupposes a high level of culture. Thus Isabelo points to pre-Spanish Filipinos having a developed culture, a "regular government," and diplomatic and commercial relations with Japan, China, and *Malasia*. In fact, he says, Filipinos were "comparable to the Japanese, their brothers in origin, in their aptitudes and intellectual attainments."[173] Their level of pre-scientific understanding augured well for their development for, as Isabelo says, "relatively speaking, ancient Filipinos had an advanced knowledge of astronomy" and their ideas of creation were "completely Darwinistic."[174]

He credits Rizal and Paterno for uncovering the Filipino God, Bathala. His arguments often seem a reprise of Paterno. Like Paterno, he exalts *Bathalismo* by attempting to show what it has in common with "high religions," thus claiming for the Tagalog/Filipino a level of social and moral attainment comparable with more "advanced" civilizations. He moves beyond Paterno, however, by constructing "Filipino Religion" along Deist and scientistic lines. Unlike Paterno, he rejects the Biblical interpretation of human history and claims a psychic unity that allows for the independent invention of religious beliefs. He rejects the belief in Hell and Purgatory and, invoking modern science, says that the age of the earth must be reckoned in millions rather than thousands of years. He gives a rationalist interpretation to the Filipino belief in souls and spirits by drawing arguments from Spiritism (*Espiritismo*). He quotes Allan Kardec: "Spirits are formed from the intelligent element (*elemento inteligente*) that exists in the Universe, they are the individualization (*individualizacion*) of the intelligent principle (*principio inteligente*) just as bodies are the individualization of the material principle."[175]

Isabelo is not interested in a return to an "ancient religion" but its development through the recovery and refinement of its core concepts. Playing the role of moral philosopher of the revolution, Isabelo says that, unlike Catholics, "we do not accept any dogma or infallible book and our only Gospel or Bible is Science, which we should study freely with the use of reason, the natural light that God gave us." Religion, he says, is nothing but morality raised to the sublime, for which reason the two are intimately connected: "Religion is the rule of conduct in relation to God and morals is the rule of conduct among ourselves."

In presenting the nobility of Filipino thought and connecting it to the inexorable advance of a regime of reason, Isabelo was building a case for the revolution Filipinos were waging. Man was born free, "complete, dignified, honorable," and with the duty to defend his liberty since there can be no progress where freedom is absent and ignorance holds sway. As sure as God exists, Isabelo says, "the triumph of our independence" is a certainty.

Isabelo expanded on these ideas in *La Religion Antigua de los Filipinos* (1909). Writing in a different moment (in 1909 he was no longer proclaiming the gospel of the revolution but that of a new church), he framed the study as part of a continuing project of cultural recovery. And though he does not declare this, he was also engaged in laying the historical and intellectual justification for the "national church" he helped establish some years earlier.

Isabelo restates his ideas on the evolution of religion. The "true foundation" of Filipino religion is animism: "The true basis of Filipino Religion, as with that of all Malays, is the cult of the souls of ancestors, called *Anitos,* from *Ani (peri-espiritu,* semi-spiritual ghost or shade*)* and from *hantu* (Sanskrit), dead, that is, soul of the dead."[176] Animism, he says, is indigenous and "the first form of religion in all lands," hence the commonalities between local religion and other religions in the world.

Elaborating on an earlier thesis, he speculates that the more "pure" form of the Filipino Religion has been conserved in the Ilocos region, in contrast to Mindanao, Visayas, and Manila, areas "converted" to Mohammedanism at the time of Spanish contact where local religion was mixed (*mezclada*) with the influence of Brahmanism and Buddhism as well. Elements of the old religion can still be found beneath layers of Hindu, Mohammedan, and Christian influence in the mythology of Tagalogs, Visayans, Bicolanos, and other lowland groups. For their part, Ilocanos, because they live close to the mountain tribes, have preserved the old religion with less adulteration.

Isabelo's arguments move from the present to the past, in an archaeology of beliefs that sets out from Christian categories. On the idea of a supreme Creator-God, *Bathala Meikapal,* Isabelo says that the word *bathala* is Sanskrit in origin (*bathara,* "lord") and variants of the same word or concept are found among the Batak, Bugis, Macasares, and the Borneo Dayak. The word was used by the inhabitants of Manila and the southern islands who had relations with Hindu and Mohammedan Malays. It is, however, unknown in northern Luzon and neither is it an indigenous Tagalog word. He says that *anito* is the more ancient word, which was replaced by *diuata* in Visayas and Mindanao and *badhala* in Manila and its surrounding areas. He speculates that *bathala* may have been a Spanish gloss on *badhala*, a word Tagalogs used to refer to the augury of birds and astronomical phenomena. He says that the "true name" for the Divine Creator among Tagalogs was *Meykapal* but this was superseded by *Bathala* after the latter was popularized by the missionaries. Such mistranslation was occasioned by a Biblical bias "to invent a Filipino cosmogony to prove the veracity of Genesis."

He considers foreign the Catholic ideas of Satan and Hell. He rejects the analogy drawn by Gaspar de San Agustin and Juan Francisco de San Antonio between the Visayan *solad* and the Christian Hell and the interpretation of the mythological creature *Pandakesita* as a Charon-like figure who ferries the soul of the dead from Hell to Paradise. Isabelo explains that *solad* is not "hell" but, as with the Ngadju of Borneo, a subterranean world to which all souls go but not necessarily to suffer. *Pandakesita*, on the other hand, is not indigenous; the word comes, he says, from *pandak* ("dwarf") and *sitan* (the Muslim "Satan"). With the possible exception of the Bagobo *kilot* and the Tagbanua *basaud*, Filipinos, believing that God is incapable of creating a place of such dire misery, have no concept or word for Hell.

Taking an intellectualist approach, Isabelo disparages Catholic beliefs in Satan. The idea of Satan, he says, came about because people customarily represented the gods of their enemies as malevolent spirits, depicting them in the imaginary figures of ferocious and terrifying animals at the same time that they represented their own idols (even if crudely made, he says) as the very model of beauty. He similarly dismisses beliefs in divine apparitions, saying these are "optical illusions" and "phenomena of the imagination and memory." Citing French astronomer Camilo Flammarion, he says there are physiological and psychological explanations for these phenomena as illustrated in the susceptibility to hallucinations of shamans and persons under the influence of hashish.

On the other hand, Isabelo claims local parallels to Christian ideas and practices. There is a Filipino conception of Paradise, he says, a place reserved for just and brave souls, usually imagined, as in the Bible, as a sacred mountain in the locality. This paradise is variously called *Makang, Kalualhatian, Ologan, Kamburagan,* or *Kamurauayan.* (He adds that the word *langit,* which the Spaniards adopted as a word for paradise, simply means "sky"; it is not an ancient *paraiso.*) Filipinos had ceremonies corresponding to the Christian baptism in indigenous rites related to naming the newborn, renaming the sick, or purifying the captive before he is returned to his family and village. Appropriating statements from missionary authors, he points to the existence of native priests and priestesses who were consecrated to the cult of *anitos* and were respected and meritorious healers. Spanish authors, he says, have erred in identifying the *sonat* (a local "bishop') as a circumciser (a specialist called *tuli* and *bating,* when the operation was done on males or females and animals, respectively) and were misled by the priest's long vestment into saying there were transvestite priests.

In the main section of *Religion Antigua,* Isabelo surveys the religion of various Philippine groups. He uses a variety of sources for this quick and summary survey: missionary dictionaries and chronicles, non-Spanish European works, and his own personal knowledge. Explaining religion in a comparativist vein, he alludes to a long line of Western travelers and scholars, from Herodotus to John Lubbock. In rationalizing the welter of data, Isabelo adopts a hierarchic, evolutionary framework. At the base of the ladder is the "primitive animism" of the aboriginal Negritos. At an intermediate level is the polytheism of groups like the Igorot, Bagobo, Tiruray, and Subano, some of whom had begun to develop a form of monotheism at the time of Spanish contact. At an advanced stage is the monotheism of the Itnegs and Tinguianes, whom he classifies as "monotheists" together with coastal Ilocanos, Tagalogs, Pangasinenses, Bicolanos, and Visayans.

In arguing for a pre-Hispanic monotheism, he isolates the belief in a "Supreme Creator" called by various names in the islands, the Igorot *Kabunian,* Tagalog *Maykapal,* Ilocano *Angngalo* or *Namarsua,* Visayan *Laon* or *Sidapa,* Pangasinan *Anagaoley,* Zambales *Malyari,* and Pampango *Suku.* This monotheism coexisted with beliefs in other deities and spirits, which Isabelo variously explains as survivals of a "primitive polytheism" or subsidiary deities that, "like the Christian saints," evolved through a logic of internal differentiation according to locus and function.

322

Isabelo highlights religious elements common to Philippine ethnic groups as well as those analogous to other religions. He universalizes the local by drawing parallels with Hindu, Egyptian, Persian, Hebrew, and Greek religions. Citing wide-ranging examples, Isabelo says that one can find among Filipinos beliefs suggestive of such ideas as reincarnation, transmigration, and totemism. He says that, "as in Japanese Shintoism," Filipinos revered the moon and sun as ancestors. He argues, however, that this had a secondary place in local religion and may have been Hindu or Mohammedan in origin. He relates the curing ritual performed by the *baylan* to the literature on shamanism, citing an eclectic set of sources that includes Vilhelm Graah and David Crantz (on Greenland), John Williams (Fiji), and Richard Burton (Africa). Marking parallels in Egyptian, Greek, Malay, and other mythologies, he calls the Ilocano god Angngalo, a giant who raised the sky and created the seas and mountains, *el Atlas filipino*, and describes Maguayan, a Hiligaynon deity who ferries the soul in a boat to the other life, *el Caron filipino*.

He acknowledges that the theogonies of the *tribus* remain to be fully studied to disentangle the confused genealogical relations and religious nomenclature. He maintains, however, that the seeming anarchy of local gods is a matter of language. As elsewhere in the world, he says, one finds neighboring communities giving different names and attributes to the same deity or combining two deities as one. "The diversity of names only arises from the difference of languages and traditions; at bottom our religion is the same as Christianity."[177] He says that from the "evidence" he has gathered the "civilized peoples" of the archipelago had only one religion (*una sola Religion*). In this connection, he remarks that this indicates that the people then were not disorganized, perennially warring tribes (as represented by Spanish writers) but a "confederated nation" (*un gran pueblo confederado*).[178]

When Isabelo wrote *Religion Antigua* in 1909 he was already interested in the literature on Spiritism. With its use of nineteenth-century research in thermodynamics and the ideas of the seventeenth-century mathematician Gottfried Liebniz, Spiritism's claims of a scientific basis appealed to Isabelo. Invoking Spiritism, Isabelo says that humans and animals are animated by "a fluid, plastic bond" called *Peri-espiritu* or *Meta-espiritu*.[179] This "spirit" is different from the "soul" since one is incorporeal while the other has an "airy body visible like the shadow, and at times palpable." For this reason people come to believe that these "spirits" dwell in forests, fields and abandoned houses; molest travelers; and enter the body of the living and cause sickness. Animism is "nothing else but modern Spiritism (*Espiritismo*)," Isabelo says.[180] He then proceeds to draw similarities between the two: the belief in the existence of a "semi-material soul" (which animists call *anioaas* or *karkarma* when the body is living and *anito* or *kalulua* when the body is dead, and the spiritists *alma* when it is still united to the body and *espiritu* when it is separated from the body); the belief that not only persons but objects have a *sombra* or spirit; that the spirit can enter other living bodies; and that shamans and mediums conjure spirits when they are in a "hysterical, visionary, and hallucinatory" state.

While Isabelo says his aim is "scientific" and not merely "patriotic," his criticism of those he calls "myopic, exclusivist Christians" is a clear subtext. Catholic sacraments have pagan origins, and the veneration of divinized ancestors is not too different from the Catholic cult of saints. Spanish chroniclers say Filipinos worship human remains, but how about the veneration of the remains of saints and friars of dubious sanctity? Claiming a superior rationality for local beliefs, Isabelo argues that the ideas of Devil and Hell are foreign to Filipinos since this contradicts the idea of God's infinite mercy. On morality, he says there are differences since it varies according to the people's "customs and psychology." He expresses optimism in the continual refinement of morality despite religious doctrines that suppress the natural instincts—such as the practices of chastity and castration, which run counter to nature, hence God's will since Nature is God-ordained.

Reviewing theories on the history of religion, Isabelo takes the stance of an interlocutor, criticizing, for instance, John Lubbock's developmental stages (atheism, fetishism, totemism, shamanism, anthropomorphism, supernaturalism, and "moral religion"). He takes issue with Lubbock's view that there was a stage when man had no religion, saying this has been refuted by "eminent ethnographers." He likewise questions Lubbock's concept of fetishism, saying that Philippine examples (such as the rain-making ritual of submerging sacred images in water, called *holom*) do not mean that objects were considered "deities."

Explaining local deities in terms of fundamental mental processes, Isabelo claims a "universality" for Filipino religion. While he says that there is little consensus on the stages in the history of religion, he has firm notions on what should go into such a theory. Religion begins with vague, embryonic notions that man perfects as abstract, elevated conceptions as his intelligence develops. First came the stage of *infantil inconsciencia* when the child experienced the mysterious in the universe as natural and spontaneous and was not preoccupied with attributing it to a god or gods. The *causa determinante* of the "religious idea," he says, was fear over nature's destructive power (such as hurricanes and volcanic eruptions) and the experience of death, a fear at first instinctive and then translated into ideas about the presence of animate spirits. The belief in spirits, *anitismo*, was fostered by the experience of such phenomena as dreams, shadows, reflections, and emanations, that suggested a *semi-espiritu* surviving after death, the idea of a force, *anito*, that gave life to a body and the material world. Isabelo speaks of it as an *energia*, comparing it to "ether, gas, electricity, psyche (*psiquis*), plasma." These ideas form the matrix in which dead ancestors are worshipped, objectified in natural things, assigned to particular domains. Out of this matrix came ideas of anthropomorphism, fetishism, reincarnation, polytheism and then monotheism.

Isabelo does not go beyond the suggestive, at times contradictory sketch. On one hand, he offers a sociological explanation of religious ideas, as in his hypothesis that the combination of tribes may have occasioned polytheism, or that the mixing of peoples occasioned the need for a "political" unification of gods in a single pantheon. On the other, he suggests that the "law of selection" (*ley de la seleccion*) may have given rise to the dominance of a figure like the Sun and later the idea of monotheism. In the main, however, he hews to a mentalist interpretation that bases religious development on the expansion of reason. The sway of the senses gives way to the rule of reason, and the powers of the shaman yield to the knowledge of the scientist.

Isabelo's rationalism does not lead him to materialism but Deism. He believes that as the mind develops, man discovers not only that the sun is just a planetary body but, with a new sense of the immensity of the universe, he comes to comprehend that God is everywhere and cannot be fully imagined. The ground is thus set for the formulation of social and moral rules, morality develops and comes to be associated with religion and, as this process evolves, man finds God among the gods and monotheism emerges.

Isabelo constructs a religion at once scientific and mystical. In "moral religion," Isabelo says, God is the First Cause that science cannot fully comprehend. He is what animates nature but is above and beyond it. God is the Supreme Intelligence (*Bondad Suprema*) and Nature is God's law impressed on the universe. God gave man sentiment, conscience, and intelligence to follow the road of Reason and Science that conduces him to God. "Each scientific advance represents another advance in the understanding of the Eternal."[181]

THE EARLY ISABELO showed an embracive openness to tradition best represented in his *Folk-Lore Filipino* project. Historical and personal circumstances, however, involved him in institutionalizing projects— first as self-styled philosopher of the Katipunan, briefly as theoretician of the labor movement, then as theologian of a new church—in which he had to order, rationalize, and convert a surplus of data into usable theory. Driven by the specific urgencies of these tasks and his personal ambitions, he foreshortened the work of cultural recovery, aligned local realities to institutional needs, and subordinated them to Western frames of intelligibility.

His involvement in the Iglesia Filipina Independiente (IFI) cast him in the role of church theologian. Almost singlehandedly, he wrote and published the basic doctrinal documents of the new church. He drew from his Catholic education, his writings on "Filipino Religion," and eclectic book learning. He was aided by the work he did translating for Protestant Bible societies. In 1899, while in Madrid, he translated the Gospels to Iloko under contract with London's British Bible Society and under the supervision of an English Protestant minister. Back in Manila in 1902, he translated the rest of the New Testament under the direction of a Protestant minister. These translations were printed in Yokohama. In 1903, he reprinted the Gospels and the Acts, also in Japan, under the name of the Iglesia Filipina Independiente.

Isabelo produced five foundational books for the Aglipayan Church: *Doctrina y Reglas Constitucionales de la Iglesia Filipina Independiente* (1904), *Catecismo de la Iglesia Filipina Independiente* (1905), *Lecturas de Cuaresma para la Iglesia Filipina Independiente* (1906), *Oficio Divino de la Iglesia Filipina Independiente* (1906), and *Biblia Filipina* (1908).[182] With the exception of *Biblia Filipina*, these books were adopted by Iglesia

Filipina Independiente as official church documents. Together with other writings attributed to Isabelo—*Catequesis* (1911), *Libro de Oraciones* (1929), *La Libre Razon* (1930), and *Catedra* (1932)—*Biblia Filipina* had quasi-official status as an Aglipayan text.[183] Due to IFI's urgent need for guiding documents, these were not written or published according to a clear, systematic plan, and are harried and repetitive.

At its inception, IFI stayed Catholic except in its break from the authority of Rome. Aware of the entrenched Catholicity of its members, IFI retained the liturgy and externalities of the Catholic Church. Beginning with the Epistles and *Doctrina y Reglas*, however, Isabelo tried to define for the IFI a doctrinal position apart from Roman Catholicism.

Doctrina y Reglas consists of the basic doctrines of the church (*Doctrina*), the IFI Constitution (*Gobierno*), and six Fundamental Epistles (*Epistolas*). The Epistles were basic doctrinal statements Isabelo earlier published in *La Iglesia Filipina Independiente* between September 22, 1902 and August 17, 1903. *Doctrina y Reglas* states that IFI was "principally" founded to "obey the imperative necessity of reestablishing in all its splendor the worship of the one God and the purity of His Holy Word which under the influence of obscurantism has been garbled and disfigured." It likewise states that the new church aims at "liberating the conscience from all anti-scientific error, exaggeration and scruple."[184] The clear reference in these statements is that the Roman Catholic Church has disfigured the true teaching and that it is IFI's mission to return to a Christianity purified of the "abuses" of the friars and Rome. *Epistolas* distances the IFI from the Catholic Church by denying Marianism, the cult of saints, the possibility of miracles, and the trinity of Persons (explaining the Holy Trinity in a Sabellian sense, i.e., that the Father, Son, and Holy Ghost are three different names or aspects of one and the same Divine Person). It assumes a liberal stance by adopting a relativist and subjectivist morality and asserting the equality of all religions.

These ideas are developed in *Catecismo*, a "textbook" for IFI presbyters that explains the doctrines stated in *Doctrina y Reglas* and *Lecturas*, a collection of Lenten sermons. *Oficio Divino* was adopted as IFI's official liturgical manual though it appears to have been compiled as an experimental effort rather than a service book for practical use. Billed as the "Philippine Gospel," *Oficio Divino* is a free translation of the four Gospels, with additions, subtractions, and commentaries introduced in footnotes or into the main text. It also sets forth the ceremonies of the Aglipayan Mass and the ritual for administering the sacraments and other religious services.

The fundamental doctrine espoused in these first books was the Unitarian tenet: "One God, One Essence, One Person." As propounded in Epistle III, first issued on October 17, 1902, barely two months after IFI was established:

> There is only one God. In so far as He is Power who created us and assists us in all things with His loving providence, we lovingly call Him celestial Father. . . . In so far as He became man to redeem us and to teach us to love all creatures including our enemies, we call Him Son because such humanity proceeded from His Divinity itself. . . . And in so far as He is sublime Love who unceasingly attracts us towards God for our sanctification, and in so far as He is eternal Truth who illumines our intelligence, we call Him Divine Spirit.
> All, however, is one God.[185]

The harried composition of these texts undermines their status as canonical documents. Isabelo makes the pretentious (and inaccurate) claim in *Oficio Divino* that he is presenting the Gospel on the basis of "very ancient codices preserved in the libraries of Jerusalem, Rome, England, France and Spain," and asserts authority by saying he has visited churches of Roman, Greco-Russian, and Anglican Christians; the temples of Brahma and Buddha in Colombo, Singapore and Japan; and the Confucianist temples in Canton, Macao and Hongkong. But the texts are careless and digressive. The full title of *Oficio Divino* mentions that the work has two parts but it actually has three. Isabelo's provisional exposition of dogma is filled with unsubstantiated claims and a hodgepodge of citations from Voltaire, Michelet, Kant, Fichte, Schopenhauer, Renan, Tolstoi, Haeckel, and—perhaps more relevantly—the freethinker David Friedrich Strauss (1808–1874) and Protestant theologian Adolf von Harnack (1851–1930), German rationalists who criticized the historical basis of the Gospel.

Biblia Filipina (1908) marks a further shift to what Catholic writers have called the "agnostic phase" of Aglipayan doctrinal development. The work's extravagant title page reads:

Iglesia Filipina Independiente. —Biblia Filipina. Primera piedra para un genesis cientifico, espuesto segun las rectificaciones de Jesus. — Por primera vez se traducen literalmente al Castellano el Hebreo original (esto es, el Caldaico) de la Sinagoga y el Griego de la Septuaginta, tales como se conservan en la famosa Biblia Poliglota Complutense de la Biblioteca de la Universidad de Barcelona, que fue aprobada por el Papa Leon X, en 1520 y se completan en notas con otros originales y las tradiciones analogas de Caldeo-Asiria, Persia, Egipto, Syria, Fenicia, India, China y otros pueblos tan antiguos como el Hebreo. Tambien se da la debida importancia a las leyendas cosmogonicas de Filipinas. —La dedica al pueblo Filipino nuestro sabio Obispo Maximo Emmo. Sr. Gregorio Aglipay y Labayan, Barcelona 1908.

It is reported that while the book contains only 192 pages, Isabelo had prepared another 300 or 400 pages which could not be published for lack of funds.[186] Boasting that his was the first literal Spanish translation of the Bible from the "Hebrew original" and Septuagint Greek, Isabelo in fact used the Alcala Bible at the University of Barcelona, the *Biblia Complutense*, a famous polyglot Bible published in 1520. Jesuit historians Pedro Achutegui and Miguel Bernad say of Isabelo's work: "It is impossible to think of greater scholarly temerity than is displayed in the 192 pages of the *Biblia Filipina*."[187]

In *Biblia Filipina*, Isabelo turns even more pronouncedly rationalist, denying such central Catholic principles as Christ's divinity, the immortality of the soul, and the divine authority of sacred scripture. Turning to an evolutionist rather than creationist view of the world, Isabelo turns agnostic, reducing God to a natural Force or Energy. In a letter to Father Miguel Saderra Maso, S.J., on June 18, 1929, Isabelo declared:

I take the opportunity to assure you on my word of honor and before God that before I set myself to writing these Aglipayan books, I went down on my knees to pray, humbly begging God to guide my pen, because I knew that thousands of people would follow me, and that I have written nothing in those religious books against my good faith and sincerity.[188]

He boasted about his competence in theology in a letter from Barcelona to American historian James Robertson in 1908:

I had read not only the best works of the Romanists while in the seminary in Ilocos Sur and at the Romanist University in Manila, where I was a student and a fervent and loyal Romanist, but also the works of the protestants and of Strauss, Renan, Tolstoi, Voltaire, Darwin, Haeckel and other eminent rationalist theologians of Germany. These catapulted me beyond protestantism into rationalism. But it is an idealist rationalism, original with the Filipinos . . .[189]

Robertson forwarded the letter to fellow American historian James LeRoy, who remarks on Isabelo's writings: "It is the usual mixture of falsehood, half-truths and truths, of ignorance and egotism lifted up by an occasional flash of discernment that his pen produces. He is no scholar at all, properly speaking. . . . Don Isabelo really has brains. But he cannot be taken seriously at all."[190] The judgment of Achutegui and Bernad is just as severe. Isabelo's readings, they write, are "omnivorous but not well chosen, and not assimilated but merely regurgitated without order and without due regard for coherence or interior logic." They add: "It is not a well-thought out, well-integrated and well-articulated theology. Indeed, it is far from being a theology. It is rather an enormous scrap-heap of doctrinal fragments, often at variance among themselves."[191]

These are statements from unsympathetic sources. Yet they underscore Isabelo's overreaching in theorizing a new church. A more sympathetic critic similarly finds *Oficio Divino* disordered and unorthodox: "The total impression given by this material is one of marked political intent, and of quite limited knowledge of the theological disciplines on the part of the writer."[192] Written by a layman at a troubled time for an infant church, it is not clear what status Isabelo's Aglipayan texts enjoyed in the church and how and to what extent they were used. Written at a time of great personal and political distraction and stress, Isabelo's performance was not only daring, it was reckless.

The early Iglesia Filipina Independiente was borne along by the surge of patriotic, anti-friar sentiments. Its leaders were involved in the revolution and the militantly nationalistic stance the church took appealed to many even as its outwardly Catholic appearance, its rites and liturgical practices, assured followers that they remained "Catholic." Its Filipinism was expressed in the Aglipayan priest wearing the Philippine flag in lieu of vestments when celebrating Mass and the veneration of Filipino heroes with the "canonization" of Rizal, Gomez, Burgos, and Zamora, on September 24, 1903. Isabelo tried to "Filipinize" liturgy by innovating ceremonies that did not appear in the Roman rubrics but were popular usages in the Philippines; introducing a native sensibility to the prayers; and departing from Latin by getting *Oficio Divino* translated into Ilocano, Visayan, and other local languages.

Its nationalism was its strength as well as weakness. As revolutionary nationalism waned so did the church. As Joseph Ralston Hayden writes: nationalism could not make up for "its relative lack of the spiritual and ethical vitality which are essential to the permanence of any religious movement."[193] The initial surge in church membership declined, particularly after 1906 when the Supreme Court handed down the decision returning to the Roman Catholic Church the contested buildings and properties the Aglipayans occupied.

Isabelo dared to define for the fledgling church an autonomous doctrinal position. He articulated a "Newtonian deism" that departed radically from Catholic doctrines, denying the possibility of revelation and taking science and reason as the only sources of truth. Various reasons however—institutional weakness, uneven indoctrination, divergence between theory and practice, contradictions and gaps in the theory itself— undermined the appeal of the new church.

Isabelo lived to witness the dissension and enervation of the church he helped bring into being. After his death, his doctrinal and devotional texts were revised, "cleaned up," or discarded as the IFI, struggling to survive by gaining new legitimacy, established relations with Unitarian and Anglican theologians and, in 1961, entered into a concordat with the American Episcopal Church. In a stroke of irony, the "reform" of the church was carried out under new IFI supreme bishop Isabelo de los Reyes, Jr., Isabelo's son.

HE WAS AT HIS BEST when he was the free intellectual working the realms of popular culture. He demonstrated this in journalism, in the periodicals he founded, *El Ilocano* (1889-96) and *La Lectura Popular*

331

(1890–1892), and numerous articles he wrote under his name or the pseudonyms *Kasalo, Deloserre,* and *Platanos.*

La Lectura Popular (1890–1892) illustrates his interest in popular education and social improvement. Dedicated to contributing to "the education and progress of the *pueblo indigena,*" its masthead announced it was going to publish "judgments concerning ways to avoid sickness, medicine, modern farming, laws and decrees published in *Gaceta* [the government bulletin], news from other places, and other useful items."[194] In line with this devotion to the propagation of "useful knowledge," the periodical published texts of laws, commodity prices, and articles on popular science, agricultural methods, and new inventions, spiced with a miscellany of stories, poetry, and lottery results. In a maiden article, Isabelo stressed the role of the press in social improvement, defending public interest, conveying useful knowledge, and inculcating such values as the desire for study and being socially informed. He defended the use of Tagalog as medium for reaching a wider audience and weaning people away from wasteful ideas of "spells, romances, goblins and other mythical creatures, marvels and other nonsense" (*mga encanto, corrido, asuang at tianac, mga catacataca at iba pang mga caululan*). In item after item, the periodical taught such values as the need for savings and cooperative associations and criticized wasteful practices like lavish fiestas, gambling, and smoking. Isabelo also published articles of historical and cultural interest, such as a piece on the "language" of Philippine flowers and a long article in which, within the frame of a romantic story, he discusses the Ilocano "class system" and various other matters of local interest.[195]

In 1894, he also founded *El Municipio Filipino*, a "popular review of legislation and jurisprudence." Launched on July 16, 1894, and lasting until 1896, this twice-monthly journal aimed to popularize, explain, and comment on laws, "to make them accessible to all minds."[196] Stimulated by municipal reform in the wake of the Maura Law of 1893, *Municipio Filipino* covered topics like the bureaucracy, property relations, and civil rights.

Isabelo pioneered in Iloko literature. He promoted the use of a new Iloko orthography, preserved and popularized the epic poem *Lam-ang*, translated foreign poetry, and wrote fiction and verse in Iloko, Tagalog, and Spanish. He wrote *Ang Singsing nang Dalagang Marmol* (1905), a

Tagalog novel set against the background of the Filipino-American War, and "*Ti langit ti inanamatayo*" (Heaven is our Hope), published as a supplement to his *Biag ni Aida* and considered "the first Iloko short story."[197] In the late nineteenth century, he wrote numerous half-essayistic, half-narrative *cuadros* of native life which are important markers in the emergence of prose fiction in the Philippines. His place in the history of Philippine literature is greater than has been acknowledged. He remained active in promoting Iloko literature until late in his life, serving as vice-president of the *Gimong Dagiti Umiiloko* (Society of Ilokanistas) convoked in 1927. His status as a literary figure, however, has been limited by the fact that he was in too many places at the same time.

He produced almanacs as part of his campaign for social reform. Almanacs are cheap, vernacular chapbooks that contain a calendar (the main text, consulted for meteorological and astrological information as well as religious feast days and observances), usually supplemented by a miscellany of items for information and amusement that often mix modern and folk knowledge. Together with the Catholic *novena*, almanacs were the most popular form of printed literature in the country.[198]

Isabelo innovated by using the form for social and political criticism. This is illustrated in *Kalendariong maanghang* (1911), subtitled "*Sili araw-araw datapuwa't birong kapatid lamang, kadiabluhang malaki ni Isabelo de los Reyes.*"[199] Its title page carries a satiric poem that lampoons the Philippine Assembly as a "Great Shadow-Play" (*dakilang carrilio*) in which the assemblymen are depicted as puppets of "the great bald Governor-General" (William Cameron Forbes) who holds the script (*dichong original*) and cooks up a lot of special effects (*magia*). A brief article by Isabelo, which he calls "pepper to whet the appetite," attacks leaders like Sergio Osmeña and T.H. Pardo de Tavera as "fake nationalists" (*mga nacionalistang tanso*). In the calendar itself (which readers consult for baptismal names, usually those of saints whose feast days fall on the child's birthday), Isabelo enters names of what he calls "true" and "false" heroes, in which he cites among "true" heroes not only Filipino revolutionaries but obscure personalities like "Miguel Ayatumo" (a sixteenth-century Visayan catechist) and "Rufino Baltazar" (author of a Tagalog *Aritmetica* in 1868). For good measure he throws in names of foreign "heroes" like Proudhon and Kropotkin.

Taking advantage of the almanac's form as space that can be "filled up" with miscellaneous information, Isabelo uses it for irreverent political and theological messages. In *Kalendariong maanghang*, he inserts such calendar entries as, for January 1: "A new year, a new life. Let's hope that politicians will get over being cowards and for once defend the interests of our country." For Lent: "It's time that you repent, you public officials who do nothing but deceive our people." For May 22: "*Makupa*. The host was copied from the sun-shaped cakes that the pagans offered to the Sun that was their deity."

Isabelo's partisan passions often took the better of him. He used the almanac as medium for Aglipayan and anti-Catholic propaganda. An example is a 1908 almanac that shows, on its title page, a lurid print illustration, captioned "*Horrores de la Inquisicion*," showing friars burning heretics at the stake in Spain.[200] Isabelo loads the almanac with adverse editorial comments on Biblical history and theology and incorporates into the calendar a medley of names that includes those of scientists like Isaac Newton, John Locke, and John Stuart Mill, and, prominently, notable Aglipayans and Protestant and Unitarian theologians.

Though Isabelo's performances are sometimes reckless, his transgressive combinations of forms of knowledge are immensely instructive. Around 1893, he adapted to Iloko Giuseppe Verdi's *Aida*, producing what may be the first Philippine-language "opera." *Aida, Opera nga uppat ti pasetna* first appeared in *El Ilocano* (October–December 1893) and was issued as a chapbook, *Biag ni Aida*, by "Imprenta de Isabelo de los Reyes" in Manila.[201] Published in prose, combining the song-element of the zarzuela and the exotic costumes and characters of the comedia, this romance of Egypt in the time of the Pharaohs became very popular in the Ilocos. Verdi's *Aida* (1871) lent itself well to adaptation into what was the most popular theatrical form in the Philippines at this time, the *komedya*: an exotic Middle Eastern setting, evocation of ancient history, and plot conventions like costumed characters of the nobility, royal marches, a love triangle, melodramatic declamations of sentiment, and battle scenes.

Even with *Aida*, Isabelo's modernizing impulse was at work. He appends a note to the play's published text that people in the Ilocos love it for its "armed clashes" though these may not be realistic, for which reason he has included them

against our own wishes, for it is our intention in translating the best
dramas or comedias of Europe to modify your comedias which have
now become very ridiculous; so that you will not feel an abrupt
change, however, we are gradually cutting off the malpractices of
your comedias and now we are still putting in a "clash" and its gim-
micks; but if you feel that this is not badly needed, we advise you
not to play it as a comedia, for this will ruin this celebrated life of
AIDA.[202]

Typically, Isabelo locates himself in the interface between inside and
outside, foreign and local, interpreting both and the possibilities that
arise when they combine. This is shown in *Ang Comediang Tagalog* (1904),
his response to a controversy over the art and utility of the *comedia* or
moro-moro.[203] Part of a wider debate on modernity at the turn of the
century, the controversy was sparked in 1902 when the playwright
Severino Reyes expelled from his theater troupe actors who had appeared
in the *comedia*, which he considered a vulgar and degenerate form. This
escalated when some town governments moved to either ban or raise the
license fees of *comedia* performances and the country's literati debated
the issue in the press. Isabelo joined the fray when he interceded for
comedia performers by drawing up a petition (August 20, 1904) addressed to civil governor Luke Wright and Rizal provincial governor
Arturo Dancel, protesting the suppression of *moro-moro* theater by the
Malabon municipal government.

Against charges that the *comedia* is backward and absurd, Isabelo
"normalizes" the form by arguing that it enacts customs and conventions found in the Philippines and other countries. He justifies the
"absurdities" of slow royal marches, the apparatus of *magia* (marvelous
stage effects), and stylized battles by saying that these replicate the ceremonial marches of European monarchs (as he himself witnessed in
Europe, he says); that *magia* is also used in European theater (as in the
staging he saw of Richard Wagner's operas in Paris, Richard Strauss's
Elektra, and *Don Juan Tenorio* in Madrid); and that the *comedia*'s pecu-
liarities of character presentation, voice delivery, and length of staging
are also characteristic of Chinese and Japanese theater ("that I have observed" in Hong Kong, Macao, China, and Japan). Moreover, he adds,
comedia conventions correspond with local cultural practices, as shown

in the martial dances of Muslims in Mindanao and Igorots in Luzon and the supernatural marvels in Filipino mythology.

More important, what may be foreign in the *comedia* has been "naturalized." He says that "though the *Moro-moro* was brought to the country by the Spaniards, it has become different from its source and now appears as truly our own (*tunay na ating atin*)."[204] Isabelo, however, contents himself with a few suggestive remarks on how the form has become "truly our own." He cites the incorporation of local material ("the authors have 'mixed in' Tagalog customs") and cultivation of a distinct style and sensibility, as shown in the "arrangement of expressions," intonation, and use of local styles of courtship and mourning. Isabelo draws the analogy of a boat drawn by a Spaniard but constructed by a Tagalog using local materials and "according to our own wisdom and ways." Hence, it becomes "Tagalog." He says that the value and authenticity of a form must be sought not just on the surface but in its true and inner spirit (*los verdaderos espiritus*).[205]

It is clear that Isabelo does not privilege some pristine, original form. He praises the *comedia* for "its pleasing and most curious mix of *opera*, *drama*, and *comedia*," a hybridity not quite found in the modern *zarzuela*, the form favored by the educated. He points out though that even the Tagalog *zarzuela* has become "truly Tagalog" and has absorbed in its turn elements of the *comedia*. This adulteration is not to be lamented since "the Tagalog, like the Japanese, if there's anything from other lands that they imitate, they dress it up (*binibihisan*) according to their own customs or notions of what is human."[206]

Isabelo does not "museumize" cultural forms. Interested in reform, he offers his ideas on how the *moro-moro* can be improved. It must remain "Filipino" in character and retain its distinctive virtues as a genre, such as its "tone" (*tono*) and use of the marvelous. It must be renovated, however, with new stage technology, better training of actors and directors, and the methods that have enriched new European theater (such as avoiding "vulgar mixing" of elements, padding of scenes, and use of obscene and uncouth movements and speech). Isabelo has "nationalist" improvements in mind as well: cleaning up the language of corrupt Hispanisms, replacing exotic, fictional settings with local or actual geographic place names, introducing old Filipino customs into the material, and dropping the name *moro-moro* since it is a Tagalog and not a Muslim creation. The *comedia*, he asserts, is superior to such Western amusements as the *can-can*, pantomimes, and other "absurdities" that he saw when he visited the Aquarium at Regent's Park in London.

Isabelo assumes a scholar's stance, underscoring the need for careful study, praising the *Orientalista*, scholars of "ancient curiosities," for the studiousness they bring into their work, and saying that he has himself watched *moro-moro* performances and read some thirty metrical romances (*romances o aleluyas antiguas*) in Spanish and local languages. He criticizes the elite and educated for their bias against popular culture. He recalls Jose Felipe del Pan telling his young writers in the 1880s, "Don't think that the readers are all dumb because among those we take to be dumb are people more knowledgeable than we are, and they are the ones we should defer to and respect." The mass appeal of the *comedia*, Isabelo says, argues in its favor since the "intuition" of the mass often turns out to be true. We must respect the people's freedom and not just follow the pedant (*mapagdunungdunungan*), "they are the true pestilence!"[207]

Isabelo was not awed by Western knowledge (though he often brandished his cosmopolitanism to enhance his authority) but neither was he into cultural "purity" and "authenticity." He relished the hybrid, confident that in and through it the Filipino will create his own form of modernity.

PRODUCING ISABELO

ISABELO DE LOS REYES was a product of the nineteenth-century "Filipino Enlightenment." Conditions that enabled the rise of intellectuals like Isabelo included the new economic opportunities that created an urban bourgeoisie (as in the case of the Paterno and Pardo families) and a provincial gentry (that included the Rizals and de los Reyeses); expanding educational opportunities (the first Filipino nationalists came out of the colony's secondary institutes and university); and the spread of Enlightenment ideas through such channels as an emergent local press.

The conventional representation of the Propaganda Movement has located its center of gravity in Europe where young Filipinos, freed from colonial constraints, imbibed the ideas of science and reason. This has diverted attention from a fuller consideration of the formation of intellectuals in the colony itself. The case of Isabelo de los Reyes is instructive. He waged a campaign for the ascendancy of reason and freedom, using the opportunities and resources available to him, contending with the obstacles and dangers of working within the colony, and deploying the advantages of his peculiar position. His gains as well as losses are instructive.

The story of Isabelo and his generation "pluralizes" the Enlightenment by grounding our understanding of the rise of modern knowledge within local society instead of seeing it simply as the effect of a late-arriving diffusionary wave from Europe.

HE WORKED against the grain and was mocked as an unpolished amateur by Spaniards contemptuous of his scholarship. Wenceslao Retana was the most choleric and scathing in his remarks. Churning out choice epithets, Retana calls Isabelo "a redemptorist petty politician" (*politiquillo redentorista*) with delusions of competence, presumptuous for one who has not even been out of the country, whose writings, in "indigestible Spanish," are fit for dealers of fodder (*zacateros*). While some of his books are not without value, Retana condescends, they merely compiled data from other authors, disorganized, sometimes plagiarized, written without knowledge of key primary sources, and written with politically suspect motives (*marcadamente nacionalista*). On Isabelo the journalist: "Isabelo de los Reyes, though he lives a thousand years, can never be a journalist: he lacks the brains, he lacks notions about many things, he lacks the talent, and he does not even know how to write in Spanish."[208] Isabelo the historian: He does not have the "serenity of spirit" needed for the practice of a discipline that requires abstraction and critical distance; he violates the historiographic principle that the person of the author should be hidden, to be discerned only in the "aims, intention, and tendency" (*fines, intencion, tendencia*) of the work. Isabelo burlesques history by constantly referring to himself, *Yo, yo, y yo*. Retana calls *Historia de Filipinas* "a veritable historical, literary, and typographic disaster." *Folk-Lore Filipino* is "written with the feet," filled with "vulgarities and foolishness in abundance," and *El Ilocano* printed "innumerable hoaxes of all kinds."[209] Retana catalogues Isabelo's "absurdities":

[H]e speaks about the work of P. Grijalva, of which there has not been a single copy in the Philippines for many years now; he speaks of some Conquistas of P. San Agustin, printed in 1725 (*Hist. de Ilocos*, II, 21), something that will leave the bibliophiles staring with wide open mouths; of the Historia of P. Rivadeneyra, Barcelona, 1601, he says (*Articulos Varios*, p. 91) it disappeared (I have a magnificent copy); he quoted Morga, not knowing him, before Rizal reprinted

Morga's most rare book; he mentioned Pigafetta, and still mentions him, without knowing the real text of his Viaje; P. Gonzales de Mendoza he takes to China, where he never went, and talks about his book with the greatest ease, without having seen one of the many editions that exist of his book; he makes mention, without knowing it, of the work of P. Garcia about the Origen de los Indios, ignoring that these indios are the Americans; of P. Adyarte [Aduarte], who died in 1636, he says that he wrote in 1693 (*Articulos Varios*, p. 34) . . . Poor Isabelo! Perhaps it is not his fault that he did not have books at his disposal. However, if his erudition is a resource obtained second, third or fourth hand, why does he not admit that his quotations are . . . quotations from quotations?[210]

Underlying Retana's attack on Isabelo's competence is a personal and racist animosity. Retana and de los Reyes were co-workers and competitors in the Philippine press and the Spaniard, schooled in the peninsula, viewed the ambitious native with contempt. He calls him a "vain, showy politicaster" and "an ingrate" (a charge commonly made by Spaniards against educated Filipinos). He scoffs at Isabelo's "political" ambitions and claims of popularity. He describes Isabelo as

a new Don Quixote, of pure breed . . . Malay, with a weakness for matters he should not touch; a wretch who never tires of looking at himself as an indio, and who, due to having so poor an opinion of himself, one cutting remark, a joke, or a correction in connection with any of his errors, is sufficient to appear to him as data for the proceedings for his exile; he talks of the civil guards; what he detests in the Spaniards; he thinks he knows everything . . . Poor Isabelo![211]

Retana condescendingly credits Isabelo with "some predilection for study," and that he has contributed "acceptable data although he lacks the scientific training which he may not be expected to have in his lifetime." He goes on, however, to say that "whatever he is worth today he owes it to the Spaniards"— the friars who gave him an education and the Spanish publishers and editors who provided him with an income. Retana mentions *Comercio* editor Francisco Diaz Puertas, *Eco de Panay* publisher Francisco Gutierrez Creps, *Diario de Manila* owner Luis de

Elizalde, *España Oriental* publisher Manuel Schiednagel, and, in particular, Jose Felipe del Pan who gave Isabelo a start by hiring him as assistant, typesetter, and scribe, and gave him "books, lessons, advice, boosting and copy editing." Retana laments the tolerance and praise given Isabelo, saying that "in another colonial country, Isabelo would be discredited."[212]

For Retana, Isabelo is the overreaching native, archetype of the ambitious, half-baked *Pobletes e Isabelos* who are infected with "the two great defects of the *indios*," vanity and ingratitude. Cultivated by Spanish patrons, Isabelo's character and limited capacity corrupt what he has learned and prevent him from advancing any further. While he writes too much, he is not a man of action: "Isabelo is timid, distrustful, irresolute; he is an *indio* in all respects."[213] Recalling Max Muller's statement that "we cannot fix the precise point at which the ape ended and man began," Retana says that in Isabelo it is impossible to determine the exact point where the "poor wretch" was transformed into the hypocritical "little politician." He ends by asking: "Who is the greater idiot, Don Isabelo or those who pay attention to him? I believe the latter since Don Isabelo, poor fellow, was born that way. And how can he be blamed for that?"[214]

Retana would later soften his opinion of Isabelo, conceding that he was a *progresista* who loved his country and worked for its welfare. His *Sensacional Memoria*, the Spaniard admitted, "is a sincere work that reveals in its author a patriot of daring."[215] Retana wrote: "Reyes was in all times a fighter. Until 1896, a cunning fighter, tricky; after that, outspoken, resolute." He continued to have a low estimate of Isabelo's intellectual abilities, calling him a "journeyman," "a little Rizal" (*un pequeño Rizal*).[216]

While Retana's comments are difficult to match for their biliousness, they expressed a common colonialist view of the ambitious native. There were Americans who shared Retana's superior attitude. The historian James LeRoy called Isabelo "a hopeless craver of notoriety and a fluent but shallow demagogue," "a Socialist of the Latin-European school (so nearly as he knows what he is) and a freethinker so far as religious faith or practice is concerned."[217]

MORE IMPORTANT, fellow Filipinos were dismissive of Isabelo's scholarship. Filipino émigré intellectuals saw themselves, and their location in

Europe, as the center of the Propaganda Movement. Isabelo's local education and rural origins marginalized him in this view. Emigres like Rizal and Pardo were discomfited by Isabelo, finding him erratic and poorly schooled.

Pardo likened Isabelo to Paterno in disseminating "falsehoods and absurdities" in glorifying an ancient Tagalog civilization. He dismissed Isabelo's scholarship, calling it "infantile in character" (*Historia de Filipinas*), "of little worth" (*Historia de Ilocos*), "curious" (*Folk-Lore Filipino*), "a string of inaccuracies and credulities" (*Apuntes para un ensayo de teodicea Filipina*), "a heap of exaggerations and nonsense" (*Filipinas: Independencia y Revolucion*).[218] While these comments were made at a time when Pardo and Isabelo were adversaries on the issue of U.S. rule, it is clear Pardo had a low regard for Isabelo's intellectual abilities.

Jose Rizal had a dim, dismissive view of Isabelo's work. On April 30, 1888, Rizal wrily wrote to Blumentritt that "many folklorists and future anthropologists are appearing in Ilocos," foreigners may think Filipino lore is "Ilocano." He remarked that Isabelo has committed some errors because "he does not speak well Tagalog."[219] Writing to M.H. del Pilar from London on February 4, 1889, Rizal was sarcastic:

> Congratulating myself and everyone for having a countryman as well informed, intelligent, and active as Mr. Isabelo de los Reyes, I have nevertheless to deplore his excessive Ilocanism, which as you suspect, can one day chop us, as an argument against us. Though he may have first-rate works, on the other hand, some seem to be written by Spaniards—so superficial, light, and of little discernment.[220]

Rizal was responding to a letter from del Pilar complaining about Isabelo's piece on Diego Silang in *Diario de Manila* (December 16, 1889) "praising the friars on the occasion of that rebellion." Thinking that it undercuts an anti-friar article on the same subject he was planning to write, del Pilar lamented: "Isabelo is going to mutilate my work with his deplorable fecundity."[221] In his reply, Rizal agreed and proceeded to criticize Isabelo's idealization of Silang in *Historia de Ilocos*. For Rizal, Silang's uprising had "a fanatical character, though Silang himself was not so, because he seemed to be a grand politician, but a rogue without honor or civic virtues, for which reason he failed." Rizal said

Isabelo erred in assuming that "Jesus Nazareno" was the name of a real person instead of a symbolic figure and mistaken as well in attributing too great an importance to the role of the friars. He said that without Silang's assassination "this uprising would not have been extinguished, not even with all the belts that are found in the convents, nor even supposing that the skins of the friars were made into belts and their greasy habits into scapulars. The importance that the friars give themselves in all uprisings should be interpreted with a grain of salt..."[222]

This disagreement came into the open when Rizal wrote an article in *La Solidaridad* (October 31, 1890) reacting to what he perceived was an attack against his competence in *Historia de Ilocos*. The "well-known Filipino historian Don Isabelo de los Reyes," an acerbic Rizal wrote, had flattered him for his patriotism and the "scientific and historical evaluation" contained in his edition of Morga. But Isabelo, Rizal quoted, had gone on to say:

> But this very same very laudable patriotism of his, in my opinion, blinds him at times and a historian should be scrupulously impartial. I do not say that the Filipinos along the coasts were entirely the same in culture to our contemporary tribes in the interior; but even if this were so, the optimism of the said author becomes emotional at some points. He takes the exception to be the general rule and vice versa. The common opinion of authors who have no motive for lying should be taken into consideration in these cases: the true character of that culture and that which is still preserved of it in the customs of the people. I say this to explain the divergence [of opinion] which exists between some of his observations and those of mine in this and in the succeeding chapter.[223]

Piqued, Rizal rapped Isabelo for presumptuousness in assuming he is the better judge and proceeded to point out flaws in *Historia de Ilocos*. Isabelo, he said, has Morga speaking of the office of *agturay*. "I have read Morga some seven times and I do not recall that he had ever spoken of any *agturay*." Isabelo errs in calling the petty chief of Cebu *Hamubao*; "the original text of Pigafetta in the Ambrosian library," Rizal pointedly said, "has *Humabon* and perhaps it was *Humabong*." Isabelo misinter-

343

prets certain Tagalog words and, instead of critically reading the sources, disparages the morals of pre-Hispanic Filipinos. Decorating his polemic with praise for the enemy and displays of false modesty, Rizal reveals a mean, supercilious streak. Dropping phrases in Italian as he cites Pigafetta, Rizal claims for himself a superior understanding not only of a wider range of sources but knowledge of these sources in the original or in a form close to it. He says of Isabelo: "I respect and admire the sincerity of the noted historian who labors to teach his people, in spite of the many difficulties which the task entails."[224] But Rizal is supremely confident he is the better scholar:

> I regret that this question has provoked Don Isabelo for I have always thought of him with admiration and although I was not in agreement with many of his ideas, I have always believed that I cannot sit in judgment of his work and that in historical matters, only the testimony of eye-witnesses can decide—testimonies which have to be subjected to critical analysis.
>   . . . On the subject of the history of civilization of the ancient Filipinos, I think I have read from cover to cover all the works of contemporary writers, except that of Father Plasencia and that of another author which had been lost. Never have I stated anything on my own authority; I quote sources and when I do, I have them before me.[225]

In a letter to Rizal on November 8, 1890, Juan Luna agrees with Rizal that Isabelo "has done harm, but a great harm" in criticizing Rizal's Morga edition but laments that the conflict had to escalate since "this discord will make the Spaniards in Manila burst with joy."[226] Blumentritt told Rizal it would have been "more proper politically" for Rizal to publish his reply to Isabelo in Madrid's *Boletin de la Sociedad Geografica*, which the *Quioquiaps* (anti-Filipino Spaniards) do not read, instead of publishing it in a manner the Spaniards could use to "create enmity between you and Reyes." Blumentritt says: "Pardo and I have kept silent in the interest of the Filipinos when Reyes did us some injustice." Isabelo is bold and rash, Blumentritt adds, but he "acts always in good faith."[227]

On November 14, 1886, Blumentritt had written to Rizal: "Your Ilocano countryman, my dear and esteemed friend I. de los Reyes is working incessantly. I'm pleased with his very valuable ethnographic works. It is a pity that he has not studied ethnography which would make his studies even more brilliant."[228] Blumentritt had his reservations and, on December 22, 1890, wrote Rizal urging him to publish on pre-Spanish Filipino civilization "and correct in it the mistaken opinions of I. de los Reyes."[229] Blumentritt, however, kept his reservations private. An ardent advocate of the Filipino cause, he was supportive of Isabelo, citing him as one of those Filipinos who belied colonial accusations of native incapacity.

UNDERLYING THIS ATTACK on Isabelo de los Reyes, from Spaniards and even Filipinos, is the attitude that he was a "half-baked" pretender to European scholarship with its canons of objectivity, accuracy, and truth, and its rites of passage (such as high education and cosmopolitan location). What invited criticism was that Isabelo was unapologetic in claiming European knowledge as his own and politically uninhibited in using it. For his critics, his utter lack of any sense of inferiority made him unpredictable. While much in his scholarship invited comparison with Pedro Paterno, Paterno, the decorous conservative, could be dismissed as a harmless aesthete. Isabelo was a provocateur.

Isabelo cannot be dismissed as a mere mimer of Western learning. For someone who worked within the confines of the colony and did not have the educational opportunities Paterno, Pardo, and Rizal had, Isabelo's display of scholarly knowedge was impressive. He was familiar with the protocols of European scholarship and assumed its stance of "objectivity." In *Prehistoria de Filipinas* (1889), he declared his commitment to historical truth (*verdad historica*): "We know that a historian ought to ruthlessly and impartially judge past actions, condemning the bad and exalting only the good without consideration for the status of the actors."[230] He takes authority from the conscientious research he has done in writing *Historia de Ilocos* (1890): "I read more than a hundred historical and non-historical works just to cull two or three times from each of them for that *History*, and then oral traditions for more recent events."[231]

Like Rizal or Paterno, he liberally draws from missionary reports and dictionaries, European travel compendiums (such as John Pinkerton's *General Collection of Voyages and Travels*, 1808-1813), and European scientific work on the Philippines. His writings on religion and folklore are decorated with a potpourri of citations on Southeast Asia (A.R. McMahon's *The Karens of the Golden Chersonese*, 1876), South Asia (T.H. Lewin's *The Hill Tracts of Chittagong*, 1869; John Davy's *An Account of the Interior of Ceylon*, 1821), Africa (James Sibree's *Madagascar Before the Conquest*, 1896; E. Casalis's *Les Bassutos*, 1859); the American Indians (Henry Schoolcraft, George Gibbs, Horatio Hale) and an exotic mix of other cultures and places. Going by his source citations, he was aware of key thinkers in the disciplines he traverses: David Hume (*Natural History of Religion*, 1755), Ernest Renan (*La Vie de Jesus*, 1863), Baruch Spinoza (*Tractatus Theologico-Politicus*, 1670), Charles Darwin (*Descent of Man*, 1871), John Lubbock (*The Origin of Civilization*, 1870), Edward Tylor (*Primitive Culture*, 1871), Max Muller (*Essay on Comparative Mythology*, 1856), Lord Kames (*Sketches of the History of Man*, 1774), Herbert Spencer ("The origins of animal worship," 1874), and Andrew Lang (*Modern Mythology*, 1897).

Self-taught, his readings were unsystematic and indiscriminate. He was criticized for pompous display of erudition, plagiarism, and writings that simply pile up borrowings from other sources. His style of bibliographic citation does not quite make clear how he accessed the sources he cites. He cites works that may not have been available to him in Manila, citing them in languages he may not have been familiar with. As in the case of Paterno, one suspects that many of the authors and titles he cites may have been culled from secondary sources and encyclopedias.

He could be the naïve enthusiast. In *Apuntes para un ensayo de la teodicea filipina* (1900), he states that Filipinos have ideas on the creation that are "completely Darwinist" (*completamente darwinistas*). This is suggested, he says, by the fact that the Philippines abounds in mineral and vegetal forms that "seem to resemble human and animal forms" as well as origin myths that trace life's beginning to primordial earth and water, out of which came plants, animals, and the first humans. He adds that, among Ilocanos and other Filipinos, there is the common belief that certain mountain peoples still have tails though (Isabelo says) he has not been able to ascertain this during his stay in the mountains of Abra.[232] He claims respectability for this view by saying that Alfred Russel Wallace (1823–1913)—the British scientist who devised the theory of natural selection independently of Darwin while collecting natural specimens

346

in the Moluccas in 1858—made a similar deduction in developing his own ideas on evolution. Though he states that his views should not be confounded with the "exaggerations" of Haeckel and other "distinguished Darwinists," Isabelo was not above the most transparent naivete.

In a manner reminiscent of Paterno, he speculates that *Bat-ha-la* may have been constituted out of the words *imbag* (Ilocano, "good"), *hangan* (Tagalog, "limit"), and *uala* (Tagalog, "none"), thus "Good without limit."[233] He imagines undiscovered artifacts in caves and mountains that would prove his theories on ancient religion and urges student excursionists to form societies to explore caves in places like Tayabas and Camarines Sur. Just as grand ruins were discovered on Christmas Island in the Indian Ocean, he believes that if excavations were made at the mouth of the Pasig, Mt. Madiaas in Iloilo, and other local sites, there will be found precious fossils, perhaps the remains of "ancient burial chambers and dolmens (*hipogeos y dolmenes*)."[234]

He was given to certain enthusiasms, as in his use of Spiritism in elaborating ideas on Filipino religion. While in Spain, he became interested in Spiritism, apparently participated in séances, and read such literature as *La Revista Espiritista de Barcelona* and, more important, Spanish editions of Allan Kardec's *Le Livre des Esprits* (1856) and *Le Livre des Mediums* (1861). Called "the Father of French Spiritism," Kardec (1804–1869) enjoyed a wave of popularity in the late nineteenth century (particularly in France and Brazil) with his ideas on the soul, reincarnation, spiritual evolution, and communicating with spirits. The pseudo-scientific character of "Kardecism" appealed to Isabelo, who used its ideas about unknown psychical forces in his own disquisitions on Malay animism and "Filipino religion." (It must be pointed out that Isabelo's dalliance with Spiritism was not peculiar. "Scientific spiritism" appealed to certain scientific circles in Europe in the late nineteenth century. Kardecism was popularized by the French astronomer Camille Flammarion [1842–1925]—an author Isabelo cites—who tried to provide spiritism with a scientific basis through his research on hallucinations, telepathy, and apparitions. Other scientists involved in spiritism were the physicist Oliver Lodge [1851–1940], a pioneer in wireless telegraphy, and Alfred Russel Wallace, who attended séances and published on psychical research after his return to England from Southeast Asia in 1862.[235])

347

Isabelo's critics conceded he was a voracious reader and indefatigable collector of data. Set in context, he deserved greater credit than his critics allowed him. More than Paterno, he had a genuine, practical interest in the emancipative value of science. He propagated modern, useful knowledge in agriculture, industry, and health, advocating it not only in words but in action. Like the European philosophes and contemporaries like Rizal, Isabelo believed that education was a primary instrument for social progress. He wielded his pen and newspapers as educative tools not only in practical affairs but for a general education grounded in a person's knowledge of his milieu. Addressing his Ilocano readers, he devoted a lot of space to teaching local history and culture at the same time that he instilled in them a knowledge of wider worlds.

He knew as well that the people's intellectual emancipation was inescapably implicated in questions of politics. Obliquely or directly (depending on the situation in which he wrote), he called for racial equality, press freedom, municipal autonomy, Filipino representation in the Spanish Cortes, and the grant to the Philippines of the political and economic concessions given to the Antilles.

Isabelo's writings on these subjects are scattered, unsystematic, and not quite consistent. Unlike Paterno, Pardo, or Rizal, Isabelo earned his living as a journalist and wrote in a spontaneous, occasional, and polemical mode. Unlike them, too, he worked in the colony, under the close surveillance of censors and authorities. Hence, in his early writings, when he had to disguise his sympathies with the obligatory praise for the religious orders and the Church, his intentions were misconstrued by colleagues based outside the country. Even then it was not in the character of Isabelo to be timorous. His contemporary Jose de Lacalle called him *"hombre que lleva el corazon en la mano"* ("a man who carries his heart in his hand").[236] He propagandized for Filipino representation in the Cortes at a time when few others were bold enough to do so. Retana was reported to have said: "My dear fellow, neither Rizal nor anybody on *La Solidaridad* has dared to tackle that subject here."[237] Later, during his sojourn in Spain, his anti-friar attacks in the press were so virulent Bishop Martinez Vigil of Oveido reportedly wrote to him that "Lopez Jaena, Rizal, and Marcelo H. del Pilar themselves would have been frightened had they read them."[238]

AMONG HIS CONTEMPORARIES, Isabelo de los Reyes had the strongest sense of where he was coming from. In contrast, Pardo was the cosmopolitan outsider and Rizal—though he frequently looked towards Laguna as home—always imagined himself as being of a "nation" instead of a locality or region. Paterno invented an identity out of local coordinates ("on the banks of the Pasig River") but, born and raised in the colonial center, could unproblematically conflate "Tagalog" and "Filipino" identities.

No one was as *local* as Isabelo. He bannered his being Ilocano and identified not only with his home region but the despised "tribes" of the islands, calling himself "brother of the wild Aetas, Igorots and Tinguians" (*hermano de los selvaticos aetas, igorrotes y tinguianes*)."[239] He proclaimed his identity with such aplomb that colleagues deplored his excessive *Ilocanism* and the Spanish press twitted him as "professor of savages."[240] He enacted his sympathies by publishing a newspaper for Ilocanos, writing in Iloko, promoting knowledge of the region, and embarking on projects for its social and economic welfare. More than Rizal and the other propagandists, he addressed a local audience and helped create it.

Born in the hinterland, nurtured in speech and mores distinct from those of the center, Isabelo was conscious of the difference in being *provinciano* and *Ilocano*. It was a difference he deployed to his advantage. He assumed the authority of someone who had "inside" knowledge of a region and addressed distinct territorial and ethnic readerships. With *El Ilocano*, he pioneered in developing a regional "public" and, based in Manila, did not only speak *to* this public but *of* and *for* them to outside readers. In his works on history and folklore, he assumed the stance of one with direct knowledge of "the field," introducing his personal experience and eyewitness observations, conversations with local informants, and knowledge of particular towns and villages. When he said that the *pacto de sangre* of the Katipunan has its origin in an old marriage rite, he assured his readers he was not inventing this but had personal knowledge of the rite as practiced in central and northern Luzon.[241] Such was his appetite for the local that when he glossed Morga's *principales* as the Ilocano *agturay* ("one who governs"), Rizal pettishly remarked: "I have read Morga some seven times and do not recall that he ever spoke of any *agturay*; I do not know whether Don Isabelo, in his laudable desire to Ilocanize the Filipinos, believes it profitable to make Morga speak Ilocano."[242]

Yet, he was always conscious of the Ilocos as part of a nation. A wider nationhood was his starting point and destination. He did not limit his writings to the Ilocos. Working as correspondent for *Eco de Panay*, he cultivated an interest in the Visayas and published *Las Islas Visayas* with the same sense of the region as constituent of the nation. He incorporated much of this material into *Historia de Ilocos* and his unfinished *Historia de Filipinas*. When he embarked on folklore research, he conceived of Ilocano folklore as part of *Filipino Folk-Lore* and tried to bring into the project contributions from other regions and language groups. While he took pride in Ilocos and Ilocanos, he could concede to the word *Tagalog* an expanded meaning of referring to "all of Malay-Chinese origin, that is to say, all the indigenes of the country."[243]

His sense of location shaped his political sympathies. More easily than other *ilustrados*, he identified with the plebian character of the Katipunan. Compared to other *ilustrados*, he had a more pluralist and inclusive view of nation-formation. In 1900, while he was still in Spain, he proposed (against the dominant "unitary" thinking of Filipino leaders) forming the nation-state out of a "confederation" of regions under a federal constitution. To avoid divisive ethnic distinctions, he recommended the formation of seven federal states named after Filipino heroes: *Estado de Burgos* (northern Luzon), *Estado de Marcelo del Pilar* (central Luzon), *Estado de Rizal* (southern Luzon), *Estado de Aguinaldo* (Bicol), *Estado de Lopez Jaena* (western Visayas), *Estado de Andres Bonifacio* (central and eastern Visayas), and *Estado de Soliman* (Mindanao). He argued that decentralization (*decentralizacion*) favored the rapid development of provinces, promoted bureaucratic efficiency, and guaranteed "in time" a defense against *caciquismo*."[244]

While Isabelo was not beyond sentiments of parochialism, his Ilocanism was neither a simple case of nativism. It was his own medium through which he could deploy the local against the foreign, the "popular" against the elitism of the ilustrados of the capital. It was material and base for his democratic sympathies. He enjoyed subverting racial and ethnic biases among Filipinos themselves, pointedly making statements like "Filipinos had long hair like Igorots" at the time of the Conquest or that "Visayan pirates were more terrible than even the Mohammedans of Jolo and Mindanao." He outraged readers when he wrote, "There are Aetas who surpass the Tagalogs in intelligence, and it is recognized that the Tagalogs are at the same intellectual level as the Europeans."[245] He repeatedly expressed the conviction that the differences separating the Ilocano or Tagalog from the Tinguian or Igorot were not innate but a matter of history and environment.

He took his local origins and sympathies as a sign of privilege. When Pardo publicly referred to him as *mi paisano*, he mischievously asked: "You say you are my countryman; were you perhaps born in the mountains of Abra?"[246]

He expressed this "cultural insiderism" in his study of Filipino religion, a field in which (he loved to point out) foreign observers are often caught in "an intricate labyrinth of contradictions" because of their ignorance of local languages. Only Filipinos, he says, are best positioned to "deepen" (*profundizar*) this ancient religion because they are "the only ones who can penetrate into the secrets and traditions of their own home" (*los unicos que pueden saber los secretos y tradiciones de su propio hogar*).[247] Retana criticized him for an arrogant insistence on "the native point of view," saying that Isabelo thinks that simply by "being an *indio*" all he says has superlative merit.[248]

Isabelo is not above displays of chauvinism but the problem is more complex than Retana suggests. In a wonderful essay on *Folk-Lore Filipino*, Benedict Anderson addresses the question of positionality.[249] What was Isabelo to himself and how did he position himself in the task of writing about the Philippines? Isabelo places himself, Anderson says, as one "inside," "outside," and "outside inside" the subject of which he writes. As one positioned "inside" the Ilocano world, he possesses privileged knowledge outsiders (foreigners and non-Ilocanos) do not have. As one standing "outside" his home community, Isabelo speaks from the ranks of the world's savants, objectifying the Ilocos for disinterested investigation, claiming access to a form of knowledge other Ilocanos do not have. As one located "outside inside," he mediates both worlds, slipping in and out of *I* and *they*, *we* and *you*, as he addresses Ilocano and non-Ilocano readers, claiming power from being able to look at the world from multiple locations.

These positional shifts are not always free of contradictions. It is interesting that in these shifts it is the local that Isabelo ultimately privileges when he confesses that there are things in the "inside" even he does not know though he is an Ilocano. Isabelo takes the tack of assuming Western ("outside") knowledge as knowledge already "revealed" while problematizing the local as that which harbors the as yet "unknown." This "unknownness" exposes the incompleteness of Western knowledge and undercuts its totalizing claims. It threatens the hegemony of the other's knowledge by virtue of its being as yet unexplained and unincorporated. The potential of the argument for a critique of Western knowledge, and the power it authorizes in the Philippines, is great. It remains, however, to be judged as to how well Isabelo enacts it.

HIS PRIMARY CONTRIBUTION lies in the trails he opened up in the study of culture. His investigation of *folk-lore* was the central project. In embarking on it he was impelled by the same motives that drove folklore studies elsewhere in the world: filling a psychic need for "national" identity, claiming a privileged site for the "soul" of a people, creating a "national" tradition. As the folklorist Roger Abrahams remarks on folklore's intimate connection to nationalism: "What colonialism is to the history of anthropology, nationalism is to the study of folklore."[250]

The circumstances surrounding Isabelo's work are quite specific. The lack of powerful, centralized and literate states or a strong Islamic or Hindu presence in precolonial Philippines left Filipino nationalists without a precolonial written archive to invoke and mine. Hence the inevitability and urgency to Isabelo's turn to folklore. There were more immediate enabling factors. One was the interest in *costumbrismo* in Manila's literary and journalistic circle at the time when Isabelo was starting out as a writer and journalist. Jose Felipe del Pan, Isabelo's editor-patron, was a leading *costumbrista*; it was del Pan who encouraged Isabelo to write articles on folklore and sent them as an exhibit to Madrid's *Exposicion General de las Islas Filipinas* in 1887. It may have been del Pan who supplied him with readings and put him in touch with folklorists in the peninsula. If del Pan imagined the project as a collecting of charming curiosities, Isabelo quickly carried it in directions quite his own.

In Spain, *costumbrismo* rose as a literary mode in the early nineteenth cenury, blending romanticism and realism in the portrayal of local or regional manners, customs, and characters in literary sketches or essays (*cuadros* and *articulos de costumbres*) and novels (*novelas de costumbres*).[251] Its motives ranged from regional nostalgia, cultural revivalism, and "local colorism" to social commentary and the criticism of manners. Carried over into the Philippines, *costumbrismo* became a medium for peninsular and creole desires to exoticize and idealize the land of their birth or residence. This occasioned the popularity of touristic prints and art works depicting *tipos del pais* ("social types" or specimens of the local population), pastoral landscapes, and "typical" scenes of local life, as well as literary sketches and novels of local customs.

This was the time when peninsulars and creoles—like del Pan, Antonio Vasquez de Aldana, Francisco de Paula Entrala, and Patricio Montojo—started to publish novels about the Philippines in such papers as *Porvenir Filipino* (1865), *Oceania Española* (1877), and *Diario de Manila* (1860-99). Written in Spanish for a Spanish and urban readership, these novels dealt with local realities for their anthropological interest and as stage for moral and social commentary.[252] Philippine *costumbrismo* distanced its object, fed the appetite for the consumption of new facts and images, and nourished sentiments of nostalgia, a delicate horror at the bizarre, or a vague romantic identification with the *other*. It was "knowledge" produced for Europeans.

Isabelo rearranged this structure of expectations. Among the earliest pieces he wrote were *costumbrista* sketches and articles, examples of which came out in *Lectura Popular* and other periodicals. These did not pander to the picturesque and strange but cultivated *costumbrismo*'s critical, satiric vein in its interest in the correction of manners and "social improvement." In this Jose Felipe del Pan (who wrote *novelas de costumbres* distinguished for their reforming, utopian zeal) was obviously an influence but it is easy to see why Isabelo would take to *costumbrismo* and *folk-lore* with alacrity. In what concerns the local he had "inside" knowledge Spaniards did not have. He was a native writing about his own society, a fact that was not only an intellectual advantage but one with important political implications as well.

The political implications would become manifest in *Folk-Lore Filipino*. He saw his work in folklore as a *Filipino* project, one that did not only primarily address Filipinos but involved them in a collective endeavor. He conceived it as an emancipatory project, one that did not exoticize the native or the past but was fully engaged in the realities of the present and the possibilities of the future. In a series of transgressive acts, he "de-exoticizes" local customs by pointing to parallels elsewhere in the world and, in a more overtly political move, arguing that "backward" superstitions may have been introduced into the country by the Spaniards themselves. He "de-primitivizes" folklore by focusing on its living presence in the Philippines of his own time, expanding the "folk" to include the "popular" such that the workings of an irrational colonial bureaucracy are as much the people's lore as a Tinguian ritual. In the process what he calls into view are not mere relics or survivals but the entire range of a people's lived experience.

Combining the authority of a "new science" (*ciencia nueva*) and "popular knowledge" (*saber popular*), he embarked on folklore studies not only out of a modernizing desire to contribute to world science but for distinct political reasons. He subverts the pretensions to intellectual and moral superiority of Spaniards and friars by citing not only analogues between local and European superstitions but, in his style of radical mischief, positing that some of the local "barbaric" beliefs (even the Devil himself) may have been invented by the Spaniards themselves. Raising the example of a "savage" in southern Ilocos who may discover in a local fruit a better antidote to cholera, he points to what local knowledge can add to Western medical science. Alluding to the depth of indigenous knowledge about flora and fauna or soils and climatic variations, he unsettles the reign of Western knowing by boasting of what remains "hidden."

More important, he looks toward the future—of Ilocos and the "nation"—by claiming folklore as a means for establishing a history deeper and longer than that framed by Spanish coloniality and uncovering a cultural unity for groups characterized as an anarchy of tribes and races. He presents folklore as fount for a cultural renaissance, imagining, for instance, the flowering of a *poesia filipina* inspired by local subjects and "born in the mind" of local bards and the genius (*ingenio*) of the people. Moreover, he sees his project as a means for social self-criticism since, seeing themselves in the mirror of their own practices, people can then proceed to reform what in their culture does not conduce to their common progress.

In claiming for the people a shared "tradition," hence the basis of nationality, Isabelo denies the colonial claim that the country is "nothing" without Spain. In refusing to exoticize tradition and consign it to the past, he claims for tradition a living presence and power for culture-making. By embarking on a project that claims for tradition an openness to "reform" and validity as medium for a distinct kind of modernity, Isabelo stakes out for his people a resource for building a common future.

Isabelo anticipates Antonio Gramsci's view of folklore as the people's "conception of the world and life" standing in opposition to "official" knowledge. Like Isabelo, Gramsci takes a dynamic, expansive view of folklore, one encompassing not only residues of earlier dominant cultural forms (like romances of chivalry) but emergent forms and practices, including the "common sense" (what Gramsci calls "philosophical folklore") of peasants and workers. "Isabelian" as well is Gramsci's radical, rationalizing project of "raising" popular knowledge by a process of intellectual and moral reformation. For Gramsci, folklore—fragmentary, non-systematic, stratified—must be taken seriously to bring about the "birth of a new culture" among the masses "so that the separation between modern culture and popular culture of folklore will disappear."[253]

UNLIKE GRAMSCI Isabelo was not part of a movement. Nor did he generate one. The planned Philippine Folklore Society did not materialize. While folklore collecting sparked wide interest in the early twentieth century, folklore was sanitized and "disciplined" as a resource for state nationalism in the U.S. era. Filipino folklorists after Isabelo did not have his bold, expansive vision of the field.

Isabelo, unlike Gramsci, did not elaborate a theory of popular culture. His innovations exist mostly at the level of textual practices rather than systematic theory. *Folk-Lore Filipino* is an archive animated by mixed, inchoate, and polyvalent impulses. While Isabelo praises popular knowledge, he also assumes a superior position from which he makes facile, essentializing statements about the naïve and ignorant in local culture. He may be brother to the wild but he is not one of them. His distance from tradition is illustrated in the difficulties he had "translating" his mother Leona Florentino to a foreign audience. Leona wrote to satisfy a personal need and a local demand and thought little of publishing or preserving her work for posterity. Isabelo sensed that exposing them to an alien, public light was a transgression. Taken out of their contexts, inserted into "universal folklore," the poems resisted Isabelo's efforts to objectify and "explain" them.

Isabelo's populist instincts, however, served him in good stead. This is shown in his defense of the *comedia*, an eminently Orientalist form in its textual origins (the European medieval romance) and its exoticization of other cultures. Isabelo's comments on the form resonate because Tagalog theater was the subject of a heated debate between Spaniards and Filipino nationalists on the larger issue of the natives' originality and creativity. This was sparked by a series of articles by Vicente Barrantes on Tagalog theater in Barcelona's *La Ilustracion Artistica* in 1888 which held up native theater as proof of the *indio*'s intellectual ineptness and penchant for lower-order mimicry. (Barrantes was a Spanish academic who served as a high colonial official in the Philippines.) The theme of mimicry was picked up by Retana who wrote of Tagalog theater and romances:

> to what should be attributed the fact that in the artistic productions of Filipinos there is scarcely a genuinely Filipino note? There are dozens of works in prose and verse that treat of battles between Moros and Christians in Europe, part of the unknown world of the authors of such works, and not a single work describes the battles which in the course of entire centuries occurred between Moros and Christians in Mindanao, in Bisayas, in Jolo, and even in Luzon. Why this tendency to emigrate, why this systematic exoticism in the artistic conception of the Filipinos?[254]

Rizal responded with a scathing criticism of Barrantes in *La Solidaridad* in 1889 in which Rizal engaged in two discursive moves characteristic of the response of Filipino intellectuals (including Isabelo) to Spanish criticism. Rizal argues that, first, Barrantes is parochial and deficient in 'world-knowledge' (he does not know enough of the relevant literature, commits basic errors in history and geography, and lacks comparative knowledge of, say, Chinese and Japanese theater). Second, Rizal says that Barrantes does not have the "local" knowledge (he does not know, for instance, that there is a difference between *awit* and *corrido* or that the *pasyon* has a staged version).[255]

Rizal does not discuss Tagalog theater itself, saying that he is going to leave it for another time. In another characteristic move in which he plays with the notion of a local knowledge "hidden" or withheld from outsiders (a move Isabelo also makes), Rizal writes:

> We are going to give more careful attention to Filipino art and Philippine literature when more serene days shine. Then we shall say which stage representation was purely indigenous, which was exotic, brought by the Spaniards, which was the product of this mixture, which were the most notable works, etc. In the meantime, Your Excellency [Barrantes] may please excuse me if I do not now reveal these glories or little manifestations of the spirit of my country. Frankly, I do not want to see mentioned the name of Your Excellency in the history of the arts of my native land. However poor and crude they might be, however infantile, ridiculous, and puny Your Excellency may hold them, nevertheless they preserve for me much poetry and a certain aureole of purity that Your Excellency could not understand. The first songs, the first farces, the first drama, that I saw in my childhood and which lasted three nights, leaving an indelible remembrance in my mind, in spite of their crudity and absurdity, were in Tagalog. They are, Most Excellent Sir, like an intimate festival of a family, of a poor family. The name of Your Excellency which is of superior race would profane it and take away all its charm.[256]

The "serene days" did not come for Rizal or, perhaps, he decided to continue playing on the Barranteses the native's tricks of invisibility.[257] Isabelo, however, picks up the problem in *Historia de Ilocos* (1890), which appeared shortly after the Barrantes-Rizal exchange though Isabelo makes no reference to it. Here Isabelo defends the *komedya* on the grounds that, far from being aberrant or exotic, it has been indigenized and exhibits artistic values comparable with the great literatures of the world. While these romances, he says, were introduced by the Spaniards "all have been adapted to a *sui generis* mold (*molde*)" and are of "singular composition" (*composicion singular*), some of them "abounding in passages analogous to those of Marc Anthony and Cleopatra, to those of India, particularly those of the famous *Reconocimiento de Sacantala* of Calidasa, ancient Indian dramatist who has been compared with Shakespeare."[258]

He unsettles the form from a specific originating point by globaliz-
ing it, seeing in it a simultaneity of traits to be found in William
Shakespeare as well as in Kalidasa (c. A.D. 400), the great Sanskrit poet
who elaborated an episode from Mahabharata in his drama *Sakuntala*.
At the same time, Isabelo localizes the form by pointing to plot elements in the *komedya* (kingdoms, royal courts, religious wars) that can
be located in the Philippines. It has characters like the prince's confi-
dant or *hazme-reir* that Filipinos call *bulbul-lagao* (the jester, also known
in the *komedya* by names like *pusong*, *locayo*, and *gracioso*). Kings and
princes are portrayed as valiant "like the *baganis* of the Manobos of
Mindanao." "In the processional marches are imitated the order followed by the Igorots when they walk." Even though there is much in
the play that appears European and exotic, it reveals something of local
history and traditions in its "wars, love-making in Ilocano style, en-
chantments, wondrous absurdities."[259] The *comedia* is a traveling, hybrid
form that can be claimed as *Filipino*.

His *Ang Comediang Tagalog* (1904) recapitulates his defense of the
komedya as a "Filipino" form. (This time he was not defending the form
against Spaniards contemptuous of local art but a modernizing Filipino
elite embarrassed by what they considered "backward" in their culture.)
His explanation of how the form has been "Filipinized" (like his apology
for Leona Florentino's poetry) remains undeveloped. He points to the
substitution of contents, the "reflection" of local customs and practices,
the infusion of a local sensibility, and the aesthetic and spiritual empa-
thy it evokes in the local audience, an experience (Rizal's "intimate festival
of a family") not quite accessible to outsiders. Isabelo, however, was mostly
indifferent to fixing the form's essence, whether *European* or *Filipino*. As
in his views on folklore, he had a vision of constant renovation. He spoke of
the need to retain and strengthen indigenous elements in the play but was
interested as well in learning from other nations for improvements in
stage technology, acting methods, and refinements of plot and language.

He was no respecter of boundaries. As early as 1893, he demonstrated this in his own attempt to convert an Italian opera, Giuseppe
Verdi's *Aida*, into an Ilocano *komedya*, *Biag ni Aida*. Unfortunately, we
cannot examine Isabelo's performance because of the unavailability of a
text.[260] Isabelo's comments on the play, however, show what he was about.
He wanted to enrich local culture by introducing a great foreign play,

translated into Iloko, and adapted to a form, the *komedya*, popular with the local audience. He aimed, by this act of translation or combination, to "improve" local theater and "elevate" the taste of its audience. Isabelo could be prescriptive in his views on how local theater could be improved but, ultimately, he trusted in the people's "intuition" or wisdom, saying, for instance, that the fact that the *komedya* was popular and had become rooted in the culture was an argument that it has its virtues and is *Filipino*.

Dislocating *comedia* or *opera* from its "origins," Isabelo opens it up to incarnations of local meaning. Reincarnated in another form, language, and musical repertoire, the staging of Verdi's *Aida* by local performers in an Ilocos village in the 1890s generated fantasies we cannot fully document. For sure, they were not quite what Verdi intended—or, for that matter, what Edward Said imagined of that imperial spectacle at the Cairo Grand Opera House in 1871.[261]

One assumes they were not quite what Isabelo proposed either but this would not have bothered him all that much. How it was experienced by Ilocanos in the 1890s was just a moment in a dynamic process of culture-making.

HISTORICALLY MINDED, Isabelo was not into primordial "authenticities." By stressing analogues, borrowings, and adaptations across cultures, he undermines notions of purity and difference. By citing the Filipino's "Malay" origins, he begins with a moment already dynamic and compromised since *Malay* was not an essence but a construct of historic movement and exchange.

His approach to ideas was more instrumental than systematic, resulting in texts that were discontinuous, inconsistent, and undeveloped. Isabelo himself had a word for this kind of writing: *centon*, crazy-quilt style. His writings go through several textual incarnations: newspaper articles become parts of a book, parts of which enter into other books. A book is literally pieced together out of articles, documents, letters, footnotes, addenda, and captioned photographs. Such textual performances are not peculiar. They are implicated in nineteenth-century ideas of literary "unity" and "variety" as well as older conceptions of the book as "space" to be filled up or an artifact cobbled out of parts. They are shaped as well by material conditions of production and authorship.

Isabelo belonged to the first generation of Filipinos raised in a print culture. While printing was introduced in the Philippines before the seventeenth century, a culture of print literacy did not come about until the mid-nineteenth century when newspapers and books began to be published in greater numbers and a reading public started to emerge. Native apprenticeship in printing came early with the work of printers (and occasional authors like Tomas Pinpin), engravers, translators, priest-authors (like Gaspar Aquino de Belen), and the first lay intellectuals to have their works published (like Francisco Baltazar). They worked, however, in the manner and form authorized by the religious orders that monopolized printing, produced works for a readership that did not extend too far beyond the religious communities, or uneasily used print as adjunct for essentially oral compositions. It was not until the printing press was secularized and journalism emerged that intellectuals of Isabelo's type appeared.

We do not know enough of the nineteenth-century world of print in the Philippines, its economics, circulation, or publishing practices. Some aspects of this world, however, seem clear. Book publishing was marginal, occasional, and opportunistic. Readership was small (particularly since Spanish was the dominant print medium) and censorship was in force. However, in Isabelo's time, a living could be made writing for the papers and peddling books. A native could even own a printing press and publish a newspaper. There were gaps in censorship and the cost of a press was not too prohibitive, as instanced by the existence of *imprentillas* (small presses) in the 1890s, including the clandestine press of the revolutionary *Katipunan*, partly equipped (it is said) by types stolen from the press of *Diario de Manila* and others bought from Isabelo himself.

This was Isabelo's world. He was a printshop worker, ephemeral bookseller, pamphleteer, printing press owner, and publisher. His books were issued from the printing presses of the newspapers (like *Imprenta de "El Eco de Panay"*) in which the textual material first appeared; through cooperative arrangements with printer-friends (Jose Ramos, Jose de Jesus); from his own printshop; or by commissioned commercial printers. Publishing practices occasioned quick, improvisational forms: chapbooks (like the popular almanacs Isabelo produced), compilations (like his *juguetes literarios*), the luxuriant, open-ended *bibliotheque* (*Folk-Lore Filipino*), composites and hybrids (*Sensacional Memoria*), and *papeles volantes* (like the anti-friar broadsides Isabelo was accused of producing in the 1890s). These practices favored a form of discourse that was extemporaneous, reiterative, and chameleonic, rather than sustained and systematic.

The formative conditions are not just technical but political. Colonial intellectuals like Isabelo were not writing from the center but in the interstices and margins. Unlike Rizal, who did his writing and publishing outside the country, Isabelo wrote and published under direct surveillance by colonial authorities. Hence the value of the mobile and improvised and the recourse to such strategies as the comic and doublespeak and devices like the innuendo and aside. He played games of evasion with power at the same time that he addressed it. M.H. del Pilar and Rizal, reading Isabelo's works from a distance, misunderstood some of his discursive moves, and Retana would excuse some of his excesses as the rashness of *un chiquillo*. Isabelo was not always deliberate about what he was doing. He was punished for his carelessness but there were times, too, when even carelessness was a saving device.

The colonial intellectual is placed in a position where he has to learn and interpellate the discourse of the Other. This made the annotation an exemplary form of nationalist writing. It is interesting (and perhaps inevitable) that Rizal, Paterno, Pardo, and de los Reyes all did annotations of European texts. Annotating Morga's *Sucesos*, Rizal corrects "official" Spanish history by exposing its errors, gaps, and exclusions. Annotating Maura's Decree, Paterno claims that Spanish reforms were what he had already independently envisioned. Annotating Plasencia's *relacion*, Pardo uses a Spaniard's testimony against the Spaniards. Annotating Spanish legislation in *Municipio Filipino*, Isabelo puts himself "above" colonial law by assuming the authority of publicly commenting on it. Far from being parasitic, the critical annotation is a form at once necessary and radical.

The multiform character of Isabelo's works says something about how the colonial intellectual confronts the dominant knowledge of the West, how, speaking from the interstices of this knowledge, the forms readily available and congenial are the quick, interrogatory forms of the journalistic sketch, anecdote, annotation and commentary. It says something about the kinds of political engagements that leave works like Isabelo's provisional and unfinished.

ISABELO RECOGNIZED the need for a fuller, more autonomous discourse. This was what he attempted in *Historia de Filipinas* but, like Rizal and Paterno (who conceived similar projects), he ran into the impossibilities and contradictions of writing the history of a subject (the nation-state) that did not exist. Such a history could only take the partial, fragmentary forms of an ethnohistorical tract or an open-ended annalistic chronicle instead of an autonomous national narrative. There were no precolonial kingdoms to resurrect and to write a history of the people apart from Empire required—beyond political boldness—the imagining of what, at the time, was not as yet fully imaginable. Rizal sketched a shadow-history by annotating Morga and then turned to writing *Noli me tangere* and *El Filibusterismo*. De los Reyes embarked on *Folk-Lore Filipino*.

More provocateur than systematizer, Isabelo broke fresh ground but, restless and interested in too many things, did not proceed to tend it. The imperatives of the moment pushed him to foreshorten the process as he tried to "institutionalize" a national revolution and a national church in his writings on the religion of the Katipunan and the Aglipayan Church. It was in this institutionalizing phase that he was weakest.

In *Religion Antigua de los Filipinos* (1909), he returned to the folklore project and repeated the call: "Come, compatriots, assist me in this study." Philippine *etnografia* and *folk-lore* are a "virgin" field, he said, and there is need to fill gaps in knowledge and rectify errors. He announced that he had written a hundred letters to Filipinos for data and photographs on local culture; advised correspondents not to invent or "disfigure" legends but preserve them exactly; urged well diggers to look for animal fossils and stone arrows; and stressed the importance of collecting traditions in the hinterland. He asked for data to be sent to his home or the Manila newspaper *El Renacimiento*. "None" responded to his call, Isabelo said, but in publishing *Religion Antigua* he asked readers to read it "for the love of our Country, for the affectionate veneration that we must show to our ancestors."[262]

His best work was behind him. At this time he was already deeply involved in producing a theology for the Philippine Independent Church, combining his interpretations of indigenous religious beliefs, his faith in modern science (including its more esoteric expression in Spiritism), and the Roman Catholic base of the new church. It was a forbidding project that failed. (It is deeply ironic that in his attempt at creating an "autonomous" discourse his final work remained a project of annotation, his version of the Holy Bible.)

The career of Isabelo de los Reyes is remarkable for its dynamic positional shifts. These shifts are not peculiar to Isabelo. This comes with the bordered condition of being a colonial intellectual, caught in the power relations between inside and outside, the conflicting desires of establishing at once both sameness and difference, universality and specificity in one's relation with the Other, learning from outside sources of knowledge at the same time as one interrogates them, driven by the imperatives of addressing *them* and *us*.

One can mark this dynamic in colonial intellectuals like Rizal, Paterno, and Pardo. What distinguishes Isabelo is the degree to which he was more rooted in the *local* than any of them, the way in which he consciously worked out of the inside to envision a future for his people. More so than any of his contemporaries, he stressed the value of popular knowledge (*saber popular*), seeing in it the "genius" out of which modern science itself has evolved, arguing that it is out of its specificities that Filipinos can make their own distinctive contribution to world knowledge.

Writing at the time that he did, his effort to harness popular knowledge was shaped by the imperatives of anti-colonial nation formation. His work on the country's *religion antigua* begins as an exercise in personal education and historical salvage, develops as a defense of the ideological basis of the Katipunan-led revolution, and culminates as a doctrinal blueprint for an independent Philippine Church. His writings on other topics—literature, labor, politics—are animated by the same indigenizing impulses.

It is a problematic "indigenism." Isabelo was no folk bard or rural intellectual. He "discovered" local culture as much by way of a European education as by his own personal experience. Such an education fostered an "outsideness" he could not quite bridge as when he vainly struggled to explain the incommensurable virtues of his own mother's Iloko poetry. This same outsideness afforded him the virtues of perspective, and the comparative knowledge and theoretical resources to construct out of the particulars of lived experience the "long view" in which this experience, the Ilocos and the "nation" could be imagined.

363

There are perils in this endeavor. Trained in the Enlightenment, Isabelo had a vision of the future, a future of rationality and modernity, to which the specificities of the local are realigned and subordinated. One finds a process in which the unfamiliar is familiarized, difference tamed, and the local delocalized through an interpretive logic in which local beliefs are "rationalist," "evolutionist," or "Darwinistic." While he ultimately trusted in the people's "good sense," he did not fully account for the fact that their power to create culture and themselves is not unconstrained.

Isabelo looked to the future and, despite the pride he took in his ethnic roots, he knew that it did not lie in the mountains of Abra but somewhere else. The young Isabelo, however, had such tricks of bilocation we could never be sure. This was his virtue.

NOTES

1. Isabelo de los Reyes, Jr., "Isabelo de los Reyes y Florentino," *Philippine Colophon*, 4:1/2 (1966), 28.

2. I am indebted to William Henry Scott's "Isabelo de los Reyes, Father of Philippine Folklore," "Isabelo de los Reyes: *Provinciano* and Nationalist," and "A Minority Reaction to American Imperialism: Isabelo de los Reyes," *Cracks in the Parchment Curtain* (Quezon City: New Day Publishers, 1982), 245–99, and *The Union Obrera Democratica: First Filipino Labor Union* (Quezon City: New Day Publishers, 1992).

Other biographical sources: *Enciclopedia Universal Ilustrada Europeo-Americana* (Bilbao: Espasa-Calpe, 1920), LI:203; Jose de los Reyes, *Biography of Senator Isabelo de los Reyes*, trans. C. Osias (Manila: Nueva Era Press, 1947); Jose L. Llanes, "The Life and Labors of Isabelo de los Reyes," *Comment*, 11 (1960), 62–81; Gregorio F. Zaide, *Great Filipinos in History* (Manila: Verde Book Store, 1970), 457–63; Erlinda Bragado, "*Sukimatem:* Isabelo de los Reyes Revisited," *Philippine Studies*, 50 (2002), 50–75.

3. Leona Florentino (1849–1884) is immortalized in her town with a monument and a street named in her honor. Her works were exhibited at the Exposicion General de Filipinas in Madrid in 1887 and Paris International Exposition in 1889. See Zaide, *Great Filipinos in History*, 184–86; Leopoldo Y. Yabes, *A Brief Survey of Iloko Literature* (Manila: The Author, 1936), 35–38; *CCP Encyclopedia of Philippine Art* (Manila: Cultural Center of the Philippines, 1994), IX:604.

4. Zoilo M. Galang, *Encyclopedia of the Philippines* (Manila: Exequiel Floro, 1951), III:409–10.

5. Tomas de los Reyes & Frederick Scharpf, "Rizal's Relatives in Vigan—the Florentino Clan," *Ilocos Review*, 15 (1983), 113–19; E. Arsenio Manuel, *Dictionary of Philippine Biography* (Quezon City: Filipiniana Publications, 1955–86), II:151.

6. On Crisologo: Alejandrino G. Hufana, *Mena Pecson Crisologo and Iloko Drama* (Quezon City: University of the Philippines, 1963), 14–26; William Henry Scott,

Ilocano Responses to American Aggression, 1900–1901 (Quezon City: New Day Publishers, 1986), 13–18, 74, 91–92.

7. See Pedro R. Lora, Jr., "The Seminary of Vigan (Philippines) (Spanish Period: 1822–1900)," *Ilocos Review*, 4:1&2 (1972), 44–97; Marcelino A. Foronda, Jr., "Education in the Ilocos during the Spanish Colonial Period, 1574–1898," *Kailukuan: Historical and Bibliographical Studies* (Manila: Philippine National Historical Society, 1976), 13–23.

8. Quoted in Llanes, "Life and Labors," 64; also De los Reyes, *Biography*, 2.

9. Scott, "Isabelo de los Reyes: *Provinciano*," 271; Jesus Z. Valenzuela, *History of Journalism in the Philippine Islands* (Manila: [The Author], 1933), 43.

10. Wenceslao E. Retana, *Sinapismos (Bromitas y Critiquillas)* (Madrid: Manuel Minuesa de los Rios, 1890), 18; Scott, *Union Obrera Democratica*, 8; *Idem.*, "Isabelo de los Reyes: *Provinciano*," 271.

11. *The Rizal-Blumentritt Correspondence* (Manila: Jose Rizal National Centennial Commission, 1961), II:136, 144.

12. *Catalogo de la Exposicion General de las Islas Filipinas* (Madrid: Est. Tipografico de Ricardo Fe, 1887), 584, 589.

13. "Letter from Austria-Hungary," *La Solidaridad*, trans. G.F. Ganzon & L. Mañeru (Metro Manila: Fundacion Santiago, 1996), I:4 (March 31, 1889), 119; "News," *Solidaridad*, I:10 (June 30, 1889), 381; "News," *Solidaridad*, I:17 (October 15, 1889), 653.

14. W.E. Retana, *El Periodismo Filipino: Noticias Para Su Historia (1811–1894)* (Madrid: Imprenta de la Viuda de M. Minuesa de los Rios, 1895), 366–76. English translation: *El Periodismo Filipino (1811–1894)*, trans. R.L. Nazareno & M.E. Peña (Manila: Philippine Press Institute, 1991), 118–21. See "El Padre del Socialismo Filipino," *Renacimiento Filipino*, I:13 (October 7, 1910), 9; Scott, "Isabelo de los Reyes: *Provinciano*," 268–69; W.E. Retana, *Aparato Bibliografico de la Historia General de Filipinas* (Madrid: Imprenta de la Sucesora de M. Minuesa de los Rios, 1906), III, 1653.

15. Scott, "Isabelo de los Reyes: *Provinciano*," 269; Retana, *Aparato Bibliografico*, III, 1654.

16. "From the Philippines," *Solidaridad*, V:108 (July 31, 1893), 367.

17. Isabelo de los Reyes, *El Folk-Lore Filipino*, trans. S.C. Dizon & M.E.P. Imson (Quezon City: University of the Philippines Press, 1994), 14.

18. See for journalism, Retana, *Periodismo Filipino*; for theater, Cristina Laconico-Buenaventura, *The Theater in Manila, 1846–1946* (Manila: De La Salle University Press, 1994); for literature, Resil B. Mojares, *Origins and Rise of the Filipino Novel* (Quezon City: University of the Philippines Press, 1983).

19. On Jose Felipe del Pan: "From the Philippines," *Solidaridad*, V:108 (July 31, 1893), 365; *Enciclopedia Universal*, 41:635–36; Galang, *Encyclopedia*, 4:429–31; Manuel, *Dictionary of Philippine Biography*, 2:167–70.

20. On his novels, see Lilia Hernandez Chung, *Facts in Fiction: A Study of Peninsular Prose Fiction, 1859–1897* (Manila: De La Salle University Press, 1998). Also Retana, *Aparato Bibliografico*, II, nos. 1502, 1568, 1620, 1691, 1938, 2048–50, 2137, 2244, 2370, 2390; III, nos. 2492, 2513–15, 2636–38, 2767.

21. Retana, *Aparato Bibliografico*, III, nos. 4480, 4483; *Idem.*, *Periodismo Filipino*, 83n, 160–72, 184–98.

22. Isabelo de los Reyes, *La Religion Antigua de los Filipinos* (Manila: Imprenta de 'El Renacimiento', 1909), ii–iii.

23. See Richard Drayton, *Nature's Government: Science, Imperial Britain, and the 'Improvement' of the World* (New Haven: Yale University Press, 2000), 92–94, 104–5, 228–29.

24. Retana, *Aparato Bibliografico*, III, 1678.

25. See Retana, *Periodismo Filipino* (1991), 162–63.

26. Isabelo de los Reyes (*Kasalo*, pseud.), "The Equality of Rights," *Solidaridad*, II:30 (April 30, 1890), 283–93; *Idem.*, "Civil Registration," *Solidaridad*, II:32 (May 31, 1890), 349–61; *Idem.*, "Church and Civil Marriages," *Solidaridad*, II:34 (June 30, 1890), 417–29; *Idem.*, "The Penal Code and Censorship," *Solidaridad*, IV:82 (June 30, 1892), 311–13.

27. Isabelo de los Reyes, "Delegates to the Cortes for the Philippines," *Solidaridad*, I:13 (August 15, 1889), 471–73; "News," *Solidaridad*, I:12 (July 31, 1889), 459. Also Isabelo de los Reyes, "Cortes Representation: The Historical Truth," *Solidaridad*, V:102 (April 30, 1893), 119–203.

28. Ferdinand Blumentritt, "A Tribute to Quioquiapism," *Solidaridad*, IV:74 (February 28, 1892), 93–99; *Idem.*, "Homage to Quioquiapism," *Solidaridad*, IV:77 (April 15, 1892), 173–79; *Idem.*, "What Fury you Show, oh Araucans!," *Solidaridad*, I:13 (August 15, 1889), 477.

29. Isabelo de los Reyes, "A la Voz de Espana," *La Lectura Popular*, I:8 (October 22, 1890), 120–22.

30. Ferdinand Blumentritt, "The Confessions and Errors of Father Jose Rodriguez," *Solidaridad*, I:14 (August 31, 1889), 509–19.

31. *Rizal-Blumentritt Correspondence*, IIb:385, 387.

32. Scott, *Ilocano Responses*, 14–18.

33. These recollections are in Llanes, "Life and Labors," 66; Hufana, *Mena Pecson Crisologo*, 17; Jose de los Reyes, "He Lived a Full Life," *Weekly Graphic* (July 8, 1964), 20, 77.

34. *La Sensacional Memoria de Isabelo de los Reyes sobre la Revolucion Filipina de 1896–97* (Madrid: Tip. Lit. de J. Corrales, 1899). Also De los Reyes's letter to Wenceslao Retana, September 14, 1897, reprinted in Pedro S. de Achutegui, S.J., & Miguel A. Bernad, S.J., *Religious Revolution in the Philippines: The Schism of 1902* (Quezon City: Ateneo de Manila University [ADMU] Press, 1972), IV:98.

35. Hufana, *Mena Pecson Crisologo*, 17.

36. De los Reyes, *Sensacional Memoria*, 101; Scott, *Ilocano Responses*, 14; Bragado, "Isabelo de los Reyes," 57–59.

37. De los Reyes, *Memoria* (2001), 93–94; Scott, "Isabelo de los Reyes: *Provinciano*," 276.

38. De los Reyes, *Sensacional Memoria*, 106. Nakpil was involved in procuring arms for the Katipunan but there is no reference to de los Reyes in his published biography: Encarnacion Alzona, ed. & trans., *Julio Nakpil and the Philippine Revolution* (Manila: Carmelo & Bauermann, 1964), 15.

39. Llanes, "Life and Labors," 67.

40. For the text of the manifesto: John Foreman, *The Philippine Islands* (New York: Charles Scribner's Sons, 1906), 542–43.

41. Mariano Ponce, *Cartas Sobre la Revolucion*, trans. M.L. Camagay & W. de la Peña (Quezon City: Office of Research Coordination, University of the Philippines, 1997), 26.

For the complicated story of *Memoria*: Scott, "Isabelo de los Reyes: *Provinciano*," 276–79; W.E. Retana, *Vida y Escritos del Dr. Jose Rizal* (Manila: Nueva Era Press, n.d.; first published in 1907), 94–95n; John R.M. Taylor, comp., *The Philippine Insurrection Against the United States* (Pasay City: Eugenio Lopez Foundation, 1971), I, 372–73.

42. See Ponce, *Cartas Sobre la Revolucion*, 43–44, 45–46.

43. *Nueva Era* (September 12, 1949); cited in Pedro S. de Achutegui, S.J., & Miguel A. Bernad, S.J., *Religious Revolution in the Philippines: The Life and Church of Gregorio Aglipay, 1860-1960* (Manila: Ateneo de Manila, 1960), I:167.

44. De los Reyes, *Biography*, 11.

45. The text of the letter is in Llanes, "Life and Labors," 68.

46. Llanes, "Life and Labors," 68.

47. Isabelo de los Reyes to Wenceslao E. Retana, Barcelona, September 14, 1897. Reprinted in Achutegui & Bernad, *Religious Revolution*, IV:95–104, 356–57.

48. Achutegui & Bernad, *Religious Revolution*, IV:96, 97.

49. "El Senador Isabelo de los Reyes habla de Acracia y de sus ideales," *La Opinion* (March 30, 1927); in Scott, *Union Obrera Democratica*, 15. I have based my account

of Isabelo's association with the anarchists on Scott's *Union Obrera Democratica* and Benedict Anderson's "Jupiter Hill" (Ms., c2004). I thank Anderson and Patricio Abinales for a copy of the manuscript.

The French translation of *Noli me tangere* was done by Sempau in collaboration with Henri Lucas: *Aux Pays des Moines* (Paris: P.V. Stock, 1899). Sempau also annotated an edition of the novel in Spain: *Noli me tangere* (Barcelona: Casa Editorial Maucci, 1903; 2d.ed.).

50. G.D.H. Cole, *The Second International, 1889–1914* (London: Macmillan & Co., 1960), 744–74.

51. Manuel Artigas, *Galeria de Filipinos Ilustres* (Manila: Imprenta de Gabino A. Pobre, 1918), II:23–25; *Manifiesto-Programa de la Colonia Filipina Reformista en Madrid* (Madrid: Establecimiento Tipografico de Pedro Nuñez, 1898).

52. Danilo R. Laeda, "The Bible in Iloko," *The Ilocos Review*, 13 (1981), 40–82.

53. James A. LeRoy, *The Americans in the Philippines* (Boston: Houghton Mifflin Company, 1914), II:268n; Esteban A. de Ocampo, *First Filipino Diplomat* (Manila: National Historical Institute, 1978), 103n.

54. Isabelo de los Reyes, *Filipinas. Independencia y Revolucion* (Madrid: Imp. y Lit. de J. Corrales, 1900).

55. Retana, *Aparato Bibliografico*, III, no. 4073.

56. Scott, *Ilocano Responses*, 91–92.

57. Letter, I. de los Reyes to Pardo de Tavera (Madrid, November 30, 1899). In Achutegui & Bernad, *Religious Revolution*, IV:105–08.

58. De los Reyes, *Sensacional Memoria* (1899), iii–vii.

59. Achutegui & Bernad, *Religious Revolution*, I:175–76; *Idem., Religious Revolution in the Philippines: The Religious Coup d'Etat, 1898–1901* (Manila: ADMU Press, 1971), III:48–51; *Idem., Religious Revolution*, IV:817.

60. Achutegui & Bernad, *Religious Revolution*, III, 105–106.

61. See Sister Mary Dorita Clifford, R.V.M., "*Iglesia Filipina Independiente*: The Revolutionary Church," *Studies in Philippine Church History*, ed. G.H. Anderson (Ithaca: Cornell University Press, 1969), 228–29, 232–33.

62. Achutegui & Bernad, *Religious Revolution*, I, 157–58, 177–79; IV, 58–63.

63. Achutegui & Bernad, *Religious Revolution*, I, 159–61; IV, 88–91; Isacio R. Rodriguez, O.S.A., *Gregorio Aglipay y los Origenes de la Iglesia Filipina Independiente (1898–1917)* (Madrid: Departamento de Misionologia Española, 1960), 394–96.

64. Taylor, *Philippine Insurrection*, V:381 (Exhibit 1180); Scott, "Minority Reaction," 289; S.V. Epistola, *Hong Kong Junta* (Quezon City: University of the Philippines Press, 1996), 163–64.

65. De los Reyes, *Biography*, 18.

66. See texts of the letters in Achutegui & Bernad, *Religious Revolution*, IV, 111–13.

67. Quoted in Clifford, "*Iglesia Filipina Independiente*," 233–34.

68. *Estrella de Antipolo* (October 26, 1901); cited in Achutegui & Bernad, *Religious Revolution*, I, 172.

69. *Report of the Philippine Commission* [hereinafter cited as *RPC*] (Washington, D.C.: Government Printing Office, 1903), III:39–41; Maximo M. Kalaw, *The Development of Philippine Politics (1872–1920)* (Manila: Oriental Commercial Co., 1926), 286–87; Michael Cullinane, "Ilustrado Politics: The Response of the Filipino Educated Elite to American Colonial Rule, 1898–1907" (Ph.D. diss., University of Michigan, 1989), 112 (published by ADMU Press, 2003).

70. On Gomez and Poblete: *Filipinos in History* (Manila: National Historical Institute, 1990), II:114–15; III:110–11.

71. See the document entitled "The Christmas Eve Fiasco and a Brief Outline of the Ricarte and Other Similar Movements from the Time of the Breaking Up of the Insurrection of 1899–1901," *Memoirs of General Artemio Ricarte* (Manila: National Heroes Commission, 1963), 157–216.

72. Cullinane, "Ilustrado Politics," 194–95.

73. *Llueven palos!* (Manila, 1905), quoted in Scott, "Minority Reaction," 291–93.

74. On de los Reyes and the labor movement: Scott, *Union Obrera Democratica*; Melinda Tria Kerkvliet, *Manila Workers' Unions, 1900–1950* (Quezon City: New Day Publishers, 1992), 6–30.

75. *La Opinion* (March 30, 1927), in Scott, *Union Obrera Democratica*, 20.

76. See Scott, *Union Obrera Democratica*, 43–45.

77. See [Felix M. Roxas], *The World of Felix Roxas* (Manila: Filipiniana Book Guild, 1970), 239–41.

78. *Muling Pagsilang* (January 2, 1903), in Scott, "Minority Reaction," 298–99.

79. *El Debate* (October 11, 1938); "Christmas Eve Fiasco," 176.

80. Scott, *Union Obrera Democratica*, 73.

81. Scott, *Union Obrera Democratica*, 74.

82. Clifford, "*Iglesia Filipina Independiente*," 234; Homer C. Stuntz, *The Philippines and the Far East* (Cincinnati: Jennings & Pye, 1904), 489–90.

83. Achutegui & Bernad, *Religious Revolution*, I, 182–90.

84. Quoted in Achutegui & Bernad, *Religious Revolution*, I, 189–90.

85. Achutegui & Bernad, *Religious Revolution*, IV, 4. Also see Rodriguez, *Gregorio Aglipay*, 381–469; Richard L. Deats, *Nationalism and Christianity in the Philippines* (Dallas: Southern Methodist University Press, 1967), 73–79.

86. "Christmas Eve Fiasco," 176.

87. *Memoirs of General Artemio Ricarte*, 125, 133.

88. *El Renacimiento* (January 14, 1908), quoted in Scott, "Minority Reaction," 294.

89. See J. Romero Maura, "Terrorism in Barcelona and its Impact on Spanish Politics, 1904–1909," *Past & Present*, 41 (December 1968), 130–83.

90. "Entierro de una Filipina en Tokyo," *Renacimiento Filipino*, II:78 (February 14, 1912), 1059–60; De los Reyes, Jr., "Isabelo de los Reyes," 28–29.

91. Quoted in Scott, "Minority Reaction," 295.

92. Isabelo de los Reyes, *Solidaridad Filipina* (Manila, January 4, 1911). Leaflet, copy in IFI [Iglesia Filipina Independiente] Archives (OM15, Box 50), St. Andrew's Theological Seminary, Quezon City.

93. On his marriages and children: De los Reyes & Scharpf, "Rizal's Relatives," 118–19.

94. Achutegui & Bernad, *Religious Revolution*, I, 479–80. On the election of 1935: Joseph Ralston Hayden, *The Philippines: A Study in National Development* (New York: Macmillan Company, 1942), 401–35.

95. Quoted in Scott, *Union Obrera Democratica*, 49.

96. Scott, *Union Obrera Democratica*, 13; De los Reyes, *Biography*, v.

97. On the controversy, see Achutegui & Bernad, *Religious Revolution*, I, 501–10; Rodriguez, *Gregorio Aglipay*, 466–69; Isabelo de los Reyes, Jr., *The Religious Retraction of Isabelo de los Reyes y Florentino* [no pub., 1960]; "Clippings from various newspapers pertaining to Isabelo de los Reyes, Sr." (OM20 Ag-Rey, Box 68), IFI Archives, St. Andrew's Theological Seminary, Quezon City.

98. In Scott, "Isabelo de los Reyes: *Provinciano*," 266–67.

99. Scott, "Isabelo de los Reyes: *Provinciano*," 268.

100. Scott, "Isabelo de los Reyes: *Provinciano*," 267, 270. See Retana, *Sinapismos*, 42; *Idem., Periodismo Filipino* (1991), 121n.

101. Retana, *Sinapismos*, 41; Scott, "Isabelo de los Reyes: *Provinciano*," 272.

102. Quoted in Scott, "Isabelo de los Reyes: *Provinciano*," 270.

103. Scott, "Isabelo de los Reyes: *Provinciano*," 270–71.

104. Isabelo de los Reyes, *Filipinas. Articulos varios . . . sobre etnografia, historia y costumbres del pais* (Manila: J.A. Ramos, 1887),

105. De los Reyes, "El Tinguian," *Filipinas*, ii, 3–4.

106. De los Reyes, "Li-Ma-Hong," *Filipinas*, 39–65.

107. De los Reyes, "Los Regulos de Manila," *Filipinas*, 87–111. On this subject, see Luciano P.R. Santiago, "The Houses of Lakandula, Matanda and Soliman (1571–

1898): Genealogy and Group Identity," *Philippine Quarterly of Culture & Society* [hereinafter cited as *PQCS*], 18:1 (1990), 39–73.

108. Isabelo de los Reyes, *Triunfos del Rosario o los Holandeses en Filipinas* (Manila: Establecimiento Tipografico de Ramirez y Comp., 1888). First published in *Diario de Manila*, this also appeared in De los Reyes, *Filipinas*, 66–86.

109. Retana, *Aparato Bibliografico*, III, no. 2652.

110. De los Reyes, *Triunfos del Rosario*, 29. Isabelo probably accessed the Spanish edition of Blumentritt's work, translated by Enrique Ruppert: *Filipinas: Ataques de los holandeses en los siglos xvi, xvii y xviii* (Madrid, 1882).

111. De los Reyes, "El Diablo en Filipinas," *Filipinas*, 115–38.

112. De los Reyes, "Diablo en Filipinas," 128.

113. Isabelo de los Reyes, *Prehistoria de Filipinas* (Manila: Imp. de Sta. Cruz, 1889).

114. Isabelo de los Reyes, *Las Islas Visayas en la Epoca de la Conquista* (Manila: Tipo-Litografia de Chofre y C.a, 1889).

115. Isabelo de los Reyes, *Historia de Ilocos* (Manila: Establecimiento Tipografica La Opinion, 1890), 2 vols.

116. De los Reyes, *Historia de Ilocos*, I:14.

117. De los Reyes, *Prehistoria*, 44.

118. De los Reyes, *Islas Visayas*, 43n.

119. De los Reyes, *Prehistoria*, 76; *Islas Visayas*, 19; *Historia de Ilocos*, I:104.

120. De los Reyes, *Islas Visayas*, 36.

121. Retana, *Aparato Bibliografico*, III, no. 2528.

122. De los Reyes, *Islas Visayas*, 25, 55.

123. De los Reyes, *Prehistoria*, 1; *Islas Visayas*, 57.

124. De los Reyes, *Prehistoria*, 1; *Islas Visayas*, 57.

125. De los Reyes, *Prehistoria*, 2; *Islas Visayas*, 58.

126. De los Reyes, *Prehistoria*, 2–3; *Islas Visayas*, 58–59.

127. De los Reyes, *Prehistoria*, 8; *Islas Visayas*, 67; *Historia de Ilocos*, I:35–36.

128. Wallace considered the Malay, Papuan, and Negrito as distinct races. See Alfred Russel Wallace, *The Malay Archipelago* (Singapore: Graham Brash, 1983; first published in 1869), 446–57. The argument that all Oceanic races are modifications of the same type was made by Wilhelm von Humboldt and James Cowles Prichard.

129. De los Reyes, *Prehistoria*, 9–10; *Islas Visayas*, 68.

130. De los Reyes, *Prehistoria*, 10; *Islas Visayas*, 69. Current scholarship lends credence to the hypothesis that the earliest Austronesians originated in Southern China and moved to Indonesia via the Philippines around 2000 B.C. See Peter Bellwood,

Prehistory of the Indo-Malaysian Archipelago (Honolulu: University of Hawaii Press, 1997), 87–89, 105–06, 119–20, 241–42.

131. De los Reyes, *Historia de Ilocos*, I:63, 74–75. Francisco Colin's views on the origin of Filipinos were particularly influential as we find them repeated by other missionary chroniclers: Gaspar de San Agustin, O.S.A., *Conquistas de la Islas Filipinas, 1565–1615*, trans. L.A. Mañeru (Manila: San Agustin Museum, 1998; first published in 1698), 48–49; *The Philippine Chronicles of Fray San Antonio*, trans. P. Picornell (Manila: Historical Conservation Society, 1977; translation of Juan Francisco de San Antonio, O.F.M., *Cronicas de la Provincia de San Gregorio Magno*, 1738–44), 128–38.

132. De los Reyes, *Islas Visayas*, 70.

133. De los Reyes, *Islas Visayas*, 72; *Historia de Ilocos*, I:26.

134. De los Reyes, *Memoria* (1899), 103.

135. De los Reyes, *Historia de Ilocos*, II:104.

136. De los Reyes, *Historia de Ilocos*, II:173. The Silang revolt is a subject of conflicting interpretations: see David Routledge, *Diego Silang and the Origins of Philippine Nationalism* (Quezon City: University of the Philippines, Philippine Center for Advanced Studies, 1979); Fernando Palanco, "Diego Silang's Revolt: A New Approach," *Philippine Studies*, 50:4 (2002), 512–37.

137. De los Reyes, *Historia de Ilocos*, II:173.

138. Retana, *Aparato Bibliografico*, III, no. 2937; Retana, *Periodismo Filipino*, 120–21; *Rizal-Blumentritt Correspondence*, II: 385.

139. De los Reyes, *Islas Visayas*, 79; *Historia de Ilocos*, I:38–39.

140. The volumes were published as part of the "*Biblioteca de 'La Espana Oriental'*" and carried the imprint of two printers: Imprenta de Santa Cruz and Tipo-Litografia de Chofre y Compania. I have used *Folk-Lore Filipino* (1994), the Spanish-English edition of volume one translated by Dizon and Imson, and *El Folk-Lore Filipino* (Manila: Imprenta de Santa Cruz, 1889), v. 2.

141. De los Reyes, *Historia de Ilocos*, I:180.

142. *El Comercio* (March 21, 1885). See "Panawagan tungkol sa Folklorismo," *Efemerides Filipinas*, 428–38.

143. De los Reyes, *Folk-Lore Filipino*, I:255, 407.

144. See William Thoms, "Folklore" (1846), *The Study of Folklore*, ed. A. Dundes (Englewood Cliffs, N.J.: Prentice-Hall, 1965), 4–6; Stith Thompson, *The Folktale* (Berkeley: University of California Press, 1977), 391–405.

145. De los Reyes, *Folk-Lore Filipino*, I:7.

146. De los Reyes, *Folk-Lore Filipino*, I:23, 31.

147. De los Reyes, *Folk-Lore Filipino*, I:7.

148. De los Reyes, *Folk-Lore Filipino*, I:24. Also Isabelo de los Reyes's prologue to Claudio R. Miranda, *Costumbres Populares* (Manila: Imp. "Cultura Filipina," 1911), i–x.

149. De los Reyes, *Folk-Lore Filipino*, I:458–59.

150. See *El Comercio* (March 21, 1885), quoted in Ponce & De Veyra, *Efemerides Filipinas,* 431.

151. He uses in the book such previously published material as *Mitologia Ilocana* (part of his *Historia de Ilocos*), which Blumentritt translated into German, *Die Religiusen Anschauungen der Ilocanen* (Wein, 1888); and his "Tradiciones Filipinas sobre la Creacion del Mundo," *El Comercio* (March 26, 1888), published under his pseudonym *Deloserre*.

152. De los Reyes, *Folk-Lore Filipino*, I:294, 304–5.

153. De los Reyes, *Folk-Lore Filipino*, I:276–77, 312–13.

154. De los Reyes, *Folk-Lore Filipino*, I:330–31.

155. Miguel Zaragoza, "Al Rededor de Un Cadaver," in de los Reyes, *Folk-Lore Filipino*, II:7–39.

156. Mariano Ponce, "El Folk-Lore Bulaqueño"; Pedro Serrano, "Folk-Lore Pampango"; and Pio Mondragon, "Folk-Lore Tayabeño," in de los Reyes, *Folk-Lore Filipino*, II:41–80, 81–109, 110–72.

157. Serrano, "Folk-Lore Pampango," 81.

158. De los Reyes, *Folk-Lore Filipino*, II:173. For a discussion of the authenticity of these documents: Scott, "Isabelo de los Reyes: Father of Philippine Folklore," 260–62.

159. "Vida de Lam-ang (Antiguo Poema Popular de Ilocos," *Folk-Lore Filipino*, II:235–97. On *Lam-ang*, see Kenneth E. Bauzon, *Lam-ang in Transition: A Historical Re-appraisal* (Quezon City: University of the Philippines, 1973).

160. De los Reyes, *Folk-Lore Filipino*, I:444–45.

161. De los Reyes, *Folk-Lore Filipino*, I:20–21, quoting what he earlier said of himself in an article published in Madrid's *Boletin de la Institucion Libre de Ensenanza* (August 31, 1885).

162. Isabelo de los Reyes, "Folk-Lore Administrativo?," *Folk-Lore Filipino*, I:540–615; *Idem., Sensacional Memoria* (1899), 103.

163. Isabelo de los Reyes, *Apuntes para un ensayo de Teodicea Filipina: La Religion del "Katipunan"* (Madrid: Tipolit. de J. Corrales, 1900), 34.

164. De los Reyes, *Apuntes para un ensayo*, 35–36. On the Katipunan initiation rite: Teodoro A. Agoncillo, *The Revolt of the Masses* (Quezon City: University of the Philippines Press, 1996; first published in 1956), 50–52; Reynaldo C. Ileto, *Pasyon and Revolution: Popular Movements in the Philippines, 1840–1910* (Quezon City: Ateneo de Manila University Press, 1979), 114–21.

165. De los Reyes, *Apuntes para un Ensayo*, 37; *Memoria* (2001), 98, 100–01.

166. Isabelo de los Reyes, *The Religion of the Katipunan*, trans. A. de Roma (Manila: National Historical Institute, 1980).

167. De los Reyes, *Religion of the Katipunan*, 42.

168. De los Reyes, *Religion of the Katipunan*, 14.

169. De los Reyes, *Apuntes para un Ensayo*, 18, 49.

170. De los Reyes, *Religion of the Katipunan*, 10, 15, 16.

171. De los Reyes, *Apuntes para un Ensayo*, 20–21; *Religion of the Katipunan*, 26.

172. De los Reyes, *Religion of the Katipunan*, 26, 27.

173. De los Reyes, *Apuntes para un Ensayo*, 29.

174. De los Reyes, *Apuntes para un Ensayo*, 23–24; *Religion of the Katipunan*, 32, 41, 42.

175. De los Reyes, *Apuntes para un Ensayo*, 53.

176. De los Reyes, *Religion Antigua*, 39.

177. De los Reyes, *Religion Antigua*, 64.

178. De los Reyes, *Religion Antigua*, 109.

179. De los Reyes, *Religion Antigua*, 98.

180. De los Reyes, *Religion Antigua*, 141.

181. De los Reyes, *Religion Antigua*, 248.

182. *Doctrina y Reglas Constitucionales de la Iglesia Filipina Independiente* (Manila: Imprenta Tipografia de Modesto Reyes y Cia., 1904); *Catecismo de la Iglesia Filipina Independiente* (Manila: Imprenta de Fajardo y Cia., 1905); *Lecturas de Cuaresma para la Iglesia Filipina Independiente* (Barcelona: [Isabelo de los Reyes], 1906); *Oficio Divino de la Iglesia Filipina Independiente* (Barcelona: [Isabelo de los Reyes], 1906); *Biblia Filipina* (Barcelona: [Isabelo de los Reyes], 1908).

These works attribute authorship to Aglipay or cite de los Reyes as "editor," but de los Reyes himself affirmed he authored these works. On this question, see Achutegui & Bernad, *Religious Revolution*, I:266–69.

183. *Catequesis de la Iglesia Filipina Independiente* (Manila: [Isabelo de los Reyes], 1911); *Catedra (Sermonario) de la Iglesia Filipina Independiente* (Manila: [Isabelo de los Reyes], 1932). *Catequesis* was approved by the IFI Supreme Council apparently in 1911; it was declared "not an official book of the church" in 1940.

184. Quoted in Achutegui & Bernad, *Religious Revolution*, I:257. In the analysis of IFI doctrine, I have relied on Achutegui & Bernad: see their *Religious Revolution*, I:256–70; II:149–55, 315–20. For a critical review of the literature on the IFI: Paul A. Rodell, "The Founding of the Iglesia Filipina Independiente (the "Aglipayan" Church): An Historiographical Review," *PQCS*. 16 (1988), 210–34.

185. Quoted in Achutegui & Bernad, *Religious Revolution*, II:152.

186. Achutegui & Bernad, *Religious Revolution*, I:265n.

187. Achutegui & Bernad, *Religious Revolution*, I:266.

188. Quoted in Achutegui & Bernad, *Religious Revolution*, I:269.

189. Quoted in Achutegui & Bernad, *Religious Revolution*, I:269.

190. Quoted in Achutegui & Bernad, *Religious Revolution*, I:262.

191. Achutegui & Bernad, *Religious Revolution*, I:171, 279.

192. H. Ellsworth Chandlee, "The Liturgy of the Philippine Independent Church," *Studies in Philippine Church History*, 262.

193. Hayden, *Philippines*, 573–74.

194. See *La Lectura Popular*, II:21 (May 28, 1891); Retana, *Aparato Bibliografico*, III, no. 4518; Retana, *Periodismo Filipino*, 452–54.

195. See Isabelo de los Reyes, "Ilao, Ilao, Pacailao-ilauan!," *La Lectura Popular*, I:1 (September 4, 1890), 2–3; *Idem.*, "El Amor y las Flores Filipinas," *La Lectura Popular*, II:36 (September 22, 1891), 886–88; *Idem.*, "La Esclavitud Ilocana," *La Lectura Popular*, II:31 (August 13, 1891) – II:33 (August 28, 1891).

196. See Retana, *Aparato Bibliografico*, III, no. 4550.

197. *Ang Singsing nang Dalagang Marmol* (Manila: Tip. Santos y Bernal, 1912); first published in *Ang Kapatid ng Bayan* in 1905, ADMU Press edition, 2005; See Yabes, *Brief Survey*, 39; Marcelino A. Foronda, Jr., & Juan A. Foronda, *Samtoy: Essays on Iloko History and Culture* (Manila: United Publishing Company, 1972).

198. On the almanac and its uses: Maureen Perkins, *Visions of the Future: Almanacs, Time, and Cultural Change* (Oxford: Clarendon Press, 1996). In the Philippines, the almanac has gone largely unstudied. See A.F. Paredes, "Old Almanac Maker," *This Week* (January 13, 1957), 36–37; Quijano de Manila, "Don Honorio Lopez and his Calendar," *Philippines Free Press* (January 6, 1968), 6, 63–65.

199. *Kalendariong Maanghang sa taong 1911. Sili araw-araw datapwa't birong kapatid lamang, kadiabluhang malaki ni Isabelo de los Reyes* (Maynila: Limbagang Magiting ni Honorio Lopez, 1911).

200. Isabelo de los Reyes, ed., *Calendario de la Iglesia Filipina Independiente para el año bisiesto del Senor, 1908* (Barcelona: Imp. A. Virgili, 1908).

201. See Hufana, *Mena Pecson Crisologo*, 96–98. The adaptation credits Camille du Locle as author of the original. Du Locle, a French librettist with whom Verdi collaborated in some of his works, sent Verdi in 1870 the scenario by Egyptologist Auguste Mariette, based on an invented story set in Egyptian antiquity. Based on this scenario, the libretto was produced by Antonio Ghislanzoni. Verdi and du Locle

collaborated on revisions in the scenario until *Aida* was premiered in Cairo on December 24, 1871. See *New Grove Dictionary of Opera*, ed. S. Sadie (London: Macmillan, 1992), I:43–46.

202. Quoted from *The Ilocos Times* (1936) in Hufana, *Mena Pecson Crisologo,* 97–98.

203. Isabelo de los Reyes, *Ang Comediang Tagalog (1904)*, Typescript copy of a *folletin*, Ateneo de Manila University Library, 68, [3] pp.

204. De los Reyes, *Comediang Tagalog*, 3.

205. De los Reyes, *Comediang Tagalog*, 16, 48.

206. De los Reyes, *Comediang Tagalog*, 15, 18.

207. De los Reyes, *Comediang Tagalog*, 38–39.

208. Retana, *Sinapismos*, 22–23.

209. Retana, *Sinapismos*, 20, 21, 25–26; *Idem., Aparato Bibliografico*, III, no. 2789.

210. Retana, *Periodismo Filipino* (1991), 120n.

211. Retana, *Periodismo Filipino* (1991), 119.

212. Retana, *Sinapismos*, 16–18; *Idem., Periodismo Filipino* (1991), 120–21.

213. Retana, *Periodismo Filipino* (1991), 121.

214. Retana, *Sinapismos*, 15, 44.

215. Retana, *Aparato Bibliografico*, III, no. 4089.

216. Retana, *Aparato Bibliografico*, III, no. 4506.

217. James A. LeRoy, *Philippine Life in Town and Country* (New York: G.P. Putnam's Sons, 1906), 166.

218. T.H. Pardo de Tavera, *Biblioteca Filipina* (Washington: Government Printing Office, 1903), 358, 359.

219. Rizal to Blumentritt, April 30, 1888. In *Reminiscences and Travels of Jose Rizal*, 295.

220. Rizal to M.H. del Pilar, London, February 4, 1889. In *Rizal's Correspondence with Fellow Reformists* (Manila: National Heroes Commission, 1963), 273. Also *Epistolario de Marcelo H. del Pilar* (Manila: Imprenta del Gobierno, 1955), I:24–27.

221. M.H. del Pilar to Rizal, Barcelona, January 1889. In *Epistolario de Marcelo H. del Pilar*, I:20–21; *Rizal's Correspondence with Fellow Reformists*, 266–67.

222. *Rizal's Correspondence with Fellow Reformists*, 274.

223. Jose Rizal, "A Reply to Don Isabelo de los Reyes," *Solidaridad* (October 31, 1890), 717–19.

224. Rizal, "Reply to Don Isabelo de los Reyes," 719.

225. Rizal, "Reply to Don Isabelo de los Reyes," 723.

226. Juan Luna to Rizal, Paris, November 8, 1890. In *Rizal's Correspondence with Fellow Reformists*, 503–504.

227. Blumentritt to Rizal, Leitmeritz, December 16, 1890. In *Rizal-Blumentritt Correspondence*, II:385–86.

228. Blumentritt to Rizal, November 14, 1886. In *Rizal-Blumentritt Correspondence*, IIa, 20. See Retana's response to Blumentritt's praise of de los Reyes in Wenceslao E. Retana, *Reformas y Otros Excesos* (Madrid: Libreria de Fernando Fe, 1890), 50–51.

229. Blumentritt to Rizal, Leitmeritz, December 22, 1890. In *Rizal-Blumentritt Correspondence*, II, 388.

230. De los Reyes, *Prehistoria*, viii.

231. *La Ilustracion Filipina* (March 7, 1892), quoted in Scott, "Isabelo de los Reyes: Father of Philippine Folklore," 246.

232. De los Reyes, *Apuntes para un Ensayo*, 23; De los Reyes, *Sensacional Memoria*, 100; Achutegui & Bernad, *Religious Revolution*, I:170.

233. De los Reyes, *Religion of the Katipunan*, 40n.

234. De los Reyes, *Religion Antigua*, 15.

235. On Kardec and Flammarion: *Encyclopedia of Occultism and Parapsychology*, ed. L. Shepard (Detroit: Gale Research, 1991), I:595–96, 891; II:1580. On Wallace's involvement in spiritism: Andrew Berry, ed., *Infinite Tropics: An Alfred Russel Wallace Anthology* (London: Verso, 2002).

236. Quoted in de los Reyes, *Folk-Lore Filipino*, I:194.

237. Quoted in Isabelo's letter to Retana, September 14, 1897, in Achutegui & Bernad, *Religious Revolution*, IV:97.

238. Quoted in de los Reyes, *Sensacional Memoria* (1899), 118–19.

239. De los Reyes, *Filipinas*, 156; a statement said to have first appeared in a Madrid periodical and reprinted in *El Comercio*.

240. De los Reyes, *Filipinas*, 156.

241. De los Reyes, *Apuntes para un Ensayo*, 26–27.

242. *Solidaridad*, II:42 (October 31, 1890), 719.

243. De los Reyes, *Apuntes para un Ensayo*, 33–34; *Memoria* (2001), 92.

244. De los Reyes, *Filipinas. Independencia y Revolucion*, 131–32.

245. Quoted in Retana, *Sinapismos*, 43.

246. De los Reyes, *Filipinas*, 155.

247. De los Reyes, *Apuntes para un Ensayo*, 6–7.

248. Retana, *Sinapismos*, 26.

249. Benedict Anderson, "The Rooster's Egg: Pioneering World Folklore in the

Philippines," *New Left Review*, 2 (2000), 47–62; also in *Debating World Literature*, ed. C. Prendergast (London: Verso, 2004), 197–213.

250. Roger D. Abrahams, "The Foundations of American Public Folklore," *Public Folklore*, ed. R. Baron & N.R. Spitzer (Washington: Smithsonian Institution Press, 1992), 253.

251. See Richard E. Chandler & Kessel Schwartz, *A New History of Spanish Literature* (Baton Rouge: Louisiana State University Press, 1961), 203–4, 517–27; E. Allison Peers, *A History of the Romantic Movement in Spain* (New York: Hafner Publishing Company, 1964), 69–73, 152–59.

252. On these novels and *costumbrismo* in the Philippines: Hernandez-Chung, *Facts in Fiction*, esp. 57–59; Mojares, *Origins and Rise of the Filipino Novel*, 116–17. For an interesting comparison with a Latin American example: Elisa Sampson Vera Tudela, "Hearing Voices: Ricardo Palma's Contextualization of Colonial Peru," *Debating World Literature*, 214–32.

253. *The Antonio Gramsci Reader: Selected Writings, 1916–1935*, ed. D. Forgacs (New York: New York University Press, 1999), 360–62.

254. W.E. Retana, *Noticias Historico-Bibliograficas de el Teatro en Filipinas desde sus Origenes hasta 1898* (Madrid: Libreria General de Victoriano Suarez, 1909), 122. See Vicente Barrantes, *El Teatro Tagalo* (Madrid: Tipografia de Manuel Gines Hernandez, 1889).

255. Rizal, "Vicente Barrantes' *Teatro Tagalo*," *Political and Historical Writings*, 94–108.

256. Rizal, "Vicente Barrantes' *Teatro Tagalo*," 105.

257. Jose Rizal presented a paper on Tagalog metrics at a meeting of Berlin's Ethnographical Society in April 1887. His views on art are to be found scattered in his writings but he never discussed the subject at great length. See his "*Arte metrica del Tagalog*" in Virgilio S. Almario, ed., *Poetikang Tagalog* (Quezon City: Sentro ng Wikang Filipino, Sistemang Unibersidad ng Pilipinas, 1996), 47–57.

258. De los Reyes, *Historia de Ilocos*, I:116.

259. De los Reyes, *Historia de Ilocos*, I:116. On the *komedya*: Nicanor G. Tiongson, *Kasaysayan ng Komedya sa Pilipinas: 1766–1982* (Manila: De La Salle University, 1982); *Idem.*, *Komedya* (Quezon City: University of the Philippines Press, 1999).

260. I have not been able to locate a copy of de los Reyes's *Aida*. The most substantial study of Iloko theater does not mention the play: Mario G.R. Rosal, "The Drama in Iloco: A Critical Survey of the Ilocano Comedia and Zarzuela" (Ph.D. diss., University of the Philippines, 1980), 2 vols.

Foreign theater companies staged Verdi's *Aida* in Manila as early as 1894. Opera's popularity as a sign of cosmopolitanism in Manila is indicated by the publication in 1906 by "Imprenta de Quiapo" of a series of pamphlets containing scene-by-scene synopses of Verdi's operas, including *Aida. Opera en 4 actos del Maestro Verdi* (Manila: Imp. de Quiapo, 1906).

261. Edward W. Said, *Culture and Imperialism* (New York: Alfred A. Knopf, 1993), 111–32.

262. De los Reyes, *Religion Antigua*, i.

THE FILIPINO ENLIGHTENMENT

Grupo de Filipinos Ilustres (1911), drawing by
Guillermo Tolentino, transferred to lithographic
stone by Jorge Pineda, pulled in sepia and printed by
Carmelo & Bauermann. It became the best-known
gallery of "illustrious Filipinos." Seated (L-R): Jose
Burgos, Antonio Luna, Jose Rizal, Andres Bonifacio,
M.H. del Pilar, and Apolinario Mabini. Standing (L-
R): Clemente Jose Zulueta, Jose Ma. Basa, Pedro
Paterno, Juan Luna, Graciano Lopez-Jaena, Miguel
Malvar, and Antonio Ma. Regidor. Limited to
posthumous figures, the composite portrait leaves
out such personalities as T.H. Pardo de Tavera and
Isabelo de los Reyes.

ENTANGLED GENEALOGIES

THE NATIVE ENCOUNTER with European knowledge did not begin with Pedro Paterno, T.H. Pardo de Tavera, or Isabelo de los Reyes. When in 1521 Ferdinand Magellan plied chief Humabon of Cebu with gifts, thrilled him with words extoling the power of the Spanish King and God, and proceeded to convert him and his followers, thought worlds collided. Humabon did not have a Pigafetta to record the native side of the encounter. The events that followed however—Magellan's death in the shallows of Mactan, the massacre of his men—illustrated what has been demonstrated time and again: acts of conquest and conversion are not always what they seem.[1]

Magellan's death was a temporary setback. Spanish colonization would begin four decades later and did not end until 333 years after. In the course of this time, the intellectual encounter took forms more systematic and unequal but always in ways neither side fully imagined.

It is here that our story begins.

EUROPEAN MISSIONARIES laid the foundation of Western scholarship in the Philippines.[2] The most pervasive form of colonial authority, the Catholic Church generated new knowledge through the institutions and practices missionaries initiated. Missionaries spread a new religion, established churches and schools, organized devotional associations, introduced crops and technology, and built towns. Moreover (and this is what primarily concerns us here) they "textualized" the Philippines in a body of written texts that did not only underwrite how colonialism was conducted, it has become an indispensable archive for students of the Philippines even today. They wrote these texts as necessary aid for pastoral work and social control and because they saw themselves as "men of learning" and privileged agents in advancing knowledge of the world. Working out of a Euro-Christian tradition and enmeshed in the politics of colonial domination, they did not produce disinterested knowledge. Yet their textualization of the country formed much of the basis for how the Philippines would be represented and counter-represented.

By the start of the seventeenth century, five religious orders had established missions in the country: Augustinians (1565), Franciscans (1578), Jesuits (1581), Dominicans (1587), and Recollects (1606). Needing to learn local languages for mission work, missionaries produced grammars (*artes*) and dictionaries (*vocabularios*). They studied the most important languages as well as lesser-known ones like Gaddang, Ibanag, and Bagobo. By 1776 there were more than twenty kinds of grammars written of Tagalog alone. Writing in 1860 that he had read thirty-seven of these grammars, Pedro de Sanlucar wrote that "there are so many grammars in this language [Tagalog] that it alone surpasses in number (being so limited in territorial extension) the number of grammars of the spoken and dead languages of Europe."[3] Missionaries introduced Romanized writing, enriched native lexical systems with Latin and Spanish, did translations and palaeographic studies, and laid the basis for scientific linguistics. They analyzed indigenous literary forms. A chapter on Tagalog poetry in Augustinian Gaspar de San Agustin's *Compendio del arte de la lengua tagala* (1703) was praised by Epifanio de los Santos as "the first work that dealt with Tagalog poetry and its metrics."[4]

European missionaries did groundbreaking work in geography, medicine, and the natural sciences. Moved by the urge to organize, classify, and thus render the unfamiliar familiar, they mapped territories, studied plants and animals, inventoried products, and classified persons and "tribes." They needed to know the people they sought to convert and wrote about their origins, racial characteristics, social organization, religion, and customs. In the absence of indigenous written records, the early accounts of Juan de Plasencia, Pedro Chirino, and Francisco Colin preserved valuable ethnological data that Filipinos themselves would later use. It is remarkable for instance how Plasencia's *Costumbres de los Tagalos* (1589)—a work that Pardo and Paterno were the first to publish—became the primary source (rather than oral tradition itself) for such themes in early nationalist writings as the barangay and precolonial social system.

Missionaries introduced a new historiographic mode by rendering written and printed reports on their mission territories and the labor of their orders.[5] The most notable examples are the Augustinian Gaspar de San Agustin's *Conquistas de las Islas Filipinas* (1698) and Joaquin Martinez de Zuniga's *Historia de las Islas Philipinas* (1803), Franciscan Marcelo Rivadeneira's *Historia de las Islas Filipinas, Japon, China, Tartaria, Cochinchina, Malaca, Siam y Camboja* (1601) and Juan Francisco de San Antonio's three-volume *Cronica de la apostolica provincia de San Gregorio* (1738–1744); Jesuit Pedro Chirino's *Relacion de las Islas Filipinas* (1604) and Francisco Colin's *Labor evangelica* (1660); the Dominican Diego Aduarte's *Historia de la provincia del Sancto Rosario de la Orden de Predicadores* (1640); and Recollect Juan de la Concepcion's fourteen-volume *Historia general de Philipinas* (1788–1792). Missionary histories took various forms (*memorias, informes, cartas*) and often covered other parts of Asia since the Philippines was base for Christian evangelization in the region.

An archetype of the missionary-scholar was the Augustinian Manuel Blanco (1779–1845), who produced local histories, maps, a manual on the use of weaving looms, and published samples of Tagalog *dalit* poetry. Teaching himself botany with Linnaeus's *Systema vegetabilium* (1774) and Antoine de Jussieu's *Genera plantarum* (1789), he published the monumental *Flora de Filipinas; segun el sistema sexual de Linneo* (1837). Botany also attracted the German Jesuit Georg Josef Kamel (1661–1706) who worked on medicinal herbs, established the first apothecary in Manila, opened a botanical garden, wrote scientific reports, and corresponded with English and Dutch physicians in India and the Netherlands Indies. The Jesuits' crowning achievement in Philippine science was *Observatorio de Manila* (1865), which won international renown for meteorological studies at a time when meteorology was just emerging as a science in Europe. It published the monthly *Boletin del Observatorio de Manila*, carried out astronomical, seismological, and magnetic investigations, and communicated with scientific institutions in Europe and America.[6]

Missionaries worked out of prior European knowledge. As agents of a grand civilizing project, they were less interested in understanding a strange, new people in their own terms as in marking the "lack" or "absence" they would fill. In recording the people's history and traditions, they worked within received intellectual frames of Biblical history and Europe's speculative sciences on race and religion. They explained grammatical features of local languages in terms of Latin structures and categories and evaluated native poetry in the grid of Spanish and Latin phonetics and metrics. As a result, written grammars differed considerably from actual native speech. Disquisitions on indigenous poetics imperfectly preserved the dynamics of local practice.

Their writings were not completely homogeneous. There were differences in assessments of local culture and colonial policies according to the time and circumstances of writing. A religious, institutional perspective, however, dominated missionary scholarship. The Spaniard Juan Alvarez Guerra summed up the ubiquity of the Church in the spread of new knowledge when he said in 1872: "The convent in the Philippines does not only synthesize the arts and sciences but also the laboratory, the infirmary, and the model country house."[7]

The late rise of civil government and modern commerce delayed the formation of secular-scientific discourse outside the religious communities. Before 1887, the only lay historian of note was Antonio de Morga (1559–1636), a High Court judge whose *Sucesos de las Islas Filipinas* (1609) Rizal annotated and reprinted in 1890. Before and after Morga, non-missionary texts were produced in the form of exploration narratives, military and economic reports, and civic chronicles. Many of these did not become available until the nineteenth century. Among the earliest to be published were Tomas de Comyn's *Estado de las Islas Filipinas* (1820), Sinibaldo de Mas's two-volume *Informe sobre el estado de las Islas Filipinas en 1842* (1843), and Jose Montero's three-volume *Historia general de Filipinas* (1887–1895).

The European Enlightenment primed the production of scientific knowledge. Bourbon reforms inspired the first Spanish botanical expedition to the Philippines in 1786–1801. Under Juan Cuellar, the expedition collected botanical and zoological specimens for Spain's scientific institutions and tried to establish the teaching of chemical botany to some students in Manila.[8] In 1792 came the expedition led by Italian-born Spanish navigator Alejandro Malaspina, the most thoroughly equipped scientific expedition at the time, which conducted botanical, zoological, meteorological, and hydrographic studies. It produced the first modern nautical chart of the Philippines published in Madrid in 1808.

Western interest in science brought to the Philippines such visits as those of the French naturalist Pierre Sonnerat (1771–1772), the Romanzoff-von Chamisso expedition (1817–1818), the British Hugh Cuming expedition (1831, 1840), and Charles Wilkes's U.S. Exploring Expedition (1842).[9] Working out of their interest in the Netherlands Indies, Dutch scholars, like the linguist Hendrik Kern, studied the Philippines. Among non-Spanish Europeans, the most notable were the Germans. They came to collect specimens and write about the country, like Carl Semper, Fedor Jagor, and Adolf Meyer. Others took up residence in the country, like the pharmacist Alexander Schadenberg who devoted himself to such scholarly labors as collecting zoological specimens and compiling Negrito vocabularies. Others were never in the Philippines but wrote about it, like the eminent Rudolf Virchow and Ferdinand Blumentritt, the Austrian schoolmaster who was not only the most prolific non-Spanish European author on the Philippines but was deeply involved in the Philippine anti-colonial movement.

Imperial knowledge-building was driven by motives of reconnaissance, conversion, and conquest. There were immediate, pragmatic ends served by identifying and classifying populations, studying languages, and investigating local resources. Scientific expeditions enhanced the collections of European and American museums and botanical gardens, augmented the West's knowledge of the world, and built up the prestige of sponsoring nations. Undergirding the practical necessities of establishing ecclesiastical or military control were ideological reasons: enforcing a European conception of order on a primitive "anarchy" of facts, converting natives to a "superior" way of life (and death), marking the differences of biology and culture that authorize racial and political hierarchies.

It must be stressed that while natives felt the practical results of the textualized knowledge Europeans produced, they did not themselves have access to the texts. Well into the nineteenth century, practically the only type of printed literature circulated among natives were religious pastoral works in the vernaculars (prayerbooks, catechisms, saints' lives). The Bible was not circulated. What passed for it was the *pasyon*, the "Filipino Bible," a versified vernacular account of the life of Christ that was more often chanted than read. Until 1800, popular publishing on secular topics was limited to a few manuals on literacy, numeracy, and health.

Written in foreign languages, European texts were either unpublished documents or books printed abroad or circulated in a very limited way. The problem was not just one of access. Natives were the object rather than subject of this kind of knowledge. European scholarship was knowledge produced *for* Europe.

UNTIL THE END of the eighteenth century, Spanish rule was discontinuous and uneven. Comparing the Philippines to a more intensely colonized Spanish America, John Leddy Phelan argued that for a host of reasons—geographical particularism, distance from the imperial center, lack of Spanish personnel—the archipelago's inhabitants "survived the 'shock' of the conquest with far less psychological and material damage to themselves than did many native races of the Americas." He believed that the cultural changes wrought by colonialism were of "a more orderly, a more selective, and a less demoralizing character."[10] Even as this may be so (at least when considering the archipelago as a whole), it must also be pointed out that there was no countervailing force approaching the Inca or Aztec kingdoms in America or the more developed polities elsewhere in Southeast Asia.

When the Spaniards came the most developed polities were Islamized communities in Mindanao and parts of Luzon. In Mindanao, Spanish encroachments met with considerable resistance, as illustrated in the career of Sultan Kudarat (c1580–1671), who rallied the Maguindanao, Maranao, and other inhabitants to preserve "the most extensive indigenous political dominion in the history of the Filipinos."[11] Muslim resistance, however, was largely defensive and there was no concerted effort to establish Muslim political hegemony in the wider archipelago.

In Manila in the 1580s, where the Spaniards had begun to rule, the chiefs of Tondo and surrounding villages, smarting over their loss of power and Spanish exactions, hatched an ambitious conspiracy to drive out the Spaniards that would involve chiefs in Pampanga, Bulacan, Batangas, and Laguna. Indicating the extensive networks of maritime chiefs at the time, the conspirators sought Japanese assistance, anticipated an imminent British attack on Manila after hearing of the capture of a Spanish galleon by the English privateer Thomas Cavendish in 1588, and sent an envoy to the Sultan of Borneo to seek an alliance against the Spaniards. While the networks were wide, they were fragile. The Tondo chiefs had problems building local alliances; the conspiracy was discovered and brutally suppressed; and its leaders were hanged or exiled.[12]

In the main, resistance was localized and where it was more sustained and organized, as in the Muslim sultanates, it was contained and kept at the margins of the colonial state-in-the-making. The native response to colonialism involved not only active resistance but ranged from acts of avoidance and selective engagement to collaboration and alliance-building. Spanish colonialism was not the product of unilateral action by Iberian *conquistadores* and *frailes* but alliances with local chiefs who provided the resources, manpower, local knowledge and leadership that made possible the extension of Spanish power. Chiefs were coopted with titles, positions, and privileges, but, more important, were actively engaged in calculations of risk and benefit in the face of a new power.

The inchoate character of precolonial polities is to be seen in indigenous culture. Compared to Spanish America or other parts of Southeast Asia, traditions of scriptural, architectural, or iconographic representation were not richly articulated. While a precolonial writing system existed, this was neither deep in use nor widely diffused. Jesuit chronicler Pedro Chirino wrote in 1604: "For none of these three things, religion, idolatry, and superstition, nor for matters appertaining to government and polity do they make use of their written characters; for they have never made any use of these latter save only for writing letters to each other. The whole of their government and religion is based on oral tradition." Sinibaldo de Mas wrote that "no books nor any kind of literature in this character (alphabets) may be met with, except for a few amatory verses written in a highly hyperbolic style, and hardly intelligible."[13]

It became a commonplace in early nationalist polemics to blame Spanish missionaries for destroying precolonial writings but while there were recorded instances of such destruction it was not widespread. The writing craft was incipient at Spanish contact. Its relative newness and material constraints (bamboo, stones, palm leaves) were such that writing was limited to recording verse fragments and short messages rather than epics or chronicles. More important, local communities did not have the scale or level of articulation of indigenous states elsewhere with their need for the legitimating uses of writing, such as the production of royal chronicles and legal treatises. In brief, sufficient conditions did not exist for the expanded use of writing.

With Islam, Arabic was introduced by the fifteenth century. This cultural infusion may have generated new literary forms, such as genealogies (*tarsila*), legal codes (*luwaran*), and religious orations (*hutbah*). Bishop Domingo de Salazar reported in 1588 that he had been informed that Muslim preachers in Mindanao "have erected and are now building mosques" and that "there is a school where [boys] are taught the *Alcoran*."[14] There was no organized effort however to establish mosques or religious schools (*madrasas*) outside Muslim communities. A substantial written literature in Arabic or the local languages did not develop. As historian Samuel Tan remarks, "no indigenous Muslim written materials earlier than the late 18th century exist to account for early origins before colonial contact."[15]

A wealth of indigenous knowledge existed, as Jose Rizal and his contemporaries set out to prove. The proof however—the kinds of proof Western discourse privileged—was not readily evident. Indigenous traditions of knowledge were most vital in oral, ritual, and localized forms. While translocal affinities were such that larger cultural complexes were developing at Spanish contact, this dynamic of expansion and elaboration was stalled, scattered, or suppressed. Precolonial society had "persons of knowledge," bards, seers, and ritual specialists. Viewed by the Spaniards as bearers of "superstitions" and agents of resistance, they were persecuted or coopted. Local cultural forms, like epic narratives, were pushed to the margins of colonial society. While these forms constituted an ideological resource for numerous revolts during the colonial period, they would not enter into the discourse of "nationhood" until late in the nineteenth century.

390

The "loss" of tradition—a familiar lament among nineteenth-century nationalists—is poignantly illustrated by a few examples. It was not until the close of the nineteenth century that the first fragments of folk epics were recorded. The first to be published, the Iloko *Lam-ang*, was written down (and obviously edited) by a Spanish Augustinian, Gerardo Blanco, and given to Isabelo de los Reyes who published the 947-line Iloko text in *El Ilocano* (1889) and *Folk-Lore Filipino* (1890). The Bikol *Ibalong* was jotted down by Franciscan Bernardino de Melendreras (1815–1867) from the performance of a local minstrel. Melendreras translated it into Spanish and a 240-line fragment of this translation appeared in Wenceslao Retana's *Archivo del Bibliofilo Filipino* in 1895.[16]

In attempting to reconstruct the genealogy of Manila's ancient rulers, Isabelo de los Reyes did not have much to go by except some nineteenth-century Spanish-colonial wills and testaments. In reaching back into the precolonial past, T.H. Pardo de Tavera turned to Malay chronicles from neighboring countries, accessing them by way of Europe. Similarly, Rizal studied the Philippines in libraries in Europe. Discovering the Ambrosian codex of Pigafetta in the British Museum in 1888—more than three centuries after Pigafetta wrote his account— Rizal read it in Italian, copied it, and excitedly wrote to a friend saying that one of the Filipinos should learn Italian and translate the manuscript to Tagalog or Spanish "so that it may be known how we were in 1520."[17]

IN 1555, King Charles I issued an edict on education in the empire: "To serve God, our Lord, and for the general welfare of our vassals, subjects and natives, there should be established in our realm universities and general studies where they may be educated and graduated in all the sciences and faculties."[18] The ambition behind the edict was not matched by realities on the ground. Earlier than in most of Asia, the country saw the introduction of institutions of modern, European learning but, for political and practical reasons, natives could not fully participate in these institutions.

European-style mission schools appeared in the sixteenth century. These developed slowly and unevenly and were almost exclusively devoted to teaching Christian doctrine and the most rudimentary learning skills. In 1595, the first secondary school, the Jesuit Colegio de Manila (later renamed San Ignacio) was established. Tertiary education started in the seventeenth century when the first baccalaureate and doctorate degrees in arts, philosophy and theology were granted by Colegio de Manila and Colegio de Santo Tomas. Higher education was "only for Spaniards" as was the case at the time in Latin America, the model for colonial and missionary policies in the Philippines. The *colegios* of San Jose (1601), Santo Tomas (1611), and San Juan de Letran (1620) admitted an inconsequential trickle of Chinese-mestizo and *indio* students by the end of the seventeenth century. Santo Tomas—which became a "royal and pontifical university" in 1645—graduated a few "Filipinos" (possibly Chinese mestizos) at the close of the eighteenth century but Filipinos attended the university in significant numbers only in the nineteenth.

In brief, higher education was not available to Filipinos (indigenes and Chinese mestizos) on equal terms with the Spaniards for more than 200 years of Spanish rule. Academic programs were focused on the training of priests and the ecclesiastical sciences of philosophy, theology, and canon law. Admission was racially restricted and biased in favor of those who could pay tuition. Women were even more disadvantaged. The first schools for girls, the *colegios* of Santa Potenciana (1594) and Santa Isabel (1632), were meant for those of Spanish descent and prepared them for motherhood or a religious life, with little academic instruction. Though teacher-training schools for women appeared after 1871, higher education was effectively denied women until the twentieth century. Santo Tomas did not admit women students until 1924. It is a remarkable fact nevertheless that in Santo Tomas the Philippines had what was Asia's first and oldest European-style university.

Printing came in the sixteenth century with the xylographic production in Manila of *Doctrina Cristiana* in 1593. Between 1593 and 1800, a total of 541 books was published.[19] Until the end of the eighteenth century, however, printing was a monastic monopoly, devoted almost exclusively to producing pastoral and language texts, mostly intended as an aid for the religious. It was not until the nineteenth century that a "print culture" emerged with the circulation of more and new kinds of books, the emergence of lay authors, and the widening of readership. There were no public libraries before 1887. Various civil and ecclesiastical decrees and instructions restricted the publication and circulation of printed matter in the islands. Censorship was in force except for a few years during the period 1813–1824.[20]

To visitors from Europe, the country seemed caught in a medieval warp. Writing from the Philippines to a friend in France in 1766, the French scientist Guillaume Le Gentil remarked: "I am writing you, sir, from the other side of the world, and I might even add, <u>from the fourteenth century</u>." Of the state of education in the colony he wrote: "All the ancient prejudices of the schools would appear to have been abandoned in Europe only to take refuge in Manila, where they will probably survive for a long time . . . Spain is a hundred years behind France in science, and Manila is a hundred years behind Spain."[21]

Seeing the country in terms of a European chronology as a place stranded in space and time will be expressed time and again. With its "discovery" by Europe, the country comes into the ken of Western eyes, constructed in Eurocentric relations of distance, difference, and subordination. Looking for signs of "modernity" in the colony, visitors found little. Before 1870 (when the first steamer arrived from Barcelona via the Suez), news from Europe took all of four months to arrive in the Philippines. Fedor Jagor observed in the 1850s: "The traffic with Spain was limited to the conveyance of officials, priests, and their usual necessaries, such as provisions, wine and other liquors; and, except a few French novels, some atrociously dull books, histories of saints, and other works."

> Manila offers very few opportunities for amusement. There was no Spanish theatre open during my stay there, but Tagalog plays (translations) were sometimes presented. The town possessed no clubs, and contained no readable books. Never once did the least excitement enliven its feeble newspapers, for the items of intelligence, forwarded fortnightly from Hong Kong, were sifted by priestly censors, who left little but the chronicles of the Spanish and French courts to feed the barren columns of the local sheets. The pompously celebrated religious festivals were the only events that sometimes chequered the wearisome monotony.[22]

Englishman Robert MacMicking made a similar observation of the reading habits of Manilans in 1850. "Books are scarce and expensive," he said, "and are in little demand by most of the residents." Austrian visitor Karl von Scherzer complained in 1858 that there was only one newspaper at the time of his arrival and Manila's two printing houses produced almost nothing but religious works. In the same year, English official John Bowring said: "Literature is little cultivated: the public newspapers are more occupied with the lives of saints, and preparation for, or accounts of, religious fiestas, than with the most stirring events of the political world." Of the state of education, he remarked: "Public instruction is in an unsatisfactory state in the Philippines—the provisions are little changed from those of the monkish ages."[23]

These observations refer largely to Manila and its citizens. One imagines that the "lag" must have been greater in the countryside where, often, the only contact natives had with Europe was limited to the *cura*, who was not always the finest specimen of this world. Unlike the case of Latin America, the natives' direct contact with Spanish culture, outside religion, was limited. Spaniards constituted less than one percent of the population at any time during Spanish rule.[24] Less than two percent of the population could speak Spanish that was not pidgin.

That the country remained relatively isolated, imperfectly penetrated by Europe, meant that well into the colonial period much of local life unfolded according to its own imaginaries and historicities. To speak of "country" and "society" is misleading since what obtained at the time was something much less than unitary but more like a conglomeration of zones of indeterminate, shifting boundaries defined by the degree of local autonomy or, conversely, control by the colonial state in its incestuously mixed ecclesiastical and civil forms. Until the nineteenth century, life in many parts of the country—with its own forms of knowledge, its production and transmission—unfolded apart from, parallel to, or lightly touched by the new regime of truth into which the Spaniards sought to incorporate natives.

Though a world of difference existed between Spain's civilizing ambitions and realities on the ground, significant cultural interaction did take place. How quickly and diversely natives engaged the new power is shown in the remarkable story of the Banals. One of the leaders of the Tondo Conspiracy of the 1580s was Juan Banal, apparently a son-in-law of Lakandula, the "king" of Tondo. After the conspiracy was suppressed he was sentenced to exile in Mexico for six years and disappeared from the records. Fourteen years later, Miguel Banal, who may have been Juan's son, had already been incorporated into the Spanish colonial order as *gobernadorcillo* of Quiapo. He would speak to power differently. Seeking redress for having been forcibly dispossessed of his family's lands by the Jesuits, he sent petitions addressed directly to the Spanish King on July 2, 1603, and July 25, 1609. In his letter of July 25, 1609, he lamented that nothing had been done about his complaint and that instead a Jesuit brother came with armed "negroes and Indians" and burned his house and threatened him. Addressing the King, he asked for protection "since we are Indians, who cannot defend ourselves by suits, as we are a poor people, and it would be a matter with a religious order." Describing the assault on his property, he said that "after seeing his [the Jesuit] intention to seize all my property and bind me, I did not raise my eyes to behold him angered, because of the respect that I know is due the ministers who teach us the law of God." He went on to say: "I have been unable to find anyone who dared write this letter for me. The letter is therefore written by my own hand and in my own composition, and in the style of an Indian not well versed in the Spanish language." After the standard courtesies, he closes with: "The useless slave of your royal Majesty, Don Miguel Banal."[25] Whether or not Banal in fact composed the letter, it is clear that natives learned to negotiate in the language of colonial power very early.

There is a postscript to this story. In just a few decades, another Banal, Marcelo (1632–1697), would join the Augustinian Order as a lay brother. (Earlier, Lakandula's own son, Martin, also became an Augustinian brother but died in 1590 before he could profess the monastic vows.) Ostensibly Miguel Banal's grandson, Marcelo was adopted by the Augustinians to be trained in their convent, not only because of the boy's musical talent but out of appreciation for the fact that the Augustinian church complex in Manila stood in what used to be land owned by the Banals. Having spent years with the Augustinians, Marcelo pronounced the perpetual vows of poverty, chastity and obedience as a lay brother (*hermano lego*), the first native to do so, on September 5, 1652. He took the name Brother Marcelo de San Augustin in honor of the founder of the Order.[26]

AS REPRESENTATIVES of a new regime of knowledge and power, Spaniards set the ground in which a native "intelligentsia" began to emerge. It was the practice of missionaries to recruit talented young men, usually from the local elite (later called *principalia*), as informants, translators, copyists, catechists, *cantores* (singers), *fiscales* (parish secretaries), and *sacristanes* (acolytes). A Recollect chronicler wrote in 1756 of this class of natives:

> The holy orders of Philipinas are wont to take account of the sons of the chief Indians of the villages under their charge, in order to teach them good morals from childhood, and rear them with those qualities which are considered necessary to enable them to govern their respective villages afterward with success, since the administration of justice is always put in charge of such Indians. They live in the convents from childhood in charge of the gravest fathers. The latter are called masters, although in strictness they are tutors or teachers . . .[27]

Documentation on these early encounters is sparse. It is clear, however, that we do not only have a case of young, compliant natives conscripted as mission assistants but natives actively engaging Spaniards to protect old prerogatives or appropriate new sources of power. Members of the indigenous elite parlayed their status and wealth to gain preferments in colonial church and government. They became *donados* and *beatas* (auxiliaries of the religious orders) and, later, priests, local officials (*cabezas*, *gobernadorcillos*), soldiers and lower-rank officers, and the first university students. When the occasion or need arose, they were also leaders of local protest actions and revolts. How natives manipulated colonial relations was a subject of continuing anxiety among Spanish authorities who complained about the various stratagems natives employed to influence local elections, sabotage government projects, or take control of church affairs. *Principales* parlayed "local knowledge" and control of manpower and resources to bolster their position vis-à-vis the Spanish priest. They proved quite skillful in exploiting to their advantage the instruments of the colonial regime. The Jesuit Pedro Murillo Velarde ruefully observed in 1749:

> In almost all the towns there are usually certain individuals who have clerked for the Spaniards in Manila, and there familiarized themselves with pleadings and actions at law. They have no diffi-

culty in persuading the natives to make a thousand false affidavits, for their intimate association with the Spaniards has given them a great fondness for stamped paper. And if the father tries to restrict their activities, a meeting is organized on the instant, and a petition drawn up against the priest is fairly covered with signatures and crosses. . . .

Natives who wish to file a suit against the priest go to one of these quondam clerks, who carefully keeps a number of old dossiers, complaints, and bills of particulars for just such a purpose. The higher the fee, the more outrageous the accusations, which he prepares in much the same way as a purgative, the dosage being increased in the measure that a more complete evacuation is desired. Signatures are affixed to the petition by people who have no idea of what it contains; instead of its being read to them, a convivial glass of wine is drunk instead. The document, covered with flourishes and crosses, is now brought to the appropriate official, to wit, the official who has the least love for the priest; for they are most expert in this. No navigator can tell how the wind blows better than these natives can predict where their petition will be received with approval. And if the official to whom it is presented happens to be of some importance, a great deal of suffering lies in store for the innocent father until the truth is finally revealed.[28]

The first known native intellectuals appeared "in the light" of Western learning—and, one might add, the grace of European record-keeping. The story of the Talangpaz sisters of Pampanga—Dionisia (1691–1732) and Rosa (1693–1731)—as pieced together by Luciano Santiago, is richly suggestive of native agency in local encounters with the new religion.[29] *Beaterio de San Sebastian de Calumpang*, the beguinage founded by the Talangpaz sisters in 1725, had a troubled existence. The first such community founded by *indias*, its story is conventionally read as proof of the transcendental power of the new faith. Yet it can be read as well as the story of native initiative in accessing new sources of power. The authorities' anxieties over the control of such groups as the community of the Talangpaz sisters, their fear of contaminations of culture and race, point to realities of syncretic practice of the new faith. (Consider, for instance, the stricture against the Talangpaz beatas speaking in Tagalog "within the walls" of their community house.) Unfortunately, we do not have much information on this case than what is allowed by the Spanish records.

The more celebrated cases are those of Tomas Pinpin and Pedro Bukaneg. Born in Abucay, Bataan, "between 1580 and 1585," *plebeyo de origen*, Pinpin worked in the Dominican printshop ran by the missionary-linguist Francisco Blancas de San Jose. (The printshop was located in Binondo in 1602 and moved to Abucay in 1608 when Blancas de San Jose was assigned as *cura* of the town.) Pinpin's skills won him fame as a printer, credited with such products as Blancas de San Jose's *Arte y reglas de la lengua tagala* (1610), the first published Tagalog grammar; Francisco Lopez's *Arte de la lengua iloca* (1627), the first Iloko grammar; and *Succesos Felices* (1637), a report on the Spanish campaign in Mindanao and Ternate in 1636–1637 that, some claim, is "the first Philippine newspaper." Pinpin was not just a printer but an avid student of languages. He wrote *Librong pagaaralan nang mga Tagalog nang uicang Castilla* ("A Book in Which Tagalogs May Study the Spanish Language") (1610), the first book to be authored by a native.[30]

Bukaneg was a ward in the Augustinian priory in Bantay, Ilocos, where he studied Spanish, taught the friars Iloko, and helped the Augustinian Francisco Lopez in producing *Libro a naisuratan ami a bagas ti Doctrina Cristiana* (1621), the first book to be printed in Iloko, and *Arte de la lengua iloca* (1627). A tradition has built around him even though little documentary evidence exists on his life. It is told that he was an Isneg baby found "early one morning in March 1592" in a basket drifting in the river separating Vigan and Bantay and then taken to an Augustinian priest who baptized him Pedro Bukaneg, from *buka* + *neg*, or "Christianized Isneg." He was born blind and ugly ("like Socrates"), facts that may have been interpreted (like the Moses-story of his origins) as part of his numinous qualities. In any case, he won renown as a lexicographer "who mastered Latin, Spanish, Iloko, and Isneg," skills that reportedly won the "admiration of the court of Philip II of Spain [who was in fact long dead when Bukaneg reached adulthood] and the Holy Father of Rome." A gifted musician and preacher, he was also reputed to be a seer who once identified a murderer by just placing his hand on the man's chest.[31]

Pinpin and Bukaneg represent the first generation of *ladinos* (the Spanish term for natives literate in Spanish and a local language), who were among the first natives to appear in the European record. These included lay catechists (like the Visayans Miguel de Ayatumo [1593–1809] and Pedro Calungsod [c1654–1672] and Tagalog Lorenzo Ruiz [c1605–1637]), tertiaries of the religious orders (like the Pampangan Felipe Sonson [1611–1686] and Tagalogs Marcelo Banal and Ignacia del Espiritu Santo [1663–1748]), as well as the printers, engravers, and artists (Diego Talaghay, Domingo Loag, Francisco Suarez, Nicolas de la Cruz Bagay) who helped missionaries in running printshops, producing maps, and executing the new art forms the church needed (like statuary, paintings, and church decorations).[32]

Ladino is commonly used with reference to authors, like the Tagalogs Fernando Bagongbanta, who wrote an adulatory verse preface to Blancas de San Jose's *Memorial de la vida cristiana en lengua tagala* (1605); Pedro Suarez Ossorio, whose poetry appeared in Alonso de Santa Ana's *Explicacion de la doctrina Christiana en lengua tagala* (1628); and Felipe de Jesus, who contributed a complimentary poem to Antonio de Borja's *Barlaan at Josaphat* (1712).[33] Little is known about these early cultural intermediaries, the country's first visible writers. Usually recruited from the native elite, they were the kind of men and women who in another time might have been the bards and priestesses of a different tradition.

From extant reports, an impression of dynamic foreign-native interaction, of much assimilation and hybridization, can be drawn. Bukaneg's case is suggestive. Straddling two traditions, he aided friars in producing Christian texts and preached (it is said) the Spaniards' religion, yet was also steeped in indigenous lore. It is claimed that he composed the Iloko epic *Lam-ang* by renovating an old Isneg narrative in the style of a Euro-Christian romance, substituting Christian elements for the pagan in the narrative.[34] Unfortunately, we cannot examine Bukaneg's oral performance or the written text into which it was purportedly rendered. While Bukaneg's example may be hypothetical, the metamorphosis of indigenous material into Christian forms was central to the drama of religious and social conversion. Spanish missionaries did not only introduce new verbal forms but used indigenous literature as vehicle for new messages. It is said of Francisco Blancas de San Jose, Pinpin's patron, that he "composed many songs in their (the natives') language after their own manner of verse, but on sacred themes."[35] This was a two-way process since natives themselves, as in the case of Pinpin and Bukaneg, did their own translation of European matter whether under or outside the friars' supervision.

Vicente Rafael has given us a finely detailed view of this process in his analysis of Pinpin's *Libro*, documenting the strategies of evasion, containment, and appropriation in the act of translating language and domesticating the strangeness and danger of what it intends.[36] Rafael shows the unexpected possibilities for assertions of autonomy in the local translation of alien thought systems, whether encoded in grammar, arithmetic, or religion. Where Pinpin enters into a foreign medium—the printed book, the language manual—and contaminates it with other meanings, Bukaneg (our imagined composer of *Lam-ang*) assimilates the foreign into an indigenous form, the chanted epic narrative.

In either case, we have historical moments in a long, drawn-out engagement in which cultural forms do not remain fixed and relations of power unchanged. In 1911, T.H. Pardo de Tavera did not only call Pinpin "the first philologist, the first humanist, the first author and the first Filipino printer," he conscripted him as a figure in a Spencerian narrative of modernization.[37] Taking Pinpin as prototype of the printers and engravers who appeared with the emergence of typography in the seventeenth century, Pardo calls Pinpin the exemplar of the "industrial type," a new class of persons in Philippine history. Pinpin was "the *first* to have an occupation and a social situation by virtue solely of his *capacity*." With productive, specialist skills, he cooperates voluntarily in social life and exemplifies "*liberty in the free man.*" Concerned with a theory of "social types," Pardo overstates the historical break as well as the autonomy of seventeenth-century artisans. He is one of the first, however, to mark the deep epistemological changes generated by Spanish colonialism.

Cultural intermediaries like Pinpin occupied an ambivalent position in society since it was not always clear how and in what directions their loyalties were shaped. Persons with access to two worlds, as signified by bilingualism, they were viewed either (or both) as persons to be emulated or persons not to be trusted. This ambivalence is preserved in the history of the word *ladino*. Originating in Spain (from *latino*) where it referred to Old Castilian and Romance languages and, later, to a bilingual or polyglot, the word traveled to Spanish America where it named the *indio* or *negro* who could speak Spanish and, more broadly, had become versed in Spanish ways. In the Philippines as in Spanish America, the word also preserved its Iberian connotation of someone who was crafty and cunning. The *ladino* (*larino*) is not the indigenous sage (*paham*, *pantas*). What defines him is not so much wisdom or knowledge (*alam*, *dunong*) as fluency of speech, often in a new language. It is a skill at once attractive and dissembling, admired and mistrusted. This double signification would recur as a theme in the history of intellectuals in the Philippines.

IF SOMETHING of the shock of the colonial encounter is exemplified in the hybridities of Pinpin and Bukaneg, a further turn is taken by Gaspar Aquino de Belen, a native of Rosario, Batangas, who ran the Jesuit printshop in Manila (1703–1716). He has been hailed as "the first great Tagalog poet" for his *Mahal na Passion ni Jesu Christong P. natin na tola* ("The Sacred Passion of Jesus Christ Our Lord in Verse") (1704), an original work in the venerable Spanish tradition of verse accounts of Christ's Redemption.[38] Many vernacular versions of the *pasyon* exist but de Belen's 984-stanza text, the first printed narrative poem by a native author, was one of the most influential. It is remarkable for the sureness with which it indigenizes a foreign form in the folk rhythms of its verse and the manner in which it infuses a local sensibility to its depiction of scene and character. This indicates a sense of confidence and ease with which a native inhabits a foreign form and, as it were, speaks out of it. Contrasted to Pinpin's work a century earlier, the text conveys an earnestness of voice and faith that demonstrates the advance of Christian conversion in Tagalog society.

Despite de Belen's seeming Christian orthodoxy, Spanish missionaries were wary about local renderings of Christian texts like the *pasyon*. After de Belen, there was a turn—the critics Bienvenido Lumbera and Nicanor Tiongson point out—from "indigenization" to "standardization" as clerical authors "cleaned up" the popular pasyon of "errors" in style and doctrinal content. This is illustrated in the anonymous *Casaysayan nang Pasiong Mahal ni Jesucristong panginoon natin* ("Account of the Sacred Passion of Jesus Christ Our Lord") (1814), known as *Pasyong Pilapil* (because it was falsely attributed to Mariano Pilapil, a learned Filipino secular priest), and *El libro de la vida* (1852) by Aniceto de la Merced, a Filipino priest from Bulacan. Both versions are attempts at "codifying" the *pasyon* as a response to the rampant, popular reinterpretations of the form in the oral tradition. In de la Merced's dry and erudite version, in particular, a turn was made (Lumbera argues) towards "urbanity" and "correctness" in a time of increasing Christianization and urbanization.

Pilapil and de la Merced signify the emergence of a new class of intellectuals, the native clergy. The priesthood was the first avenue to higher education and social status in the colonial system for Filipinos. For practical, institutional, and ideological reasons, the avenue was exceedingly narrow. In the eighteenth century, however, the first Filipino seminary, Seminario de San Clemente (1705), was opened and the first indigenes and mestizos broke through the *limpieza de sangre* barrier to obtain a university education. As educational opportunities opened up, a fair number of *indio* secular priests was produced by 1762 (fifty to sixty in the archdiocese of Manila). Luciano Santiago has listed twelve "Filipinos" (indios and mestizos) who earned doctorates in the ecclesiastical sciences (sacred theology, philosophy, canon law) between 1772 and 1796.[39]

There is a remarkable continuity between the precolonial elite and the early native clergy, as shown in the case of "the first *indio* priest," Francisco Baluyot, who was ordained in 1698. The Baluyots were an old and prominent Kapampangan family involved in a revolt in Pampanga in 1660 that was sparked by oppressive Spanish economic exactions. The revolt spread to neighboring provinces and was suppressed after its leaders, including a Baluyot, were hanged. It is ironic but not completely surprising that in the decades that followed several Baluyots would join the priesthood.[40] When they were not involved in local uprisings, the local elite took the initiative in accessing the privileges of the clerical estate, thus aiding the rise of the native clergy. This was done particularly through the practice of the *capellania* (chaplaincy), a private pious grant to the church, usually in the form of tilled or residential land, the income of which was applied for the support of a priest or *capellan* (chaplain). The donor usually determined the choice of chaplain and may reserve the post for blood relatives (in which case it is called *capellania de sangre*). Meant as an act of piety, the *capellania* was also a medium for "capitalizing" family members in the priesthood.[41]

The careers of native priests illustrate, on one hand, the impressive abilities of natives in learning the new culture and, on the other, the consciousness of colonial subalternity that would seed nationalism in the nineteenth century. Illustrating the former is Bartolome Saguinsin (c1694–1772), said to be of prehispanic Tagalog nobility, who was educated in the Jesuit college of San Jose, ordained priest in 1717, and rose by virtue of his merits to become synodal examiner in moral theology and parish priest of the prestigious district of Quiapo in Manila. Fluent in Tagalog, Spanish, and Latin, he was part of the "Congregation of Tagalista Priests" created by the Manila archbishop in 1748 to select and edit the best Tagalog translation of the *Doctrina Cristiana* among many versions already in print or manuscript form. Saguinsin's only surviving book—which makes him, according to Luciano Santiago, "the first Indio priest-poet and writer"—is *Ilustrissimo doctori d.d. Simoni Anda et Salazar olim in Manilensi curia senatori dignissimo causarum criminalium auditori aequissimo in laboriosissimo tempore belli a britannis* (Sampaloc, 1766), a collection of twelve Latin epigrams that honor the gallantry of governor Simon de Anda during the British Occupation of Manila (1762–1764), an event in which Saguinsin participated as chaplain under Anda.[42] The astonishing fact of an indio publishing a book of Latin odes in the eighteenth century shows the remarkable precocity with which natives assumed the idioms and symbols of the new culture.

European "matter" had seeped into the imaginings not only of native priests but local literati as shown in an interesting episode narrated by the missionary Joaquin Martinez de Zuniga. In 1796, a high Spanish naval official, visiting Lipa, Batangas, was honored in an elaborate welcome ceremony in which a local resident delivered a Tagalog verse eulogy (*loa*) replete with references to the voyages of Ulysses, the travels of Aristotle, and other incidents in ancient history, garnished with such flights of poetic license as Aristotle drowning himself in chagrin at not being able to measure the depths of the sea and Pliny throwing himself into the mouth of Vesuvius in his zeal to investigate the cause of its eruption.[43]

Disciplined by their vows, the native clergy occupied a subordinate role in the church. It is said that they began to assume a race-based group identity as early as 1771–1777 when they were caught up in conflicts between church and state and the archbishop and religious orders over issues of visitation, royal patronage, and restrictions on the powers of the religious orders.[44] We know little, however, about what the first native priests thought, wrote, or said.

The rise of the Filipino priest as writer came in the mid-nineteenth century with the expansion and improvement in the training of the native clergy. This nineteenth-century clerical intelligentsia included the Tagalog Vicente Garcia, Pampangan Anselmo Jorge de Fajardo, Iloko Justo Claudio, and Hiligaynon Anselmo Avanceña. For the first time (with the rare exception of Pinpin and Saguinsin), Filipinos wrote and published books in their own name. A benchmark work is Modesto de Castro's *Pagsusulatan nang dalauang binibini na si Urbana at si Feliza na nagtuturo ng mabuting caugalian* (1864), the most popular example of the *manual de urbanidad* or book of conduct, a genre popular in the late colonial period. It went through several editions and was translated into other Philippine languages. A manual aimed at regulating social and moral behavior, *Urbana at Feliza* is wholly orthodox in its religious and moral prescriptions but, as the first example of an extended vernacular prose narrative by a local author, it points to the advent of the novel in the Philippines in the decades that followed. De Castro (1819–1864), a native of Laguna and graduate of Colegio de San Jose, was a secular priest with a reputation as an *autor clasico* for his sermons and "precise and elegant" writings.[45]

In sum, the first "modern" native intellectuals emerged in the shadow of the Church. These included catechists, scribes, printers, and artists. They were followed by native clergymen, who began to be prominent by the mid-nineteenth century. They constituted a social formation intimately complicit in the twin project of Christianization and colonization although, as Pinpin and de Belen show, they were not passive transmitters of new knowledge but creative agents in its dissemination. Conditions, however, were such that one could not speak of a "Filipino intelligentsia" prior to the mid-nineteenth century, not only because the Filipino as *national* had not yet evolved but because an "intelligentsia" as a self-aware, secular community of persons did not exist. The early printers, translators, and church poets were few in number and operated as independent artisans and literati, linked individually to friar-patrons instead of horizontally to each other. The contemporaries Pinpin and Bukaneg may have been vaguely aware of each other, if at all. Pinpin's *Libro* is remarkable for its stance—a Tagalog openly addressing "fellow Tagalogs" in print—but it is doubtful whether it was widely circulated since the early books, for such reasons as cost and scarcity of paper, were not meant for popular distribution but reference use by missionaries.

Monastic control of publishing inhibited the formation of a secular literature. There was, however, much creative work outside the orbit of print and the surveillance of authorities. This is indicated in the anxieties frequently voiced by Spanish observers about "mistranslations" of doctrinal works and the "heretical" and "profane" activities engaged in by natives even during Church-related events. The creation of the "Congregation of Tagalista Priests" in 1748 signified that unauthorized redactions of Christian texts, mainly in manuscript form, had proliferated. In 1842, Sinibaldo de Mas observed how young men and women had converted the singing of the Lenten pasyon into "a carnival amusement, or to speak more plainly, into a pretext for the most scandalous vices, and the result of these canticles is that many of the girls of the village become *enceinte*."[46] In 1878, an Augustinian complained about the "bad trends of the times and anti-Christian ideas" carried in hybrid local renderings of European metrical romances and religious tales.[47] Writing in the 1880s of pasyon performances in and around Manila, Vicente Barrantes described all-night sessions in which the chanting of religious verses contended with the irreverent sounds of people gossiping and playing music more evocative of a popular dance than a religious occasion.[48] Such was the "profaning" of the *pasyon* that *curas* went out with a whip to disperse revelers and censors had to act to control the proliferating folk versions of the *pasyon*.

There were realms of culture that could not be effectively monitored or policed because they took private, oral, and ephemeral forms, or took place outside the reach of *iglesia* (church) and *tribunal* (government hall). These did not exist as a separate tradition but were constituents of a dynamic and evolving colonial culture. They determined the more visible, canonical cultural texts (like books) or problematized them by indicating what was silenced or suppressed.

HORACIO DE LA COSTA calls 1760–1860 "the formative century."[49] In the main population centers, the construction of churches and schools, introduction of printshops and other technologies, and changes in ways of life stimulated new forms and styles of thinking about the world. The country's increased integration into empire and the world economy irrevocably changed local society, creating ground in which people had to define themselves in relation to a changed lifeworld and the disturbing presence of the other.

In 1762–1764 the British Occupation of Manila shook the colony's isolation. Although it was short and the British controlled only Manila and Cavite, it opened to foreign trade the port of Manila (which was closed to the world except the Manila-Acapulco galleon and Chinese traders), liberalized commerce, and dented Spanish power in the eyes of the inhabitants. While part of the population remained loyal to Spain, certain sectors (like the Manila Chinese and the Sultanate of Sulu) supported the British and sections of the country descended into lawlessness or rose in revolt (as in the insurrection led by Diego Silang in the Ilocos).

In the decades that followed the Philippines was transformed by a changing world economy and what was a politically turbulent nineteenth century in Spain. The Spanish Enlightenment (*Ilustracion*) under Carlos III (1759–1788) strengthened the civil state against the powers of the Church and nourished secular forces in the colony. Under governors Simon de Anda and Jose Basco, efforts to foster economic self-sufficiency encouraged the expansion of cash-crop agriculture, the most dramatic instance of which was the tobacco monopoly (1782–1882). The termination of the galleon trade in 1813 sealed the end to an era of isolation. Manila was formally opened to the trade of all nations in 1835, followed by the ports of Iloilo in 1855 and Cebu in 1863. The exclusion of non-Spanish foreign residents, a policy already eroded by the early nineteenth century, officially ended in 1863 when non-Spanish foreigners were permitted to take up residence in the provinces and engage in any economic activity. All these took place during a politically tumultuous time in Spain. The South American wars of independence (1808–1825) signaled the breakup of the Spanish Empire and a complex struggle of liberal and conservative forces plunged Spain into a prolonged state of civil unrest as coups and civil war led to a bewildering succession of governments.

With the opening of the Suez Canal in 1869, the voyage from Europe to the Philippines was cut down from three to four months to just a month. In 1870 the first steamer arrived in Manila direct from Barcelona via the Suez. The "opening up" of the colony did not only mean that the Philippines was linked more closely to the outside world but that the "inside" was changed as well as commercial agriculture expanded and domestic commerce intensified. Life quickened not only in Manila and the major ports but in large sections of the country as the state bureaucracy expanded, patterns in the use of land and labor changed, the circulation of persons, goods, and ideas accelerated, and population grew. By 1887 the Philippines had a population of seven million.[50]

Economic exploitation and social inequality were exacerbated by these changes yet bound people in a world of grievance and aspiration that was no longer locality-specific. At the same time, the changes created an economically empowered *principalia* with the appetite for cultural and social advancement. Of this rising elite, T.H. Pardo de Tavera wrote:

> Bigan, Taal, Balayan, Batangas, Albay, Nueva Caceres, Cebu, Molo, Jaro, Iloilo, began to be covered with solidly constructed buildings; their wealthy citizens would come to Manila, make purchases, become acquainted with the great merchants, who entertained them as customers whose trade they needed; they visited the Governor-General, who would receive them according to the position that their money gave them; they came to know the justices of the Supreme Court, the provincials of the religious orders . . . and, on returning to their pueblo, they took in their hearts and minds the germ of what was subsequently called subversive ideas and later still "filibusterismo". . . Already the "brutes loaded with gold" dared to discuss with their curate, complain against the alcalde, defend their homes against the misconduct of the lieutenant or sergeant of the police force. . . . Their money permitted them to effectively defend questions involving money first, then, those of a moral character.[51]

A native, secular literature began to emerge. This is shown in the careers of two early nineteenth-century poets, Jose de la Cruz (1746–1829) and Francisco Baltazar (1788–1862). They were masters of local versions of medieval European romances and hagiographical tales, called *awit* and *corrido* when they were chanted or circulated in chapbooks, or *comedia*, when they were adapted to the stage. Probably introduced in the sixteenth century by Spanish and Mexican soldiers and sailors, these romances became popular in the nineteenth century, produced by mostly anonymous bards and authors. Unlike Pinpin and de Belen, who worked under the missionaries' patronage, or de la Merced and de Castro, who wrote as part of their vocation as churchmen, de la Cruz and Baltazar were "free-floating" intellectuals. Writing for a living, they were part of an emerging town culture in which persons with learning and literary skills could earn both prestige and an income by producing verses and plays for theater and other occasions. Our first known examples of writers operating outside the domain of the church, they were precursors of the professional men of letters in the nineteenth century.

Of the petty elite of Tondo in Manila, Jose de la Cruz (called Huseng Sisiw, from the practice of his being gifted chicks, *sisiw*, in exchange for his poetic compositions) was an autodidact who is said to have taught himself Spanish, Latin, philosophy, and theology. He headed an itinerant troupe of *comedia* players and lived off commissions producing poetry for private and public purposes. He is credited with having authored numerous lyrics, plays, and romances (none of which has survived except for fragments published in 1933). Remembered for his legendary skills in verse-making, he was a poet in the oral tradition as well as child of an emerging book culture. He is reported to have said: "My library is my own mind. A rich library is not what is needed but to put in the mind what it contains."[52]

Baltazar (also Balagtas) apprenticed as a versifier under the Tondo bard.[53] The son of a village blacksmith in Bulacan, he moved to Manila when he was eleven and entered into the domestic service of a family who paid for his secondary education at Colegio de San Jose. His stay in Manila introduced him to an expanding native literati that included his teacher Fr. Mariano Pilapil, a well-regarded Latin scholar. Baltazar had a troubled and unhappy life. After being jailed in 1838, reputedly on a trumped-up charge filed by a *cacique* who was a rival in love, he left Manila for Bataan where he married, worked in the lower civil service, and raised a large family. He was imprisoned again for having cropped the hair of an *alferez's* housemaid and probably something else besides since he spent nearly four years in prison. Driven in part by his need to make a living from commissions, he wrote "more than a hundred" *comedias* and *corridos*, of which only barely a dozen titles are known today and only three of which have survived intact.

His masterwork, *Pinagdaanang Buhay ni Florante at ni Laura sa Cahariang Albania* (The History of Florante and Laura in the Kingdom of Albania) (1838) is a long romance in dodecasyllabic quatrains.[54] It shows a poet versed in Greek and Roman classics, "universal history," and Europe's courtly love tradition. In the manner of metrical romances, it claims to have been "based on various 'historical scenes' or portraits relating to events in ancient times in the Greek Empire" (*Quinuha sa madlang "cuadro historico" o pinturang nagsasabi sa mga pangyayari nang unang panahon sa Imperio ng Grecia*). Its literate orientation is signified in the poet's address to the "reader" (*sa babasa nito*) in the 1861 edition, asking that his lines not be altered and that readers refer to his footnotes and analyze the "deeper" sense of his lines. It is not a mere miming of European erudition. *Florante at Laura* is an original composition. By the force of his language and skill in shaping his characters' subjective life in a woeful tale that condemns unjust powers, Baltazar localizes the exotic, stamps his personality on a foreign form, and gives to the Enlightenment faith in reason a native voice. Taken as a veiled indictment of colonial oppression, *Florante at Laura* has been regarded as a text that marks the transition from folk realism to the more vigorous and overtly political realism of the Propaganda Movement.

Baltazar was a favorite among early nationalists. When Rizal left for Europe in 1882, he carried with him a copy of an 1870 edition of *Florante at Laura*. Its status as a political allegory, however, has been debated given the poem's exotic material and cryptic relations to actual events. In this respect, it is important to stress how it was read or heard in its own time. *Florante at Laura* was not just a printed text: it circulated in manuscript copies, entered the oral tradition, sung by amateur and semiprofessional bards, and generated meanings in ways now difficult to document. In a sensitive study of the poem's language, Virgilio Almario points to the semantic and affective values of the poem's Tagalog words that may have suggested covert "sociopolitical" meanings to its Tagalog readers.[55]

What has gone largely unrecognized by critics is that the poem was composed at a time when the country witnessed a convulsion of rational-critical dissent and the earliest manifestation of a "national" consciousness. A conjunctural moment was the promulgation of the Cadiz Constitution of 1812 which set Spain on the road to a parliamentary monarchy in the troubled context of a domestic revolution and the war against France.[56] In providing that laws were to be the same for all citizens on both sides of the Atlantic and in the Philippines, the 1812 Constitution gave impetus to revolution in Latin America and the beginnings of autonomist politics in the Philippines. In Manila (when Baltazar was in the city), a brief spell of press freedom (1813–1824) stimulated the expression of liberal ideas. *Ramillete Patriotica Manilense* (May 27, 1821) reported that "clandestine publications are multiplying in a scandalous manner." "Five or six of this class are being circulated in these parts."[57] Manila's weekly *La Filantropia* (1821–1822) criticized pedantic school education, discrimination against indios and creoles in student admission, and book censorship (citing the ban on the importation of Rousseau's *Social Contract*). These papers had a small, precarious existence but, for the first time, political dissent was openly expressed in print.

How "Filipino" intellectuals engaged the realities of the time is indicated in the stories of four diverse contemporaries of Baltazar, the indios Mariano Pilapil and Apolinario de la Cruz and the creoles Luis Rodriguez Varela and Domingo Roxas.

A secular priest, Mariano Pilapil (1759–1818) belonged to a prominent Bulacan family.[58] Illustrating the process by which the indigenous elite carved out space for itself in the colonial system, the Pilapil family invested in education, produced priests, and donated land to the church for a *capellania* on condition that Pilapils in the clergy take precedence in being appointed its chaplain. Mariano Pilapil earned a doctorate in sacred theology from Santo Tomas (making him the first native to earn a doctorate) and built a distinguished clerical career, publishing pastoral and pedagogical texts, and serving as ecclesiastical censor and philosophy professor at Colegio de San Jose. Though the most accomplished native priest of his time, he found his ascent in the church hierarchy blocked for racial reasons, a fact he did not suffer in silence but protested with formal appeals to higher authorities, including the Spanish Crown.

After the Constitution of 1812 was proclaimed in Manila on April 17, 1813, Pilapil was one of the four delegates elected to represent the Philippines in the Spanish Cortes. (The others were two Spanish-mestizo priests and a creole layman; another *indio tagalo*, also a priest, was chosen as an alternate.) It was the first election of its kind in which the electors (albeit small and mostly priests) included indios. The election stunned colonial authorities already quite aware of the role creoles and priests played in revolutionary movements in Spanish America. The archbishop and other church dignitaries snubbed the proclamation of the elected delegates in the Manila Cathedral on September 19, 1813. Critical pieces against Pilapil were anonymously circulated (but traced to friars), eliciting a response from Pilapil and his students at San Jose who published their riposte in verse form in *Dos mascarados descubiertos* (1813).[59] For reasons that are not known Pilapil did not leave for Spain together with the other delegates. When the decree of the Cortes secularizing parishes reached Manila in December 1814 it was Mariano's cousin, Domingo Pilapil (1755–1822), parish priest of Bacoor, who led others in boldly petitioning the archbishop to publish and implement the decree. Instead Domingo and his co-signers were imprisoned in the city's convents and released only two months later, in March 1815, when news of the abolition of the Cortes on May 4, 1814, finally reached the Philippines. We know little of what the Pilapils did subsequently, but the rights of the native and secular clergy they espoused would widen into a movement in the decades that followed.

The "liberal space" that opened up under the 1812 Constitution also revealed the tensions between creoles and peninsulars in the colony.[60] Spanish authorities were suspicious of the loyalty of creoles—called "Filipino Spaniards" (*españoles Filipinos*) or simply "Filipinos"—because of the role of creoles in the Spanish-American revolutions. Discriminated against by peninsulars, creoles—many of whom had never been to Spain and had neither friends nor personal relations there—proudly identified with the land, calling themselves *hijos del pais* (sons of the country).

The most vocal advocate of native rights was the creole Luis Rodriguez Varela (1768–1826), a Manila-born Spaniard who was educated in France, served in Manila's Ayuntamiento and received in 1795, for reasons that are not clear, the title of *Conde Filipino* from Charles IV. Author of several works, including a patriotic tract on the French invasion of Spain, *Proclama Historial* (1809), he called for expanding education in the colony and defended the rights of the native clergy in the controversy surrounding the election of Pilapil and other delegates to the Cortes. In *El Parnaso Filipino* (1814), a book of poems he published in the flush of enthusiasm that followed the 1812 Constitution, he stirred debate with his extravagant claims of the artistic and scientific accomplishments of indios and creoles in the land he called *Perla del Oriente*. Retana dismisses him as a "pedestrian writer, scurrilous, an occasional poetaster, a patriot in his own mind," but credits him as "the precursor of redemptorist politics," "*precursor de los Rizal, los Lopez Jaena, los del Pilar.*"[61] Retana exaggerates but Varela was not inconsequential.

In 1815, news of the abolition of the Cadiz Constitution in 1814 sparked a bloody uprising that started in Sarrat, Ilocos, and spread to neighboring towns. It was, however, suppressed in a matter of days. Enmity between peninsulars and creoles, was behind a plot in 1822 of creole military officers—led by the brothers Manuel, Jose, and Joaquin Bayot—to take over the government and declare Philippine independence. The conspiracy was discovered and its leaders punished. The following year, another conspiracy of Mexican and creole officers, led by the Spanish mestizo Andres Novales, sparked a mutiny in which the mutineers arrested Spanish officials, took control of installations, including the Governor's Palace, and declared Novales (in the manner of General Agustin de Iturbide of Mexico) "Emperor of the Philippines." The coup was crushed on its first day and its leaders executed. A French eyewitness to the events, Paul de la Gironiere, wrily wrote of Novales: "At midnight he was outlawed; at two o'clock in the morning proclaimed Emperor; and at five in the evening shot."[62]

These were short-lived events that mostly involved Spaniards, Mexicans, and creoles. They were, however, more than military mutinies. Leading creole citizens, like Varela, businessman Domingo Roxas, and lawyer Jose Maria Jugo, had been under surveillance on suspicion of subversive activities. Roxas (1782–1843) was one of the country's wealthiest businessmen. Jugo (1780–1855), a Manila-born Spaniard, was a law professor at Santo Tomas and (with Varela and Roxas) active in *Real Sociedad Economica de Amigos del Pais.*[63] Varela, Roxas, and Jugo were taken under custody in the aftermath of the Novales revolt and, together with the Bayot brothers who had languished in prison since their abortive conspiracy in 1822, shipped off to Spain on February 18, 1823, to stand trial. They were exonerated after more than a year's appeal. (Varela died in Spain while Roxas returned to the Philippines.)

While the unrest was quickly contained, the interregnum saw the racist foundations of colonial rule publicly attacked in print, perhaps for the first time. Responding to an article in *Noticioso Filipino* (August 5, 1821), an anonymous political tract, *El Indio Agraviado*, published in Sampaloc in 1821, denounced the oppression of indios.[64]

This is what you (Spaniards) are saying among yourselves: If we allow the Indians to learn Spanish, some of them may turn out to be satirists and scholars who will understand what we say, dispute with us and write things against us. If we allow them to prosper they will become rich, they will mix with us freely, sit beside us, eat at the same table, aspire to high and important offices, become persons of distinction. Is it not shameful that they should be on the same level as ourselves? And so, that they may never rise from their miserable condition, that they may always be poor, that we may have them to serve us always, let us not teach them Spanish; let us leave them in their ignorance; let us not help them correct the barbarous speech and stupid ideas that among them pass for polite conversation; let us not provide them with money, that being always needy they may learn to steal. Thus we shall be able to call them thieves and they will have nothing to say in their defense because they <u>will</u> be thieves. And if by a miracle they refrain from stealing, being in need they will do what work they can for whatever wage they can get. By this method or system we will always be the masters and they will always be poor, miserable and ignorant, bearing all injuries, unable to defend themselves. We will possess all, and all will have need of us. Was this not what your lordships had in mind from the beginning, that you may always have the better of us, as you do? There is not doubt at all about it. What then is left for the poor Indian? If he tries to reason with you, he is impertinent; if he keeps his peace, he is a dolt.

A state of nervousness characterized the period. When a cholera outbreak hit Manila in 1820, rumors spread that the epidemic was caused by foreigners poisoning the waters. A riot broke out on October 9 that killed 39 Europeans in Manila. A British naval officer writing about the situation in 1822 noted the anti-Spanish feeling among natives and creoles. Some of the disaffected, he said, "are rapidly spreading doctrines gleaned from the works of Voltaire, Rousseau, Tom Paine, etc. . . . stimulating [the populace] with songs of liberty and equality." Such remarks as "the country belongs to the Indians, *La tierra es de los Yndios*" are common "even amongst the lowest orders." Referring to the xenophobic riot of October 1820, he lamented that a crisis will surely come now that "the doctrine of *El Pueblo Soberano* ["the sovereign people"] is hourly echoed in [the native's] ears by those who are least capable of managing him when once aroused."[65]

Concern for public order occasioned moves to strengthen press censorship and regulate the movements of people. An edict in 1826, for instance, provided for the registration of vagrants and the arrest of persons caught posting anonymous *pasquines* or satirical posters.[66]

Several tendencies were at work in the early formation of a critical intelligentsia—assertion of the rights of the secular clergy, Enlightenment liberalism, "creole patriotism," and the economic empowerment of local *principales*. Sinibaldo de Mas, in his 1842 *informe*, raised the dire prospect of creoles forging common cause with indios and recommended that "the Spaniards born in the Philippines must be reduced as much as possible in number." He warned against the spread of liberal ideas: "It is indispensable that we avoid the formation of liberals, because in a colony, *liberal* and *rebellious* are synonymous terms." Saying that for the colony's maintenance "the colored population must *voluntarily* respect and obey the whites," he recommended the closure of Manila colleges and an end to the ordination of native priests. Mas bewailed the increased assertiveness of indios and mestizos and the many instances of insubordination he suffered from natives during his stay in Manila. "I have traveled among Turks, Egyptians and Bedouins, without pomp nor escorts and I can say that in no place have I been object of less respect and deference than in the Philippines." To "break the pride of the natives," he exhorted, "it is necessary to keep [them] in such an intellectual and moral state that despite their numerical superiority they may weigh less politically than [the Spaniards], just as in a balance a pile of hay weighs less than a bar of gold."[67]

Critical public discourse was restricted. Priests (like the Pilapils) worked in a disciplined institutional setting that militated against autonomous debate. Philippine creoles (like Varela)—compared to creoles in Latin America—were few in number and could only issue quixotic declarations or mount pocket mutinies that were readily suppressed. They constituted a collection of individuals rather than a social movement. Their aims were limited, advancing the rights of the secular clergy *within* the church and the prerogatives of the local-born *within* the imperial system.

Other, deeper forces were, however, at work as indicated in the Apolinario de la Cruz "rebellion" of 1841. The son of fairly well-to-do peasant parents in Tayabas, de la Cruz (1815–1841)—also Hermano Pule—went to Manila in 1830 with the desire to enter the religious orders.[68] This was an avenue closed to *indios* at the time. He could have gone the route taken by the Pilapils but his family may not have been prosperous enough to capitalize a clerical profession for the young Apolinario. Working as a *donado* in San Juan de Dios Hospital, driven by an exceptional religious zeal, he became a lay preacher and in 1832 organized *Cofradia de San Jose*, a confraternity devoted to the practice of piety and works of charity. By 1840 the *cofradia* had expanded to include a few thousand members in several Tagalog provinces and acquired a life of its own outside the control of the church. Its phenomenal expansion, and the fact that the organization specifically excluded those other than "pure-blooded" natives, alarmed the authorities. Harrassed and persecuted, Hermano Pule and his followers (who, it was reported, hailed their leader as "King of the Tagalogs") withdrew to establish a "commune" in the hinterland. Government forces attacked the encampment in late 1841, killing "almost a thousand" Cofradia members. Pule was captured, summarily tried, and executed, his body cut into pieces, his head publicly displayed in a cage on top of a pole.

The bloodbath raised a hail of public criticism in Manila. A year later, on January 20, 1843, soldiers of the "Tayabas regiment" based in Malate—who had relatives and friends among the victims in the Cofradia massacre—mutinied under the leadership of Sergeant Isidro Samaniego. The mutiny was brutally suppressed. The French consul in Manila reported to his superiors a few days later that at the height of the mutiny the rebels "were heard to cry out to their countrymen to rise in arms and fight for independence." "This was the first time that the word, independence, had been uttered in the Philippines as a *rallying cry*." With Gallic aplomb, the consul reported: "It is a milestone, Your Excellency, on the road to freedom."[69]

The Hermano Pule revolt was not the country's first religious revolt but may be the first to directly engage the institutions and forms of colonial authority. De la Cruz was not a *babaylan* preaching a return to precolonial religion. He aspired to join a European religious order, used as vehicle a European medieval organization (*cofradia*), and adopted

415

European ritual and verbal genres (*pasyon, novena*). While Reynaldo Ileto has shown that these took effective form to the degree that they were animated by indigenous notions of virtue, power, and community, it was an indigenized Christianity rather than, say, a Christianized animism that provided de la Cruz a "language" for articulating local notions of renewal and resistance.[70]

It is interesting that a key devotional text Cofradia members chanted in their gatherings, *Dalit sa caluwalhatian sa langit na cararatnan ng mga banal*, was copied from *Meditaciones, cun manga mahal na pagninilay na sadia sa Santong pag Eexercisios* (1645) by Pedro de Herrera, an Augustinian praised by his confreres as a "Horace" in the Tagalog language. Herrera's *dalit* compositions were meant to supersede (and thus suppress) "bad" native poetry. They were, Virgilio Almario says, "the first truly successful insertion (*pagsisilid*) of Christian doctrine into indigenous form and language."[71] The irony of its use by the Cofradia illustrates the recurrent fact in local intellectual history that a Spanish appropriation of an indigenous language (Tagalog) and form (*dalit*) as medium for colonial-Christian evangelizing would be reappropriated by natives who, in recuperating older meanings "hidden" in the language, would perform versions of community and salvation other than what the Spaniards intended.

De la Cruz withdrew to the wilderness only after the persecution began and his petitions to "legalize" the cofradia (addressed to the bishop of Nueva Caceres, the archbishop, and the Manila Audiencia) were denied or set aside by the authorities. In these petitions he was counseled or aided by prominent liberals in Manila, including the landowner Iñigo Gonzalez Azaola and merchant Domingo Roxas. Azaola was one of the delegates elected to the Spanish Cortes in 1813. Roxas, who was persecuted for the Bayot and Novales mutinies in 1822–1823, was a dynamic businessman with investments in such enterprises as mining in Cebu, a water-powered spinnery, and a gunpowder factory in Laguna. Implicated again in the Hermano Pule revolt and Samaniego mutiny (it was alleged that he supplied gunpowder to the rebels), the sixty-year-old Roxas was imprisoned with his two sons in Fort Santiago. He died in prison on June 10, 1843.[72]

Roxas's association with de la Cruz appears bizarre in the light of the binary divide historiography has constructed between folk rebels like Hermano Pule and men like Roxas (who sired ascendants of today's Roxas,

416

Ayala, Zobel, and Soriano families). The connection may have been concocted or magnified during de la Cruz's trial to convict an influential creole with a "subversive" record. Government paranoia was such that in the wake of the Hermano Pule revolt authorities even considered an ordinance that would permit only Spaniards to reside in the walled city, the creoles being sent out to live in the suburbs.[73] The Roxas-Pule link, however, should be taken not just as a product of paranoia but a sign of dynamic interrelations within local society.

While much of de la Cruz's career remains unclear what is known signifies an important aspect in the native encounter with foreign power. Saguinsin and Pilapil worked under the rules of established colonial institutions; Balagtas and Huseng Sisiw operated at the margins of colonial power. Rejected and persecuted, Hermano Pule took instruments the Spaniards created and deployed them in dangerously subversive ways. This was not a lament in the wilderness (as critics have falsely represented in the matter of Balagtas, Pule's contemporary) but a bold claim to the right to interpret power, and to power itself.

THE INTERRELATED STORIES of Pilapil, Varela, Roxas, and de la Cruz are sketchily documented and the relations somewhat tenuous. They signify, however, the social and political intersections that formed the *national* intelligentsia of the nineteenth century. There are four intertwined strands in this emergent formation: clerical intellectuals (Pilapil), creole patriots (Varela), an empowered bourgeoisie (Roxas), and folk-popular intellectuals (de la Cruz).

They constitute an uneven discursive terrain owing to differences in social location, conditions of emergence, and the nature of their grievances and aspirations. They are all, however, formed and shaped by colonial processes—Christian evangelization, Hispanic acculturation, and colonial economic expansion. They all had their own grievance: discriminations against natives and seculars in the Church; the bias against mixed-blood and "local-born" Spaniards; the constraints on an ascendant bourgeoisie; and the oppression of peasants and rural dwellers. They expressed these grievances differently and were energized by domestic and external events in different ways. Creoles were the most directly affected by the Latin American revolutions and expressed themselves in forms of "creole patriotism," in assertions of parity ("we are as much

Spaniards as the peninsular-born") or dreams of autonomy. Peasant rebels, on the other hand, were not unaffected by "large events" (as shown in the uprisings triggered by the British Occupation and the abolition of the Constitution of 1812)—even the Hermano Pule rebellion was not a case of pure indigeneity—but they drew sustenance from a more indigenous body of ideas that, throughout the colonial period, expressed itself in various forms of resistance.

These intersections were remembered. Four decades after Pilapil and Varela, another creole, Jose Burgos, would expand Pilapil's tentative advocacy of the native clergy and invoke Varela in a brief on native abilities that would, for the first time, enlarge on *Filipino* as name for a multiracial, proto-national community. Jugo was one of the liberals surveilled by the authorities at the time of the Cavite Mutiny of 1872. Joaquin Pardo de Tavera was Jugo's law partner and Jugo's daughter would figure as benefactress of expatriate Filipinos in Spain, Isabelo de los Reyes among them. Rizal would acknowledge Pilapil and Jugo among the nationalists' intellectual antecedents. And Pedro Paterno would, in his own fashion, live out the *ancien regime* dreams of *Conde Filipino*.

Their great wealth and status as "not quite Spanish" exposed the Roxas family to persecution. Domingo Roxas's son, Jose, was a member of the *Comite de Reformadores* headed by Joaquin Pardo de Tavera in 1872. Domingo's grandson, Pedro, was tagged together with his cousin Francisco and brother-in-law Jacobo Zobel as the highest leaders of the Katipunan in 1896.[74] Pedro's properties were embargoed at the outbreak of the 1896 revolution and he would have been arrested had he not jumped ship in Singapore on his way to Europe. Francisco was arrested in August 1896 and executed by firing squad. The government confiscated his properties. Zobel, a wealthy German pharmacist married to Trinidad de Ayala, Pedro's sister-in-law, was associated with the 1872 *reformadores* and imprisoned in 1874 for alleged involvement in a separatist plot. He died of a heart attack at the revolution's outbreak in 1896.

The Hermano Pule revolt would inspire other acts of insurrection. And turn-of-the-century *ilustrado* historians would trace the beginnings of the Philippine revolution (if for reasons of their own) to such events as the Pule revolt. The linkages are tenuous but they would thicken in the decades that followed.

THE RISE OF AN INTELLIGENTSIA

FEDOR JAGOR observed in 1873: "The colony can no longer be kept secluded from the world. Every facility afforded for commercial intercourse is a blow to the old system."[75] The expansion of the colonial state and market economy stimulated new needs and new ways of looking at the world. Urbanization, improved communications, and a larger, more mobile population opened spaces for the circulation of ideas and formation of a "public." Schools, newspapers, voluntary associations, and other sites of what Jurgen Habermas calls "the public sphere" expanded as networks for rational-critical discourse.[76]

After the 1860s *Filipino* increasingly came to refer not only to creoles but natives and Chinese and Spanish mestizos. An intelligentsia was formed that was *modern* in the manner in which it engaged Western knowledge and *Filipino* in its sense of location and nationality, one that was shaped by a consciousness of difference and "outsideness" in relation to the knowledge it had to confront and possess in the process of defining itself.

COLONIAL EDUCATION expanded despite material and ideological constraints. Already in 1846 Jean Mallat wrote, if too optimistically, that "the education of the Indios is far from backward, if it is compared to that of the lower classes in Europe; almost all Tagals know how to read and write." Mallat added, however, that "as for the sciences properly called, they have made very little progress."[77]

On June 24, 1821, in the wake of the Liberal revolution in Spain, a plan for an all-level public educational system for the colony was approved but the defeat of the Liberals in 1823 aborted the plan's enactment. The plan was revived in 1863 with an educational decree that laid the ground for a colony-wide public school system. The decree prescribed curricula with Spanish as medium of instruction and provided for teacher-training schools. While the decree was never fully implemented, the school system grew. A source published in 1876 stated that there were 1,004 primary schools for boys and 775 for girls, or a total of 1,779 with a combined attendance of 385,907. The same survey, however, gave the less sanguine view that of the primary school attendance in 1876, only 28.46 percent knew how to write, 18.36 percent knew how to read and write, 2.16 percent knew how to speak Spanish, and 51.02 percent knew "nothing at all."[78]

The key factor in the spread of education was social demand rather than government progressivism or ecclesiastical altruism. The expansion of state and civil society made the production of educated citizens both feasible and necessary. Hence the late nineteenth-century surge of educational reforms. In 1865, Madrid decreed the establishment of secondary schools, placing them under the supervision of Universidad de Santo Tomas. San Juan de Letran and Ateneo Municipal were elevated to first-class secondary schools and obliged to offer the same basic curriculum prescribed in Spain. By the 1890s there were seven other first-class secondary schools and more than 178 other secondary institutes, for boys and girls, throughout the Philippines. (First-class secondary schools offered a five-year course leading to the degree of *bachiller en artes*, a degree conferred after an examination by Santo Tomas, the only degree-granting educational institution in Spanish Philippines.)

Enrolment expanded at Santo Tomas. Between 1861 and 1898, some 40,158 students, mostly Filipinos, attended the university. Eighty-nine percent of these students sought a secular education, particularly in the fields of jurisprudence (34 percent), medicine (22 percent), and philosophy (22 percent).[79] While these students made up less than one

420

percent of lowland Christian Filipinos, the period saw a growing class of educated Filipinos. By this time, too, Filipinos began to seek higher education in Europe in such fields as law, medicine, and engineering.

Religious-run schools were highly disciplined sites where the program of studies was controlled and rote learning the rule. The character of the system was such that its reform was a major issue among Filipino propagandists. Yet, despite its constraints, it offered opportunities denied the colonized elsewhere in Southeast Asia. Moreover, it provided an arena in which Filipinos came together and exchanged experiences and ideas (even if much of this took place outside classrooms or school premises).

What is particularly important (and mostly unstudied) is that Filipinos took the initiative in opening private, mostly home-based secondary schools. These schools existed in the early nineteenth century but proliferated after 1865. By 1895, there were around a hundred of these institutes, called "Latinity schools" or *escuelas de latinidad*. They were authorized by the government, supervised by Santo Tomas, and followed prescribed textbooks and curricula. Typically run by a government-licensed schoolmaster (usually a graduate of Santo Tomas, Ateneo, or Letran) and housed in a private residence, these preparatory schools became training ground for future nationalists. There is scant information on the schoolmasters and what actually transpired in these schools. It has been remarked that, prior to the reforms of 1865, they often had "incompetent teachers—oftentimes university flunkers without any authorization."[80] While this may be true, their native character and relative autonomy suggest there may have been more interaction and openness in these institutes than in the Dominican or Jesuit-controlled classrooms.

At the secondary level after 1863, subjects included elementary Greek, universal history, logic, moral philosophy, French and English. At Santo Tomas, students studied philosophy, physics, chemistry, Spanish literature, history of Spain, colonial legislation, and political economy. Philippine history *was* taught, as illustrated by schoolbooks like Jesuit Francisco Baranera's *Compendio de la Historia de Filipinas* (1877) and Felipe Govantes's *Compendio de la Historia de Filipinas* (1877) and *Lecciones de Geografía Descriptiva de Filipinas* (1878).[81] These rudimentary texts dealt with Spain in the Philippines rather than the Filipinos themselves (as the nationalists would point out). Yet they gave students the framework of a colonial state in which or against which they could place themselves. It is interesting, for instance, that Baranera's treatment of precolonial society already contains the themes (aboriginal Aetas, primitive monotheism, Malay migrations) that Filipino historians like Paterno and de los Reyes would develop. They would diverge in their interpretation of the "facts" but much of the basic plot remained.

Education was not as expansive as the list of subjects indicates. Something of the period's pedagogical style can be glimpsed in a primary-school textbook, Ricardo Diaz de Rueda's *La Escuela de Instruccion Primaria* (1844), an all-subject compendium of lessons in a tiny book of 334 pages.[82] Intended as a teaching crib, it ranges from the Old Testament and Spanish grammar to such subjects as arithmetic, geography, botany, mineralogy, physics, and zoology. It contains the barest information, a litany of dogmatic assertions in question-and-answer format. One-sentence answers are given to a series of questions: What is geometry? What is an angle? What is a circle? On the subject of history, the book offers a short, schematic survey of civilizations, with the focus on Europe and Spain. Its perspective is shown in editorial assertions on Mohammedanism as a religion founded by an "impostor" and on the "anarchy and misfortunes" caused by the French Revolution. Yet the book does illustrate the recognition that "modern" knowledge could no longer be excluded or ignored.

In spite of the nationalist attack on colonial education, the educational system was remarkable. Santo Tomas was the only real university in nineteenth-century Southeast Asia. No country in the region at the time had such a large number of Western-educated native students as the Philippines. *Cristianismo* and *Ilustracion* bound Spaniards to goals of humanism and enmeshed them in contradictions that undermined their rule. Colonial education constrained but had effects the colonialists could neither fully predict nor contain. Curricula and textbooks did not account for what students made out of the books they read and their experience in school.

THE ELABORATION of the civil bureaucracy raised the semblance of a rationally organized state, created a demand for new professional and technical skills, and became an arena for the encounter of native and foreign knowledge.[83]

State and private institutions stimulated an appetite for science and modernity. The utilitarian aspects of science, such as mining and agriculture, received government attention because of their practical benefits in the control and use of the population and environment. The need to promote and regulate the exploitation of natural resources led to the creation of *Inspeccion General de Minas* (1837), *Inspeccion General de Montes* (1862), and *Comision Agronomica* (1884). State agencies undertook scientific research, theoretical and practical training, and publications (like *Boletin Oficial Agricola de Filipinas* [1894–1898] and *Boletin de la Estadistica de la Ciudad de Manila* [1895–1898]). Examples of research generated are the pioneering works in geology of Jose Centeno and Enrique Abella, who headed the Spanish mining bureau in 1876–1886 and 1889–1897, respectively. Significant work was done by Sebastian Vidal, inspector general of the forestry bureau (1871–1889), who established a botanical library and herbarium, communicated with the Kew Herbarium and other European institutes, and published works like *Reseña de la Flora del Archipielago Filipino* (1883).[84]

There were agencies like the Meteorological Service (provided by the Jesuit Observatory, which was declared an official state institution in 1884), Central Commission of Statistics (1877), and Central Administration of Communications (1882), which regulated postal and telegraphic services. Public health was an important area of colonial work. Spaniards introduced hospitals from the beginning of their rule. These included the dispensary (1596), founded for the treatment of poor Spaniards, which evolved into the Hospital of San Juan de Dios, the first general hospital in the Far East. A pioneering effort was *Instituto Central de Vacunacion* (1806), founded as a result of the Francisco Xavier de Balmis expedition (1805) that introduced smallpox vaccination to the Philippines at a time when the merits of vaccines were still being debated in Europe. This institute was later placed under *Inspeccion General de Beneficencia y Sanidad* (1834), which performed such functions as the supervision of doctors, midwives, hospitals, and quarantine services. Other innovations included *Laboratorio Municipal de Manila*, established in 1887 to conduct chemical and bacteriological analyses of food, water, and drugs, in support of public health and legal medicine.

In 1887, the first public library, *Museo-Biblioteca de Filipinas*, was opened. Antedating it were special libraries like the Spanish Army's

Biblioteca Militar (1847), the library of *Real Sociedad Economica de Amigos del Pais* (1878), and libraries of private clubs and recreational societies. The more significant libraries were the holdings of the religious orders. Santo Tomas library had the largest library, with 12,000 volumes, and had, in addition, 5,747 specimens in its natural history museum and 330 instruments in its physics laboratory.[85]

The most ambitious attempt by the colonial government to promote science and progress came in the reign of Carlos III when governor-general Jose Basco (1778–1787) launched a series of economic reforms. Basco envisioned two institutions to spur development: *Real Compania de Filipinas*, a development company, and *Sociedad Economica de Amigos del Pais*, an association that would generate ideas and plans to be implemented by *Real Compania*.[86] Established in 1785, Real Compania stimulated cash crop cultivation (particularly, the tobacco monopoly that ran from 1782 to 1882) but, beset by indifference and factional rivalries, it was dissolved in 1834.

Sociedad Economica was an offshoot of the *sociedades economica* in Spain and Latin America that were inspired by the example of Europe's royal academies of science. In Manila, *Sociedad* was founded by a small group of Spanish peninsulars in 1781. It was active in 1781–1782, stagnated in the years that followed, and stirred back to life after 1820. Focused on promoting the colony's economic self-sufficiency and value for the Empire, the society held its first public meeting in Manila on May 6, 1781, at which Basco gave a speech in which he invoked the ideals of the Enlightenment in transforming the colony into *la perla del Oriente*.[87]

Sociedad was divided into five committees: natural history, agriculture and rural economy, industry and manufactures, foreign and domestic trade, and industrial technology and popular education. The society tried to stimulate agriculture and exports by offering awards to outstanding plantation owners and supporting training for artisans. It was, however, beset by factionalism, a sluggish bureaucracy, and competition from cheap manufactures from China and India. The committee on natural history did not function; "there was not a single Spaniard in all Filipinas who could explain to the members what natural history was." The other committees lacked experts and equipment for the few skills training programs they managed to conduct in towns around

Manila. *Sociedad* became "little more than a discussion group" and was moribund by 1787.[88]

There were some achievements. One was Juan de Cuellar's Scientific Commission to the Philippines (1786–1801), which collected botanical and zoological specimens for Spain's scientific institutions. While Cuellar attempted to teach chemical botany to some students in Manila, his initiatives in this regard did not seem to have gone far. Revived in the 1820s, *Sociedad* became more active, sponsoring lectures, distributing free books on grammar and reading, offering prizes for inventions, and supporting the training of Filipinos in dyeing and mechanics. It organized arts-and-trades schools called *escuelas patrioticas* (i.e., "patriotic" to Spain) in Manila and neighboring towns. With its support a nautical school (1820), school of drawing (1824), museum (1850), agricultural school (1858), and library (1878) were established. It issued the periodicals *Registro Mercantil* (1824–1833) and *Boletin de la Real Sociedad Economica Filipina de Amigos del Pais* (1882–1884). *Sociedad* supervised Manila's *Jardin Botanico* (1861), which was maintained until the end of Spanish rule though it never attained the prominence of botanical gardens in other European colonies.

Sociedad's training programs expressed a bias for the utilitarian and a particular conception of native abilities. Spanish writers commonly refer to the *indio*'s abilities in mechanical and mimetic arts, that they make excellent copyists, calligraphers, and illustrators, but that, conversely, they are weak and ill-suited for abstract forms of knowledge, like theology and philosophy. In the eighteenth century, the Franciscan Juan Francisco de San Antonio wrote that the natives were mechanically gifted and such skillful imitators that there were many printers, musicians, and clerks. For San Antonio, this natural disposition (*genio*) came with an incompetence in intellectual matters: "their understanding appears to be fastened to them (as it were) with pins and is always limited to materialistic subjects because it does not extend to matters of depth."[89]

Ideas about what was suited to the native's abilities as well as useful—and, one may add, politically harmless—underlie the support given by church and state to *artes* (like music, embroidery, and drawing) and *oficios* (like bookkeeping, engraving, and construction). Between 1742 and 1893, fifteen schools in arts-and-trades, agriculture, business, nautical science, and telegraphy were opened. Music and painting were cultivated, albeit along lines relevant to the liturgical, ceremonial, and prestige-building activities of church and state. As early as 1742, a *Colegio de Tiples* was established, teaching piano, organ, violin, vocalization and composition in a program patterned after that of the Madrid Conservatory of Music. In 1823, *Sociedad* established *Academia de Dibujo*, the country's "first official Philippine art academy," which ran until 1889, mostly administered by Spaniards in the Spanish "academic art" tradition. Government and privately endowed scholarships enabled Filipinos (like Juan Luna, Melecio Figueroa, and Felix Pardo de Tavera) to study art in Spain.[90]

Native arts and crafts figured prominently in the Philippine exhibits organized by the Spanish government in international expositions in London (1859), Philadelphia (1876), Amsterdam (1882), Madrid (1887), and Paris (1889), as well as local expositions like the *Exposicion Regional de Filipinas* in 1895. These events paraded examples of "native ingenuity" (samples of woodcraft, embroidered *piña*, the books of Paterno and de los Reyes). More important, of course, these expositions were designed not just for the practical benefits of scientific and commercial promotion but as ideological showcases for the "enlightened imperialism" of Western nations.

It must be stressed that the transition to modern, scientific institutions was neither immaculate nor sequential. This is shown in the introduction of Western medicine. The lack of doctors, supplies, and facilities was such that the Spaniards either tolerated or relied on the expertise of local healers. Missionaries like Fernando Santa Maria, author of *Manual de Medicinas Caseras* (1768), compiled data on traditional medicine and made them available for people in places "without doctors or pharmacies." In the absence of doctors, local *curanderos* were sought to treat Spanish soldiers wounded in battle or allowed to practice in the infirmaries of the Spanish Army and Navy. There are indications that herbalists were even given permits to operate local pharmacies (*botiquin*), and as late as July 21, 1843, a governor-general's decree granted permits to *mediquillos* and *herbolarios* to minister to the native population although they were barred from treating Spaniards and other foreigners.[91]

Though Europeans dominated activities in knowledge-production Filipinos were involved in these activities. Natives worked for botanical expeditions and such undertakings as the Jesuits' Manila Observatory.

Blanco's *Flora de Filipinas* (1877–1883) featured botanical plates executed by twelve gifted Filipino artists (like Lorenzo Guerrero, Felix Resurreccion Hidalgo, and Miguel Zaragoza), some of whom (like the botanist Regino Garcia) had scientific interests as well. The work of artist Damian Domingo (1790–c1832) and composer Marcelo Adonay (1848–1928) belied Spanish preconceptions about the native's "lower-order" skills. A Tondo-born Chinese mestizo, Domingo did not only direct *Academia de Dibujo* in its early years, it was his private art school that paved the way for the academy's formation. A musical prodigy from Laguna, Adonay became choirmaster and music teacher in Manila's San Agustin Church and amazed Spaniards with his mastery of Western musical traditions as performer and composer of original music in such forms as the Gregorian chant.[92]

By the late nineteenth century, Filipinos taught at Santo Tomas, carried out state-sponsored scientific studies (as did T.H. Pardo de Tavera), published on scientific and cultural topics, and headed government agencies (as did Pedro Paterno and Anacleto del Rosario, directors of *Museo-Biblioteca de Filipinas* and *Laboratorio Municipal de Manila*, respectively). Filipinos participated in professional and civic societies, like *Camara de Comercio* (1886), *Colegio Farmaceutico de Filipinas* (1891), and *Colegio Notarial* (1891). Normal school graduates formed an association called "Academy of Pedagogy" which published *Boletin Oficial del Magisterio Filipino* (1895–1897), devoted to pedagogical trends and information useful to teachers.[93] Filipinos wrote for scientific journals like *Boletin de Medicina de Manila* (1886–1887), *Revista Farmaceutica de Filipinas* (1893), *La Correspondencia Medica* (1893), and *Cronica de Ciencias Medicas* (1895). In the pages of these journals and elsewhere, Filipino scientists like Fernando Benitez, Leon Ma. Guerrero, and Manuel Zamora published on medicine, chemistry, and botany. An outstanding figure in this group was Anacleto del Rosario (1860–1895) who won the competitive post of director of Manila's *Laboratorio Municipal*, conducted bacteriological studies, and published scientific reports. Both Rizal and Pardo, it must be remembered, also worked in the medical and natural sciences.[94]

It remains to be studied as to what interactions occurred between indigenous knowledge and early Filipino scholarship in the natural and physical sciences. One may cite the example of Edilberto Evangelista

(1862–1897), a remarkable Tagalog who finished his studies in engineering at University of Ghent in Belgium in 1895, returned to Manila on the eve of the revolution in 1896, and designed and supervised the building of trenches and fortifications for Aguinaldo's army.[95] More broadly, however, training in the sciences had implications beyond the acquisition of professional and technical competencies. It oriented individuals to a rational, secular view of the world and built confidence in the powers of the mind and the possibilities of progress.

The emancipative effects of scientific knowledge are amply demonstrated in the careers of the physicians Jose Rizal and T.H. Pardo de Tavera. Further illustration is the case of Antonio Luna (1866–1899), who earned a licentiate in pharmacy in Barcelona and a doctorate in the same field in Madrid in 1890. He was the first Filipino to earn the latter degree. It is said that he apprenticed in medical laboratories in Paris, including that of Louis Pasteur, and that he "worked with" such pioneers in bacteriology as Ilya Mechnikov, Shibasaburo Kitasato, and Emile Roux.[96] While these claims may have been inflated, Luna was well-trained. He published a study of malaria, *El Hematozoario del Paludismo* (1893), and contributed scientific articles to *Siglo Medico* and *Farmacia Española* in Spain and *Revista Farmaceutica* and *Ilustracion Filipina* in the Philippines. Part of the Propaganda Movement, he wrote for *La Solidaridad* and published a book of sketches, *Impresiones* (1891). In 1894, he returned to the Philippines and became "chemist expert" of Manila's Municipal Laboratory. Though he was not involved in the revolution of 1896, which he denounced after he was taken prisoner, he was shipped off to Madrid where he was imprisoned until 1897. He returned to the Philippines in 1898 to play a leading role in the war against the Americans.

THE RISE OF THE PRESS was among the most important in the ensemble of nineteenth-century cultural transformations. In colonial Philippines, it represented a rationalizing, secularizing force vis-à-vis the religious orders and even the state.

The newspaper made its appearance in the Philippines with *Del Superior Gobierno* (1811–1812), a government newssheet that carried European news for Manila Spaniards. Though more than a dozen newspapers appeared between 1821 and 1862, these were ephemeral papers dealing mainly in government notices, commercial information, European affairs and intra-Spanish community gossip. By mid-nineteenth century, however, journalism had expanded as a social institution. Retana lists at least 97 newspapers and journals launched between 1875 and 1894.[97] Newspapers like *Diario de Manila* (1860–1898), *El Comercio* (1869–1925), *La Oceania Española* (1877–1899), and *La Opinion* (1887–1890) were substantial vehicles of news and opinion. With the founding of printshops in the provinces (Cebu in 1873, Iloilo in 1875, Vigan in 1883), provincial journalism also made its appearance (*Eco de Vigan* in 1884, Iloilo's *Porvenir de Visayas* in 1884, *Boletin de Cebu* in 1886, *El Eco del Sur* in Nueva Caceres in 1893). The field diversified with special interest publications like *Revista del Liceo Artistico-Literato de Manila* (1879–1881), *Revista Filipina de Ciencias y Artes* (1882–1883), and *El Foro Juridico* (1882–1888).

The establishment of *Comision permanente de censura* on October 7, 1856 was a response to the increasing availability of printed matter. Subject to censorship were printing presses, periodicals, books for commercial circulation and "personal use," prints and engravings, and theatrical presentations. Grounds for censorship were often specious and arbitrary: "false" interpretations of the Bible and history, dangerous intellectual tendencies (like "pantheism" and "materialism"), and obscenity. Among works banned were those of Hugo, Dumas, Eugene Sue, and Oliver Goldsmith. A work of Francisco de Quevedo was censored for satirizing the sacrament of matrimony. Sue's *El Gitano* suffered the same fate for "containing ideas conducive to fomenting profane love." Even Cervantes's *Don Quixote* was initially banned for portraying "immoral customs in minute detail." It was later approved with "corrections."[98]

Printing ceased to be a friar monopoly and, despite censorship, liberal ideas found print in newspapers and other publications. While early journalism was a distinctly Spanish or creole phenomenon, the complexion of ownership, content, and readership was changing, as indicated by the appearance of native-owned, local-language papers, like the partly Tagalog *El Pasig* (1862); M.H. del Pilar's *Diariong Tagalog* (1882); Pascual Poblete's *Revista Popular de Filipinas* (1888); and Isabelo de los Reyes's *El Ilocano* (1889).

Autonomous public spaces opened up since colonial policing of ideas was far from efficient. As early as 1827, a Spanish official expressed concern over foreigners who had entered the country and "clandestinely introduced impious, revolutionary, and obscene books printed in the Spanish language, but pirated in France, with which they have caused atrocious injury in the morals of families there."[99] Censorship, a Spanish author wrote in 1883, only stimulated the traffic in contraband literature:

> To ban the books of Victor Hugo, Sue, Dumas, Paul de Kock [novelist of seamy Parisian life] and other French writers, as well as the great majority of Spanish novelists, excepting only [Enrique] Perez Escrich [popular Spanish novelist] serves no other purpose but to arouse a passion for possessing them. We are reminded of a mestizo . . . who once showed us his little library. It contained, besides the novels mentioned above, the complete works of Renan, Volney, Voltaire, Rousseau and Talleyrand.[100]

Rizal said that the works of Dumas, Sue, Hugo, and Schiller were read in the colony though he admitted that most of the books in circulation were "religious and narcotizing in character." His own family home in Calamba had a library of "more than one thousand volumes."[101] Rizal wrote that at twelve he had read Spanish editions of Chateaubriand's *Les aventures du dernier Abencerrage*, Dumas's *Le comte de Monte Cristo*, and Cesare Cantu's *Storia universale*. And Isabelo de los Reyes, though he may have used "quotations from quotations" (as Retana said) to conjure an aura of erudition, had a book-learning remarkable for one who did not study abroad.

The careers of professional *literatos* like Joaquin Tuason (1843–1908), Mariano Perfecto (1853–1912), and Pascual Poblete (1857–1921), attest to the increased traffic of ideas through the medium of print. They were of the petty principalia, fairly well educated for their time. (Tuason was the son of a landowner-merchant in Pateros, outside Manila; Perfecto a rich merchant's son in Ligao, Albay; and Poblete a native of Naic, Cavite) They were indefatigable producers of journalistic articles and chapbooks, like romances, religious manuals, and almanacs. Among his numerous works, Tuason published *Bagong Robinson* (1879), a Tagalog translation of a Spanish edition of Joachim Heinrich von Campe's Daniel Defoe-inspired *Robinson der Jungere* (1779–1780).[102] Perfecto was a publisher-bookseller in Iloilo and Nueva Caceres, a newspaperman in Bikol and Hiligaynon, and, with Tuason, the most prolific book author of his time. Poblete was the publisher of around nine newspapers, including *El Bello Sexo* (a pioneering women's periodical established in 1891) and the more successful *Ang Kapatid ng Bayan* (1899–1907). Unlike Huseng Sisiw and Baltazar (who straddled folk and proto-urban cultures), these men were denizens of a world of print. They represented the aspirations for urbanity in their generation and the strengthening of empirical tendencies in the literature of the period.[103]

With Spanish as dominant medium, limited literacy, and urban bias, periodical circulations were not large. The influence of newspapers, however, extended beyond readers, they were relay points in the oral transmission of news, rumor, and gossip. Words traveled wide. As Manila papers carried news from Europe and other parts of the world, provincial papers transmitted articles from Manila. Isabelo de los Reyes is a prime example of a writer who reached out to a "national" audience, writing not only for Manila (and Madrid) newspapers but *Eco de Panay* in the Visayas and *El Ilocano* in Ilocos. In the virtual space of books and newspapers, readers in various parts of the country imagined others like them and created that "imagined community" that was the nation.[104]

THE NINETEENTH CENTURY saw the formation of modern, voluntary associations. The earliest examples, like *Sociedad Economica de Amigos del Pais*, were associations of Spaniards rather than Filipinos. In *Sociedad*, *indios* figured as workers and apprentices; even the prizes went to Spanish priests and hacienda owners. In Spain, together with the *sociedades economicas*, the Enlightenment inspired *sociedades patrioticas*, clubs of political discussion that were open to the public. While the former were dominated by conservatives (*moderados*) and focused on economic development, the latter were more openly liberal and political.[105] In the Philippines, what existed were not *sociedades patrioticas* but *escuelas patrioticas* devoted to training natives in arts and crafts.

The most significant association in this period was Freemasonry.[106] No institution in colonial Philippines expressed as directly the idea of the European Enlightenment as a moral and political project. Masonic lodges had existed in the Philippines since the late eighteenth century, possibly from the time of the British Occupation (1762–1764), but these were European in membership. While there may have been creoles and mestizos in these lodges by the nineteenth century, they remained distinctly European until Filipino lodges were introduced in 1891 by Filipino Masons returning from Spain. Banned by the Catholic Church in 1738 and the Spanish Crown in 1812, anathemized as villain in the loss of the Spanish American colonies and various outrages against the Church in Spain, Freemasonry (while legal by the late nineteenth century) had a discontinuous, subterranean existence.

In Spain, Filipinos joined Masonic lodges in the 1880s, usually in lodges that included Spaniards, Cubans, and Puerto Ricans. In 1889–1890, the first Filipino lodges, *Revolucion* and *Solidaridad*, were founded. Among the first members were Graciano Lopez-Jaena, M.H. del Pilar, Mariano Ponce, and Jose Rizal. Schumacher remarked: "It is a fact that almost every Filipino nationalist leader of the Propaganda Period was at one time or another a Mason."[107] Almost from the time these expatriate lodges were formed there were efforts to organize similar groups in the Philippines. Through Masons Jose Ramos, Pedro Serrano, and Moises Salvador, the first Filipino lodge in the Philippines, *Nilad*, was established on January 6, 1891. By 1893, there were 35 Filipino Masonic lodges in the country, nine in Manila and some in Visayas and Mindanao. An auxiliary lodge for women, *La Semilla*, was organized in 1893 with Rosario Villaruel, the daughter of a mason, as the first Filipino woman initiated to Masonry.[108]

It is easy to see why Freemasonry proved attractive to Filipinos. Masonic lodges were "schools" of Enlightenment thought, forward points of a "modernity" emancipated from traditional forms of authority. Resolutely civil and secular, oriented towards ideas of republicanism and constitutionalism ("Liberty, Equality, Fraternity"), Freemasonry was a model for what colonial society was not. As Margaret Jacob says of Freemasonry in Europe, lodges were "microscopic civil polities, new public spaces, in effect schools for constitutional government."[109] They were key sites in the formation of a modern civil society.

Freemasonry's appeal was enhanced by its values of comradeship amd exclusivity (initiation ceremonies, mystical symbols), aura of learnedness (meetings routinely invoked Voltaire, Locke, and Montesquieu), and a stress on ethicality that mystified lodges as "temples" in which "new persons" were formed. While egalitarian in principle, Masonic lodges were distinctly male, educated, and bourgeois despite Freemasonry's historic roots in Europe in guilds of craftsmen and artisans. Freemasonry's original constitutions explicitly excluded women (on such grounds as the view that women were indiscreet and endangered secrecy) and it was only around 1760 in France that women (typically, spouses, sisters or daughters of Masons) were first accepted into "lodges of adoption" that had to operate under the supervision of a male lodge.[110]

Of particular relevance in the Philippine case was the political utility of Freemasonry. Filipino lodges were cells for nationalist, anti-friar agitation. Lodge meetings were devoted not only to the inculcation of Enlightenment principles but the discussion of Philippine issues (such as representation in the Cortes and the teaching of Spanish). They were centers for diffusing libertarian ideas and, given Freemasonry's international character, vehicles for enlisting the support of foreign lodges and Spanish politicians for Filipino causes. The politically militant character of Filipino lodges is conveyed by Teodoro Kalaw:

> Speeches and lectures, letters and circulars, banquets and meetings, newspapers, friendly ties, in short, all the best means of propaganda were utilized, zealously and with great skill. The lofty humanitarian principles of the Fraternity were taken from the realm of thought and applied to the sad Filipino reality.[111]

Freemasonry was so important for staging ideas of rationalism and nationalism that *Frac-Masoneria* became for friars and conservatives a symbol for all that was morally and politically pernicious, a product of the French Revolution and chief cause of Spain's loss of her American colonies. A Spanish official wrote: "The Masonic lodges gave the Indios the secret and mysterious way of organizing themselves and weaving under cover of darkness their separatist schemes."[112] In the violent fits of repression in the late nineteenth century, Masons or suspected Masons were targets of domiciliary searches, torture, exile, and execution. Masonry's phantom loomed so large that the authorities imagined Masons everywhere. An official report during the revolution said that "along the banks of the Pasig River alone there are 17,000 native Masons."[113]

While Masonic lodges and other associations were important in the formation of a "public sphere," it is crucial to underscore the role of provisional, informal sites where discussions took place and a "public" germinated. Though John Foreman called nineteenth-century Manila "a dull capital," the city was not a medieval outpost. In the 1870s, Manila and its environs had around ten hotels and pension houses (with names like *De Europa* and *La Fonda Francesa*), general stores, two theaters (*Teatro Español* and *Circo de Bilibid*), a dance hall (*El Kiosko*), and the Manila Jockey Club race course. Visitors and locals could repair to cafes and partake of coffee and pastries, pass time at gaming tables, or read the local papers. In a few years, the city would have the beginnings of a telephone system (1890), electricity (1893), and a railroad service (the 120-mile Manila-Dagupan Railway inaugurated in 1891). A cable telegraph service connected Manila to the provinces (1873) and the outside world (1880). In 1891, Manila had thirteen printing presses, nine bookstores, and fifteen newspapers and magazines.[114]

As early as the 1870s, there were workers' organizations, *gremios* of woodcarvers, carpenters, lithographers, and other workers, usually focused on shops or neighborhoods, organized for mutual aid and fraternal purposes. The *imprenta*, in particular, gathered persons not along kinship and ethnic lines but shared intellectual and technical interests. As an axis for the circulation of ideas and information, it was a forward point in intellectual change. It is not surprising that printers, lithographers, and bookbinders were the first to form trade guilds in the Philippines. There were other sites. In military arsenals, tobacco factories, and shipyards, workers shared aspirations and expressed grievances in strikes and work stoppages. The first of these stoppages (which William Henry Scott calls the country's "first proletarian strike") took place on September 2, 1872, just months after the Cavite Mutiny, when 1,189 workers of the Cavite arsenal did not report for work. Unnerved authorities had the strike leaders promptly arrested. Governor-General Rafael Izquierdo voiced concern that the strike was the sign of a vast socialist conspiracy, warning that "the International has spread its black wings to cast its nefarious shadow over the most remote lands." He was thinking of the International Working Men's Association the Spanish Cortes declared illegal on November 10, 1871.[115]

Events like a religious procession, theatrical performance, or cockfight, and groups like orchestras and theatrical troupes, were sites where people gathered and traded news, opinion, and gossip. While much "political" talk took place at the edges to escape surveillance and censor-ship, the medium presented by public gatherings was crucial in the production and circulation of ideas. In Rizal's novels, scenes like a boat ride or cockpit assembly provide us with a kinetic sense of how ideas traveled in colonial society.

In the Philippines, unlike countries in Europe, the boundaries be-tween public and private were much more porous. Home-based gatherings (from wakes and baptisms to literary soirees or *tertulias*) were important in cultivating civic consciousness. *Tertulias* were gatherings at which patriotic poetry was recited and political discussions took place. Masonic meetings and much of the organizing work of the Katipunan were done in the privacy of homes. To avoid surveillance, Masons posted lookouts, used secret passwords, and seldom met in the same house twice. A dance or card game was usually held as a cover and furnishings of the Masonic "temple" were kept simple so they could be removed quickly. Family members provided "cover" and women presided over the ameni-ties of setting and refreshments. Not quite the ritualized Parisian *salonniere*, the Filipina kept to the margins of male discourse (though not completely out of it) even as her presence as the invisible hostess symbolized the harmonious sociability important to these meetings. That the home was important in the spread of nationalist thought is sug-gested by the prominence of kinship ties in political mobilization. Rosa Sevilla (1879–1954), for instance, recalls that she had her first lessons in patriotism listening to discussions held in her aunt's house by young men headed by M.H. del Pilar. She would later join the revolution as one of only two women staffers in Antonio Luna's *La Independencia*. Sevilla became a leading educator, suffragist, and civic leader in the early twentieth century.[116]

Informal sites and circuits were channels not only for disseminating the ideas of propagandists like Rizal. This was the ground where oper-ated "folk" intellectuals, the vernacular poets and writers who played a major role in the spread of ideas in towns and villages.[117] While there is little information on this "proto-public" realm, its significance can be gleaned from the authorities' anxieties over popular dissidence. As early as 1840, local society was no longer (if it ever was) the genteel, colonial Eden envisioned by such authors of religious conduct books as Modesto de Castro. In 1842, Sinibaldo de Mas wrote: ". . . the *cura* and government employees were ridiculed in pantomimic dances in Gapan in 1841; a comedy was to have been enacted at the feastday celebrations at Santa Cruz, Laguna, in 1840, in which the *alcalde-mayor* and his court were to be held up to ridicule, but it was avoided by the arrest of the actors." Mas warned against *principales* holding meetings (*consejo*) outside the priest's supervision right in the parish house or even in church during which they plot to discredit the priest and other officials. Spaniards expressed concern over the circulation of "manuscript newspapers" and the trouble caused by ambitious *indios abogadillos* ("little indio lawyers") and *apoderadillos* ("men with a little power").[118]

In an 1843 report to the governor-general, Juan Manuel de Matta expressed alarm over the colony's restiveness in the wake of the uprisings of Hermano Pule (1841) and the Tayabas Regiment (1843). Recalling the role of priests and lawyers in fostering revolution in Spanish America, he recommended "the suppression of the colleges of Santo Tomas, San Jose, and San Juan de Letran of this capital [Manila], and the conciliar seminaries of the bishoprics, as perpetual nurseries of corruption, laziness, or subversive ideas. . . . From them come the swarms of ignorant and vicious secular priests, and the pettifogging lawyers, who stir up so much trouble among the natives, and cause the provincial chiefs so great inconvenience." He wrote: "Ideas of emancipation are sheltered in many bosoms. Discontent swarms in all places."[119]

James LeRoy wrote that Spanish censorship was such that one could "look almost in vain in [local] periodicals prior to 1898 for expressions of the Filipino point of view, or, till the close of 1897, for any frank expression of liberal political views on the part of Spanish editors."[120] LeRoy—who thought the Americans inaugurated "modernity" in the country—is not entirely correct.

SPANIARDS AND CREOLES were the most visible figures in the public sphere by virtue of their advantages of access and education. With the expansion of the state and economy and increased influx of Spaniards, non-clerical Europeans became, vis-à-vis the church, an axis of secular modernity and alternative source of authority. Agents of a "colonial Enlightenment," they built up journalism, promoted scientific knowledge, and popularized new literary and cultural forms. By 1851, for instance, European novels by writers like Alexandre Dumas, Alphonse Daudet, and Hendrik Conscience, were serialized in the Manila press. More important, peninsulars and creoles began to publish novels about the Philippines in local periodicals. While their ambit is circumscribed by facts of production and authorship (authored as they were by writers conscious of their *prestigio de raza*), they signified that opening up to the "world" that animated cultural work in the nineteenth century.

This secular modernity is well illustrated in *Ilustracion Filipina* (1859–1860) and *Revista de Filipinas* (1875–1877), periodicals that promoted an ethos combining the "enlightened despotism" of Bourbon rule and the Victorian ideology of "social improvement."[121] The fortnightly *Ilustracion Filipina*, the country's first illustrated periodical, declared its aims in its maiden issue thus:

> The Philippines is one of the countries least known in Europe and of which the most misinformation exists, because of the erroneous description of some of the few travelers who have visited here. Not having remained long enough to form a correct idea, they have credited absurd stories, generally unfavorable to the islands, in an effort to give interesting accounts of their voyages, and have created erroneous impression. We have had investigators, laboring for the good of the country, without result, because they saw what the titled officials wanted them to see and got little actual knowledge of the country. We venture into this field of journalism to contribute what we can toward the dissemination of information concerning this land where the hand of providence has scattered blessings with such abundance. We shall try to do what has never been done here before, publish a paper combining the artistic, scientific and the literary, in harmony with the march of progress. We shall endeavor to make it useful as well as entertaining.[122]

It was a distinctly Spanish and creole publication. Lithographs of *costumbres* and *tipos del pais* romanticized the colony; scientific articles conveyed elite notions of social improvement. Augustinian Antonio Llanos contributed barometric and pluviometric observations and a scientific study of Mount Arayat. Ricardo de Puga, a colonial officer, wrote historical and literary pieces. There were articles on sanitation and health, a plan for a water supply system for Manila, and other "useful" contributions. *Revista de Filipinas* displayed the same appetite for modern knowledge. The review carried items on geography, history, law, and science, contributed by Jose Felipe del Pan, Sebastian Vidal, Jose Centeno, Federico Casademunt, Fernando Benitez, and others. Articles included Pedro de Govantes's "Religion primitiva de los Filipinos"; Jose Felipe del Pan's "El Darwinismo y las razas Papua y Malaya"; Fr. Ramon Martinez Vigil's "La escritura propia de los Tagalos"; translations of Pigafetta and Carl Semper; and diverse information on economics, medicine, and geography. A consciousness of location in the Southeast Asian region was conveyed by articles on the Dutch and British experience in Java, Sumatra, and the Malay peninsula.

Further illustration of this type of Spanish patriotism was the launching on May 22, 1891, of *Biblioteca Historica Filipina*, an ambitious project to publish rare historical sources on the Philippines. Billed as a "national monument to the glories of Spain," it was inspired by the arrival in Manila of a new director-general of civil administration, Jose Gutierrez de la Vega (1824–1899), a litterateur who, as governor of Granada and Madrid, initiated similar literary-civic projects. With the combined support of civil officialdom and the religious corporations, a subscription drive netted around 2,460 institutional and individual subscriptions from Batanes to Jolo, that included not just the clergy and local officials but a large number of citizens.[123] In 1892, the association issued in rapid succession Jesuit Juan Delgado's *Historia General Sacro-Profana, Politica y Natural de las Islas del Poniente llamadas Filipinas*, Franciscan Francisco de Santa Ines' *Cronica de la Provincia de San Gregorio Magno*, and Augustinian Juan de Medina's *Historia de los Sucesos de la Orden de N. Gran P.S. Agustin de estas islas Filipinas*. Apparently, the project did not survive its first burst of enthusiasm.

These manifestations of "colonial Enlightenment" expressed Spanish patriotism, a colonial elite's aspirations for modernity, and a new rhetoric of legitimacy vis-à-vis the earlier one of Christianization. Yet these also inspired an appetite for new kinds of knowledge as well as the growing awareness among Spaniards and, in particular, creoles of an intellectual and emotional stake in the land. Creole identification with the land would merge with the increasing self-assertion of indigenes and Chinese mestizos to forge a new social consciousness. This is shown in the examples of the peninsular Jose Felipe del Pan and the creole Juan

Atayde. A stalwart in Philippine journalism and a man of liberal sympathies, del Pan (1821–1891) actively promoted scholarship on the Philippines. He cultivated a coterie of local adepts (including Isabelo de los Reyes) and left behind a son, Rafael, who would cast his lot with Filipinos in the struggle for Philippine independence. Born in Manila in 1838, of Spanish and Aztec descent, Atayde was a retired Spanish army officer who headed *Circulo Hispano Filipino* (1882–1883), the first organization of Filipinos in Madrid. He ran a printing house in Manila, financed such papers as *La España Oriental, Revista Mercantil de Filipinas*, and *Ang Pliegong Tagalog*, and combined in his work as publisher and writer a Bourbon-style Spanish patriotism and a pronounced sympathy for Filipino culture and reformist ideas.[124]

Further example of the creole's intellectual evolution is the lawyer Manuel Regidor.[125] Born in Manila, the son of a Spanish colonial official, he was in Spain at the onset of the revolution of 1868 and was radicalized by the experience and his links to *progresistas* in the Philippines, among them his brother Antonio Regidor, also a lawyer. In Madrid, he founded the anti-clerical *La Discusion* (1860) and *El Correo de España* (1868–1870) and edited *El Eco Filipino* (1871–1872), periodicals that advocated the secularization of parishes and Filipino representation in the Cortes. Under the Moret ministry, he was named deputy of the *Junta consultiva de reformas de Filipinas*, in which capacity he made bold proposals for reform. The fall of the Moret ministry scuttled his appointment to the Cortes in 1873 as deputy for Quebradillas (Puerto Rico). When his brother Antonio and other *reformadores* were exiled to Guam, he was one of the lawyers who worked for the release of the deportees.

Regidor is interesting in a history of thought for a book attributed to him, Raimundo Geler's *Islas Filipinas: Reseña de su organizacion social y administrativa y breves indicaciones de las principales reformas que reclaman* (1869), which took up the Philippine cause as a contribution to the debate on liberal reforms in Spain.[126] *Islas Filipinas* is a spirited, anti-friar defense of the capacity of the *indio*. In an apologetics that foreshadows Paterno, Regidor frames the native in a "deep" and dynamic history that includes Hindu occupation (*invasion India*) and Arab and Chinese migrations. Using modern science in defending the *indio*, he deploys the race studies of German anatomists Carl Vogt and Friedrich Tiedemann and, in particular, the French surgeon Paul Broca.

Broca, founder of the Anthropology Society of Paris (1859), had obtained from Parisian cemeteries a large number of skulls representing the twelfth, eighteenth, and nineteenth centuries, classified according to gender, social status, and chronology. Interested in the relationship between intelligence and brain size, he argued that the brain is larger in superior races (with the white European as the pinnacle), in men than in women, and in higher over lower social classes. Subsequent studies would debunk this racist ranking of mental worth as misguided and highly injurious. In the nineteenth century, however, this was very "modern," authoritative knowledge. Regidor accepts Broca's basic premises but highlights two facts in his defense of the *indio*. First, he distinguishes the *indio* from the aboriginal Aeta by stating that the former are of the "Malay race" and have further intermixed with Arabs, Chinese, Japanese and Europeans. And, he pointedly adds, it has been shown that the Malay's skull measurements are "similar to the European Latins and near that of the Germans." Second, he invokes Broca's thesis that brain size increases as the influence of European civilization advances. (Broca asserted inferiority is not a permanent condition, arguing that women and primitives have small brains because of socially enforced underusage.) Highlighting this thesis, Regidor argues that even if one admits that the Filipino's intelligence is inferior, "[c]an this not be the natural result of the stagnation of their intellectual faculties due to the paralyzation of the monastic theocratic element that has reigned there with a force unknown in Spain even under the reign of Philip II?"[127]

Citing craniometric "evidence" that the skull capacity of a "Negro born in Africa is bigger than that of a Negro slave born in America," he argues that mental inferiority results from conditions of social brutalization. If the Filipino has not reached the level of "the cultured peoples of Europe and America," this can only be blamed on conditions created by the country's "theocratic element." Speaking the language of positivist science, Regidor defends the indio's potential for progress which, despite the lack of incentives, he has already demonstrated in his aptitude for reading, writing, and the arts. The friars indict themselves, he says, when they point to their policy of educating women as proof of their commitment to education. "Science" has shown, he says, that the male skull develops faster than the female with the influence of civilization.

440

Regidor accepts the assumptions of racialist science, with its class and gender bias, but bends them in a defense of the "Filipino." This application of European science to Philippine politics, while perverse today, was not peculiar at the time. It was ammunition for reformists. While Regidor's book circulated in a very limited way (Spanish officials and friars reportedly tried to stop its publication and then bought the whole edition and had it destroyed), Rizal and Paterno used the book extensively. Rizal highly recommended the book to Blumentritt, saying: "If only there were 50 Spaniards like Geler, I would give and shed my blood for Spain."[128]

In other respects Manuel Regidor was marginal to Philippine political and intellectual life and, like his brother Antonio, he stayed more European than Filipino. By the time, however, *Islas Filipinas* appeared in 1869 the focal site of intellectual work had shifted from Spaniards to more local actors.

A NATIONAL INTELLIGENTSIA was formed in the second half of the nineteenth century. It became a visible formation in the liberal interregnum of 1868–1871 that began with the revolution that toppled Isabel II and ended with the proclamation of King Amadeo in 1871. In the Philippines, this was an opening for more aggressive, public manifestations of discontent that simmered below the surface even before 1868.

The first overt manifestation came with the struggle over the rights of the native clergy. This struggle harks back to the 1820s but came to a head in the 1860s when the intra-Church dispute took on a racial and nationalist character. The "secularization movement" was first led by the creole Pedro Pelaez (1812–1863), a respected academic and church official, before leadership passed on to Fr. Jose A. Burgos (1837–1872) after Pelaez died in the great Manila earthquake of 1863. With Burgos, the Ilocos-born son of a Spaniard and Spanish mestiza, the secularization issue went beyond just an institutional debate over policies and prerogatives. As John Schumacher writes:

For Pelaez the major question is the rights of the secular clergy being violated by the Friars. For Burgos, there is an even more important point—that parishes were being denied to Filipinos because of their race and its alleged inferiority to Europeans. Burgos clearly writes as a Filipino, and if he does not preach disloyalty to Spain—indeed he strongly disclaims it—he is clearly conscious of his nationality, and ready to defend his people.[129]

Burgos did not leave behind a substantial body of writings—some documents, articles in the Madrid newspaper *La Discusion* (1870), and *Manifiesto que a la noble nacion española dirigen los leales filipinos* (1864), anonymously issued and signed "Los Filipinos."[130] Burgos drew authority from his status as a respected creole priest and his local knowledge as someone of the country. Speaking of *nuestra raza, nuestra clase*, by which he encompassed creoles, mestizos, and indios, he defended the capacities of the country's inhabitants and criticized the friars for denying them opportunities for advancement. His boldness was not just occasioned by the moment. He was not only trained in canonical jurisprudence but steeped in Enlightenment ideas as shown in his allusions to Montesquieu, Adam Smith, and Benjamin Franklin and studies on race by scientists like Franz Josef Gall and Ludwig Teichmann.

Burgos's Enlightenment rhetoric on *nuestra raza, nuestra clase* was not his alone. Encouraged by the liberal pronouncements of governor-general Carlos Ma. de la Torre, who assumed office on June 23, 1869, members of the local elite, mainly lawyers, civil servants, businessmen, and priests in Manila and neighboring provinces, surfaced as the *Comite de Reformadores* that organized "popular manifestations" for reforms. Called "the first Liberal Party in the Philippines," the committee (led by such men as Antonio Regidor, Joaquin Pardo de Tavera, Ambrosio Rianzares Bautista, and Maximo Paterno) included secularization advocates in the clergy (Jose Burgos, Mariano Sevilla) and students (Felipe Buencamino, Gregorio Sancianco, Paciano Rizal). The *reformadores* were linked to liberals in Spain. Manuel Regidor's *La Discusion*, the Cuban intellectual Rafael Labra's *El Correo de España*, and former Philippine resident Federico de Lerena's *El Eco Filipino* propagandized for such causes as secularized parishes, a liberalized school system, and representation in the Cortes. Copies of these papers were surreptitiously distributed in Manila through such *reformadores* as Burgos, who was in communication with Regidor and Lerena, and Jose Basa, Lerena's brother-in-law. The students Buencamino, Sancianco, and Paciano Rizal, helped distribute the papers by concealing copies in bundles of grass and posing as *zacateros* (peddlers of fodder).[131]

For the first time, a reform movement emerged that cut across sectoral and racial lines. Two streams of liberalism intersected. One gravitated around Spanish and creole elements in the colony, espousing pro-gressivist Enlightenment principles, often anti-clerical but "patriotic" in their adherence to a modern, reform-minded Spain. The other was a "native" stream of indigenes and Chinese mestizos who shared the reformist principles of progressive Spaniards but were more inward-oriented in their aspirations. It was a wider, more coherent movement than the political actions of 1813–1822, and while it remained assimilationist in its aims it was anchored on a more widely shared, if still inchoate sense of "national" community.

Expectations ran high. De la Torre set up commissions to propose reforms in the colony. In 1870, Overseas Minister Segismundo Moret issued decrees aimed at secularizing Philippine education. Santo Tomas was to be renamed *Universidad de Filipinas* and placed under state su-pervision, and the principal secondary schools (Ateneo, San Jose, and Letran) were to be merged as one body called *Instituto Filipino*. In late 1869, anonymous anti-friar leaflets (*pasquin*) appeared on the campus of Santo Tomas as a group called *Juventud Escolar Liberal* criticized anti-quated instructional methods and called for the use of Spanish instead of Latin as medium of instruction. The disturbance caused the impris-onment of student leader Felipe Buencamino and the arrest of others, including parents of students.[132]

The fall of the Moret ministry and replacement of de la Torre as governor in 1871 unleashed the forces of reaction. The new governor, Rafael Izquierdo, reversed the liberal initiatives of his predecessor and clamped down on the circulation of Spanish liberal papers.

On January 20, 1872, a mutiny of soldiers and workers in the arse-nal of Cavite, over what appears to be work-related grievances, was seized upon by the authorities as part of a vast revolutionary conspiracy. All kinds of rumors spread, including talk that two ships flying foreign flags were coming with smuggled arms. Reformers were portrayed as separat-ists and subjected to house searches, arrested, banished, or executed. The crackdown climaxed with the public garroting, on February 17, 1872, of the three priests, Jose Burgos, Mariano Gomez, and Jacinto

Zamora. The deportation of leading *reformadores* virtually decapitated the reform movement.

An obscure episode in the campaign of repression was the wholesale arrest of the Cavite company of *Guias de la Provincia* (state-authorized rural guards) under Casimiro Camerino, who was executed by garrote nine days before the execution of Burgos, Gomez and Zamora. Twenty-two of his men were sentenced to ten-year prison terms. In his chronicle of the events of 1872, Manuel Artigas cites the Camerino episode as part of the "agrarian issue" that, he says, was one of the roots of the reform movement. Artigas, however, disclaims any actual link between the *reformadores* and such groups as the Cavite arsenal workers or Imus Hacienda peasants.[133] That a link existed is intriguing because Cavite was a seedbed of rural unrest close to Manila. In the mid-1860s, Camerino was a peasant rebel whose activities wreaked havoc on the Recollect-owned Imus Hacienda and won him a following among peasants. After he surrendered on August 15, 1869, under an amnesty program introduced by de la Torre, Camerino and his men were integrated into the *Guias de la Provincia*. The martyred Mariano Gomez (1799–1872), long-time parish priest of Bacoor in Cavite, must have known Camerino. As early as the agrarian uprising of Cavite in the 1820s, Gomez was an active mediator in the grant of amnesty to peasant rebels in the province.[134]

The authorities imagined (or anticipated) a much broader rebellion that included not only soldiers and workers in the Cavite arsenal but restive rural elements. Government ordered all provinces to concentrate military forces and mobilize volunteer militias. In Cebu, where news of the mutiny arrived only when a Belgian naval corvette called on the city, things were quiet. Artigas wrote that "the people in Cebu did not understand what took place in Manila nor know the events in Kawit." "There was no report of public disorder in Cebu nor in the other provinces of the Archipelago."[135] Yet, it was clear that the situation was far from stable. There were outbreaks late in 1872 in places like Pampanga and Zamboanga. In 1884, the arrest of prominent citizens in Santa Maria, Pangasinan, after they complained about being harassed for not paying their tributes on time, triggered rumors of an uprising. The friars reportedly seized upon the disturbance to instigate arrests of known liberals in Manila and several provinces. Among those arrested were Felipe Buencamino and Gregorio Sancianco, and the father, brother, and uncle of Antonio and Juan Luna (the uncle, Andres Novicio, was named leader of the conspiracy). Buencamino wrote that there were "more than 1,700" of them brought to Lingayen, Pangasinan, for detention.[136]

The colonial order had cracked and the momentum for change could not be stopped. As governor-general Izquierdo wrote to the Overseas Minister in 1872: "Today the *Indios* are not what they once were."[137] The generation of 1872 did not only remain active in the years that followed, they sired a new crop of leaders in a remarkable pattern of succession. The connections are multistranded. Rizal, Paterno, Pardo, and M.H. del Pilar had parents and elders who were involved in the events of 1872. Rizal remarked on this fact of intellectual descent when he said in 1889: "Without 1872 there would not now be a Plaridel, a Jaena, a Sanciangco, nor would the brave and generous Filipino colonies exist in Europe." He warned: "Before the catastrophe of 1872 there were fewer thinkers, fewer anti-friars. They sacrificed innocent victims and now you have the youth, women, girls, embracing the same cause. Let the hecatomb be repeated and the executioners shall have sealed their own sentence."[138]

UNTIL 1872, reformist activities were creole-led, class-based, assimilationist, and opportunistic. A deeper drama was played out in the folk and popular uprisings that made of the Spanish era a state of almost permanent insurrection. These were, however, localized revolts that, at best, aimed at creating ethnic kingdoms rather than a modern nation. In spite of such intriguing signs as the Pule revolt and Camerino episode, folk rebellion and urban reformism were parallel rather than interconnected phenomena.

After 1872, a "national" movement began to emerge. The change is shown in the career of Marcelo H. del Pilar (1850–1896). In 1872, del Pilar was a law student in Santo Tomas though he does not seem to have taken part in *Juventud Escolar Liberal.* He entered Santo Tomas in 1866 after his secondary studies at San Juan de Letran; earned a bachelor's degree in 1871 and enrolled in Law in the same year. Though little is known of his activities he lived close to the events. Born in Bulacan to a family with roots in old Tagalog nobility, del Pilar was of the native literati: his father Julian was a grammarian-poet and thrice-*gobernadorcillo* of Bulacan and his uncle Alejo (for whom Marcelo worked as *escribano* in

Quiapo) was a noted *awit*-writer. His elder brother Toribio was a priest associated with Burgos in the secularization campaign and one of those deported to the Marianas in 1872. At Letran, his teacher was Mamerto Natividad, a member of *Comite de Reformadores*. In Manila, Marcelo reportedly lived with Fr. Mariano Sevilla, another Burgos associate and Marianas *deportado*. On February 16, 1871, Burgos himself, in one of his last official acts as member of the Santo Tomas faculty, presided over the examination Marcelo took to earn his bachelor's degree.[139]

Mariano Ponce related that as a high school student, he was already one of those who gathered around del Pilar to listen to his political ideas. It is said that del Pilar participated in meetings of the *reformadores* although he escaped notice and prosecution in the aftermath of the Cavite Mutiny. The events of 1872 left del Pilar shaken. He skipped school through much of 1872–1876 and, sometime in this period, spent thirty days in jail after he engaged a priest in a quarrel over arbitrary church fees. He, however, resumed his studies and earned his licentiate in law in 1881.

The reprisals ushered in a new phase in the reform movement. More young Filipinos left the country for Europe where they pursued their studies and pushed the reform movement forward. Oppositional work remained alive in the colony. Much of this took place outside public notice and has not been closely looked at but we have clues from del Pilar's activities. In 1882, the Tagalog-Spanish *Diariong Tagalog* was founded, ostensibly by peninsular official Francisco Calvo but it was actually run by del Pilar with the help of Basilio Teodoro, a member of *Juventud Escolar Liberal*. The paper lasted less than a year but among the items it published was "El Amor Patrio" (August 20, 1882), contributed by Rizal, newly arrived in Spain, indicating transoceanic contact among a new generation of reformers. Addressed to Filipinos, with the events of 1872 lurking in its subtext, the article affirms *amor patrio*, "the most heroic and sublime of all loves," as one to which one can dedicate one's life and death. Vivid in its invocation of the "tenacious ghost" of home, it is less so in its final statement about how *amor patrio* now calls not for violence or fanaticism but for the native son to follow "the arid but peaceful and productive paths of Science which lead to Progress."[140]

For his part, del Pilar was already engaged in more daring tasks. A vigorous polemicist, he used all opportunities, like fiestas and funeral wakes, to spread liberal, anti-friar ideas. In Malolos, he ran the local cockpit where he propagandized among those who frequented it. Using multiple connections (kinship, occupational, personal), he mobilized the entire Malolos *principalia* in asserting its rights over the town friar. By 1885, this group had grown strong enough to challenge the friar-*cura* for control of the town's affairs. Linked to Manila *progresistas* as well as reform-minded individuals in other parts of the province, they held clandestine meetings in private houses and the local town hall, coordinated protest actions, and circulated propaganda materials. As center of reformist activities, Malolos "was undoubtedly one of the best organized and effective in the entire archipelago."[141]

Others helped prime the ground for another bold public challenge against the colonial authorities. As in 1869–1872, the opportunity was presented by the ascension in Spain of a new liberal regime that named the Mason Emilio Terrero as governor-general in 1885. The 1880s saw initiatives to strengthen the colonial state. These included the abolition of the tobacco monopoly in 1884, the introduction of a uniform system of personal taxation in 1885 (which abolished the racial and class distinctions of the old tribute system), and the extension to the colony of the Spanish Penal Code in 1887. The moves to strengthen the state, joined to anti-clerical sentiments in Spanish officialdom, created church-state conflicts over jurisdiction and, more importantly, opportunities for Filipinos to exploit the breach and openly advocate reforms. In 1887, the appointment of the Masons Jose Centeno and Benigno Quiroga as Manila civil governor and director of civil administration, respectively, sparked a year of clashes between civil and religious authorities.

As in 1869–1872, Spanish liberals in the peninsula contributed to the agitation. This time, however, Filipino expatriates played the primary role in the debate. A pioneering figure was Gregorio Sancianco (1851–1897). A Tagalog-Chinese mestizo, he was part of *Juventud Escolar Liberal* in 1872 but escaped persecution when he left for Spain after the Cavite Mutiny. He earned a doctorate in civil and canon law in Spain and wrote *Progreso de Filipinas* (1881), a scholarly treatise on economic policies needed to stimulate progress in the Philippines.[142] Addressed to the government and Filipino property owners, it is "assimilationist" in its position but at the same time an angry, well-reasoned rebuttal of the claimed inferiority of the *indio*, with Sancianco declaring himself "as native as those" who have been impugned by ignorant authors. Within months of his return to the Philippines, he was imprisoned for alleged complicity in the Pangasinan "rebellion" of 1884. Released after several months, he served as judge in Nueva Ecija and Pangasinan, hounded by trouble until his death in Nueva Ecija on November 17, 1897, when revolutionary hostilities had began in that province.[143]

The situation in Manila came to a boil when Rizal returned to the Philippines on August 5, 1887. Rizal had just published *Noli me tangere* (1887) which the church declared "heretical, anti-patriotic, and subversive" on August 30 and the *Comision permanente de censura* banned shortly after. The publication of *Noli me tangere* was a pivotal moment in Philippine intellectual history. John Schumacher writes: "Until 1887, the Filipinos had assailed the colonial administration and the predominance of the friars in the Philippines in a sporadic, unorganized, and more or less veiled manner."[144] No work before it had so directly, fully, and effectively engaged colonial power in the country. It was radically seditious in having been written by a native in a manner that actualizes, in Europe's own discursive form, the capacity of the *Filipino* to comprehend, represent, and hence direct his own society.

Written in Spanish, published in a print run of 2,000 copies in Germany, stymied by distribution problems, banned and confiscated— not many in the Philippines read the novel in the year after it came out. In a generous estimate Leon Ma. Guerrero says that not more than a thousand copies may have reached Filipino readers in Rizal's lifetime.[145] Yet, out of sight, people recognized its importance. What effect it had at the time of its appearance owes a lot to the fact that there was a readiness for it that goes back, at least, to 1872 and what happened in the colony in Rizal's absence. Manila was in a state of agitation when Rizal came home. Men like del Pilar worked under and above ground to spread liberal ideas. The secular-minded *La Opinion* (1887–1890)—before the editorship was taken over by Wenceslao Retana in 1889—tussled with pro-friar papers like *La España Oriental* (1888–1889) and *La Voz Española* (1891–1893).

Fearing arrest, pressured by family and friends, Rizal left the country in February 1888. Days later, the popular demonstration of 1888 took place. On March 1, some 300 demonstrators marched through the streets of Manila to the office of governor Centeno and submitted to him for transmittal to the Crown a printed manifesto that petitioned

Queen Regent Maria Cristina for the transfer of Archbishop Pedro Payo, suppression of the religious orders, and secularization of parishes. Written in impeccable Spanish, assuming the highminded stance of reason and respect for the Crown, the manifesto blamed the friars for fomenting instability by willfully manipulating the law and obstructing progress. Disclaiming any separatist aspiration, the petitioners accused the friars of treason for driving a wedge between the people and the Crown. Friars denigrated the native clergy, accusing them of "consecrating host made of rice flour," invoking Darwin to make them out to be descendants of the monkey. They denounced as subversives citizens who tried to bring the Enlightenment to the colony. "It is enough to be a man of science, of letters, or speak at least Spanish, to be considered a *filibustero*."[146]

The unprecedented anti-friar demonstration shook the authorities. Reaction was swift. Terrero's term, which expired in April, was not extended. Centeno was forced to resign and Quiroga stayed in office only a few months more. *La Opinion* was forced to close shop. Leading citizens were imprisoned and more were persecuted in the years that followed.

The momentum for change could not be stopped. Though the 1888 demonstration focused on friar rule it signified a much wider base of discontent. It was more broadly based than the manifestation of 1872. The 810 manifesto signatories—indios and mestizos from districts in greater Manila—identified themselves as "proprietors, merchants, industrialists, lawyers, and residents." The leader was Doroteo Cortes, a Chinese-Filipino lawyer who had served as *gobernadorcillo* in Santa Cruz. Spanish authorities suspected that the real author of the manifesto was either del Pilar or the businessman-mason Jose Ramos. Loath to assign any credit to natives, Retana believed that Cortes was just an *amanuense* and the real author was Centeno. Examining the signatories, Retana debunked the manifesto by saying that 218 of the 810 signatories were fictitious, deceased, underaged, or did not know what they had signed, and that the rest (592) were "fodder cutters, scribes, laborers, fishermen, carpenters, tailors," 384 of whom "do not know Spanish."[147] Yet, from the data he presents, Retana chose not to highlight the fact that 305 of the 592 signatories were past or present *cabezas de barangay* and eighteen were or had been *gobernadorcillos*. While Retana was contemptuous of the social types represented, it is clear that the rural gentry and urban bourgeoisie of greater Manila were well represented.

The Manila petitioners expressed the grievances of Filipinos elsewhere in the country, as indicated in the case of Calamba and Malolos. In Calamba, the town gentry feuded with the Dominican owners of the Calamba hacienda, the largest in Laguna, over rent and ownership. This escalated after Rizal (whose family was one of the hacienda's biggest leaseholders) helped Calambeños draw up a petition addressed to the government on January 8, 1888.[148] In Malolos, the crackdown after the 1888 demonstration did not deter twenty young women of the local elite from boldly presenting to the new governor-general, Valeriano Weyler, visiting the town on December 12, 1888, a signed petition seeking permission to open a school where they could learn Spanish under a professor they would themselves hire. While it all seemed harmless (an article lauded them for aspiring to be model "Spanish women"), it was clearly meant to defy the wishes of the local friar and demonstrate the women's—and "Filipino'"—readiness to take their education into their own hands.[149] Calamba and Malolos were punished for their show of autonomy. On September 6, 1890, troops entered Calamba and evicted about thirty families (including Rizal's family); by the beginning of 1891 forty heads of families had been deported and 300 families left landless and destitute. On May 15, 1895, the governor-general deported to Mindanao the entire municipal council of Malolos, together with other prominent citizens, on the charge that they were engaged in Masonic activities.

Despite the reform movement's setback in 1888, intellectuals were convinced that historical change was inevitable. A new power had accumulated and it was not a question of whether change would take place but who would stand at its head and shape it. T.H. Pardo de Tavera was sojourning in Manila as a government-sponsored scientist when the demonstration of 1888 took place. Disturbed by the events, a somber Pardo returned to Paris telling friends he was convinced the colony was headed for a revolution. Rizal wrote at the time: "There is no example whatever in history that says that a people in the process of enlightenment can be made to go backward."[150]

THE SENSE that the future is astir is voiced by the old rural sage Tasio in Rizal's *Noli me tangere* (1887). Tasio admitted to a friend that "the country today is no longer the same as it was twenty years ago." Though colonial

450

education is mired in narrow scholasticism, young men have been stirred by new ideas. No longer will you find, he said, "the metaphysical youth of our own times, with prehistoric learning, who, with brains tortured, died philosophizing in some provincial nook without beginning to understand the attributes of being, without resolving the matter of essence and existence, pretentious concepts which have made us forget what is essential, our own existence and proper self." "Look at the child of today: full of enthusiasm at the sight of broader horizons, he studies History, Mathematics, Geography, Physics, Literature, Physical Sciences, Languages—all subjects which we in our own time listened to with horror as if they were heresies."

> Choke Progress, the potent offspring of Time and Action? When was Progress ever choked? Dogma, the gallows and the bonfires, in trying to stifle it, pushed it. "*E pur si muove;* nevertheless it moves," said Galileo when the Dominicans obliged him to declare the earth did not move; the same phrase can be applied to human progress. Some wills may suffer violence, some individuals may be sacrificed, but it does not matter: Progress will follow its course and from the blood of those who fall now, vigorous shoots will sprout.[151]

No decade in Philippine intellectual history has been as productive and consequential as the 1880s. This period saw the appearance of Rizal's novels, *Noli me tangere* (1887) and *El Filibusterismo* (1891), and his critical edition of Morga's *Sucesos de las Islas Filipinas* (1890); the books of Paterno, Pardo de Tavera, and de los Reyes; del Pilar's *La Soberania Monacal en Filipinas* (1889) and *La Frailocracia Filipina* (1889), Lopez Jaena's *Discursos y Articulos Varios* (1891), and an important mass of periodical and ephemeral literature. In 1889, Filipinos launched, in the center of the empire, that remarkable document of anti-colonial literature, *La Solidaridad* (1889–1895). As Rizal declared in 1884, speaking at the banquet honoring the artists Juan Luna and Felix Resurreccion Hidalgo in Madrid: "The patriarchal era in the Philippines is waning . . . The Oriental chrysalis is leaving the cocoon."[152]

Though connected by a sense of a shared undertaking, intellectuals pursued their work independently of each other. It was Rizal who had the clearest sense that they constituted a distinct and strategic formation, defined not by ethnicity, race, or class but a "nationality" standing in opposition to imperial power.

Rizal saw the importance of a national discourse and repeatedly urged Filipinos to "buy books by Filipinos; mention now and then names of Filipinos like [Pedro] Pelaez, [Vicente] Garcia, [Jose] Burgos, Graciano [Lopez Jaena], etc.; quote their phrases." He told Mariano Ponce: "Try in every number [of *Solidaridad*] to speak of some ancient or modern Filipino, and to cite their works . . . Cite Pilapil, Pelaez, Burgos, etc., etc." Commending M.H. del Pilar for his articles, he reminded del Pilar that "only, when you cite the names of Filipinos you have forgotten much more deserving ones, such as Pelaez, Burgos, Garcia, Jugo, etc." Thanking Filipino priest Vicente Garcia for his defense of *Noli me tangere*, he wrote: "We have had very great intellects, we have had a Pinpin, a Dr. Pilapil, a Father Pelaez, a Father Mariano Garcia, a Dr. Joson [pharmacist Feliciano Jocson], etc." "We have to bring forward our first ranks," Rizal repeatedly urged, so that Filipinos may be better known. Resurrecting the earliest examples of local intellectual accomplishments, Rizal even invoked the obscure, seventeenth-century Marcelo Banal as a "great organist, choirmaster" who composed many choral books.[153] While Rizal had his preferences, he imagined an inclusive formation that harked back to Pinpin and Pilapil and included creoles, mestizos, and indios, and a mix of professions and vocations.

What Rizal wished to make visible was a formation of Filipino intellectuals staking out their claim over knowledge and its enabling power, exercising intellectual authority over their country. In 1884, Rizal already proposed that members of *Circulo Hispano-Filipino* in Spain collaborate to produce a collection of essays on the Philippines. He dreamed of being a professor in the home country where he "would stimulate these Philippine studies which are like the *nosce te ipsum* [know thyself] that gives the true concept of one's self and drives nations to do great things."[154] And in 1889 he took the bold, unprecedented step of initiating *Association Internationale des Philippinestes*. Its aim, as drafted by Rizal, was to gather Filipino and non-Filipino scholars "to study the Philippines from the historic and scientific point of view" through such projects as conferences, competitions, and the establishment of a Philippine library and museum. He proposed an international roster of officers, with the Austrian Ferdinand Blumentritt as president, Frenchman

Edmund Plauchut as vice-president, and Anglo-German Reinhold Rost, Filipino-Spanish Antonio Regidor, German Adolf Meyer, and Dutch J.G.F. Riedel, as counselors. Rizal (calling himself *malayo-tagalo*) offered to serve as secretary.

It was planned to have the first "international congress" on the Philippines in Paris to coincide with the Paris International Exposition in August 1889. For this purpose, Rizal drew up a program that covered a wide range of historical and ethnological topics. The core was history, with Rizal dividing Philippine history into three broad periods: the precolonial era, the period from 1521 to "the loss of Philippine autonomy and her incorporation in the Spanish nation" in 1808 (referring to the first time the Philippines was granted representation in the Spanish Cortes), and the period from 1808 to the Cavite Mutiny in 1872.[155]

The conference (and the association) did not push through due to logistical and other reasons but it is clear what Rizal was about. He wanted to create a "voice or authority" apart from the colonial power (as he indicated in the preface to Morga's *Sucesos*, which he published at this time). He recognized the contributions of foreign scholars in this endeavor but repeatedly stressed that Filipinos themselves, mainly and ultimately, had to assume authority over their own country. Addressing Filipinos in Barcelona in 1889, he said: "It is necessary that you study the questions that concern our country. Knowledge of a thing prepares for its mastery: knowledge is power. We are the only ones who can acquire a perfect knowledge of our country because we know both languages [the Spanish and the local] and besides we are informed of the secrets of the people among whom we had been raised."[156]

It was M.H. del Pilar who gave Rizal's vision a political organization. On October 31, 1888, fearing arrest, del Pilar hurriedly left for Spain. Before he left he made plans to continue the struggle. As early as 1885, del Pilar, with his associate Mariano Ponce, had formed a group with a religious name, *Caja de Jesus, Maria y Jose*, purportedly to raise money to support bright but indigent students. Whether this was indeed what it was about, it was quickly transformed, on the eve of del Pilar's flight, into what was called *La Propaganda* or *Comite de Propaganda*, which aimed to finance and distribute liberal, anti-friar propaganda. Principal members were Doroteo Cortes (lawyer), Deodato Arellano (army armory clerk), Numeriano Adriano (clerk and notary),

Timoteo Paez (shipping clerk), Pedro Serrano (teacher), Mariano Crisostomo (lawyer), Mamerto Natividad (lawyer), Ambrosio Rianzares Bautista (lawyer), Basilio Teodoro (journalist), and Jose Ramos (businessman).[157]

An examination of the lives of these men shows how people were mobilized and ideas circulated in the colony. Natividad was del Pilar's teacher in Letran and, with Rianzares Bautista, a member of the 1872 *Comite de Reformadores*. Teodoro was from Malolos, a member of *Juventud Escolar Liberal* in 1872 and del Pilar's associate in *Diariong Tagalog*. Adriano met del Pilar while he was working as a clerk of court; he had his notarial office in a building that may have been owned by Cortes. As clerk of court, Adriano's assistant was Apolinario Mabini who would later emerge as the principal ideologue of the revolution. Crisostomo, another clerk of court, was del Pilar's nephew and apprenticed in his law office. Arellano was del Pilar's brother-in-law and had as a helper in distributing propaganda materials the young Gregorio del Pilar, Marcelo's nephew, who would become a revolutionary general. Serrano came from the same Bulacan village as Marcelo. These men participated in the anti-friar demonstration of 1888, joined Masonic lodges, and were variously involved in the *Liga Filipina* organized by Rizal in 1892, the *Katipunan* founded in 1892, the *Cuerpo de Compromisarios* formed in 1894, and the revolution that broke out in 1896. There were tensions as these groups evolved and shifted but there was remarkable consistency in the personalities and social types involved.

Del Pilar envisioned staying in Spain for a few years to organize the campaign for reforms there and then return to continue the struggle in the Philippines. He already had his "advance party" in Spain in fellow Bulaqueño Mariano Ponce to whom he had been sending articles for publication in Spanish newspapers. (Ponce studied at Letran and Santo Tomas before he left in June 1887 for Spain where he earned a medical degree at Universidad Central de Madrid.) Even while in transit to Spain del Pilar furiously worked on propaganda materials addressed to people at home. These were printed in Barcelona when he arrived in early January 1889 and copies sent to the Philippines for distribution. The same or similar materials were also printed in Hong Kong and smuggled to the Philippines. Transiting in Hong Kong, del Pilar had conferred with Jose Basa, a Marianas *deportado* who had established residence in the

British colony where he acted as key overseas link in Filipino propaganda activities.

These materials included del Pilar's *Dasalan at Tocsohan* (1888), *Pasyong Dapat Ipag-alab nang Puso nang Tauong Babasa sa Kalupitan nang Fraile* (1888), *Sagot nang España sa Hibik nang Filipinas* (1889), and *Arancel de los Derechos Parroquiales* (1889). These works signified a distinct aspect of nationalist writing. Del Pilar wrote in Tagalog and addressed Filipinos in a manner the likes of Rizal, Paterno, and Pardo did not. He carried folk genres (*duplo, dalit*) and colonial religious forms (*catecismo, pasyon*) beyond what Baltazar and de la Merced attempted with these genres by deploying them for overtly political ends. Mining familial sentiments and indigenous antiphonal poetry in *Sagot nang España sa Hibik nang Filipinas*, del Pilar expresses political ideas hitherto unheard in this type of poetry. Similarly, he appropriates the *pasyon* in *Pasiong Dapat Ipag-alab nang Puso* and the catechism in *Dasalan at Toksohan* as vehicles of anti-clerical propaganda. A provocateur with a feel for the public nerve, he even translated to Tagalog the official Church schedule of stole fees for services like baptisms and funerals, *Arancel de los Derechos Parroquiales*, to stoke public indignation over commercialized religion. Printed as small-size *libritos* (like Catholic novenas), or circulated in oral and manuscript form, del Pilar's verses break away from the formal refinement and lachrymose mode of "learned" Tagalog poetry. Epifanio de los Santos writes of del Pilar's poems:

[T]hey purge Tagalog literature of a literary mannerism of long standing, invigorating it with purely popular elements, indigenous to the soil, and endowing it with harmony, number, and measure characteristic of the Tagalog tongue, to the extent that the acidity and mordant wit of the roguish sentences convert the very dung into earth from which springs the beautiful *camantigue*.[158]

Del Pilar's writings tapped into a living tradition. Teodoro Agoncillo writes: "Rizal spoke from the pulpit; del Pilar spoke in the cockpit."[159] Locating the works of del Pilar in a stream of Tagalog poetry that goes back to Baltazar, Epifanio de los Santos writes that the "revolutionary pamphlets and catechisms" of the period 1888–1895 "added greater luster to the glory of the rich Tagalog tongue and the essays of that epoch seemed to Rizal himself models of Tagalog satire and grace; in fact, the language was created and established in this sense."[160] This literary underground has not been adequately studied. The patriotic poetry and revolutionary songs that have been preserved from the 1890s and 1900s indicate that popular intellectuals, now mostly anonymous, were active even at an earlier period.

Del Pilar's presence in Spain was a catalyst in the advance of the propaganda movement. Filipinos in Spain were active in cultural and political propaganda since 1880 but their activities were individual and sporadic. Attempts were made in coordinating these activities, as in the formation of *Circulo Hispano-Filipino* in 1882 under the leadership of Juan Atayde; Rizal's aborted project in 1884 to get the expatriates to publish a collective work to make the Philippines better known to the world; and the launching in Madrid of the newspaper *España en Filipinas* on March 7, 1887. These did not gain much headway. *Circulo Hispano-Filipino* was "little more than a social club" and its *Revista del Circulo Hispano-Filipino* (1882) lasted less than a year. *España en Filipinas* collapsed in a matter of months. Leadership was a problem. Rizal was too focused on his own work to be an organizer. Graciano Lopez Jaena, one of the most politically active Filipinos in Spain, was notoriously unreliable. Pardo stayed at the margins of the movement and Paterno was in a world of his own.

The founding of *La Solidaridad* (1889–1895) was a turning point. It provided Filipinos a medium for expressing their collective aspirations and the symbol of a "movement," with what this implies of numbers and a shared identity, form, and purpose. Declaring its commitment to democracy and progress, *Solidaridad* aimed to air liberal ideas in politics, science, arts, commerce, and other fields in so far as these concerned Spanish "overseas provinces" (Cuba, Puerto Rico) and, in particular, the Philippines.[161] Its international outlook is shown in its articles on European and Latin American politics. It lists correspondents in places like Havana, New York, and Saigon. Mainly addressing the colonial power, Spain, it was a major vehicle of Filipino *ilustrado* thought.

Mariano Ponce had a key role in preparing the ground for the paper.[162] He was in communication with del Pilar and other reformers in Manila on plans to either revive *España en Filipinas* (which ceased publication on July 7, 1887) or start a new paper. He was involved in organizing the Filipino association in Barcelona called *La Solidaridad* on January 1, 1889, apparently an effort to mobilize support for the new paper. Del Pilar's arrival in Barcelona in January hastened the appearance of the paper on February 15, 1889 with Lopez Jaena as editor and Ponce as business manager. With Ponce, del Pilar played the main role in sustaining the paper, writing for it, soliciting contributions, and drumming up financial support in Spain and the Philippines. When the paper moved from Barcelona to Madrid in November 1889, he took over as editor.

Solidaridad was envisioned as part of a multi-pronged program of political action that included *Asociacion Hispano-Filipina*, founded on January 12, 1889, as forum for building alliances with progressive Spanish intellectuals and politicians, and the *Comite de Propaganda* in Manila. Masonic lodges played a supportive role as nodes of recruitment, training, and communication. They cultivated alliances with Spanish Masons in the metropolis, contributed money to propaganda work, and served as distributing points for propaganda materials. Del Pilar and Ponce were at the core of these activities: they represented the Manila *Comite*, ran *Solidaridad*, staffed *Asociacion Hispano-Filipina*, and were active Masons.

Comite may have been responsible for the large number of anti-friar broadsides or *proclamas* that circulated in Manila and neighboring provinces in the 1880s. Materials smuggled in from Spain were shipped via Singapore or Hong Kong to a Chinese house on Plaza Jolo in Manila and distributed from there. Another distributing center was "La Gran Bretaña" bazaar in Intramuros owned by *Comite* member Jose Ramos, a London-educated Mason. Ramos, who owned a printing press, wrote and printed anonymous anti-friar broadsides that were secretly distributed on the streets or left at doors of houses. He is said to have been involved as well in Pascual Poblete's *El Resumen* (1890–1892), a paper with "nationalist" tendencies, and *Amigo del Pueblo* (1893), a paper Spaniards mocked as "*Le Petit Marat.*" Reference is made to issues of *Solidaridad* being reprinted in an *imprentilla clandestina* in Nueva Ecija. Isabelo de los Reyes himself was tagged around 1890 as the author of anonymous, pro-reform handbills that provoked the anti-*indio* Camilo Millan, *La España Oriental* editor, to launch vicious attacks against natives.[163]

It appears that *Comite* did not extend too far beyond greater Manila and provincial centers like Malolos. As in 1813–1823, 1868–1872, and 1885–1888, reformist activities remained bourgeois in composition and aims. What is remarkable nevertheless is the extent to which the various strands of earlier reformist activities came together in a relatively coordinated and self-consciously *Filipino* political movement. Earlier activities had either been issue-oriented (the rights of the native clergy) or race-based (creole patriotism). But with what is properly called the "Propaganda Movement"—which, if one must mark a beginning, began with the formation of the *Comite de Propaganda* in 1888—domestic racial categories (indio, mestizo, creole) were subsumed under the identity of *Filipino* and various issues encompassed by the goal of emancipation (which if expressed in "autonomist" terms was one that opened out to other possibilities).

THE CONTEST over authority is shown in the Spanish reaction to Filipino dissent. Examples are the anonymously published *Filipinas ante la razon del indio* (1874) and Franciscan Miguel Lucio's didactic novel *Si Tandang Basio Macunat* (1885), both of which pretend to convey the views of enlightened and "patriotic" indios.[164] Written in response to the clamor for better education, *Tandang Basio Macunat* attacked natives for seeking an education not proper to their race and status. Authored by the Augustinian Casimiro Herrero, *Filipinas ante la razon* was even more vituperative. It deploys a fictional indigene called "Capitan Juan" who visits Manila in 1871 and is distressed by unrest in the capital over issues of "liberty, equality and individual rights." Concerned that this threatened the benefits Spain brought to the islands, he writes a treatise on the "true" meanings of liberty, equality and fraternity; attacks the "monstrous" distortion of these ideas by Lutheranism, evolutionism, socialism, and the French Revolution; and defends the legitimacy of Spanish domination. In a catechism-style primer ("*Catecismo racional y social para la utilidad de los indios*"), the book characterizes what Filipinos amounted to without Spain: indigenous religion was "an ensemble of ridiculous superstitions," indigenous government was "absolutist and tyrannical," what the precolonial Filipinos had of culture, wealth, and liberty was "what the Manobos of Mindanao and the hillfolk of the Caraballo have today," that Filipinos have advanced only because of "the mercy of God and the coming of the Spaniards."[165]

Comision permanente de censura (the same body that censored Cervantes) judged *Filipinas ante la razon* "excellent" and earnestly recommended its circulation. Thousands of copies were to be distributed "freely and profusely" but the authorities came to their senses and restricted the book's circulation to the religious communities, fearing it would inflame Filipinos.[166]

A basic theme in the attack against natives was the racist denigration of their mental and moral abilities. Natives are biologically deficient in the abstract and philosophical forms of knowledge, it was argued. They are adept only in mimetic, mechanical skills and hence make fine clerks, bookkeepers, musicians, embroiders, and cobblers. "They are capable of imitating the most curious works but they can invent nothing, for they lack imagination and fancy, and are very obtuse in the abstract sciences because they lack understanding." Thus, an Augustinian questions the investments being made in higher education, asking: "How many scientific notabilities have resulted from the natives up to the present from the university cloisters? How many Indian theologues, canons, philosophers, moralists [have graduated] from the conciliar seminaries?" Not one, he replies, except for some mediocre canon, lawyer, pharmacist, or physician. "What does this signify," he concludes, "if not that the deficiency exists in the race, and not in the professors or in the books." Raising the race issue even more pointedly, he says that if the native does attain some intellectual distinction it is because he is a mestizo and "it must be because another blood inoculates in his own blood the divine breath of wisdom" that he "advances somewhat when the cross whitens his olive-colored face, has lowered his prominent cheekbones, and elevated his flat nose a trifle."[167]

It was in this context that Filipino reformists were typically named in the derisive diminutive as *politiquillos*, *ilustradillos*, *abogadillos*, or *mediquillos*. Spaniards blamed native resistance on deficient, misguided, and warped native minds. Education has produced *filosofos*, "no more than ignorant and presuming fellows, pettifoggers, intriguers," who, arrogant in their shallow learning, have turned towns into "a workshop of intrigue, and give a numerous contingent to the [Masonic] lodges and to separatism."[168]

A siege mentality infected the religious corporations. A Dominican warned: "Liberalism is invading us. Secularization is approaching with gigantic steps." The Santo Tomas rector reportedly declared that "medicine and the natural sciences are materialistic and impious studies," and when a Filipino student proposed a thesis on economic reasoning he was warned that political economy was a "science of the devil."[169] The religious orders, however, responded to counter-claims of authority at the level of institutional change and scholarly discourse and not just scurrilous propaganda. A confidential report for the Dominican Provincial Chapter of 1886 urged the adoption of the "accidental variations of the century" to offset the challenge of secularization. It recommended, among others, that Santo Tomas offer courses of higher mathematics, upgrade its library and laboratories, hire better trained science professors, and publish a scientific-literary journal for studies in medicine, pharmacy, law and literature. Long tied to a medieval curriculum of philosophy, theology, and canon law, Santo Tomas expanded to include faculties of Medicine and Pharmacy (1871), Notary Public (1878), Philosophy and Letters (1896), and Sciences (1896). It also opened schools for midwives (*matronas*) and medical aides (*practicantes*) in 1877 and 1879, respectively.[170]

The contentious mood of the times is indicated in the lectures that opened the academic year at Santo Tomas. Themes of harmonizing science and religion, the dangers of positivism, and the role of Thomism as answer to the errors of the age run through these discourses. Started in 1866, these *discursos de apertura* featured Dominican professors (it was not until 1907 that the series began to have lay speakers) and took the character of Catholic apologetics against the threat of philosophies like rationalism, utilitarianism, and materialism.[171] Examples are the lectures by Manuel Puebla ("Catholic instruction is the only sure and easy way for scientific progress in all its forms," 1872), Jose Garcia Navacerrada ("The great advantage of Christian principles over rationalist principles concerning the fundamental problems of philosophical science," 1879), Evaristo Fernandez Arias ("The doctrine of positivism is absurd and anti-scientific because its principles contradict sound reason and deny the sources of all science," 1885), and Gabriel Martin Tembleque ("Theology is the only science that offers a firm and sure solution to the great philosophical and social problems," 1893). In the 1901 lecture, professor Florencio Llanos, reporting on a scientific conference in Cambridge, said that the discovery in 1891 of the *Pithecanthropus erectus* ("Java man") by Dutch physician Eugene Dubois has not proved the theory of human evolution. Llanos praised modern science while (an unfriendly observer writes)

460

"wiping Darwin, Haeckel, and other such men off the slate with quotations from the Bible and the saints of the church."[172]

These were skirmishes in the wider battle the Catholic Church waged against a European Enlightenment that, particularly in the work of the French Encyclopedists, took a decidedly anti-Catholic cast. Catholic apologists confronted intellectual trends that exalted the powers of science and reason and rejected the traditions of truth represented by the Church. Pope Gregory XVI rejected Liberalism in 1832; Pius IX's *Syllabus* condemned all errors arising from Enlightenment philosophies; and in 1870 Vatican Council I censured rationalism, pantheism, and naturalism. To establish a philosophical basis for defending the order on which the Church was built, the philosophy of St. Thomas Aquinas was revived and promoted under the name Neo-Scholasticism or Neo-Thomism. Far from being a closed, medieval system, it was argued, Catholicism was a tradition of thought capable of renewing itself and assimilating modern science.

It is not surprising that Dominican-owned Santo Tomas, in farflung Manila, saw itself locked in a mighty ideological struggle. The Dominican Order was founded to combat heresies and Aquinas was a Dominican. A Dominican at Santo Tomas, Ceferino Gonzalez (1831–1894), who was in the Philippines in 1849–1866 and had Jose Burgos, Mariano Sevilla, and Toribio del Pilar among his students, would in fact become a leading light in Thomistic philosophy in Europe.[173]

Santo Tomas and other religious schools were buffeted by anti-friar policies from the peninsula and unrest within the colony. There was frenzied lobbying on both sides in Spain (the Filipinos and their Liberal allies and the Dominicans and religious orders) on secularizing the university, teaching Spanish, and other reforms. Writing in *Solidaridad* in 1889, Santo Tomas graduate Jose Panganiban criticized the university's medievalism. Elsewhere in the world, Panganiban wrote, "the principle of freedom of *scientific inquiry*" has been accepted but Santo Tomas "continues to require candidates for degrees to take the oath, kneeling down, to defend and to remain loyal to Thomistic doctrines; thus it keeps science chained to the immobility of dogmatism forever." To expect radical reform in Philippine education, he direly concluded, is tantamount to a "meditation on death."[174] The sharpest remark was Rizal's, who wrote in *Noli me tangere* that Dominican scholastic philosophy was "now dead

461

for all that Pope Leo XIII may say or do." "There is no Pope who can resurrect what common sense has executed." Rizal acknowledged that the religious corporations had done great work in science but asserted that "science is not progress itself, but only its material component." "It is only the acceptance of its principles which actually constitutes progress."[175]

John Schumacher points out that for all its defects "Philippine higher education was not far behind, or, under certain respects, was even superior to the general level of higher education in Spain, at least outside Madrid." Schumacher argues that "against their explicit desire" colonial educational institutions contributed to the awakening of Filipino national consciousness.[176] Colonial schools bred not just docile colonials and tidy scholastics but freethinkers and rebels.

Filipino nationalists were not themselves above falsehood and exaggeration nor were they completely free of the intellectual biases of the Spaniards they criticized. Graciano Lopez-Jaena and M.H. del Pilar were often disingenuous in their attacks on the friars. The style of nineteenth-century Spanish polemics occasioned rhetorical excess, and one should not in all instances demand from victims disinterested analysis and literary polish. Rizal raised this argument when, responding to Spanish academician Vicente Barrantes's criticism of *Noli me tangere*, he said (with some false modesty), "if it is not the conic, nickel-plated, and polished bullet that an academician can shoot but only a rough pebble picked from the brook, on the other hand it has hit the mark, hitting on the head that double-faced Goliath that in the Philippines is called *frailismo* and bad government."[177]

There is, however, little excuse for bad faith. This is shown in the case of Graciano Lopez Jaena (1856–1896). Lopez Jaena was an effective polemicist for Philippine causes because of his oratorical and debating talent (of his writings it was said that they were like speeches, they "gesticulate"). He was, however, a politician on the make. Declaring himself "a Spaniard by sentiment, a Spaniard by conviction," he was intent on a career in Spain, addressed a Spanish audience, pandered to liberal, anti-friar sentiments in the metropolis, and advocated colonial reforms as a Spanish republican rather than a Filipino nationalist. He was Paterno's twin except that Paterno, with his wealth, could craft for himself the Olympian image of a Spanish grandee; Lopez Jaena, the penurious college dropout, had to work the fringe of Spanish intellectual life and in the end could not quite parlay his literary gifts for a career in Barcelona politics.[178]

LA PROPAGANDA unraveled as a political network after 1892. Men like Lopez Jaena and Antonio Luna resented del Pilar's leadership and Rizal sulked. The purported Rizal-del Pilar rivalry highlighted problems over money and personalities within the Manila *Comite* itself. Aggravated by financial difficulties, personal and factional differences splintered the movement in Madrid and Manila. Many felt that *Solidaridad's* campaign for reforms was futile and the time for talk was done.

Hounded by a sense of fatality, Rizal surprised many with his daring move to accelerate the reform campaign by bringing it back to the Philippines. In a letter to Filipinos in Barcelona in October 1891, he wrote in Tagalog: *Ang gamot ay dapat ilapit sa may sakit... Ang parang na paglalabanan ay ang Filipinas: doon tayo dapat magtatagpo* ("The medicine should be brought close to the patient. The field of struggle is the Philippines: there is where we should meet").[179] His return was a pivotal moment. A week after he arrived in Manila on June 26, 1892, he founded *Liga Filipina* in a meeting in the district of Tondo. Under the motto *Unus instar omnium* ("One like all"), *Liga* aimed to "unite the whole archipelago into one compact, vigorous, and homogeneous body," foster mutual protection against violence and injustice, encourage instruction, agriculture, and commerce, pursue reforms, and organize "popular councils" in all provinces.[180] It was nothing less than an attempt at forming what amounted to a national political party. It triggered a series of highly consequential events.

Four days after *Liga* was founded, Rizal was arrested, jailed at Fort Santiago, and sent to the isolated Spanish outpost of Dapitan in Mindanao for an exile that would last four years. Dissolved after Rizal's arrest, *Liga* was revived in October 1893 but, divided over methods, lasted only until mid-1894 when it was reduced to a 50-man *Cuerpo de Compromisarios*, a group pledged to raise money to continue *Solidaridad's* work in Spain. *Cuerpo* effectively replaced the dormant *Comite*. In May 1895, Apolinario Mabini, *Cuerpo's* secretary, wrote to del Pilar asking that shipment of *Solidaridad* be suspended. A shipment of the paper had been seized; there was ominous talk that "governmental action is under way"; and in Malolos the town's leading citizens had just been arrested for deportation to Mindanao. Mabini wrote, "these are unusual days: although one cannot be sure if they are an omen of a cataclysm or a simple change in atmospheric equilibrium." In August, Mabini wrote del Pilar saying that the decision had been reached to stop the publication of *Solidaridad*. Intimating that the mood had turned insurrectionary, Mabini wrote that many people have lost hope in the paper and "have transferred it [hope] wholly to another direction."[181] (Within a few years Mabini himself would change direction and become the leading theoretician of the Philippine Republic.)

Solidaridad folded up with its issue of November 14, 1895. Del Pilar and Ponce were informed that a meeting would take place in Hong Kong to discuss plans (including *Solidaridad's* possible revival somewhere outside Spanish jurisdiction). To escape persecution at home and solicit Japanese assistance for the movement, Jose Ramos was already in Japan in August 1895 and was joined there by Doroteo Cortes in May 1896.[182] Del Pilar and Ponce were preparing to leave Barcelona for Hong Kong when del Pilar was taken ill. He died in Barcelona on July 4, 1896.

What Mabini meant by "another direction" was the *Katipunan*. On the night Rizal was arrested, July 7, 1892, Andres Bonifacio, a member of *Liga*, and others founded *Kataastaasan Kagalang-galang na Katipunan ng mga Anak ng Bayan* (Highest and Most Respectable Society of the Sons of the People), a secret revolutionary society committed to uniting Filipinos to wage a revolution for Philippine independence. The society did not seem to have been very active until the breakup of the *Liga* in mid-1894 forced a final split in the movement. In 1894 the Katipunan purchased an old handpress for 650 pesos from a Manila bazaar and fitted it out it with types bought from Isabelo de los Reyes and stolen from the shop of *Diario de Manila* by employees who were Katipunan members. With the press, the Katipunan issued its organ *Kalayaan* in January 1896 (with a claimed circulation of 1,000) and tried to mislead authorities with a masthead saying it was printed in Yokohama with M.H. del Pilar as editor. Within a year, membership in the Katipunan was estimated at 20,000.

Andres Bonifacio (1863–1897) has been variously described as a vendor of canes and paper fans, warehouseman, and agent or employee of English and German trading firms. His associate Emilio Jacinto (1875–1899), the son of a poor bookkeeper, briefly studied at Santo Tomas. Though they did not have the education of the likes of Rizal and Paterno, neither were they of the "unlettered folk." They were part of that segment of clerks, artisans, students, and petty merchants who formed the backbone of the first organized groups of Filipino reformers. Their in-between location in society invested them with entry to both "outside" and "inside" but Katipunan, unlike the reformist associations, was dedicated to addressing the masses (*las masas*). Isabelo de los Reyes spoke of it as a "plebeian society": "the people speak little and perhaps think little, and I wish to say, perhaps without the artificial complication of a cultivated intelligence, but the little they think is intense, forms their second nature, and that which they believe is their faith is fanaticism in them and works miracles, moves mountains, creates new worlds and other prodigies."[183]

Later historians would claim an Enlightenment lineage for Bonifacio by suggesting that he read Victor Hugo, Eugene Sue, and works on the French Revolution and U.S. history. Moved by the impulse to "intellectualize" the revolution, the earliest portrayals of Bonifacio draw attention to his literateness. These range from the repeated mention of the Katipunan library to Francis St. Clair's disparaging remark that Bonifacio was "a great reader" who, like Don Quixote, "passed many a night burning away oil and candles, sacrificing needed sleep in reading, until his brain was turned and his whole mind given up to ideas of revolutions."[184]

Others ground Bonifacio in indigenous tradition. It may be closer to the available evidence to locate him in an intermediate cultural zone. Raised in colonial-urban Tondo in a milieu of sailors, artists, merchants, and lower-order bureaucrats, he was the type of person involved in the manifestation of 1888 and addressed by del Pilar's Tagalog propaganda and the anonymous broadsides and pasquinades of the 1880s. In the same way that the *pasyon* was not pure indigeneity, the revolutionary poetry and manifestoes attributed to Bonifacio and Jacinto appropriated Spanish-colonial forms (*cartilla, pasyon*), Masonic themes, and *ilustrado* interpretations of history. It is likely, for instance, that such symbols and practices as the *pacto de sangre* and *baybayin* may have entered into the Katipunan through the mediation of *ilustrado* texts rather than directly from folk tradition. What is important of course is that they infused these forms and symbols with a revolutionary semantic content and affective power.[185]

The discovery of the Katipunan by the authorities on August 19, 1896, precipitated the start of the insurrection. Hostilities quickly spread such that, on August 30, the governor-general declared a state of war in eight Luzon provinces (Manila, Cavite, Laguna, Batangas, Bulacan, Pampanga, Nueva Ecija, and Tarlac). Rizal's execution on December 30, 1896, further inflamed the colony.

For Filipinos, revolution was not just a crash course in warfare, it was a school of learning. The forms of writing and composition corresponded to the exigencies of the time: proclamations, manifestoes, improvisatory theater, verses, and songs. The literature produced was not just war propaganda but texts that aimed to constitute a nation. The revolution (as in France) gave rise to the writing of moral "catechisms" and "decalogues" and the framing of constitutions that showed Filipinos quite skilled in the modern discourse on state and republicanism.[186]

It was the country's most complex and politically turbulent period. The revolution stalled with the treaty of Biyak-na-Bato in 1897, gathered new force in 1898 against the background of the Spanish-American War, widened into a war of resistance against the U.S. occupation in 1899–1901, and was suppressed in the years that followed. These events exacted their toll. Marcelo del Pilar and Graciano Lopez Jaena died stranded in Barcelona in 1896, Jose Rizal was executed in Bagumbayan in the same year, Andres Bonifacio and Antonio Luna were killed in 1897 and 1899, respectively, in fratricidal struggles within the revolution. More perished in the war. Others—like Pedro Paterno, T.H. Pardo de Tavera, and Isabelo de los Reyes—survived and tried, with varying degrees of sense and success, to ride out and direct the changes. A generational change of leaders took place, a new colonial order was established, and the challenge of creating a nation remained.

WRITING ABOUT OURSELVES

WRITING IN 1889, Jose Rizal saw the spread of the Enlightenment within and without the colony as vital in the emancipation of the Filipino. Alluding to "Filipino writers, free thinkers, historiographers, chemists, physicians, artists, jurists, etc.," Rizal said: "This class whose number is increasing progressively is in constant communication with the rest of the islands, and if today it constitutes the brains of the country (*cerebro del pais*), within a few years it will constitute its entire nervous system and demonstrate its existence in all its acts."[187]

This was both a boast in the face of colonial power and a statement of Enlightenment faith. Rizal was a realist in whom hope and despair fiercely contended; he was acutely conscious of the dangerous powers of unreason. Yet, Rizal and his generation lived in a time when the colony, though fettered, seemed poised to break free.

WHEN RIZAL spoke of "the brains of the nation," men like Pedro Paterno, T.H. Pardo de Tavera, and Isabelo de los Reyes had begun their careers as intellectuals. Established in Madrid, Paterno was entertaining the Spanish literati in his home and writing on the "ancient Tagalog civilization." Pardo

467

had returned to Paris after a two-year home visit that was intellectually productive even as it was politically distressing because of the civil turmoil in Manila. The young Isabelo had just founded *El Ilocano* and was furiously writing and publishing. They represented many others in and outside the colony.

Who were the *ilustrados* ("enlightened")? As educational and professional opportunities expanded in the nineteenth century, the word came into use to broadly refer to the educated and, loosely, the upper class due to the close association of education and wealth. "However," Cesar Adib Majul writes, "in its more restricted and correct sense, the term *ilustrado* referred to a person who had a profession, spoke and wrote Castilian well, and had been educated in any of the colleges."[188] Michael Cullinane adds that *ilustrados* are a subset of the larger elite and not a separate or monolithic class: "Not all educated Filipinos were recognized as *ilustrados* and not all *ilustrados* were from wealthy families."[189] Differences within this formation are occasioned by such variables as location, scale and type of wealth, and ethnic, social, and familial networks, as illustrated in the examples of Paterno, Pardo, and de los Reyes. The association with wealth, however, is strong, particularly if one limits the category to those with higher education from the university or *colegios* and were fluent in Western intellectual culture.

There was one other important distinction. The idea of the *ilustrado* arose in the context of the rise in Spain of *progresistas*, the "progressives" who emerged during the revolutionary period of 1808–1814 and rose in influence during the "Glorious Revolution" of 1868. Hence, the association of *ilustrado* with progressive, reform-minded individuals. It is interesting to note that, Majul points out, "colloquially, the term as a collective did not denote any Spaniard, however cultured or educated he might have been."[190]

Even if broadly defined, *ilustrados* constituted a minuscule part of the population. William Howard Taft opined in 1902 on the matter of political competence: "Political conception must be generally confined to less than 10 per cent who speak Spanish, and the discussion of political parties must be limited to that 10 per cent." The rest of the population, he said, was credulous, susceptible to any show of authority and force, and expressed "very little political sentiment of any kind." Another American, David Barrows, broke down Filipino society into two "classes,"

468

the *gente ilustrada* (the "controlling dominant class") and *gente baja* ("the subordinate class"), and concluded that the former, "though very small," was "the only class we have to consider.[191] Such views are part of the familiar discourse of the colonialist defining and isolating a political "problem." This was, however, a view of social formation shared by the Filipino elite. The directive role of the educated (Felipe Calderon's "oligarchy of intelligence") is a given in the discourse of Rizal and other propagandists.[192] Such belief was part of the intellectual climate in Europe, expressed by thinkers like Edmund Burke, Alexis de Tocqueville, and Juan Donoso Cortes. It was part of a whole philosophy of organic social growth with its distrust of popular democracy, confidence in the elite's stabilizing authority, and assumption that "liberty" and "equality" are not synonymous.

There is a racial complexion to the *ilustrado* formation because of the socioeconomic advantages of the Spanish creoles and Chinese mestizos who dominated the commercial and landowning class in the colony. They constituted a very small minority in the population. In a reported Philippine population of 5,151,423 in 1876, there were only 3,823 peninsular Spaniards (nearly half of whom were Philippine residents for five years or less), 9,910 creoles (*españoles filipinos*), 177,570 Spanish and Chinese mestizos, and 23,252 Chinese and other Asians. Close to five million were *indios* (Christian and non-Christian *indigenas*). Ninety-seven percent of the entire population could not speak Spanish.[193]

Racial distinctions, however, can be overdrawn. Spanish creoles were such a minuscule part of the population that they could emerge as a significant political force only to the extent that they identified with Chinese mestizos and *indios*. Chinese mestizos blurred into the native population by depth of residence, kinship ties, and inculturation. Common causes were forged across social and racial lines. The secularization campaign, agrarian conflicts, and struggle over the civil bureaucracy were not separate but interconnected issues. The secular clergy, in which creoles and mestizos were prominent, typically came from the *principalia* that had as well begun to assert their civil prerogatives and rights to land and property.

What of the *indios*? A derisive term Spaniards applied to indigenes in their American colonies, *indio* was the Spanish term for natives of the Philippines though it was later confined to Christianized natives since

469

Muslims were called *moros* and the pagan tribes *infieles*. *Indio* was not a term the inhabitants themselves used (though Rizal would, in a familiar reversal, turn it into a badge of honor by forming the group *Indios Bravos* in Paris in 1889). They continued to think of themselves in locality or ethnic-specific categories. The nineteenth century, however, brought about an unprecedented degree of integration in the archipelago as the countryside was carved out for cash-crop cultivation, provincial trading centers expanded, communications accelerated, and population grew and became more mobile. While many hinterland areas remained isolated and a large part of Mindanao was unintegrated into the Spanish colonial system, a significant population inhabited the proto-national space where they began to imagine themselves not only as *Tagalog, Bisaya,* or *Iloko,* but *Filipinos.*

The opening up of a "national space" is indicated by the phenomenal increase in the number of towns in the nineteenth century, growth in interisland shipping, and the appearance of provincial newspapers and colleges. By 1896, for instance, there were at least 110 secondary schools outside Manila. Seven of these (in Cebu, Iloilo, Vigan, Dagupan, Bacolor, Naga, and Guinobatan) were "first-class secondary schools" that offered courses leading to a bachelor's degree, mostly *colegios-seminarios* that developed out of the diocesan seminaries in the provinces. By 1896 provincial newspapers had appeared in Iloilo, Cebu, Vigan, and Nueva Caceres. All these indicated the presence of a communications network that encompassed large sections of the country. If it was not quite the vitally functioning "nervous system" Rizal envisioned, it explains why the insurrection that began in the environs of Manila in 1896 would expand, in just a few years, into a national revolution.

THE PRODUCTION of modern knowledge in the Philippines was driven by shifting and overlapping motives. Early exploration and missionary narratives reported to Europe knowledge about a new land and glorified projects of discovery, conquest, and conversion. Mercantilist and administrative histories served aims of colonial consolidation through inventories of local wealth, descriptions of administrative structures, and recommendations on matters like trade and taxation. The Spanish vision of an "enlightened imperialism" inspired a "colonial Enlightenment" driven by ideas of political reformism, science promotion, and the paternalistic advocacy of native rights. These themes would persist but a pivotal shift occurred when Filipinos themselves began to write their own history and carve out their own specific version of "Enlightenment" and "modernity."

The production of modern knowledge by Filipinos was determinative in the rise of Philippine nationalism. In the late nineteenth century, Filipinos, increasingly self-aware in their nationality, started to lay the local foundations of such disciplines as history, anthropology, linguistics, political science, and sociology. Filipinos were engaged in cultural self-definition in the context of anti-colonial nation-formation. There was excitement in the challenge of creating a "national" body of knowledge encompassing such fields as literature, history, language, and politics. Disciplines were cultivated not as specialized, abstract systems but as instruments and ways toward understanding and "organizing" society. Varied in their creative and critical practices, Filipino intellectuals engaged Western knowledge from their own specific site of work, worried about their relation to the country *from*, *of*, and *for* which they spoke, and traced the possibilities of an autonomous, critical voice in dialogue with the West.

The establishment of the Malolos Republic in 1898 provided nationalists with the stage to create an educational system that conformed to their aspirations for an education that was secular, scientific, patriotic, and democratic. The Malolos Constitution and various decrees provided for free and compulsory elementary education and a reformed higher education system. A state university, *Universidad Literaria de Filipinas*, was established on October 19, 1898, with programs in law, medicine, pharmacy, and notary public, and leading *ilustrados* (like Paterno and Pardo) in the faculty. Short-lived and ambulatory because of the war, the university awarded its first degrees on September 29, 1899, in Tarlac (given to students who began their studies at Santo Tomas). At the graduation ceremony, botanist Leon Ma. Guerrero, the university's dean, delivered a stirring address in which he called on the graduates to "help create a free country."

The soldier faces a shower of bullets and shots and repulses the enemy; the doctor and the pharmacist strengthen the body that it may better fight for life, and they cure the wounds of the wounded heroes; the engineer will build fortifications; the priest will console the dying; and you, men of the law, will uphold the empire of justice and defend from every attack the glorious liberty of our people.[194]

The country's first autonomous educational system was distinctly *ilustrado* in orientation. This was not surprising since the first national congress was a veritable roster of the Filipino intellectual elite: 43 lawyers, 18 physicians, 5 pharmacists, 7 businessmen, 4 agriculturists, 3 educators, 3 soldiers, 2 engineers, 2 painters, and a priest. Its orientation to Western-style modernity is shown in the educational plan the congress drafted (which, it may be noted, reflected Rizal's own philosophical bias about what constituted modern education).[195] It did not substantially expand education for women. The new system continued to give primacy to Spanish language and literature, retained Latin, and provided for the teaching of French and English (even German and Italian). Significant departures were the elimination of Religion from the curriculum and the emphasis placed on teaching the Philippines in subjects like geography and history (specifying, for instance, that the textbook in Philippine history must be prepared by a Filipino).

It must be noted that other ideas on educational reform were floated in this tumultuous period. Isabelo de los Reyes, writing from Spain in 1900, called for a system that builds on the privately initiated schools and sociopolitical clubs that mushroomed in the country in the wake of the revolution.[196] Out of these *academias, centros, circulos, clubs, ateneos, casinos o katipunans*, he proposed forming an "academy of the country," called *Aurora Nueva* ("New Dawn"), that will be guided by the principles of Honor, Science, Liberty and Progress. With his usual enthusiasm, Isabelo drew up the organizational structure, statutes, and plan of studies of a network of semi-autonomous groups and institutes (up to the university-level) that will be "adopted" or initiated by *Aurora Nueva*.

The central aim of this system (which, Isabelo claimed, continued Rizal's *Liga Filipina*) was to perfect the Filipino through an education that was "virile, scientific, and free." Its program would stress individual and social rights, patriotism and civic spirit, free inquiry, and the spread of useful, modern knowledge. It would be non-sectarian and democratic in character, encompassing all social, ethnic, and racial groups. Isabelo looked toward the assimilation of the best in Western culture (what he calls *europeizacion*) but combined this with the revival of what was positive in "ancient Filipino civilization." Suggesting by this combination the formation of a distinct kind of Filipino modernity, Isabelo, however, did not pursue the idea in a sustained way. Moreover, in 1900, the initiative had already moved away from men like Isabelo.

The building of a Filipino government was made in a time of war and aborted with the U.S. annexation of the Philippines. The admirable effort at forming the political and intellectual apparatus of an independent state did not quite mask the discursive contradictions of "nationhood" at the time. This is shown in the changing complexion of the revolution as the center of gravity shifted from Tondo to Cavite to Malolos and the leadership passed from lower-class urban elements (represented by Bonifacio) to provincial gentry (led by Emilio Aguinaldo) to a national bourgeoisie (represented by men like Pedro Paterno). Perhaps, given the historical conditions, it could not have been otherwise but the contradictions and discontinuities in the formation of the nation would remain in the decades that followed.

THE TURN of the century was a time of great intellectual excitement. Private schools, Masonic lodges, and other associations were venues for discussions and intellectual comradeship. In the early 1890s, young intellectuals like Clemente Zulueta, Epifanio de los Santos, Rafael Palma, and Jaime de Veyra gathered in private houses to talk about European and Latin American literature (from Spanish novelist Benito Perez Galdos to the Cuban poet Jose Marti), recite poetry, and discuss philosophy and the sciences. It was a time of great effervescence in Filipino-Spanish poetry as writers like Fernando Guerrero and Cecilio Apostol brought Filipino writing in Spanish—ironically, in Castilian's twilight in the country—to new heights of refinement.

The burst of civic enthusiasm that followed the collapse of Spanish rule is shown in the remarkable case of Lipa, Batangas.[197] In January 1899, local *principales* launched a political club, *Club Democratico Independista*; a women's Red Cross auxiliary, *Cruz Roja de Damas*; a secondary school, *Instituto Rizal*; and a periodical called *Columnas Volantes de la Federacion Malaya*. Led by Gregorio Aguilera and Baldomero Roxas (who had studied in Europe and knew Rizal and the propagandists), they turned Lipa into a cosmopolitan, republican haven. The club held political banquets and had its own library and fencing salon. *Instituto Rizal*, with a modified Ateneo Municipal curriculum, was authorized to grant degrees by the Malolos government. (Teodoro Kalaw was one of its students.) Patriotism ran high. Instead of religious images, *Instituto Rizal* was decorated with political posters that caricatured the Americans. Pledging support for the Malolos government, the school declared it will teach students "positive knowledge, with philosophical basis, of the latest achievements of modern science" and instill *nacionalismo* and desire in students to fight for *Patria Filipinas*. *Columnas Volantes* (a Spanish-Tagalog weekly that lasted from March 1899 to January 1900 when Lipa fell to the Americans) had its own press and was run on volunteer labor. Publishing national and provincial news, literary pieces, and editorial articles, the paper announced that it aimed to contribute to the "struggle for liberty and independence" and that it has called itself *Federacion Malaya* because it is moved by "noble sentiments that cherish the beautiful idea of seeing Filipinas not only independent but progressing at the front and in union with all the peoples of *Malasia*."[198]

It was a time pregnant with possibilities. The intercolonial transition saw a flourishing of the press, the birth of the vernacular novel, and "the golden age" of vernacular letters. The anti-American resistance sparked a burst of creative energy, particularly in literature and music. The surge of creative work did not abate with the collapse of the Republic. Its most dramatic instance was the appearance of "seditious" plays between 1902 and 1906 not only in Manila and its environs but as far away as Laoag and Cebu. These vernacular plays stirred crowds and challenged censors with their use of allegory, symbolism, and stage improvisation in criticizing the U.S. occupation. The Americans cracked down by arresting playwrights, actors, stagehands, and, in one case, an entire audience.[199]

After the Americans shifted from military to civil rule, and the more repressive measures of military occupation were repealed, there was greater latitude than in the Spanish era for open cultural work. Writers' organizations mushroomed and literary publishing was more vigorous than at any other period. Theater companies, musical societies, and art associations were formed. Filipinos set up colleges, such as *Instituto de Mujeres* (1900), *Liceo de Manila* (1900), *Colegio Filipino* (1901), and

Centro Escolar de Señoritas (1907, now Centro Escolar University). Labor organizations were founded. *Asociacion Feminista de Filipinas* was organized on July 23, 1905. Led by Concepcion Felix (who studied law at Escuela de Derecho under Felipe Calderon whom she later married; she also taught at *Instituto de Mujeres*), members included the Rizals (Trinidad, Narcisa, Saturnina, Josefa), Paternos (Agueda and Jacoba), and Concepcion Pardo de Tavera.[200]

No one illustrates the time's intellectual excitement better than Felipe G. Calderon (1868–1908).[201] Of a wealthy Manila family, Calderon earned a licentiate in Law at Santo Tomas in 1893 and traveled abroad to observe colonial administrations. He was not involved in the revolution but played a key role in framing the Malolos Constitution, drawing from his knowledge of European and Latin American constitutions. Like Pardo, his relative, he dissociated himself from the Aguinaldo government and participated in U.S. "pacification" efforts to reorganize local governments. His knowledge of Spanish and republican laws made him an invaluable consultant to the Americans.

Stirred by a passion for "building a new educational edifice upon the ruins of a lost cause," Calderon was a most energetic advocate. In 1899, he organized *Colegio de Abogados de Manila*, a bar association, and in the same year established *Escuela de Derecho*, the first law school outside of Santo Tomas, which had its first classes in the offices or homes of the professors (among them, Rafael Palma and Juan Sumulong). Calderon managed the school and taught civil law, constitutional law, and comparative legislation. He introduced non-law subjects, like sociology, political economy, and statistics, and developed textbooks suited to the local situation, among them his *Lecciones de Derecho Civil Filipino* (1905). *Escuela* accepted women students and sent students to their towns to research local conditions. Asserting that juridical science should be humane and holistic in orientation, Calderon said: "I do not want to train mere defenders of law suits, I want to produce *men*." "It is imperative to turn out not only lawyers, but men, citizens, true Filipinos."[202] Calderon left a deep imprint on his students. One of them, Teodoro Kalaw, wrote: "His lectures in class were like oracles."[203]

Calderon conducted classes in his house, opened his personal library to the public, organized lectures, and taught in several Manila schools. He wrote *El ABC del Ciudadano Filipino* (1905), a question-and-answer manual on the citizen's rights and duties that was translated into Philippine languages. He published an important memoir of the revolution, *Mis Memorias Sobre la Revolucion* (1907).[204] A member of the American Academy of Political and Social Science, he was, according to Ignacio Villamor, "the first who seriously made sociological studies in the Philippines, maintaining scientific connections with the most reputed sociologists in Europe and America."[205] In 1904, he initiated *Samahan ng mga Mananagalog*, the forerunner of the Institute of National Language, and acted as its first president. In 1905, he launched *Asociacion Historica de Filipinas*, the country's first historical association.

His intellectual zeal deeply impressed those who knew him. Guided by the belief that the American era was a field of opportunities to be exploited, he said: "We have need of two kinds of work—one of ejection and the other of acquisition. We must eject the old and acquire the new."

> With our defective inheritance, and now with an equally unsatisfactory environment, we awake to discover that our greatest enemies are our own selves. Our work of acquisition must consist in the formation of that ideal which should make each one of us not merely a lawyer, or a doctor, or a Federal, or an Independista, or a Catholic, or an Aglipayano, but into a MAN, a true FILIPINO.[206]

Calderon stressed the importance of practical, locally relevant knowledge: "The foundation of all the sciences is in the country. What we need are *lessons* on *things*. Our knowledge will then be neither bookish nor useless."[207] In the lecture that opened the school year in *Escuela de Derecho* in 1903, he called for "the blending of systems of laws and legal institutions in the Philippines against the background of surviving customary laws and traditions."[208] Endorsing the plan of a Manila college in 1905 to establish a "pedagogical academy," he called for "laboratories of ideas" that will carry out philosophical and sociological studies in a "historical, positivist, and experimental" mode. He warned against a dogmatic pedagogy that teaches students such irrelevancies as the number of times Vesuvius erupted instead of the configuration of Mayon and Taal volcanoes. The needed laboratory is one where the "real Filipino" investigates according to "truly scientific criteria" instead of the "garrulity of the pedant." Education must be "realist and local" and not "generalized and theoretical," he said.[209]

LANGUAGE AND LITERATURE were key sites in the creation of a *national* discourse. This was most visible in the creative field, particularly in poetry, drama, and the novel. The release of creativity in the early twentieth century was remarkable. A survey of printed literature in 1916 cites 3,290 books and pamphlets and 175 periodicals published in Philippine languages, the great bulk of them in Tagalog. More than a thousand novels in Philippine languages were published in book or serial form between 1900 and 1940. As that realm where the nation was most intimately and intensely imagined, literature had an importance greater than academic scholarship in the shaping of popular consciousness.[210]

In Manila and the provinces, language societies appeared and issues of language were avidly debated in the press. In 1903, leading Tagalog writers, scholars, and journalists formed *Kapulungan ng Wikang Tagalog*, ostensibly to work for the creation of a national language through a fusion of the major local languages. In 1904, Felipe Calderon initiated *Samahan ng mga Mananagalog*, which aimed to "study, purify and enrich the Tagalog language." Many of those involved in these groups (like Lope Santos, Rosa Sevilla, Hermenegildo Cruz, Jaime de Veyra, and Patricio Mariano) were also active in promoting the study and dissemination of Tagalog literature. The most notable in this group was Epifanio de los Santos (1871–1928), a nephew of Gregorio Sancianco and graduate of Santo Tomas. In 1898, he was Clemente Zulueta's associate in putting out *Libertad* and was in the staff of Antonio Luna's *La Independencia*. He was, in the early twentieth century, the country's most eminent biographer and literary scholar.[211]

De los Santos and his cohorts built on unfinished work. In the nineteenth century, the propagandists had initiated the move to construct a "national philology" through palaeographic and linguistic investigations and orthographic reform. Rizal wrote *Arte metrica del Tagalog*, a paper read before the Ethnographical Society in Berlin in April 1887, the first formal treatise on Tagalog metrics written by a Filipino. He engaged the Spanish author Vicente Barrantes in a discussion of the nature of Tagalog theater and left behind a study of Tagalog grammar, *Estudios sobre la lengua tagala* (1893), published posthumously in *La Patria* (December 19, 1899).[212]

Philological work was carried into the twentieth century by Pedro Serrano Laktaw (1853–1928), a teacher educated in Manila and Spain, who was himself continuing work done by his father Rosalio Serrano (1802–1867), a pioneering Filipino lexicographer who authored *Diccionario de terminos comunes tagalo-castellano* (1854) and *Nuevo diccionario manual español-tagalo* (1872). In 1889, Pedro Serrano joined the move for a "new orthography" initiated by Pardo and Rizal by publishing *Diccionario hispano-tagalog*, which he continued with *Diccionario tagalog-hispano* in 1914.[213] Another transitional figure was the German Otto Scheerer (1858–1938). A Philippine resident since the early 1880s, he joined the University of the Philippines faculty in 1911 and succeeded Pardo as head of the university's Department of Oriental Languages in 1924. He edited and published *The Archive: A Collection of Papers Pertaining to Philippine Linguistics* (1924–1932), a series of monographs written by students in a Philippine linguistics seminar Scheerer taught in the state university. The aim, Scheerer said, was to encourage research by students and make available "such valuable information as lies as yet untouched or hidden within the confines of our archipelago, and which can be brought to light by nobody better than by properly guided students hailing from the very speech-groups that are of interest to science."[214]

Several impulses lie behind language promotion activities at the time. There was the interest, at once scholarly and patriotic, in "recovering" language by producing grammars and dictionaries, addressing a local audience, and correcting Spanish-colonial philological studies on the basis of local understanding and practice. There was the modernizing interest in standardizing, "purifying," and enriching language as medium for modern communication. This was particularly true of languages that developed late as print languages. (For instance, newspapers in Cebuano, Kapampangan, and Leyte-Samar did not appear until after 1900.) Finally, there was the interest in popularizing and officializing the use of local languages in media, schools, and government, as expressed in the call for a "national language," mainly envisioned at the time either as Tagalog or a fusion of Philippine languages.

These moves carried with them certain hazards. Building a "national" language or literature involves rearticulations of tradition by selecting, discarding, or recombining elements in the culture in a discourse on what "represents" the collective values of the nation. Such acts of promotion are a form of "disciplining" as hierarchies of style, taste, and practice are set up. This is illustrated by a meeting of leading Tagalog writers in Manila on March 8, 1905, at which they chose the poet Francisco Baltazar (*Balagtas*) as symbol in the campaign to promote Tagalog language and culture. This initiated the literary movement the critic Virgilio Almario calls *balagtasismo* that, while laudable in its promotion of Tagalog models, also became a codifying project that privileged certain varieties of form and speech over others. It was not only a project focused on the language of the center, Tagalog, it was—given the formation of its proponents—biased in favor of European and Spanish poetics in its critical vocabulary and the premium placed on formalism and "high," literate poetry.[215]

Moreover, moves to develop autochthonous traditions of language and literature were compromised by the U.S. imposition of English as medium of education and government and the Filipino intellectuals' ambivalence towards the new colonial language and the national language issue. While the aborted Biyak-na-Bato Constitution (1897) declared Tagalog as the republic's official language, the Malolos Constitution (1899) made no decision on the national language, choosing instead to continue the use of Spanish as official medium and make the use of local languages in government optional. There was no marked aversion toward Spanish at the time. For nineteenth-century intellectuals, Spanish was the link to centers of world-knowledge. For a nationalist movement oriented towards assimilation and modernity, the possession of Spanish rather than its abolition was the goal. In 1889, *Solidaridad* expressed the prevailing view among intellectuals when, speaking of the benefits of Spanish, the paper said that "the people look forward to the time when they can voice their needs themselves without the intervention of others."[216] While the rest of the population may not have shared the *ilustrados'* zeal for learning Spanish, they were mostly indifferent rather than hostile to it since Spanish was not dominant enough to be viewed as a menace.

The aggressive propagation of English under the Americans presented the elite with what they had so actively sought: linguistic access to modernity and power. Yet, nationalism and the revolution—as shown in Rizal's changing views on language and the use of Tagalog by the Katipunan—fostered attachments to the native language as marker and resource of national identity and medium of popular communion. Hence intellectuals were caught between the cultural and moral suasion of a "national language" and the practical and ideological benefits of English. By the 1920s, however, the country had an English-speaking elite that profited from expanding economic, administrative, and educational systems under the Americans. Division and deferral characterized the intelligentsia's attitude towards the national language. The adoption of a national language did not become public policy until the 1935 Constitution, which led to the creation of the Institute of National Language in 1936 and government's declaration of Tagalog as "the basis for the national language" in 1937.

In the intercolonial space of the early twentieth century, local languages and literatures flourished. An English-based educational system derailed this development. There was a dramatic change in the language of print, as shown in the shifts in the medium of newspapers from Spanish to Spanish-Tagalog or Spanish-Tagalog-English, to dominant Tagalog, and then dominant English. Cultural energies released at the century's turn were domesticated or channeled into state-sponsored and academic projects of codification and formalization. *Balagtasismo*, which began as a nationalist response to the threat of "Anglo-Saxonization," turned nativist and conservative. The national language movement, on the other hand, was safely institutionalized with the creation of the Institute of National Language, intellectualized in such acts as the adoption of Lope Santos's *Balarila ng Wikang Pambansa* (1940) as "official grammar," and postponed to some indefinite future.[217] In both language and literature, Tagalog and other Philippine languages were subordinated to English and the culture it represented. Writing in the "vernaculars" was deprivileged as "literature" in the English-based literary education under the Americans. As in the Spanish period, but in ways more complex, a split was preserved between the language of popular discourse and the language of "high" literature and scholarship.

THE NEED to create a *Filipino* social science was a recurrent theme at the turn of the century. Historiography was an exemplary case. Colonialism, it was argued, erased the Filipino as a historical subject,

480

caricaturing him as a creature of contradictions that defied definition, an "emptiness." The archetypal story told is that of the friar and his blank book. In one version, the friar is the Augustinian botanist Manuel Blanco who, it is said, retired to a monastery outside Manila after his monumental labor on *Flora de Filipinas* to write the history of the Filipino. He sequestered himself in his cell and left orders he should not be disturbed and that his book was to be opened only after his death. When he died years later, his fellow Augustinians searched his cell for the manuscript on which he had labored. When they found his opus, entitled *El Indio*, they saw a book of blank pages.[218]

The need to define the nation as a sovereign subject was already the motive behind Rizal's annotated edition of *Sucesos de las Islas Filipinas* (1890). Though sketchy and flawed, the edition contains a veritable grammar of anti-colonial rhetorical moves. Here Rizal traced the basic outline of a Filipino historiography when, speaking to fellow Filipinos in his preface, he positioned his work as one addressed to Filipinos and one that has for its subject "our country" (*patria*). He sounded the call for the recovery of a lost past ("to awaken your consciousness of our past, already effaced from your memory"), rectification ("to rectify what has been falsified and slandered"), assumption of authority ("Born and brought up... without voice or authority to speak of what we neither saw nor studied"), and orientation to the future ("we shall [then] be able to study the future"). Earlier, in his preface to *Noli me tangere* (1886), he made the problem of authorial location quite clear. Conflating nation and self ("Desiring your well-being, which is our own"; "as your son, I also suffer in your defects and failings"), Rizal was acutely conscious of what "writing about ourselves" means. He would infuse into scholarship something of the existential necessity and force of a confessional narrative.[219]

The call for a history focused on "the Filipino people themselves" was made by Pardo, Calderon, and others. In 1903, the Exposition Board (of which Paterno was a member), preparing for the St. Louis Exposition, planned to have a Filipino history written by Calderon "from the standpoint of Filipinos, in contrast to other historical works which were written from the Spaniards' standpoint, being unjust in giving no credit to Filipinos in the past." As late as 1926, introducing his *Development of Philippine Politics* (1926), a pioneering work in political science, the

U.S.-educated Maximo Kalaw lamented that previous books on the subject were written "from the standpoint of the outsider and have been mostly a record of foreign administrations, Spanish and American, which have been established in the Islands."[220]

Clemente J. Zulueta (1875–1904) addressed this problem.[221] A law student at Santo Tomas, he belonged to a group of literati that met regularly to discuss poetry and politics, and knew the Luna brothers when he took lessons in the fencing school Antonio Luna opened after he returned from Europe in 1894. (Mabini, before he was paralyzed, was one of the fencing students.) In 1896, he was secretary of the Katipunan's section in Manila's Paco district. To hide his involvement when hostilities began, he presented his services as a military historian to the Spanish authorities. With a safe-conduct pass, he crossed battle lines, did interviews in the field and, it is said, passed intelligence to the rebels. He served as Paterno's private secretary in the Biyak-na-Bato negotiations and, when war resumed in 1898, joined the Aguinaldo forces and participated in the takeover of the Augustinian-run Asilo de Huerfanos in Tambobong. Put in charge of the orphanage-owned press, Zulueta published *La Malasia* (1898) and *La Libertad* (1898). These periodicals were cut short when he was ordered by the revolutionary authorities to move out and close down the press. In September 1898, he joined the cream of the country's literary intelligentsia in publishing Luna's *La Independencia*.

Opting out of the war in late 1899, he taught history at Liceo de Manila, acted as librarian for Manila clubs, and helped collect materials for the St. Louis Exposition. In 1903, apparently through Pardo's intercession, he was tasked by the Philippine Commission, as "collecting librarian," to undertake research and procure Philippine-related books and manuscripts "with the view to the foundation in Manila of a public historical library upon the subject of the Philippine Islands."[222] For fifteen months, he visited foreign archives and libraries, brought home a trove of source materials, and upon his return called for a "general compilation of historical sources" as an aid to writing the country's history. At this time, American historians Emma Blair and James Robertson had just begun to publish the 55-volume documentary series *The Philippine Islands, 1493–1898* (1903–1909), an ambitious private enterprise aimed at enlarging American knowledge about the new U.S. colonial possession.[223] Zulueta did not believe this fully satisfied the need and urged not only more work in foreign archives but the collection of local materials, including literary works. To promote these aims, Zulueta had started to form *Asociacion Historica de Filipinas* when he died on September 9, 1904, at the age of twenty-nine.

In "*El elemento indigena en la Historia de Filipinas*," a lecture delivered on June 19, 1902, at Liceo de Manila, Zulueta outlined the need for a new Philippine history.[224] The country, he lamented, has been treated as a mere "appendix" to Spanish history. Spanish-colonial histories glorify "Providence," record only "the acts of the dominant caste," contain "a superabundance of details even on the most insignificant details," and do not amount to "a real critical and philosophical history." Denigrating the natives, Spaniards claimed for themselves and "the dominant class" sole agency in the creation of history.[225]

Historians have neglected, Zulueta argued, "the substantivity of the indigenous element (*elemento indigena*)" in Philippine history. Though "hidden," the indigenous "not only forms an integral portion but the very base and substructure, the main element of Philippine society, not alone during prehistoric times but during the very height of Spanish dominion." The victories against Dutch and English incursions, for instance, "are inconceivable without the effective and devoted cooperation of the people." The indigenous barangay shows that "our people had evolved and enjoyed a degree of social interrelationship not demonstrable by races judged more favorably than ours, since this very fact demonstrates most emphatically the depth and stability in the race of a spirit of order and justice as its very foundation concept."[226]

While not beyond nativism, Zulueta stressed that the indigenous had an "assimilating power" as shown in the way native arts and industries were dynamized through precolonial contact with other countries. Spain's "tutelary regime," however, excluded the indigenous from the "political or intellectual spheres" and reduced it to passivity. The native "was obliged to have recourse to an introspective concentration of his faculties until was lost, together with former contact and relations with neighboring countries, much of its own sociability." Because its assimilative power was not allowed full play, its evolution was arrested even as it conserved "its individuality, its personality of race characteristics." Colonial relations were such that between "the indigenous and the dominating element" there could be no social evolution since these two "heterogeneous groups failed to interpenetrate each other reciprocally in their respective spheres of activity." Zulueta concluded by saying "it is fully time that the native element take its proper place in Philippine history, to which factor has belonged not alone the initiative but as well the accomplishment of many great events."[227]

What Zulueta suggests by the *elemento indigena* is the spirit of the "people," the motivations and acts that generate their distinctive customs, arts, and industries. This factor "powerfully affected" the course of events and "gave to history a heroic character." He calls for a holistic history that includes all human activities and not just the political. History, he quotes Spanish historian Rafael Altamira, must rest on "the consideration of social life as an *organism* in which every part and manifestation has its own proper and essential value; for this reason it becomes necessary to study peoples as corporate units, organized in every aspect of their activities and all the manifestations of energy which they show, of which one only, politics, cannot claim in all cases and absolutely, the supremacy." In this regard, Zulueta cites the value of folklore, which has "only one adept in the Philippines, D. Isabelo de los Reyes, who, most certainly has not exhausted the subject." Folkloric investigations, he says, "can give us a view of the inner life of our people, indispensable for a fundamental understanding of our society."[228]

Zulueta, Gregorio Zaide writes, was "among the first Filipino historians who advocated the need of interpreting the history of the Philippines from the Filipino point-of-view and not from the biased viewpoint of the Spanish chroniclers."[229] Indeed, Zulueta was probably the first to give a formal, programmatic statement to a theme foreshadowed by Rizal and Paterno. He does not, however, go too far beyond exhorting historians to give primacy to native agency. What this required remained imperfectly articulated both as an intellectual project as well as a mode of engagement in society and the times.

In 1905, Felipe Calderon gave a more theoretical statement of the new history in "*Por la Historia de Filipinas,*" a lecture at Manila's Club Internacional.[230] (Meant to inaugurate a series of public lectures in history, this may have been part of the activities launching *Asociacion Historica de Filipinas* that year.) Calderon takes off from a review of modern philosophies of history in which he discusses such versions of "universal history" as Jacques-Benigne Bossuet's Bible-based providential history of mankind, Giambattista Vico's theory of historical cycles, Condorcet's rational-scientific framework of "organic perfectability," the ideas of Montesquieu and Henry Thomas Buckle on the materialist basis of human institutions, and the historicism of Johann Gottfried Herder.

Calderon rejects the systematists who write to demonstrate *a priori* theses on history as well as the determinists who reduce social phenomena as products of nutrition and environment. Natural forces, he says, determine institutions and events in culturally mediated ways. Human history is the product of a "double activity," not just the influence of external phenomena on our "spirit" (*espiritu*) but the action of the spirit on physical nature. Taking the Herderian view, Calderon stresses human agency and creativity ("spirit," a word Herder uses for what he also calls "culture"), the organic interrelation of everything, and the need to understand human actions genetically in terms of their history. Like Herder, Calderon believes that history's proper subject is the life of communities and not the deeds of great individuals. Human achievements encompass everything from "the modest labor of the most obscure worker to the lucubrations of the scientist, the victories of the *caudillo* and the successes of the nation." Using organic metaphors to show how great natural cataclysms result from a mass of obscure, cumulative changes, Calderon says that history must encompass "all the manifestations of the activity of social life." Rhetorically, he asks: How could Bonifacio have set into motion the Katipunan if the people were not already yearning for greater liberties they could not obtain by other means? How was it possible that the seeds sown by Hermano Pule in 1833 should bear fruit in 1898 if people had remained passive?[231]

An "organic conception of society," he asserts, requires that "the true content of the history of the Philippines should embrace the study of the sciences, the arts, industry, customs, religion, laws, etc., of our nation to appreciate the entire ensemble of organs and functions with their respective dependencies and relationships in the unity of the Subject (*Sujeto*), which is no other than the Filipino people." History must not only be an organic history (what German historians called "cultural history"), it must be based on the agency of the "people," which Zulueta calls the "indigenous element" and Calderon (appropriating Herder's populism) anchors in "the laboring and underprivileged mass of the nation."[232]

Organized to stimulate interest in history, *Asociacion Historica de Filipinas* was conceived as a forum that included historians and scholars like Paterno, Pardo, and de los Reyes.[233] The primary movers were Zulueta (who died before the association could be launched) and Calderon (whose death in 1908 effectively ended the association). Three aims animated the association: the cultivation of history as a discipline, archive-building, and popularization. In 1905, the association published the Spanish-English monthly, *Revista Historica de Filipinas*. The review ceased in 1906 and was succeeded in February 1908 by *Enciclopedia Filipina*, a monthly that expanded the scope of *Revista Historica* by covering government, economics, finance, and sociology.[234] Calderon's death cut it short at four issues. It was Calderon who edited *Enciclopedia Filipina*, headed the editorial committee of *Revista Historica*, and virtually capitalized both publications.

Influenced by Western positivist historiography, these publications gave primacy to the collection of documents. As *Revista Historica*'s maiden editorial stated, "we are tired of hearing it stated that the time is not ripe to write the history of the Philippines" since the material is not yet sufficient in quantity and quality "to permit the minute analysis . . . which must precede all attempts at the historical synthesis of our civilization."[235] *Revista Historica* and *Enciclopedia Filipina* published primary sources (such as the sermons of Pedro Pelaez, Chao-ju-kua's account of the islands, and a Tayabas document on the Hermano Pule revolt), bibliographies by Pardo and Ponce, and such foreign contributions as a comparison of Tagalog and Malagasy by the Swiss scholar Renward Brandstetter. It carried an article on *feminismo* and the lecture "*La mujer Filipina*" given by Concepcion Felix at a gathering held in honor of Alice Roosevelt on August 11, 1905.[236] *Enciclopedia Filipina* published book reviews and notices on academic congresses, including a list of papers presented at the 1906 conference of the American Political Science Association in Providence, Rhode Island, as well as an article on the definition of sociology as a discipline.[237]

The ideas of Zulueta and Calderon lie behind both publications. A "true history" has emerged, *Revista Historica* said, in which "the subject of history is not solely comprised by political events . . . nor its only proper subjects certain selected individuals, however great these may seem . . . but that it should include *all events,* the manifold and varied manifestations of human activity as conditioned upon the state of social conceptions and the medium surrounding the same"—that is, "our history as people in this large and complete sense." The "indigenous," the review affirmed, "constitute[s] the true subject of Filipino history and research." To know the indigenous, *Revista Historica* editors underscored the need to look to the precolonial past as "that broad substructure upon which must rest the substantivity (*substantividad*) of this essential historical factor of our past."[238]

The Filipino historiographical project would primarily involve Filipinos. However, *Revista Historica* also invited Americans, "the countrymen of a Prescott, Schoolcraft," to contribute to the project "knowing that a proper and just understanding of the character of any people is essential before it is possible to so govern it that both governors and governed are happy."[239] In 1908, Calderon even enlisted the help of Wenceslao Retana in drawing up a "schema of Philippine historiography" for *Enciclopedia Filipina*.[240] A rabid anti-nationalist, Retana modified his views after the fall of the Spanish regime and devoted himself to Philippine causes. Despite his political past, Filipinos recognized his considerable bibliographic contributions. Responding to Calderon's invitation, Retana presented an outline for an ambitious thirteen-volume history of the Philippines. This history, he writes, should be done by Filipinos but adds that it must not be undertaken for at least ten years since "indispensable" sources are not all available and "bias and prejudice have not entirely disappeared."[241] Commenting on Retana's plan in 1918, Epifanio de los Santos, lauding Retana for his "new state of mind," praises the plan as useful in outlining "a connected historical dissertation of the evolution of the Filipino people." Endorsing the view that the country's history should be written by and for Filipinos, de los Santos agrees that "the time for writing that history has not yet come" as there is still a need for authentication, synthesis and perspective.[242]

After *Revista Historica* ceased publication, Manuel Artigas tried to continue its initiative by publishing *Biblioteca Nacional Filipina* (1908–1909). A Spanish creole, Artigas (1866–1925) studied medicine at Santo Tomas, worked as a civil servant, and, having set up his own press, took up the work that Jose Felipe del Pan pursued before him, producing the twice-monthly review, *El Faro Administrativo* (1892), the two-volume *El Municipio Filipino* (1894), and *Diccionario Tecnico-historico de la*

Administracion de Filipinas (1894).[243] The political situation drove him to Spain in 1897 but he returned in 1902. (At the time of *Biblioteca Nacional Filipina*, he was a librarian at the National Library; he became its acting director in 1921–1922.) Artigas was basically a compiler. *Biblioteca Nacional Filipina*, also called *Philippine National Library Historical Review*, displayed his appetite for documentation.[244] A Spanish-English monthly, it was virtually a one-man publication. It carried biographies, texts of documents, and monographs (such as histories of Filipino parliamentary representation, agriculture, journalism, and the Tagalog language) so formatted that they could be taken out as separates and bound as books. In his maiden editorial, Artigas said that he had taken up the task of building a bibliographic archive "up to now left in the hands of those who did not feel toward the Philippines that love which everyone must feel toward the mother." Hence the need for Filipinos ("we") to collect reliable sources to counter "the prejudices which were allowed in the past to disfigure completely all that related to these islands."[245]

The need to build a *national* body of scholarly knowledge animated initiatives in education, cultural organizing, and publishing. Newspapers in Manila and the provinces carried historical sketches, literary and folkloristic works, and bibliographies. Intellectuals who began their careers in the nineteenth century, like Paterno, Pardo, and Mariano Ponce continued to be active. Reviving a series he started in *Solidaridad* in 1892–1893, Ponce produced, with Jaime de Veyra, a series of historical and cultural articles called *Efemerides Filipinas* in *El Renacimiento* and *El Ideal* in 1911–1912. He also helped organize *Sociedad Orientalista de Filipinas* in 1918 together with Pardo, Artigas, Jose Alejandrino, Macario Adriatico, and Teodoro Kalaw. The society published a short-lived monthly journal of Asian affairs, *Boletin de la Sociedad Orientalista de Filipinas* (1918).[246]

After Calderon's death, however, much of the philosophical ambition behind Filipino historiography that he and Zulueta had was dissipated. Even at the outset, despite Calderon's professed populism, one discerns the drift towards academism and formalism. While the proponents of the new history were lawyers, doctors, and poets, the idea of "discipline" was pronounced. In his 1902 lecture, Zulueta lamented that schools had not kept up with theoretical advances and that the country lacked the kind of scholarly authority scientific societies in other countries had. While the revolution had given impetus to historical work, he said, the passions of the day were such that "this impulse was twisted into channels determined by the passions aroused." A positivist bias put the premium on the collection of written documents. While history was seen as an instrument for "organizing" society there was a mood of deferral premised on the belief that "reliable sources" were not yet sufficient for writing Philippine history.

The "cultural history" project pointed to a new way of conceiving the country's past and reclaiming what colonialism had suppressed. It may be said that in proposing an organic history that placed at its center the structuring principle of the "indigenous," Zulueta and his colleagues strategically displaced U.S. dominance in the "political" realm by asserting the primacy of the "cultural." The project, however, also signified *ilustrado* accommodation to U.S. rule. Like many intellectuals, Zulueta and Calderon believed that the American order was propitious for the pursuit of knowledge and did not quite confront the contradictions between native agency and the new colonial domination. In steering historiography away from an exclusive concern with "politics," men like Calderon and Zulueta expressed the postrevolutionary mood of gradualism, of turning away from a politics of confrontation to one of "nation-building." The avoidance (or acceptance) of U.S. rule rendered the new historiography problematic since it ignored the materially and ideologically constitutive effects of the new colonialism.

THE INTERCOLONIAL TRANSITION derailed the development of an "indigenous" intellectual tradition. Private initiatives like *Asociacion Historica de Filipinas* were swamped by the U.S. colonial state's program of reorganizing government, establishing an English-based national educational system, and renovating the national culture.

The American colonial state embarked on producing a new fund of knowledge about the archipelago. As anthropologist Daniel Brinton said in 1899, now that the Philippines are "definitely ours," knowledge of the country is essential for its "proper management."[247] The Washington-based Bureau of Insular Affairs, America's "colonial office," functioned as a research and information bureau for the U.S. government on civil affairs connected to Cuba, Puerto Rico, and the Philippines. BIA collected economic intelligence, recruited experts in finance, labor, and economics (and the first American teachers sent to the Philippines), produced maps and gazetteers, and archived captured records of the Aguinaldo government. In Manila, the Philippine Commission interviewed Filipino experts, initiated the first modern census of the Philippines (1902), established museums and libraries, and laid the groundwork for a countrywide public school system.

Building on earlier Spanish institutions, the Americans established bureaus of Forestry (1900), Agriculture (1901), Mines (1901), and Science (which began as Bureau of Government Laboratories in 1901). The U.S. Coast and Geodetic Survey (1900) completed work done by the Spaniards in charting the coast and waters of the archipelago. The American Circulating Library (1900) evolved into the Philippine Public Library in 1908 and Philippine Library & Museum in 1916. (The museum, which incorporated the Insular Museum of Ethnology, Archaeology and Commerce established in 1901, became the National Museum in 1928.) The Bureau of Archives created by the Philippine Commission in 1901 gave rise to the National Archives. A Bureau of Non-Christian Tribes was created in 1901 and charged with undertaking "the Ethnological Survey for the Philippine Islands" which launched expeditions and reconnaissance work, did translation and photographic documentation, organized exhibits, and published monographs.[248]

The U.S. occupation opened up a "research field" for American scholars. Bureau of Non-Christian Tribes engaged the services of anthropologists and scientists, like David Barrows, Albert Jenks, Fay Cooper Cole, William Jones, and Laura Watson Benedict. Within months of the invasion of the Philippines, the American Historical Association, American Economics Association, and American Association for Political and Social Science each formed its "Committee on Colonies," while Smithsonian and the Bureau of American Ethnology maneuvered to claim a leading role in colonial investigation.[249] At Johns Hopkins University a course in Philippine linguistics, under Frank R. Blake, was opened in 1900 under the Oriental Seminar directed by Paul Haupt. There were plans for U.S. government support for courses in Tagalog and Visayan, and Blake went on to become a prolific scholar on Philippine languages.[250]

More than anything else the sweep of intellectual changes is indicated by the phenomenal expansion of the public school system.

Between 1903 and 1940, the number of schools increased from 3,000 to 13,000; the number of teachers from 2,500 to 42,000; and school enrolment from under 300,000 to 1,860,000.[251] A new higher education system, at the apex of which was a new state university, University of the Philippines (1908), introduced far-reaching intellectual reorientations. English-based, modeled after American universities, and manned by Americans and U.S.-educated Filipinos, the university became the standard for higher education in the country. Women were admitted from the time the university opened in 1908. Student enrolment rose from 67 in 1908 to 7,849 in 1929. The university's expansion can be seen in the succession of colleges established: Medicine (1907), Agriculture (1909), Fine Arts (1909), Liberal Arts (1910), Forestry (1910), Engineering (1910), Pharmacy (1911), Law (1911), Education (1913), Tropical Medicine and Public Health (1914), Dentistry (1915), Nursing (1916), Music (1916), Surveying (1925), and Business Administration (1929).

Disciplines were institutionalized with the establishment in the state university of such departments as History (1910), Anthropology (1914, the first such department in Southeast Asia), Political Science (1915), and Linguistics (1922). Americans did not only run the university but headed academic departments, as in the examples of H. Otley Beyer, Dean Fansler, and George Malcolm. The Department of History, for instance, had an all-American faculty when it was established in 1910. The Department of Political Science did not have a Filipino head until Maximo Kalaw became its chairman in 1920. In 1910–1911, there were six American deans and only one Filipino and the faculty list named 72 Americans and foreign nationals and only 15 Filipinos.[252]

Filipinism was a major theme in discussions of the university's role at its inception. In his inaugural address on December 20, 1911, as the first U.P. president, Murray Bartlett, an Episcopalian minister with a Doctor of Divinity degree from University of Rochester, raised the aim of building a university "which shall measure up to world-standards" but stressed at the same time that U.P. will be a "University for the Filipino."

The world-centers of knowledge are essentially national. With students from all parts of the world, Berlin is essentially German

and Oxford essentially English. This university should not be a reproduction of the American university. If it is to blossom into real
fruit, it must grow in Philippine soil, it must not be transplanted
from foreign shores. It can serve the world best by serving best the
Filipino.[253]

What this mostly meant at the time, however, for American and
Filipino intellectual leaders, was the gradual expansion of the role of
Filipinos both in the university and the government through the pro-
duction of educated and efficient professionals in various fields.

What must be stressed is the easy accommodation of the Filipino
intellectual elite to the new order. There were skirmishes on issues of
political independence, U.S. economic domination, and the cultural perils
of Anglo-Saxonization. A celebrated case was the storm over *El
Renacimiento*'s "Birds of Prey" editorial (October 30, 1908) that attacked
Dean C. Worcester for using his scientific expeditions to further personal business interests. (A University of Michigan zoologist, Worcester
was Secretary of Interior in 1901–1913.) Convicted of libel, publisher
Martin Ocampo and editor Teodoro Kalaw were heavily fined and escaped serving jail terms only because of an executive pardon. *El
Renacimiento* was forced out of existence. The case raised not only the
issue of press freedom but the use of colonial science to camouflage commercial exploitation and misrepresent a people. Worcester's advocacy
and promotion of Philippine "tribals," it was said, were meant to disparage Filipinos and undermine their claims of competence for independence.
The *Renacimiento* libel suit became a rallying cry for nationalists.[254]

Yet, despite such irritants, the intellectual elite saw much in the
new order that satisfied their aspirations for secularism and libertarian-
ism. "Filipinization" under the Americans opened up many opportunities
for intellectuals. Filipinos had their own legislature by 1907. By 1913,
they filled 71% of national civil service positions, 99% of all municipal
and 90% of all provincial posts.[255] While it was not until the Commonwealth that a Filipino headed the Department of Public Instruction,
Filipinos actively participated in the execution of educational policies.
In 1920, there were only 385 American teachers compared to 17,244
Filipinos. As early as 1915, the University of the Philippines had Filipinos as president (Ignacio Villamor, acting presidents Jose Escaler and

Alejandro Albert, Rafael Palma, Jorge Bocobo). After an almost exclusive diet of Americana in the early years, public school textbooks were "Filipinized" in authorship and content. Textbooks narrated the life-stories of national heroes and stimulated a juvenile appetite for "native culture." In the country's schoolhouses, pictures of Rizal, Bonifacio, and other heroes graced schoolrooms, the Philippine flag floated side by side with the Stars and Stripes, and the Philippine National Anthem was daily sung.

State cultural agencies were in Filipino hands almost from their inception. Filipino intellectuals directed the National Library and Museum (Manuel Artigas, Teodoro Kalaw, Epifanio de los Santos, Jaime de Veyra) and Institute of National Language (de Veyra, Lope Santos). They conducted research, collected "Filipiniana," wrote on history and culture, and speculated on the Filipino personality. While the intelligentsia had expanded and diversified it is remarkable that the time's most influential scholars formed a small, homogeneous formation. Epifanio de los Santos, Lope Santos, Jaime de Veyra, Rafael Palma, and Teodoro Kalaw were middle-class, Manila-based postrevolutionary cohorts enthused over the challenge of participating in the U.S.-guided nation-building project. They were mostly allied with the ruling Nacionalista Party (and personally associated with Manuel Quezon and Sergio Osmeña) and served as governors, assemblymen, senators, or held Cabinet-level posts. Scholar-bureaucrats, they exercised considerable influence in shaping public memory and "national identity" in this period.

Unlike the nineteenth-century propagandists, who worked outside the state, the leading early twentieth-century intellectuals were positioned within it. They imagined themselves "organic" (though not quite in Gramsci's sense) to a state-guided nation-building enterprise that, they believed, represented the people's aspirations.[256] While there were dissident and unincorporated voices, the prevailing mood among intellectuals was one of complacent acceptance of power.

When the twentieth century began, the basic themes of a national historiography had been enunciated. The nation is narrativized as a single and coherent entity with a "long" and "high" past embedded in an ancient "Malay civilization" leavened with centuries-long Hindu, Arab, Chinese, and European influences. While Spanish colonialism stunted its growth, the nation did not lose its capacity for "modernity" and

493

"progress," a capacity the nation now exercised as it prepared for full nationhood under American auspices. It is a teleological narrative guided by an elite vision of a future blazed by the West but one that Filipinos, by the specific force of their "culture," are making their own.

Writing history and politics from the "Filipino point of view" was the norm though it was not always clear what this meant. On one hand, it meant making visible the actions of the "people" vis-à-vis the colonial masters. Yet, it also involved the strategic move of incorporating these actions into the elite's view of the evolution of the nation. Hence, historians illustrated the "substantivity of the Filipino race" by tracing the lineage of the ilustrado revolution back to such episodes of resistance as the "separatist" revolt of Diego Silang in 1814 and Hermano Pule's "religio-political" uprising in 1841.[257] On the other hand, claims for an autonomous history stressed the rich indigeneity of local culture. Thus the preoccupation of the cultural nationalists with the problem of the "Filipino Soul." The discourse on "soul" however—like that of a romanticized, abstract "people"—was not one that could not be harmonized with acceptance of U.S. rule.

As formulated, the project of Filipino-centric scholarship lent itself to nation-building under U.S. "stewardship." Public school textbooks "officialized" a modular narrative of the country's historical evolution that inserted the period of U.S. rule as the culmination of the people's struggle for democracy and progress. Scholars (most notably, Teodoro Kalaw and Epifanio de los Santos) built a canonical understanding of the revolution and its pantheon of heroes as mental and moral foundation of the new nation. Research and promotional activities created a "national" canon of literature, dance, music, painting, and architecture. Such texts as the "Code of Calantiao," Andres Bonifacio's "Duties of the Sons of the People," and Apolinario Mabini's "True Decalogue" were invented or wrested out of their contexts and deployed for citizenship-building. Departing from the dynamic claims de los Reyes made for folklore studies, works like Kalaw's *Cinco Reglas de Nuestro Moral Antigua* (1935) harnessed folklore for strengthening state nationalism.[258]

Revolutionary nationalism mutated into "Filipinism" (*filipinismo*), a benign and conservative view of recovering, preserving, and promoting native traditions in combination with the best in Western (specifically, American) culture. Distinctly culturalist rather than political or economic, its spirit is summed up in Teodoro Kalaw's words: "Let me write the songs of a nation and I do not care who makes its laws."[259] Diffuse and non-aggressive, Filipinism was a form of nationalism perfectly congruent with the dominant politics of "constructive partnership" with America. It was congenial to leaders who invoked nationalism to distance themselves from the Americans as well as deflect the radical demands of those who could not abide with U.S. rule. It played into the U.S. policy of "Filipinization" under the country's directing class.

In the cohabitation of "Americanization" and "Filipinization," a canonical, civic nationalism was formed. It is not surprising that a high American official, Joseph Ralston Hayden, would claim Filipino nationalism as product of the American colonial project. In 1941, Hayden boasted that "only within the last generation have they [Filipinos] become generally conscious of a national history, national heroes, and common aspirations for a national destiny."[260]

THE CULTURAL SHIFT under the Americans was a disjunction in Philippine intellectual history. Much was left out in the construction of a national intellectual tradition. To cite the example of scholars in the mainstream of nineteenth-century thought, the break is illustrated by the virtual erasure of Pedro Paterno, T.H. Pardo de Tavera, and Isabelo de los Reyes from canonical disciplinary histories in the Philippines.

Paterno was, whether we like it or not, one of our first "modern" intellectuals, author of the first Filipino novel, pioneer scholar in the cultural sciences. He was the first to consciously position himself in the emerging Western discipline of anthropology, harnessing its theories and methods in understanding his country in relation to the world. This has gone virtually unacknowledged. Histories of Philippine anthropology barely mention Paterno, if at all. Where he is mentioned, he is quickly dismissed as a credulous and careless amateur.

Like Paterno, Pardo is an odd figure in the pantheon of "great Filipinos." His intellectual reputation has earned him a place in history but his intellectual *work* has not been adequately studied. His work as precursor in medical science, anthropology, history, and sociology has received scant notice from today's scholars. He was a trained linguist who wrote well-informed studies in his time, yet he figures marginally in histories of Philippine linguistics. These accounts have instead privi-

leged as foundational the contributions of American linguists like Carlos
Everett Conant and Leonard Bloomfield. Scholars on Sanskrit elements
in Philippine languages have given notice to his works but treat them
without benefit of context in nineteenth-century linguistic science and
colonial politics. Pardo's polemical essays had the better fortune of surviving but have been culled for contextless ideas on themes like culture
and education.[261]

Isabelo de los Reyes's work has fared better, particularly in his role as
"Father of Filipino Folklore" and theologian of the Philippine Independent Church (in no small measure due to the scholarship of William
Henry Scott). The totality of his many-sided intellectual contributions,
however, has not been carefully examined.

Histories of Philippine anthropology begin with such U.S. state-
sponsored projects as the work of Dean Worcester and the Bureau of
Non-Christian Tribes, and professionals like Alfred Kroeber and Laura
Watson Benedict, or the discipline's institutionalization in the state
university after 1914. While reference is made to the "enormous amount"
of ethnological data generated by Spanish and other European authors,
American anthropologists and the Filipinos who trained under them
mainly approached the Philippines as virgin territory. In a summation
of knowledge about Philippine "ethnography, ethology, idiomography,"
authorized by the Philippine Commission in 1901, Paterno is ignored
while only passing mention is made of Pardo and de los Reyes.[262]

In a survey of the state of knowledge about the Philippines as of
1898, James LeRoy, one of the most influential of U.S.-colonial scholars, mentions the contributions of Filipinos but is dismissive of their
value. Calling Paterno a person with "a lively imagination, too lively for
politics and history," he dismisses as "ridiculous" Paterno's writings
on "an imaginary primitive religion and civilization of the Filipinos." He judges de los Reyes's writings as "commonly unreliable"
and, elsewhere, writes that, on the subject of mythology and folk-
lore, "the writings of Pedro A. Paterno are virtually worthless, being in
fact discreditable to his race, and the pamphlets of Isabelo de los Reyes,
while better, do not deserve the name of 'researches'." LeRoy believed
that the "modern era" in the Philippines "in certain respects, did not
really begin until after the establishment of American rule." On ethnology, he writes that "the real foundations of that science are only now

being laid in the Philippines." He dismisses pre-American scholarship as biased and confused. Spanish ethnological writings were, "speaking strictly from the scientific point of view, unreliable or, in some cases, worthless." LeRoy concludes that "the science of Philippine ethnology proper is still in its infancy."[263]

The claim of American beginnings has persisted. Karl Hutterer illustrates the break by pointing out that Kroeber's *Peoples of the Philippines* (1919) does not mention a single primary Spanish (or, for that matter, Filipino) source outside of what was made available in the Blair and Robertson *Philippine Islands* series. Honoring the work of H. Otley Beyer (1883–1966), hailed as the "father of Philippine anthropology," E. Arsenio Manuel writes: "Before Beyer came there was no Philippine prehistory to speak of. When he started his career in research he practically did so from scratch." Similarly, Filipino students came to believe it was Beyer who first theorized that the Philippines was once part of the Asiatic mainland, ignoring the fact that this was an idea already found in Paterno and early Spanish authors.[264]

The American divide stranded the works of Paterno, Pardo, and de los Reyes in the past. The promotion of the English language, which Pardo ironically pushed, severed a new generation of readers from the Spanish works Pardo and his contemporaries wrote. Language and access, however, were not the only reasons for the genealogical break. Increased professionalization, changing orientations in the disciplines and the hegemonic claims of American education propagated new approaches and methods. The premium on "objectivity" and empirical, fieldwork-based research devalued the philosophical and speculative style of Victorian anthropology. Anthropology demarcated its field apart from the expansive and philosophical ambitions of early ethnology; modern linguistics weaned itself from its roots in nineteenth-century philology; and sociology shifted from a European preoccupation with social philosophy to American positivism.

The postrevolutionary order inculcated values of civic tutelage and academic apprenticeship. The political moment was ripe for a new scientific outlook that stressed disciplinary specialization, empirical research, and detachment from political concerns. Anthropology moved towards cultural relativism, setting the premium on understanding a culture "in its own terms," in effect discrediting the "universal history of mankind"

Paterno was engaged in. While all these advanced knowledge about Philippine society, the new cult of "objective" scholarship masked its own historical groundedness and bias in the treatment of "other peoples." It disguised the continuing complicity of Filipino intellectuals in Western forms of knowledge.

ON THE ADVENT of the Western disciplines in colonial India, Partha Chatterjee (drawing from Michel Foucault) says that differences could appear at four levels in the dispersal of the disciplines in the colony: the formation of objects of knowledge, modalities of enunciation, concept-formation, and thematic choices.[265] Here the question of "modalities of enunciation" (who is authorized to speak and how, from which institutional site and subject position, and for what ends) is crucial, informing as it does what and how objects and concepts are selected, shaped, and deployed. It brings into play other discursive factors: the location one occupies in existing communication networks, the real and imagined audiences one addresses, and the discursive mode or medium one uses. This makes intellectual biography—with its focus on the specificities of human enunciation—a productive axis for understanding larger discursive formations.

Though the intellectual constitutes discourse, he comes into a field already constituted by others. It is a system of reference with determinative effects, orienting those engaged in cultural production by defining the universe of problems, models, and references. It is both a "space of possibilities" as well as one that subjects the intellectual to "the structured constraints of the field" (in Pierre Bourdieu's words, a field of "positions-taken").[266] The constraints are not just intellectual (though it is at this level that they are most insidious, lying so deep we are scarcely aware of them) but material (lack of educational opportunities and leisure, censorship, repression).

This is most evident in a colonial situation. By definition, a colonial intellectual is one already compromised. Once one is drawn into the orbit of a colonizing power, the groundwork of one's existence has changed. The "outside" is already part of the "inside" and one is no longer innocent. There is no pure, originary, Archimedean position from which one can interrogate the Other. To be an "intellectual" is to assume a role already contaminated. To begin to speak of the "modern" is to deny a pure indigeneity. The idea of the "local" already presupposes a relation to a wider, englobing outside.[267]

Yet these very same experiences, of "nativization" and subordination, are markers of difference that can be mined as source of an autonomous, empowered identity. Mediating knowledge, the local intellectual does not leave it unchanged. His principal advantage is location and difference: of being so situated he knows things the other cannot know, deploying the power of the "hidden" to interrogate the claims of what the other has "revealed," or, conversely, posing the "evident" against what the other has "concealed."

Edward Said writes: "An interlocutor in the colonial situation is by definition either someone who is compliant and belongs to the category of what the French in Algeria called an *evolue, notable,* or *caid...* or someone who, like Fanon's native intellectual, simply refuses to talk, deciding that only a radically antagonistic, perhaps violent riposte is the only interlocution that is possible with colonial power." Said dramatizes for effect the contrast between the "scrubbed, disinfected interlocutor" who discourses in the master's handsomely appointed salon and the one who is outside, clamoring on the doorstep, making such an unseemly disturbance as to be let in "guns or stones checked in with the porter."[268] Between one and the other—mimicry and silence, genteel repartee and violent riposte—the acts of interlocution are in fact quite complex.

What of the Filipino interlocutor? How does the Filipino intellectual engage Western knowledge? Where relations of dominance and subordination are perceived as existing between cultures, in what specific ways are ideas and categories conceived in the context of the dominant culture received and transformed in the subordinate? What local or indigenous resources are deployed in this engagement with the Other?

Examining the works of Paterno, Pardo, and de los Reyes reveals the varied, dynamic ways in which Filipino intellectuals positioned themselves in relation to Western knowledge. Such variety and dynamism derive from the specificities of their location and formation, the stance they took in relation to the object and audience of their discourse, the refractions of the languages and forms they used, and the shifts in the moments of enunciation. Such an investigation shows that the binaries of collaboration and resistance, acceptance and rejection, are reductive polarities that flatten out historical reality. This is not to deny the utility of notions of resistance and collaboration, to descend into particularism and relativism and refuse judgments of political consequence. The discourse of rulers and ruled is not an academic conversation in a parlor but a deep, assymetrical struggle for power. One needs to acknowledge, however, that the realm of intellectual acts is a tricky, complex field and must always be historicized both at the point of enunciation as well as reception.

The particularities of the Philippine case are important. Nineteenth-century Filipino intellectuals developed in the belly of colonialism. Typically, they were of the urban bourgeoisie and landed gentry, social formations produced by colonialism and capitalism. They were almost exclusively male, mostly creole and mestizo, the racial types that, owing to their spatial and social location, were the earliest to access economic and cultural advantages under colonial rule. Like their counterparts in Latin America, they associated with Europeans, attended European-style schools, entered the modern professions, became proficient in metropolitan languages, traveled widely, and avidly consumed Western culture. (Unlike Latin American intellectuals, however, among whom there was a great deal of cross-border contact among Chileans, Argentinians, Uruguayans, and others, Filipinos largely worked by themselves.[269])

Empowered by wealth and education, they nevertheless remained subordinate in a colonial order that privileged Europeans over indigenes, peninsulars over creoles, and the "pure-blooded" over the mixed. They were conscious, however, that they were the leading elements of the colonized. They parlayed this "in-between" position into a space of knowledge and power, authorizing them to speak for the dominated and excluded. As cultural translators, they had the privilege of access to both sides. They exercised a double authority (one more chameleon-like than Janus-faced), claiming on one hand the "authenticity" of the native and moral high ground of the victim, and, on the other (or at the same time), access to the European world and its levers of power. They drew authority from their being well-read, well-traveled lawyers, physicians, or writers, yet claimed power from being "native" (as did—even if dissimilar in intent—Paterno when he assumed the title of *maguinoo* or Rizal when he invented *indios bravos*).

Their positionings were biased in favor of the West. There was little of an autochthonous tradition out of which they could speak or engage the West. Unlike other parts of Asia, there were no large, powerful precolonial "kingdoms," no well-articulated corps of royal scribes and religio-literary specialists, no archive of written histories or legal treatises. Islam was incipient at Spanish contact and while it maintained its influence in the archipelago's unincorporated southern end, it did not seriously challenge Spanish hegemony in the rest of the country. There were, despite Paterno's fantasies, no ancient kingdoms to restore, no "past" to summon into the present. The "nation" did not even have a name. Tagalog nationalists dilated *Tagalog* to refer to the nation (and even then it did not quite include the unsubjugated Muslims and "tribes," who were not encompassed by the term *indio* but were classed as *moros* and *infieles*). *Tagalog* did not catch on for those who thought of themselves as *Bisaya* or *Ilokano*. Thus the recourse to the name the Spaniards invented for the country, after the King of Spain, *Filipinas*.

When Rizal's generation was born, Spanish colonialism was already three centuries deep. Men like Paterno may have descended from "old Tagalog nobility" but this did not invest them with real symbolic or material power beyond the nostalgic and decorative. Despite the nationalists' wishful theme of the lost *codice* of palmleaf manuscripts and Rizal's lament over "our vanished nationality," the challenge for Filipino intellectuals was, in a sense more apt and urgent than elsewhere, the "invention" of the nation. They used Western frames and sources in this endeavor. It could not have been otherwise given their intellectual formation and available resources. It could not have been otherwise given the primary audiences they addressed (Spaniards, Europeans, fellow *ilustrados*), the language and verbal genres they used, and the assimilationist aims that guided the Propaganda Movement.

It simplifies to say that theirs was a "derivative discourse." It is less derivative (with what the word suggests of the handed-down and imitated) as appropriated and reconstituted.[270] If the West's discourse had to be appropriated it was because colonialism *happened*. Filipino intellectuals had to work *through* it and not outside of, or apart from, it. They worked out of their particular location, framing the object ("nation") in their own way, deploying themes and concepts to their advantage, making their own strategic choices. They claimed the best of what the West had to offer as their own. Trained in the modern professions, exposed to Europe, adept in its language and textual practices, they appropriated the authority of its best minds, seeing themselves in the same simultaneous order as Voltaire and Darwin. They did not only claim parity with Europeans, they did something more radical. They "provincialized" the Spaniards in the colony by claiming they knew "Europe," what it represented, better than these Spaniards did. They, and not the Spaniards, were the moderns.

To a certain extent, as in Paterno's case, this was mimicry. Yet even mimicry has an unstable, dangerous quality. While it reinforces the mystique of the original, it can slide into parody and subvert it. In more positive ways, it was not just mimicry but an assumption of the theoretical premises of Enlightenment thought, the promise of science and reason. Such men as Rizal were acutely aware of the perils of "foreign" knowledge. In his message to the young women of Malolos in 1889, he endorsed the value of learning from others but warned, "may you not gather in the garden of knowledge the unripe fruit but select what you pick, think about it, taste it before swallowing it, for on the face of the earth all are mixed and it is not unusual for the enemy to sow weeds together with the good seeds in the middle of the field."[271]

In staking out their claim to knowledge they constructed the agency of a nation. In arguing that Filipinos had an ancient and noble past, Rizal and his contemporaries mostly relied on Spanish sources but selected, recontextualized, and stressed statements and themes to advance their thesis. They developed European "migration wave" theories of the peopling of the islands into a theme of historic dynamism and progressive advance at the crest of which they stood. They used to their advantage the Spanish chroniclers' Eurocentric observations about petty states, a local priesthood, and beliefs analogous to Christianity, using them to show that the elements of "civilization" and "high religion" existed in precolonial times. They turned Spanish observations about similarities in local languages, customs, and racial types into "proof" of the existence of a definable *nacion*.

They expanded this argument in two directions. They excavated Malay and Asian sources outside the Philippines to link the country to broader, better-documented civilizations in the region, the "Malay" or an *Ur*-civilization that Filipinos shared with other Asians, like the Japanese (in Paterno's extreme case, even the civilizations of the Near East). And, in the case of Isabelo de los Reyes, they attempted the recovery of *folk-lore* in a bid to resurrect and replenish a storehouse of indigenous traditions and popular thought.

Both projects were flawed and unfinished. There was a pronounced bias for Western frameworks of modernity and progress (naïve and mendicant as well as critical and pragmatic) in which local phenomena were explained according to Western categories and local history realigned to fit a Western teleology. Equally important, much was left unrecognized or unfinished with respect to accessing and building a local knowledge-base and expanding the scope of the people's substantive participation in intellectual life.

Leading theoreticians of the nation died young or were lost and coopted in the shift to the U.S. colonial order. De los Reyes was consumed by many enthusiasms and did not push forward the project of a *folk-lore Filipino*. Pardo grew impatient with the past and devoted himself to the pursuit of an American vision of the present. Despite the populism of de los Reyes and the commitment to public education of Rizal and Pardo, the work of the intellectuals (in a time when the "directing" role of an educated elite went largely unquestioned) remained elitist in range and assumptions.

The elite's historical formation carried with it ethnic, territorial, economic, and political biases. It would be a mistake to overstress racial and class divisions. Racial categories like "mestizo" and "creole" are blurred by such facts as depth of residence, density of local blood and social ties, or (in the case of creoles) the lack of numbers to sustain an autonomous, corporate identity. Polarities of "elite" and "masses," on the other hand, do not account for the dynamic specificities of social formation in nineteenth-century Philippines, particularly in the places where revolutionary activities were intense. The *ilustrados'* version of the "nation," however, remained inchoate and provisional, one shaped out of their own locations. It is limited in the ways they imagined the nation's body in terms territorial (in its bias for a Tagalog center), social (in its marginalization of Muslims and "tribes"), and political (in its misrecognition of the agency of the "people" they presumed to lead).

Nationalist thought is a process. Today—with the interest in the historical "situatedness" of knowledge and "the native viewpoint"—the examples of writers like Paterno, Pardo, and de los Reyes are immensely instructive. They were, after all, among the first "natives" in Southeast

Asia to engage Orientalist scholarship in its homegrounds. Inserting themselves into a European discursive formation, they selected and used topics, methods, and theories dominant in European scholarship at the time. In the process, it may be said that they created a derivative discourse that affirmed the ideas of racial, social, and political hierarchies that underwrote Orientalism. However, to dismiss their works as a simple case of complicity is reductive. The figures of Paterno in Salamanca, Rizal at the British Museum, and Pardo at the Sorbonne are signs not only of complicity, but the critical engagement of Filipinos in Western structures of knowing the world.

There are important lessons to be learned from looking at the enunciative modalities that informed how they dealt with local realities and positioned themselves in relation both to European knowledge and the national community with which they identified themselves. Rizal, Paterno, Pardo, and de los Reyes are instructive not just for how they engaged European Orientalism but—and this is part of the same process—how they located themselves in relation to the country *from*, *of*, and *for* which they tried or pretended to speak. There is much to be learned from the unfinished, strange and wondrous itineraries they took.

A PHYSICIAN in the Age of Reason, Jose Rizal was fond of speaking of society in medicophysiological terms. His image of the nation as a nervous system expressed his hope in the formation of an integral, coordinated, vitally functioning body. It is not a bad metaphor. As in the human nervous system, a nation cannot be self-sufficient. It is nourished by a constant flow of impressions from the outside world, otherwise, deprived of contact and starved of stimulation, the body falls disoriented and prey to hallucinations. It is not only turned outwards but inwards, alive to what goes on inside the body, parts sensitive and interconnected, the system's sensory receptors receiving and processing information, alerting the body to what dangers lie within or may sneak in from the outside. It is a centered system, with the brain and spinal cord as main base of operations from which neural impulses travel through a wondrously intricate network, stirring emotion, thought, such that the body acts as one.

There are limits to the analogy as well as dangers, as in the specter it raises of the center as a malign controlling intelligence.[272] Rizal, however, was not thinking of hierarchy and control as much as he was of circulation and exchange. Elsewhere (to stay with his medical analogies), he spoke of free commerce and communication as an index of progress "just as the index of a man's health is the perfect circulation of the blood through the vessels of the anatomy; because without those routes there cannot exist relations between the different parts of the country and the other nations; without these relations the bonds between men and nations cannot be understood; without these bonds there cannot be either unity or strength; and without strength or unity man cannot attain perfection or even progress."[273] Of colonialism, he similarly wrote: "The existence of a foreign body in another endowed with strength and activity is against all natural and moral laws. Science teaches us that either it is assimilated, it destroys the organism, it is eliminated, or it is encysted. The encystment of a conquering people is impossible, whenever it means complete isolation, absolute inertia, adynamia of the victorious element. Encystment here signifies the tomb of the foreign invader."[274]

When Rizal spoke of intellectuals as the "brains of the nation," by what alchemy of history did he imagine that the brain could become one with the body itself? Rizal was enough of a realist to know the extreme difficulty, even essential impossibility, of the dream but he understood that nations live on such dreams.

NOTES

1. See Resil B. Mojares, "The Islands According to Pigafetta," *Waiting for Mariang Makiling: Essays in Philippine Cultural History* (Quezon City: Ateneo de Manila University [ADMU] Press, 2002), 20–51.

2. On the intellectual contributions of the missionaries: Pablo Fernandez, O.P., *History of the Church in the Philippines (1521–1898)* (Metro Manila: National Book Store, 1979), 365–84; Policarpio F. Hernandez, O.S.A., *The Augustinians in the Philippines* (Makati: Colegio de San Agustin, 1998).

On colonial linguistic studies: Pedro Serrano Laktaw, "Breve Observaciones," *Diccionario Tagalog-Hispano* (Manila: Imp. y Lit. de Santos y Bernal, 1914), i–xxxv; Otto Scheerer, "Outlines of the History of Exploration of Philippine Languages and their Relatives in the East and West," *Philippine Review*, III:1&2 (1918), 56–67; John Leddy Phelan, "Philippine Linguistics and Spanish Missionaries, 1565–1700," *Mid-America*, 37:3 (1955), in *Readings in Philippine Linguistics*, ed. A.B. Gonzalez, et al. (Manila: Linguistic Society of the Philippines, 1973), 54–69, 70–82. See Joseph Errington, "Colonial Linguistics," *Annual Review of Anthropology* 30 (2001), 19–39.

3. Quoted in Hernandez, *Augustinians in the Philippines*, 39.

4. Epifanio de los Santos, "Literatura Tagala," *Cultura Social,* II (1914), 273. In E. Arsenio Manuel, *Dictionary of Philippine Biography* (Quezon City: Filipiniana Publications, 1955–1986), IV:491.

5. See C.R. Boxer, "Some Aspects of Spanish Historical Writing on the Philippines," *Historians of Southeast Asia*, ed. D.G.E. Hall (London: Oxford University Press, 1961), 200–12.

6. See Manuel Blanco, O.S.A., *Flora de Filipinas* (Manila: San Agustin Convent, 1993; reissue of 1877–1883 edition), 3 vols.; Hernandez, *Augustinians in the Philippines*, 160–62; Leo A. Cullum, "Georg Joseph Kamel: Philippine Botanist, Physician, Pharmacist," *Philippine Studies,* 4:2 (1956), 319–39; John N. Schumacher, "One Hundred Years

of Jesuit Scientists: The Manila Observatory, 1865–1965," *Philippine Studies,* 13:2 (l965), 258–86.

7. Juan Alvarez Guerra, *De Manila a Marianas* (Madrid: Libreria Universal de Cordoba, 1883; first ed., 1872), 57.

8. *Botanical Plates: Juan de Cuellar's Scientific Commission, Philippines (1786–1801)* (Manila: National Commission for Philippine Culture and Art, 1995).

9. Ferdinand Blumentritt, "Lo que Escribieron los Extranjeros sobre Filipinas," *La Solidaridad,* trans. G.F. Ganzon & L. Mañeru (Metro Manila: Fundacion Santiago, 1996) (March 31–August 15, 1893; September 30, 1894); Hermogenes E. Bacareza, *The German Connection* (Manila: [The Author], 2003); Reg Zell, *A Bibliography of Works About the Philippines in German* (Munchen: Verlag Almuth Petersen-Roil, 1996); Denis Nardin, *France and the Philippines,* trans. M.J. Cruz (Manila: National Historical Institute, 1989); Otto van den Muijzenberg, *Dutch Filipiniana: An Annotated Bibliography of Dutch Publications on the Philippines* (Leiden: KITLV Press, 1992).

10. John Leddy Phelan, *The Hispanization of the Philippines: Spanish Aims and Filipino Responses, 1565–1700* (Madison: University of Wisconsin Press, 1959), 26, 135.

11. Cesar Adib Majul, *Muslims in the Philippines* (Manila: Saint Mary's Publishing, 1978), 157; also 124–25, 129–31, 134–36, 139–51, et passim. Also see *The Philippine Islands, 1493–1898,* ed. Emma H. Blair & James A. Robertson [hereinafter cited as *BR*] (Cleveland: Arthur H. Clark Company, 1907), XXXV:92–112; O.D. Corpuz, *The Roots of the Filipino Nation* (Quezon City: AKLAHI Foundation, 1989), I:151–57.

12. *BR,* VII:95–111; Corpuz, *Roots of the Filipino Nation,* I:111–19.

13. Pedro Chirino, S.J., *Relacion de las Islas Filipinas,* trans. R. Echevarria (Manila: Historical Conservation Society, 1969), 296; Sinibaldo de Mas, "Informe de las Islas Filipinas en 1842," *BR,* XL.

14. "Letter to Felipe II," *BR,* VII:69.

15. Samuel K. Tan, *Filipino Muslim Perceptions of Their History and Culture as Seen Through Indigenous Sources* (Zamboanga City: SKT Publications, 2003), 2. See Najeeb M. Saleeby, *Studies in Moro History, Law and Religion* (Manila: Bureau of Printing, 1905), xiii, 1–66; William Henry Scott, *Prehispanic Source Materials for the Study of Philippine History* (Manila: University of Santo Tomas Press, 1968), 83–85.

It is interesting that Sultan Kudarat's oft-cited speech—which Corpuz cites as a "rare and profound" native statement on "concepts that modern intellectuals discuss as political obligation and political liberty"—has survived as an indirect recording by a Jesuit missionary. See Corpuz, *Roots of the Filipino Nation,* I:153. On the use of reported speech, see Carlo Ginzburg, "Alien Voices: The Dialogic Element in Early Modern Jesuit Historiography," *History, Rhetoric, and Proof* (Hanover: University Press of New England, 1999), 71–91.

16. On these epics: Damiana L. Eugenio, *Philippine Folk Literature: The Epics* (Quezon City: University of the Philippines Press, 2001); Merito B. Espinas, *Ibalong: The Bikol Folk Epic-Fragment* (Manila: UST Publishing House, 1996).

17. *Rizal's Correspondence with Fellow Reformists* (Manila: National Heroes Commission, 1963), 275.

18. See Luciano P.R. Santiago, "The Beginnings of Higher Education in the Philippines (1601–1772)," *Philippine Quarterly of Culture & Society* [hereinafter cited as *PQCS*] 19 (1991), 135.

On colonial education: Encarnacion Alzona, *A History of Education in the Philippines, 1565–1930* (Manila: University of the Philippines Press, 1932); Evergisto Bazaco, O.P., *History of Education in the Philippines* (Manila: University of Santo Tomas Press, 1953); Domingo Abella, "State of Higher Education in the Philippines to 1863—A Historical Reappraisal," *Philippine Historical Review*, 1:1 (1965), 1–46; Fidel Villaroel, O.P., "The University of Santo Tomas of Manila (1611–1987)," *Philippiniana Sacra*, 23:67 (1988), 81–119.

19. See Resil B. Mojares, *Origins and Rise of the Filipino Novel* (Quezon City: University of the Philippines Press, 1983), 45–46. On the first book: *Doctrina Christiana, The First Book Printed in the Philippines, Manila, 1593* (Washington, D.C: Library of Congress, 1947).

20. On censorship: W.E. Retana, *La Censura de Imprenta en Filipinas* (Madrid: Libreria General de Victoriano Suarez, 1908); *Idem.*, "Press Censorship in the Philippines," *Philippine Colophon,* 3:1/2 (1965), 26–52 (Translation of an article in *Nuestro Tiempo*, Madrid, November 1907). Also *BR*, V:256–73; LI:37, 71; LII:139; Vicente S. Hernandez, *History of Books and Libraries in the Philippines, 1521–1900* (Manila: National Commission for Culture & the Arts, 1996), 55–58.

21. Guillaume Le Gentil, *A Voyage to the Indian Seas*, trans. F.C. Discher (Manila: Filipiniana Book Guild, 1964), xx, 75.

22. Fedor Jagor, *Travels in the Philippines* (Manila: Filipiniana Book Guild, 1965; first published in 1873), 4, 18.

23. John Bowring, *A Visit to the Philippine Islands* (Manila: Filipiniana Book Guild, 1963), 84, 118; Lafond de Lurcy, et al., *Travel Accounts of the Islands (1832–1858)* (Manila: Filipiniana Book Guild, 1974), 231; Robert MacMicking, *Recollections of Manila and the Philippines* (Manila: Filipiniana Book Guild, 1967), 48–49.

See the remarks of an English traveler in 1828: *BR*, LI:98–99.

24. In 1870, there were 3,823 Spaniards from the Peninsula (all but 516 of them males) and 9,710 "Filipino-Spaniards" (mestizos and creoles). The 1903 Census listed only 3,888 Peninsular Spaniards in the archipelago. On these and other estimates: James A. LeRoy, "The Philippines, 1860–1898—Some Comments and Bibliographical Notes," *BR*, LII: 115–116n.

25. "Petition of a Filipino Chief for Redress," *BR*, XIV:327–29; "Letter to Silva," *BR*, XVII:151–52. Also Corpuz, *Roots of the Filipino Nation*, I:96–97.

26. Luciano P.R. Santiago, "Brother Marcelo Banal de San Augustin, O.S.A. (1632–1697): First Indio Lay Brother," *Unitas*, 63:1 (1990), 26–33.

27. Pedro de San Francisco de Assisi, "Recollect Missions in the Philippines, 1661–1712," *BR*, XLI:194–95. Also see Nicholas P. Cushner, "Early Jesuit Missionary Methods in the Philippines," *The Americas*, 15:4 (1959), 371, 375.

28. Quoted in H. de la Costa, S.J., *The Jesuits in the Philippines, 1581–1768* (Cambridge: Harvard University Press, 1967), 533.

29. Luciano P.R. Santiago, "Talangpaz: The Foundresses of the Beaterio de San Sebastian de Calumpang (now the Congregation of the Augustinian Recollect Sisters), 1691–1732," *PQCS*, 17:3 (1989), 212–51.

30. W.E. Retana, *Origenes de la Imprenta Filipina* (Madrid: Libreria General de Victoriano Suarez, 1911), 60–61, 81–87, 199–203; Jose Lopez del Castillo, *Disquisiciones Historico-Bibliograficas* (Manila: Imprenta del Gobierno, 1956), 9–11; Bienvenido L. Lumbera, *Tagalog Poetry, 1570–1898: Tradition and Influences in its Development* (Quezon City: ADMU Press, 1986), 38–39.

See *Sucesos Felices, que por mar y tierra ha dado N.S. a las armas Españolas en las Islas Filipinas contra el Mindanao y en las de Terrenate, contra los Holandeses, por fin del ano de 1636 y principio del de 1637* (Manila: por Tomas Pinpin, 1637). Only two or three issues are known and authorship has been ascribed to the Jesuit Pedro Gutierrez. The claim that it is "the first Philippine newspaper" and its author is Tomas Pinpin is made in Carlos Quirino, "First Newsletter in the Philippines," *Journal of History*, V:3/4 (1957), 169–78. See *BR*, XXIX:116–34; Retana, *Origenes de la Imprenta Filipina*, 123–24, 165; *Early Philippine Imprints in the Lopez Memorial Museum* (Pasig: Lopez Memorial Museum, 1961), 10–13.

31. Gaspar de San Agustin, O.S.A., *Conquistas de las Islas Filipinas*, trans. L.A. Mañeru (Manila: San Agustin Museum, 1998; original ed., 1698), 990–91; Marcelino A. Foronda, Jr., & Juan A. Foronda, "Bukaneg and the Early Books in Ilocano," *Samtoy: Essays in Iloko History and Culture* (Manila: United Publishing, 1972), 81–115. Also Zoilo M. Galang, ed., *Encyclopedia of the Philippines* (Manila: Exequiel Floro, 1951), III:198; *Filipinos in History* (Manila: National Historical Institute, 1990), I:131–33.

32. For biographies of early converts: Santiago, "Brother Marcelo Banal de San Augustin," 26–33; John N. Schumacher, S.J., "Felipe Sonson, Seventeenth-Century Filipino Jesuit: Missionary to the Marianas," *Landas*, 9:2 (1995), 266–85; Marcelino A. Foronda, Jr., *Mother Ignacia and her Beaterio* (Makati, Rizal: St. Paul Publications, 1975); Mojares, *Waiting for Mariang Makiling*, 87–108, 109–39.

33. See Lumbera, *Tagalog Poetry*, 36–38, 43–45, 66–70. On Bagongbanta: Manuel Artigas, *Galeria de Filipinos Ilustres* (Manila: Imprenta de Gabino A. Pobre, 1918), II:59–60.

34. See Kenneth E. Bauzon, *Lam-ang in Transition: A Historical Re-appraisal* (Quezon City: University of the Philippines, 1973).

35. Diego Aduarte, O.P., "Historia de la Provincia del Sancto Rosario de la Orden de Predicadores" (Manila, 1640), *BR*, 32:52; Mojares, *Origins and Rise of the Filipino Novel*, 25–27.

36. Vicente L. Rafael, *Contracting Colonialism: Translation and Christian Conversion in Tagalog Society Under Early Spanish Rule* (Ithaca: Cornell University Press, 1988), 55–83 (also published by ADMU Press, 1988).

37. Pardo, "Imprenta en Filipinas," in Epifanio de los Santos, *Trinidad H. Pardo de Tavera* (Manila: Imprenta "Cultura Filipina," 1913), 89.

38. W.E. Retana, *Aparato Bibliografico de la Historia General de Filipinas* (Madrid: Imprenta de la Sucesora de M. Minuesa de los Rios, 1906), I, no. 317; T.H. Pardo de Tavera, *Biblioteca Filipina* (Washington: Government Printing Office, 1903), nos. 92–93; Lumbera, *Tagalog Poetry*, 57; Rafael, *Contracting Colonialism*, 194–209.

39. See Horacio de la Costa, "The Development of the Native Clergy in the Philippines," *Studies in Philippine Church History*, ed. G.H. Anderson (Ithaca: Cornell University Press, 1969), 65–104; John N. Schumacher, "Some Historical Considerations on the Evangelization of the Philippines," *Contemporary Studies*, 2:4 (1965), 222–37; *Idem.*, "The Eighteenth Century Filipino Clergy: A Footnote to de la Costa," *The Filipino Clergy: Historical Studies and Future Perspectives*, ed. H. de la Costa & J.N. Schumacher (Manila: Loyola Papers No. 12, 1980), 60–78; *Idem.*, "The Early Filipino Clergy, 1698–1762," *Philippine Studies*, 51:1 (2003), 7–62.

Also Luciano P.R. Santiago, *The Hidden Light: The First Filipino Priests* (Quezon City: New Day Publishers, 1987); Hernando M. Coronel, *Boatmen for Christ* (Quezon City: Reyes Publishing, 1998). For a critical summary of the scholarship on the early Filipino clergy: John N. Schumacher, S.J., "The Early Filipino Clergy: 1698–1762," *Philippine Studies*, 51:1 (2003), 7–62.

40. On the Baluyots and the Pampanga uprising: Luciano P.R. Santiago, *Kapampangan Pioneers in the Philippine Church, 1592–2001* (Angeles City: Holy

Angel University, 2002), 26, 28, 30–31, 106–10, 114–20; *Idem.*, *Hidden Light*, 27–30; "Insurrections by Filipinos in the Seventeenth Century," *BR*, 38:139–215.

41. See Luciano P.R. Santiago, "The Capellania of Padre Mariano Gomes," *Philippine Studies*, 32 (1984), 325–34; *Idem.*, *Kapampangan Pioneers*, 1–9, 35–38.

42. Santiago, *Hidden Light*, 145–51.

43. Joaquin Martinez de Zuniga, *Estadismo de las Islas Filipinas*, ed. W.E. Retana (Madrid: Imprenta de la Viuda de M. Minuesa de los Rios, 1893), I:60–61.

44. Luciano P.R. Santiago, "The Struggles of the Native Clergy in Pampanga (1771–1777)," *Philippine Studies*, 33 (1985), 176–202.

45. Salvador Pons, *El Clero Secular Filipino* (Manila: Imp. La Democracia, 1900), 25–26; Luciano P.R. Santiago, "Of Prose and Souls: Padre Modesto de Castro (1819–1864)," *PQCS*, 13 (1985), 51–67.

46. *BR*, XL:321. The same observation about the "profaning" of the *pasyon* is made by John Bowring in 1858 (Bowring, *Visit*, 82–83).

47. Toribio Minguella, "Estilo Poetico," *Ensayo de Gramatica Hispano-Tagala* (1878), reprinted in Retana, *Aparato Bibliografico*, II:872.

48. Vicente Barrantes, *El Teatro Tagalo* (Madrid: Tipog. de Manuel Gines Hernandez, 1890), 23–24.

49. Horacio de la Costa, S.J., "The Formative Century, 1760–1860," *Archipelago*, 2:19 (1975), 8–13.

50. The 1887 census, the only completed population census during the Spanish period, placed the country's population at 6,462,875. See O.D. Corpuz, *An Economic History of the Philippines* (Quezon City: University of the Philippines Press, 1997), 143; *Idem.*, "The Population of the Archipelago, 1565–1898," *Roots of the Filipino Nation*, I:515–70.

51. T.H. Pardo de Tavera, "The results of the economic development of the Philippines" [1912], *Philippine Agricultural Review*, 18 (1925), 151–78.

52. Jose Ma. Rivera, *Huseng Sisiw* (Manila: Balagtasiana, 1933), 17. See Lumbera, *Tagalog Poetry*, 72–82; Mojares, *Origins and Rise of the Filipino Novel*, 63–65.

53. On Baltazar: Patricia Melendrez-Cruz & Apolonio Bayani Chua, *Himalay: Kalipunan ng mga Pag-aaral kay Balagtas* (Manila: Cultural Center of the Philippines, 1988).

54. The best edition is Francisco Balagtas, *Florante at Laura*, ed. V.S. Almario (Quezon City: Adarna House, 2003), based on the 1861 edition, which clarifies problems arising from the printing history of the text.

55. See Virgilio S. Almario, *Kung Sino ang Kumatha Kina Bagongbanta, Ossorio, Herrera, Aquino de Belen, Balagtas, atbp.* (Metro Manila: Anvil Publishing, 1992).

56. See Richard Herr, "The Constitution of 1812 and the Spanish Road to Parliamentary Monarchy," *Revolution and the Meanings of Freedom in the Nineteenth Century*, ed. I. Woloch (Stanford: Stanford University Press, 1996), 65–102.

57. See Retana, *Censura de Imprenta*, 2; Carson Taylor, *History of the Philippine Press* (Manila: no pub., 1927), 10–11; Jesus Z. Valenzuela, *History of Journalism in the Philippine Islands* (Manila: The Author, 1933), 47–49.

58. On Pilapil and his family: Luciano P.R. Santiago, "Doctor Don Mariano Bernave Pilapil (1759–1818): Passion and Transformation," *PQCS*, 16 (1988), 19–43; *Idem.*, "The Filipino Priest-Delegates to the Spanish Cortes of 1813," *PQCS*, 13 (1985), 221–34.

59. *Dos mascarados descubiertos. Contestacion juiciosa del Sor. Dor. D. Mariano Pilapil, Diputado en Cortes por esta Provincia de Manila . . .* (Manila: Carlos Francisco de la Cruz, 1813). See Angel Perez and Cecilio Guemes, *Adiciones y Continuacion de "La Imprenta en Manila" de D.J.T. Medina* (Manila: Imprenta de Santos y Bernal, 1905), 249–50.

60. "Sinibaldo de Mas' Exposition on the Creoles of the Philippines," in Gregorio F. Zaide, comp., *Documentary Sources of Philippine History* (Metro Manila: National Book Store, 1990), 7:3–13; Eliodoro G. Robles, *The Philippines in the Nineteenth Century* (Quezon City: Malaya Books, 1969), 40–43.

61. W. E. Retana, *El Precursor de la Politica Redentorista* (Madrid: Viuda de M. Minuesa de los Rios, 1894); Nick Joaquin, *A Question of Heroes: Essays in Criticism on Ten Key Figures of Philippine History* (Makati: Ayala Museum, 1977), 27–36; Luciano P.R. Santiago, "Philippine Titles of Spanish Nobility (1761–1897)," *PQCS*, 19 (1991), 281–87. For the text of Varela's *Proclama Historial*: W.E. Retana, *Archivo del Bibliofilo Filipino* (Madrid: Imprenta de la Viuda de M. Minuesa de los Rios, 1895–98), II:243–67.

62. Paul P. de la Gironiere, *Twenty Years in the Philippines* (New York: Harper & Brothers, 1854), 51.

63. On Varela, Roxas, and Jugo: Clarita T. Nolasco, "The Creoles in Spanish Philippines" (M.A. thesis, Far Eastern University, 1969), 150–54, 215–18, 219, 260–61; Luciano P.R. Santiago, "The First Filipino Lay Doctors of Philosophy and of Laws (1785–1871)," *PQCS*, 16 (1988), 83–92.

64. *El Indio Agraviado contra El Noticioso Filipino* (Sampaloc, 1821); quoted in Artigas, *Events of 1872*, 37; Horacio de la Costa, S.J., *Readings in Philippine History* (Makati: Bookmark, 1992), 186. See Retana, *Archivo del Bibliofilo Filipino*, 5:189–210.

65. "Remarks on the Philippine Islands, 1819–1822" (by "An Englishman," Calcutta, 1828), *BR*, LI:178–81.

66. Corpuz, *Roots of the Filipino Nation*, I:476–77.

67. Sinibaldo de Mas, *Report on the Condition of the Philippines in 1842* (Manila: Historical Conservation Society, 1963), 121, 133, 159. This is the confidential third volume of *Informe sobre el Estado de las Islas Filipinas en 1842* (1843). Also see the memorial of Spanish official Manuel Bernaldez Pizarro on April 26, 1827: *BR*, LI:182–273.

68. The career of Apolinario de la Cruz is the prototype in Reynaldo C. Ileto's *Pasyon and Revolution: Popular Movements in the Philippines, 1840–1910* (Quezon City: ADMU Press, 1979).

69. De la Costa, *Readings in Philippine History*, 188.

70. Ileto, *Pasyon*, 15–16.

71. See Almario, *Kung Sino ang Kumatha*, 107–27; Ileto, *Pasyon*.

72. On the Roxas family: Salvador Araneta, "Introduction," *The World of Felix Roxas* (Manila: Filipiniana Book Guild, 1970), xi–xviii; Manuel Artigas, *The Events of 1872*, trans. O.D. Corpuz (Quezon City: University of the Philippines Press, 1996), 35, 79; Benito J. Legarda, Jr., *After the Galleons: Foreign Trade, Economic Change and Entrepreneurship in the Nineteenth-Century Philippines* (Quezon City: ADMU Press, 1999), 229–30, 317–18, 331–33; Nolasco, "Creoles in Spanish Philippines," 150–54, 276–78, 282–83.

73. De la Costa, *Readings in Philippine History*, 187.

74. Teodoro Agoncillo says that Bonifacio and Jacinto implicated the Roxases and other wealthy businessmen through forged documents to punish them for their non-support of the Katipunan and force them to take the side of the revolution. See *The Revolt of the Masses* (Quezon City: University of the Philippines Press, 1996; 1st ed., 1956), 146.

75. Jagor, *Travels*, 264–65.

76. Jurgen Habermas, *The Structural Transformation of the Public Sphere*, trans. T. Burger (Cambridge: MIT Press, 1991). Also see Dorinda Outram, *The Enlightenment* (Cambridge: Cambridge University Press, 1995), esp. Ch. 2.

77. Jean Mallat, *The Philippines: History, Geography, Customs, Agriculture, Industry and Commerce*, trans. P. Santillan-Castrence (Manila: National Historical Institute, 1983; Original ed., 1846), 434.

78. Agustin de la Cavada Mendez de Vigo, *Historia* (Manila, 1876), extracted in Abella, "Higher Education in the Philippines," 29–30. See Alzona, *History of Education*, 97–98. Alzona provides a different set of figures, saying that by 1877 there were 1,016 state-supported primary schools for boys and 582 for girls, with a combined enrolment of 177,113.

79. See Alzona, *History of Education*, 122–45; Villaroel, "University of Santo Tomas," 92, 96–97; Michael Cullinane, "Ilustrado Politics: The Response of the Filipino Educated

Elite to American Colonial Rule, 1898–1907" (Ph.D. diss., University of Michigan, 1989), 63–64 (published by ADMU Press, 2002).

80. On Latinity schools: Alzona, *History of Education*, 123–33; Bazaco, *Education in the Philippines*, 304–10, 321; Fidel Villaroel, O.P., *Marcelo H. del Pilar at the University of Santo Tomas* (Manila: UST Publishing House, 1997), 17–19; *Idem., Apolinario Mabini: His Birth Date and Student Years* (Manila: National Historical Institute, 2000), 12–17.

The role of these schools as relatively autonomous sites is suggested by Retana who cites *profesores de latinidad* among the leading elements of the anti-monastic movement in the Philippines. See Wenceslao E. Retana, *Frailes y Clerigos* (Madrid: Libreria de Fernando Fe, 1891), 54–55, 118.

81. Francisco X. Baranera, S.J., *Compendio de la Historia de Filipinas* (Manila: Imprenta de los Amigos del Pais, 1877); Felipe Ma. de Govantes, *Compendio de la Historia de Filipinas* (Manila: Imprenta del Colegio de Santo Tomas, 1877); *Idem., Lecciones de Geografia Descriptiva de Filipinas* (Manila: Imprenta del Colegio de Santo Tomas, 1878). On history in the curriculum: Bazaco, *Education in the Philippines*, 337–38, 396.

82. For a survey of primary-school textbooks in 1863–1896, see Alzona, *History of Education*, 108–21, 125–29; Bazaco, *Education in the Philippines*, 233–36, 335–39.

83. On the nineteenth-century bureaucracy: Robles, *Philippines in the Nineteenth Century*. A useful source is *Guia Oficial de Filipinas, 1891* (Manila: Tipo-Litografia de Chofre y Comp.a, 1891), and other volumes in this series.

84. See Lorenzo Rodriguez, O.P., "The Botanical Garden of Manila and Sebastian Vidal Soler," *Unitas*, 50:2/3 (1977), 60–74.

85. Fidel Villaroel, O.P., *Jose Rizal and the University of Santo Tomas* (Manila: University of Santo Tomas, 1984), 76; *Idem.*, "University of Santo Tomas," 96.

86. Corpuz, *Economic History*, 90–93. On the promotion of science under Charles III: Jorge Cañizares Esguerra, "Spanish America: From Baroque to Modern Colonial Science," *The Cambridge History of Science* (Cambridge: Cambridge University Press, 2003), IV:718–38.

87. Maria Luisa Rodriguez Baena, *La Sociedad Economica de Amigos del Pais de Manila en el Siglo XVIII* (Sevilla: Escuela de Estudios Hispano-Americanos de Sevilla, 1966), 64–65.

88. Baena, *Sociedad Economica*, 71; Corpuz, *Economic History*, 94.

89. *The Philippine Chronicles of Fray San Antonio*, trans. P. Picornell (Manila: Historical Conservation Society, 1977), 141. Also San Agustin, *Conquistas de las Islas Filipinas*, 99, 101.

90. Frederick Fox, "Philippine Vocational Education: 1860–1898," *Philippine Studies*, 24 (1976), 261–87. On the fine arts: Raymundo C. Banas, *The Music and Theater of the*

Filipino People (Manila: The Author, 1924); Luciano P.R. Santiago, "Damian Domingo and the First Philippine Art Academy (1821–1834)," *PQCS*, 19 (1991), 264–80; *Idem.*, "Philippine Academic Art: The Second Phase (1845–1898)," *PQCS*, 17 (1989), 67–89.

91. Lorenzo Rodriguez, O.P., "Chronicle of Philippine Pharmacy During the Spanish Period," *Unitas*, 27:3 (1954), 489–90, 493–94, 497–99.

92. Luciano P.R. Santiago, "The Painters of *Flora de Filipinas* (1877–1883)," *PQCS*, 21 (1993), 87–112; *Idem.*, "Damian Domingo"; *Filipinos in History*, III:4–6.

93. Alzona, *History of Education*, 76–77. In 1893, *La Voz Española* also published a weekly supplement devoted to the teaching profession (*Suplemento dedicado al Magisterio Filipino*). See *La Voz Española*, I:1 (January 1, 1893) – I:9 (February 26, 1893).

94. On Rizal's scientific work: J.P. Bantug, "Rizal and the Progress of the Natural Sciences," *Philippine Studies*, 9:1 (1961), 3–16. On medicine and pharmacy: Manuel Artigas, *Bibliografia medico-farmaceutica de Filipinas* (Manila: Imprenta de I.R. Morales, 1915); Jose P. Bantug, *Bosquejo Historico de la Medicina Hispano-Filipina* (Madrid: Ediciones Cultura Hispanica, 1952); Rodriguez, "Chronicle of Philippine Pharmacy," *Unitas*, 27:3 (1954), 465–529; 28:1 (1955), 5–75; 28:2 (1955), 219–60.

95. *Filipinos in History*, I:181–84.

96. Luciano P.R. Santiago, "The First Filipino Doctors of Pharmacy (1890–1893)," *PQCS*, 22 (1994), 90–102; Vivencio R. Jose, *The Rise and Fall of Antonio Luna* (Quezon City: University of the Philippines, 1972). See *Solidaridad*, V, 111 (September 15, 1893), 429–31; Retana, *Archivo del Bibliofilo Filipino*, 3: n63; 4: n82, 83, 106, 115.

97. W.E. Retana, *El Periodismo Filipino* (Madrid: Viuda de M. Minuesa de los Rios, 1895; English ed., 1991).

98. Retana, *Censura de Imprenta*, 7, 9, 12–13, 22–23, *passim*.

99. "Reforms Needed in the Philippines," *BR*, LI:207–8.

100. Francisco Javier de Moya, *Las Islas Filipinas en 1882* (Madrid, 1883); quoted in de la Costa, *Readings in Philippine History*, 188.

101. *Rizal-Blumentritt Correspondence*, II:209–11.

102. *Bagong Robinson* (1879) is a Tagalog translation of Tomas de Iriarte's Spanish translation of Joachim Heinrich von Campe's *Robinson der Jungere* (1779–1780), a book for young readers based on Daniel Defoe's novel. See Joaquin Tuason, *trans.*, *Ang Bagong Robinson; Historiang Nagtuturo nang Mabubuting Caugalian* (Manila: Imprenta del Colegio de Santo Tomas, 1879), 2 vs.; Mojares, *Origins and Rise of the Filipino Novel*, 80–83.

103. Perfecto ran a grammar school and the bookshop *Libreria La Panayana* (1877) in Iloilo, set up the first printshops in Bicol (*Imprenta de Nuestra Señora de Peñafrancia* [1890] and *Imprenta La Sagrada Familia* [1892]), and published the first Bicol newspapers in 1899 (*La Union* and *Parabareta*). See Maria Lilia F. Realubit, "Mariano Perfecto:

Writer, Translator and Publisher," *Katipon: Gawad Bonifacio sa Panitikan*, ed. D.G. Landicho (Manila: National Commission for Culture & the Arts, 1998), 121–30.

On Poblete and Tuason: Francis St. Clair, *The Katipunan or the Rise and Fall of the Filipino Commune* (Manila: Tip. "Amigos del Pais," 1902; reprint ed., 1991), 178–80; Manuel Artigas, "Pascual H. Poblete," *Journal of History*, V:3/4 (1957), 190–204; Manuel, *Dictionary of Philippine Biography*, I:461–68.

104. Benedict Anderson, *Imagined Communities: Reflections on the Origin and Spread of Nationalism* (Metro Manila: Anvil Publishing, 2003; Rev. ed.).

105. Valero, "Intellectuals, the State, and the Public Sphere," 213–14.

106. See Teodoro M. Kalaw, *Philippine Masonry: Its Origin, Development, and Vicissitudes Up to the Present Time (1920)*, trans. F.H. Stevens & A. Amechazurra (Manila: McCullough Printing Company, 1956; Original ed., 1920); John N. Schumacher, S.J., *The Making of a Nation: Essays on Nineteenth-Century Filipino Nationalism* (Quezon City: ADMU Press, 1991), 156–67, 168–77; Reynold S. Fajardo, *The Brethren: Masons in the Struggle for Philippine Independence* (Metro Manila: Enrique L. Locsin / Grand Lodge of Free and Accepted Masons of the Philippines, 1998).

107. Schumacher, *Making of a Nation*, 156.

108. Manuel, *Dictionary of Philippine Biography*, I:475–77.

109. Margaret C. Jacob, *Living the Enlightenment: Freemasonry and Politics in Eighteenth-Century Europe* (New York: Oxford University Press, 1991), 20.

110. Dena Goodman, *The Republic of Letters: A Cultural History of the French Enlightenment* (Ithaca: Cornell University Press, 1994), 253–55.

111. Kalaw, *Philippine Masonry*, 23.

112. Bores, *Philippine Insurrection*, 139.

113. Quoted in Kalaw, *Philippine Masonry*, 125.

114. John Foreman, *The Philippine Islands* (New York: Charles Scribner's Sons, 1899), 165; *Guia Oficial de las Islas Filipinas para 1891* (Manila: Tipo-Litografia de Chofre y Comp.a, 1891); Vicente Castañeda, *Manila en 1875* (Offprint from *Bibliofilia*, IX, 1957), 1–12; Gregorio F. Zaide, *Manila During the Revolutionary Period* (Manila: National Historical Commission, 1973).

115. William Henry Scott, *The Union Obrera Democratica: First Filipino Labor Union* (Quezon City: New Day Publishers, 1992), 5–11.

116. Fely I. San Andres, *Woman of Molave (A Biography of Mrs. Rosa Sevilla Alvero)* (Manila: [Alumnae Association of the Instituto de Mujeres], 1948).

117. Perhaps the first scholar to point to the importance of these informal sites and the role of "folk" and "proletarian" intellectuals is Epifanio de los Santos: De los Santos, *Trinidad H. Pardo de Tavera*, 29, 36–38.

118. Mas, *Report on the Condition*, 157–58, 166–67; Retana, *Periodismo Filipino*, 571–79.

119. *BR*, LII:60, 95.

120. *BR*, LII:139.

121. See *Revista de Filipinas* (Manila: Imp. de Ramirez y Giraudier, 1876–1877), I (July 1875–June 1876) & II (July 1876–July 1877); Retana, *Periodismo Filipino*, 50–73.

These expressions of a conservative Enlightenment can be profitably compared with the Latin American experience: Arthur P. Whitaker, ed., *Latin America and the Enlightenment* (Ithaca: Cornell University Press, 1961); R.A. Humphreys & John Lynch, eds., *The Origins of the Latin American Revolutions, 1808–1826* (New York: Alfred A. Knopf, 1965).

122. Quoted in Taylor, *History of the Philippine Press*, 17. See Isagani R. Medina, *Index to Ilustracion Filipina* (Quezon City: University of the Philippines Library, 1962); *Idem.*, "La Ilustracion Filipina," *Philippine Colophon*, 3:3/4 (1965), 6–9.

123. See Juan J. Delgado, S.J., *Historia General Sacro-Profana, Politica y Natural de las Islas del Poniente llamadas Filipinas* (Manila: Imp. de El Eco de Filipinas, 1892), i–viii, 961–1009, for the prospectus and list of subscribers. On Gutierrez de la Vega: *Enciclopedia Universal Ilustrada Europeo-Americana* (Bilbao: Espasa-Calpe, S.A., 1920), 27:372. Also see Pardo, *Biblioteca Filipina*, nos. 281, 824, 2567, 2808.

124. Schumacher, *Propaganda Movement*, 28; Retana, *Periodismo Filipino* (1991), 99–101, 104–05, 153; Nicanor G. Tiongson, "Juan Atayde and 'Los Teatros de Manila'," *Philippine Studies*, 30 (1982).

On del Pan: *Enciclopedia Universal*, 41:635–36; *Solidaridad*, V, 108 (July 31, 1893), 365.

125. On Manuel Regidor: Retana, *Aparato Bibliografico*, II:764; *Enciclopedia Universal*, 50:160. On Antonio Regidor: *Enciclopedia Universal*, 50:160; Artigas, *Events of 1872*, 157–62; Manuel, *Dictionary of Philippine Biography*, I:367–70.

126. Raimundo Geler, *Islas Filipinas: Reseña de su Organizacion Social y Administrativa y Breves Indicaciones de los Principales Reformas que Reclaman* (Madrid: J.E. Morete, 1869). Gregorio Zaide identifies Geler as Manuel Regidor but Retana is silent on the subject. Rizal believed Raimundo Geler (anagram for *Manuel Regidor*) to be Regidor though Regidor denied it.

See translated excerpt from Geler in Zaide, *Documentary Sources*, 7:219–38; also *Rizal-Blumentritt Correspondence*, II:218; Retana, *Aparato Bibliografico*, II, no. 1206; Nolasco, "Creoles in Spanish Philippines"; Manuel, *Dictionary of Philippine Biography*, II:49, 65–66; Leandro Tormo Sanz, *1872*, trans. A. Molina (Manila: Historical Conservation Society, 1973), 26, 35, 51; John N. Schumacher, S.J., *Revolutionary Clergy: The Filipino Clergy and the Nationalist Movement, 1850–1903* (Quezon City: ADMU Press, 1981), 19–22.

127. Geler in Zaide, *Documentary Sources,* 7:227. For Broca and craniometry: Stephen Jay Gould, *The Mismeasure of Man* (New York: W.W. Norton, 1996; Rev. ed.), 105–41.

128. *Rizal-Blumentritt Correspondence,* II:205–06.

129. John N. Schumacher, S.J., *Father Jose Burgos: Priest and Nationalist* (Quezon City: Ateneo de Manila University Press, 1972), 23–24. On Pelaez: Artigas, *Events of 1872,* 43–45.

130. These writings are in Schumacher, *Father Jose Burgos.* Also see Schumacher, "The Authenticity of the Writings Attributed to Father Jose Burgos," *Making of a Nation,* 44–70; Fidel Villaroel, O.P., *Father Jose Burgos: University Student* (Manila: University of Santo Tomas, 1971).

131. Felipe Buencamino, Sr., "Sixty Years of Philippine History," trans. A. Lecaros, in *Historical Bulletin,* XIII (1969), 317, 338 (first published in *La Opinion* in 1929); Sanz, *1872;* Carlos Quirino, "El Eco Filipino," *Philippine Colophon,* 3:3/4 (1965), 2–5.

132. See John N. Schumacher, S.J., "Nationalist Student Activism in Manila in the Eighteenth and Nineteenth Centuries," *Philippine Historical Review,* 4 (1971), 189–200. Also Buencamino, "Sixty Years of Philippine History"; Villaroel, *Father Jose Burgos,* 93–106.

133. Artigas, *Events of 1872,* 58–62, 107–08. For a critical review of sources on the Cavite Mutiny: Schumacher, "Published Sources on the Cavite Mutiny," *Making of a Nation,* 71–90.

134. Artigas, *Events of 1872,* 60–61, 99–100.

On Camerino: Isagani R. Medina, *Cavite Before the Revolution (1571–1896)* (Quezon City: University of the Philippines, College of Social Sciences & Philosophy, 1994), 74–75, 83, 86, 115. On Gomez: Santiago, "Capellania of Padre Mariano Gomes," 325–34; *Idem.,* "Before Bacoor: The Initial Career of Padre Mariano Gomes (1822–1824)," *Philippine Studies,* 33 (1985), 87–92; *Idem.,* "The Last Will of Padre Mariano Gomes," *Philippine Studies,* 30 (1982), 395–407.

135. Artigas, *Events of 1872,* 106–07.

136. Artigas, *Events of 1872,* 29–31; Buencamino, "Sixty Years of Philippine History," 321–23; Corpuz, *Roots of the Filipino Nation,* II:111–13.

137. Quoted in Schumacher, *Father Jose Burgos,* 253.

138. Jose Rizal, *Political and Historical Writings* (Manila: National Historical Commission, 1972), 91.

139. See Magno S. Gatmaitan, *Marcelo H. del Pilar, 1850–1896* (Quezon City: The Author, 1965); Villaroel, *Marcelo H. del Pilar.*

140. The article also appeared in *La Solidaridad*, II:42 (October 31, 1890), 722–29. On *Diariong Tagalog*: Retana, *Periodismo Filipino* (1991), 81–82.

141. Jaime C. de Veyra, "La situacion de Malolos," *Epistolario de Marcelo H. del Pilar* (Manila: Imprenta del Gobierno, 1955), I:273–306; Gatmaitan, *Marcelo H. del Pilar*, 158–61, 166–70; Nicanor G. Tiongson, *The Women of Malolos* (Quezon City: ADMU Press, 2004), 48.

142. Gregorio Sancianco, *The Progress of the Philippines: Economic, Administrative and Political Studies*, trans. E. Alzona (Manila: National Historical Institute, 1975). Original ed.: *El Progreso de Filipinas; Estudios economicos, administrativos y politicos* (Madrid: Imprenta de M. Perez, 1881).

143. Artigas, *Events of 1872*, 29–31; Angeles S. Santos, *Ang Malabon* (Malabon: Dalubhasaang Epifanio de los Santos Press, 1975), 133–34.

144. Schumacher, *Propaganda Movement*, 74–80.

145. Leon Ma. Guerrero, *The First Filipino* (Manila: National Historical Commission, 1974), 146–48.

146. Marcelo H. del Pilar, *Monastic Supremacy in the Philippines*, trans. E. Alzona (Quezon City: Philippine Historical Association, 1958), 76–87.

147. W.E. Retana, "La Manifestacion Patriotica de 1 Marzo 1888," *Cuestiones Filipinas. Avisos y Profecias* (Madrid: Imprenta de la Viuda de M. Minuesa de los Rios, 1892), 161–367. Also St. Clair, *Katipunan*, 52–53.

148. On the Calamba case: Austin Coates, *Rizal: Philippine Nationalist and Martyr* (Hong Kong: Oxford University Press, 1968), 139–43, 167–68, 183–84.

149. Tiongson, *Women of Malolos*; "Ecos de Ultramar," *Solidaridad*, I:1 (February 15, 1889), 12–18; Rizal, *Political and Historical Writings*, 56–66.

150. Rizal, *Political and Historical Writings*, 92.

151. Jose Rizal, *Noli me Tangere*, trans. M.S. Lacson-Locsin (Makati: Bookmark, 1996; first published in 1887), 350–52.

152. Rizal, *Political and Historical Writings*, 18.

153. *Epistolario Rizalino* (Manila: Bureau of Printing, 1931–1933), II:273, 302, 308; III:137; *Rizal's Correspondence with Fellow Reformists*, 273, 302, 308, 514. Rizal's reference to Banal (who is not cited by name) is in Antonio de Morga, *Sucesos de las Islas Filipinas… nuevamente sacada a luz y anotada por Jose Rizal* (Manila: Comision Nacional del Centenario de Jose Rizal, 1961; first published in 1890), 331n.

154. *Rizal-Blumentritt Correspondence*, II:1, 71–72.

155. *Rizal-Blumentritt Correspondence*, II:1, 229–32.

156. *Rizal's Correspondence with Fellow Reformists*, 254.

157. See Manuel, *Dictionary of Philippine Biography*, I:39–42 (Adriano), 59–61 (Arellano), 138–40 (Crisostomo), 353–61 (Ramos); II:360–62 (Serrano); IV:135–37 (Cortes); Galang, *Encyclopedia of the Philippines*, III:459 (Cortes); *Filipinos in History*, I:17–18 (Adriano), 103–06 (Bautista), II:71–73 (Paez), III:25–27 (Arellano), IV:317–20 (Serrano).

158. Epifanio de los Santos, *Marcelo H. del Pilar, Andres Bonifacio, Emilio Jacinto* (Maynila: Kapisanang Pangkasaysayan ng Pilipinas, 1957), 64.

159. In del Pilar, *Monastic Supremacy*, 1.

160. Epifanio de los Santos, *The Revolutionists: Aguinaldo, Bonifacio, Jacinto* (Manila: National Historical Institute, 1993), 164.

161. "Nuestros Propositos," *Solidaridad*, I:1 (February 15, 1889), 2–5.

162. On Ponce's role in *Solidaridad*: Mariano Ponce & Jaime C. de Veyra, *Efemerides Filipinas*, trans. E.M. Tiamson, et al. (Quezon City: University of the Philippines, Office of Research Coordination, 1998), 257–61, 569–74.

163. Retana, *Archivo del Bibliofilo Filipino*, III:132; Taylor, *History of the Philippine Press*, 25. On Ramos: Manuel, *Dictionary of Philippine Biography*, I:353–61.

164. *Filipinas ante la Razon del Indio, Obra Compuesta por el Indigena Capitan Juan para Utilidad de sus Paisanos y Publicada en Castellano por el Español P. Caro* (Madrid: Imprenta de A. Gomez Fuentenebro, 1874); Miguel Lucio y Bustamante, *Si Tandang Basio Macunat* (Manila: Lap. de Amigos del Pais, 1885). See Retana, *Censura de Imprenta*, 37–40.

165. *Filipinas ante la Razon del Indio*, 259–93.

166. Retana, *Censura de Imprenta*, 37, 39; *Idem.*, "Press Censorship," 50–51.

167. "The Friar Viewpoint," *BR*, XLVI:272–363. (Excerpts from Augustinian works published in 1897 and 1901.)

That conceptions of grades and categories of intelligence were dominant is shown in the fact that Graciano Lopez-Jaena, in urging the establishment of more arts-and-trades schools in the Philippines, conceded that the Filipino is inferior to the European in "speculative science" due to "the climate, temperament and the influence of other physical and moral causes." See Graciano Lopez-Jaena, *Speeches, Articles and Letters*, trans. E. Alzona (Manila: National Historical Commission, 1974), 94–97.

168. "Friar Viewpoint," 315–19; Retana, *Frailes y Clerigos*, 54–55.

169. See Villaroel, *Jose Rizal and the University of Santo Tomas*, 51, 249; John R.M. Taylor, comp., *The Philippine Insurrection Against the United States* (Pasay City: Eugenio Lopez Foundation, 1971), I:498; James A. LeRoy, *Philippine Life in Town and Country* (New York: G.P. Putnam's Sons, 1906), 207.

170. Villaroel, *Jose Rizal and the University of Santo Tomas*, 247–49. See Jesus C. Bacala, "The First 'Nursing' School in the Philippines," *Unitas*, 33:1 (1960), 179–85.

171. See Alberto Santamaria, *Estudios Historicos de la Universidad de Santo Tomas de Manila* (Manila: Tip. Pont. de la Univ. de Sto. Tomas, 1938); Megan C. Thomas, "Orientalist Enlightenment: The Emergence of Nationalist Thought in the Philippines, 1880–1898" (Ph.D. diss., Cornell University, 2002), 59–74.

172. LeRoy, *Philippine Life in Town and Country*, 213–14.

173. Villaroel, *Jose Rizal and the University of Santo Tomas*, 50.

174. See [Jose Ma. Panganiban], "The University of Manila: Its Plan of Study," *Solidaridad*, I, 5 (April 15, 1889), 149–55; I, 6 (April 30, 1889), 189–95; I, 8 (May 31, 1889), 281–85.

175. Rizal, *Noli me Tangere*, 352. Also see Rizal, *Filibusterismo*, Chs. 13 & 27.

176. Schumacher, *Making of a Nation*, 36, 39.

177. Rizal, *Political and Historical Writings*, 192.

178. On Lopez-Jaena's character, see Joaquin, *Question of Heroes*, 37–50; Lopez-Jaena, *Speeches, Articles and Letters*, xvi, 41, 335–38, 343–45.

179. *Rizal's Correspondence with Fellow Reformists*, 629–30.

180. For the text of the constitution: *BR*, XLII:217–26.

181. *The Letters of Apolinario Mabini* (Manila: National Heroes Commission, 1965), 10, 12, 14, 32–33, 34, 38; Agoncillo, *Revolt of the Masses*, 37–41. On Mabini: Cesar Adib Majul, *Mabini and the Philippine Revolution* (Quezon City: University of the Philippines Press, 1996; first ed., 1960).

182. *Letters of Apolinario Mabini*, 34–35; Ponce & de Veyra, *Efemerides Filipinas*, 569–74. On the *Comite*'s attempts to secure Japanese assistance: Josefa M. Saniel, *Japan and the Philippines, 1868–1898* (Quezon City: University of the Philippines Press, 1969), 171–75, 254–55.

183. In Taylor, *Philippine Insurrection*, I:210.

184. St. Clair, *Katipunan*, 87; de los Santos, *Revolutionists*, 91–93; Taylor, *Philippine Insurrection*, I:107.

185. Ileto, *Pasyon*; de los Santos, *Revolutionists*; Glenn Anthony May, *Inventing a Hero: The Posthumous Re-Creation of Andres Bonifacio* (Madison: University of Wisconsin-Madison, Center for Southeast Asian Studies, 1996); Bernardita Reyes Churchill, ed., *Determining the Truth: The Story of Andres Bonifacio* (Manila: Manila Studies Association, 1997). Also see Reynaldo C. Ileto, "Bonifacio, The Text, and the Social Scientist," *Philippine Sociological Review*, 32:1–4 (1984), 19–29..

Tondo's urbanization is indicated by the following figures: 40% of men and women in Tondo in 1893 were born outside Manila and at least 40% of adult males native to Tondo-Sampaloc in 1889–1893 were in white-collar jobs (esp. clerk), commerce (agents, dealers, storekeepers), skilled production trades (printers, machinists, blacksmiths), skilled construction trades, transport, and others (tailors, artists, cigar workers). See Daniel F. Doeppers & Peter Xenos, eds., *Population and History: The Demographic Origins of the Modern Philippines* (Quezon City: ADMU Press, 1998), 165, 256.

186. See Cesar Adib Majul, *The Political and Constitutional Ideas of the Philippine Revolution* (Quezon City: University of the Philippines Press, 1996; first ed., 1967).

187. Jose Rizal, "The Philippines a Century Hence," *Solidaridad*, I, 18 (October 31, 1889), 667.

188. Cesar Adib Majul, "*Principales, Ilustrados*, Intellectuals and the Original Concept of a Filipino National Community," *Asian Studies*, XV (1977), 12.

189. Cullinane, "Ilustrado Politics," 35, 42, 44. Also see Artigas, *Events of 1872*, 166n; Majul, *Mabini and the Philippine Revolution*, 51.

190. Artigas, *Events of 1872*, 166n; Majul, "*Principales, Ilustrados*, Intellectuals," 12.

191. *Affairs in the Philippine Islands* (Washington: Government Printing Office, 1902), I:308–09, 680–81.

192. See the remarks of Felipe Calderon in *Report of the Philippine Commission* [hereinafter cited as *RPC*] (Washington: Government Printing Office, 1900), II:68–70.

193. In Abella, "Higher Education in the Philippines," 30.

194. Quoted in Teodoro M. Kalaw, *The Philippine Revolution* (Mandaluyong, Rizal: Jorge B. Vargas Filipiniana Foundation, 1969), 149–50n. On education under the Malolos Republic: Cesar Adib Majul, *Education During the Reform Movement and the Philippine Revolution* (Offprint from *The Diliman Review*, XV:4, 1967), vii, 185–257; Alzona, *History of Education*, 180–85.

195. See "Jose Rizal's Plan of a Modern School," in Alzona, *History of Education*, 367–71.

196. De los Reyes, *Filipinas. Independencia y Revolucion*, 118–36. De los Reyes's plan for *Aurora Nueva* was announced in *Boletin de la Aurora Nueva*, a special section of *Filipinas ante Europa*, on April 10, 1900.

197. Max Bernard [Bernardo Solis], *Columnas Volantes de la Federacion Malaya (Contribucion a la Historia del Periodismo Filipino)* (n.p., 1928); Teodoro M. Kalaw, *Aide-de-Camp to Freedom*, trans. M.K. Katigbak (Manila: Teodoro M. Kalaw Society, 1965), 16–19. On Gregorio Aguilera: Manuel, *Dictionary of Philippine Biography*, III:14–15.

198. Bernard, *Columnas Volantes*, 2.

199. See Arthur S. Riggs, *The Filipino Drama (1905)* (Manila: Intramuros Administration, 1981); Amelia Lapeña-Bonifacio, *The "Seditious" Tagalog Playwrights: Early American*

Occupation (Manila: Zarzuela Foundation of the Philippines, 1972). On the situation in Cebu: Resil B. Mojares, *Vicente Sotto: The Maverick Senator* (Cebu: Cebuano Studies Center, 1992), 24–25.

200. See Tiongson, *Women of Malolos*, 203–9.

201. See Ignacio Villamor, *Industrious Men* (Manila: Oriental Commercial Company, 1930), 169–76; E. Arsenio Manuel, *Felipe G. Calderon: A Biographical Portrait* (Manila: Filipiniana Publications, 1939).

202. Quoted in Manuel, *Felipe G. Calderon*, 34–36, and Teodoro M. Kalaw, "The First Filipino Law School," *Philippine Magazine*, 36:1 (1939), 17.

203. Kalaw, "First Filipino Law School," 17.

204. Felipe G. Calderon, *El ABC... del Ciudadano Filipino* (Manila: Imp. de Quiapo, 1905); *Idem.*, *Mis Memorias Sobre la Revolucion (Segunda Etapa)* (Manila: Imp. de El Renacimiento, 1907).

205. Villamor, *Industrious Men*, 174.

206. Quoted in Kalaw, "First Filipino Law School," 17.

207. Quoted in Kalaw, "First Filipino Law School," 17.

208. Felipe G. Calderon, *Discurso leido en el dia de la apertura del curso escolar de 1903 a 1904* (Manila: Imp. de Quiapo, 1903); Manuel, *Felipe G. Calderon*, 53.

209. Felipe G. Calderon, "Laboratorios de ciencias filosofico-sociales," *El Renacimiento*, IV:209 (May 20, 1905), 2.

210. H. Otley Beyer, *Population of the Philippine Islands in 1916* (Manila: Philippine Education Co., 1917), 27–31; Teodoro Agoncillo, *Tagalog Periodical Literature* (Manila: Institute of National Language, 1953); Mojares, *Origins and Rise of the Filipino Novel*, 6n.

For an overview of the novel in this period: Mojares, *Origins and Rise of the Filipino Novel*; Soledad S. Reyes, *Ang Nobelang Tagalog (1905–1975): Tradisyon at Modernismo* (Quezon City: ADMU Press, 1982). An important study of the relationship between literature and nationalism is Caroline S. Hau, *Necessary Fictions: Philippine Literature and the Nation, 1946–1980* (Quezon City: ADMU Press, 2000).

211. See Ernest J. Frei, *The Historical Development of the Philippine National Language* (Manila: Institute of National Language, 1959), 63–65; Teodoro A. Agoncillo, "The Development of the Philippine National Language," *History and Culture, Language and Literature: Selected Essays of Teodoro A. Agoncillo*, ed. B.R. Churchill (Manila: University of Santo Tomas Publishing House, 2003), 193–207.

For early examples of literary scholarship: Epifanio de los Santos, "Literatura Tagala, 1593–1886," *Philippine Review*, I:8 (August 1916); *Idem.*, "Nuestra Literatura a traves de los siglos," *Builders of a Nation*, ed. M.M. Norton (Manila: E.C. McCullough, 1914); Hermenegildo Cruz, *Kung Sino ang Kumatha ng "Florante"* (1906); *Poetikang Tagalog:*

Mga Unang Pagsusuri sa Sining ng Pagtulang Tagalog, ed. V.S. Almario (Quezon City: Sentro ng Wikang Filipino, Unibersidad ng Pilipinas, 1996), 59–159.

On de los Santos and his writings: Manuel, *Dictionary of Philippine Biography*, IV:463–518; Teodoro A. Agoncillo, "Epifanio de los Santos, Pioneer Historian," *History and Culture*, 239–45.

212. Jose Rizal, "Arte Metrica del Tagalog," *Poetikang Tagalog*, 47–57; [Jose Rizal], *Ang Balarila ni Rizal*, trans. C. Lopez (Manila: Benipayo Press, 1962; Spanish ed., 1943).

213. Pedro Serrano Laktaw, *Diccionario hispano-tagalog* (Manila: Estab. Tipografico "La Opinion," 1889); *Diccionario tagalog-hispano* (Manila: Imp. y Lit. de Santos y Bernal, 1914). On Rosalio Serrano: Manuel, *Dictionary of Philippine Biography*, I:404; II:360–62.

For an evaluation of the works of Rizal, Serrano, and Tagalog grammarians: Lydia Gonzales Garcia, *Mga Gramatikang Tagalog/Pilipino, 1893–1977* (Quezon City: Sentro ng Wikang Filipino, Unibersidad ng Pilipinas, 1992).

214. Otto Scheerer, "Introduction," *The Archive: A Collection of Papers Pertaining to Philippine Linguistics* (Manila, 1924). Paper No. 3. On Scheerer: Manuel, *Dictionary of Philippine Biography*, II:350–54.

215. Virgilio S. Almario, *Balagtasismo versus Modernismo* (Quezon City: ADMU Press, 1984); *Idem.*, *Kung Sino ang Kumatha*, 159–76.

See Lope K. Santos, *Tinging Pahapyaw sa Kasaysayan ng Panitikang Tagalog* (Manila: Bureau of Printing, 1938); J.C. Balmaseda, *Ang Tatlong Panahon ng Tulang Tagalog* (Manila: Bureau of Printing, 1938).

216. *Solidaridad*, I:1 (February 15, 1889), 9.

217. On the INL and the *Balarila*: Andrew B. Gonzalez, *Language and Nationalism: The Philippine Experience Thus Far* (Quezon City: ADMU Press, 1980).

218. The earliest reference I can find to this story is in Juan Alvarez Guerra, *Viajes por Filipinas. De Manila a Tayabas* (Madrid: Imprenta de Fortanet, 1877), 135–36. Also Ponce & De Veyra, *Efemerides Filipinas*, 435; Alejandro Roces, "Guide," *Archipelago*, A-31 (1976), 39–41.

219. Morga, *Sucesos de las Islas Filipinas*, v–vi; Rizal, *Noli me tangere*, i.

220. *RPC*, 1903, I:413. See Felipe G. Calderon, "De 1521 a 1921," *Revista Historica de Filipinas*, I:3 (July 1905), 1; T.H. Pardo de Tavera, "Antiguas costumbres de los Pampangos," *El Ideal* (July 18, 1919), 3; Maximo M. Kalaw, *The Development of Philippine Politics (1872–1920)* (Manila: Oriental Commercial Co., 1926), vii.

221. On Zulueta: Retana, "Revista Historico-Bibliografica," *Archivo del Bibliofilo Filipino*, V:93; "El Aniversario de Zulueta," *Revista Historica de Filipinas*, I:5 (September

1905), 73; Jaime C. de Veyra, "Sino si Peping Zulueta?," *Efemerides Filipinas*, 600–606; Manuel Artigas (pseud., *Sagitra*), "Filipinos ilustres: Clemente J. Zulueta," *Renacimiento Filipino*, I:35 (March 21, 1911), 3–7 – I:36 (March 28, 1911), 10; Villamor, *Industrious Men*, 161–66; Manuel, *Dictionary of Philippine Biography*, II:458–62; Gregorio F. Zaide, *Great Filipinos in History* (Manila: Verde Book Store, 1970), 638–42.

222. *RPC*, 1903, I:691–92; Manuel, *Dictionary of Philippine Biography*, II:458–62. For a report on the collecting trip: Clemente J. Zulueta, "Fuentes historicas de Filipinas," *Cultura Filipina*, I:11 (February 1911), 405–45; also in *Alzina Papers* (Chicago: University of Chicago, Philippine Studies Program, n.d.), v.p.

223. See the prefatory materials in *BR,* I:1–93; Carlos Quirino, "The Philippine Story: Blair and Robertson," *Philippines Free Press* (December 9, 1961), 50, 158–59.

224. Clemente J. Zulueta, "El Elemento Indigena en la Historia de Filipinas," *Revista Historica de Filipinas*, I:1 (May 1905), 6–7 – I:6 (October 1905), 82–83.

225. Zulueta, "Elemento Indigena" (June 1905), 28.

226. Zulueta, "Elemento Indigena" (May 1905), 7; (July 1905), 36–38; (September 1905), 67.

227. Zulueta, "Elemento Indigena" (September 1905), 67–69.

228. Zulueta, "Elemento Indigena" (July 1905), 38; (September 1905), 69.

229. Zaide, *Great Filipinos in History*, 641–42.

230. Felipe G. Calderon, "Por la Historia de Filipinas," *El Renacimiento*, IV:201 (May 11, 1905), 202 (May 12, 1905), 206 (May 17, 1905). There are apparently five parts to this series but I have consulted the only three issues available at the National Library.

231. Calderon, "Por la Historia de Filipinas" (May 12, 1905), 3.

232. Calderon, "Por la Historia de Filipinas" (May 12, 1905), 3. On Herder's populism: Isaiah Berlin, *Three Critics of the Enlightenment: Vico, Hamann, Herder* (London: Pimlico, 2000), 170–71, 176–79, 208–9.

233. "Bases de la Asociacion Historica de Filipinas," *Revista Historica de Filipinas,* I:1 (May 1905), 15.

234. *Revista Historica de Filipinas*, I:1 (May 1905) – I:12 (April 1906); *Enciclopedia Filipina*, I:1 (February 1908) – I:3 (April 1908).

235. "Nuestro Fines," *Revista Historica de Filipinas*, I:1 (May 1905), 1.

236. See *Revista Historica Filipinas*, I:8 (December 1905), I:11 (March 1906).

237. See *Enciclopedia Filipina*, I:1 (February 1908), 55–56; "Sobre la Definicion de la Sociologia," *Enciclopedia Filipina*, I:3 (April 1908), 234.

238. "Nuestro Fines," 2–3.

239. "Nuestro Fines," 4.

240. W.E. Retana, "Philippine Historiography," *Philippine Review*, III:8 (1918), 599–608. Reprinted in Galang, *Encyclopedia of the Philippines*, XV:405–28.

Retana's proposal assigns eleven of the thirteen volumes to the Spanish colonial period. Aspiring to a "Filipino" viewpoint, Retana insinuates that the "awakening of the political spirit" of Filipinos is the main thread that runs through Philippine history. Vain and prescriptive, Retana refers to his *Aparato Bibliografico* (1906) as containing "the references to all the elements necessary to write the general history of the Philippines." Giving prominence to Spanish authors, his citations of works of what he calls "Filipino intellectuality" are minor.

See John N. Schumacher, "Wenceslao E. Retana: An Historiographical Study," *Philippine Studies*, 10 (1962), 550–76.

241. Retana, "Philippine Historiography," 605.

242. In Retana, "Philippine Historiography," 607.

243. On Artigas: Mariano Ponce, "Prologo," *Galeria de Filipinos Ilustres*, II:5–40; Artigas, *Events of 1872*, x–xv; Villamor, *Industrious Men*, 179–82; Manuel, *Dictionary of Philippine Biography*, I:68–79.

244. *Biblioteca Nacional Filipina*, I:1 (October 30, 1908) – II:12 (September 30, 1909).

245. "Porque Venimos," *Biblioteca Nacional Filipina*, I:1 (October 30, 1908), 1–2.

246. See Ponce & de Veyra, *Efemerides Filipinas*; Manuel Artigas, "Un esforzado obrero de la Log. 'Sinukuan': Mariano Ponce," *Acacia*, 1:16 (November 30, 1920), 525–48.

See *Boletin de la Sociedad Orientalista de Filipinas*, I:7 (July 1918).

247. Daniel G. Brinton, "Professor Blumentritt's Studies of the Philippines," *American Anthropologist*, I:1 (N.S.) (1899), 122.

248. *RPC*, 1900–03 (1904), 606–10, 706–09.

249. Paul A. Kramer, "The Pragmatic Empire: U.S. Anthropology and Colonial Politics in the Occupied Philippines, 1898–1916" (Ph.D. diss., Princeton University, 1998), 73–74.

250. Frank R. Blake, "The Part Played by the Publications of the United States Government in the Development of Philippine Linguistic Studies," *Journal of the American Oriental Society*, 42 (n.d.), 147–70; Frei, *Historical Development of the Philippine National Language*, 44–45.

251. Teodoro M. Kalaw, ed., *The Social Integration of the Philippines* (Manila: Philippine Commission of Independence, 1924); Joseph Ralston Hayden, *The Philippines: A Study in National Development* (New York: Macmillan Company, 1942), 609–17.

252. Cristino Jamias, *The University of the Philippines: The First Half Century* (Quezon City: University of the Philippines, 1962), 231–36.

253. The text of the address is in Jamias, *University of the Philippines*, 238–47.

254. Kalaw, *Aide-de-Camp to Freedom*, 69–79; Kramer, "Pragmatic Empire," 293–97; Rodney J. Sullivan, *Exemplar of Americanism: The Philippine Career of Dean C. Worcester* (Ann Arbor: University of Michigan, Center for South & Southeast Asian Studies, 1991), 159–64, 239–40.

255. Michael Cullinane, "Implementing the 'New Order': The Structure and Supervision of Local Government During the Taft Era," *Compadre Colonialism*, ed. N.G. Owen (Ann Arbor: University of Michigan, Center for South & Southeast Asian Studies, 1971), 16–17.

256. *The Antonio Gramsci Reader: Selected Writings, 1916–1935*, ed. D. Forgacs (New York: New York University Press, 1999), 196–99. Also Edward W. Said, *Representations of the Intellectual* (New York: Pantheon Books, 1994), 4; Terry Eagleton, *Scholars & Rebels in Nineteenth-Century Ireland* (Oxford: Blackwell, 1999), 2–3, 6–7, 36–37.

257. Felipe G. Calderon, "Documentos Relativos a la Epoca de la Revolucion," in Retana, *Archivo del Bibliofilo Filipino*, V:319; Artigas, *Events of 1872*, 67–68.

258. Agoncillo, "Philippine Historiography in the Age of Kalaw," *History and Culture*, 3–29; Teodoro M. Kalaw, *Cinco Reglas de Nuestra Moral Antigua* (Manila: Bureau of Printing, 1947; first published in 1935). See Resil B. Mojares, "The Formation of Filipino Nationality Under U.S. Colonial Rule, 1900–1940." Paper presented at "*Sangandaan*: International Conference on Arts and Media in Philippine-American Relations, 1899–2002," Quezon City, July 9, 2003.

259. Quoted in Alfredo R. Roces, *Amorsolo (1892–1972)* (Makati: Filipinas Foundation, 1975), 90.

260. Hayden, *Philippines*, 515.

261. See Maria Luna Vico, "Investigacion Analitica de los Valores Promovidos por el Doctor Trinidad H. Pardo de Tavera en sus Ensayos Dirigidos a la Juventud Filipina y a sus Educadores" (Ph.D. diss., University of the Philippines, 2000); Maria V. Luna, "Building the Filipino Nation in the Mind and Heart of Dr. Trinidad H. Pardo de Tavera," *Philippiniana Sacra*, 35:105 (2000), 535–46.

262. *RPC*, 1901, III:329–412. The history of the disciplines in the Philippines is scattered in many sources. On anthropology: Ricardo E. Galang, "Anthropological Work in the Philippines," *Encyclopedia of the Philippines*, 13:529–35; Frank Lynch, S.J., & Mary R. Hollnsteiner, "Sixty Years of Philippine Ethnology: A First Glance at the Years 1901–1961," *Science Review*, 2:11 (1961), 1–5; Eufracio C. Abaya, Ma.

Luisa Lucas-Fernan, & Daisy Y. Noval-Morales, "Shifting Terms of Engagement: A Review of the History of Anthropology in the Philippines," *The Philippine Social Sciences in the Life of the Nation*, ed. V.A. Miralao (Quezon City: Philippine Social Science Council, 1999), I:1–10. Also see David G. Brinton, "The Peoples of the Philippines," *American Anthropologist*, 11:10 (1898), 298, 304; Charles O. Houston, Jr., "A Preliminary Bibliography of Philippine Anthropology, Linguistics, Ethnology and Archaeology," *Journal of East Asiatic Studies* (University of Manila), 2:2 (1953), 55–110.

On linguistics, history, and other disciplines: Miralao, *Philippine Social Sciences; Philippine Encyclopedia of the Social Sciences* (Quezon City: Philippine Social Science Council, 1993), I & II; Ernesto Constantino, "Some Problems in Philippine Linguistics," *Asian Studies*, 1 (1963), 23–30; Nobleza Asuncion-Lande, "Theoretical and Methodological Trends in Philippine Linguistics Research: 1560–1970," *Readings in Philippine Linguistics*, 1–17; Benicio T. Catapusan, "Development of Sociology in the Philippines," *Philippine Sociological Review*, V:4/5 (1957), 53–57; Isabel S. Panopio & Ponciano L. Bennagen, "The Philippines," *Sociology and Social Anthropology in Asia and the Pacific* (New Delhi: Wiley Eastern, 1985), 218–64; George H. Weightman, "Sociology in the Philippines," *Sociology in Asia*, ed. M.S. Das (New Delhi: Prints India, 1989), 35–62; Remigio E. Agpalo, "Political Science in the Philippines, 1880–1998," *Philippine Social Sciences Review*, 55:1/4 (1998), 1–72; Patricia B. Licuanan, "Psychology in the Philippines: History and Current Trends," *Philippine Studies*, 33 (1985), 67–86.

263. LeRoy, "Philippines, 1860–1898," 154n, 161n, 189–90; *Idem., The Americans in the Philippines* (Boston: Houghton Mifflin, 1914), II:215n.

264. Karl Hutterer, "Dean C. Worcester and Philippine Anthropology," *PQCS*, 6:3 (1978), 125–56; E. Arsenio Manuel, "H. Otley Beyer: His Researches and Publications," *Studies in Philippine Anthropology*, ed. M.D. Zamora (Quezon City: Alemar-Phoenix, 1967), 30; Juan Salcedo, Jr., "H. Otley Beyer: Anthropology and the Philippines," *Studies in Philippine Anthropology*, 3.

265. Partha Chatterjee, ed., *Texts of Power: Emerging Disciplines in Colonial Bengal* (Minneapolis: University of Minnesota Press, 1995), 24–25. See Michel Foucault, *The Archaeology of Knowledge and the Discourse on Language*, trans. A.M. Sheridan Smith (New York: Pantheon Books, 1972), 50–55, 116.

266. Pierre Bourdieu, "Principles of a Sociology of Cultural Works," *Explanation and Value in the Arts*, ed. S. Kemal & I. Gaskell (Cambridge: Cambridge University Press, 1993), 173–89.

267. On "double-consciousness" as the origin of nationalism, see Benedict Anderson,

The Spectre of Comparisons: Nationalism, Southeast Asia and the World (London: Verso, 1998), 2, 229.

268. Edward W. Said, "Representing the Colonized: Anthropology's Interlocutors," *Critical Inquiry*, 15:2 (1989), 209–10.

269. For these intellectual exchanges, see nineteenth-century Chilean intellectual Jose Victorino Lastarria's *Literary Memoirs*, trans. R. K. Washbourne (Oxford: Oxford University Press, 2000).

270. See Partha Chatterjee, *Nationalist Thought and the Colonial World: A Derivative Discourse* (Minneapolis: University of Minnesota Press, 1986).

271. Rizal, *Political and Historical Writings*, 66.

272. Using the same metaphor of society as a nervous system, Michael Taussig presents a menacing vision of a nerve center hidden and remote and a body caught up in an indeterminate nervousness without system, a chronic state of emergency. See Michael Taussig, *The Nervous System* (New York: Routledge, 1992).

273. Jose Rizal, "On Travel," *Rizal's Prose* (Manila: Jose Rizal Centennial Commission, 1962), 27.

274. Rizal, *Political and Historical Writings*, 155.

APPENDIX

PEDRO PATERNO BIBLIOGRAPHY*

1876

Influencia Social del Cristianismo; Discurso Pronunciado ante la Academia de Teologia Dogmatica y Polemica del Seminario Central de Salamanca. Madrid: C. Moliner, 1876. 23p.

> Cited as "2d. ed." because this was first published in a periodical in Spain. Third ed.: Colegio de Sto. Tomas, 1917.

1880

Sampaguitas. Madrid: Imprenta de F. Cao y D. de Val, 1880. 22p.

> Offered as the first volume of "Biblioteca Filipina." Other editions cited: 1881, 1885, and 1890 ("ninth"). Colegio de Sto. Tomas published a "3rd ed." in 1917.

Poesias Liricas y Dramaticas. Madrid: Establecimientos Tipograficos de M. Minuesa, 1880. xlii, 128p.

> Also announced as first volume of "Biblioteca Filipina." Prologue by Daniel Balaciart.

---

* It cannot be determined whether some titles announced by Paterno in the bookcovers of his works were actually published. These include: *Genesis Filipino, Haz el Bien y no Mires a Quien, Musica Tagalog: El Kumintang, El Kundiman, El Balitao y La Sampaguita, Gat-Maitan: Heroe de Kainta (Leyenda Filipina), Matando Fanatismos (Novela filipina), El Codice de Bathala, El Dolor de Amor, S.M. La Usura. Las Espureas, Reglas del Juego de Chongka, El Fruto de dos Educaciones, Amores del Colegio, Matando Precausiones, El Martir de Golgota, El Ultimo Celaje.*

530

1885

Ninay (Costumbres Filipinas). Madrid: Imprenta de Fortanet, 1885. 352p.

Second ed.: Colegio de Sto. Tomas, 1917. English translation by E. F. du Fresne; dedicated to Mrs. William H. Taft: Imprenta "La Republica," 1907. Tagalog translation by Roman Reyes: Limbagan nang La Republica, 1908; reprint by De La Salle University Press, 2002.

1887

La Antigua Civilizacion Tagalog (Apuntes). Madrid: Tipografia de Manuel G. Hernandez, 1887. [8] 411, [3] p.

Second ed.: Colegio de Sto. Tomas, 1915. Dedicated to Overseas Minister German Gamazo.

1890

Los Itas. Madrid: Imprenta de los Sucesores de Cuesta, 1890. viii, 439p.

Dedicated to Rafael M. de Labra, a member of the Spanish Cortes. Second ed.: Colegio de Sto. Tomas, 1915. Cited as Part I of *Historia de Filipinas*.

1892

El Cristianismo en la Antigua Civilizacion Tagalog. Contestacion al M.R.P. Fr. R. Martinez Vigil . . . Obispo de Oviedo. Madrid: Imprenta Moderna, 1892. 88p.

Serialized in *La Solidaridad*, IV:81–88 (June 15–September 30, 1892), 90–91 (October 31–November 15, 1892). See the English translation of this periodical by G. F. Ganzon and L. Mañeru: *La Solidaridad* (Metro Manila: Fundacion Santiago, 1996).

El Barangay; con la relacion de Fr. Juan de Plasencia escriba en 1589 de como se gobernaban los tagalos en la antiguedad y una carta de D. Miguel Villalba Hervas. Madrid: Imprenta de los Sucesores de Cuesta, 1892. [4] 122, [1]p.

Villalba Hervas was a member of the Spanish Cortes.

La Familia Tagalog en la Historia Universal con un apendice; contestacion al M.R.P. Fr. R. Martinez Vigil de la orden de predicadores, obispo de Oviedo. Madrid: Imprenta de los Sucesores de Cuesta, 1892. [8] 152p.

Dedicated to Ezequiel Ordoñez, a deputy of the Cortes. There is a reference to the separate publication of its *Apendice* by Imprenta Moderna (Madrid) in 1892. Reviewed in *Oesterreichische Monatsschrift fur den Orient* (Vienna, 1892).

1893

El Individuo Tagalog y su Arte en la Exposicion Historico-Americana. Madrid: Sucs. de Cuesta, 1893. 108p.

Dedicated to Segismundo Moret y Prendergast.

El Regimen Municipal en las Islas Filipinas. Real Decreto de 19 de Mayo de 1893 con notas y concordancias. Madrid: Estab. Tipog. de los Sucesores de Cuesta, 1893. [8], 280p.

A commentary on the reforms of the Maura Law of 1893; reproduces the text of the decree.

"The Kumintang: Its Music, Its Dance," *Solidaridad*, V:111 (September 15, 1893), 439–41.

With original Spanish text.

1894

Los Tagalog. Madrid: Sucesores de Cuesta, 1894. 112p.

Contains *Individuo Tagalog, Familia Tagalog*, and *El Barangay*. Also referred to as Part II of *Historia de Filipinas*.

1895

"Philippine Art," *Solidaridad*, VII:147 (March 15, 1895), 119–21.

With original Spanish text.

"A Reply," *Solidaridad*, VII:149 (April 15, 1895), 177–81.

With original Spanish text; a reply to the criticism of *Boletin de Museo-Biblioteca de Filipinas* by *La Voz de España* (February 10, 1895).

1898

"The All Saints' Day Speech of Dr. Pedro A. Paterno (Paco Cemetery, Manila, November 1, 1898)," in Gregorio F. Zaide, *Documentary Sources of Philippine History* (Metro Manila: National Book Store, 1990), 9:342–44.

From Gregorio F. Zaide, "All Saints' Day in 1898," *Graphic* (October 26, 1932); reprinted in *The Evening News* (October 29, 1952).

"La Muerte de Rizal" (December 31, 1898). In: *Poesias Dedicadas a Jose Rizal* (Manila: Comision Nacional del Centenario de Jose Rizal, 1961), 78.

1899

"Speech of Dr. Pedro A. Paterno, President of the Malolos Congress, on the Inauguration of the First Philippine Republic (Malolos, January 23, 1899)," in Zaide, *Documentary Sources*, 10:57–60.

Published in Spanish in *Heraldo Filipino* (formerly *El Heraldo de la Revolucion*) (Malolos), II:8 (January 26, 1899). Also in John R. M. Taylor, comp., *The Philippine Insurrection Against the United States* (Pasay City: Eugenio Lopez Foundation, 1971), III:533–36, Exhibit 409.

1900

El Problema Politico de Filipinas. Manila: Imp. y Estereotipia de J. Alemany, 1900. 42p.

Text of the plan for a "free Filipino state" proposed by Paterno to the Americans in 1900.

1902

La alianza sonada, opera filipina en un acto dividido en cinco cuadros. Musica por L[adislao] Bonus. Manila: Estab. Tipog. de M. Paterno y Cia., 1902. 28p.

Premiered at Zorilla Theater, Manila, on August 2, 1902, by the Molina-Benito Company.

English translation: *The Dreamed Alliance, Philippino Opera in One Act,* trans. Walter H. Loving (Manila: Impr. de "R. Mercantil," 1902), 22p.

Tagalog translation: *Sangdugong panaguinip, operang filipina na isang bahagui, ikinalat sa limang timbon; isinalin sa uicang tagalog ni Roman Reyes at nilapatan nang tugtuguin ni Ladislao Bonus.* Manila: Imprenta de Quiapo, 1902. 26p.

1903

Magdapio o la Fidelidad Premiada. Manila: Imprenta de la Patria, 1903. 16p.

Staged at the Zorilla Theater in 1903 and 1904; an opera in four acts; translated into Tagalog by Roman Reyes; music by Alejo Carluen. The Tagalog translation was published by Limbagan ng "La Patria" in 1903. Undated English translation by E. F. Allen, printed by Imprenta de La Patria. Both the Tagalog and English translations are in Arthur Stanley Riggs, *The Filipino Drama (1905)* (Manila: Intramuros Administration, 1981), 338–48, 652–66.

1905

Gayuma, operang Filipina. Isinalin sa uicang Tagalog ni Roman Reyes at nilapatan nang tugtuguin ni Gabino Carluen. Manila, 1905. 23p.

Opera staged at Teatro Zorrilla in 1902; music by Gavino Carluen.

Ang Buhay ni Rizal.

Zarzuela in four acts; staged in Manila on January 14, 1905. Translated from Spanish to Tagalog by Roman Reyes; music by Alejo Carluen.

1906

Discurso de don . . . pronunciado en la asamblea de señoras a favor de la union de los partidos politicos nacionales. Manila: Imprenta "La Republica," [1906]. 8p.

Los Amores de Rizal.

Zarzuela in four acts; staged at Manila's Grand Opera House on December 30, 1906; music by Alejo Carluen.

1907

En Automovil por el Primer Distrito de la Laguna de Bay. Manila: Imp. "La Republica," 1907. 116p.

> Account of a trip through Laguna in 1907; with data on the province and its towns.

A los Electores del Distrito de la Laguna de Bay. [n.p., n.d.], 116p.

> Copy at University of Santo Tomas Library.

1908

Historia Critica de Filipinas. Manila: Imprenta "La Republica," 1908. 3 vols.

> I. "Los Negritos" (146p.); II. "Los Tagalog. El Individuo. La Familia" (183p.); III. "La Sociedad Tagalog. El Barangay. El Cristianismo en la Civilizacion Tagalog" (117p.). A second edition of volumes 1–3 was published by Colegio de Sto. Tomas in 1920.

Historia de Filipinas: Apuntes de obras y documentos ineditos escritos por Españoles, copiados y coleccionados por . . . Manila: Imp. La Republica, 1908–1912. 7 vols. [2,906p.]

1909

Synopsis de Historia de los Estados Unidos (Apuntes). Manila: Imprenta "La Republica,"1909. [viii], 200p.

1910

El Pacto de Biyak-na-Bato. Manila: Imprenta "La Republica," 1910. 207p.

> Excerpts in English translation: "Excerpts from Pedro Paterno's *El Pacto de Biyak-na-Bato*," *Colloquia Manilana*, II (1994), 72–84.

Gobierno Civil de las Islas Filipinas; o manual del ciudadano Filipino. Manila: Imprenta "La Republica," 1910. 2 p.l., 7–360p.

> Second ed.: 1911.

Los Amores en Antipolo. (Leyendas). I. Las delicias (baños). Manila: Imprenta "La Republica," 1910. 58p.

> Also listed as *Leyendas de Antipolo*. A Tagalog translation, *Ang pagiibigan sa Antipolo*, was published by Imprenta "La Republica" in 1910 (see below).

En el Pansol de Kalamba. Amor de un Dia. Manila: Impr. "La Republica," 1910. 83p.

El Alma Filipina. Manila: Imprenta "La Republica," 1910. 65p.

> Part of a series of short novels called *Aurora Social*.

La Dalaga Virtuosa y El Puente del Diablo. Maring, Amor de Obrero Filipino. Boda a la Moderna. Manila: Imp. "La Republica," 1910. 85p.

> A series of short novels called *Aurora Social*.

Maring, amor de obrero Filipino (novela corta). Manila: Imp. "La Republica," 1910. 124p.

Ang Pag-iibigan sa Antipolo; salita at buhay na nasapit ni Bitwin at ni Batis sa parang ng Bosoboso at sa bayan ng Antipolo. Sinalin sa wikang Tagalog ni Rosa Sevilla. Manila: Imprenta "La Republica," 1910. 19p.

La Dalaga Virtuosa y el Puente del Diablo; Leyenda Filipina, novela corta. Manila: Imp. "La Republica," 1910. 34p.

La Braveza de Bayani; obra premiada con 4,137 votos; en el concurso de novelas cortas abierto por El Ideal. Manila: Imp. "La Republica," 1910. 23p.

"El Puente del Diablo: Leyenda Filipina," *Cultura Filipina*, 1:2 (May 1910), 119–22.

1911

Synopsis de Historia de Filipinas. Manila: Imprenta "La Republica,"1911. 367p. [v.p.]
   The synopsis ends with a brief mention of the Philippine Revolution.

La Fidelidad (novela Filipina). Manila: Imp. "La Republica," 1911. 69p.

Los Heraldos de la Raza (Novela Corta). Manila: Imp. "La Republica," 1911. 41p.

Los Ultimos Romanticos en la Erupcion del Volcan de Taal, 30 Enero 1911. Manila: Imp. "La Republica," 1911. 2 p.l., 55p.

T. H. PARDO DE TAVERA BIBLIOGRAPHY*

1881

"Sobre el Mal de Pott," *El Siglo Medico* (Madrid) (August 21, 1881), 534.
   Clinical observations on "Pott's disease"; written in Paris.

1884

Contribucion para el Estudio de los Antiguos Alfabetos Filipinos. Losana: Imprenta de Juanin Hermanos, 1884. 30p.
   Dedicated to Ferdinand Blumentritt; reviewed by Friedrich Muller in *Oesterreichische Monatsschrift fur den Orient* (Vienna, 1885) and *Journal of the Straits Branch of the Royal Asiatic Society*, 17 (1886), 158.

---

*   For manuscripts, clippings, and catalogues, see the Pardo de Tavera Collection (*PTC*), Pardo de Tavera Special Collections Archives, Rizal Library, Ateneo de Manila University, Quezon City, Philippines.

French translation by Meyners de'Estrey: "Les Anciens Alphabets des Philippines," *Annales de l'Extreme-Orient* (1885), 204–10, 232–39.

English translation: "A Contribution to the Study of the Old Filipino Alphabets," *Readings in Philippine Linguistics*, ed. A.B. Gonzalez, et al. (Manila: Linguistic Society of the Philippines, 1973), 40–53.

"La Medecine a l'Isle de Lucon (Archipel des Philippines), *Journal de Medecine* (Paris), 6:2231 (March 31, 1884).

Spanish translation by Pedro Govantes de Azcarraga: "La Medicina en la Isla Luzon," *Los Dos Mundos* (Madrid) (September 28–October 8, 1884).

German translation by Ferdinand Blumentritt: "Die Medicinischen Kenntnisse der Eingeborenen der Insel Luzon," *Globus*, 47:20 (1885).

1886

Contribution a l'etude de la Periarthrite du Genou (Affections de la bourse sereuse de la patte d'oie). Paris: A. Parent, Imprimeur de la Faculte de Medecine, 1886. 128p.

Dedicated to the author's mother and the memory of his father and uncle.

1887

El Sanscrito en la Lengua Tagalog. Paris: Impr. de la Faculte de Medecine, A. Davy, 1887. 55p.

Dedicated to Segismundo Moret y Prendergast, minister of State.

Reprinted in *Filipiniana* (ed., Z. M. Galang), 2 (1938), 260–300.

"Apuntes sobre la Medicina en China," *La Opinion* (October 9, 1887).

1888

"Ortografia del Tagalog," *Diario de Manila* (August 5, 1888).

1889

Catalogo Memoria de la Exposicion de Productos de las Islas Filipinas. Paris: Biblioteca de Europa y America, 1889. 26p.

Imp. V. Goupy et Jourdan has also been cited as publisher: W. E. Retana, *Aparato Bibliografico de la Historia General de Filipinas* (Madrid: Imprenta de la Sucesora de M. Minuesa de los Rios, 1906), III:2769.

Consideraciones sobre el Origen de Nombre de los Numeros en Tagalog. Manila: Tipo-litografia de Chofre y Ca., 1889. 26p.

Dedicated to Pierre Favre; first published in *La España Oriental* (Manila), 1889.

Reprinted in *Filipiniana* (ed., Z.M. Galang), 2 (1938), 301–19.

[Prologue], Manuel Xerez y Burgos, *La Eclampsia Infantil en Filipinas y Medios para Reducir la Excesiva Mortalidad de los niños*. Manila: Tipo-Litografia de Chofre y Comp.a, 1889. p. xv–xviii.

"Una Opinion Filologica," *La España Oriental* (November 7, 1889).
> Spanish and Tagalog texts

[Letter to the Editor], *Diario de Manila* (November 13, 1889).
> Datelined Paris, October 4, 1889.

1891

[Barbilampino, *pseud.*], "La Tierra de Quioquiap," *La Solidaridad* (March 31, 1891).

1892

Las Costumbres de los Tagalos de Filipinas, segun el Padre Plasencia. Madrid: Tipografia de Manuel Gines Hernandez, 1892. 20p.

> Appeared originally in *Revista Contemporanea* (Madrid), June 15, 1892.

> Dutch translation by Hendrik Kern: "De Gewoonten der Tagalogs de Filipijnen Volgens Pater Plasencia," *Bijdragen tot de Taal- Land-en Volkenkunde van Nederlandsch-Indie*, 8 (1892).

> German translation by Ferdinand Blumentritt: "Die Sitten und Brauche der alten Tagalen. Manuscrip des P. Juan de Plasencia, 1589," *Zeitschrift fur Ethnologie* (Berlin), 25 (1893), 1–21.

Plantas Medicinales de Filipinas. Madrid: Bernardo Rico, 1892. 341p.

> English translation by Jerome B. Thomas, Jr.: *The Medicinal Plants of the Philippines.* (Philadelphia: Blakiston, 1901). 269pp.

> A new edition, together with the Thomas translation, was published by Ayala Foundation and Filipinas Heritage Library in 2000.

> An English translation of the book's preface appears in Eliseo Quirino and Vicente M. Hilario, eds., *Thinking for Ourselves: A Collection of Representative Filipino Essays* (Manila: Oriental Commercial Company, 1924), 370–75.

"Correspondencia Medica," *El Comercio* (May 11, 1892).

"Correspondencia Medica," *El Comercio* (June 7, 1892).

> Datelined "Paris, Abril 1892: 14 Avenue de Wagram."

"Correspondencia Medica," *El Comercio* (April 9, 1892).

1893

Noticias Sobre la Imprenta y el Grabado en Filipinas. Madrid: Tipografia de los Hijos de M.G. Hernandez, 1893. 48p.

> Published in *Revista Contemporanea* (Madrid, 1892), nos. 426, 427, and 428.

1894

El Mapa de Filipinas del P. Murillo Velarde. Manila: Tipo-litografia de Chofre y Comp., 1894. 19p.

1895

Arte de Cuidar Enfermos. Manila: Tipo-Litografia de Chofre y Comp., 1895. 45p.

Tagalog translation by Iñigo Regalado: *Paraan sa Pag-aalaga sa Maysaquit* (Manila: Imprenta de J. Atayde y Comp., 1895). 37pp.

"Algo sobre el Colera," *El Comercio* (July 7, 1895).

"El 31 de Marzo," *El Comercio* (1895).

On the location of the first Mass in the Philippines.

"Adiciones y rectificaciones," W. E. Retana, *El Periodismo Filipino: Noticias para su Historia (1811–1894).* Madrid: Imprenta de la Viuda de M. Minuesa de los Rios, 1895, 561–64.

1896

"El Beriberi—su Etimologia," *La Correspondencia Medica de Filipinas*, IV:32 (May 1896), 71–73.

Reprinted in *Revista Filipina de Medicina y Farmacia*, 14:9 (September 1923), 284–87.

1899

Una Memoria de Anda y Salazar. Manila: Imprenta "La Democracia," 1899. 102pp.

1901

"A History of the Federal Party," *Report of the Philippine Commission, 1901.* Washington: Government Printing Office, 1902, I, Appendix A, 161–72.

Etimologia de los Nombres de Razas de Filipinas. Manila: Establecimiento Tipografico de Modesto Reyes y C.a, 1901. 20p.

Dedicated to Dean C. Worcester.

Los Frailes en Filipinas. Conferencia dada en el Club International el dia 9 de Junio [1901]. Manila: Estab. Tip. de Modesto Reyes y Ca., 1901. 19p.

[T. H. Pardo de Tavera to General Licerio Geronimo, Dumaguete, April 9, 1901], *La Democracia* (April 17, 1901).

1903

Biblioteca Filipina. Washington: Government Printing Office, 1903. 439p.

Also in *Bibliography of the Philippine Islands* (Washington: Government Printing Office, 1903).

1904

"Discurso del Dr. Pardo de Tavera," *La Democracia* (November 7, 1904).

Speech delivered at Hotel Metropole, Manila. English translation of the speech in *The Manila Cablenews* (November 10, 1904).

1905
"Opiniones sobre el lenguaje oficial," *El Renacimiento*, IV:209 (May 20, 1905), 3.

1906
Reseña Historica de Filipinas desde su Descubrimiento hasta 1903. Manila: Bureau of
Printing, 1906. 80p.

English translation in *Census of the Philippine Islands*, 1903, I (Washington:
U.S. Bureau of Census, 1905), 309–88. This English translation was in turn
translated into Spanish in *Censo de las Islas Filipinas, 1903*, (Washington, 1905),
I:333–440.

"Adiciones a la *Reseña Historica de Filipinas*" (TS, 59 leaves). Written by Pardo de
Tavera in answer to criticisms in *Libertas* later published as *Sobre Una "Reseña
Historica de Filipinas"* (Manila: Imp. de Santo Tomas, 1906), 206p.

"El Alma Filipina," *El Renacimiento* (May 17, 1906).

Reprinted in Epifanio de los Santos, *Trinidad H. Pardo de Tavera* (Manila:
Imprenta "Cultura Filipina," 1913), 50–66; English translation in Hilario and
Quirino, *Thinking for Ourselves*, 172–90, and Zoilo M. Galang, ed., *Encyclopedia of
the Philippines* (Manila: Exequiel Floro, 1951), I:302–16.

1909
*Discurso del Dr. T. H. Pardo de Tavera en el Banquete de despedida ofrecido en Manila por sus
Amigos en la noche del 17 de Abril de 1909.* Manila: Bureau of Printing, 1909. 18p.

Spanish and English texts; in E. de los Santos, *Trinidad H. Pardo de Tavera*, 66–
77, with the title "Autoridades Sociales." Reprinted, with the title "Nacionalista
Party does not rule," in *The Independent* (September 14, 1929), 12–13, 15.

1910
"Notas para una Cartografía de Filipinas," *Cultura Filipina*, 1:8 (November 1910),
102–76.

1911
"La Imprenta en Filipinas," *La Vanguardia* (June 20, 1911).

Reprinted in E. de los Santos, *Trinidad H. Pardo de Tavera*, 77–92.

"Desarrollo Industrial," *Merchants Association Review*, 1:4 (August 1911), 7–9.

Letter to John S. Hord of the Manila Merchants' Association, dated July 26, 1911.
Reprinted in E. de los Santos, *Trinidad H. Pardo de Tavera*, 171–78, and *Philippines Free Press* (August 5, 1911) in both the Spanish original and English translation.

1912

"Por Donde y Como Debemos Ir," *Revista Economica* (February 1912).

> Reprinted in E. de los Santos, *Trinidad H. Pardo de Tavera*, 178–83.

"Porque se Suicido el General Nogi," *Philippines Free Press* (September 28, 1912).

> Reprinted in E. de los Santos, *Trinidad H. Pardo de Tavera*, 112–16.

"El Japon Moderno," *Revista Economica* (October 1912).

> Reprinted in E. de los Santos, *Trinidad H. Pardo de Tavera*, 93–111.

"La Nueva Mentalidad Filipina," *El Comercio* (November 14, 1912).

> Reprinted in E. de los Santos, *Trinidad H. Pardo de Tavera*, 116–38.

"Resultados del Desarrollo Economico de Filipinas," *Revista Economica* (November 1912).

> Lecture before the Philippine Columbian Association, Manila, 1912.
>
> Reprinted in E. de los Santos, *Trinidad H. Pardo de Tavera*, 138–71.
>
> Translated into English with the title "The Economic History of the Philippines," *Philippines Free Press* (29 March, 5, 12, 19 & 26 April 1913); Reprinted with the title "The Results of the Economic Development of the Philippines," *Philippine Agricultural Review*, 18 (1925), 151–78. Also in *The Philippines Herald* (February 15 and 22, 1925).

"La Agricultura y la Inmigracion," *Revista Economica*, 8 (September 1912).

1913

"Estudios Sobre la Vida Actual," *El Ideal* (April 11, 1913), 2.

"Carta de nuestro presidente al Gobernador General," *Revista Economica* (May 1913).

> Letter addressed to Governor-General W. Cameron Forbes, dated May 14, 1913.

1915

"La Guerra Europea," *El Comercio* (July 7, 1915), 2–4.

> Under the title "Interesante Trabajo"; datelined Barcelona, May 24, 1915.

"Why Did Jones Bill Fail?," *The Independent* (August 7, 1915), 3–5.

"Coalicion Necesaria de los Partidos Politicos," *The Independent* (September 25, 1915), 12–14.

> Letter from Llavaneras, Barcelona, dated July 3, 1915.

1916

"Recuerdos de Argentina," *Philippine Review*, 1:6 (June 1916), 42–59.

"Los Chinos (de Mis Recuerdos)," *Philippines Free Press* (July 8, 1916).

> Reprinted in *The Citizen*, 3:20 (September 17, 1920), 18–20, 30.

"Pulcritud del Lenguaje."

Newspaper clipping; periodical and issue not indicated; datelined "Barcelona, Mayo 1916."

"El Alma Filipina," *La Democracia* (May 15, 1916), 1–2

Speech before the Teachers' Summer Institute.

1917

"El 'Don Juan Tenorio,'" *Philippine Review*, 2:3 (March 1917), 14–18; 3:1–2 (January-February 1918), 68–72.

"El Caracter de Rizal," *Philippine Review*, 2:5 (May 1917), 27–42.

English translation: "The Character of Rizal," *Philippine Review*, 2:6 (June 1917), 41–56; Galang, *Encyclopedia of the Philippines*, III:88–124; Trinidad H. Pardo de Tavera, *The Character of Rizal and the Legacy of Ignorantism* (Quezon City: U.P. Publication Office, 1960).

"Los Estudiantes Filipinos de Chicago," *Philippine Review*, 2:11 (November 1917), 14–15.

With parallel Spanish text.

"America's Work in the Philippines," *Philippine Review*, 2:12 (December 1917), 60–68.

With parallel Spanish text.

1918

El Caracter de Rizal. Manila: Imprenta Manila Filatelica, 1918. 83p.

See 1917 entry above.

Cebuano translation by Marcos Trinidad: *Ang Gawi ni Rizal* (Cebu: Barili Press, 1926), 71pp.

"España y la Gran Guerra," *La Vanguardia* (February 14, 1918).

Translation of an article published in *The Century* (New York) (January 1918).

"Japan Redentor," *Boletin de la Sociedad Orientalista de Filipinas,* I:7 (July 1918), 13–15.

1919

"Recuerdos de Hongkong, Kowloon, Macao y Canton," *Philippine Review*, 4:5 (May 1919), 342–58.

English translation: *Philippine Review*, 5:11 (November 1920), 765–78.

"Antiguas Costumbres de los Pampangos," *El Ideal* (July 18, 1919).

Reproduces and annotates a section of a manuscript by Juan de Plasencia (1589).

"Elogio a la Bandera Americana," *La Nacion* (October 31, 1919).

Text of a speech; also in *El Debate* (October 31, 1919).

"La Bandera Filipina," *Philippine National Weekly* (November 8, 1919), 17.

"Dr. T. H. Pardo de Tavera's Message to the Youth of Cebu and his Ideas on Birth-limitation and Immigration," *The Freeman* (Cebu), I:28 (November 16, 1919), 1, 3.

> Text of an interview; follow-up article: "Dr. Pardo de Tavera reiterates procreation theory," *The Freeman*, I:32 (December 14, 1919), 1–2.

"Taiwan como Obra Civilizadora del Japon," *Philippine Review*, 4:12 (December 1919), 787–819.

> English translation: "Taiwan: a Product of Japanese Civilization," *Philippine Review*, 5:2 (February 1920), 106–33.

1920

"Patriotismo Constructivo," *Philippine Oriental Exposition* [1920], 3–4, 13, 39–41.

> Spanish and English texts; article written for the Chamber of Commerce of the Philippines.

"Discurso sobre Inmigracion en el Junior Philippine Senate (University of the Philippines)."

> Notes for a speech delivered on September 25, 1920.

[Prologue], Enrique Altavas, *Impresiones de Viaje*. Manila: Imp. La Comercial, 1920. p. iii–xiv.

"Recuerdos Personales de Rizal," *El Espectador* (Cebu) (February 9, 1920).

"Documentos Historicos de Filipinas: Pardo no es Anti-Español," *The Independent* (February 28, 1920), 23–24.

> Letter written from Barcelona, December 30, 1915.

"Liliw, Laguna," *The Citizen*, 2:46 (March 19, 1920), 19–20, 22; 2:47 (March 26, 1920), 25.

> Offprint: Manila, Times Press, [1920], 16p.

"En Retraso," *Philippines Free Press* (May 15, 1920).

"La Masoneria por Kalaw" [1920].

> Review of T. M. Kalaw's *Masoneria Filipina*, dated April 5, 1920; original manuscript in *PTC*.

"El Trabajo Mas Util," *Philippine Oriental Exposition* (June 1920), 42–45.

> Speech at the assembly of *Comite de Defensa Social*, Manila Opera House, May 30, 1920. Also in *El Ciudadano*, 3:6 (June 11, 1920), 25–27.

El Legado del Ignorantismo. Manila: Bureau of Printing, 1920. 40p.

> English edition: *The Legacy of Ignorantism (Ignorantismo)* (Manila: Bureau of Printing, 1921), 41p.
>
> Spanish original published in *El Debate* (May 4, 1920); *Philippine Oriental Exposition*, 3:13 (May 1920), 43–75; *Dia Filipino*, 8:10 (June 19, 1920), 32–

49; *Acacia*, 1:7 (July 15, 1920), 174–214; *The Citizen*, 3:23 (October 7, 1920), 1, 9–15, 17–18.

> English translation reprinted in Hilario and Quirino, *Thinking for Ourselves*, 1–17; Pardo de Tavera, *The Character of Rizal and the Legacy of Ignorantism* (1960).

"Cuatro Cositas," *El Adalid* (Iloilo) (June 26, 1920).

"Pensamiento," *Hojas Sueltas* (July 9, 1920).

"El Problema de la Inmigracion," *Revista Economica* (September 1920), 7–18.

> Also in *Philippines Free Press* (September 11, 1920).

"El Reloj," *The Citizen* (September 3, 1920).

"Mentalidad Pueril," *The Rising Filipina*, 2:21 (October 9, 1920).

> Also in *The Independent* (October 30, 1920).

"Moral Laica," *Acacia*, 1:16 (November 30, 1920), 508–10.

"La Lengua Inglesa en Filipinas," *El Debate* (December 12, 1920).

"Porque Debemos Aprender Bien el Idioma Ingles," *El Ciudadano* (December 24, 1920), 25–27.

1921

"La Independencia Individual," *Philippines Free Press* (January 8, 1921), 35, 38, 43, 46.

"La Labor de Harrison por el 'Self-government,'" *La Vanguardia* (January 19, 1921).

"El Viaje de Magallanes," *Celebracion del Cuarto Centenario del Descubrimiento de Filipinas por Fernando de Magallanes, 1521–1921* (Manila: Bureau of Printing, 1921), 83–103.

> Speech on the occasion of the Fourth Centenary of Magellan's Discovery of the Philippines, February 5, 1920. Also published as a separate title by the Bureau of Printing in 1921.

"Las Tres Fuerzas Empleadas por el Ignorantismo," *El Ciudadano* (February 4, 1921).

The Conservation of the National Type. Manila: Bureau of Printing, 1921. 33p.

> With Spanish text; delivered in the commencement exercises of the University of the Philippines, April 4, 1921.

> Spanish text in *La Vanguardia* (April 6, 1921). English text reprinted in Hilario and Quirino, *Thinking for Ourselves*, 341–66; *Filipiniana Reference Shelf* (August 1941), 180–81, 191; (September 1941), 205–6.

1922

"La Capacidad de Ganar y Gastar el Dinero," *El Debate* (February 11, 1922).

"Material Progress," *The National Forum*, 1:1 (July 1922).

> With Spanish text.

"La Enseñanza de la Religion en la Universidad de Filipinas," *The Alumni News*, 2:1 (July 1922).

"La Enseñanza de la Religion," *The Independent*, 8:390 (September 23, 1922), 22.

"The Commercial Awakening of the Philippines," *The National Forum*, 1:2 (August 1922).
> Spanish translation, "El Despertar Comercial de Filipinas," in *La Vanguardia* (March 8, 1922); also in *El Debate* (March 9, 1922).

"The New Filipino Mentality," *The National Forum*, 1:4 (October 1922), 24–44.
> Also see *The Independent*, 8:405 (December 9, 1922), 8–10.

"Hay que Empesar Imitando," *Philippines Free Press* (October 28, 1922).

"Peor es el Otro," *The Woman's Outlook*, I:1 (October 1922).

"Las Nihilistas," *The Woman's Outlook,* 1:2 (November 10, 1922).

"La Tuberculosis y su Significacion Economica en la Nacion," *The Citizen* (November 11, 1922).
> With English translation.

"Moros y Cristianos" [1922].
> Manuscript; sent to *Philippines Herald* for publication, November 14, 1922.

"El 'Desideratum' de la Pedagogia Moderna," *Philippines Free Press* (February 4, 1922).

1923

"Lest We Forget! Lest We Forget!" *The Manila Times* (March 11, 1923).

"La Medicina Casera y Sus Peligros," *Revista Filipina de Medicina y Farmacia* (June 1923).
> Reprint: Manila: Imp. Manila, 1923, 12p.

"Los Filipinos Necesitamos de Tres Cosas Esenciales: Instruccion, Educacion y Fe en Nuestro Propio Esfuerzo," *El Debate* (June 17, 1923).

1924

"Lo que Necesitan los Filipinos," *The Independent* (March 1924), 24.

"Deberes Sociales," *La Vanguardia* (March 22, 1924).
> Speech before the members of the Central Student YMCA, Manila, March 14, 1924.

"La Civilizacion y Cultura Filipina," *El Debate* (May 11 and 15, 1924).

"One Language Here Utopian," *Philippines Herald* (October 4, 1924).

"Conferencia pronunciada por el Dr. T. H. Pardo de Tavera en el 'Rizal Hall' de la Universidad de Filipinas el 25 de Febrero de 1924, ante los estudiantes de Economia Politica de dicha Universidad." Manila, 1924. 28pp.
> Manuscript copy in *PTC*.

1925

"La 'Rising Generation,'" *La Vanguardia* (February 21, 1925).

Speech before the Law faculty and students at the University of the Philippines, January 31, 1925.

"La Postuma Disquisicion del Dr. Tavera Sobre el Ingles," *La Vanguardia* (March 21, 1925), 1, 7.

N.D.

"The Filipino Youth," *The Filipino Students' Journal*, 20–35.

Undated periodical clipping; address delivered at the Sampaloc Intermediate School, Manila.

ISABELO DE LOS REYES BIBLIOGRAPHY*

1887

Ilocanadas. Varios trabajos literarios. Iloilo: Imprenta de "El Eco de Panay," 1887. 167p.

Contains literary and ethnological articles published in *El Eco de Panay.*

Las Islas Visayas en la epoca de la conquista. Iloilo: Imprenta de "El Eco de Panay,"1887. 83p.

Enlarged and corrected second ed.: Manila: Tipo-Litografia de Chofre y Cia., 1889. 114p.

Filipinas. Articulos varios . . . sobre etnografia, historia y costumbres del pais. Manila: J.A. Ramos, 1887. [v], 208p.

Prologue by Cesareo Blanco y Sierra. Part 1, The Tinguians; Pt. 2, Account of Lima-hong; Pt. 3, Dutch in the Philippines; Pt. 4, Early rulers of Manila; Pt. 5,

---

* This list does not include numerous articles, stories, and poems de los Reyes published in Iloko and other vernacular publications. Other works that have been cited, though it is not clear in what form they appeared: *Memoria sobre los productos comerciales de Filipinas, Teogonia Ilocana, El Partido Republicano de Filipinas, Tipos y Cuadros de Manila* (Iloilo: El Eco de Panay, 1888), and *Los Antiguos Regulos de Filipinas.*

Other works with de los Reyes cited as editor: *Catequesis dela Iglesia Filipina Independiente* (1911), *Al Padre de todos; Libro de oraciones y enseñanzas de la Iglesia Filipina Independiente* (1929), *La Libre Razon: descubre los grandes abusos del catolicismo (controversias entre Aglipayanos y Catolicos)* (1930).

"Juguetes sobre costumbres e historia."
    Second ed., 1888.
Die Tinguianen (Luzon). Vienna [Wien]: Eduard Holzel, 1887. 32p.
    Translation from Spanish to German by Ferdinand Blumentritt, published in *Mittheilungen der Kaiserlich-konigliche geographische Gessellschaft* (Wien, 1887).
    See the Spanish text in de los Reyes, *Filipinas.*

1888

"*Die Religiosen Anschauungen der Ilocanen (Luzon),*" *Mittheilungen der Kaiserlich-konigliche geographische Gessellschaft*, 552–75.
    Published by the Bulletin of the Geographical Society of Vienna (1888), with comments by Ferdinand Blumentritt and Adolf Meyer. This is an annotated German translation by Blumentritt of de los Reyes' *Mitologia Ilocana*, published in *La España Oriental* in 1888.
Expedicion de Li-Ma-Hong contra Filipinas en 1574. Manila: Estab. Tipog. de Ramirez y Compania, 1888. 24p.
    First published in *Diario de Manila* in 1882; see de los Reyes, *Filipinas.*
    Tagalog edition: *Ang pagsalacay ni Li-Mahong dito sa Maynila at sa mga bayan nang iba,t,ibang Provincia sa sangcapuluang ito*. Manila: Imp. de Sta. Cruz, 1889. 52p.
Triunfos del Rosario, o los Holandeses en Filipinas. Manila: Est. tip. de Ramirez y Compania, 1888. 38p.
    Originally appeared in *Diario de Manila*; also in de los Reyes, *Filipinas*, 66–86, where it is dedicated to one of the author's teachers at University of Santo Tomas, Fr. Prudencio Vidal.

1889

Historia de Filipinas. Manila: Imprenta de D. Esteban Balbas, 1889. viii, 101p.
    First volume of a planned two-volume work; the second volume did not appear. The book also carries another title, *Prehistoria de Filipinas*, and printer, Imprenta de Sta. Cruz. Dedicated to Victor Balaguer.
El Folk-Lore Filipino. Manila: Imprenta de Santa Cruz, 1889. 2 vs (345, [5] p. + 300, [3] p.)
    Awarded a silver prize in the Exposicion Filipina in Madrid in 1887.
    Produced by two printers, hence "Tipo-Litografia de Chofre y C.a" is also cited.
"La Vida de Lam-ang; Daan a Sarita," *El Ilocano* (December 1889-February 1890).
    See De los Reyes, *Folk-Lore Filipino.*

"Delegates to the Cortes for the Philippines," *Solidaridad*, I:13 (August 15, 1889), 471–73.

With Spanish text; originally published in *La España Oriental.*

1890

Historia de Ilocos. Manila: Establecimiento Tipografico de "La Opinion," 1890. 2 vs. (239 + 235, [5] p.)

Dedicated to Juan Luna. Cited as second edition since this was earlier published as articles, some under a pseudonym, in *Diario de Manila, El Comercio, España Oriental,* and *Eco de Filipinas.*

An earlier version, "Historia de Ilocos," was published in Iloko translation in *El Ilocano*, I:1 (June 28, 1889)–II:26 (June 27, 1890).

El Regulo de Tondo Lacandola, Documentos oficiales (ineditos) Apendice al Folklore Filipino, publicado por esta revista. Manila: Imp. de Santa Cruz, 1890. 92, [3] p.

Also appears in De los Reyes, *Filipinas; Idem., Folk-Lore Filipino.*

"The Equality of Rights," *Solidaridad*, II:30 (April 30, 1890), 283–93.

Spanish and English texts; published under the pseudonym *Kasalo.*

"Civil Registration," *Solidaridad*, II:32 (May 31, 1890), 349–61.

Spanish and English texts.

"Church and Civil Marriages," *Solidaridad*, II:34 (June 30, 1890), 417–29.

Spanish and English texts.

1892

"The Penal Code and Censorship," *Solidaridad*, IV:82 (June 30, 1892), 311–13.

Spanish and English texts. Article addressed to Antonio de Santisteban, "Press Censor of Manila."

1893

"Cortes Representation: The Historical Truth," *Solidaridad*, V:102 (April 30, 1893), 199–203.

Spanish and English texts; written for *La Ilustracion Filipina.*

1894

Biag ni Aida. Manila: Imp. de Isabelo de los Reyes, [ca. 1894].

This translation or adaptation of Verdi's *Aida*, entitled *Aida, Opera nga uppat ti pasetna*, was published in *El Ilocano* (October-December 1893); also appeared in *The Ilocos Times* (June 10, 1936), 3, 7; (June 20, 1936), 3, 6; (June 30, 1936), 5, 6; (July 20, 1936), 4.

Calendario ti El Ilocano iti taoen á 1895. Manila: Imprenta de Isabelo de los Reyes, [1894]. [48 p.]

An 1893 edition has been cited.

N.D.

Evangelio wenno ti nasantuan a biag ni nasam-it unay a Jesus kas insurat ni San Marcos. Manila: Imp. ni Isabelo de los Reyes, n.d., 139p.

De los Reyes's translation from Spanish to Iloko of St. Mark's Gospel.

See Leopoldo Y. Yabes, *A Brief Survey of Iloko Literature* (Manila: The Author, 1936), nos. 81, 87, 92, 95, 99.

Ipacaammo cadaguiti taga Iloco. Dagdaga ni D. Isabelo de los Reyes idiay Tarlac. Manila: Imp. de I. de los Reyes, n.d.

See Retana, *Aparato Bibliografico*, III, no. 4254.

1899

Apuntes para un Ensayo de Teodicea Filipina. La Religion del "Katipunan" o sea la antigua de los Filipinos tal como ahora la resucita la asociacion de los hijos del pueblo ("Katipunan"), la promovedora de la revolucion filipina. Madrid: Imprenta Palma Alta, 1899. 39p.

La Sensacional Memoria de Isabelo de los Reyes sobre la Revolucion Filipina de 1896–1897, por la cual fue deportado el autor al castillo de Montjuich. Madrid: Tipo-Litog. de J. Corrales, 1899. 128p. illus.

Published by "*Delegacion Filipina en Europa*"; prologue by Miguel Morayta.

1900

Filipinas. Independencia y Revolucion! Coleccion de los principales articulos de propaganda. Madrid: Imp. y Lit. de Jose Corrales, 1900. 160p.

La Religion del "Katipunan"; o sea la antigua de los Filipinos tal como ahora la resucita la Asociacion de los Hijos del Pueblo (Katipunan), la promovedora de la Revolucion Filipina. Madrid: Tipolitografia de J. Corrales, 1900. 64p.

Revised second edition; first edition: *Apuntes para un ensayo de teodicea filipina* (1899).

Also *The Religion of the Katipunan or the Old Beliefs of the Filipinos*, trans. J. M. Yap, in *Views on Philippine Revolution* (Quezon City: Toyota Foundation-UP Press, 2002), I:197–299. A translation of the second edition.

Translated excerpt from the 1900 edition: "Isabelo de los Reyes on the Katipunan," in Taylor, *Philippine Insurrection*, I:202–11.

1903

"Biografia del Emmo. Sr. Gregorio Aglipay y Labayan, Obispo Maximo de la Iglesia Filipina Independiente," *La Iglesia Filipina Independiente: Revista Catolica*, 42 (May 29, 1903), and succeeding issues (nos. 43, 46–47, 53–55).

Unfinished; annotated and edited version in Pedro S. de Achutegui, S.J., and Miguel A. Bernad, S.J., *Religious Revolution in the Philippines: The Schism of 1902* (Quezon City: Ateneo de Manila University Press, 1972), IV, 292–311.

A condensed version appears in *El Renacimiento Filipino*, I:46 (June 14, 1911), 1–5, under the pseudonym "Isabelo de Leon." Also in Achutegui and Bernad, *Religious Revolution*, IV, 307–11.

1904

Ang Comediang Tagalog. 1904. 68, [3] p.

This chapbook may have been published after 1904 since an appendix contains summaries of plays produced as late as 1918. Typewritten copy at the Rizal Library, Ateneo de Manila University.

First serialized in *Ang Kapatid ng Bayan* (August 2 –September 21, 1904); also in *El Defensor de los Obreros* (August 9, 1904).

"Historia Documentada de la Iglesia Filipina," *La Iglesia Filipina Independiente: Revista Catolica*, 43, 44, 53 (1904).

Unfinished; reprinted, with editorial note, in Achutegui and Bernad, *Religious Revolution*, IV, 312–20.

Doctrina y Reglas Constitucionales de la Iglesia Filipina Independiente. Manila: Imprenta Tipografia de Modesto Reyes y Cia., 1904. 87p.

Serialized in *La Iglesia Filipina Independiente* (October 11, 1903–January 17, 1904).

1905

Ang Singsing nang Dalagang Marmol. Manila: Tip. Santos y Bernal, 1912. 32p.

A translation by Carlos B. Raimundo from the Spanish version, published in *El Grito del Pueblo* in 1905, written by de los Reyes based on his lost Tagalog original published in *Ang Kapatid ng Bayan* in 1905.

Reprinted with Precioso Palma's *Ipaghiganti Mo Ako* in a single volume by Ateneo de Manila University Press in 2004.

Catecismo de la Iglesia Filipina Independiente. Manila: Imprenta de Fajardo y Cia., 1905. 50p.

Serialized in *La Iglesia Filipina Independiente* (April 10–May 1, 1904).

1906

Oficio Divino de la Iglesia Filipina Independiente. Barcelona: n.p., 1906. 240p.

Attributed to de los Reyes; appears to have been published in 1907 despite its publication date.

Gregorio Aglipay y otros prelados de la Iglesia Filipina Independiente; lecturas de cuaresma para la Iglesia Filipina Independiente. Barcelona: n.p., 1906. 40p.

Lecturas de Cuaresma para la Iglesia Filipina Independiente. Barcelona: [Isabelo de los Reyes], 1906.

Earlier version appeared serially in *La Iglesia Filipina Independiente* (February 21–May 1, 1904).

1908

Biblia Filipina. Primera piedra para un Genesis cientifico, expuesto segun las rectificaciones de Jesus. Barcelona, 1908.

Author not cited but attributed to de los Reyes.

Calendario de la Iglesia Filipina Independiente para el año bisiesto del Señor, 1908. Barcelona: Imp. A. Virgili, 1908. 66p.

Prologue by Gregorio Aglipay.

1909

La Religion Antigua de los Filipinos. Manila: Impr. de El Renacimiento, 1909.v, 249 [3] p.

1911

Kalendariong Maanghang sa taong 1911; Sili araw-araw datapwa't birong kapatid lamang, kadiabluhang malaki ni Isabelo de los Reyes. Maynila: Limbagang Magiting ni Honorio Lopez, 1911. 63p.

There is a 1921 edition with the same title, containing an article by Dominador Gomez on Chinese immigration and items by de los Reyes criticizing the U.S. government and the Quezon-Osmeña leadership.

De los Reyes published other almanacs or *calendarios* in Iloko, Tagalog, and Spanish, usually containing articles and miscellaneous items he and others authored. See "An Iloko Bibliography,"in Yabes, *Brief Survey of Iloko Literature*, nos. 1705, 1821; Marcelino A. Foronda, Jr., *An Iloko Bibliography* (Manila: De La Salle College Library, 1972), nos. 1511, 1561, 1574–78; Maxima M. Ferrer, ed., *Union Catalog of Philippine Materials* (Quezon City: University of the Philippines Press, 1976), II, nos. 16277–79, 16290, 16292.

[Prologue], Claudio R. Miranda, *Costumbres Populares.* Manila: Imp. "Cultura Filipina," 1911. pp. i–x.

1915

"Documentos Historicos de Filipinas," *The Independent*, 1:31 (November 6, 1915), 11–12.

    Letters of de los Reyes and Felipe Buencamino on the surrender of Aguinaldo.

Calendario de la Iglesia Filipina Independiente para el año bisiesto de 1916. Maynila: Limbagan at Litograpya ni Juan Fajardo, 1915.

    Other editions: 1918, 1924, 1925.

1918

"El Beso de Carcar," *Nueva Fuerza* (Cebu), IV:323 (July 18, 1918).

    Legend of Cebu place names, with an anti-friar theme.

1926

"The Legend of Angalo," *The Ilocos Review*, 1:1 (1969), 37–39.

    Translation from the Spanish original in *El Norte* (February 1926); also see de los Reyes's account of this legend in *Consolidacion Nacional*, 3:756 (October 12, 1915).

"Da Dongguial ken Namicqui," *Kutibeng: Philippine Poetry in Iloko, 1621–1971*, ed. M. A. Foronda, Jr. Manila: De La Salle University Press, 1976. pp. 37–41.

    Iloko and English texts. Poem published in *Sangcareppet a Dandaniw (Parnaso Ilocano)*, ed. M.A. Peña and A. Fogata (Manila: Filipino Publishers, 1926).

1929

[Prologue], Vicente Sotto, *Mga Sugilanong Pilipinhon*. Barili: Barili Press, 1929. p. 1–9.

    Spanish and Cebuano texts; datelined Barcelona, April 8, 1908.

1932

Catedra; sermonario de la Iglesia Filipina Independiente. Manila: n.p., 1932. 132 [1]p.

    De los Reyes is cited as editor.

1970

"Ilocano Thriftiness," *The Ilocos Review*, II:1 (January-June 1970), 7–16.

NAME INDEX

552

Pardo de Tavera, Joaquin II, 130
Pardo de Tavera, Juan (Cardinal), 122, 231n 3
Pardo de Tavera, Juan (Marques de Magahon), 122, 158
Pardo de Tavera, Julian, 122
Pardo de Tavera, Pacita (Paz), 123, 130, 134, 135
Pardo de Tavera, Trinidad, 15, 22, 25, 43, 84, 91, 121–230, 260, 272, 282, 289, 294, 296, 300–2, 333, 342, 345, 348, 349, 351, 361, 363, 381, 383, 385, 391, 400, 407, 427, 428, 445, 450, 451, 455, 466, 467–68, 471, 475, 478, 481, 482, 486, 488, 495–97, 499, 503
Paredes, A. F., 376n 198
Paredes, Ruby, 152
Pastells, Pablo, 53, 76
Pasteur, Louis, 428, 127, 128, 220
Paterno, Adelaida, 5, 6
Paterno, Agueda, 5, 6, 475
Paterno, Antonio, 5, 7
Paterno, Concepcion, 5, 6
Paterno, Dolores, 5, 6, 38
Paterno, Feliciano, 5
Paterno, Jacoba, 5, 6, 475
Paterno, Jose, 5
Paterno, Luisa. See Pineyro, Luisa
Paterno, Maria de la Paz, 5, 6
Paterno, Mariano, 5
Paterno, Maximino, 5, 7, 18, 21, 31, 107n 49
Paterno, Maximo Molo, 4, 5, 6, 7, 8
Paterno, Narciso, 5
Paterno, Pedro, 3–102, 138, 141, 260, 265, 266, 275, 285, 289, 292, 294,

296–98, 300–2, 318, 319, 342, 345, 347–49, 361–63, 381, 383, 385, 418, 422, 426, 427, 439, 441, 451, 455, 462, 465, 466, 467, 471, 473, 484, 486, 488, 495–98, 499, 500–2, 504
Paterno, Rosenda, 5
Paterno, Trinidad, 5
Payo, Pedro, 131, 449
Paz, Octavio, 217
Peding, Lorenzo, 290, 303
Pelaez, Pedro, 441–42, 452, 486
Perez Escrich, Enrique, 430
Perfecto, Mariano, 430–31
Philip II, 122, 398
Philipps, P. Lee, 174
Pi y Margall, Francisco, 14
Pickering, Charles, 88
Pigafetta, Antonio, 340, 343, 383, 391, 438
Pilapil, Domingo, 411, 414, 417, 418
Pilapil, Mariano, 401–2, 408, 410–11, 414
Pineda, Maria, 5
Pineda, Silvino, 5
Pineda, Valeriana, 5, 6
Pinedas, 6
Pineyro, Antonia, 12
Pineyro, Luisa, 12, 20, 34
Pineyro de Lugo family, 12
Pinkerton, John, 345
Pinpin, Simon, 173
Pinpin, Tomas, 173, 360, 398–401, 404, 407, 452
Pius IX, 461
Plasencia, Juan de, 49, 76–77, 132, 171–72, 385
Plato, 80

Rizal, Narcisa, 475

Rizal, Paciano, 475

Rizal, Saturnina, 475

Rizal, Trinidad, 475

Robertson, James, 151, 203, 282, 330, 482, 497

Rodell, Paul A., 375n 184

Rodriguez, Eulogio, 158, 226

Rodriguez, Jose, 314, 367n 30

Romanzoff-von Chamisso, 387

Roosevelt, Alice, 486

Roosevelt, Theodore, 149, 155, 158

Root, Elihu, 35

Rosal, Mario G. R., 379n 260

Roskoff, Gustav, 292

Rosny, Leon Prunol de, 304

Rost, Reinhold, 453

Rousseau, Jean-Jacques, 100, 304, 410, 430

Routledge, David, 373n 136

Roux, Emile, 428

Roxas, Baldomero, 473

Roxas, Domingo, 412, 416, 417, 418

Roxas family, 416

Roxas, Felix, 5, 280

Roxas, Pedro, 8, 18, 418

Rueda, Ricardo Diaz de. *See* Diaz de Rueda, Ricardo

Ruiz, Lorenzo, 399

Ruiz, Manuel "Prin," 280

Sacy, Silvestre de, 211

Saderra Maso, Miguel, 329

Saguinsin, Bartolome, 403, 417

Said, Edward, 70, 359, 499

Saint-Simon, Henri de, 215, 216

Sakay, Macario, 276

Salazar, Domingo de, 390

Salcedo, Juan de, 255, 290

Salvador, Moises, 432

Samaniego, Isidro, 415

San Agustin, Gaspar de, 49, 75, 166, 296, 321, 384, 385

San Antonio, Juan Francisco de, 45, 75, 321, 385, 425

San Buenaventura, Pedro de, 77

San Jose, Francisco de. *See* Blancas de San Jose, Francisco

Sanciangco, Gregorio, 43, 73, 442, 444, 447–48

Sanger, Joseph, 178

Sanlucar, Pedro de, 54–55, 168, 384

Santa Ana, Alonso de, 399

Santa Ines, Francisco de, 438

Santa Maria, Fernando, 163, 165, 426

Santiago, Luciano, 371n 107, 397, 402, 403

Santos, Lope K., 480, 493

Schadenberg, Alexander, 387

Scheerer, Otto, 26, 230, 478

Scherzer, Karl von, 394

Schiednagel, Manuel, 341

Schiller, J.C.F. von, 430

Schlegel, Wilhelm, 301

Schoolcraft, Henry, 346

Schopenhauer, Arthur, 328

Schumacher, John, 10, 43, 205, 206, 432, 441–42, 448, 462

Scott, William Henry, 280, 291, 365n 2, 368n 41, 434

Sebillot, Paul, 306

Selgas, Jose, 45

Sempau, Ramon, 268, 269, 369n 49

Semper, Carl, 299, 387, 438